Christianity in Eurafrica

Steven Paas

Christianity in Eurafrica

A History of the Church in Europe and Africa

CHRISTIAN LITERATURE FUND PUBLISHERS
CHRISTELIKE LEKTUURFONDS UITGEWERS

Christian Literature Fund, Wellington, South Africa
2016

Copyright© 2016 Steven Paas

All rights reserved. No part of this publication may be reproduced, stored in a retrieval system, or transmitted in any form or by any means, electronic, mechanical, photocopying, recording or otherwise, without prior permission from the author.

ISBN: 978-1-86804-350-7

Layout: Wim Paas

Cover Design: Amanda Carstens

Publisher: Christian Literature Fund, Private Bag X19, Wellington 7654, SA. Phone: 0027 (0)21 873 6964; email: info@clf.co.za

Table of contents

Preface	18
1. Characteristics of Church History	20
1.1. Defining Church History	20
a. Church History Belongs to Secular History	21
b. Church History Belongs to Theology	24
1.2. African Church History	25
a. Southern Christianity	25
b. Received from the Outside	26
c. Textbooks	26
d. Ideological bias	27
1.3. The Sources of Church History	28
a. Categories of Sources	29
b. Writers of Source Material	30
1.4. The Branches of Church History	32
a. History of Christian Missions	32
b. History of Persecutions	33
c. History of Church Polity	33
d. History of Church-State Relationship	33
e. History of Church Praxis	33
f. History of Christian Life	33
g. Histories of the Branches of Theology	34
1.5. Reasons for Studying Church History	34
a. Understanding the Present	34
b. Noticing God's Providence	34
c. Seeing Satan's Attempts	34
d. Examples for Present Training	35
e. Source of Tools for Learning	35
f. Guide for Exegetics	35
Bibliography: Historiography	36
PART I	39
FROM GALILEE TO THE ATLANTIC	39
A. ANTIQUITY 60-500	40
2. The Fullness of Time	41
2.1. The Covenant	41
2.2. Contributions of the Roman Empire	42
a. Imperial Rule	42
b. Pax Romana	42
c. System of Communication	43
d. Economic development	43
e. Sense of Unity	43
f. Legal System	43
g. The Religion of the Romans	43
2.3. Greek Contributions	45
a. The Greek Language	45
b. Greek Philosophy	46
2.4. Contributions by the Jews	48
a. The Septuagint	48

    b. The Diaspora   49
3. Expansion inside the Roman Empire   50
  3.1. The Church is rooted in Christ   50
  3.2. The Church in Palestine   50
  3.3. The Church outside Palestine   51
    a. Inside and outside the Empire   51
    b. Paul: from Jerusalem to Rome   51
    c. Four early Centres of Christianity   52
    d. Figures, and Characteristics of Growth   54
4. The Life of the Earliest Church   57
  4.1. The Government of the Church   57
  4.2. The Doctrines of the Church   59
  4.3. The Conduct of Christians   59
5. The Church and the Roman State   61
  5.1. Persecutions   61
  5.2. Reasons for Persecution   62
  5.3. The Christians' Answer   63
  5.4. Threats to the Church   64
  5.5. The End of Persecutions   66
6. Expansion beyond the Roman Empire   68
  6.1. 'Southern Christianity'   68
    a. The Term   68
    b. Edessa   68
    c. Armenia   69
    d. Parthia and Persia   69
    e. Arabia   71
    f. India   71
  6.2. Christianity in the North   72
    a. The Huns   72
    b. The Goths   73
  6.3. Christianity in the North West   73
    a. Two Missionary Movements   73
    b. Mission by the Celtic Church   73
7. Conflicts and the Definition of Dogma   76
  7.1. Before 313   76
    a. Dualism   76
    b. Legalism   78
  7.2. After 313   79
    a. Theological Heresies   79
    First phase: attacks on the Trinity of God   79
    Second phase: struggle about the two natures of God the Son   80
    Third phase: God the Holy Spirit   81
    b. Anthropological Heresies   81
8. The Church Fathers   83
  8.1. Apostles and Apostolic Fathers   83
  8.2. Apologists and Polemicists   83
  8.3. Post-Nicene Church Fathers   85
  8.4. Tertullian, a North African Church Father   86
9. Cyprian   88
  9.1. Decian Persecutions   88
  9.2. The Lapsi   89

10. Augustine	92
10.1. On the City of God	92
10.2. Augustine's Life	92
10.3. Dichotomies	94
10.4. Dualism	94
10.5. Pelagianism	95
10.6. Donatism	96
11. Monasticism	98
11.1. Ascetism	98
11.2. Antony and Pachomius	98
11.3. Benedictine Rule	99
11.4. Celtic Monasticism	99
11.5. Significance	100
12. Collapse in the West	101
12.1. West and East drifting apart	101
12.2. Golden Age of the Church Fathers	101
12.3. Causes of the Collapse	101
12.4. The Rise of Papacy	102
12.5. Africa and Europe	103
a. Maurice, 'the first black saint'	103
b. Inward looking	103
Bibliography: Antiquity	105
B. MIDDLE AGES 500-1500	108
13. The Rise and Expansion of Islam	109
13.1. Attractive to many	109
13.2. Pre-Islamic Arabia	110
13.3. Muhammad	110
13.4. Shi'ites	111
13.5. The Arabian Movement	112
13.6. The Turkish Movement	113
13.7. The Expansion in Sub-Saharan Africa	114
13.8. Expansion in the Western World	114
14. Expansion in North West Europe 590-800	115
14.1. Mission by the Church of Rome	115
a. Extension of Christianity	116
b. Extension of Papal Power	116
14.2. Romanising of European Christianity	117
14.3. Christianisation of North Germany and Scandinavia	118
a. Charlemagne and the Saxons	118
b. Liudger and Charlemagne	119
15. Church and State in Competition	121
15.1 The Frankish Holy Roman Empire	121
a. Merovingians and Carolingians	121
b. Charlemagne Extends his Empire	122
c. Charlemagne's Church Policy	123
15.2. The German Holy Roman Empire	123
a. Emperors and Popes	123
b. Investiture Controversy	124
c. Summit of Papal Power	125
16. Monastic Reforms	126
16.1. Degradation of Monasticism	126

16.2. The Cluniac Reforms	126
16.3. Cluniacs Boost Papal Power	127
16.4. The Cistercians – Bernard of Clairvaux	127
16.5. Mendicant Orders	128
17. Eastern Orthodox Church	**131**
17.1. The terms EC and EOC	131
17.2. Before the Fall of Rome	131
17.3. The Iconoclastic Controversy	132
17.4. Photius, Filioque, Hesychasm, Paulicians	132
17.5. The Final Breach, 1054	133
17.6. Moscow, the 'Third Rome'	134
17.7. Different from the West	134
17.8. Lack of Reformation	135
18. The Crusades	**136**
18.1. Pilgrims Threatened	136
18.2. Who Joined and Why?	137
18.3. First Period: Conquests 1095-1204	137
18.4. Second Period: Defence 1204-1291	139
18.5. Third Period: Against Turkish Expansion 1291-1464	140
18.6. Consequences of the Crusades	140
19. Medieval Papacy	**142**
19.1. Emerging Papalism	142
19.2. Growing Power	142
19.3. Innocent III and Boniface VIII	143
19.4. Babylonian Captivity of the Popes (Avignon Period)	143
19.5. Popes and Antipopes (Great Schism)	144
19.6. Conciliar Movement and Extreme Papal Decay	144
20. Education and Learning	**146**
20.1. Schools and Universities	146
20.2. Faith and Reason	146
20.3. Realism	147
20.4. Nominalism	147
20.5. Conceptualism	148
21. Reform and Dissent	**150**
21.1. External dangers	150
21.2. Internal causes	150
21.3. Reform Movements	151
21.4. Forerunners of the Reformation	152
Bibliography: Middle Ages	**154**
C. REFORMATION ERA 1500-1650	**160**
22. An Era of Great Change	**161**
22.1. Political Changes	161
22.2. Social Changes	162
22.3. Economic Changes	162
22.4. Psychological Changes	163
22.5. Cultural changes	163
a. Art	163
b. Science	163
22.6. Spiritual Changes	164
a. Papal Claims Criticised	164
b. Ecclesiastical Claims Criticised	164

c. Ethical Abuses of the Church Criticised	164
d. Doctrinal Heresies Attacked	165
22.7. The Reformation	165

23. Martin Luther 1483-1546 — 166
- 23.1. His Childhood — 166
- 23.2. Luther joins the Monastery — 166
- 23.3. His Conversion — 167
- 23.4. The 95 Theses against Indulgences — 167
- 23.5. His Publications in 1520 — 168
- 23.6. Condemned by Pope (1520) and Empire (1521) — 170
- 23.7. At the Wartburg — 170
- 23.8. The Prophets of Zwickau — 171
- 23.9. The Lord's Table — 172
- 23.10. The Government of the Church — 173
- 23.11. Bound Will — 173
- 23.12. His Last Years — 173

24. Huldrych Zwingli 1484-1531 — 175
- 24.1. His Early Years — 175
- 24.2. Reformation in Zürich — 176
- 24.3. Political Climate — 177
- 24.4. Radical Tendencies — 178
  - a. The Lord's Supper — 178
  - b. Anabaptists — 178
- 24.5. Zwinglianism and Calvinism — 178

25. Martin Bucer 1491-1551 — 179
- 25.1. His Early Years — 179
- 25.2. Reformation — 179
- 25.3. Christian Unity — 180
- 25.4. In England — 181
- 25.5. The Communion of Saints — 182
- 25.6. Pastoral Care — 183
  - a. The civil authorities — 183
  - b. The congregation — 183
  - c. The office-bearers — 183

26. John Calvin 1509-1564 — 184
- 26.1. Initial Period — 184
- 26.2. Wandering Refugee — 184
- 26.3. First Period in Geneva — 185
- 26.4. Period in Strasbourg — 186
- 26.5. Second Period in Geneva — 186
- 26.6. Calvin's Theology — 187
  - a. The Honour of God — 187
  - b. The Third Use of the Law — 187
  - c. Presbyterian Church Government — 188
  - d. The Lord's Supper — 188
  - e. Aspiring Unity — 188
- 26.7. Calvin's Political Views — 188
- 26.8. The reception of Calvin's Thought — 189
  - a. Writings — 189
  - b. Correspondence — 189
  - c. The Spread of Calvinism — 189

27. The Radical Reformers — 190

27.1. The Kingdom	190
27.2. Kinds	190
27.3. Peasants' Revolts	190
27.4. The First Anabaptists	191
27.5. Violent Anabaptists	192
27.6. Mennonites	193
27.7. Reformers and Anabaptists	193
28. Reformation in France	**194**
28.1. The European Context	194
28.2. Forerunners	195
28.3. Spreading	195
28.4. Night of St. Bartholomew 1572	196
28.5. Edict of Nantes	196
28.6. Huguenots legalised 1802	197
29. Reformation in The Netherlands	**198**
29.1. Terms	198
29.2. Spanish 'Possession'	198
29.3. Preparation	199
29.4. Reformation	199
29.5. Liberation Struggle	200
29.6. Education	200
30. Reformation in England	**203**
30.1. Spirit of Independence	203
30.2. John Wycliffe	203
30.3. Henry VIII's Divorce Problems	203
30.4. Reformation and Counter Reformation	204
30.5. The Puritan Movement	204
30.6. Protectorate and Restoration	206
30.7. The Glorious Revolution	207
31. Reformation in Scotland	**208**
31.1. Antiquity and Middle Ages	208
31.2. Patrick Hamilton, the Martyr	208
31.3. The Death of George Wishart	209
31.4. John Knox in England	209
31.5. John Knox in Geneva	210
31.6. John Knox, Reformer of the Church of Scotland	210
31.7. Andrew Melville	211
31.8. Kirk versus King	211
32. The Counter Reformation	**213**
32.1. Terms	213
32.2. The Inquisition	214
32.3. Council of Trent	214
32.4. The Jesuits	215
Bibliography: Reformation	**217**
D. MODERN AGE 1650–2000	**233**
33. The Enlightenment	**234**
33.1. Renaissance and Humanism	234
33.2. Enlightenment	234
33.3. Influence on the Church	235
a. Orthodoxy	235
b. Pietism	235

33.4. Rationalism as Deism	235
33.5. Romanticism	237

34. Roman Catholicism 1648-1800 — 238
- 34.1. Nationalism — 238
- 34.2. Conquests — 238
- 34.3. Jesuits and other New Orders — 239
- 34.4. Jesuitism versus Mysticism and Quietism — 239
- 34.5. Gallicanism — 240
- 34.6. Jansenism — 241

35. Roman Catholicism 1800-1900 — 243
- 35.1. Revolutions — 243
  - a. The French Revolution of 1789 — 243
  - b. The Revolution of 1830 — 244
  - c. The Revolution of 1848 — 244
  - d. The Industrial Revolution — 244
- 35.2. Victories and Losses — 245
- 35.3. Birth of Anglo-Catholicism — 247

36. European Protestantism 1648–1800 — 249
- 36.1. Expansion outside Europe — 249
- 36.2. Enlightenment and Decay — 249
- 36.3. Pietist Reactions — 249
  - a. Streams — 249
  - b. Extremism — 250
  - c. Fruits of Puritanism — 250
- 36.4. German Pietismus — 251
  - a. Spener — 251
  - b. Francke — 251
  - c. Bengel — 252
  - d. Von Zinzendorf — 252
- 36.5. Evangelical and Methodist Revivals after 1700 — 253
  - a. Anglican Decay — 253
  - b. The Wesleys — 253
  - c. Whitefield — 254

37. European Protestantism 1800-1900 — 255
- 37.1. Effects of the Revivals — 255
- 37.2. Reform of Church and Society — 256
- 37.3. The Awakening of Mission — 256

38. North American Protestantism 1600-1900 — 259
- 38.1. Beginnings — 259
- 38.2. The Pilgrim Fathers — 259
- 38.3. Slavery and Mission — 260
- 38.4. Awakenings and Revivals — 260
- 38.5. War and Abolition — 261
- 38.6. Other Groups — 262
- 38.7. Finney and Hodge — 262

39. Theological Developments 1800-2000 — 263
- 39.1. Modernism in Theology — 263
- 39.2. Classical Liberalism — 263
  - a. Philosophies — 263
    - Immanuel Kant — 263
    - Friedrich Schleiermacher — 263
    - Georg Hegel — 264

Albrecht Ritschl	264
b. 'Higher' Criticism	264
c. The Roman Catholic Church	266
d. Decline	266
39.3. Neo-Orthodoxy	267
39.4. Radical Theologies and Revivals	268
39.5. Post-Modernism	269
40. Cooperation and Unity	270
40.1. The Reformed-Evangelical Movement	270
40.2. The Ecumenical Movement	271
a. Faith and Order (FO)	271
b. Life and Work (LW)	272
c. International Missionary Council (IMC)	273
d. World Council of Churches (WCC)	274
41. Church and Ideology	276
41.1. Left and Right	276
41.2. The Church under Communism	277
41.3. Western Opinion and Persecution	279
41.4. The Church and the Nazis	280
41.5. Church in Crisis	281
a. Secularisation	281
b. 'God is dead'	282
c. Extreme Israelism	282
d. Waves of church leavers	283
41.6. Revivalism and Evangelism	283
a. Pentecostalism and the Charismatic Movement	283
b. Reviving Reformed and Evangelical Churches	284
Bibliography: Modern Age	286

PART II — 290

THE FAITH MOVES SOUTH — 290

E. AFRICA IN GENERAL	291
42. Africa on the Eve of Change	292
42.1. Earliest Regions of Christianity in Africa	292
a. Egypt	292
b. North Africa	292
42.2. A New Era of Contact	294
42.3. The Situation of Traditional Religions	295
42.4. The Situation of Islam	296
a. Two Gateways	296
b. The Islamisation of Egypt	297
c. The Islamisation of North Africa	298
42.5. The Fullness of Time	299
42.6. The Situation in Sub-Saharan Africa	300
a. West Africa	300
b. East Africa	303
c. South-Central Africa	304
d. South Africa	305
43. *Nubian and Ethiopian Christianity*	307
43.1. Nubia excavated	307
a. Archaeological Findings	307

b. Monophysitism	307
c. Royal Power	308
d. Decline	309
43.2. Ethiopia	310
a. Ethiopia until 1100	310
b. The Zagwe Kings	311
c. Decline and Survival	313
d. Jesuit Attempt Fails	314
e. Conflicts and Disintegration	314
f. The First Protestant Missionaries in Ethiopia	316
g. Another Roman Catholic Attempt Fails	317
h. New Protestant Missions	317
i. Ethiopia Maintains its Independence	318
44. Africa and Early Portuguese Missions	**321**
44.1. Henry the Navigator	321
44.2. Islands and the West Coast	322
44.3. The Congo	323
44.4. Angola	325
44.5. Southern and Eastern Africa	326
45. Africa and the Dutch until 1800	**329**
45.1. Gold Coast, the Congo, Angola	329
45.2. Boers and Khoikhoi	331
45.3. Nguni and Tswana	332
45.4. Planting of the Dutch Reformed Church	333
45.5. Early Mission Work	333
46. Africa and the British until 1885	**336**
46.1. The Empire extends to Africa	336
a. Competition	336
b. Triangular Trade	336
c. Southern Africa	337
46.2. Effects of the Great Awakening	337
a. Rediscovery of the Centrality of Christ	337
b. Missionary Movement	338
c. Anti-Slavery Movement	339
d. The Classical Missions	340
47. Western Africa 1800-1900	**341**
47.1. Sierra Leone	341
47.2. The Niger Mission	342
47.3. Liberia	345
47.4. Ghana, Cameroon, Senegal, Gabon, Zaire	346
a. Ghana and Cameroon	346
b. Senegal, Gabon and Zaire	346
47.5. Angola	347
a. Comparative Roman Catholic Weakness	347
b. Opportunities for Protestant Mission	348
48. Southern Africa 1800-1900	**351**
48.1. The Dutch-Speaking Settlers	351
48.2. The English-speaking Missions	353
48.3. Andrew Murray	356
a. Scottish-Dutch descent	356
b. Missionary Strategist	356
c. Writings	358

  d. Theological Significance   358
 48.4. Johannes van der Kemp   359
  a. With the London Missionary Society   359
  b. Work among Khoikhoi, San and Xhosa   359

49. Eastern Africa 1800-1900   361
 49.1. Swahili-Arab rule   361
 49.2. Rebmann and Krapf   361
 49.3. Kenya   363
 49.4. Tanzania   365
 49.5. Uganda   366
 49.6. Mozambique   367
 49.7. Madagascar   368
  a. First Roman Catholic Attempts   368
  b. Start of Protestant Mission   369
  c. Persecution   369
  d. Freedom Restored   370
  e. French Colony   371
  f. Independence   371

50. Africa's Old Colonisers after 1885   373
 50.1. The Scramble   373
 50.2. The British   374
  a. Egypt and the Sudan   374
  b. South Africa   375
  c. Sierra Leone   376
  d. Ghana   376
  e. Nigeria   376
  f. East Africa   376
  g. Decolonisation   377
 50.3. The Portuguese   378
  a. Extension   378
  b. Lusitanianism   378
  c. Between Concordat and World Council of Churches   379
  d. Wars and Independence   379

51. Africa's New Colonisers after 1885   381
 51.1. The Belgians   381
  a. Congo Free State   381
  b. Congo Colony   383
  c. Independence   383
 51.2. The French   384
  a. Before Berlin 1885   384
  b. From Berlin 1885   384
  c. Decolonisation   385
 51.3. The Germans   385
  a. The German Scramble   385
  b. The Cameroons and Togo   386
  c. German East Africa   387
  d. South-West Africa   387
  e. Defeat   387

52. Missions and Colonialism 1885-1960   389
 52.1. Protestant and Roman Catholic Missions   389
 52.2. Competing Missionary Movements   391
 52.3. Accusations   393

- 52.4. Neither Soulmates nor Antagonists — 394
- 52.5. The 'Heyday of Missions' 1885-1918 — 395
  - a. Growth — 395
  - b. Cooperation — 396
  - c. Aggressiveness — 397
- 52.6. Strained Partnership 1918-1945 — 398
- 52.7. Final Period 1945-1960 — 399

53. African Instituted Churches — 401
- 53.1. Two Traditions — 401
- 53.2. Early African Initiatives — 402
- 53.3. The Rise of Ethiopianism 1890-1910 — 403
- 53.4. The Rise of Prophet-Healing Churches — 405
- 53.5. The East Africa Revival — 409
- 53.6. The Golden Age of Independency — 410
- 53.7. Continuing Independency after 1960 — 411

54. Church and Mission in Independent Africa — 413
- 54.1. The Joy and the Pain of Change — 413
- 54.2. Churches Responding to Independence — 414
- 54.3. Theology Responding to Independence — 416
  - a. African Theology — 416
  - b. Liberation Theology — 417
  - c. Evangelical and Reformed Theology — 418
  - d. Other Theologies — 420
- 54.4. Africa and Mainstream Theologies — 420

55. Faith Missions — 421
- 55.1. Pre-Classical Missions — 421
- 55.2. Classical Missions — 421
- 55.3. Revival Ferment — 421
  - a. Brethren Movement — 422
  - b. Prophetic Movement — 422
  - c. Holiness Movement — 423
- 55.4. Faith Missions — 423
- 55.5. Special Characteristics of Faith Missions — 424
- 55.6. Faith Missions in Africa — 427
  - a. Livingstone Inland Mission — 427
  - b. Africa Inland Mission — 427
  - c. Sudan Missions — 428

56. Unity and Cooperation — 431
- 56.1. What is Unity? — 431
  - a. Diversity and Truth — 431
  - b. Analogy Qualified by Scripture — 432
  - c. Restoration through Salvation by Christ — 432
- 56.2. Syncretism — 433
- 56.3. Examples in Malawi — 434
- 56.4. Ecumenism and Christian Cooperation — 435
- 56.5. The Situation in Africa — 437

Bibliography: Africa — 440

F. SOUTH-CENTRAL AFRICA — 449

57. The Church in Malawi — 450
- 57.1. David Livingstone — 450
- 57.2. Classical Missions — 451

- a. Universities' Mission to Central Africa — 451
- b. Livingstonia Mission — 452
- c. Blantyre Mission — 456
- d. Dutch Reformed Church Mission — 458
- e. Church of Central Africa Presbyterian — 459
- f. The Roman Catholic Mission — 460
- 57.3. Post-Classical Missions — 463
  - a. Joseph Booth and the Industrial Missions — 463
  - b. Africa Evangelical Church of Malawi — 465
  - c. Providence Industrial Mission — 465
- 57.4. From Mission to Church — 466
  - a. Forms of Cooperation — 466
  - b. Matchona churches — 467
- 57.5. Independent Malawi — 468
  - a. Church and State — 468
  - b. New Missions after the 'End of Missions' — 470
  - c. Revival — 471
  - d. Women's Organisations — 471

58. The Church in Zambia — 473
- 58.1. East Zambia — 473
- 58.2. South Zambia — 473
- 58.3. The Copperbelt — 474
- 58.4. Unity and Dissent — 475
- 58.5. Reformed and Presbyterian Churches — 476
- 58.6. Independent Zambia — 477

59. The Church in Zimbabwe — 480
- 59.1. Jesuit and Dominican Attempts — 480
- 59.2. Mission before 1890 — 481
- 59.3. The Era of Colonialism — 482
- 59.4. The Reformed Church of Zimbabwe — 483
- 59.5. The CCAP in Zimbabwe — 483
- 59.6. Independence — 484

60. Pentecostals and Charismatics — 486
- 60.1. Five Streams — 486
- 60.2. Beginnings of Pentecostalism — 486
- 60.3. Pentecostal Churches in Malawi — 488
- 60.4. Features of the Charismatic Movement — 490
- 60.5. The Charismatic Movement in Malawi — 492
- 60.6. Politics — 493

61. The Position of Africa's Women — 495
- 61.1. Biblical Pattern — 495
  - a. Together with Man — 495
  - b. Equal to Man — 496
  - c. Different from Man — 496
- 61.2. Cultural Patterns — 496
  - a. Philosophy — 496
  - b. Western Culture — 497
  - c. African and Islamic Cultures — 499
  - d. Christ is more than Culture — 500
- 61.3. Christian Women Today — 501
  - a. Situation before Independence — 501
  - b. Present situation — 502

    61.4. The Way Forward   505
62. Conversion   507
    62.1. Conversion in Context   507
    62.2. God and the African Past   508
    62.3. New Perspectives on an Encounter   508
        a. Adaptation   509
        b. Functions in Society   510
        c. Mediators of Modernity   510
        d. Position towards the State   510
        e. Agents of Cultural and Social Change?   510
    62.4. African Conversion   511
    62.5. The Character of the 'Continuum'   512
    62.6. Lessons from History   513
Bibliography: South Central-Africa   515
63. Europe and Africa in the Post-Modern Age   522
    63.1. Minority and Majority positions   522
        a. Shift of appearances   522
        b. Post-Christian culture   522
    63.2. The Faith Moves North   523
        a. The Blessed Reflex   523
        b. Racist tensions   525
        c. Christian Zionism and Antisemitism   526
        d. Enlightenment suspicions   528
    63.3. European Christians and Africa   528
        a. Hospitality   528
        b. Muslim Mission   528
        c. Harmful influences   529
        d. Conditions   529
        e. Education   529
        f. Church and Mission   530
        g. Church and Diaconia   530
    63.4. The Militant Church   530
O God, our help in ages past   532
Register   533

Preface

Nothing has bound Africa and Europe more together than the history of Christianity. From Paradise onwards the Church has been the communion of believers. As the Body of Jesus Christ she started in Jerusalem. Through the proclamation of the Gospel the Church reached soon parts of Africa and the Atlantic Coast, from where – after the Middle Ages and particularly in the 19th and 20th centuries – she took deep root in Sub-Saharan Africa. Today, in post-modern times African Christianity is being challenged to re-plant the Church in secularized Europe.

This textbook for learners and teachers of the History of the Church focuses on the West and the South, on Europe and Africa, the continents whose histories have been increasingly intertwined since Antiquity. Since the 1960s the classical dependence of the South on the North has changed dramatically. Kalu, when stressing the growing importance of African Church History, refers to the Afro-American Liberian missionary and statesman Edward Wilmot Blyden (†1912), who 'foresaw the coming shift in the centre of gravity of Christianity from the north to the south Atlantic, and its import for African Christianity'.[1] I would add that the future of European Christianity largely depends on a much-needed shift to mission-mindedness in the African churches.

The present book is based on two textbooks[2] that I composed before 2007 for theology students in an African context. They have been widely used at various institutions for theological and pastoral training, particularly in Malawi. Their titles are used for the two parts in the present work, *From Galilee to the Atlantic*, and *The Faith Moves South*. The idea was born when I taught at Zomba Theological College, an institute for the training of ministers of the Word of God in South-Central Africa, mainly in Malawi. I arranged the text in such a way that it may be profitable for students at tertiary institutions of theological education. The prescribed curricula of theological colleges in Central Africa were taken into account. However, I trust that the book will also serve students in a wider region within or outside Africa. It is meant as an introduction to the study of the field of Church History from the New Testament era to the end of the 20th century, especially targeting Western Europe and Southern Africa. I am confident it is a tool for (future) pastors who are called to proclaim the wonderful acts of God, who in Jesus Christ, through the Word and the Holy Spirit, planted His Church, and continues to look after it. Moreover, I trust that any individual having an interest in the History of the Church will find the book useful.

Writing a textbook is not possible without using the work of others, which I have profusely done, as can be seen in the footnotes. Bibliographies and footnotes contain literature for further study. In the bibliographies, I have consciously mentioned English titles only, except for a few titles in Chichewa, as this book was originally written for students in South-Central Africa. The illustrations I mainly collected from various free sites at the Internet. Specific sources were only mentioned when apart from the website address more details were given and when copyright-regulations were referred to. If

---

[1] Kalu, 'Ethiopianism', in: Kalu, O.U. (ed.), *African Christianity: An African Story*, University of Pretoria, 2005, p.272.

[2] Steven Paas, *From Galilee to the Atlantic: A History of the Church in the West*, Zomba: Kachere 2006 [first 2004] and *The Faith Moves South: A History of the Church in Africa*, Zomba: Kachere, 2006.

unintentionally some pictures have not been duly accounted for, please accept my apologies.

Remarks and questions from students throughout the years have helped me to improve the text. Zikomo kwambiri abale![3]

I am especially indebted to Mr. Andrew Goodson, Head of Classics at *Kamuzu Academy*, in Mtunthama, Malawi. He contributed greatly to the weeding out of writing errors and style mistakes while his critical questions and remarks enabled me to improve the logical flow and content of the text.

I gratefully cite Rev. Mark Thiesen (MA), formerly Director of *Namikango Mission* in Thondwe, Malawi, now Church of Christ pastor in the USA. He carefully checked most of the text and he made various suggestions for correction and clarification.

Rev. Dr. Willie Zeze, Presbyterian minister of the Malawian CCAP, now teaching at *Mukhanyo Theological Seminary* in South Africa assisted by proofreading some chapters and he suggested important additions to chapter 1, on historiography, which I gratefully incorporated.

Rev. Willem-Henri, den Hartog, Director of the Distance Department of the *Namibia Evangelical Theological Seminary* obliged me with some valuable corrections and additions.

For part II, on Africa, I owe particular gratitude to Prof. Dr. Klaus Fiedler, of the *University of Malawi* (now of *Mzuzu University*), who is an experienced teacher of Church History and Missiology, specialised in Africa. He helped by advising, proof reading, and making corrections and improvements, showing his hand especially in sections of chapters 51, 55, 57, and 60.

Dr. Harvey Kwiyani – the Executive Director of *Missio Africanus*, a Journal of African Missiology – contributed meaningfully to the concluding part of the book. I also thank Dr. Gideon van der Watt of *Christian Literature Fund*, the Publisher of this book, for weeding out writing errors and punctuation mistakes.

At early stages of the composition of this work the following persons, mentioned in alphabetical order, read parts of the text, made corrections and gave valuable advice: Ms Elizabeth Ritchie (MA), Rev. David Kawanga (MA), Mr. Frackson Ntawanga, Mr. Arie van der Poel (MA).

Despite these important contributions, of course, the responsibility for the contents and the language of this book is mine.

My brother Wim Paas made the layout of the book and assisted in finding useful illustrations and inserting them properly into the text.

My wife Rita has played an important role. In many aspects she has facilitated my functioning. I owe her much for her love, loyalty and practical wisdom.

We praise God who in Christ, through the Word and the Spirit, is known to us as our dear heavenly Father. In Jesus Christ He revealed Himself by entering human history as the Son of Man, the Alpha and the Omega. His Name be glorified in the lives of the readers of this book.

Steven Paas

Veenendaal 2016

---

[3] Chichewa for: Thank you very much brethren!

1. Characteristics of Church History

1.1. Defining Church History

This book is an introduction to the study of Church History. It is particularly focused on Western Europe and Africa, but the birth site of the Church in the Holy Land and its early extension to other parts of the Near East and later to America[1] have certainly not been left out of sight. Students who are entirely new to the field of Church History may feel like strangers in a foreign land. They need an introduction to the introduction. Therefore, the first chapter provides some preliminary notes and remarks, which will hopefully facilitate a first encounter with the subject.

Definitions of Church History differ greatly, depending on the writer's view of Theology, of the Church and of History. At the outset we should take note that the compound term Church History suggests that the Church unquestionably has a story. Let us look at how some writers have defined the term.

H.M. Gwatkin defines Church History as the 'spiritual side of the history of civilized people ever since the Master's coming.'[2] One would wonder how the word 'civilized people' could be a synonym of the Christian community, because those parts of the world that have become known as civilized often have not behaved in a Christian manner. Therefore, a more neutral definition should be preferred, for example describing Church History as the story of the wider Christian community and its relationship to the rest of the world throughout the ages.

Eusebius of Caesarea (c.260-c.340) is called the 'Father of Church History', because of his Ecclesiastical History, which is seen as 'the principal source for the history of Christianity from the Apostolic Age to his own day'.

For A.M. Renwick and A.M. Herman Church History is 'an account of a success and failure of the Church in carrying out Christ's great commission to go into all the world and preach the gospel to every creature and teach all nations.'[3] The use of the word 'account' intelligibly indicates that Church History is both a process and a product of past events, both in and with regard to the Church.

Earle E. Cairns suggests that Church History is 'the interpreted and organised story of the redemption of mankind and the earth.'[4] In this definition, Church History comprises interpreted historical data of the origin, process and impact of Christian faith on society, based on organised information gathered by scientific method from

---

[1] For example: the Middle East, Eastern Europe, America.
[2] H.M. Gwatkin, *Early Church History to A.D. 313,* London: Macmillan, vol.1, p.4.
[3] A. M. Renwick and A.M. Herman, *The Story of the Church*, Leicester: Intervarsity Press, 1997. p.7,8; cf. Mk.16:15; Mt.18:19.
[4] Cairns, E.E., *Christianity through the Ages: A History of the Christian Church*, Grand Rapids: Zondervan, 1996, p.17,18.

archeological, documentary, or living sources. Given this, studying Church History is much more than an analysis of past data, because it is connected to the story of salvation of people through the blood of Jesus Christ.

Philipp Schaff considers Church History in an academic sense, as a theological discipline, a faithful and lifelike description of the origin and progress of the heavenly kingdom, aiming to reproduce in thought and to embody in language its outward and inward development down to the present time. On the one hand, Church History shows how Christianity spreads over the world and how it penetrates, transforms, and sanctifies the individual, communities and societies. On the other hand, it records the deeds of the heroes of faith as well as the acts of agents of the devil against the Kingdom of God. Considering these descriptions, we suggest the following definition.

> Church History is a comprehensive description of the past progress of the Church of God, through Jesus Christ in the midst of this world, by the power of the Word and of the Spirit.

Some readers might question the word *progress* in this definition. Perhaps they would prefer the word *development*. We have not chosen *development*, because we want to evade its *evolutionary connotations*. In our view, the Church of the 21st century is not more advanced in quality than the Church of Antiquity. The term progress seems more fitting, because it denotes deployment, expansion or extension, which does not necessarily include qualitative evolutionary progress. Our definition implies that Church History belongs to *Secular History* in general (a), and also that it belongs to *Theology* (b). Let us look at these two aspects.

a. Church History Belongs to Secular History

Whether history in general should be defined as Secular History is debatable. It cannot be doubted, however, that history in general is intertwined with Church History or the other way round. But first we should address this question: What is History? We follow Elliot, who distinguishes three elements: (1) historical events themselves, (2) communication of historical events, and (3) historiography.

Historical Events

These are significant events that happened at certain dates in connection with certain persons. Some events have meaning in themselves; other events need to be highlighted and explained for their full meaning to be understood. Among historians, the choices of events and opinions on their effects can be very different.

> Which events are significant? Those that influenced, or are influencing people? Those that are recorded and communicated most? Those that produced, have produced or are producing ideas?[5]

Christians are right in saying that History in some way or another reflects God's Providence, i.e. God's acts in the world. But how does God act in the History of the world? Does He act in History only through His Church, or also through other agents? Does God follow or lead events? Is History worked out by Him from a *starting point* in the past, as most historians have assumed? Or is it the reflection of an *aim* in the future?

---

[5] Cf. M.W.Elliot, 'The Meaning of History', an address at Schloss Mittersil, August 1997.

Some Church historians such as J. MacIntyre believe that there is in History a *telos* (or purpose) which is being worked out and which is a projection in time of the *eschaton* (the last days), which stands at the end or at the edge of time.[6]

The Communication of Events

This is the written or oral account of events. Its quantity and quality depend on the geographical and chronological place of the teller or describer, and on his or her scholarly abilities. Accounts of events also depend on the researcher's philosophical and religious assumptions and concepts. For example, among scholars there are different expectations as to the end of History. Will all events end by a man-made disaster or by divine interference, or is there no end to history?

Meaningful communication of historical accounts ends when historians are unable to see patterns, an intelligible order. This can happen when researchers are lacking information, because they are too far from events and primary sources. It can also happen, though, when they have too much information, because they are too close to the events. Some researchers are so biased by pre-determined conclusions or outlook that they can relate events only from a skewed perspective and not see other interpretations.

Terms Used in Historiography

Historiography is critical reflection on the way historical events have been studied and communicated throughout history. Elliot describes two extreme views in historiography: historismus and historicism.

What Elliot calls *Historismus* is the belief that history is essential for understanding human beings and developments within cultures. *Historicism* is the idea that the only meaning we can get from history is what we already think. Historiography has shown the important difference between circular and linear views of history. History writers in Antiquity generally considered the cohesion of events as a circular pattern, in which history is more or less repeated. From Augustine onwards there has been an awareness of continuation from one set of events to another as a linear movement. Historiography also accounts for the many attempts that have been made to divide history into periods.

> Here are some examples: (a) the Kingdoms prophesied by Daniel; (b) six periods of 1000 years; (c) three periods of successively: God the Father, God the Son, God the Holy Spirit of the Law; (d) division according to the centuries; (e) Antiquity (before 500 AD); Middle Ages (Early-/ High-/ Late-, 500-1500 AD); Modern Times (after 1500); (f) division into a period of allegedly uncritical history writing, and the Enlightenment (17th and 18th century) as the beginning of the era of supposedly critical history writing.

Depending on their varying views as to events, communication of events, and historiography, historians have come to very different conceptions of history. We would suggest the following definition:

> History is a comprehensive survey of past events and movements in the divinely created reality of nature and humanity, a survey which within the framework of God's providence has significance for our understanding of the past and of the present, and that guides us when thinking about the future.

Let us have a closer look at this tentative definition of the subject of history and assess how its readers can benefit from it.

---

[6] J. MacIntyre, *Christian Doctrine of History*, Oliver & Boyd, Edinburgh, 1957, pp.88,89.

History is a comprehensive survey. This means that the science of history aims at giving an intelligible story of events, dealing with as many aspects as possible, written, oral, pictorial, image, and even musical.

History concerns previous facts and movements. Historians study the events and movements of the past that we are able to know and to assess from the various sources of history. They keep in mind that these sources are varied and also limited. This also applies to the historian's ability to research them.

History is about the facts of divinely created nature and humanity. Historical facts derive their significance from God's creation of heaven and earth.

History presupposes God's providence. Although often not seen or not acknowledged by man, history happens within the framework of God's plan.

History aims at understanding the past. Students of history have to realise that the past has its own right, and that it has to be understood as being detached from the present.

History leads to understanding the present. When understood in its own right the past makes the present situation more transparent. Knowledge of the present is inseparably interwoven with comprehension of the past.

History facilitates thinking about the future. Without an understanding of past and present, man is blind with regard to the future.

Secular History cannot deny its dependence on the Bible, nor can it deny its connection with Church History. The account of God's revelation in the Holy Scriptures and in nature is the pilot history. There would have been no history without it. All history is rooted in it.

From a Christian perspective, Church History sheds light on other branches of the history of humanity and nature. The significance and place of Secular History in its varied aspects become clearer in the light of Church History. This helps to realise that 'the Church is the cork on which the world floats'. Church History also profits from Secular History. Knowledge of aspects of Secular History is indispensable when describing the history of the Church. In the conception of a Christian Secular History and Church History, both serve the honour of God and His Kingdom. This is not to deny the principal difference between Secular History and Church History.

The Church is a plantation by God in the midst of the world of Secular History. It is the most important reminder of the presence and of the advent of the Kingdom of God. As such, the Church is unique, and so is its history. Secular History, rightly understood, also acknowledges God, but it reflects the Kingdom of God in a less comprehensive and in a more indirect way. In the last analysis Secular History and its many branches and sub-branches, such as political history, cultural history, economic history, history of science, natural history, history of literature and even history of Christianity, have to be distinguished from Church History.

Secular History does not belong to the field of Theology, whereas Church History does. This 'dual home' of Church History is not an unhappy incident; it is of great theological significance. It runs parallel to the greatest fact of salvation: Christ's incarnation made Him to be fully man and fully God. Man's salvation hinges on this duality. The history of God's Church is fully divine and fully human. Only in that way can it reflect the work of Triune God in history.

b. Church History Belongs to Theology

The Church is God's plantation in this world. It is the product of His revelation through the Word. Theology is the Church's scholarly approach of God's revelation. The main emphasis is on the Church. Church History being part of Theology aims at describing the history of the Church, not the *history of Christianity,* which aims at describing Christian culture, and as such belongs to Secular History. Although Church History and the history of Christianity are related, they differ fundamentally. Christian culture and the Christian Church are not identical; sometimes they even oppose one another. Students should notice the tendency among many writers to underestimate the Church in favour of *Christianity.*

The term Church itself does not appear in Scripture. But the words from which the English 'Church', Scottish 'Kirk' and French 'Église' derive, *kuriakè* (Greek: of the Lord) and *ekklesia* (Greek: *ek-kalein* = to call out), show that it designates the congregation of the people of God, as it has existed since creation in its various modes of existence, militant, triumphant, visible, invisible.

The Church has existed since Paradise. As God's revelation continued to fulfilment in Jesus Christ, there developed a difference in appearance between the Church of the Old Testament and the Church of the New Testament. Since Pentecost, in the *Apostles' Creed*, the Church has come to understand itself as the 'one, holy, catholic, Christian Church, the communion of saints'. This understanding of the Church has been the criterion of Christian faith, and the foundation of theological study.

The Church is one. This refers to the unity of the Church, spiritual unity in the first place, not necessarily unity in a geographical, organisational, visible sense. Disunity is caused by sin and error. The Church can be torn by disunity, although it appears as a geographical, organisational and visible unity.

The Church is holy. It is set apart; it does not belong to the world, although it is *in* it. It is not man's creation, but it is God's plantation through the Word and the Spirit. The Church is the most important sign of the existence and of the approaching of the Kingdom of God.

The Church is catholic. This means that the Church is common to all or universal.[7] As representations of the universal Church, every local church in principle has all characteristics of the Church. This rejects every claim of limitation of the Church to a specific geographical area or to a certain ethnic group of people.

The Church is Christian. Christ is the King of the Church. He is the Head and also the Body of the Church. There is no Church without Him being the beginning, the end, the foundation, the top, the inside, and the outside of it.

The Church is the communion of saints. The Church is a fellowship, a brotherhood of saved sinners, an unbreakable bond between men and women, rooted in fundamental relationship with God, that is to say in God's covenantal promises through Christ.

The scholarly study of God's revealed relationship with His creation and with His people comprises the various branches of Theology, including the study of Church History. Like all Theology, Church History is connected to the Bible in a special way. The Bible contains history. God has revealed Himself in two ways, in a particular sense by using history as recorded in the Holy Scriptures, and in a general sense in nature. The

---

[7] '*catholic*' contains the Greek word *holos*: whole.

Bible contains the history of the revelation of God's plan with world and humanity, the *historia sacra Divinae revelationis*. This includes the history of salvation. Church History overlaps with salvation history, is rooted in it, and continues describing it in the post-Biblical era. At the same time, Church History and salvation history are different.

The Bible is inspired by the Holy Spirit, and is therefore holy, infallible (trustworthy), authoritative, the highest rule for life and faith. This does not apply to Church History, nor does it apply to any history described by man. Written and oral accounts of Secular History and Church History can even oppose God's revelation. At best, they are guided by the Scriptures and enlightened by the Holy Spirit. This is also true for studies in any other field of Theology.

All other branches of Theology have historical aspects, although they remain distinguished from Church History.[8] However, the fact that all branches of Theology are embedded in history should not be confused with the position of the subject of Church History itself, which specifically deals with the history of the Church in all its aspects. The scholarly subject of Church History can be broken up into various fields and sub-fields. Some examples of the branches of Church History are:

> the histories of Dogma, Ecclesiology, Old Testament research, New Testament research, Biblical archaeology, Mission, Preaching, Historiography (the history of writing Church History), Church art (e.g. iconography, painting, sculpture, architecture), State-Church relationships, Denominations, Awakenings, Schisms, Church music, Church leaders, Church Fathers, Popes, Monasticism, Reformers, common church members.

1.2. African Church History

a. Southern Christianity

In terms of *Historiography* I have consciously tried to avoid bias and to honour *African Church History* in its own right. I am inclined to follow Verstraelen, who uses the term *Southern Christianity* for a great variety of churches and Christian cultures that came into being east and south of the *Roman Empire*. In the title of Part II of this book, *The Faith Moves South*, I have expressed this sentiment. Verstraelen stresses that 'Christianity was not an exclusive phenomenon in the *Roman Empire* in the North, but struck roots in different socio-cultural contexts in the Southern Hemisphere'. He pleads for 'new modes of rethinking and rewriting Christian History' by telling the full story of this non-Roman and non-Greek Christianity, 'and making it part of Christian history as a whole'.[9] Extending this thought, other historians derive from the flourishing

---

[8] The other main branches of Theology include: the Bible itself (Old Testament and New Testament), Biblical Languages, Dogmatics (Systematic Theology), Ecclesiology (knowledge of the organisational structures and offices of the Church), Missiology, Exegetics, Hermeneutics, Homiletics, Pastoral Theology.

[9] F.J. Verstraelen, 'Southern Perspectives on Christian History', in: *Neue Zeitschrift für Missionswissenschaft*, 53-1997/2, pp.100,101; F.J. Verstraelen, 'The Teaching of Christian History and Ministerial Formation Today', in: *Association of Theological Institutions in Southern and Central Africa* (ATISCA), Bulletin 2, 1993, pp.3-25. Verstraelen developed the ideas of his deceased wife, published in: Gerdien Verstraelen-Gilhuis, *From Dutch Mission Church to Reformed Church in Zambia: The Scope for African Leadership and Initiative in the History of a Zambian Mission Church*, Franeker: Wever, 1982, pp.13-21: 'Recovering the African Perspective of Mission History', and 'Written and Oral Sources'; Gerdien Verstraelen-Gilhuis, *A New Look at Christianity in Africa*, Gweru: Mambo Press, 1992, pp.77-98: 'Rewriting the History of Christianity in Africa'.

Christianity of today's Africa the idea that the epicentre of Christianity has critically 'shifted from the North to the South'.[10]

b. Received from the Outside

An important consequence of this observation is that African Christianity should not be considered as an appendix or an extension of Western Christianity. It is rightly stressed that 'Christianity was a non-Western religion in the first place'. For that matter, it is a non-Southern religion too. However, some historians have developed their ideas to the opposite extreme, suggesting that the beginnings of Christianity are in Africa, geographically and religiously. They have come to adhere to a completely 'new historiography' in which African Christianity is presented as 'an extension of African primal religion'. This approach is not helpful, because, as Kalu admits, it is 'based on many unarticulated assumptions'.[11] It distorts the picture of the course in history that Christianity took. But there is nothing wrong in emphasising that the Gospel of the joyful events of salvation went from Jerusalem either directly to the North and the North East of Africa, or much later, indirectly to sub-Saharan Africa through the churches in the West. After all, Christians, anywhere in the world, have received the Gospel from the 'outside'. The Church is rooted in a message that is imparted from the outside, spiritually, and for most of the Church geographically as well.

There is need to remember that the Christian Church did not start in Africa or the West, but in Jerusalem, and its foundation is located even outside history, it is not possessed by any world view, however primal it may be. Through Christ God has shown his love for the world, so that people of all nations, world views and religions may realise the superiority and the uniqueness of the Gospel of salvation, join together in His Church, and be saved, now in principle, and presently, after the *Parousia*, in perfection. This – in my view – is the perspective for the Historiography of Church History.

Given this, I need not apologise that this book is shaped in a European mind that is groomed by classical Biblical beliefs as re-iterated in the 16th-century Reformation and in the ensuing reformed and evangelical awakenings in the 18th and 19th centuries. My starting point is that Church History is not only part of Secular History, but that it is also an aspect of Theology, and that in both cases, from the perspective of divine Revelation in the Holy Scriptures, it shows the deployment or progress of the Church as herald of the ever approaching Kingdom of God. Elsewhere I have explained this view in more detail.[12]

c. Textbooks

African Church History is part of the discipline of Church History in general. Therefore, at the same time, it is a branch of Theology. To its descriptions belong the older works

---

[10] Chukwudi A. Njoku, 'The Missionary Factor in African Christianity 1884-1914', in: Kalu (ed.), *African Christianity: An African Story*, p.220. He refers to David B. Barrett, 'AD 2000: 350 million Christians in Africa', in: *International Review of Mission*, 59 (1970), pp.39-54, and to: Kwame Bediako, *Jesus in Africa: The Christian Gospel in African History and Experience*, Akropong-Akuapem: Regnum Africa, 2000, pp.3,4.

[11] Ogbu U. Kalu, 'Ethiopianism in African Christianity', in: Kalu (ed.), *African Christianity*, p.259.

[12] Steven Paas, *Digging out the Ancestral Church: Researching and Communicating Church History*, Zomba: Kachere, 2006³, pp.11-22.

by Latourette[13] and Groves,[14] written in the period 1935-1960. They are still valuable secondary sources, but as pre-independence literature, they are limited in that they perceive *African Church History* largely from a European or American angle. They were important sources for Hildebrandt, who first published his concise survey of the history of the Church in Africa in 1981.[15] Hildebrandt tries not to neglect the African contribution to Mission. He is apparently sympathetic to the object of his survey, the Church. His main focus is the loyalty of the Church to Jesus Christ as reflected by classical Christian teaching. Didactically his book remains a helpful tool for beginners, because of its brevity, its clarity and its well defined Biblical position.

Recent textbooks have increasingly tried to consider *African Church History* in its own right. Six volumes have drawn special attention, Kalu (2005), Sundkler and Steed (2000), Shaw (1996), Isichei (1995), Baur (1994), and Hastings (1994). Some of them, Sundkler and Hastings followed at some distance by Baur, are fat handbooks constituting rich sources for finding details on practically all missions and churches. They try to be neutral from a scholarly point of view, although they cannot always hide their respective Protestant (Sundkler) and Roman Catholic (Hastings, Baur) preferences. Shaw and Isichei are not lacking interesting details, but they are smaller and concentrate more on the general lines of African Church History. Shaw looks from an Evangelical angle and operates from the interesting idea that *African Church History* can be grasped by kingdom concepts. Kalu's book takes a special position. He serves as the editor. Except for his own contributions, the book consists of valuable studies by 18 other writers, almost all of them Africans.[16]

d. Ideological bias

Kalu explicitly defends a way of writing Church History that excludes histories written from an institutional or denominational angle, or written by 'missionaries and their protégés'. Probably that is why he only mentions Shaw's book once, in a rather depreciatory manner, and even does not include the title in his bibliography of 32 pages.[17] Hildebrandt's book stands perhaps even lower in Kalu's hierarchy, because it is not mentioned at all! Kalu thinks it is possible for a church historian to eliminate in his mind the images of the Church going 'beyond the Biblical images' in the myriad denominations and the 'unique claims of Christianity'. He also claims that this position

---

[13] Kenneth Scott Latourette, *A History of the Expansion of Christianity*, 7 volumes, Exeter: Paternoster/ Grand Rapids: Zondervan, New York: Harper and Row, 1971 [first 1935-1946; on Africa parts of all volumes, except 4]; Kenneth Scott Latourette, *Christianity in a Revolutionary Age*, 5 volumes, Exeter: Paternoster/ Grand Rapids: Zondervan/ New York: Harper and Row, 1970 [first 1955-1965; on Africa: parts of volumes 3 and 5].

[14] Charles P. Groves, *The Planting of Christianity in Africa*, 4 volumes, London: Lutterworth, 1948-1964 [vol. I: before 1840, vol.II: 1840-1878, vol III: 1878-1914, vol. IV: 1914-1954].

[15] J.Hildebrandt, *History of the Church in Africa, A Survey*, Achimota (Ghana): African Christian Press, 1990 (first 1981].

[16] Ogbu U. Kalu (ed.), *African Christianity: An African Story*, Pretoria: University of Pretoria, 2005; Bengt G.M. Sundkler and C. Steed, *A History of the Church in Africa*, Cambridge: Cambridge UP, 2000; Mark R.Shaw, *The Kingdom of God in Africa: A Short History of African Christianity*, Grand Rapids: Baker,1996; E. Isichei, *A History of Christianity in Africa: From Antiquity to the Present*, London: SPCK, 1995; J. Baur, *2000 Years of Christianity in Africa: An African History 62-1992*, Nairobi: Paulines, 1994; A. Hastings, *The Church in Africa: 1450-1950*, Oxford: Clarendon, 1994.

[17] Ogbu U. Kalu, *African Christianity*, Preface, p.xi: 'Shaw's [book] is rather marred by the extreme application of the kingdom motif, but the maps are very helpful'.

makes it possible for him to write a history of the Church that is genuinely 'ecumenical', showing the 'unique Christian perception of reality'. In Kalu's idea of ecumenicity not only individual church traditions are excluded; he also seems to exclude the outward-derived and uniquely imparted character of the Christian faith, by suggesting that there is 'continuity' between the traditional non-Christian religions of Africa ('primal religions') and African Christianity. According to him, this idea of continuity does not pose the danger of opening the door to *syncretism*. Yet it is not clear how Kalu can evade this danger when he wants Christians to 'engage the interior of the non-Christian worldview and reclaim it from Christ', which to him is 'not merely breaking with the past'.[18]

Kalu says that he is 'ideologically-driven' to 'tell the story as an African story'. Of course, in the descriptions from European and American angles we are dealing partly with African history. But accepting and honouring this reality does not need the help of an ideology. The conclusion about the character of African Church History must be the result of scholarly deliberation, by both Africans and non-Africans, without limiting the study to any particular group. People who forget this are failing to heed Ki-Zerbo's warning that historians should go for historical truth in a scholarly way in order 'to be sure of not exchanging one myth for another'.[19] Kalu seems to take a new position on the line of 'Africo-liberal ecumenism' (cf. chapter 54.3.a), which finds it difficult to admit to its own disposition to bias. While I appreciate the important issue Kalu is raising, I do not think that Scripture requires church historians to erase denominations and to accept that 'African Christianity is essentially rooted in primal religion'. It certainly would run against the ideas of Byang Kato, the 'founding father of African Evangelical Theology'. Kato is convinced that African Christian self-identity, which is rooted to any extent in pre-Christian or non-Christian religious tradition, will not be able to maintain itself because it compromises the Gospel.[20] I am of the opinion that the History of the Church of Christ can be accounted for in a genuinely catholic spirit that does not first denounce the histories of denominations and institutions, but describes and evaluates them in the light of the Gospel, just as the writing of Church History involves and evaluates the meeting of the Church with traditional non-Christian worldviews and religions. This may be in disagreement with Kalu's view. Yet I have gratefully used information in the volume by Kalu and his co-writers, in order to balance possible over-representation of the Western element in my account and in the descriptions by other authors that I have used.

1.3. The Sources of Church History

How do students of Church History obtain knowledge of the facts and developments of the past? Definitely, they search for sources and study their contents. A student should look at any source from two angles (a) the kind of source, and (b) the person who created it.

---

[18] Ogbu U. Kalu, 'The Shape and Flow of African Church Historiography', in: (ed.), *African Christianity*, 2005, pp.2-23.

[19] J.Ki-Zerbo (ed.), *General History of Africa*, p.3 [through: Verstraelen Gilhuis, *A New Look at Christianity in Africa* pp.4,84].

[20] Byang Kato, *Theological Pitfalls in Africa*, Kisumu: Evangelical Publishing House, 1975. See also Keith Ferdinando's DACB article on Kato [Internet].

a. Categories of Sources

Sources can be (1) written and non-written, or (2) primary and secondary, or (3) direct and indirect.

Written and Non-written Sources

Written material consists of any written witness of historical events. Examples of written sources: manuscripts, letters, memoranda, laws, books, questionnaires, etc. Written sources can be found on modern paper, papyrus, parchment (vellum), clay-tablets, potsherds (= fragments of earthenware), walls, and rocks. Written materials are often kept in in libraries, archives, museums.

Non-written historical material is transmitted orally, in music, in drawings and paintings of the landscape, of buildings, of roads, of customs, and of all other things that humanity has made or done. The characteristics of nature (such as the presence of deserts or mountains) must also be taken into account when studying history.

Writing African Church History largely depends on oral sources. There is a growing consciousness of the need to collect information that has not yet been reduced to writing. Many accounts given by Africans themselves or other people's accounts about agents of African Church History are in the process of being recorded. A commendable work is being done by the organisers and writers of the *Dictionary of African Christian Biography* (DACB). Their accounts of recorded oral history, some of which I have gratefully used, are not published in books, but digitally on the DACB-Website.[21]

DACB is not the only source facilitated by the Internet. Fortunately, the number of useful websites is growing. This is important in view of the factors that limit the possibilities for studying African Church History: time, money, and distance. These factors especially limit the availability of books, libraries, and archives. That is why students in an African context increasingly resort to websites on the Internet.[22]

Coin with the image of Emperor Titus, who occupied, and destroyed Jerusalem in the year 70.

Primary, and Secondary Sources

Primary sources are the contemporary witnesses of historical facts, and movements. Secondary sources are later accounts of the same. For example, a letter, a drawing, or carved wooden objects made by your late great-grandparent are primary sources for his life, whereas a story, song or description made by your mother about that parent are secondary sources. However, a song made by your great-grandmother and recited by your mother is a primary source for the former's life! Church Father Augustine's

---

[21] http://www.dacb.org
[22] The number of helpful websites is growing rapidly. See: Bibliography, Africa, 'Various countries', after chapter 56.

biography *Confessiones* is a primary source; later books on his life are secondary sources.

Direct, and Indirect Sources

Direct Church History sources comment directly on the things of God, the Church, and the Christians. Indirect Church History sources are provided by other disciplines.

> Examples of *indirect sources* to the student of Church History: the various branches of Secular History, the other branches of Theology, chronology, geography, archaeology, linguistics, numismatics (the knowledge of coins), heraldry, genealogy, graphology, the sciences of books, libraries, archives, and manuscripts.

From this survey of categories, it can be concluded that there is a great variety in the sources of Church History. This especially applies to the category of books. There are handbooks (often in more than one volume), dissertations, theses, editions of manuscripts, monographs, biographies, topical books, popular books, schoolbooks, novels, television/radio scripts, collections of newspaper and magazine articles, and/ or archived manuscripts. They differ in various aspects. Let us look at some criteria.

Size. Handbooks are often fat, popular books are not. A lengthy dissertation or thesis is not necessarily a good one.

Scholarliness. Scholarly works are based on independent research of primary sources. The writers acknowledge their sources, mostly in footnotes.

Organisation of the contents. The table of contents of a book should be studied first. It shows the order, or lack of order, and reflects the *what – when – why – how* of a study or a story.

Intended group of readers. Books differ greatly depending on the category of readers that the writer had in mind, for instance: age group (children or adults), professional group (theologians or non-theologians), students or holiday-readers.

Title page of a much used collection of important original documents.

b. Writers of Source Material

New students of Church History mainly work with written, secondary or direct sources found in textbooks, teachers' handouts, published texts of lectures, and documents on the Internet. Students have to realise that the writers of these texts (1) reflect differences in faith and abilities, (2) are not necessarily Christians, and (3) if they are Christians they still may have differing opinions.

1.Writers differ in Faith and Abilities

A writer cannot create an intelligible survey of previous facts and developments without a certain faith. Moreover, writers have a certain level of natural abilities and experiences, and they differ in knowledge and expertise.

This inevitability or necessity of having a basic faith or starting point and natural skills is not only true for history writers but for any writer of scholarly or scientific work. Work by any Church History writer reflects openly or indirectly belief in certain truths, values, ideas, stances, cultural, ethnical, and political views, and also a degree of natural giftedness. It is of great importance that the student of Church History is aware of this. Students should assess the Christian character, the scholarly level and the practical use of a Church History book. Good Christians are not necessarily Church History experts, nor are they necessarily able authors who write intelligibly. A Church History book that has no scholarly pretensions can be very useful at times, especially if it is the only available record.

2. Non-Christian Writers

A Writer of Church History is not necessarily a Christian. Many writers of Church History denounce the essentials of the Christian faith or even belong to other religions. Some are Muslims, Buddhists, African Traditionalists, Liberalists, Socialists, and Communists. They are not able to write Church History in faithful loyalty to the Church of Christ and they often aim to undermine the Church. Nevertheless, students of Church History should not neglect their work. Here are some reasons:

Non-Christians can be excellent experts, and well-informed sources of information concerning aspects of Church History. Non-Christian writers sometimes very ably show weaknesses and faults in Churches, Christians, and Christian Church History writers. The study of work by non-Christians can strengthen the apologetic character of Christian Church History writing. In order to defend the true Church, Christian students and writers need to know what the opponents of the Church write and from what angle they operate.

3. Disagreement among Christian Writers

Christian Church History Writers do not necessarily agree with one another. Parallel to the differences in Christianity there are a great many differences among Christian Church History writers. These differences apply to the basic beliefs underlying their work, to the method of their research, and to their ways of communicating. Here are some examples.

Roman Catholic writers, especially those who formed their views before Vatican II, tend to look upon Church History as the history of the Roman Catholic Church. Hence, they emphasise antique and medieval developments of papacy, hagiography, and monasticism, the spread of Roman Catholicism in Southern Europe, Latin America, and Roman Catholic mission to other parts of the world. Protestant writers tend to emphasise certain negative aspects of the Medieval Church, the positive significance of the 16th-century Reformation, and the developments caused by subsequent Awakenings and Schisms.

Aurelius Augustine (354-430). He changed the way of history writing from applying a circular principle, which is circulating different facts around the same theme, to writing from a linear angle, looking upon history as a movement from a starting point to its fulfilment.

Pentecostal and Anabaptist writers often look upon

the event of the outpouring of the Holy Spirit in *Acts* 2 as the beginning of Church History, whereas others are of the opinion that essentially Church History begins with the Creation of Man in *Genesis* 1. This arises from a different view on the unity of Scripture. Pentecostal and Anabaptist writers also tend to emphasise, more than others do, the History of the 16th-century Radical Reformation and its consequences.

Eastern Orthodox writers tend to accept the hegemony of the State over the Church, and often serve nationalistic aims, whereas Roman Catholic writers stress the supra-nationality of the Church.

Most *Protestant* writers emphasise the independence of State and Church from one another.

African, Asian, and Latin American writers have gradually come to describe the history of the Church from a different angle than Western writers. They realise their churches are not imitations of the churches in the countries that first sent missionaries there or colonised them.[23]

Ecumenical Church History writers tend to underestimate the differences between Churches because they envisage a growth in the global unity of Churches. In the opinion of some scholars, Church History can only be written in conjunction with the histories of other world religions. However, such a radical ecumenical approach runs against the authority of Scripture and Christ as the only Way of salvation, and therefore does damage our conviction of the uniqueness of the Christian faith.

1.4. The Branches of Church History

Church History has various departments, corresponding to the different branches of secular history. It is an account of the aspects natural life in their relationship to the scriptural imperatives, especially where Jesus commands his followers to be the salt and the light of the world[24] and make disciples of all nations.[25] Some principal divisions of Church History are:

a. History of Christian Missions

The history of missions concerns the development of the spread of Christianity among unconverted nations, whether 'barbarous savages' or 'civilized'. The history of mission traces the outward expansion as well as the penetration and the transforming power of Christianity. Through the history of Christian mission we have access to information about the conversion of the elect remnant of the Jews, the Greeks and the Romans in the first three centuries; the conversion of the barbarians of Northern and Western Europe, in the Middle Ages; and last but not least the combined efforts of various churches and societies for the conversion of the heathen peoples in America, Africa, and Australia mostly before 1900, and of the semi-civilized nations of Eastern Asia in our own time. The whole non-Christian world, including the Muslims, Buddhists, Hindus and secularized Western agnostics and atheists, is now open to missionary labour. Domestic or home mission work embraces the revival of Christian life in corrupt or neglected

---

[23] Cf. Kwame Bediako, *Theology and Identity: The impact of Culture on Christian Theology in the 2nd century*; F.J. Verstraelen, 'Southern perspectives on Christian History', in: *Neue Zeitschrift für Missionswissenschaft*, 52-1979/2, Immensee, Switzerland.

[24] Mt 5:13-16.

[25] Mt 28:16-20.

portions of various communities, societies and countries. Here it also includes the planting of a purer Christianity among the Christian sects and cults.

b. History of Persecutions

This concerns the story of the persecution of Christians by hostile peoples, religions and ideologies. For instance, the anti-Christian activities of Judaism and Heathenism in the first three centuries, and by Islam from the Middle Ages onward. This is another important branch of Church History. Persecutions on one hand proved a purifying process, bringing out the moral heroism of martyrdom, and thus means for the spread and establishment of Christianity: 'The blood of martyrs is the seed of the church.' On the other hand, the persistent persecution has crushed and rooted out the Church in parts of the world.

c. History of Church Polity

The Church is both the invisible communion of saints and a visible body, which needs office bearers, laws, and structures to regulate its activity. To this branch belongs the history of developments of various forms of church government: the episcopal, the congregational and the presbyterial, and the history of the law and the discipline of the Church. Various systems of governing the Church have generally resulted into the serious strife and division within Christendom. The question that we need to ask is whether there is a system of governing the Church that is as close as possible to the teaching of Scriptures, or is such a system just a human invention?

d. History of Church-State Relationship

Throughout the history of Christianity, the Church has been either under or above the state or at par with it. All these relationships have had great impact on the work and the influence of the Church. Thus, this branch sheds light on how the Church and the State have been relating to each other and how they have influenced one another. Also included in this branch are the reforms of civil law and of government with regard to Christianity and the Church, the spread of civil and religious liberties, and the progress of civilization under the influence of Christianity.

e. History of Church Praxis

This branch is the history of the development of Worship and of how the Church celebrates, revives, and strengthens her fellowship with Jesus Christ. Among its sub-divisions are the histories of preaching, catechismal training, liturgy, rites and ceremonies, and religious art, particularly sacred songs and music.

f. History of Christian Life

This branch of Church History concerns the development of Christian morality and the role Christians in the society, for instance the exhibition of the distinguishing virtues and vices of different ages, of the development of Christian philanthropy, the regeneration of domestic life, the gradual abolition of slavery and of other social evils, and the mitigation and diminution of the horrors of war.

g. Histories of the Branches of Theology

Each branch of Theology has a history of its own: Biblical studies (Hermeneutics, Exegetics), Systematic Theology or Dogmatics, Christology, Pneumatology, Ecclesiology, Practical Theology, and even the study and understanding of Church History itself (Historiography). The history of doctrines or dogmas is most important, and its object is to show how the Church has gradually found and unfolded the divine truths of revelation. This branch describes how the teachings of Scripture have been formulated and shaped into dogmas and grown into Creeds or Confessions of Faith, or how systems of doctrine have been stamped with public authority. The history of dogmas shows the growth of the Church in the faith and in the knowledge of the infallible Word of God in a continuous struggle against error, misbelief, and unbelief. For that reason, the history of heresies is an essential part of the history of doctrine. Every important dogma now professed by the Christian Church is the result of a severe conflict with error. For example the doctrines of Trinity, the Natures of Christ, the Person and work of the Holy Spirit, the structure and government of the Church, the doctrinal symbols of the various churches, from the Apostles' Creed down to the confessions of Dort and Westminster, and the more recent standards, embody the results of the theological battles of the Militant Church. As such, they reflect sub-divisions of Church History.

1.5. Reasons for Studying Church History

Many students have studied Church History only because it is one of the core subjects of the curriculum. Some institutions of theological training have completely neglected this subject, for various reasons. But there is great value in studying the subject. Let us look at some reasons why studying Church History is important.

a. Understanding the Present

The first reason is that Church History helps students to understand the events that led up to the present situation. Through the study of Church History they understand why there are various churches, various creeds, various forms of church government, and various alliances and hostilities against the Church.

b. Noticing God's Providence

The reading of Church History enables students to see how God operates in his providence toward the Church. This is another value of Church History and reason for studying it. The subject greatly enriches our spirituality, increases our faith and comforts us when facing discouragements, for they provide us with a wide and a long perspective.

c. Seeing Satan's Attempts

The third value is that Church History assist students to clearly see how Satan has attempted to destroy the Church. It is very true to assert that the current situation is the result of how the Church responded to attacks by the Devil. In addition, the discipline of Church History will help the Church to avoid surprise, to be prepared for assaults and to recognize evil forces within its environment.

d. Examples for Present Training

The fourth reason for studying Church History is that it provides rich material for training of church workers and church leaders. Students encounter the life and struggles of great heroes of the faith. They particularly learn how these Christians of the past faithfully constituted and led the Church and rigorously defended Christian truth.

e. Source of Tools for Learning

The study of the subject offers students some important practical tools of evaluating methods of Christian work, observing failures and successes of those who served the Lord before us, assessing root causes and results of their strengths and weaknesses.

f. Guide for Exegetics

Finally, the study of Church History is necessary for the explanation of Scripture and the formulation of doctrine. Some theological topics cannot be thoroughly grasped without a knowledge of Church History. Unless a student has ample information about the Council of Nicaea (325), the Council of Constantinople (381), and the Council of Chalcedon (451), he or she will not understand the theological development in the doctrine of Trinity. Behind the number 666 in *Revelation* 13:11-18, there is the history of persecution of the Church in the first century as well as the vision of future suffering of believers.

In this brief introduction we have tried to locate Church History by defining it, and by indicating its sources. For further study of definitions and the use of sources, students will find more details in the introductions to other textbooks, and also in handbooks.[26] After some progress, students will discover the need for knowing about methods of researching and communicating Church History. We refer them to the existing literature in this field.[27]

---

[26] E.g. E.E. Cairns, *Christianity through the Centuries: A History of the Christian Church*, Grand Rapids: Zondervan, 1996³, pp.17-35; T. Dowley, The History of Christianity, Oxford: Lion, 1990², pp.14-54; S. Paas, *Digging out the Ancestral Church: An Introduction to Researching and Communicating Church History*, Blantyre: CLAIM, 2000, pp.9-46.

[27] Cf. Paas, *Digging*, pp.47-64, where I describe a workable plan for research-projects, and a survey of widely accepted notation and lay-out for writing theses. I also summarised some other writers on methodology.

Bibliography: Historiography

a. General, and Reference Books

Aland, K., *A History of Christianity*, 2 vols, Minneapolis: Fortress, 1986.

Barrett, D.B., *World Christian Encyclopedia*, New York: Oxford UP, 1982.

Bodenkotter, T., *A Concise History of the Catholic Church*, New York: Doubleday, 1990.

Bowden, H. (ed.), *A Century of Church History*, Southern Illinois UP, 1988.

Bradley, J.E., and R.A. Muller, *Church History: An Introduction to Research, Reference Works, and Methods*, Grand Rapids: Eerdmans, 1995.

Brauer, J.C. (ed.), *The Westminster Dictionary of the Christian Church*, Westminster Press, 1971.

Cairns, Earle E., *God and man in Time*, Grand Rapids: Baker, 1979.

Cairns, Earle E., *Christianity through the Centuries: A History of the Christian Church*, Grand Rapids: Zondervan, 1996^3.

Case, S.J. (ed.), *A Bibliographical Guide to the History of Christianity*, Chicago UP, 1931.

Chadwick, O., *A History of Christianity*, London: Weidenfield & Nicholson, 1995.

Chadwick, H., and G.R. Evans (eds), *An Atlas of the Christian Church*, London: Macmillan, 1987.

Collingwood, R.G., *The Idea of History*, Oxford UP, 1956^2.

Comby, J., *How to Read Church History* (2 vols), London: SCM, 1985^2.

Cross, F.L., and E.A. Livingstone, *The Oxford Dictionary of the Christian Church*, Oxford UP, 1997^3.

Dowley, T. (ed.), *The History of Christianity*, Oxford: Lion, 1990^9.

Gaustad, E.S., *Historical Atlas of Religion in America* (revised ed.) New York: Harper, and Row, 1976.

Guilday, P. (ed.), *Church Historians*, New York: Kennedy, 1926.

Gwatkin, Henry Melville, *Early Church History to A.D. 313*, 2 vols, London: Macmillan, 1912.

Hastings, A. (ed.), *A World History of Christianity*, London: Cassel, 1999 [Bibliography, pp.537-571].

Houghton, S.M., *Sketches from Church History: An Illustrated Account of 20 Centuries of Christ's Power*, Edinburgh: The Banner of Truth Trust, 2000^4.

Johnson, P., *A History of Christianity*, Harmondsworth: Penguin, 1984.

Jedin, H., and J. Dolan, *The Handbook of Church History*, New York: Herder, 1965-1981.

Latourette, Kenneth Scott, *A History of the Expansion of Christianity*, Grand Rapids: Zondervan 1970 [first: New York: Harper and Brothers, 1937]; 7 volumes: 1.*The first five Centuries*; 2. *The Thousand Years of Uncertainty: AD 500-AD 1500*, 3. *Three Centuries of Advance 1500-1800 A.D*; 4. *Europe, and the United States*; 5. *The Americas, Australasia, and Africa*; 6. *North Africa and Asia*; 7. *Advance Through the Storm*.

Livingstone, E.A. (ed.), *The Concise Oxford Dictionary of the Christian Church*, Oxford UP, 1977^2.

MacCulloch, D., *Groundwork of Church History*, London: Epworth, 1987.

McGrath, A.E., *An Introduction to Christianity*, Oxford: Blackwell, 1997.

McGrath, A.E. (ed.), *The Christian Theology Reader*, Oxford: Blackwell, 2001^2 [an anthology of extracts from primary sources].

McManners, J. (ed.), *Oxford Illustrated History of Christianity*, Oxford UP, 1992.

Needham, N.R., *2000 Years of Christ's Power*, 2 vols, London: Grace Publications Trust, 1998, 2000.

Paas, Steven, *Digging out the Ancestral Church: Researching and Communicating Church History*, Zomba: Kachere, 2006³ [first 2000], [bibliography pp.107-109].

Petry, R.C., and C.L. Manschreck (eds.), *A History of Christianity* (2 vols), Englewood Cliffs: Prentice-Hall, 1964.

Pillay, G.J. and J.W. Hofmeyr (eds), *Perspectives on Church History: An Introduction for South African Readers*, Pretoria: De Jager-HUM Publ. 1991.

Rapozoh, I.B., and Malemu Bambo Dirkx, *Ulendo Wathu monga Mbumba ya Mulungu*, Limbe: Popular Publ., 1992.

Renwick, A.M., and A.M. Harman, *The Story of the Church*, Nottingham: IVP, 1998.

Schaff, Ph., *History of the Christian Church*, vols I, II, III, Grand Rapids: Eerdmans, 1955.

Shelburne, G.B., *Mbiri ya Mpingo,* Thondwe: Namikango Bible School, 1994².

Sykes, N., *The Study of Ecclesiastical History*, Cambridge: Emmanuel College, 1945.

Websites

Historiography Resources, http://legacy.fordham.edu/halsall/sbook2.asp#hist2
Christian History Institute: https://www.christianhistoryinstitute.org/
Church History by the Century, http://www.christianity.com/church/church-history/
Linguistic Tools, http://www.prdl.org/reference.php?ref_type=Linguistic%20Tools
Post-Reformation Reference Sources, http://www.prdl.org/reference.php

b. In an African Context

Barnes, H.E., *History of Historical Writings*, University of Oklahoma Press, 1937.

Barrett, D., *World Christian Encyclopedia: A Comparative Survey of Churches, and Religions in the Modern World AD 1900-2000*, Nairobi/ Oxford/ New York, 1982.

Bediako, K., *Christianity in Africa: The Renewal of a Non-Western Religion*, Edinburgh UP, 1995.

Bediako, Kwame, *Jesus in Africa: The Christian Gospel in African History, and Experience*, Akropong-Akuapem: Regnum Africa, 2000.

Bradley, J.E., and R.A. Muller, *Church History: An Introduction to Research, Reference Works, and Methods*, Grand Rapids: Eerdmans, 1995.

Cairns, E.E., *God, and man in Time*, Grand Rapids: Baker, 1979.

Case, S.J. (ed.), *A Bibliographical Guide to the History of Christianity*, Chicago UP, 1931.

Collingwood, R.G., *The Idea of History*, Oxford University Press, 1956².

Davidson, Basil, *Africa in History*, Phoenix, 2013 [first 1969].

Denis, Ph., *Orality, Memory, and the Past: Listening to the Voices of Black Clergy under Colonialism, and Apartheid*, Pietermaritzburg: Cluster Publ., 2000.

Guilday, P. (ed.), *Church Historians*, New York: Kennedy, 1926.

Jewsiecki, B., and D.Newbury (eds), *African Historiographies: What History for Which Africa?*, Beverly Hills: Sage, 1986.

Kalu, O.U. (ed.), *African Church Historiography: An Ecumenical Perspective*, Bern: Evangelische Arbeitsstelle Oekumene Schweiz, 1968.

Kalu, Ogbu, U., 'The Shape, and Flow of African Church Historiography', in: O.U. Kalu et al. (eds), *African Christianity: An African Story, University of Pretoria*, 2005, pp.2-23.

Livingstone, E.A. (ed.), *The Concise Oxford Dictionary of the Christian Church*, Oxford UP, 1977².

Kwiyani, Harvey C., *Sent Forth: African Missionary Work in the West, American Society of Missiology*, book 51, Orbis Books, 2014.

McIntyre, C.T., *God, History, and Historians: An Anthology of Modern Christian Views of History*, New York: Oxford UP, 1977.

Olubumehin, O.O., *Issues in Historiography*, Ibadan: College Press Publ., 2001.

Oyemakinde, Wale, *An Introduction to Church Missionary Society Manuscripts*, Ibadan: Sunlight Syndicate Ventures: College Press Publ, 2001.

Paas, Steven, *Mtanthauziramawu: Dictionary of Chichewa/ Chinyanja – English, and English – Chichewa/ Chinyanja*, Blantyre: CLAIM/ Veenendaal: Foundation Heart for Malawi, 2013^4 [first 2009].

Paas, Steven, 'Working with Oral Sources' [and a bibliography], in: Idem, *Digging out the Ancestral Church: Researching and Communicating Church History*, Zomba: Kachere, 2006^3, pp.89-106, 109-112.

Smith, Ken, *The Changing Past: Trends in South African History Writing*, Athens: Ohio University Press, 1989.

Sykes, Norman, *The Study of Ecclesiastical History*, Cambridge UP, 1945.

Verstraelen, Frans J., 'Southern Perspectives on Christian History', in: *Neue Zeitschrift für Missionswissenschaft*, 53-1997.

Verstraelen, Frans J., *History of Christianity in the Context of African History: A Comparative Assessment of Four Recent Historiographical Contributions*, Gweru: Mambo Press, 2002.

Verstraelen, Frans J., Kenneth R. Ross, P. Gundani, and I. Mukonyora, *The Teaching of Church History, and Ministerial Formation,* in: Association of Theological Institutions in Southern, and Central Africa (ATISCA) Bulletin no 2 (1993).

Verstraelen-Gilhuis, Gerdien, *A New Look at Christianity in Africa*, Gweru: Mambo Press, 1992 [pp.77-98, 'Rewriting the History of Christianity in Africa'].

Verstraelen-Gilhuis, Gerdien, *From Dutch Mission Church to Reformed Church in Zambia: The Scope for African Leadership and Initiative in the History of a Zambian Mission Church*, Franeker: Wever, 1982 [pp.13-21, 'Recovering the African Perspective of Mission History', and 'Written, and Oral Sources'].

Websites

See after chapter 56.

Part I

From Galilee to the Atlantic

A. Antiquity 60-500

2. The Fullness of Time

2.1. The Covenant

'When the time had fully come God sent forth his son' (*Galatians* 4:4). God wanted to gather up people of all nations in His Church. Therefore, He sent Jesus Christ, who is the Saviour of the world. So the Church of God continues in the name of Christ. The beginning of the history of the Christian Church is the day of Pentecost in the *Acts of the Apostles*, chapter 2.[1] Since that day up to this, many people have been added to the communion of the saved. Before the day of Pentecost, God prepared the preaching of the Gospel so that the Church should continue on earth, and that many people should accept Christ. The arrival of the Church of Christ was prepared for in a number of ways through God's work. Scripture witnesses this.

The holy Scriptures reveal the covenant of grace. It is a kind of pact or contract by which God has pledged to offer salvation to fallen humanity. The covenant has two sides, *the work of humans*, and *the work of God*. In the Garden of Eden people spoilt this covenant, by giving themselves over to the powers of sin, death, and hell. However, God did not leave His Church alone. He continued the covenant by way of grace, in *Genesis* 3:15. This renewed covenant also has two sides, *the faith of humans,* and *God's promise of grace*. This covenant of grace was also given to Noah, Abraham, Isaac,

Fishermen on the Lake of Galilee. Here the preaching of the Gospel began.

Jacob, Moses, and the people of Israel. In this covenant, God said, 'all the families of the earth shall be blessed' (*Genesis* 12:3). In the final implementation of this, He sent his Son to the earth. God the Son became man. Through Him, the Messiah, the Anointed One, the King of Kings coming from God, the *covenant of grace* is given to the elect of all the earth. Through Christ God has given them the Word of His promises

---

[1] It happened in probably the year AD 29. *AD* = Anno Domini (Latin) : Year of the Lord, an indication of the years which came after the birth of Jesus Christ

and the Holy Spirit. Many are gathered together in His Church, which is the symbol of the presence of the coming of the Kingdom of God. So through the covenant, which is fulfilled in Christ, the age of the Church, or the age of the Holy Spirit, has begun.

God also prepared for this age in other ways. He used the Roman Empire, founded by Romulus more than 700 years before Christ was born. During the republican period[2] (509-31 BC[3]), Rome conquered Italy and many other lands. The goodness of God used the Roman Empire to help the spread of the Christian faith[4].

2.2. Contributions of the Roman Empire

a. Imperial Rule

At the time of Jesus' birth, Palestine and many other countries were provinces of the Roman Empire. This empire spread around the Mediterranean Sea, from the Sahara Desert in Africa to the rivers Rhine and Danube in Germany, and from Syria in the east to Spain in the west. The prophecy of Jesus' birth found its fulfilment in a decree by Caesar (Emperor) Augustus, who ordered that every male citizen in his Empire should be registered in his original home.[5] One of the interesting things is that God though the decree made it possible for Joseph and Mary to be present in Bethlehem, the birthplace of Jesus.[6]

A Roman cargo ship in the first century A.D.

b. Pax Romana

Wherever this empire was, peace was enforced by military subjection. In Latin this peace was called *Pax Romana*[7]. An important contributor to this situation of relative peace was Gaius (Caius) Octavianus. At the sea-battle of Actium in 31 BC he succeeded in bringing to an end the dangerous civil wars that had weakened the empire. The Senate in Rome named him Augustus, meaning the 'revered', 'majestic', or 'holy'.[8] Through this victory, the Emperor Augustus ensured that one single man became ruler of the whole empire with no further possibility of civil war. Then, he devised a plan, which urged the tribes and peoples in his vast territory to stop their arguments, and obey the Roman law.

---

[2] *Republic* (Latin: res publica = thing of the people), a type of government of a nation without a king.
[3] *BC* = Before Christ, an indication of the number of years before the birth of Christ.
[4] See: Michael Green, *Evangelism in the Early Church*, London: Hodder and Stoughton 1970.
[5] Lk 2:1-7.
[6] Micah 5:2.
[7] *Pax Romana*: Roman Peace.
[8] Cf. Lk.2:1.

c. System of Communication

A network of roads joined all the parts of the Roman Empire. It helped the rapid movements of Augustus's armies so that they could quickly stop any revolution in the empire or any enemy that tried to enter. It should be noted that Christians among the Roman soldiers used the opportunity of spreading the Gospel in remote parts of the Empire. These roads were instrumental in fighting thieves and other criminals. Control by the army made them safe for the traffic of traders and other travellers, including Christian missionaries. The roads also helped establish contacts between different tribes and peoples, thus promoting the unity of Roman culture in the empire. Roman laws helped to establish justice in the empire.

Coin showing an image of the Emperor Augustus.

d. Economic development

In these ways Augustus's long reign (from 31 BC to AD 14) stimulated the development of wealth, which alleviated the poverty of many people. All these things assisted the work of the Apostles and other missionaries so that the Gospel could spread rapidly to all parts of the Roman Empire.

e. Sense of Unity

Being under one Emperor meant that there was a sense of unity of all Roman citizens under universal law. This sense of unity created an environment favourable to the reception of the Gospel that proclaimed the unity of the human race in the truth that all people are under punishment because they are sinners and that they all are offered salvation through the suffering of one Saviour Jesus Christ and of being part of his Body, the Church.

f. Legal System

Roman laws contributed to a good judicial system that helped establish justice in the Empire. For instance, Paul's appeal to the Emperor's Court was possible because there was a legal system that gave any citizen an opportunity to have his case tried by the highest court.

g. The Religion of the Romans

When considering the religion of the Romans, the first thing to mention is that it was extremely varied, because the Romans adopted aspects of the religions of their defeated subjects.[9] The Romans gave freedom of worship to all subdued peoples, provided they

---

[9] The official system of Roman religion consisted of many gods. Children of the gods were also gods, or half gods if they were born of a human woman and a god. All gods had Roman and Greek names, the leader was Jupiter (Zeus), who was called 'Great Lord of the earth and heaven', or the 'father and king of gods and men'. He married Juno (Hera): the queen of the gods. Among their children were Vulcan (Hephaestus: the blacksmith god), Mars (Ares: war), Minerva (Athene: the warrior goddess and patron of Athens). Other gods were Ceres (Demeter: goddess of the harvest), Vesta (goddess of the hearth and home), Neptune (Poseidon: sea), Dis (Pluto, Hades), Mercury (Hermes), Apollo (Apollon), Diana (Artemis), Hercules (Heracles), Venus (Aphrodite, the goddess of love), and so on.

2. The Fullness of Time

Emperor Domitian (†96), who decreed that he should be called 'lord, and god'.

did not oppose the political rituals of the Roman Empire. Generally, the Romans were indifferent as to the question of religious truth, but the government forced all people, except the Jews, to follow some important things in the official religion of the Roman Empire. A minimum requirement was the offering of a sacrifice before the statue of the Emperor. People were allowed to deviate from Roman polytheism only if they took part in certain ceremonies that signified Roman unity and power. Those who disobeyed were regarded as rebels who were against the Roman Empire and the Emperor. Emperors who had died were considered to be gods, and consequently entitled to receive honour and offerings. Beginning with Domitian (d. AD 96), Emperors called themselves 'lord and god' during their lifetime. They also functioned as high priests in the Roman religious system. As such, they were called *pontifex maximus*, i.e. chief bridge-makers, bridging the gulf between the gods and the people. That is why refusing to perform the essential ceremonies of Roman religion meant rebelling against the gods and the Emperors, threatening the foundations of the Roman Empire.

In this way politics and religion were strongly united. Gradually the system was corrupted. In their hearts many Romans rejected the old polytheistic religion of Rome, for they wanted to find true answers to the problems of life. Therefore, many people's hearts were opened to other religions.

First, many people turned to *monotheism*, that is to the Jewish religion, and then to Christianity. Although the religion of the Roman Empire became weak, it was strong enough for a long time to resist Christianity when it began to spread in parts of the Empire.

Secondly there was the increasing interest in popular *'folk beliefs'*. This type of faith exists among any people of any religion in any time. It is sometimes stronger than the official religion. Many people believed in the power of *fate*. They thought that it is not possible to change the destiny of man and the world, and that there is no one who can help. Everyone's fate has been destined. Popular folk-thought also comprised belief in the power of *evil spirits* or *witches* which surpassed the power of the gods.

There was also a belief in *magic*, that through the manipulation of nature, events can be influenced. There was also the idea that the future of man is ruled by signs, for example by the the position of the stars and planets or by the image of the intestines or liver of a slaughtered sheep. Christianity helped to remove these superstitions, but it could not root out completely the beliefs in fate, evil spirits, and magic.

Thirdly, in the Empire there were some fanatical religious sects that opposed the official polytheistic religion of the Romans. The leaders of the Empire feared these sects, for many Romans converted to them. The leaders called them *superstitiones*. The state intimidated these sects, which were often organised as secret fellowships. For example, there was the cult of Cybele, which came from Asia Minor, and the worship of Isis, Osiris, and Serapis from Egypt.

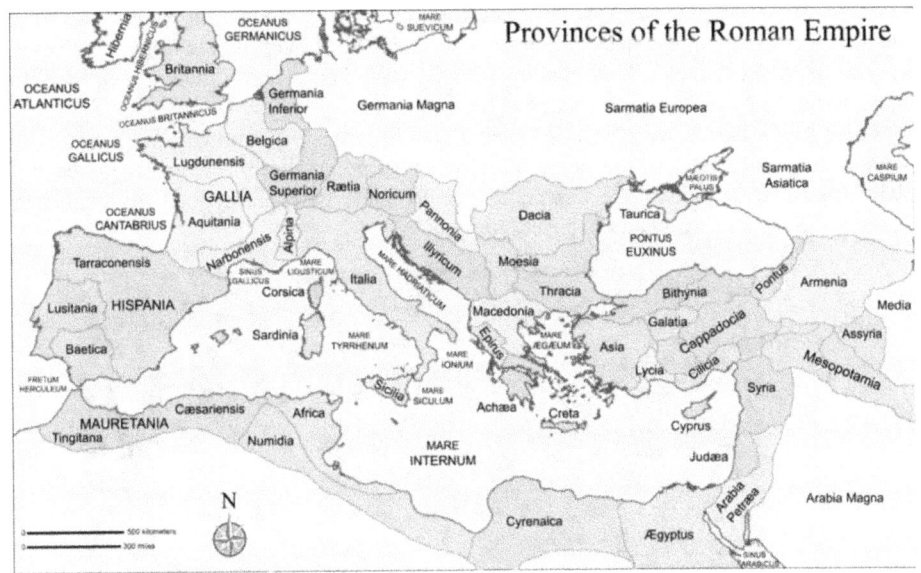

There was also the religion of Mithras. Because many soldiers followed this cult, the state did not intimidate it. The followers of this sect believed that Mithras was a saviour born in a miraculous way. The initiation rites included the killing of a bull and the flowing of the blood of that animal onto the person who was in a pit under the bull.

These sects in a way prepared for the coming of the Gospel, for some ideas are similar to Christian beliefs: they did not belittle women and slaves, they knew the importance of forgiveness of sins, they tried to remove the power of superstition, and they promised eternal life.

2.3. Greek Contributions

a. The Greek Language

The Romans adopted many aspects of the culture of the peoples they had conquered. Through this they strengthened the unity of the Roman Empire. Of great importance was the Roman conquest of Greece in 146 BC, and of Syria, Palestine, and Egypt, which had earlier been conquered by the famous Greek ruler Alexander the Great of Macedonia (356 BC-323 BC)[10].

We should realise that long before the Roman conquest Greek culture had already spread through trade and migration and was spread further, especially in Palestine, as a deliberate policy of some of the Greek kings who ruled Syria.[11] *Koine Greek*[12] became

---

[10] Greek history begins before the establishment of Rome. The Greek lived in present Greece and its surrounding islands, and in Asia Minor (today Turkey). They introduced a system of self-rule in independent cities, and they excelled in art, writing, philosophy, politics, and sports. Alexander the Great conquered Persia and other parts up to the rivers Indus and Nile.

[11] Cf. Julian Spriggs, "Antiochus IV-Epiphanes: The 'Contemptible Person' predicted by Daniel (Dan. 11:21)" [Internet].

[12] *Koine* = Common; *Koine Greek*: a dialect originating from Attic that spread to the whole Hellenistic (= Greek) world and was basic to later forms of the Greek language.

2. The Fullness of Time

the most important language in the eastern part of the Roman Empire. Earlier, Greek had also spread to some coastal regions of the West. Thus everywhere there were people who understood Greek. This made it easier for Paul, and other Greek-speaking missionaries to explain Scripture, and preach the Gospel.

Later missionaries were helped when *Latin* became the dominant language in the western provinces, and in the north of Africa. We noted that the Romans mixed their own religion with that of the Greeks. Some Romans were influenced by the famous Greek philosophers who had criticised polytheism.

The Acropolis in Athens

b. Greek Philosophy

Greek philosophy has determined Western culture to a large extent and has also deeply influenced the development of the Church. Approximately 600 BC, Greek philosophers tried to define the essence of all things. Originally, their rational explanations were strongly influenced by the religious perceptions of their polytheism. Yet gradually the Greek thinkers tried to distance themselves from the system of beliefs connected to a multitude of divine beings. However, when in the 5th century BC a satisfactory explanation of the All had not been found, Socrates defined the limit and the ability of human reason with the criterion of necessity.

In the 4th century BC the great Greek philosophers Plato and Aristotle devised their systems of thought about the world and life. Because Plato believed that there is the power of only One God or One Thing, later Christian writers regarded him as a monotheist.[13] In Plato's philosophy gods or divine powers were not absent, but he said

---

[13] Cf. Sioniossoglou, *Plato and Theodoret: The Christian Appropriation of Platonic Philosophy and the*

that they basically derive from the one Thing or Idea, which is higher and better than all other things and ideas. Aristotle did not follow Plato's idealism. He stressed the value of empirical observation and the practical concerns of life. He believed in an imperishable substance, which is the source of all and is not subject to process or change. This substance is the only 'prime mover'.[14] In Aristotle's thinking the Divine Being follows from observations and experiences here and now, whereas in Plato's thought the Divine Being or Idea is the source of all that can be observed or experienced.

Statue of the goddess Diana (Artemis) in Ephesus.

Greek schools of thought after Aristotle continued to be influential. In *Acts* 17 the Apostle Paul in Athens met with representatives of two of them, the *Epicureans* and the *Stoics*. According to the *Stoics*, the ideal man is the one who is perfectly self-controlled and displays the virtues of wisdom, courage, justice, and temperance. Basic to these virtues is for man to maintain his will, so that he can live in agreement with nature and control his emotions, which are considered destructive, and have power over his body. The Divine Being is in all material and bodily matters. The Epicureans were opposed to the Stoics. They followed the materialistic idea that everything was made of atoms and that the gods did not concern themselves with human affairs. They declared pleasure to be the sole intrinsic good. However, their morality consisted in the idea that pleasure must be moderated; the maximum pleasure is obtained when you have had enough; more of the same only leads to pain.[15] In that sense they were less radically hedonist than the school of the Cyrenaics of the 4th centuryBC, who considered pleasure the supreme good under all circumstances, especially the immediate gratifications. By Paul's time, according to the NIV Study Bible, Epicureanism 'had degenerated into a more sensual system of thought ... At its best Stoicism had some admirable qualities, but like Epicureanism ... it had degenerated into a system of pride'.[16] Yet Stoicism continued to be influential, for example through the writings of the Emperor Marcus Aurelius.[17] The Apostle Paul was familiar with Stoic ideas and even quoted from Stoic writers.[18]

Hellenistic Intellectual Resistance, Cambridge UP, p.105: [Theodoret, 5th-century theologian of the Antioch school] 'appropriated Plato as a monotheist while denouncing his successors as polytheists and apostates'.

[14] Cf. Aristotle, *Metaphysics*, chapters 6-10 [Internet].

[15] The popular idea that they allowed their bodies to be destroyed by following their every desire and lust in over-indulgence in pleasures, seems to be prejudiced. Cyril Bailey, in his edition of the Epicurean poet Titus Lucretius Carus (99-55 BC), *Titi Lucreti Cari De Rerum Natura*, vol. I, Oxford: Clarendon, 1947, writes: 'Pleasure being the end it is man's business to seek the maximum amount of pleasure ... It was this unflinching assertion which led to the popular misconceptions of Epicurean morality both in antiquity and in later times; it was regarded as a symbol for debauchery ... But this was not Epicurus' philosophy; for he did not believe that in such indulgence the maximum of pleasure could be obtained'.

[16] Note with Acts 17:18 in the NIV Study Bible.

[17] Marcus Aurelius, 121-180, expressed Stoic ideas in his *Meditations*, composed in Greek a short time before his death.

[18] In Acts 17 Paul quotes Epimenides and Aratus; cf. Donald Robertson, 'St. Paul on Stoicism: From the Acts of the Apostles' [Internet].

2. The Fullness of Time

The early Christian missionaries used the ideas of Plato, Aristotle and others in explaining the Gospel concerning the characteristics of man and the God of Scripture. Thus some thoughts of Greek philosophers paved the way for Christianity, yet their ideas differed from the teaching of the Bible. One of the differences concerns the concept of body and soul. In the Old Testament, they are one, and distinction between them is not emphasised. The same is true for the New Testament definition of man's body and soul. In Greek or Hellenistic[19] philosophies, however, a dualistic idea is in control: man is composed of two things, the soul or the spirit and the body, which are distinguished from one another. In chapters 7 and 10 we will see that *Gnosticism*, a heretical movement in Christianity, adopted this Greek idea and developed it further, thus creating distance to the Biblical concept of man and God. The soul is good, but the body is evil. The soul is chained in a dangerous jail, which is the body. When a person dies, the soul is released from its prison, and it returns to its origin, which is the great Idea. The body is left in the grave as of no value.

Many Christians thus unintentionally mixed the Christian teachings and these Greek-Gnostic ideas. However, it must be stressed again that the Bible does not teach the separation of body and soul; on the contrary, the Word of God approves their unity. Both body and soul were created by God; both fell in sin, and need justification, and sanctification through the sacrifice of Christ. Both look forward to heaven. The body will be resurrected (1 *Corinthians* 15), and be reunited with the soul and the spirit.

We conclude that on the one hand Greek culture and language helped people to understand the Gospel, not least through the influence of philosophers who criticized polytheism and recognized that there is only One God. On the other hand, we have to say that the same Greek culture was instrumental in introducing unbiblical concepts of the body and the soul of man.

2.4. Contributions by the Jews

a. The Septuagint

Since time immemorial, the Jews had spread to all parts of the Roman Empire, and other countries.[20] The spread of the Jews or the Jewish *diaspora*[21] simplified the work of the Christian missionaries who taught the monotheistic belief of the God of Scripture. There had already been Jews outside Israel or Palestine since the time of captivity. Many stayed in Egypt, especially in Alexandria. There, around 250 BC, Jews translated the Old Testament into Greek; the translation was called the *Septuagint*, often indicated by the symbol LXX.[22] It greatly helped the spread of the knowledge of God.

---

[19] *Hellenistic* comes from *Hellas*, the ancient name for Greece.

[20] Acts 2:9-11 mentions the countries to which Jews had spread: Parthians, and Medes, and Elamites, and the dwellers in Mesopotamia,and in Judaea, and Cappadocia, in Pontus, and Asia, Phrygia, and Pamphylia, in Egypt, and in the parts of Libya about Cyrene, and strangers of Rome, Jews and proselytes, Cretans and Arabians'.

[21] *Diaspora* comes from the Greek verb: to scatter about.

[22] *Septuagint* or *Septuaginta* is Latin for seventy, which is indicated by its Roman numeral acronym LXX. The name refers to the legend that 70 Jewish Rabbi's made the translation into Greek in 70 days in the early 3rd century BC.

When the Roman general Pompeius (Pompey) conquered Jerusalem in 63 BC, Palestine became a part of the Roman Empire. Under the influence of Jews, many Romans rejected polytheism, and developed a belief in a form of monotheism. The Pharisees were interested in spreading their thought among the Gentiles. Consequently, many Romans were converted to the Jewish religion. Some were circumcised, and accepted all the Jewish laws. They were called *proselytes*. Others refused to be circumcised, although they accepted the Jewish faith, and went to the synagogues. They were called *God-fearers*. And there were some people who had a general interest in the Jewish religion, but were not converted. This phenomenon of conversion to the Jewish faith is a remarkable thing, because generally Romans and Jews disliked each other. During the time of the New Testament, the Jews often rebelled against the Roman government.

b. The Diaspora

In 70 AD, a Roman army led by Vespasian and his son Titus occupied and destroyed the city of Jerusalem, including the temple. After the rebellion of the Jews led by Simon Bar Kokhba in 135 AD, the Romans chased nearly all the Jews out of Palestine, but the Jewish religion continued to be accepted as a *religio licita*, a permitted religion, in the Roman Empire. They enjoyed freedom of worship, and were not forced to offer sacrifices to the statue of the Emperor. In a way the Jews were the forerunners of the preachers of the Gospel. The beginnings of the Church of Christ were among the Jews.

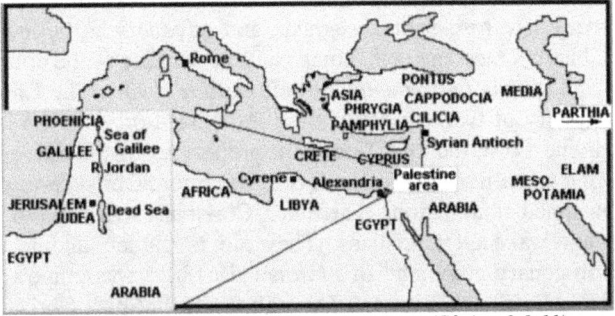
Jewish Diaspora in the time of the New Testament (Cf. Acts 2:9-11).

Many Jews, however, did not accept the message of the missionaries, and rejected Jesus Christ. During the time of the Emperor Nero they even urged the Romans to persecute the Christians. Although their particular position as bearers of the covenant of grace had ended because it had been fulfilled in Christ and had widened to all peoples of the earth, still they were by no means excluded from God's covenantal grace. Many reacted positively to the Gospel of salvation. Consequently, the Christian faith spread rapidly in the areas where there were many Jews.

3. Expansion inside the Roman Empire

3.1. The Church is rooted in Christ

The Church of God began in Paradise. With the incarnation of God the Son to be the Messiah Jesus Christ, the Church began its manifestation as the Church of Christ. The Christian Church 'arose out of the life, and work of its Lord, and became a universal witness to him at Pentecost'.[1]

The theme of Christ's preaching is the approaching of the *Kingdom of God*. The Kingdom of God is nearby, and man can enter it.[2] In order to enter people have to repent of their disobedience. People have been disobedient to God's most central law, love of God, and love of neighbour.[3] God forgives those who repent, and receives them as His children, as citizens of His Kingdom, as members of His Church. He receives them because of Christ's obedience that fulfilled the law.[4] In the place of God's children He was obedient to death. His crucifixion is a saving death, through which He redeemed many. He rose from the grave, and anyone who believes in Him shall not die.[5] The Church's message is that man can live because of the crucified[6] and resurrected[7] Lord.

Christ is *fully human* as well as *fully divine*. The Church has always professed this mystery of two aspects of the life of her Lord.[8] In the *first advent* of this human and divine Lord, the Old Testament prophecies of the universal character of the people of God come true. In His work of redemption, Christ restores creation, and this saving act is aimed at all nations. Therefore, Christ has sent out into the world His disciples, and in their wake all Christians. They are to gather, and to build His Church. The great missionary command of *Matthew* 28:18-20 was empowered by the outpouring of the Holy Spirit at *Pentecost*. Through the Holy Spirit Christ has been with His Church. At Pentecost the strictly Israelite, national, priestly church came to an end, and was replaced by a universal, international Church, in which all believers are priests. At Pentecost the expansion of the Church of Christ began. Thirty years later it had been established over a vast area, not only in Palestine, but also in Syria, Asia Minor, Greece, and Italy. The Church's expansion will go on until every member of the elect will be gathered in, and the promise of Christ's *Second Advent* will be fulfilled.

3.2. The Church in Palestine

In Jerusalem, at Pentecost, for the first time in history the Christian Church took shape. Thousands were baptised. Many of them were visitors. After they left Jerusalem, they undoubtedly contributed to the beginning of a worldwide expansion of Christianity. Others formed the congregation of Jerusalem. They lived in fellowship, worship, and

---

[1] H.R.Boer, *A Short History of the Early Church*, Grand Rapids: Eerdmans, 1988², pp.15-25, gives a survey of Christian expansion until the middle of the second century.
[2] Mk.1:14,15.
[3] Mt.22:34-40.
[4] Mt.5:17-20.
[5] John 11:25,26.
[6] 1 Cor.2:2.
[7] Acts 17:8.
[8] cf. 1 Tim.3:16.

mutual help, daily receiving new members (*Acts* 2:43-47). They proclaimed the Gospel, and were helped by miracles, and the power of the Holy Spirit. The congregation consisted entirely of Jews. There were two kinds of Christian Jews: Hebrews proper, and Hellenists. The first group came from Palestine itself. They continued to live in accordance with the laws of Moses, and other old Jewish traditions. The other group of Christian Jews came from abroad, from the *diaspora*, i.e. from the places around the Mediterranean where Jews had settled. They were more open to the ideas of the Greek. Soon tension and even conflict arose between the two groups, for example on the distribution of food to poor Hellenist widows.

Even as the Church grew, many Jews, both Hebrews and Hellenists, refused to become Christians. The Hellenists in particular, could not accept that some of their number had become followers of Jesus. The young Church suffered, mainly because of the hostile attitude of these non-Christian Hellenist Jews from the *diaspora*.[9] The Jerusalem congregation was persecuted. The stoning of Stephen is an example. Saul, a Jew from Tarsus (in Cilicia, Asia Minor) was an organiser of cruelty against Christians.

The persecutions did not stop the church of Jerusalem from sending out missionaries to surrounding regions. Philip, and later John and Peter went to Samaria. Then, Philip went to Gaza, and baptised an envoy of the queen of Ethiopia (probably Nubia, in present-day Sudan). Peter then went to the coastal city of Joppa (Jaffa), and learnt that the Gospel was to be preached to the Gentiles (non-Jews) too. Barnabas went to Antioch. The congregation in Jerusalem supervised these missionary activities, and took important decisions through a council of Apostles (*Acts* 15).

Finally, the membership of the church in Palestine became restricted to Hebrews only, and as such it was unable to progress. When the Jewish nation revolted against the Romans in the years 62-70, the Christian Jews refused to side with the revolutionaries. This was looked upon as treason to the Jewish cause. In 66 the Christians left Jerusalem. They settled in Pella, beyond the River Jordan, just outside Palestine, creating a definite separation between the Jews, and Christians. From then onwards numerically spectacular Church growth discontinued among the Jews. However, it continued to grow among the peoples outside Palestine.

3.3. The Church outside Palestine

a. Inside and outside the Empire

The work of the Apostles and of their numerous successors made the Church expand *outside* the Roman Empire, and *inside* the Roman Empire. The early expansion outside the Empire (in Edessa, Persia, Armenia, India, Ethiopia, among Huns, Goths, and Celts, etc.), is described in chapter 6. For now we will be sketching the expansion of the Church within the boundaries of the Roman Empire.[10]

b. Paul: from Jerusalem to Rome

Early Christian growth inside the Roman Empire is described in the New Testament, and also in extra-Biblical literature. Saul, the persecutor of Christians had become a

---

[9] Acts 6:8,9.
[10] Cf.: Cairns, *Christianity through the Centuries*, pp.49-85, T. Dowley, *The History of Christianity*, Oxford: Lion, 1990², pp.63-81; Foster, *First Advance*, pp.20-51 (first Christians), 36-52 (earliest Church).

3. Expansion inside the Roman Empire

Christian himself,[11] and as Paul he was to become the father of the Gentile mission, and the author of nearly one fourth of the New Testament. Paul contributed to the Church of all ages, by his stance against the heresy of *Judaism*, and by his letters to the young churches. We mention three major aspects of his work:

(1) During the three or four major journeys he made, he established congregations in the vast area of *Asia Minor* (present-day Turkey), *Macedonia*, and *Greece*. From influential congregations in cities like Ephesus and Corinth, the Gospel continued to be spread. Paul also influenced the church in *Rome*. At last, in the year 67, he was killed in the persecutions by the Emperor Nero.

(2) Paul clearly saw that the significance of the Old Testament Law had changed because of its fulfilment in Christ. That is why he withstood the Hebrew Jewish Christians, and all other Judaists who wanted Gentiles to become Jews before they could be baptised as Christians. Paul was influential at the *Apostles' convent* or meeting that debated this matter, and decided that non-Jews could be baptised as non-Jews. This was a great victory for the Gospel, but it also underlined the separation between Jews, and Christians.

(3) Paul's letters have greatly influenced teaching concerning the salvation of the Church, and the conduct of Christians.

c. Four early Centres of Christianity

Christianity first expanded in the regions around the *Mediterranean Sea*. The earliest centres were: Antioch (in northern Syria), Egypt, North Africa, and Gaul. The first two regions were Greek-speaking, the other two were Latin-speaking.

Antioch in Cappadocia (Syria). Partly due to the work of Paul, Christianity was established in this region north-east corner of the Mediterranean Sea.[12] Here lived the Church Father Ignatius, who was martyred in Rome in the year 107. Ignatius was bishop of the congregation of Antioch. Roman soldiers arrested him, and took him to Rome. On his way to the Roman capital, he sent letters to churches, also one to the congregation in Rome, asking them not to beg the authorities for clemency. Antioch (like Alexandria in Egypt) became an influential centre of Christian thinking, especially with regard to the formulation of doctrines of *Christology, and Exegetics*. The *Cappadocian Fathers*, who in the 4th century contributed to the dogma of the *Trinity*, came from this region. Antiochene theology, against the Alexandrian school of thinking, emphasised the humanity of Christ, and rejected the *allegorical* method of explaining Scripture.

Egypt. In Egypt Christianity developed in the context of the Greek culture that was dominant in the eastern part of the Roman Empire, beginning among the many Hellenised Jews living there. Soon the Church spread among the other Greek-speaking people in the urban areas. Alexandria became an influential centre of Christianity, often in opposition to the Antiochene school of thinking. Clement of Alexandria (†215), Origen (†254), and Athanasius (†373) were among the early Church Fathers who contributed to the beginnings of Christian theology in the Hellenist world. These Greek-speaking Christians were called *Melkites*. At an early stage, many non-Hellenised people in the Egyptian countryside also turned to Christianity. They were called *Copts*.

---

[11] Acts 9:1-31.
[12] Acts 11: 26.

The Copts, after the *Council of Chalcedon* in 451 (see chapter 7), stuck to the *Monophysite* position in Christology. They separated from and replaced the official Melkite church, having their own Coptic language. The Coptic Church survived the first

Fragment of Coptic Bible translation (Rev. 11: 6-8).

persecutions by pagan Roman Emperors, then conflicts with the Catholic Church, and finally oppression under Islamic rule. Egypt is part of Africa. Therefore, this subsection of course connects to and overlaps with chapter 42.1.a., belonging to the part of this book that describes the history of the Church in Africa.

North Africa. Another region of early Christian history is North Africa, like Egypt a province of the Roman Empire. The term *'Africa'* referred to the coastal area with the city of Carthage (near modern Tunis in North Africa) as the centre, and also to the highlands of Numidia, and the more remote Mauritania. The Roman province covered more or less the territories of present-day Tunisia, Algeria, and Morocco. Unlike Egypt, North Africa was influenced by the western part of the Roman Empire, where Latin gradually became the most important vehicle of culture. Latin Roman names and Latinised African names appear in reports of persecution, and condemnation of Christians of the period before 313. The theological school of Carthage became influential. Tertullian (†c.[13] 225), and Cyprian (†258) were at the cradle of the development of theology in the Latin language. Much more important, however, was Augustine (†430). Baur even calls him 'the culminating point of the whole of Western theology'.[14] At the same time, these early theologians of North Africa belong to the history of the Church in Africa, described in the second part of this book. Therefore, this subsection overlaps with chapter 42.1.b.

It is true that the Western church owes much to Africa. That is why the ancient church of North Africa still captures the imagination of many modern people. We wonder about its original rapid growth, we also wonder about the internal quarrels and schisms that contributed to its almost complete eradication. The liberation of

---

[13] c. = circa or approximately.

[14] John Baur, *2000 years of Christianity in Africa: An African History 62-1992*, Nairobi: Paulines Publ., 1994², p.28.

3. Expansion inside the Roman Empire

Christianity in 313 was followed by a hundred years of internal quarrels that damaged the Church of North Africa. These *Donatist* upheavals were followed, just after Augustine's death, by a hundred years of occupation by the Germanic Vandals, who persecuted the African Christians, forcing them to accept the heresy of *Arianism*.[15] In the meantime, in the West the Roman Empire had collapsed (476). This historic event had significant consequences for the relationship between Africa, and Europe.[16] After the invasion by Arab Muslims in the 7th-century, North African Christianity faded out.

Gaul. At the beginning of the second century Christianity had also entered the south of Gaul (present-day France), centring especially in some cities. Lyons was the place where in 177 a group of nearly 50 Christians, among them Blandina and bishop Photinus, were martyred. The Church Father Irenaeus barely escaped execution. Irenaeus came from Smyrna (on the west coast of what is now Turkey), where he was a pupil of Polycarp. He studied in Rome, and then became a presbyter in Lyons. At the time of the persecution, he had just left for Rome to deliver a letter to the pope. After his return in 178, he was made bishop of Lyons. He became famous for his attacks on *Gnosticism*. Whether he was martyred is unknown.

By the end of the third century, Christians 'appeared to be represented virtually everywhere' in the Roman Empire. That could not be said of any other part of the world. However, Christians in the Empire still were a minority.

d. Figures, and Characteristics of Growth

How can the rapid expansion of the early Church be explained? Was it a result of 'miraculous' intervention by God or was it a result of 'ordinary' human circumstances, and events? In the literature there is a discussion about the figures, and the character of Christian growth during the first centuries of the Church. How many Christians were there in the Roman Empire at the beginning of the 4th century? Hastings thinks that perhaps in a few areas they could have exceeded 20%, but 'in general the figure must be lower, and in most of the West far lower'.[17] Stark looked at the arithmetic of early Christian growth from a sociological angle.

Agreeing with the widely accepted estimate of a total population of 60 million in the Roman Empire at that time, he quotes various estimates of the number of Christians: not more than 5% (Gibbon), 15 million (Von Hertling), less than 7.5 million (Grant), 5 million (MacMullen).

Stark thinks that in 300 the Roman Empire had a little more than 6 million Christians, which is 10.5 percent of the total population. According to him,

A Roman soldier.

---

[15] *Arianism:* The principal heresy which denied the true Divinity of Christ, so called after its author Arius († c.336), who maintained that the Son of God was not eternal but was created.
[16] See also chapter 12.5.
[17] Adrian Hastings, *A World History of Christianity*, London: Cassell, 1999, p.34.

this numerical growth is in keeping with growth rates of religious movements in modern times, e.g. of the *Mormon Church*. Therefore, Stark does not seek 'exceptional explanations' and miracles when trying to understand the growth of the Church in the first centuries.[18] In his opinion, Christian growth can be explained by the methods of modern *sociological science*. These methods he applied to the investigation of phenomena that favoured the ongoing spread of Christianity. He concludes that in the beginning conversion to Christianity was attractive to the Jews. He also says that the spread of the Gospel among the Gentiles was helped by factors like Christian behaviour during epidemics; the family and other social networks of Christians; the role of women and slaves in the Church; Christianity's aptitude for adapting to city life, especially to the chaos and crises in the ancient cities; the *'rational'* attractiveness of martyrdom; Christians' ability to make use of opportunities; able organisation of Christian activities, and also Christian virtues that restored 'humanity' to many.[19]

Hastings on the other hand, tends to refer to the *'miraculous'* as an explanation for early Christian growth, because he does not see much organised Christian effort in the early Church. He says: 'There was, at least after the close of the Pauline era, no specifically missionary activity, so far as we know'. The Christians had no organising centre, no missionary task force, and no specially trained clergy. His conclusion, though, is not very far from Stark's as he thinks that Christianity spread 'through a network of family, friendship, business contacts', through the movements of migrants, through the scattering effect of persecutions, and through the impact of Christian literature.[20]

Is the expansion of early Christianity to be explained by either the *'ordinary'* or the *'miraculous'*? In chapter 2, on the *Fullness of Time*, we saw that God prepared the Jewish, and the Gentile world for receiving the message of Christ. God's hand is present in history, a miracle indeed. At the same time, God uses ordinary human means. He made His Church arise in the midst of the political, economic and sociological developments of the history of humanity. God used these events to contribute to the emergence of the Church. Green, in his account of the results of the early proclamation of the Gospel among Jews and Gentiles, shows that there is considerably more of a miracle in it than Stark thinks. Conversion, in the sense of surrendering to Christ, was 'completely foreign to the mentality of the Graeco-Roman world'. It only could be brought about by the power of divine interference through the preaching of the Word, and the work of the Holy Spirit.[21] Green seems to see more structure in the missionary activities of the early Church than Hastings does. Office-bearers and other members acted as evangelists. There was a consciousness among Christians that the example of individual and communal Christian life could attract others.

Green further refers to: (1) *missionary methods*, e.g. public preaching, street preaching, preaching in schools, evangelism in the home, and family, through marriage, among slaves, at special meetings, in personal encounters, by the spreading of literature, e.g. apologetic addresses, in the first place the books of Scripture, (2) *missionary*

---

[18] Rodney Stark, *The Rise of Christianity: How the Obscure, Marginal Jesus Movement Became the Dominant Religious Force in the Western World in a Few Centuries*, San Francisco: Harper Collins, 1997², pp.6,7.

[19] Stark, *Rise*, pp.49-216.

[20] Hastings, *World History*, p.27.

[21] Michael Green, *Evangelism in the Early Church*, London: Hodder and Stoughton 1970. See chapters 1-6, chapter 6 especially deals with 'conversion'.

motives, e.g. feelings of gratefulness, and responsibility, concern for fellow human beings, and (3) *missionary strategy*, e.g. use of geographical factors, the approach of Paul, and eschatological expectations.[22]

The spread of early Christianity in the midst of a powerful non-Christian culture required of the Church a specific organisation, faith, and exemplary behaviour of its individual members. We will be looking at these factors in the next chapter.

---

[22] Green, *Evangelism*, chapters 7-10.

4. The Life of the Earliest Church

4.1. The Government of the Church

The life of the Church in the first centuries was characterised by *growth* (see chapters 3 and 6), and also by *persecutions* (see chapter 5), *doctrinal controversies* (see chapter 7), and by *tension* between the East and the West (see chapter 17). Here we want to look at three aspects of Christian life before 313 that are related to growth, persecutions and controversies: (1) *church government*, (2) *faith*, and (3) *conduct*.

Apart from the Council of Apostles at Jerusalem, in the beginning the New Testament Church had no governmental structure of office-bearers. Only a little later, as reported in *Acts* 6, did the congregation of Jerusalem appoint deacons. There are differences between these early deacons and the office of deacon that appeared later. At least two of the first deacons were preachers of the Gospel or *evangelists*.

The basic office of the Church was the *elder*. The first reference to elders is in *Acts* 11:30, and various other references follow. The New Testament uses two words for this office-bearer, *presbyteros*[1] (elder) and *episkopos* (overseer). The terms are used alternatively for the same functionaries.[2] Together the elders are the leaders and overseers of the congregation. They are not priests in the exclusive sense of the word, as the Old Testament sacrificing priesthood is fulfilled in Christ, therefore in Christ all believers are now included in the priesthood. The New Testament office-bearers are leading the Church by administering the Word of God and the sacraments, and by looking after the discipline of its members.

Apart from these formal offices, in the first period there were the more informal offices of a specific *prophetic* and *charismatic* character, performed by men, and sometimes by women, with special gifts of leadership and guidance. We read about *prophets*, *teachers*, *pastors*, and *evangelists*. Whereas the formal office-bearers served one congregation, these prophetic and charismatic leaders often were in the general service of the Church. Lindsay says that generally authority in the Church was executed in an informal way. Even the formal leaders were more in the tradition of the prophetic office of Christ than in the royal and priestly offices of their Lord.[3] Soon after the New Testament, in the period of the *Apostolic Fathers*, this pattern changed along three lines.

The Christian Chi-Rho (X-P) symbol, the first two letters of the name Christ in Greek, was often used by the early Christians. The other characters are the Alpha (A) and the Omega (Ω), signifying Christ as the beginning and the end, Rev.22:13.

First, a priestly (*sacerdotal*) element is introduced. Office-bearers tend to be transformed into *priests*. This is because the conception of the Holy Supper as a meal of

---

[1] *presbyteros*: related to the Greek word for oldest (*presbutatos*).
[2] Cf. 1 Tim.3:1-13; 5:17; Titus 1:5-9.
[3] T.M. Lindsay, *The Church and the Ministry in the Early Centuries*, London: Hodder and Stoughton, 1867, pp.271ff.

4. The Life of the Earliest Church

remembrance is gradually changing into the idea of the Holy Eucharist as a kind of sacrifice.

Secondly, these two titles are beginning to be used for different offices, *presbyteroi* for elders, and *episkopoi* for bishops. The bishop is seen as a kind of *monarch* (a single ruler) above the congregation and also above the elders and deacons. He is said to derive his position from the Apostles whom he claims to succeed through the laying on of hands. This means that besides the thought of *sacerdotalism*, the idea of *hierarchicalism* makes inroads into the early Church.

Thirdly, the deacons are fitted into this hierarchy, ranking after bishops and elders, and still later serving as special assistants to the bishops.

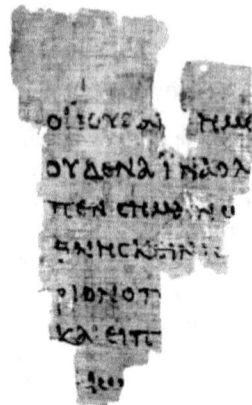

One of the oldest existent fragments of the Bible, approximately 125: parts of seven lines of John 18:31–33,

Schaff says that these changes were generally accepted by the middle of the second century AD. According to him, the first clear indication of a difference between elders and a bishop is seen in the letters of Ignatius of Antioch (†107), which he wrote in Rome, the place of his martyrdom. Ignatius says:

> 'Look up to the bishop, so that God may consider you ... We have to look up to the bishop as to the Lord himself'.

Ignatius gives to the bishop a position of unique authority. Moreover, salvation tends to be made dependent on the authority of the bishop, although sacerdotal teaching was not yet formulated in Ignatius' time. In Ignatius' conception a bishop is still the ruler of only one congregation, but his ideas are the beginning of a development that would lead to the organisation of a bishop heading a diocese of several congregations, or of *metropolitan* bishops being regional rulers, or finally of the *episcopus episcoporum* (pope) ruling the entire Church. In the third century Cyprian of Carthage (†258) would lay a theoretical foundation for the further development of these ideas. But neither he nor Ignatius intended to pave the way for the *papacy* (see chapter 9). In the meantime, the division between higher and lower bishops took shape. And some *Apostolic Fathers*, e.g. Irenaeus of Lyons (†200), joined their theory of the *apostolic succession* of bishops to the recognition of the *primacy* of the bishop of Rome.[4]

Schaff says that the development to monarchical episcopacy is understandable because the external danger of persecution and the internal danger of chaos and heresy seemed to require this type of centralised leadership. In his opinion, unbiased historians have to admit that the 'divine right of the episcopacy' was an adaptation 'to the needs of the Church'.[5] Boer considers this development as a deviation from the New Testament, although he can also understand why it happened. He mentions four reasons for the use of the office of the monarchical bishop in distinction from the elder's office:

> (a) the natural tendency in a governing group for one to become the leader, especially in difficult circumstances, (b) the need to centralise the administration because of rapid church growth, and the necessity of discipline, teaching and caring for the many poor, (c) the persecutions required wise and fearless leaders who could speak and act for all members, (d)

---

[4] Ph. Schaff, *History of the Church*, vol. II, pp.69-70, cf. pp.74-75.
[5] Shaff, *History*, p.68.

the rise of heresies required strong and faithful leaders to define and uphold the doctrines of the Church and to be its spokesman in disputes.[6]

Especially the defence against *Gnosticism* required strong leadership. This movement of *dualistic mysticism* 'mixed Christian ideas and vocabulary with all sorts of incompatible beliefs', rejecting the oneness of God and the Old Testament, and dividing reality in general in matter and spirit, and reality of man particularly in body and soul. As Gnosticism gradually developed into a powerful counter-church, the Catholic Church needed theologians with authority, like Irenaeus of Lyons, who could give a clear formulation of the anti-Gnostic position.[7]

4.2. The Doctrines of the Church

After the apostolic era, the *Apostolic Fathers*, i.e. those leaders who were taught by the Apostles in person, played an important role in defining the teachings of the Church. Letters by the most important *Apostolic Fathers* are those from Clement of Rome (approximately 95), Ignatius of Antioch (†approximately 107), Polycarp of Smyrna (†approximately 155), the writer of the letter to Barnabas (perhaps of Alexandria, between 70 and 100), Hermas of Rome (perhaps approximately 145), Papias of Hierapolis (†130), the anonymous writer of the *Didache*, or *The Teaching of the Apostles* (approximately 100), and the anonymous writer of *The Letter to Diognetus* (probably between 150 and 180). These letters show deep love for Christ, high regard for the Church, and a stern self-discipline. At the same time, there are teachings in them that tend to deviate from Scripture, and are at least preparations for later heresies.

Boer distinguishes the following tendencies: (a) an unhealthy *desire for martyrdom*, even a spirit of seeking martyrdom (especially in Ignatius' letter to the Romans; (b) the belief that repentance precedes baptism, and that *baptism removes past sins*, and also the idea that after baptism there can only be repentance once (especially in *The Shepherd of Hermas*); (c) an extremely strong emphasis on *law-keeping and good works*, giving the impression that man by good works contributes to salvation (all Apostolic Fathers) and (d) the use of *allegories* in explaining Scripture, that is 'the use of an image or figure to describe an entirely different matter than that which the image or figure represents' (especially Hermas's letter to Barnabas).[8]

4.3. The Conduct of Christians

Christians did not separate from society. Although the world did not possess them, they realised that they were living *in* the world, and that it belonged to their calling to faithfully work in and for society.

A letter by a Christian to a certain Diognetus says that 'Christians are not distinguished from the rest of mankind in country or custom'. At the same time, so the writer continues, Christians are different, they are aliens in this world, they do not condone adultery, they do not abandon their children, and their citizenship is in heaven. 'In a word, what the soul is in the body, Christians are in the world'.

---

[6] Boer, *History*, pp.27-30.

[7] cf. Hastings, *World History*, p.29.

[8] Boer, *History*, pp.33-35.

4. The Life of the Earliest Church

Generally, Christians would not take part or even attend public spectacles and amusements as these were often immoral or connected to pagan worship. Church Father Tertullian († approximately 225), who is among the most strict and profuse writers on Christian morality, even forbade Christians to join the Roman army or to take official positions in government. However, many Christians did not feel and act as strictly as Tertullian did.

Contrary to the widely accepted habit of concubinage and other forms of adultery, Christians strictly adhered to their law of monogamy. This contributed much to the improvement of the position of *women* in society. Although Christians did not condemn *slavery*, they honoured their Christian slaves as equals in the Church, and they protested against the improper treatment of slaves. In religious and moral purity the Christians differed much from the pagans. This was reflected in a very strict church discipline.

The negative side of this was that the Gospel tended to become a *new law*. There was little room for repentance and forgiveness after baptism. Sinners had to confess and repent in public, and this was followed by harsh punishments.

Those who wanted to repent because they had denied Christ before the persecutors of the Roman state caused a special problem. A considerable part of the Church refused to accept their repentance and the renewal of their membership. This question led to various schisms, mainly the one in the North African context, where in the 4th century a separate Church was formed.[9] The emergence of the Christian Church led to reactions by the surrounding pagan culture, which was reflected in the policies of the Roman state. This is the subject of the next chapter.

---

[9] Boer, *History*, pp.35-41; cf. A. Hastings, *A World History of Christianity*, London: Cassell, 1999, p.26.

5. The Church and the Roman State

5.1. Persecutions

In its earliest period the Church was under pressure by the Roman Empire. In the beginning the Roman leaders thought that the Christian Church was just another branch of the Jewish religion, although like Pontius Pilate they saw that the Jews ill-treated Christians. Some Emperors, like Claudius (d.54), did not know the difference between Jews and Christians. When Christianity began to grow rapidly, the Roman leaders became anxious. The Roman State did not like the independent way in which Christians behaved. Generally, it opposed the Christian Church. At certain times it persecuted the Christians by trying to hinder the growth of their numbers and attempts were made to root them out. Persecutions started in the year 63 and ended in 313. This era can be divided into two periods, before and after the year 250.

In the first period, which lasted until 250, persecutions did not take place all the time, and in all places. Nor were the persecutions organised campaigns. Let us look at the policy of some of the Emperors before 250. Nero (d. 68), who seemed to have gone mad, probably deliberately set the city of Rome on fire. To avoid unpopularity with the Roman citizens he accused the Christians of the act. He had many of them killed, for example by throwing them to wild animals, and by burning them. Domitian (†96) threatened the Christians by his religious pretences. He was the first Emperor to call himself lord and god (*dominus et deus*). The Emperors before Domitian were regarded as gods after they had died, through their *genius*. But Domitian decreed that the people should begin to honour him as a god during his lifetime. Through this command he especially threatened Christians, because they could never obey and were therefore liable to punishment. Domitian hated the Christians. In his opinion, the Christians had brought poverty to the Roman State. Trajan (d. 117) persecuted

Coin with the image of the Emperor Nero (37-68)

the Church in a passive way. In a letter to Pliny, the governor of a province, he forbade him to actively search out Christians. Marcus Aurelius (d. 180) was an advocate of Stoic philosophy. As such, he was looking forward to the reform and strengthening of the pagan religion of the Roman State. Some famous witnesses of Christ like Speratus and Polycarp were killed. Septimus Severus (d. 211) prohibited the conversion of Romans to Christianity or to the Jewish religion. He decreed that Christians must be actively searched out and condemned. Among the executed Christians were Perpetua and Felicitas in the province of North Africa.

A second period of persecutions started in the year 250, when the Emperor Decius issued the *Edict of Sacrifice*. This edict forced all the people in the Roman Empire to offer sacrifices to the statue of the Emperor. Only the Jews were free not to obey this law. Others who refused were punished, often by execution.

During the reign of Decius, persecutions of Christians began to take place throughout the Empire at all the times. Many Christians did not obey Decius' edict. But some Christians, fearing death, abandoned their religion. They offered sacrifices, or they rejected the Christian Church in another way. These backsliders were called the *fallen ones*, in Latin: the *lapsi* (singular: *lapsus*). Emperor Valerian (d. 260) at first behaved peacefully towards the Christians. But his policy changed suddenly, and he started confiscating Church buildings and arresting office-bearers. Among the martyrs was Cyprian, a famous bishop in North Africa. Others were not faithful. They gave in to the persecutors. Soon a special problem arose concerning these *lapsi*, when some of them wanted to rejoin the Church. This problem was going to split the Church. Opposed to those who were lenient enough to re-admit the *lapsi*, there were those, led by Novatian, who adamantly refused to accept anyone who had once rejected Christ.

The most dangerous persecution took place during the reign of the Emperor Diocletian (d. 305). He held the Christians responsible for the increasing weakness of the Roman Empire. By rooting out Christianity, so he thought, the empire would be saved. He ordered the demolition of all religious buildings of the Christians. The Bible and other Christian writings were to be handed over to the authorities. He also ordered the arrest of Church leaders, and he restated the law that all Christians had to offer sacrifices. This wave of persecution did not last very long, ending when Diocletian died. After the Emperor's death, the pagan religion and the State's ability to resist Christianity grew weaker.

Bust of the Emperor Decius (†251) who in 250 extended and systematised the anti-Christian persecutions.

5.2. Reasons for Persecution

According to the Roman laws, Christianity was a *religio illicita*, an illegal religion. This is surprising because the State generally accepted any religion, including Judaism, which did not threaten the symbols of Roman power and unity. However, the condition of this relative religious freedom was not acceptable to the Christian faith. The officially prescribed Emperor-worship was the stumbling block. Any religion was tolerated that would not forbid its members to take part in the ceremonies for worshipping the Emperor of the Roman State. The Emperor was looked upon as a *pontifex maximus*, i.e. as a bridge-builder between the gods and the people, or between heaven and earth. That is why the Emperor deserved to be honoured as a god. At times incense had to be offered to his statue by all. Those who refused were charged with rebellion against the Emperor, the empire, and humanity. Christians did not want to offer sacrifices. That is why, in the thinking of the Romans, they were enemies of the Roman Empire and hated by the human race (*odium generis humani*). It seemed as though Christians wanted to destroy the protective relationship of the gods with the Roman Empire and the protective function of the empire for humanity. In other word, the Christians were thought to threaten the foundations of unity and peace. Because of this, they deserved punishment, even execution.

In Roman opinion the Christians were also *atheists*. There were no images of the gods in their temples, and they did not respect the statues of the Emperors. So, they had no god. Because of this, the gods had become angry and they wanted the Christians killed. Besides, the Romans accused the Christians of gathering at night in *secret fellowships* to plot against the State. In Roman pagan view Christians were also *abject* and *dishonourable*. In the Roman mind there was no place for the message of forgiveness and love preached by the Christians. To them the Christian principles of forgiveness and love indicated weakness and dishonesty.

Moreover, Christians were suspected of doing evil things in their nocturnal meetings. They *killed children* so that they could drink their blood. In the view of a satirical cartoonist, Christians were praying to a *donkey-god*, who was crucified on the cross. To the Romans this was a shameful death without any positive significance. These were some of the accusations. But many Romans knew that all these things were just insults, and false allegations. Although Christians were ridiculed and persecuted, their number grew because many people showed interest in the Gospel[1].

A cartoon made by a Roman soldier. He drew a crucified donkey and compared it to the crucified Christ. He added these words: 'Alexamenos prays to his God'.

5.3. The Christians' Answer

Although they sometimes found themselves in very stressful situations, most Christians did not reject the Lord Jesus Christ. They showed faith and perseverance. Consequently, many were arrested and killed or punished in other ways. The victims of the persecutions who received capital punishment were called martyrs. This word is derived from Greek *martures* (witnesses), or *martyrion* (testimony). They were also called *confessors*. Through their testimony many people were converted. Tertullian, a bishop in North Africa, said about this: 'the blood of the Christians is seed' (*sanguis Christianorum semen est*). Christians were punished in a number of ways. Those who refused to offer sacrifice were killed: true Roman citizens were beheaded; others were crucified, burnt, thrown to wild animals, or killed in other ways. Less severe punishments were banishment, being used as slaves in mines, being jailed, or being stripped of wealth. In many places, courts heard cases against Christians. Many reports of these court sessions were kept. They are called *acts of martyrs*, and they serve as stores of information for today's students of Church History.

---

[1] Cairns, *Christianity through the Centuries*, pp.86-94 [Persecutions], Dowley, pp.83-95,121-122, 1 Foster, *First Advance*, pp.69-85, A.M. Renwick and A.M. Harman, *The Story of the Church*, Leicester: Inter-Varsity, 1985, pp.49-52.

Unfortunately, there were also Christians who lacked courage. When their faith was put to the test, they betrayed Christ. Some of these backsliders or *lapsi* rejected Christianity completely and permanently. Others, however, after a time would repent and express the wish to rejoin the Church. This especially happened when a period of persecution had ended. Then, they wanted to become members of their church community again. Church leaders and other Christians that had remained faithful realised, however, that these *lapsi* had done much damage to the Church. This made the question of accepting the lapsi a very difficult thing to the Church. It was also found difficult to assess the genuineness of a repenting lapsus.

Besides, there were several types of lapsi. There were for example, the *sacrificati*, who had offered sacrifice to the gods in a pagan temple. There were also the *thurificati*, who had offered incense before the statue of the Emperor. Others were the *libellatici*. They had not offered sacrifice but through corrupt ways, they had bought a document stating that they had. Some were called *traditores*. These people had handed over Bibles and other holy books of the Church to the Roman persecutors, who burnt them.

5.4. Threats to the Church

The persecutions threatened the Church, although indirectly they also helped the Church to grow quantitatively and qualitatively. By the year 300 AD the number of Christians had grown considerably. Rooting out the Church had become impossible. Yet the persecutions had some negative effects on the Church.

First, some people had begun to believe that being killed because of your Christian faith was profitable for salvation. They thought that suffering and being killed were the means of personally receiving the *grace of God* and *eternal life in heaven*. Consequently, some people desired greatly to die as a martyr and they voluntarily handed themselves to the pagan leaders for execution. In addition to this, slowly the idea grew that the death of martyrs created a *store of grace* from which other people could be helped in their attempts to acquire salvation. In this thought, the martyrs had become *saints*, who from their dwellings in heaven helped people on earth, functioning as a kind of mediators between Christ and the people. Because of this, Christians started venerating the martyrs and even praying to them. A special day (*saint's day*) was given to each martyr. The practice of worshipping martyrs had serious consequences for theological opinion and spiritual life. It weakened the knowledge of grace, for it encouraged a false teaching that the salvation of men depends on their good works. Gradually the Church lost sight of the true teaching that man is saved only through faith and that salvation is made possible by the sacrifice of Christ only.

Picture of the execution of Church Father Polycarp (c.69-c.155), leader of the church in Smyrna, in Asia Minor.

Secondly, the persecutions indirectly weakened the Biblical structure of the organisation of the Church. From the time of the Apostles the congregations had been governed by groups of elders. This *collegiate* form of church government was found less practical by those who thought that the Church would be stronger if it were ruled by only one leader. They were of the opinion that one leading elder (or *bishop*) would be able to protect the Church better than a number of elders through their sessions. These thoughts were realised in the church, and they developed to the practice of bishops who ruled as kings over a number of congregations (*monarchical bishops*). There were also *metropolitan bishops* who were church leaders in larger cities. Slowly the bishops of Rome received supreme authority over the other bishops, at least in the West. This order of *Episcopal* church government was supposed to protect the Church against the dangers that threatened from the outside and from the inside. Bishops had to lead the Church in times of persecution.

More dangerous, however, were the *false teachings* (heresies), which threatened the Church from within. The bishops were supposed to formulate authoritative answers to the challenges by e.g. *Gnosticism*, *Marcionism* and *Manichaeism* with their *dualistic* ideas of denying the unity of the Bible, of God and of man. There was also the heresy of *Judaism*. It weakened the Church's witness of free grace of Jesus Christ by stating that Christians can only be saved by being obedient to the laws of the Old Testament. After some time, other groups emerged, such as the *Arians* who rejected the total divinity of Christ, and *Pelagianism*, which rejected the belief that all men are born in sin. The Church denounced all these heresies through its bishops who from time to time gathered together in Church Councils.

Thirdly, although the bishops and the Councils tried to ward off heresies, at the same time teachings opposing the Bible entered the Church. For example, the teachings on

Christians put to the lions in Rome.

the *sacraments* were affected by this. The idea grew that the elements as such, the water for baptism and the bread and the wine at the Lord's Supper, give grace and new life. It was even thought that the Church itself is a sacrament, over-arching the sacraments as the great channel of grace. Some thought that the power of the sacraments depended on the hierarchy of priests.

Persecutions at times also threatened the unity of the Church. Before 200, the *Montanists* emerged, among Christians in the North Africa. They particularly stressed the work of the Holy Spirit, and said the Spirit was not at work in the Catholic Church. Their members were not allowed to evade persecution and martyrdom.

About the year 250 in the north of Africa in the time of Bishop Cyprian, the movement of the Novatians emerged. These people did not want the Church to accept the *lapsi*. They also refused to re-admit the *lapsi* who repented. After the time of persecutions, a large group of Christians in North Africa became followers of this idea. They separated from the main church and established an independent church, called after one of their leaders, Donatus, the Donatist Church. Donatists were of the opinion that a church can only be a true Church of God if its office-bearers are true and perfect Christians. Thus Donatism made the truth of the Church depend on the truthfulness and the holiness of its priests and bishops. In their view the Catholic Church was a false church because some of its bishops were ordained by *lapsi*.

5.5. The End of Persecutions

After the death of Diocletian in 311, the Roman Empire had a number of Emperors at the same time who all wanted power over the entire empire. Constantius Chlorus, an army commander in Britain, became the Emperor of the Western part. He married Helena, who was a Christian. In 306 in York their son, Constantine, succeeded his father as western Emperor. In 312 Constantine defeated Maxentius, his important competitor, probably near Rome at the Milvian bridge. Eusebius says that some time before the battle, Constantine saw a vision. 'He saw

Statue of Emperor Constantine the Great (†337).

with his own eyes in the heavens a trophy of the cross arising from the light of the sun, carrying the message, *In Hoc Signo Vinces* or: with this sign you will have victory'.

In 313, through the *Edict of Milan*, Constantine decreed freedom for the Christian religion and other religions. This meant the end of persecution in the Western part of the Roman Empire. In 324 Constantine (who later would be called *Constantinus Magnus*: Constantine the Great) defeated Licinius, who was Emperor in the Eastern part. The persecutions ended in the entire Roman Empire. Christians and their bishops were allowed to worship in freedom. In 380 the Christian religion became the religion of the Roman Empire. This meant that the political leaders favoured Christianity.

Was Constantine himself ever converted to Christianity? It is true that he legitimised Christianity in the Roman Empire and presided over the Council of Nicaea, which declared Christ's divinity. But it is also true that he killed his own son and his second wife, and that he exiled Church Father Athanasius, and also that he used pagan symbols in building the city of Constantinople. Constantine refused to be baptised until shortly before his death in 337.

Nonetheless, Constantine played a significant role for the Church, although not necessarily in a completely positive sense. The position of being the favoured religion may have helped the Church in growing numerically and in power, but this situation unfortunately also made the Church deviate from Scripture as to some of its teachings and its leadership.[2]

---

[2] Cf.: Cairns, *Christianity through the Centuries*, pp.118-124, Dowley pp.139-151.

6. Expansion beyond the Roman Empire

6.1. 'Southern Christianity'

a. The Term

The New Testament gives very little information about the expansion of Christianity beyond the boundaries of the Roman Empire. Also, the accounts of *Church History* do not give many details of the early emergence and growth of the Church outside the Empire. It is apparent, however, that missionary activity and consequent expansion of Christianity did not remain limited to the territories of the Roman Empire. There are indications that even the Apostles extended their missionary journeys beyond the boundaries of the Empire.

The Church in the Latin West and the Church in the Greek East eventually developed to respectively the *Roman Catholic Church* and the *Greek Orthodox Church*. Beside them other types of Christianity came into being. This worldwide expansion began a long time before the end of the Roman Empire in the West (476), and it continued after that. In this chapter, we will briefly look at developments East, South, North, and also West of the old Empire. For expediency's sake, we will not always limit our survey to the history before 476.

Verstraelen uses the term *Southern Christianity* for a great variety of churches and Christian cultures that came into being East and South of the Roman Empire. He stresses that 'Christianity was not an exclusive phenomenon in the Roman Empire and in the North, but struck roots in different socio-cultural contexts in the Southern hemisphere'. He is right, although south of the equator this happened much later. Verstraelen pleads for 'new modes of rethinking and rewriting Christian History' by telling the full story of this non-Roman and non-Greek Christianity, 'and making it part of Christian history as a whole'.[1] African Church History, though being a very significant aspect of 'Southern Christianity' is left out in this section, because Part II of this book is entirely devoted to it.

b. Edessa

Edessa, capital of the small kingdom of Osrhoene, was situated in Mesopotamia (modern Iraq) about 200 kilometres east of the Roman city of Antioch, where the name *'Christians'* was used for the first time. The church historian Eusebius († approximately 340) claims that he saw letters exchanged between Abgar, king of Edessa, and Jesus himself, who promised to send one of his disciples to the kingdom. According to Eusebius, in a later time Thaddeus preached the Gospel in Edessa, baptising King Abgar and many others. Apart from having the first Christian king, Edessa may have had the first church building, and well before 200 the first translation of the Greek New Testament into another language. This was the *Syriac* language, spoken in most parts of Mesopotamia, and closely related to the *Aramaic* of Palestine. Among the early

---

[1] J. Verstraelen, 'Southern Perspectives on Christian History', in: *Neue Zeitschrift für Missionswissenschaft*, 53-1997/2, pp.100,101. Our survey of *Southern Christianity* mainly follows the order given by: J. Foster, *The First Advance*, London: SPCK, 1994³, pp.88-110 (Edessa, Armenia, Parthia/Persia), pp.110-121 (Ethiopia, Arabia, India), cf. Cairns, *Christianity through the Centuries*, pp.120-14). See also: Baur, pp.21-39 (North Africa and Egypt, and beyond: Nubia, Ethiopia), Shaw, *Kingdom*, pp.11-72 (Egypt, North Africa, Nubia, Ethiopia), Tindall, *History of Central Africa*, p.20 (Romans and Africa).

Christians in Edessa was Tatian. He became a Christian in Rome, wrote against the pagan Graeco-Roman civilisation (*Address to the Greeks*), and was a pupil of Church Father Justin. After his return to Edessa about 172, he wrote a history of the life of Jesus, the *Diatessaron*. Another early Edessan Christian was Bardaisan, the first writer of Syriac hymns and author of the book entitled *Concerning Fate*, which says that the pattern of man's life consists of *nature, fate,* and *freedom*. Both Tatian and Bardaisan were counted as heretics in the West.

c. Armenia

Church historians Eusebius (4th cent.) and Sozomen (5th cent.) report about the existence of Armenian Christianity in the third century. The earliest full record is from the Armenian Agathangelos (5th cent.). Armenia, situated south of the Caucasus Mountains, tried to retain independence between the two conflicting world powers of the day, the Roman Empire in the West and the Empire of Parthia in the East. Roman *polytheism* and Parthian *Zoroastrianism* were the competing religious forces. Christianity became the third force. In a struggle between the pro-Roman and pro-Parthian parties, the child Gregory, later called the *Illuminator*, was carried off to Roman territory where he was brought up as a Christian. On his return to Armenia Gregory Illuminator started to preach the Gospel. The circumstances were favourable as the Armenians had come to mistrust the official religions of Rome and Parthia. But they were prepared to listen to the preacher of a religion that seemed to oppose one of their enemies. About the year 300 the Armenian king adopted Christianity. Gregory was made Armenia's first bishop. One of his successors developed an Armenian alphabet, which facilitated the translation of the New Testament into the Armenian language in about 400.

d. Parthia and Persia

Parthia. From 240 BC to 225 the Parthians ruled the vast area from Mesopotamia to India, including present-day Iran. Their Empire was a loose federation, the main religion being *Zoroastrianism*. The main language was *Syriac*, although Greek was in use in many cities. In some cities there were strong Jewish communities. In the *Chronicle of Arbil* there is a record of the history of a Christian church in the region of Adiabene (in what is now northern Iraq) from 99 to 540. It mentions the first convert, Paqida, who became the first bishop of the land of Adiabene. He was succeeded (in 120) by Samsun. His preaching among rural *fire worshippers* angered the Zoroastrian priests, and they put him to death, which made Samsun the first martyr in this part of the world. Under bishop Izhaq the governor of Adiabene, Raqbakht, became a Christian. However, in 148 Izhaq was murdered by Zoroastrian priests and Raqbakht was killed on the battlefield before he could further the cause of Christianity. The chronicle mentions periods of persecution by Zoroastrians after the years 160 and 179. But this could not stop the growth of Christianity. The chronicle names seventeen places where before 225 a bishop was selected.

Persia. In 225 the Persians began a revolution and took over the Parthian Empire. Their Emperors were called by their family name, the Sassanids or Sassanians. They wanted to revive the ancient Persian Empire of 500 years before. *Zoroastrianism* became the official religion. The founder of this religion is supposed to be Zoroaster or Zarathustra, who probably lived before 1000 BC. Almost nothing is known about him personally except perhaps some hymns (the *Gathas*) that are part of Zoroastrian writings. *Zoroastrianism* became influential in the Parthian epoch, which is before 225. It became the main religion after the takeover of Persia (present-day Iran) in the Sassanid era, which is 226-651. It seems *Zoroastrianism* gradually changed from some kind of monotheism to a dualistic system in which Ahura Mazda was the good god (hence, this religion is also called *Mazdaism*), and Angra Mainyu the evil god. Man has to choose between either the good god or the evil one. By choosing truth, man will pass Chinvat bridge on the day of judgment and pass into paradise. By choosing lies, however, man will be led to a razor's edge and fall into Hell. Zoroaster and his supporters are called the *sosyant* (redeemers). Their priests are called *magi*. Prayer is always done in the presence of a holy fire; hence, they were called *fire worshippers*. Influenced by Christianity, later Zoroastrians believed that a future *Sosyant* will come, born of a virgin from Zoroaster's seed which had been preserved in a lake. He will crush the devils, resurrect the dead, and restore paradise. Zoroastrianism was heavily persecuted by Islam, but it has survived in parts of Iran, Iraq, and south of the Caucasus mountains. There are also Zoroastrians in India, where they are called Parsis.[2]

The Roman Empire was seen as Persia's traditional archenemy, so the Christians were not persecuted there during the time they were persecuted in the Roman Empire. This changed after the ascension of the Emperor Constantine, who in the *Edict of Milan* (313) gave the Christians freedom in the Roman Empire. Now the Persian rulers began to mistrust the Christians. This became even worse when Constantine wrote a letter to the Persian Emperor demanding freedom and protection for Persian Christians. In 337 Constantine announced a military expedition against Persia. This greatly contributed to Persian hatred against the Christians. In 339 a period of forty years of persecutions began. The Emperor ordered the arrest of bishop Shimun and double taxation for Christians. Then, he commanded that priests and ministers should be killed as traitors to the state, and that churches be destroyed. Over these forty years, according to Sozomen, the killing of 16,000 Christians was registered. 'But beyond those is a multitude too great to be counted, whose names have not been listed'. Foster says: 'This persecution may have surpassed any of the sufferings of the Church of the Roman Empire during the previous century'.[3] There were other periods of persecution, for example the one of 420 to 422.

Gradually, however, the Persian Church came to some kind of working agreement with the government of the Persian Empire. Tolerance grew and mistrust diminished as the Persian Church got its own bishop and became more and more independent from the Church in the Roman Empire. Beside the leading bishops of Alexandria, Constantinople, Rome, and Antioch within the Roman Empire, the capital of the Persian Empire, Ctesiphon, from 291 onwards had its own leading bishop. The first one was Papa. In a later stage these primate bishops were called Catholicos. As we have seen, this growing independence of the Persian Church could not prevent heavy persecution in the beginning, but especially after 410 when bishops of Armenia and Persia were mediators for a peace agreement between Rome and Persia, toleration of Christianity gradually increased. Finally, in 424, the Persian Church declared itself completely independent from Rome. Eventually this stopped the persecutions.

---

[2] Cf. M. Boyce, *A History of Zoroastrianism*, 2 vols, Leyden: Brill, 1982 [first 1975].
[3] Foster, *First Advance*, p.103.

e. Arabia

Both from the North and from the South Christian influences entered the Arabian Peninsula, from the Roman Empire as well as from the Persian Empire. The first records are from the early fourth century, dealing with certain chieftains who became Christians. One Theotinus, 'bishop of the Arabs', was present at the Synod of Antioch in 364. Among the early converts was the king of Yemen. He adopted the Christian faith on the preaching of Theophilus, an envoy of the Roman Emperor Constantius. Later Theophilus also played a role as missionary in Ethiopia.

The Jewish community in Yemen opposed the Christians. In Himyar, which was aproximately the territory of present-day Yemen, a Jewish state existed during a few decades in the beginning of the sixth century. It was established in 522 by King Dhu Nuwas of Himyar, who converted to Judaism and forced Himyarite citizens to follow his example. Christians among them in general refused and in the city of Najran some attacked a synagogue. Subsequently the king took revenge. He sent his army and reportedly[4] four thousand Christians were slaughtered; later one of them, Arethas, was honoured as a saint. The massacre did not remain unnoticed. It became known to the imperial court of Byzantium and the royal court of Ethiopia, both defenders of Christianity. Supported by the Emperor Justinian and his fleet, in 525 the Ethiopian King Ashbeha (Caleb) and his army crossed over to crush Dhu Nuwas, thus terminating the Jewish state.

The activities of Muhammad (570-632) and the emergence of Islam caused the end of Christianity in Arabia.

f. India

According to the pseudepigraphical[5] *Acts of Thomas*, the Apostle Thomas was sent to India. After having baptised a king named Gudnaphar and his brother Gad, he continued his journey, only to be speared to death. Foster thinks the coming of Thomas to India might be true, because the journey from Alexandria to India was regularly made at that time, and there is a very early tradition of connecting Thomas the Apostle with India.

Foster lists some of the records of early Christian presence in India. Eusebius mentions one Pantaenus of Alexandria (approximately 180), who went to India as a philosopher-missionary. A Syriac document refers to one David of Basra, who 'evangelised many people' in India. John the Persian is among those who signed the Creed of the *Council of Nicaea* (325); he signed in the name of the churches of Persia and India. In 345 *Thomas the Merchant* arrived with a group of Christian immigrants, probably refugees, in Malabar (now Kerala) who were given written privileges. On his travels Foster learnt of the existence of a travel diary witnessing the existence of a Christian king, Pallivanavar of Malabar, about 350. Then, there is the witness of Cosmas, a widely-travelled Alexandrian merchant and monk, writer of *The Christian*

---

[4] Peter W. van der Horst, *Het Joodse Koninkrijk van Himyar en de Christelijke martelaars van Nadjrân: Joden en Christenen in Arabië in de zesde eeuw*, Amsterdam: Athenaeum, 2015, who used: M. Detoraki & J. Beaucamp, *Le Martyre de Saint Aréthas et de ses compagnons* (BHG 166): edition critique, étude et annotations, Paris, Association des amis du Centre d'histoire et civilization de Byzance, 2007; cf. R.L. Wilken, *The First Thousand Years: A Global History of Christianity*, New Haven/ Londen: Yale UP, 2012, p.217,218.
[5] *pseudepigraphical* is the adjective of pseudepigrapha: texts ascribed to Biblical persons but authored after their death by persons who wanted to have. them included in the Biblical canon.

6. Expansion beyond the Roman Empire

Topography (approximately 547), who said he had seen churches in Ceylon, Malabar, and Kalliana (near Bombay).[6]

6.2. Christianity in the North

a. The Huns

The homeland of the Huns was not north of the Roman Empire, but in Mongolia, North of the Gobi Desert and the Himalaya Mountains, which were natural barriers that for a time prevented them from invading China and India. Yet the acts of these Central Asian

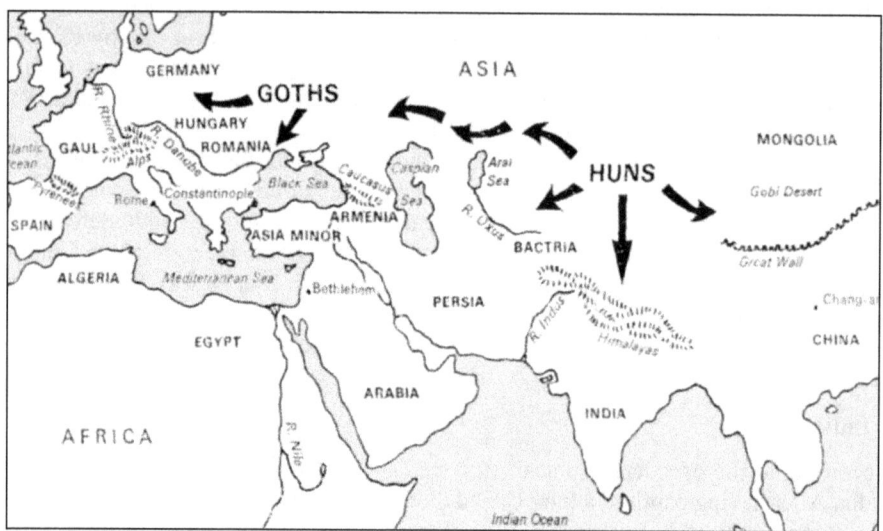

Routes taken by the Goths and the Huns.

nomads had a great impact on the peoples living north of the Roman Empire, and eventually this deeply affected the Roman Empire itself. The Huns gradually became fierce warriors who acted to rob, kill and destroy the peoples that were in their way. Some Huns invaded China and India, in both cases destroying ancient civilisations. The larger part went westwards, catching up with other wandering tribes, mostly Germanic peoples, among them the Goths. Pressed by the Huns behind them these Goths burst through the Roman frontiers in the 5th century, thus contributing to the eventual collapse of the Roman Empire in the West.

There are witnesses of early Christianity among the Huns. Foster refers to the *Chronicle of Sa'art,* which narrates how Christian Huns in Bactria helped Persian refugees. The document also mentions missionary activities by Armenian bishops Qaradushat and Makarios, among the 'White Huns' or Turks. They preached to them, applied the *Syriac alphabet* for writing their sounds, and translated the Scriptures into their language.

---

[6] For a condensed story of Christianity in India, see: R.E. Frykenberg, 'India', in: A.Hastings, *A World History of Christianity*, London, 1999, pp.147-191.

b. The Goths

From the second century Germanic tribes, foremost Goths north of the rivers Danube and Rhine, under pressure of the advancing Huns, tried to enter the Roman Empire. The Romans called them *barbarians*. The Empire was increasingly unable to ward off the swelling flood of Goth refugees. Many came in especially after 376 and often not with peaceful intentions. A revolution by Goths even led to the occupation and the looting of Rome in 410. Many Romans, Christian and pagan alike, felt the world had collapsed. However, only the Roman Empire in the West would collapse. The Church continued and even started to flourish more than before. The invading Goths, though hostile to *Graeco-Roman culture*, were not against Christianity. Long before the end of the Roman Empire many Goths had adopted Christianity. In 264 during a raid in Asia Minor, the Goths brought back with them many Christian prisoners. The example of the life of these prisoners brought many of their masters to the Christian faith. Actually, the great apostle to the Goths, Ufilas (311-383) was a descendant of one of these abducted Christians. Ufilas was an Arian. That is perhaps why he has not had much attention in books on Church History. Nevertheless, he is significant for the conversion of the Goths to Christianity, not in the least by his language work. He took Greek letters to write the Gothic sounds, and he translated the Bible into this language (341). This is the first book written in a tongue of the family of Germanic languages. There were also non-Arians who worked as missionaries among the Goths. One of them was the famous Church Father John Chrysostom.[7]

6.3. Christianity in the North West

a. Two Missionary Movements

By North-West Europe we mean the *British Isles* (= present-day England, Wales, Scotland, Ireland), *Scandinavia* (= present-day Norway, Finland, Sweden, Denmark), the *Low Countries* or *Low Lands* (= present-day The Netherlands and Belgium), and most of the territories of present-day *Germany*. Historically the conception of North-West Europe is very much connected to countries like France, Switzerland and Austria, although they belong to South and Central Europe. The spreading of Christianity in all these regions began in Antiquity and Europe in the Early Middle Ages.

Originally, the Gospel reached North West Europe from two directions, the South and the West. Missionary activities were deployed by two churches, the *Celtic Church* of the British Isles, and the *Roman Catholic Church* with its centre in Italy. Much of the history of early Christianity in North-West Europe is characterised by competition between these two missionary movements. In this chapter, the Celtic Church and its missions until the beginning of the 7th century is discussed. Chapter 14 deals with the continuation of the Christianisation of North-West Europe by missions originating in Rome.

b. Mission by the Celtic Church

Before the Roman Emperors had become Christian, and before Rome had become an authoritative centre of Christianity, some of the original Celtic people of the British Isles already had adopted Christianity. The first Celtic congregations were founded by

---

[7] Foster, *First Advance*, pp.122-131 [Huns, Goths].

6. Expansion beyond the Roman Empire

missionaries from the early Christian churches mentioned in the Bible (Palestine, Asia Minor), and by missions from Gaul. After the Roman Emperor Claudius had added Britain to the Empire in 44, Roman soldiers and traders contributed to the proclamation of the Gospel among the Celtic Brits. Many of the Picts and Scots of Scotland turned to Christianity.

Ireland was originally evangelised by Patrick, who lived in the middle of the 5th century. Born in Britain and brought up as a Christian, he was captured by Irish pirates and forcefully taken to Ireland. During his captivity he experienced conversion to Christ. He escaped to Britain, underwent training for the ministry, and went back to Ireland as a missionary. Part of his autobiography, *Confessions*, is still extant. Another early missionary in Ireland was Palladius.

The earliest church in England, Scotland and Ireland is called the *Celtic Church*. It differed from the Roman Church and was independent. In the *Celtic Church* the communities of believers were organised around monasteries on common land. Private possessions did not play an important role. Life was looked upon as a *pilgrimage*. The most important church officials were the *abbots*, to whom in practice the bishops and priests were subordinated. Clergy were allowed to marry. Papal authority was rejected. The Gregorian calendar for the celebration of the Christian feasts was not followed. Looking at the introduction of the Passover Feast in *Exodus* 12, they celebrated Easter between 14th and 21st of the first month of the year, which was a custom among Christians before the Council of Nicaea in 325.[8] The Celtic monasteries were not intended for seclusion. They were centres of missionary activity, where believers were prepared for being sent out to the mission fields, first to the rest of the British Isles, including Ireland and Scotland, then to other European countries. Celtic missionaries were said to be more adapting to local situations and cultures (i.e. more *contextual*) in their approach of pre-Christian customs, than Roman missionaries.[9]

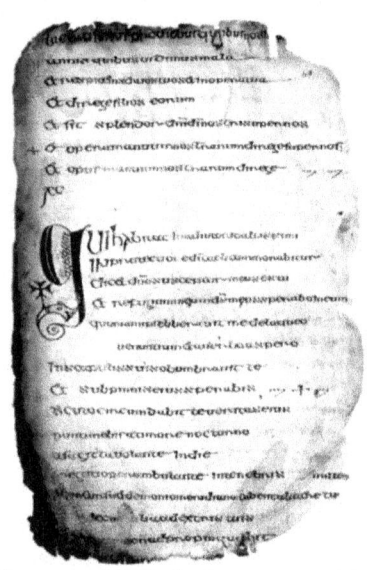

Fragment of the Cathach manuscript of the

---

[8] The Christian Feast of Easter, in remembrance of the resurrection of Jesus Christ, is the ultimate fulfilment of the Old Testament Feast of Passover when the Israelites (emulated by the present-day Jews) celebrated how God had delivered them from slavery in Egypt while punishing the Egyptians. The Old Testament Passover begins on the 14th of the month Nisan (Ex.12:6), which is the first month of the Hebrew Calendar. The Roman Empire followed the Julian calendar, introduced by the Emperor Julius Caesar and effectuated in 45 BC. Following the Julian calendar, in 325 AD the Council of Nicaea decided that Easter would be held on the first Sunday after the first full moon after 21 March. As a refinement of the Julian calendar, in 1582 Pope Gregory XIII introduced a new calendar, named after him. Gradually the Gregorian Calendar came to be accepted globally, except for the Eastern Churches, which in the ecclesiastical order still use the Julian Calendar. Consequently, Eastern Christianity celebrates the Feast of Easter on a different date than the rest of Christianity. After the Second World War Christian Zionists and others have pleaded for the introduction of the Hebrew Calendar in the Church and celebrate Easter on the 14th of Nisan.

[9] G. Noort, *Germaanse Cultuur en Christianisatie van Noordwest-Europa*, Utrecht: IIMO, 1993, pp.54.

In the second half of the 5th century the Roman administration left Britain, because of the collapse of the Western part of the Empire. Large parts of the British Isles were invaded and conquered by Germanic tribes from the Continent, e.g. Angles, Saxons, Frisians, Jutes. They were pagans. Fearing pagan dominance and persecution, many Celtic Christians fled to the fringes of the British Isles, to Cornwall, Ireland, and to the mountainous regions of Wales and Scotland. In those parts the *Celtic Church* continued its existence, and also its missionary activity. On the European Continent they often met with the Roman missionary enterprise from the South. Here are some of these Celtic missionaries:

Icon of Columba (c.543-615)

Columba: Together with 12 companions (number of the disciples) this presbyter and abbot left the Irish monastery of Bangor for Scotland, approximately 563. Off the Scottish West coast, on the island of Iona, he had his missionary centre. From there missionaries were sent out, first to the Hebrides and Scotland, then to the Continent.

Columbanus (born approximately 550): Like Columba with 12 companions he went out from the monastery of Bangor. First they went to Brittany, a Celtic region on the west coast of present-day France. Then, they were invited to Franconia, and especially worked in Burgundy. These central and eastern parts of present-day France were ruled by the Merovingians (see chapter 15). In the Vosges mountains, at Luxueil and Fontaines, Columbanus founded new monasteries, independent of the already existing Roman Catholic structures in the region. These monasteries were meant as centres of reform and mission. The existing Church had decayed since the days of King Clovis (c.466-511), who deliberately had converted to Roman Christianity, knowing that the bishops supported him in his struggle with Arian competitors. But now the Roman Church had been weakened by abuses and chaos.[10] In this situation of civil war and immorality, the people were challenged by the newly arrived missionaries of the *Celtic Church*. Celtic mission did not limit itself to France. Especially from Luxueil the Celtic mission was extended to Switzerland. Many pagans in the German-speaking northern parts of Switzerland were converted by Columbanus' work. Then, he went on to North Italy where he worked among the Arian Longobards. On the River Trebbia, the monastery Bobbio was founded. A short time before his death in 615 he met Pope Boniface IV. He warned against the claim that popes are successors of the Apostle Peter.

Gallus: He was one of Columbanus' companions and his successor in Switzerland. He worked south of the Bodensee from the centre Arbon. When he died, the monastery Sankt Gallen was built there.

---

[10] Noort, *Germaanse Cultuur en Christianisatie*, p.56.

7. Conflicts and the Definition of Dogma

7.1. Before 313

A considerable part of the history of the Church consists of attempts to overcome false or erroneous (i.e. unbiblical) teachings that have crept in, pretending to be the truth. This also applies to the history of the Early Church (1-500 AD). As the position of the Church was different in the pagan-ruled and in the Christian-ruled periods of the Roman Empire, the character of heresies in these two periods also differed. Heresies are always caused by man's conscious or unconscious disobedience to God and his Word. But there are differences in emphasis. We will first look at some heresies and germs of error that originate before the year 313, when the Emperors Constantine and Licinius met at Milan, and agreed to legalise the Christian Church. Then, we will look at the struggle against heresy in the period after 313, when the Church gradually grew to a powerful position, especially after 380 when Christianity became the favoured religion in the Roman Empire.

Before 313, in the persecuted Church, most heresies were attempts to evade the attacks by the conflicting and competing pagan and Jewish religions. They did so either by degrading the Old Testament and overemphasising the New Testament, or the other way round, thus distorting the truth in both Testaments. Basically this means that the Biblical view of God and of man is distorted. We discern two main lines of heretical thought, (a) the *dualism* and (b) the *legalism*. A trendsetter on the first line was *Gnosticism*, whereas most heresies on the second line relate to *Judaism*.[1]

a. Dualism

In trying to find an explanation for the origin of good and evil, the *dualistic sects* divided the whole of reality into two basic elements that they saw as opposed to one another, spirit and *matter*. Spiritual things are good and material things are evil. Greek philosophical and Jewish heretical thought contributed to this vision. Later it mixed with Christianity (*syncretism*).

Gnosticism. In the movement of Gnosticism this dualism became powerful, first outside and then also inside the Christian Church. One of the earliest and most influential Gnostic teachers who tried to mix these thoughts with Christianity was Valentinus (second century). Here are some of his ideas. The whole of created reality of man and nature is twofold. This created reality is in the grasp of misery, because the good spiritual things have been captured by the bad material things. The spiritual existence is imprisoned in matter, like a beautiful bird in a cage. Salvation is provided by acquiring secret knowledge about this dual reality (*gnosis* = *knowledge*). This knowledge is revealed by the spiritual world and it is given only to them who can receive it. In fact, the spiritual things are given back to the original divine Being. Thus harmony is restored. This original divine Being produced *aeons*, lower divine beings, who in their turn produced special aeons named Christ and the Holy Spirit, and finally Jesus. Together they constitute the fullness (*pleroma*) of the original divine Being. One of the aeons named Achamoth, born out of aeon Wisdom, fell out of the pleroma, and

---

[1] Cf.: Cairns, *Christianity through the Centuries*, pp.95-101, Dowley pp.84-93, 96-100 (Gnostics), 101-122 (Judaists, Marcionists).

produced the Demiurge, who is the creator of all material things. Although the Demiurge and its material creation are evil, they are controlled from the pleroma by Wisdom. Through Wisdom's influence, the Demiurge creates men in whom there are good spiritual elements. Wisdom is also the one who made aeon Jesus to be born from the Virgin Mary. At the crucifixion Jesus' aeon left his body and went back to the pleroma. Jesus did not have a real human body, although He was considered to be real man. He only appeared to have a body. This idea is called docetism (Gr. *dokein* = to seem). Consequently, He was not really crucified. Birth, death and resurrection are not historical facts. Jesus can help people by installing in them the beginning of a process of thinking that leads to discovery of secret knowledge. All who receive this knowledge are elect people, they are liberated from evil matter, and they return to the pleroma. Guided by angels and aeons the human soul finds its way via the planets to heaven. No wonder that the required secret knowledge includes the knowledge of astrology.

'Christian' Gnostics reinterpreted the Bible by discerning two gods, the Father of Jesus, who is the god of light and the origin of all good things, and the Demiurge, the origin of all bad things. This thought was applied to the Bible. The Old Testament was the book of the Demiurge, and the New Testament, or more precisely a re-worked part of it, was the book of the god of light. The same idea was applied to human beings who were said to consist of a good soul and an evil body. The Church rejected Gnosticism: especially the Church Fathers Irenaeus and Tertullian wrote against it. The need for defence against the danger of Gnosticism led to a reorganisation of the power structure of the Church, giving more authority to the bishops. It also led to a deeper consciousness about the canon of Scripture and to the formulation of creeds.

Marcionism. This type of Gnosticism was mainly a reaction against the Jewish religion and Judaist thought in Christianity. In the view of the founder, Marcion († approximately 160), the Church was following a religion that was fundamentally Jewish. This he wanted to change. In his opinion, the God of the Old Testament is different from the Father of Jesus Christ, who is the God of the New Testament. The former is inferior to the latter. The former is imperfect, vengeful, and makes mistakes. The latter is the good God who teaches and practises mercy, forgiveness and love. They are absolutely separate. Christ came to reveal the good God, but the creator God caused him to be crucified. In making up for this, the creator God gave to Christ the souls of those who were to be redeemed. Christ will not return, and there is no resurrection of the dead, and no restoration of the created world.

Manichaeism. This Gnostic sect was founded by Manes or Mani (†276), a teacher of religion in Persia. His dualism made a distinction between light and darkness. Darkness has stolen the light by imprisoning it, for example in the human body and brains. By the help of Jesus and in the way of *ascetism,* the light can be liberated.

Neo-Platonism. This was a philosophical system that originated in the Greek philosopher Plato (†approximately 347 BC), and was revived in the third century. It differed from Gnosticism in not considering the *origin* of reality to be dual. The origin is *the One* (monism), from whom emanate all things. In the beginning things are good and *spiritual.* But during a long process evil *matter* creeps in. The former has to be delivered from the latter. This thought makes Neo-Platonism also *dualistic.*

In chapter 10.4., when dealing with the Church Father Augustine (Augustinus), we will come back to the subject of *Manichaeism* and *Neo-Platonism* and look at them in more detail. Augustine for a time was a follower of *Manichaeism* and later of *Neo-Platonism.* We will notice how he answered both sects.

b. Legalism

Whereas the dualistic sects largely rejected the Old Testament, the legalists tended to stress the importance of the Old Testament, even at the cost of the New Testament. Their basic thought was that obedience to the Law is a *condition* for the effectiveness of the Gospel.

Judaism. This sect weakened the Christian belief that Old Testament ceremonial law has been fulfilled in Christ. Contrary to Christian thought, the Judaists claimed that the Old Testament laws apply to all Christians of all times in the same way they had been laws to the people of Israel. Becoming a Christian means becoming a Jew first. The Apostles rejected this view (*Acts* 15).[2]

Montanism. Its founder Montanus, before converting to Christianity, used to be a priest of some wild prophetic type of pagan religion, in which ecstasy was highly valued. On becoming a Christian, he started to express his new religion in the same manner, especially emphasising the work of the Holy Spirit. Two women, Maximilla and Priscilla, helped him in his prophetic activities. He announced that the age of the *Paraclete* had come and that the Holy Spirit spoke through him. The *New Jerusalem* was at hand. Christians had to challenge the persecutors of the Church. Escaping martyrdom was sin. Montanus and the two prophetesses could forgive sins. They propagated a complete separation from the world. Soon Montanist churches were settled in many places. After Montanus' death, the prophetic element subsided. What remained of Montanism was a strict Christian sect, emphasising obedience to the law, fasting, separation from the world, willingness to suffer for the faith. Church Father Tertullian (†approximately 225) joined the Montanist Church for a period; perhaps he saw it as a consequence of his struggle against the Gnostics who had mixed in the Catholic Church. As a reaction against Montanism the Catholic (*catholic* = common to all, universal) Church began to discourage prophecy and unusual spiritual powers.

Novatians and Donatists. According to them, the holiness of the Church is rooted in the holiness of its leaders. Not only did they form sects outside the Catholic Church, they often influenced deeply the Catholic Church itself. In chapter 10 the *Donatists* will be discussed in more detail, together with Church Father Augustine's answer to them.

In the wake of the above mentioned early heresies and as a by-product of resistance against the persecutions by the Roman state, the Christian Church very soon began to cultivate the germs of subsequent erroneous practices. All of them would harden into real heresies in later times.

> Some examples: (a) The idea that Jesus did not really come into the flesh (*docetism*); (b) The thought that seclusion from ordinary life and fasting are ways to have peace with God (*ascetism, monasticism*); (c) The assumption of an essential difference between clergy and laity (*clericalism*); (d) Concentration of ecclesiastical power in the hands of priests and bishops (*hierarchicalism*); (e) The idea that the elements of the sacraments automatically give grace (*sacramentalism*); (f) The veneration of Mary as a kind of deity (*mariolatry*); (g) The veneration of martyrs, subsequently *saints*, because of their assumed mediatory power and (h) The veneration of *relics* of saintly persons or things.

---

[2] See chapter 2.

7.2. After 313

After the Roman Emperor freed Christianity from persecution (313 *Edict of Milan*), and after 380 when the Christian Church became the powerful State Church of the Empire, the Church became tempted by heresies of a very fundamental kind. The emphasis of heresies shifted from attacks on (parts) of the Bible to distortions of the Biblical view of God and of man. This challenged the Church to formulate (a) its *theology*, and (b) its *anthropology*.[3]

a. Theological Heresies

By the term *theological heresies* we mean erroneous ideas with regard to the character of God. We discern three phases in the struggle for a Biblical view of who God is, pertaining to (1) the Trinity of God, (2) the *two natures* of God the Son, and (3) the *position* of God the Holy Spirit

First phase: attacks on the Trinity of God

The fact of the three-one-ness of God is a great mystery that cannot be rationalised. This was not always (consciously) given credit in the Early Church. The first theologian who formulated the term Trinity was Tertullian. Gregory of Nazianze tried to indicate the mystery as follows: 'As soon as I see the Unity I am enfolded by the Trinity; as soon as I discern the Trinity, I am led back to the Unity'.

Even before 313 some theological thinkers tried to adapt the relationship between the three Persons in the one God to their own rational understanding. They were led by the desire to facilitate the defence against the accusation that Christians were *polytheists*. Out of this a number of heresies emerged that would eventually develop to the *Unitarianism* of later times. On the way to that ultimate consequence there were the various types of *Monarchianism*., e.g. Paul of Samosata who said that Christ's divinity was only of an adoptive type (*Adoptionism*), and Sabellius, who taught that God manifested himself in three persons successively (*Sabellianism*). In an attempt to save the Godhead of Christ, the Church Father Origen adopted the idea that the Son, though Divine, is subordinated to God the Father. He emphasised that Christ is not a creature; He is eternal God. But this does not prevent him from positioning the Son under the Father, in a kind of hierarchical relationship; hence, his view is called *Subordinationism*.

After 313, the presbyter Arius from the Egyptian city of Alexandria, motivated by the desire to deny polytheism, went further on this erroneous line of thought. He claims that God the Father before all things created the Son; so Christ is the firstborn of all creatures, not from eternity. Subsequently Christ created the material world. In Arius' thinking Christ is neither ordinary man (has no human soul), nor God. Many people were impressed by Arius' ascetic and noble lifestyle, and they accepted his ideas. However, the bishop Alexander of Alexandria realised the serious consequences of Arius' teaching for Christ's work of salvation, and he censured him. During the ensuing

---

[3] For the attacks on the Trinity, the Natures of the Son, and the Holy Spirit, see: *Christianity through the Centuries*, pp.103-111,125-133, Dowley, pp.164-186 (Arianism), Foster, *First Advance*, pp.137-150, Renwick/Harman, pp.53-62; for attacks on the nature of man: Cairns, *Christianity through the Centuries*, pp.131,132,142,161,311, Dowley, pp.205,207-210; for attacks on the nature of the Church: Steven Paas, *A Conflict on Authority in the Early Church: Augustine of Hippo and the Donatists*, Zomba: 2005[2].

conflict the Emperor Constantine tried to mediate. The Emperor ordered a Church Council to be held, which eventually took place in Nicaea in 325. There the Alexandrian deacon Athanasius (295-373) was the main representative of the party that defended the orthodox faith that Christ together with the Father is one God. Christ is *homo-ousios* (= one with the essence) of the Father. Looking upon Christ as a half god damages the image of God himself. Later followers of Arius invented a slightly different sounding term to underline their opposing view: Christ is *homoi-ousios* (= like the essence) of the Father.

The heresy of Arianism was condemned by the Nicene Council. However, Athanasius had to continue his struggle. The Emperor Constantine supported him, but his successor favoured the Arians and made Athanasius suffer banishment in the deserts of Egypt. Athanasius' view was supported by the *Three Cappadocians*, Gregory of Nazianze, Gregory of Nyssa, and Basilius the Great. The Church tried to formulate its view of the Trinity in three confessions of faith that were born at this time. These *three ecumenical symbols* to the present-day are shared by all non-sectarian Christian churches, i.e. the *Apostolic Confession of Faith*, the *Nicene Confession of Faith*, and the *Athanasian Confession of Faith*. The last mentioned was not written by Athanasius himself. The Nicene Creed was finally adopted by the Church Council of Constantinople in 381. The Apostolic Creed attained its final form in the 5th century.[4]

Church Father Athanasius of Alexandria (296-373).

In the Middle Ages the section on the Holy Spirit in the *Nicene Creed* was to become a bone of contention between the Western Church and the Eastern Church. Who sends out the Spirit, the Father only, or the Father and the Son? In a way present-day *Jehovah's Witnesses*, *Unitarians* and *Muslims* inherited the ideas of Arius.

Second phase: struggle about the two natures of God the Son

At the Nicene Council the Church agreed to the Trinity of God. Christ is not only human but also divine. There are two natures in Him. But what and how is the relationship between these two, and to what degree is He fully man, and to what degree is He fully God? These are the questions that play an important role in the rest of the third century.

---

[4] The ecumenical symbols were consciously based on Scripture. How does God reveal Himself as Trinity in the Old Testament? Study texts like Gen.1:26,27; Gen.3:22; Gen.11:5,7; Numbers 6:24-26; Ps.33:6; Haggai 2:6; Job 28; Is.63:9-11. In the New Testament God revealed his Trinity more fully. Study texts like: Mt.3:16,17; Mt.28:19; 2 Cor.13:13; 1 John 5:7. The Creeds of the Reformation also comment on this. See the sections on the Trinity in e.g. the *Westminster Confession of Faith* and *Catechisms*, and in the *Heidelberg Catechism*.

Some taught that the natures of Christ do not constitute a unity. They are divided, so that Christ is at the one occasion only man and at the other only God (*School of Antioch*). Others maintained that the two natures are a unity, but mixed, so that Christ's humanity is absorbed by his divinity (School of Alexandria). The adherents of this thought are called Monophysites. They lost sight of Christ's humanity. The Church Council of Ephesus (431) went into the direction of this view by stating the opinion that Mary is the Mother of God (*theotokos*), which conveniently fitted to the beginnings of the veneration of the Holy Virgin, and to docetism. Nestorius, however, rejected this idea, and said that Mary is the Mother of Christ (*christotokos*), in an attempt to stress Christ's humanity. His view is known as Nestorianism.

Finally, the *Church Council of Chalcedon* (451), trying to avoid the one-sidedness of both Monophysitism and Nestorianism, found words that honour the various expressions of Scripture on this matter. Christ's divine nature and his human nature are united 'unconfusedly, unchangeably, and indivisibly, inseparably'. Actually, the Council of Chalcedon tried to say what the relationship between Christ's humanity and divinity is NOT! Fortunately, the Council Fathers realised that the rational understanding of these things is beyond human grasp.

Third phase: God the Holy Spirit

The Holy Spirit is the third Person of the Divine Trinity. He is fully God, not created, but from eternity. The Early Church and the Church of the Middle Ages developed various erroneous views on the work and the Person of the Holy Spirit. Some examples:

(a) Stressing the work of the Holy Spirit at the expense of the work of the Father and of the Son. An early example is the sect of the Montanists, to which the Church Father Tertullian turned in advanced age.

(b) The idea that the Holy Spirit is not a Person but a power.

(c) The opinion that the Holy Spirit is only sent out by the Father and not by the Son. This view was adopted by the Eastern Orthodox Church,. in Greece and in the Slavonic countries like Russia. The dispute about this question led in the West to the introduction of an addition to the Nicene Creed, i.e. the Latin word *filioque* (= and the Son), stressing that the Holy Spirit is sent out by the Father and the Son.

b. Anthropological Heresies

By anthropological heresies we mean errors with regard to the character of man. The Bible teaches how much the doctrines on God and the doctrines on man are interrelated. Erroneous doctrine on God always distorts doctrine on man, and the other way round. In other terms: theology and anthropology are two sides of the same coin. The misconception in Gnostic theology of the evil god of the Old Testament and the good god of the New Testament had to lead to an anthropology of breaking the unity of soul and body in man.

Arian attack on the Trinity and the subsequent weakening of Christology, i.e. the undermining of Christ's 100% divinity and 100% humanity, is related to the desire of putting man at too high a level. When it is supposed that God is far away and his saving acts are weak, room can be created for man's capabilities to contribute to his own salvation. Then, man can take the initial steps towards salvation by his own efforts, apart from Divine grace. This is apparent in the opinions of the British monk Pelagius who worked in Rome in the late 4th and early 5th centuries, and whose ideas have

7. Conflicts and the Definition of Dogma

become known as *Pelagianism*. Pelagius rejected the reality of *original sin*, i.e. the transmission of Adam's sin to his descendants. He claimed that man is born as a *tabula rasa* (blank writing pad). Man only sins because of the influence by bad examples. His free will enables him to choose between good and evil. He should choose to follow the good examples. Pelagius admitted that Christ is the best example. In this way, by following Christ's example, not by surrendering to Him as Saviour, man ascends to liberation. *Ascetism* is the main characteristic of the way to salvation in this view. Pelagius' great opponent was the Church Father Aurelius Augustinus, who maintained that man is born in sin. He is not saved because he chooses God, but because God chooses him. There is only salvation by Christ's redemptive work. Although the Roman Catholic Church did not follow Pelagius in his rejection of original sin, it retained the idea of the free will by which man is supposed to be able to collaborate with God in the work of salvation. This view is called *semi-pelagianism*. In chapter 10 which deals with Churchfather Augustine, we will return to this subject.

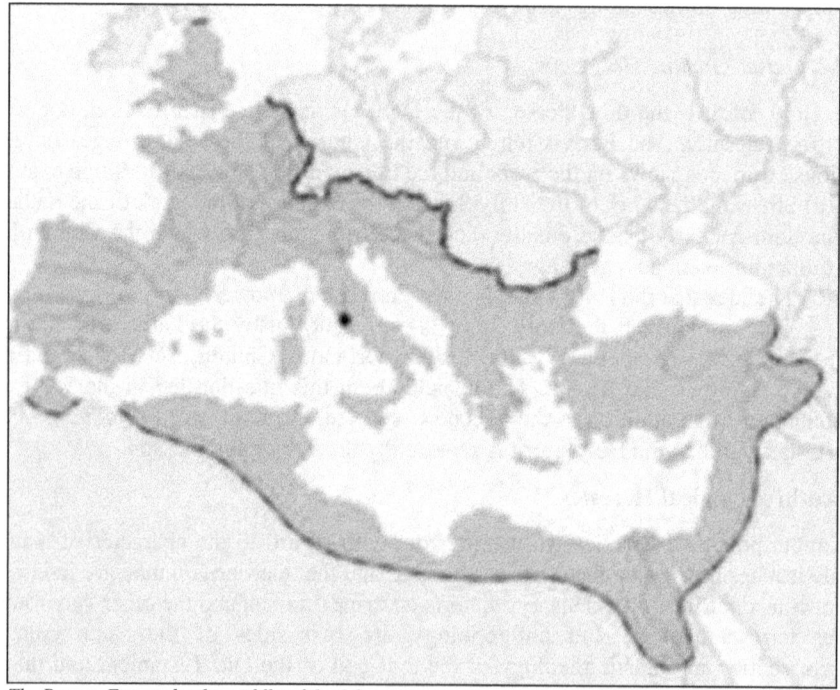

The Roman Empire by the middle of the 5th century.

8. The Church Fathers

8.1. Apostles and Apostolic Fathers

A number of influential and leading figures in the Early Church have become known as *Church Fathers*. Although they intended to serve Christ and His Church, the Church Fathers sometimes differed considerably in teaching and behaviour. In *Patristics* or *Patrology*, i.e. the branch of Church History dealing with the Church Fathers, scholars have attempted to divide them into categories. But clear cut divisions without overlapping have not been found.[1]

The first criterion for categorizing them is whether they were from the Greek culture of the East or from the Latin culture of the West. The most important group of Church Fathers were the *Apostles*. Having been brought up as Hebrew or Hellenist Jews, they were all from the East. The New Testament was completed by them before the end of the first century. As the Gospel spread gradually, differences emerged between church leaders in the East and in the West.

This was not yet conspicuously apparent in the group that followed the Apostles. They are called the *Apostolic Fathers*, because they knew the Apostles in person and were personally taught by them. One of the Apostolic Fathers is from the West, Clement of Rome. The others are from the East, Ignatius, Polycarp, Pseudo-Barnabas, the writer to Diognetus, the writer of the second letter to Clement, Papias, the shepherd of Hermas, and the writers of the *Didache*. In chapter 4 we emphasised the positive significance of the writings by Apostolic Fathers and also indicated one-sidedness and seeds of error in them.

Jerome (c.342-420) in his study, working on the Latin translation of the Bible.

8.2. Apologists and Polemicists

All fathers who were active after the apostolic era could be called *Post-Apostolic Church Fathers*. Cairns divides the *Post-Apostolic Fathers* of the second and the third centuries into *Apologists* and *Polemicists*. Let us look at them in succession.

---

[1] Cairns, *Christianity through the Centuries*, pp.73-79,103-11,134-142; Dowley, passim, see reference section; Renwick/Harman, 37-48; Paas, *A Conflict on Authority*, pp.9-15 (Augustine), pp.47-48 (Tertullian), pp.49-61 (Cyprian).

8. The Church Fathers

The word *Apologist* comes from the Greek noun *apologia*, which means speaking or defending in public, thus referring to the work of a lawyer in court. Apologists defended the Church against dangers from the side of the state and the pagan culture. They reacted to persecutions and accusations. An example of apologetic literature in the East is Origen's answer to the pagan writer Celsus who had tried to prove that the Bible cannot be true. He had stated that Jesus' real name was Ben Panthera, because he was the son of the Roman soldier Panther, that Moses was a deceiver, and that the story of creation is ridiculous. In *Contra Celsum* Origen showed the weakness of his opponent's arguments. Other Eastern Apologists were Church Fathers like Aristides, and Justin Martyr who both defended the faith in apologies to the Emperor Antoninus Pius. Justin Martyr, in his *Dialogue with Trypho*, tried to attract Jews to Christ. Justin's pupil Tatian denounced pagan pretensions in his *Address to the Greeks*. Athenagoras refuted the accusation of atheism against the Christians in his *Supplication*. Theophilus tried to win pagans to Christianity by using rational arguments.

Justin Martyr (c.100-165), apologist who taught in Ephesus and Rome, he was beheaded.

To the Apologists in the West belonged Tertullian, who in correspondence to the Roman governor ridiculed the charges against Christians and presented them as loyal subjects.

Other Church Fathers became known as *Polemicists*. They acted against heresies that undermined the Church from within. Some examples in the West are Irenaeus who wrote against Gnosticism in his work *Adversus Haereses*, Tertullian who turned against many abuses and errors, such as the *Patripassian Monarchianism*, which held that God the Father had suffered. Tertullian wrote a treatise against the Monarchianist leader, Praxeas, in which he was the first to use the term 'Trinity'. In his *Apologeticum* he criticised the Gnostics, particularly Marcion. Cyprian defended a central position of bishops in the Church.

Polemicists in the East struggled with the question of the proper method of explanation of Scripture. Two schools emerged with different views, the *Alexandrian school* and the *Antiochene School*. As to the explanation of Scripture, the *Alexandrians* defended the methods of allegory and speculation. They followed the example of the Jewish philosopher Philo who tried to bridge the gulf between Judaism and Greek wisdom. Pantaenus, Clement and Origen successively headed the catechetical[2] school in Alexandria. Clement saw Greek philosophy as a preparation for Christianity. Origen systematized various theological views in *De Principiis*. He contributed to *text criticism* of the Bible by his *Hexapla* that showed in columns nine versions of the Old Testament

---

[2] *Catechetical* (adj.), *catechize* (verb) come from catechizare (Latin) or katēkhein (Greek): to teach, especially the principles of faith. Catechism = a set of questions and answers for such teaching. Catechumen = someone who is taught about those principles in preparation for baptism.

text. In Scripture he recognised three senses: (a) a literal-historical meaning, plain to many, (b) a hidden moral meaning, not clear to all, and (c) an underlying spiritual meaning only to be understood by some.

In Origen's view, the hidden and spiritual meaning could be unveiled by allegorical explanation. This allegorical meaning was more important than the literal meaning of Scripture.

The Alexandrians were opposed by the *Antiochene School*, which advocated a literal-historical method of explanation of Scripture. They did not look for a hidden meaning, but for the intention of the writer. In the polemics on the natures of Christ in the fourth century Alexandria and Antioch differed, the one stressing Christ's divinity and the other stressing Christ's humanity.

Some Apologists and Polemicists were one-sided so that in resisting a certain accusation or error, they fell victim to another, often opposite, error. Origen adopted the view of a hierarchical order between God the Father and God the Son (*Subordinationism*). Tertullian joined the radical sect of the *Montanists*. Other Church Fathers in defending the Church against accusations from without and heresy from within, gave way to errors like: *hierarchicalism*, *veneration of martyrs and relics*, *moralism*, and *sacramentalism*. The letters, books and creeds formulated by the Apologists and Polemicists shaped the beginning of the sciences of *Apologetics* and *Dogmatics*, which in their turn were the origin of *Theology*.

Ignatius of Antioch (c.35-107). He was a bishop; the Romans took him as a prisoner to Rome. In Origen's view the hidden and spiritual meaning could be unveiled by allegorical explanation. This allegorical meaning was more important than the literal.

8.3. Post-Nicene Church Fathers

The year 325 of the Church Council of Nicaea is also used to divide the Church Fathers. The *Ante-Nicene Fathers* of the first, second and third centuries have been indicated above. They had to defend the Church against a hostile state, against legalistic sects (*Judaism, Montanism, Novatianism*) and dualistic sects (*Gnosticism, Marcionism*). The *Post-Nicene Fathers* lived with a friendly state. That is perhaps why Cairns calls their time 'the Golden Age of the Church Fathers'.[3] Being favoured changed the spiritual climate in the Church. The old problems of legalism and dualism still played a role. But the emphasis shifted to conflicts with regard to the formulation of the Trinity and the two natures of Christ. In the East there were Church Fathers like Chrysostom and Theodore of Mopsuestia. They followed the *Antiochene school* of Bible interpretation. There was also Eusebius of Caesarea, who wrote a history of the Church of the period up to 325. Some Post-Nicene Fathers of the West were Jerome (Hieronymus), the translator of the Bible into Latin, Ambrose (Ambrosius) the able administrator and

---

[3] Cairns, *Christianity through the Centuries*, p.134.

preacher in Milan, and not least the famous North African philosopher and theologian Aurelius Augustine (Augustinus).

8.4. Tertullian, a North African Church Father

In many aspects the Church Fathers of North Africa have contributed considerably to Christianity, especially to the Church of the West. As such, they are links between European and African Christianity. The *Carthaginian School* comprised Church Fathers like Tertullian, Cyprian, and Augustine. In chapters 9 and 10 Cyprian and Augustine will be discussed. Both were taught by Tertullian, either directly or indirectly. That is why we conclude this chapter with a short sketch of 'the father of theology'.

Tertullian (c.160-c.225) was born in the family of a pagan Roman centurion in Carthage. He trained as a scholar in Greek and in Latin, and he was destined for a career in the empire. After his studies, he settled in Rome as a lawyer. There he converted to the Christian faith. Tertullian was of great importance for the development of theology in the Western (i.e. Latin) world. Helped by his knowledge of philosophy and his 'fiery nature and fighting spirit'[4] he became a powerful apologist of the faith against the anti-Christian propaganda by pagan attackers. 'The blood of Christians is seed', was his famous adage against the persecutors. Besides, he became known as an able polemicist against the heretics, especially the Gnostics, who weakened the church from within. His attempt to formulate the unity of the essence of God in three persons, contributed to the acceptance of the dogma of Trinity in later times. Tertullian was convinced that the church is more than a structure of formal organisation and doctrine. In his theology and practical life there was room for the emotional side of faith and for spiritual contact with God through the work of the Holy Spirit.

Tertullian (Quintus Septimus Florens), c.160-c.225: Ante-Nicene Church Father in

He also had a keen eye for the practical issues of Christian life. Resistance against the formalisation of leadership in the church made him temporarily join the sect of the *Montanists*. However, this did not diminish his authority in the church of North Africa.

In Tertullian the tension between subjectivity and objectivity was a contradiction of 'personal holiness and the holiness that is attributed to the church as an institution'. Shaw emphasises that Tertullian's commitment to holiness was closely connected to his vision of 'the city of God to come'.[5] He enveloped the holiness of the church and the believers in eschatological expectation. Frend says that with Tertullian, unlike with Augustine, the authority of the church and its office-bearers was not yet of religious significance.[6] But Tertullian's commitment to holiness and eschatology certainly

---

[4] Cairns, *Christianity through the Centuries*, p.106.
[5] Shaw, *Kingdom*, p.46.
[6] Cf. Noordmans, *Augustinus*, pp.104,123.

motivated him in fiercely opposing the tendency of strengthening the formal leadership in the congregation. For the first time, in Tertullian's ideas we notice an *anti-clerical* element. He limited the power of bishops to a disciplining function, as an addition to the authority of the martyrs.[7]

Eventually he went much further. Facing the bishops, he appealed to freedom for the congregation. The church lives by that freedom, not by a handful of bishops. The church lives in the Spirit, in obedience to the Word of God. Personal holiness should be maintained by strict exercise of discipline.

This element is also found with the *Donatists* whom we will meet again in chapter 10. But the Donatists definitely did not adopt Tertullian's spirituality leading to the rejection of an organised ecclesiastical structure with bishops. Frend calls Tertullian 'a forerunner and father of Donatism'.[8] This statement does not find much support, although both Tertullian and the Donatists emphasised martyrdom, separation and holiness. But the Donatist church was orderly, organised in a hierarchical structure, and this would not have suited Tertullian. Tertullian eventually joined the sect of the *Montanists*, who emphatically advocated a prophetic-charismatic leadership that could not agree to church government by a rigid system of bishops and presbyters. Augustine valued Tertullian's apologetic work, but he rejected his teaching with regard to church and office.[9]

---

[7] Frend, *Donatist*, pp.114-117.

[8] Frend, *Donatist*, p.124.

[9] Von Campenhausen, *Kirchenväter*, pp.33-35.

9. Cyprian

9.1. Decian Persecutions

Cyprian (†258) was born in a pagan family. He was trained in rhetoric, and he became a Christian in c.246. Some years before the beginning of the persecutions under the Emperor Decius, he was elected Bishop of Carthage. We will look at his attitude during the persecutions of the mid third century, and at some of his writings.

We will see that Cyprian played a considerable role in the change of ideas regarding the ecclesiastical office. Before him the *charismatic* aspect was emphasised. But under his influence the emphasis on the *formal* aspect of the office began to get wide acceptance. Cyprian was in favour of powerful leadership. This is understandable, because the past had often shown the necessity of strong leaders. During the persecutions under Emperors like Nero, Domitian, Marcus Aurelius, Septimus Severus and Maximus the church and its office-bearers had been under very heavy pressure. However, this had not been the only danger. Ecclesiastical structures had also been threatened from within, because of heretical movements like those of Marcion (approximately †160), Montanus (approximately 150), and Manes (†276). The defence of the church required strong leaders.

Cyprian (Thascius Caecilius Cyprianus), c.200-258: Ante-Nicene Church Father, Bishop of Carthage.

Cyprian was born in a comparatively quiet time, without persecutions. But the heretics were very active. There was particular need for protection against the *Gnosticism* of the Marcionists. Their teachings endangered the Biblical foundation of the Church. This seemed to necessitate the creation of a solid organisational structure under formal local leaders. Tertullian had been Cyprian's teacher. But he acted against the strengthening of formal leadership. Eventually this made him join the sect of the Montanists. These followers of Montanus refused to agree to a formalising of ecclesiastical structures. They held to the classical *prophetic-charismatic* leadership in the congregations. However, soon their revolt degenerated to extreme spiritualistic forms. They were not able to prevent the development of a system in which great power was wielded by local formal office-bearers.[1]

Cyprian's work accelerated this development, and gave a theoretical foundation to it. He was helped by the wave of persecution of Christians under Emperor Decius in the years 249-251.[2] Soon after Cyprian had been elected to be bishop in the northern African city of Carthage, Christians in the entire Roman Empire were hit by a wave of

---

[1] Cf. Th.M. Lindsay, *The Church and the Ministry in the Early Centuries*, London: Hodder and Stoughton, 1907, pp.214-261.

[2] As to the activities of Cyprian during the Decian persecutions, I used: J. Baer (ed), *Bibliothek der Kirchenväter* (further BVK), vol.34, Band I. Preceding the writings of the Church Father, Baer includes a biography of Cyprian on pp.VII-XXXVII.

persecutions. The cruelty and the scope of the Decian measures exceeded those by previous Emperors. Many were surprised by the sudden character of the persecutions. For almost half a century there had been comparative quiet and tolerance. During this peaceful period the Church had grown in numbers, but its strength to resist external threats had not increased. Many had turned to Christianity, not as a matter of faith, but just because this seemed to be the fashionable thing to do. Consequently, the harsh edict of Emperor Decius brought numerous Christians to (temporary) unfaithfulness. These people were labelled as *lapsi*, fallen ones. The edict demanded at least an act of sacrificing or the partaking of other pagan ceremonies. Many Christians tried to have their names included in the registers of those who had fulfilled the obligation of sacrificing. The only way to escape the death sentence from the imperial court was to belong either to the *sacrificati*, i.e. the sacrificers, or to the *thurificati*, those who had burnt some grains of incense before the bust of the Emperor-god. The desired statement, *libellus pacis*, which confirmed one's partaking in the pagan sacrifice, was acquired by a number of Christians through bribing, without really sacrificing. This group, the *libellatici*, as they were called, never really intended to turn their back on the Church, and expected to be re-accepted as members. As soon as the mania of persecution subsided, a number of *lapsi* asked for re-admittance to the Church.

This placed a difficult question before the church leaders. How should they deal with those, who in the very hour of affliction, had not been able to stand fast, and now wanted to renew their membership? The problem was even more pressing because some of the returning *lapsi* were not very repentant, and among them also were high-ranking people like bishops and elders. The opinions differed greatly. Soon the Church was being afflicted by a serious conflict between two parties, a mild one and a strict one.

9.2. The Lapsi

Cyprian, who during the persecution had taken shelter in a safe refuge, did not join any of these parties. Perhaps neither side would accommodate a bishop who had left his flock in the time of trial. He adopted a different view, and in a sense he formed a third party. It was precisely this party-in-between the two others, that characterises the development towards the formalisation and episcopalisation of the church office.

The mild party in Carthage, led by Felicissimus and Novatus, reproached the returned Cyprian with a lack of leniency. Moreover, they blamed him for having left Carthage during the persecutions, thus escaping the executioner. The mild party maintained that the *lapsi*, after a period of repentance and penance, should be re-admitted to the Eucharistic community of the Church. They particularly wanted to open a way back for those fallen ones for whom the 'martyrs and confessors' had interceded. The 'martyrs and confessors' were the category of believers who even after torture had not denied the name of the Lord. Statements by these heroes of the faith included requests to readmit certain *lapsi* to the Church. These requests were especially valued by those who considered the 'martyrs and confessors' as exponents of the prophetic-charismatic leadership of the Church. Among the adherents to this view were many Carthaginian presbyters.[3] During the absence of their bishop they had taken over the leadership in the congregation. In their own way, taking into account the New

---

[3] Lindsay, *The Church*, pp.295f.

9. Cyprian

Testament rules, they tried to have repentant *lapsi* reconciled with the Church. Decisions were taken without directly involving the bishop.

To this Cyprian could not agree. He, the Roman rhetorician, could not accept that beside the office of the bishop other powers of authority could operate. Presbyters are not allowed to make decisions. Only the bishop is entitled to do this. Beside this formalistic issue, Cyprian had yet another objection to the activities of the elders. In his view, they did not deal in a Biblical way with the sins of the *lapsi*. Even from his shelter outside Carthage, he had reacted sharply against the idea that 'martyrs and confessors' could reconcile the sins of others. Their intercession has no value. 'It ought to be sufficient for the martyr to be cleansed of his own sins. Partly it is ungratefulness and pride to spend on others that which one has acquired for oneself for a high price. Who has been a propitiation for the death of others by his own death, but only the Son of God?'[4]

In this reaction against his elders, Cyprian criticises the position they had adopted in the organisation, as well as their stance with regard to the return of the *lapsi*. In both aspects the authority of the bishop was at stake. One should understand Cyprian well

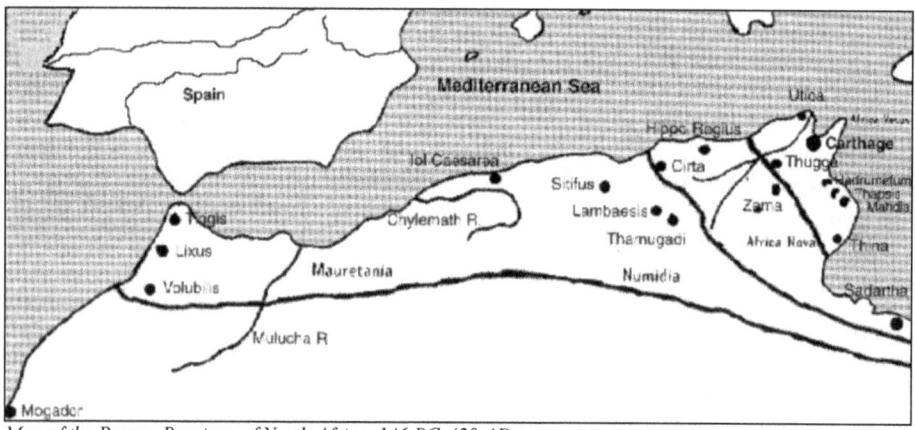

Map of the Roman Province of North Africa, 146 BC-429 AD.

here! His adverse attitude is not inspired by unwillingness to have the *lapsi*, after repentance and penance, back in the Church. This already was apparent because he definitely did not belong to the strict party in the conflict. The strict party had acquired strength especially in Rome, under the leadership of Novatianus.[5] The stance of the *Novatians* included demands and conditions that practically excluded the possibility of return for the *lapsi*. In their opinion, all those who were guilty of 'mortal sins' like murder, adultery and idolatry could not be rehabilitated by penance anymore. In this concern the Novatians connected an obsolete practice in the old Church. However, the pressure of circumstances had forced the Church to abandon this strict practice in most places in the beginning of the third century. Bishop Calixtus of Rome belonged to those who confirmed this new, more tolerant attitude, with a number of official measures that

---

[4] Baer, *BKV*, vol. 60, Band II, 'Cyprianus'; epistles 11.1, 13.5; cf. Band I, vol. 34, 'De Catholicae Ecclesiae Unitate', p.20.

[5] Novatianus should not be confused with the Carthaginian dissenter Novatus, mentioned earlier in this account, although also he – remarkably enough – adopted Novatian symphathies later.

facilitated the return to the Church by repentant committers of 'mortal sins'.[6] At the same time, this measure included the idea that the decision on re-admittance belonged to the exclusive authority of the bishops[7]. In his conflict with the Carthaginian elders and with the Novatians, Cyprian followed this new line of thought in ecclesiastical politics.

To Cyprian the problem of the fallen ones was a very important issue. He was disgusted at weak leniency, but he did not block the return of the *lapsi* to the Church, provided that the bishops of the Church would have the exclusive power of turning the key of the door to the Church. He stressed the inviolability of the *Catholic Church*, and in his opinion this was founded on the authority of the bishops.[8]

---

[6] F. Loofs, *Leitfaden zum Studium der Dogmengeschichte*, Tübingen: Max Niemeijer, 1968, pp.162, 163; Cf. K.Heussi, *Kompendium der Kirchengeschichte*, Tübingen: Mohr, 1960, p.80.

[7] Lindsay, *The Church*, p.274.

[8] Cyprian has worked out this view in a number of tracts and letters, discussed in: Paas, *A Conflict on Authority*, pp.54-61.

10. Augustine

10.1. On the City of God

The most important Church Father in the West was Aurelius Augustine (354-430 AD). He was born in the city of Thagaste, which is in what is now Tunisia. Together with other regions in Northern Africa his homeland belonged to the Western part of the Roman Empire. In this part the political and military power of the Empire was soon to collapse.[1] One of the works that Augustine wrote was in relation to what people thought about the fall of the Roman Empire. When the Visigoths sacked the city of Rome in 410, there was great anxiety. Adherents of the old pagan religion of Rome thought that the defeat of Rome was a punishment by the gods because so many Romans had accepted Christianity. And the Christians thought that this event was a sign of the downfall of the Church, and the end of the world. In his book called *On the City of God* (Latin: *De Civitate Dei*) Augustine says that the fall of Rome was not a punishment by the gods, nor did it signify the end of the Church. Like all

Oldest picture of Church Father Augustine

empires in the history of the world, the Roman Empire had to end because of its sins and unrighteousness that will meet with God's judgment and punishment. All empires shall come to an end, but one empire shall never end. That is the *City of God*. Noah, Abraham, and Israel, and the whole Church with all Christians are citizens of that city. And that city will be fully seen in the *New Jerusalem*. Augustine concluded from this that Satan has no power to bring down the Church of God.

Augustine wrote many other books. The most famous example is *Confessiones*. This book is an autobiography. He includes descriptions of his sins, and how his sinful life found peace in God[2].

10.2. Augustine's Life

Adding to and commenting on the *Confessiones*, some authors have tried to write about the life of Augustine[3]. This enables us to mention some headlines of his life. In the North African province of the Roman Empire there were roughly two kinds of people, Romans and Berbers. The Romans originated in Europe and the Berbers were from Africa. Some were Christians and others were pagans. This mixture was shown in

---

[1] See chapter 12.

[2] There are many (translated) editions. Cf., Bakhuizen Van den Brink, *Handboek*, Vol.1, p 258. I consulted C. Biggs, *The Confessions of Saint Augustine: Newly translated with notes and introduction*, London; Methuen, 1898.

[3] See especially: P. Brown, *Augustine of Hippo*, London Faber & Faber, 1967.

Augustine's parents. His mother Monnica (Monica) was a Christian Berber, and his father Patricius was a Roman pagan. So, Augustine was influenced by both Christian and pagan cultures, and also by both Roman-European and African cultures. The parents soon found that their son was very intelligent. They sent him to school in Madaura and Carthage where he studied very well. But his behaviour was not good at all. He was a womaniser. When he was 18 years old, he impregnated a girl and a male child was born, to whom the name Adeodatus was given. Mother Monnica prayed much for the conversion of her son. But Augustine did not want to become a Christian. Instead, he decided to join *Manichaeism*, a sect that followed *Gnostic* ideas.

In the meantime, his studies were successful; consequently he rose to a higher social position. He was invited to become professor of rhetoric at the Emperor's Court in Milan in Italy. At the time this city was the administrative capital of the Roman Empire. When he arrived in Milan, Augustine had stopped being a follower of *Manichaeism*, because the teaching of this group had disappointed him. Now he turned to another movement of thought, *Neo-Platonism*. At the same time, he felt attracted by the sermons of Ambrose, the bishop in Milan. It was clear that

Painting of Augustine and his mother Monnica.

his mind and heart were drifting to other positions. Then, a thing happened that would be debated by many historians. Augustine sent away the woman who had lived with him for a long time as his concubine. He developed the theory that marriage and sexuality would not be in accordance with the changes in his life. But nature is not that easily chained. Soon after this he took another woman to live with. However, this did not last long.

In the year 386 Augustine had an experience of conversion when he was in the garden of his friend Alypius. He heard little children playing. They sang the words 'take and read' (*tolle lege*). These words urged him to take up the Bible. The first verses he read were *Romans* 13:13-14:

> 'Let us behave decently, as in the daytime, not in orgies and drunkenness, not in sexual immorality and debauchery, not in dissensions and jealousy. Rather clothe yourselves with the Lord Jesus Christ, and do not think about how to gratify the desires of the sinful nature'. (NIV)

The Holy Spirit used these words to convert Augustine to the Christian faith. In 387 he was baptised. He became a very influential leader in the Church. Augustine connected his conversion to the thought of celibacy. He swore to refrain from marriage and sexual relationships.

Then he returned to Africa, to the city of Hippo Regius near Carthage. First he served the Church as a priest. In 396 he was called to be bishop. He was very active, mainly in preaching, writing books, and defending the Church against heresies. He promoted monastic life and established a monastery. Augustine died in 430. By the time of his death the Roman Empire had grown very weak. Augustine died when the Germanic Vandals, who had penetrated North Africa from Spain, were besieging the city of Hippo Regius.

10.3. Dichotomies

Augustine was the most important Church Father in the Western Church. Perhaps his influence has been so great because of some seemingly contradictory features or dichotomies in his life. He belonged to Africa and to Europe. He was born to a Christian parent and to a pagan parent. There is a sharp contrast between his former sinful life and his later life as a Christian. His theology harboured such contrasts that later it could attract both Roman Catholicism and Protestantism.

Augustine was a theologian of great significance. His writings have drawn the attention of scholars even in the 21st century. He is also known because of his stress on practical pastoral care. Augustine preached a lot and many of his sermons were jotted down by helpers. Even today these sermons are printed, re-printed and read. He especially helped the Western Church by the formulation of arguments against a number of heresies. At least two heretical movements he knew from within, the *Manichaeans* and the *Neo-Platonists* with their renewed interest in the philosophy of Plato. Before his conversion Augustine had been a member of these groups. Both were based on the principle of *dualism*.

10.4. Dualism

In chapter 7.1.a we already met with the sects of *Manichaeism* and *Neo-Platonism*. Now let us look at them in more detail. The followers of these philosophical movements were especially interested in the origins of good and evil. Their teachings were based on the thought of dualism, discerning in everything and in every person two opposing elements, the *spiritual* and the *material*. The spiritual is good, and the material is evil. This dualistic principle the Manichaeism and the Neo-Platonism share; they differed in other regards.

Manichaeism distinguished good and evil right from the beginning of the history of the created things. All the way from creation through today to the future there are the good spiritual things and the bad material things. *Neo-Platonism*, on the other hand, said that in the beginning of created reality there was the one thing or the one spirit, and that was good. All things emanate from the One. But in the process of time they gradually differentiate into good and evil. The *Manichaeans* like the *Marcionists* thought that this division also concerns divinity.

Mosaic of Church Father Ambrose of Milan (c.339-397), who was instrumental to Augustine's conversion (found in the Vittore church, Milan).

They believed that there were two gods, the spiritual god, who is the source of good, and the evil god who created the material things, including human bodies. In their teaching God cannot be Almighty. The followers of *Neo-Platonism* tried to explain reality using the ideas of the Greek philosopher Plato, who taught that both good and evil originate from One Thing or One Spirit. In (Neo-) Platonist teaching there is room for God who is one and almighty, but as both good and evil come from Him, He cannot be good.

The name *Manichaeism* came from its founder *Mani*, born in Persia in 216. He was a Jew who was converted to Christianity. Dualism radicalised his thought, and made him oppose the Old Testament, thus deviating from orthodox Christianity. His teachings spread to other parts in the Roman Empire, including North Africa. Pagan Emperors like Diocletian persecuted and executed *Manichaeans*. When Christianity became legalised and respectable the persecutions of Manichaean sects continued. The sect existed in North Africa, and spread to other countries under other names.

> Since 900 the *Manichaeans* were found in Armenia and in Bulgaria (where they were called Bogomils), and in the Balkan countries. Between 1100 and 1200 *Manichaeans* were also flourishing in North Spain, North Italy, and South France. There they were called *Albigenses* or *Cathari* (Greek: the pure ones). The court of *Inquisition* of the Roman Church together with the French State organised a crusade against them and practically rooted them out. Recently scholars found Inquisition reports in the archives of the Vatican concerning the interrogation of Cathari in some villages of France. A French historian, Le Roy Ladurie, published parts of these reports in his book *Montaillou*. This publication teaches us about the Albigenses, but also about everyday life and thought in the Middle Ages.[4]

Augustine for a time was attracted to these sects, first of Manichaeism and later of Neo-Platonism. However, he stopped following *Manichaeism* and *Gnosticism*, and he also turned away from *Neo-Platonism*. Augustine was converted and became a true Christian. But he did not remove all the effects of *dualism* from his thought and work. There is an opposition between the material or physical and the spiritual in his underestimation of the value of marriage and when he seems to relegate the whole of sexuality to the realm of sin. In Augustine's opinion, really spiritual people need to be celibates.[5] These things show a certain dualism in the teachings of Augustine. The Church would maintain this line of thought throughout the *Middle Ages*.

10.5. Pelagianism

After Augustine became a Christian, he began to defend Church and faith against the older heresies of *Manichaeism* and *Neo-Platonism*, and also of *Arianism*,[6] which spread in many parts of Europe and North Africa. He was also aware of some newer heresies that emerged during his lifetime.

He argued with followers of *Pelagianism*, which was started by Pelagius, a monk from Britain. We have met with the teachings of Pelagius already[7]. In opposition to

---

[4] Emmanuel Le Roy Ladurie, *Montaillou: Cathars and Catholics in a French Village 1294-1324*, London: Penguin, 1990.

[5] *Celibacy*: Behaviour of men or women who had vowed never to get married and have sex, often for religious reasons.

[6] *Arianism*: See Chapter 7.

[7] *Pelagianism:* See Chapter 7.

Pelagius, Augustine said that man is not born like a blank sheet of paper. Original sin is present in everyone. Consequently, he also maintained against Pelagius that man is not born with free will which is to help him choose to follow the good examples. But his freedom is spoiled. The human will is not free because of sin. It needs God to liberate him. Man is not saved by the decision of his own will, but by the will of God in Jesus Christ. Man does not choose God, but God chooses man. In this way Augustine explained the doctrine of divine *predestination*[8]. The mercy and grace of God are not in reaction to the good choices and good deeds of people, but they are a gift from the sovereign God who saves and liberates man from evil through Christ only.

Although Augustine showed the fundamental mistake in the teaching of Pelagius, the Church of the Middle Ages partly followed Pelagius. It accepted a theological principle that is sometimes called s*emi-pelagianism*. The word *semi* means *half*. This term suggests that the Church of Rome followed half of Pelagianism. The term refers to the following chain of teachings: (a) baptism removes original sin, thus liberating man's will; (b) the sacraments of the Church give the grace of God; (c) the free will of the baptised and his good works join together with God's sacramental grace; (d) this cooperation results in salvation.

This sequel of dogmas cannot be derived from Augustine. Yet looking at his view of the structure and exclusive position of the Church and its priests, the Church of Rome has honoured him as a Church Father and teacher of the Church. The 16th century-Reformers like Luther, Calvin and others, would not follow this line in Augustine's ecclesiology. Yet they considered Augustine's teachings on grace and salvation to be in accordance to Paul and the whole of Scripture. In other words, they agreed with Augustine's view of salvation in stressing that man is saved through free grace.

10.6. Donatism

Augustine became a well-known opponent to the movement of *Donatism*, which through its legalistic approach had parallels with Judaism, Montanism, and Novatianism[9]. *Donatism* was the name of a break-away movement from the Catholic Church in North Africa. The Donatists refused to accept Caecilian as bishop of Carthage on the ground that the one who had consecrated him had betrayed Christ in the time of testing. He was a *lapsus* or a *traditor*[10]. During Emperor Diocletian's persecutions this consecrating bishop was said to have handed over some books of the Church to the Roman leaders. Consequently, all his acts, including his laying hands on Caecilian, were supposed to be false and void. That is why the bishops from Numidia, a Donatist stronghold, consecrated Majorinus to be bishop instead of Caecilian. Donatus succeeded to Majorinus, and his name was given to the movement. Beside this background of theological or pastoral difference, the Donatist question was also inspired by tensions between Romans and Africans, jealousy of the people of Numidia toward the people of Carthage, and by economic differences. The Donatists generally were Berbers from the interior mountains who did not trust the people of mixed race in the flat areas along the Mediterranean coast. They thought that the Catholic Church was led by unfaithful priests who undermined the faith and the purity of the Church. They believed that the

---

[8] *Predestination*: teaching that God from eternity foreordained those who are saved.
[9] *Judaism, Montanism,* and *Novatianism*: See Chapter 7.
[10] *Lapsus, Traditor*: See Chapter 5.

Church is false if the leaders are sinful. That is why they started their own Church. Some of them even planned a revolution against the Roman State.

Augustine opposed the Donatists by emphasising that the Church does not depend on the holiness and perfection of its people and priests, but that the Church is a plantation by God and completely depends on His Word[11]. He tried to discuss with them, and help them in a pastoral way to find a solution. Around the year 400 when his conciliatory attempts proved futile, Augustine assisted the Roman government to break the *Donatist* movement[12]. But the power of the Roman government and the Catholic Church did not entirely stop the Donatist Church. It continued to weaken Christianity in North Africa, until the *Muslim* Arabs took over and conquered the whole of North Africa in the 7th century. The history of *Donatism* stresses the necessity of faith in ministers and other office-bearers in the Church, and what other qualities and abilities they should have. It also shows that a church cannot survive only because of the spiritual power of its leaders.

---

[11] See *James* 2:10, 'Whoever keeps the whole law but fails in one point has become guilty of all of it'.
[12] See: Paas, *A Conflict on Authority;* W.C.H. Frend, *The Donatist Church: A Movement of Protest in Roman Northern Africa*, Oxford UP, 1985.

11. Monasticism[1]

11.1. Ascetism

The period of persecution in the pagan Roman Empire witnessed the heroic and faithful life of many Christians. Generally, the Christians were characterised by a practical missionary attitude. According to New Testament rule, the priesthood of all believers was functioning and the prophetic element was apparent in the congregations. But gradually less sound teachings and practices crept in. Some of them we mentioned in chapter 7 on the conflicts on dogma.

After the formal *Christianisation* of Roman political and cultural institutions, a great many people flocked to the Church. Among them were many who were less interested in Christianity than in the privileges for Christians. The Church's growth enlarged its positive influence. The influx of nominal believers, however, also stimulated the acceptance of worldly lifestyles and the spread of erroneous teachings.

The practice of *ascetism*, and in its wake *monasticism*, was meant to defend the Church

Benedict of Nursia (c.480-c.550), called 'Patriarch of Western monasticism'.

against the worldly influences by nominal members. Ascetism itself, however, was founded on the Gnostic idea that the body was the cause of sin. *Ascetism* and *ascesis* come from the Greek word *askein*, which means: to exercise, to train. The term, originally used by athletes, indicated the refraining from food, sleep, luxury, pleasure, etc. This self-inflicted suffering reacted against a worldly lifestyle. To some it also took the place of the glorified martyrdom of the past.

11.2. Antony and Pachomius

Individual Monasticism. The forerunners of monasticism were the *hermits*. Antony (c 250-347) was the first famous hermit. He withdrew into the deserts of Egypt, and devoted his life to meditation and prayer. The behaviour of many hermits was quite excessive, e.g. the *pillar saints,* but it is also true that many had good and righteous intentions. Later Antony introduced a very rudimentary form of community life among these *desert fathers*. Some rules were made for such communities. Although the hermits might sometimes live close together, their monasticism was *individual* in character. For a certain period the Church Father Athanasius belonged to a community like these.

---

[1] Cairns, *Christianity through the Centuries*, pp.25,98,144-149,161,194,209,217-221,224,243; Dowley, pp.192,205,212-224,256,267-275,281,282,304,307-315,346,386,667; Renwick/Harman, pp.73-76; Foster, *First Advance*, pp.153-166; Boer, *Short History*, pp.127-133.

Communal Monasticism. The initiative to communal monasticism was taken by another Egyptian, Pachomius (c.290-346). He was a soldier in the army of the Emperor Constantine, and became converted in 313, the year of the Edict of Milan. After having been a hermit in the tradition of Antony for a time, he organised a community of hundreds of members, first at Tabennisi, and later also elsewhere. His set of rules has survived in Latin translation. It regulated the whole day. The communal activities included meditation, prayer, physical work, and meals.

11.3. Benedictine Rule

Antonian and Pachomian monasticism spread to Europe in the 4th century. Athanasius of Alexandria (c. 296-373), who was a friend of both Antony and Pachomius, did much to promote monasticism in the countries of his exile, mainly Gaul and Italy.

The Antonian type of monasticism, however, proved to be not very fitting to the European climate, so communal monasticism developed. One of the first organisers was the Italian Benedict of Nursia (c. 480-c. 550).

The Monastery of Monte Cassino before it was destroyed in 1944. It was founded by Benedict of Nursia in approximately 529.

His community of followers had so many members that had to build twelve monasteries for housing them. In 520 he established a monastery at Monte Cassino. Here Benedict created a *directory* of the spiritual as well as of the administrative life of a monastery. Everything was to be aimed at love of God and love of fellow monks. Patience, obedience, charity, and humility should be seen in every member. The monks had to promise sobriety, submissiveness to their abbot, and celibacy.

11.4. Celtic Monasticism

This *Benedictine Rule* gradually superseded a form of monasticism that already existed in Western Europe. Independent of Rome the *Celtic Church* had developed in parts of the British Isles, i.e. in Cornwall, Wales, Scotland and Ireland. Celtic Church life consisted mainly of missionary activities that were organised and carried out by the monasteries. Celtic missionaries like Columbanus travelled widely. They founded their monastic centres of religious life in various regions of the European continent, including Switzerland and the North of Italy.

Benedictine monasticism developed in the climate of the Church that centred in Rome. Due to the zealous activities of Pope Gregory the Great and men like the missionary Boniface most traces of *Celtic monasticism* vanished.

11.5. Significance

In general, both the Benedictine and Celtic monasticism were important agents for maintaining and spreading Christianity in Western Europe at the time when the Roman Empire collapsed under the pressure of less civilised invaders, i.e. the Germanic tribes. In this period of cultural and political breakdown, the monks in their monasteries became the bearers of culture and religion. They were the masters in any skill, church leaders, philosophers, architects, advisors at royal courts, agricultural specialists, builders, writers, musicians, glass-makers. Monks did not shun manual labour, but they were also active in copying manuscripts, teaching, art, and doing research. On the negative side monastic life weakened Christian spirituality and fellowship, by emphasising social isolation and celibacy. Thus, other abuses crept in gradually. The Middle Ages would see attempts to reform monasticism (see chapter 16).

12. Collapse in the West[1]

12.1. West and East drifting apart

By the end of the 5th century the Roman Empire was considerably weakened because of the collapse of its political and military structures in the West. The causes and consequences of this breakdown deeply influenced the Church. There were various causes.

The lack of unity between the West and the East was the main cause. The Roman Empire comprised the Latin world in the West and the Byzantine-Greek world in the East. Originally, the main power centres of the Empire were in the West, especially in the capital Rome. But Rome declined in political significance when the capital of the Empire, at the instigation of Emperor Constantine was removed to the East. On the banks of the Bosporus in the province of Asia Minor (present-day Turkey) he had a new capital built on the site of the Greek city of Byzantium. In 330 this place was inaugurated as Constantinople. This move had far reaching consequences for State and Church. East and West were drifting apart in political outlook. As to the Church, incipient differences between Eastern and Western Christianity (see chapter 17) grew stronger. This made the bishops of Rome and of Constantinople competing powers. Both aspired to dominance over the entire Church, thus contributing to internal strife and disunity.

12.2. Golden Age of the Church Fathers

This is far from saying that the collapse of unity in the Empire went hand in hand with a downfall of the Church. The events took shape in the 4th century, which witnessed at the same time tremendous growth of the Church. There was also much theological activity. Cairns calls this period *The Golden Age of the Church Fathers.*[2]

In the Post-Nicene era, i.e. the period after the Council of Nicaea, which dealt with the heresy of Arius, in the East there were Church Fathers like Chrysostom, Theodore of Mopsuestia and Eusebius. They were important figures in the fields of exegetics, preaching and the study of the history of the Church. In the West the work of Church Fathers like Jerome, Ambrose and Augustine was especially important for the translation of the Bible, the organisation of the Church and the development of systematic theology. Despite this flourishing of the Church there was a breaking down of the unity between West and East.

12.3. Causes of the Collapse

Apart from the crumbling of unity with the East, there are many more explanations of the termination of the Roman Empire in the West. Some have pointed to changes in the climate, exhaustion of the soil, mixture of races, the destructive effect of immoral or corruptive practices especially among the Roman élite. Others have mentioned the relative poverty of the West as compared to the East.

---

[1] Cairns, *Christianity through the Centuries,* pp.120-121,134-143,150-155; Dowley, pp.187-196.
[2] Cairns, *Christianity through the Centuries*, p.134.

12. Collapse in the West

However, the main reason is the 'barbarian' attacks on the Western Empire. These attacks had begun long before. But in the 5th century the Byzantine Emperors and their Western vassals were unable to continue resistance. Germanic tribes like the Vandals, the Burgundians and the Goths penetrated the Empire from beyond the rivers Rhine and Danube. In the South the boundaries were threatened by the Saharan Berbers. An important role was played by the Visigoths. This branch of Goths had turned to an Arian type of Christianity. From the third century they tried to enter the Empire. They eventually succeeded after the battle of Adrianople in 378 and then they continued to threaten the centres of authority. In 401 the Visigoth King Alaric invaded Italy. In 410 his troops occupied and sacked the city of Rome, to the despair of the Roman leaders. In the meantime, the provinces of Gaul (present-day France) and Spain were invaded by other barbarian tribes, e.g. the Vandals. Under King Gaisaric the Vandals passed through Spain and in 429 they entered North Africa. The province of Britain was occupied by Angles, Saxons, Danes, Frisians and other Germanic groups. By the mid 5th century, the Vandals controlled much of the North African coast and of the Mediterranean Sea. The end came in 476 when barbarian troops on the Roman side revolted. Their king, Odoacer, deposed the last Roman Sub-Emperor in the West.

A medieval illustration in Augustine's De Civitate Dei (On the City of God), which discusses the transitoriness of earthly empires and the invincibility of the Kingdom of God.

In the East the Roman Empire continued to exist for another 1000 years. In 1453 it fell to the Turkish branch of Islam. These events further divided the Church in East and West. The Eastern Church, under the supremacy of the *Oecumenical Patriarch* of Constantinople distanced itself from the West and finally seceded in 1054.

12.4. The Rise of Papacy

The collapse of the Western Roman Empire did not mean the downfall of Rome as the authoritative centre of Western Christianity. On the contrary, Rome and its bishop filled much of the power vacuum that was created after the Emperor and his administration vanished. Before 476 the power of the bishops had steadily increased. They intervened in theological disputes and the Roman see was a court of appeal. The breaking down of the political and military structures of the Empire gave more room for the increase of papal power. In fact, much of Roman imperialism was continued by the papacy. The Pope became the symbol and the reference point for Western identity and unity. Developments of refining the hierarchical structure of the Church, its rituals and its doctrines reflect the claim of papal hegemony.

Able popes like Gregory I (509-604) knew how to fill the power vacuum when Rome had ceased to be the political and military centre. His successors followed suit in aspiring to political power. In the 8th century the Popes managed to become independent rulers of a part of Italy, thus establishing the ecclesiastical state. This territorial ownership strengthened the papal claim of religious and political supremacy. Practically and theoretically, the Church of Rome was going to be looked upon as the *supra-national state* that, under the Pope, was above the nations in the world. The rulers of the new kingdoms and empires of Europe owed their position to the collapse of the Roman Empire. At the same time, they were to learn that another imperial power, the Pope of Rome, claimed authority over them.

12.5. Africa and Europe

a. Maurice, 'the first black saint'

From a very early age Christianity has been present in Africa. The flight of Joseph and Mary with the Child to Egypt[3] signifies that Jesus Christ touched Africa before His message was spread to Europe. Before the end of the persecutions by the heathen Roman Empire Egypt and North Africa had become strongholds of the Church, soon to be followed by Nubia and Ethiopia. Legend has it that one of the last heathen (co-) Emperors, Maximian (d. 310) in 286 had a full legion of his Christian Egyptian or Nubian soldiers, garrisoned in Thebe (Thebes), killed when they refused to obey the order to sacrifice to the Emperor and to attack local Christians in Agaunum, a place in present-day Switzerland, then situated in the north of the Roman Province of Gaul (Gallia). The commander of the murdered legionaries was said to be Maurice (Mauritius, Moritz, Maurikios), a black African, who is now venerated as a saint in the Roman Catholic and Coptic Churches.[4]

b. Inward looking

The collapse of the Western Roman Empire meant for Europe the beginning of a new era. The Middle Ages would focus on the restructuring of Europe's political and religious institutions. Apart from the Portuguese fascination for a supposed Christian kingdom of 'Prester John' in Central Africa, until the Crusades, in which some Nubian and/or

Statue of Martyr Maurice, 'the first black saint', at the southern wall of the chancel of the Cathedral of Magdeburg. Anachronically the 3rd-century saint is dressed here in the armour of an 12th-century crusading knight.

---

[3] Mt.2:13-15; cf.Hos.11:1.

[4] According to a letter by Eucherius, Bishop of Lyon (mid 5th century), which some historians consider as a complete fiction, the Theban Legion consisted of 6666 soldiers. They were said to have been put to death by decimation, one of ten at a time, until all were martyred. Ancient images of Maurice, known as 'the first black saint', exist in various places in the West, notably his statue in Magdeburg (Germany). In Riga (Latvia) and Tallin (Estonia) his icon still appears on the (restored) premises of the Blackheads, a medieval Brotherhood of young Hanseatic merchants, who considered him their patron saint [Internet: Agaunum, Maximian, St. Maurice and the Livonian Merchants, etc.].

Ethiopian knights were used, or rather until the Renaissance, i.e. the rebirth of interest in Greek culture, Europe would be inward looking. This was the end of the expansive mood of the Roman Empire with its aspiration to draw foreign regions within its boundaries. Soon it would be forgotten that North Africa once was a pillar of the Roman Empire.

Indeed, the downfall of the Roman Empire in the West had serious consequences for the relationship between Africa and Europe. North Africa used to be Rome's most important province, at least economically. African grain fed the Roman élites with their faltering local economies. Besides, there are traces of Roman commercial activity on the East coast of Africa. Culturally and religiously, North Africa contributed considerably to the Empire. Almost all these links were cut off. North Africa temporarily came under the influence of Byzantium and finally, in the 7th century, it was invaded by Islam. The two continents became separated politically and religiously. The Mediterranean Sea that for centuries had been a means of contact through transport and communication had become a barrier.

For a long time most of Africa seemed to be lost for the Church, apart from the presence of Eastern Christianity in early Egypt, Nubia and Ethiopia. But the voice of African Church Fathers like Tertullian, Cyprian and Augustine would never be forgotten. Much of the foundation of early Christianity was laid in Africa! In part II of this volume, *The Faith Moves South*, we will see how God has used this foundation to build His Church in the whole of the African continent.[5]

---

[5] See chapters 42-62.

Bibliography: Antiquity

Baillie, J., J.T. McNeill, and H.P. van Dusen (eds), *The Library of Christian Classics* (26 vols), Philadelphia: Westminster, 1953-1969.

Bauer, W., *Orthodoxy and Heresy in Earliest Christianity*, Philadelphia: Fortress, 1971.

Bettenson, H., and C. Maunder (eds.), *Documents of the Christian Church*, Oxford U.P., 1999.

Bieler, L., *The Life and legend of St. Patrick*, Dublin: Clonmore & Reynolds, 1964².

Bindley, T.H. and F.W. Green, *The Oecumenical Documents of the Faith*, London: Methuen, 1950.

Brown, P., *Augustine of Hippo: A Biography*, London: Faber & Faber, 1967.

Brown, P., *Religion and Society in the Age of Augustine*, London, Faber & Faber, 1972.

Brown, P., *The making of late Antiquity*, Cambridge (Mass.): Harvard UP, 1978.

Bury, J.B., *The Invasion of Europe by the Barbarians,* New York: Norton, 1967.

Campenhausen von, H.F., *The Formation of the Christian Bible*, Philadelphia: Fortress, 1977.

Chadwick, H., *The Early Church*, Harmondsworth: Penguin, 1967².

Chitty, D.J., *The Desert a City: An Introduction to the History of Egyptian and Palestinian Monasticism under the Christian Empire*, Oxford: Blackwell, 1966.

Clark, G., *Women in Late Antiquity: Pagan and Christian Lifestyles*, Oxford: Clarendon, 1993.

Comby, J., *How to read Church History?* (vol.I), London: SCM, 1995.

Cyprian, *Treatises* (transl. by Mary Hannam Mahoney. Edited by Roy D. Deferrari), New York, 1958.

Daniélou, J. and H.Marrou, *The First Six Hundred Years*, Harmondsworth: Penguin/ London: Darton, Longman and Todd and Paulist Press, 1964.

Daniélou, J., *Gospel Message and Hellenistic Culture*, London: Darton, Longman and Todd / Philadelphia: Westminster Press, 1973.

Defarrari, R. (ed.), *The Fathers of the Church* (60 vols), Washington: Catholic University of American Press, 1947ff.

Dix, G., *The Shape of the Liturgy*, Westminster: Dacre Press, 1945.

Dodds, E.R., *Pagan and Christian in the Age of Anxiety*, Cambridge University Press, 1965.

Eusebius, *The History of the Church from Christ to Constantine* (transl. by G.A. Williamson), New York UP Press, 1966.

Foakes-Jackson, F.J., *History of the Christian Church to AD 461*, London: Allen and Unwin, 1965.

Foster, J., *After the Apostles: Missionary Preaching of the First Three Centuries*, London: SCM, 1951.

Foster, J., *The First Advance: AD 29-500*, London: SPCK, 1972.

Fox, R.L., *Pagans and Christians in the Mediterranean World from the Second Century to the Conversion of Constantine*, London: Viking, 1986.

Frend, W.H.C., *Martyrdom and Persecution in the Early Church*, Oxford: Blackwell, 1965.

Frend, W.H.C., *The Rise of Christianity,* Philadelphia: Fortress, 1984.

Gibbon, E., *Decline and Fall of the Roman Empire* (an abridgement by D.M. Low), Harmondsworth: Pelican, 1963.

Grant, R.M., *Gnosticism and Early Christianity*, New York: Harper and Row, 1966².

Grant, R.M., *Gnosticism, An Anthology*, London: Collins, 1961.

Green, Michael, *Evangelism in the Early Church*, London: Hodder and Stoughton 1970

Greenslade, S.L., *Schism in the Early Church*, London: SCM, 1953.

Harnack, A., *History of Dogma* (transl.), London: Williams and Norgate, 1894.

Harnack, A., *The Expansion of Christianity in the First Centuries* (2 vols), New York: Putnam, 1905.

Hincliff, P., *Cyprian of Carthage*, London: Chapman, 1974.

Jeremias, J., *Infant Baptism in the First Four Centuries*, London: SCM, 1960.

Jonas, H., *The Gnostic Religion*, Boston: Beacon, 1963^2.

Josephus, Flavius, *The Complete Works* (transl.), Grand Rapids: Kregel, 1960.

Justin Martyr, *Writings of Saint Justin Martyr* (transl.), New York: Christian Heritage, 1948.

Kelly, J.N.D., *Early Christian Doctrines*, London: Black, 1972^3.

Kelly, J.N.D., *Early Christian Creeds*, London: Longman, 1972^3.

Kidds, B.J. (ed.), *Documents Illustrative of the History of the Church* (3 vols), London: SPCK, 1921-1941.

Lampe, G.W.H. (ed.), *A Greek Patristic Lexicon*, Oxford: Clarendon, 1961-1968.

Latourette, Kenneth Scott, *A History of the Expansion of Christianity*, 7 volumes, Exeter: Paternoster/ Grand Rapids: Zondervan, New York: Harper and Row, 1971 [first 1935-1946; on Europe vols I, II and IV];

Lightfoot, J.B., and J.R. Harmer (eds), *The Apostolic Fathers*, Grand Rapids: Baker, 1988.

McGrath, A.E. (ed.), *The Christian Theology Reader*, Oxford: Blackwell, 2001^2 [an anthology of extracts from primary sources].

McLynn, N.B., *Ambrose of Milan: Church and Court in a Christian Capital*, Berkeley/Los Angeles, London, 1994.

Momigliano, M., *The Conflict Between Paganism and Christianity in the Fourth Century*, Oxford: Clarendon, 1963.

Paas, S., *A Conflict on Authority in the Early African Church: Augustine of Hippo and the Donatists*, Zomba: Kachere 2005^2.

Prestige, G.L., *Fathers and Heretics*, London: SCPK 1954.

Roberts, A., and J. Donaldson (eds), *The Ante-Nicene Fathers* (10 vols), Grand Rapids: Eerdmans: 1989.

Schaff, Ph., *History of the Christian Church*, vols I, II, III, Grand Rapids: Eerdmans, 1955.

Stark, R., *The Rise of Christianity: How the Obscure, Marginal Jesus Movement Became the Dominant Religious Force in the Western World in a Few Centuries*, San Francisco: Harper, 1997

Stevenson, J.A., *A New Eusebius: Documents Illustrative of the History of the Church to 337*, London: SPCK, 1960.

Sordi, M., *The Christians and the Roman Empire*, London: Norman/New York: Routledge, 1988.

Treadgold, W. (ed.), *Renaissances before the Renaissance: Cultural Revivals of late Antiquity and the Middle Ages*, Stanford UP, 1984.

Trigg, J., *Origen*, Atlanta: John Knox Press, 1984/ London: SCM 1985.

Wand, J.W., *A History of the Early Church*, London: Methuen, 1963^4.

Wiles, M., *The Christian Fathers*, London: SCM, 1977.

Wilken, R.L., *Judaism and the Early Christian Mind*, New Haven: Yale, 1971.

Wilken, R.L., *The Christians as the Romans Saw Them,* New Haven: Yale, 1984.

Wilken, R.L., *The First Thousand Years: A Global History of Christianity*, New Haven/ London: Yale UP, 2012.

Young, F., *From Nicea to Chalcedon*, London: SCM/ Philadelphia: Fortress, 1983.

Websites

Augustini Opera Omnia, http://www.augustinus.it/latino/

Christian Classics Ethereal Library: The Early Church Fathers, http://www.ccel.org/fathers.html
Christian History Institute: The Early Church, https://www.christianhistoryinstitute.org/study/era/early-church/
Christianity Today: The Early Church, http://www.christianitytoday.com/ch/byperiod/earlychurch
Fordham: The Early Church Fathers, http://legacy.fordham.edu/halsall/sbook2.asp#ecf
Fourth Century Christianity, http://www.fourthcentury.com/
The Hall of Church History: The Church Fathers, http://www.spurgeon.org/~phil/fathers.htm
The Tertullian Project, http://www.tertullian.org/

B. Middle Ages 500-1500

13. The Rise and Expansion of Islam

13.1. Attractive to many

The phenomenon of Islam has affected the history of the Church. Christians have living faith in the Triune God who through Jesus Christ has come near and has become known to lost people to whom He offers His love and salvation, and in whom He works through His Holy Spirit. The faith in the fullness of knowledge and love given by this God who had deeply revealed Himself to man, was being challenged by the faith in a 'common' God who reflects the 'emptiness' that men experience when they meditate on themselves and the universe. Kohlbrugge describes how this image of God takes away real hope and leads people to mysticism and fatalism.[1] Here we only deal with some historical aspects of the spread of this religion.[2] For mission-conscious Christians the theology of Islam needs separate attention outside the framework of this survey of history.[3]

There are many reasons for the rapid and vast expansion of Islam: (a) religious zeal; (b) attraction of fatalistic predestinationism; (c) desire for power and riches; (d) ruthless methods together with clever conversion policies; (e) liberal attitude towards previously

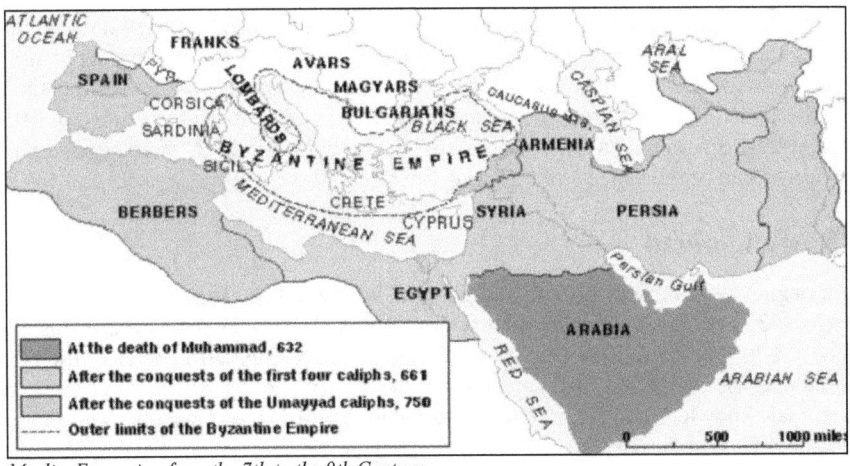

Muslim Expansion from the 7th to the 9th Century.

oppressed minorities; (f) political and military instability of invaded countries; (g) easy religious rules and obligations; (h) freedom for polygamy; (i) high intellectual and cultural level; (j) emancipation tendencies; and (k) attraction of a *Book religion* versus primitive paganism. Another reason for Muslim victory was the weakness of the Church

---

[1] H.Kohlbrugge, *De Islam aan de deur: Op zoek naar een antwoord*, Zoetermeer: Boekencentrum, 2001, pp.127-139.

[2] Steven Paas, *Beliefs and Practices of Muslims: The Religion of our Neighbours*, Zomba: Good Messenger Publications, 2006 [On the history of Islam: chapters 1-10,21,22, on the spread of Islam in Africa chapter 30, and in Malawi chapter 31; Cf. Cairns, *Christianity through the Centuries*, pp.165-171, 183; Dowley, pp.234-236; Foster, *Setback and Recovery*, pp.11-20.

[3] For an introduction to the study of Islam: Paas, *Beliefs and Practices of Muslims*, chapters 11-20,23-29. Bibliography, pp.171-176.

because of dissension and conflict. Examples are the degeneration of the Church and the Christian culture followed by the destruction of Christianity in Northern Africa, Byzantium, and Nubia.

Besides, persistent rejection of Christianity by Muslims has some reasons in Christianity itself. The Cross is a stumbling block to all religious systems that deny the necessity of redemption of personal sin by sacrifice. The Medieval Church did nothing and the Church of the Reformation did very little to witness the Gospel to Muslims. The medieval Crusades against Islam and Colonialism by Western countries in the Modern Era contributed to Muslim hatred against Christianity.

13.2. Pre-Islamic Arabia

The cradle of Islam is 7th-century Saudi-Arabia. The Persians had ended Abyssinian (= Ethiopian) rule in a large part of the peninsula. North of Persian territory was Byzantium, i.e. the *Eastern Roman Empire* where Christianity was the state religion. Before Islam emerged, the religious situation in Saudi Arabia was dominated by polytheistic Pagans, but there were also influential Jewish colonies, and especially in the South (close to *Coptic-Christian* Abyssinia) and in the North (close to *Christian Byzantium*) there lived strong minorities of Christians.

The Pagans not only worshipped many gods, but also *spirits* ('jinn') and the places, trees, stones etc. where these spirits were supposed to live. Their religious centre was the *Ka'ba* in Mecca, a cubical sanctuary containing a large black stone. Among the gods were the lunar god and three goddesses, mentioned in the *Koran* (*Surahs* 53, 19, 20). There were also remnants of monotheism, devoted to Allah. A yearly pilgrimage to Mecca was one of the aspects of religious life.

13.3. Muhammad

Islam begins with the activities of Muhammad, who was born in Mecca in about 570. At the age of 25 he married a much older widow, Khadija, who owned a prosperous trading business with commercial contacts in the Northern and Southern regions where many Jews and Christians lived. Influences by adherents of these two *Book religions* and a superficial knowledge of the Old Testament and of the Gospels contributed to Muhammad's conviction that his fellow Arabians were erring. They had lost sight of the monotheism of their ancestor Abraham. God had sent his prophets to erring people. To the Jews He sent men like Moses and David, to all the other peoples He sent Jesus. Muhammad himself would be the next prophet. He claimed that the Archangel Gabriel informed him about this in a vision in 611 (*Surah* 96, 1-5). The passages written down during Muhammad's lifetime were later put together[4] in 114

Page of the Qur'an.

---

[4] by Caliph Uthman (643-656).

sections (*Surahs*), and called *Koran* or *Qur'an*, which means 'recitation'.

After these visions, Muhammad began to preach his message. All people have to surrender (Islam = *surrender*) to the one God, Allah, who created heaven and earth and all that is in it. Predestination by Allah decides who is going to paradise and who is going to hell. On the day of judgment Allah will count everyone's deeds. A true Muslim (= *surrendered one*) will devote his life to Allah and be obedient to the *five pillars*: confession of faith, prayers (and ablutions), giving of alms, fasting, pilgrimage to Mecca.

Although Muhammad succeeded in creating a congregation of followers, his message was not well received in Mecca. Because of persecutions some of his followers fled to Christian Abyssinia in 615. After the death of his wife, Muhammad and his adherents decided to leave Mecca and to go to Jathrib, subsequently called Medina. This event is the *hijrah*. It happened in 622 and denotes the formal beginning of Islam. In Medina Muhammad started his violent campaigns of subjugation of other peoples. Pagan opposition was soon neutralised. Confrontation with the Jews, after their refusal to accept Muhammad as a Messiah, ended in the killing of Jewish opponents, the breaking of Jewish power and the confiscation of Jewish possessions. In 630 Mecca was conquered. Muhammad purified the *Ka'ba* of polytheism and made it a visible centre of his new *Book religion*. Two years later Muhammad died, after having conquered almost the whole of Saudi-Arabia.

13.4. Shi'ites

After Muhammad's death in 632, the territorial expansion of Islam continued. At the same time, Islamic power was weakened by a conflict about the question of succession. One group chose Muhammad's father-in-law Abu Bakr; he and his successors, like Omar and Uthman, were called *caliphs*. They are the *Sunnites*. After some civil wars (*fitna*), the *Sunnite* Muslims neutralised the political power of other groups, mainly of the followers of Muhammad's close relative Ali.[5] Since then the Sunnites have a majority (90%).

Other groups have remained important minorities, like the descendants of those who chose to follow Muhammad's son in law Ali. Perhaps they represent 10% in present-day Islam; they are called S*hi'ites* (*shi'at Ali* = followers of Ali). Muslims of the

The Ka'ba in Mecca, surrounded by praying pilgrims.

---

[5] A brief and helpful survey of early Islam history I found in: K. Armstrong, *Islam: A Short History*, London: Modern Library, 2002².

shi'a have introduced an almost *mystical* teaching, as opposed to the *formal* approach of the Sunnites. Ali was the first *Imam*, and his descendants succeeded him as such.[6] Imams are thought to be nominated by Allah as spiritual leaders, and keepers of the prophetic teachings, who know the hidden meaning of the Koran. Ali and after him successively his two sons Hassan and Husayn, tried to take the position of caliphs from their Sunnite competitors. But they were killed. Their suffering and death are symbolic. Later imams concentrated on their spiritual office. They behaved as theocratic rulers, opposed to any secular state. In 874 the twelfth Imam, Muhammad Mahdi, disappeared mysteriously. He had no children to succeed him. Shi'ites have had no central leader since that time. They think the real imam is invisible. He lives on in the hearts of individuals who keep his secret and who inwardly oppose any secular order. At a time decided by Allah he will make his appearance as the *Mahdi*, an immaculate saviour who will re-institute Islam in all its original purity. Until that time the *shi'a* is being ruled by the *mojtahids*, the learned men who can interpret his will.[7]

In the expansion of Islam we can discern four movements which were deployed in four periods: the *Arabian Movement*, 632-800; the *Turkish Movement*, 1080-1480; the *Expansion in sub-Saharan Africa*, beginning at the end of the 18th century; the *Expansion in the Western world* after the Second World War.

13.5. The Arabian Movement

The Arabian Movement starts with the conquest of the Arabian Peninsula. Soon after, the stronghold of Medina fell into their hands (630) Islam conquered Syria, Palestine and other parts of the Eastern Roman Empire (Byzantium) pushing the Empire back to the territory of *Asia Minor* (= present-day Turkey). During the next decade the Persian Empire was taken. In 640 Islam conquered Egypt, thus ending Christian hegemony in that country. Then, the Arabian Movement continued its expansion in two directions. In the East and in the North they penetrated into the Caucasus area, reached Lake Aral, took Turkestan and influenced the Eastern parts of China (755). The Arabian Movement by then controlled nearly the whole of Central Asia and its Turkish peoples. In the meantime, they occupied Cyprus (648) and got to Constantinople two times (668, 716).

In the West they pushed forward through present-day Libya, Tunisia, Algeria, and Morocco. Thirty years after Muhammad's death, they had conquered the whole of Northern Africa. Then they crossed over to Europe at Gibraltar, took Spain, and in the beginning of the 8th century they were in Southern France. There, at *Poitiers* in 732, the advance of Islam was stopped by the armies of Charles Martel, who pushed them back to Spain. Later Charlemagne drove them beyond River Ebro. In Spain south of that river they remained for many centuries. The last remnant of Arabian occupation in Southern Spain was removed only in 1492. In the meantime, they plundered Rome (846), occupied Crete (823), and took Sicily (878). Only by the beginning of the 12th century were they driven out of Southern Italy.

---

[6] The title *Imam* has also a much more general meaning, i.e. a leader of prayers in the mosque.
[7] Kohlbrugge, *Islam aan de deur*, pp.49-59.

13.6. The Turkish Movement

The Turkish Movement has its origin in the Central Asian regions where the Arabs had turned the Turkish peoples to Islam and had mixed with them. Gradually the Arabian centres of Islam, like Medina, Damascus, Baghdad (the seats of the *Caliphs*) lost their importance in the East to the growing Turkish influence. In 1070 the Turks occupied Palestine, and by the end of the 11th century the Turkish *Sultans* were the masters in the Islamic world from Egypt to Turkestan. First the Seljuk Turks and then the Ottoman Turks pushed eastwards, then westwards. They took Afghanistan, and then penetrated India. The territory of present-day Pakistan was conquered; then parts of present-day India. Delhi became an Islamic capital; and Bengal was taken. The violence and bloodshed by the kingdom of the Mongols (1525-1707) was notorious. In the North, these powerful Mongols almost finished the Turkish Empire before being converted to Islam themselves. Examples of a peaceful expansion of Islam are in Southern India and the present-day Indonesian archipelago.

In 1453 the Turks brought the Eastern Roman Empire to an end by capturing its last fortress city Constantinople. Then, their armies conquered the Balkans, Greece, and part of Hungary and Austria. The victorious advance of Turkish Islam in the West was stopped in the 17th century. In 1683 the Turkish armies were repulsed before the gates of Vienna. But they remained the masters of South East Europe until the Greek war of independence in the 19th century. The Peace Treaty concluding the *First World War* (1918) confined Turkish territory to the boundaries of present-day Turkey, but in South East Europe some ethnic groups, e.g. in Bosnia, remained faithful to Islam.

A 20th-century picture of the Hagia Sophia in Istanbul (Constantinople) that after 1453 was changed from a cathedral into a mosque.

13.7. The Expansion in Sub-Saharan Africa

The third movement of expansion of Islam especially pertains to sub-Saharan Africa. The occupation of North Africa in the first period was followed by the Islamic conquest of the Sahara in the second period. Then, the Eastern and Western coastal areas of sub-Saharan Africa were penetrated, Niger, East Sudan, West Sudan. The Hausa belonged to the first sub-Saharan peoples that were converted to Islam. From about 1750 the Fullah people, voluntarily joined by the Hausa, in a violent way founded a large and powerful Islamic state.[8] Gradually during the 18th and 19th centuries, Islam spread southwards, sometimes using violent, sometimes peaceful methods. In the coastal areas of East Africa the influence of Arabic Islam even reached the South of the continent, leading to the foundation of Muslim island and city states. Swahili Arabs and allied tribes were active as hunters and traders of slaves. In the East and the South of Africa[9] Islam not only spread from Arabia, but also by means of the migration of workers from India to Africa.

13.8. Expansion in the Western World

Until the 19th century western public consciousness harboured fear that the Arab and Turkish branches of Islam might threaten the heartland of Europe. This changed when in the era of *colonialism* many Muslim states became dependent on the West. For Islam this opened doors to the West. Especially after the Second World War and after the end of *colonialism*, millions of Arabic, Turkish and Indian Muslims migrated to Western Europe. The main reason was that Western industrial leaders invited them, to use as cheap labour. In the meantime, Islam has become one of the main religions in many cities of Western Europe.[10]

---

[8] K. Shillington, *History of Africa*, London: Macmillan, 1995, discusses on pp.90-106 the early spread of Islam in the Sudanic states of West Africa.

[9] Cf. J.S.Trimingham, *Islam in East Africa*, London: Oxford University Press, 1964; E.C. Mwandivenga, *Islam in Zimbabwe*, Gweru: Mambo Press, 1983; D.S. Bone (ed.), *Malawi's Muslims: Historical Perspectives*, Blantyre: CLAIM, 2000 [with bibliography].

[10] For example, in 2003 from an official statistical survey in The Netherlands we learnt that with 5% of the population the number of Muslims in that country has doubled since 1993, making Islam numerically the fourth religious denomination (*Centraal Bureau voor de Statistiek,* in: RNW 14-10-03).

14. Expansion in North West Europe 590-800[1]

14.1. Mission by the Church of Rome

In the second and third centuries many parts of the Roman Empire were 'conquered' by Christianity, although the Church was not recognised by the State, and often was persecuted. The missionary spirit of the early Christians is evident. The Church had not only to defend itself against the powers of pagan culture, but also against erroneous teachings and practices, which crept into the Christian communities right from the

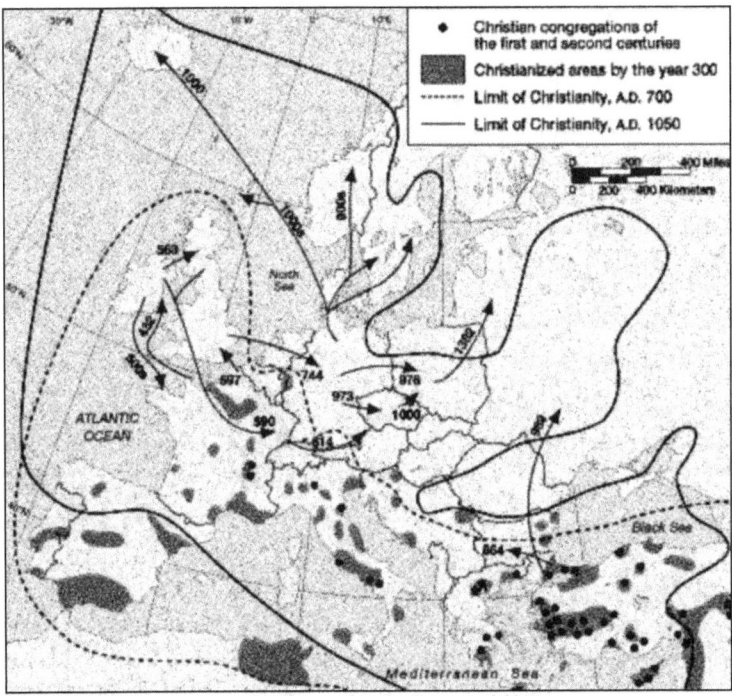

Expansion of Christianity in the West and in the East, until 1054.

beginning. After the *Edict of Milan* in 313, which gave freedom to the Church, and after 380, when Christianity became the state religion, the abuses, errors and heresies increased. C*lericalism* and *hierarchicalism* emerged gradually taking its extreme form in *papalism*. At the same time, although often mixed up with worldly elements and heretical thought, the true Gospel of Christ was spreading

After the collapse of the Roman Empire in the West in 476, most of the political and military power in Europe was taken over by the emerging Frankish Empire, and later by the German Empire. But in this process of disintegration and re-integration the Church remained the unifying factor. The influence of the bishops of Rome increased

---

[1] Cairns, *Christianity through the Centuries*, pp.120-124,159-163,171-175; Dowley, pp.217-219,226-234,236-238,298,299,302,303,307-309; Foster, *Setback and Recovery*, pp.22-37; Renwick/Harman, pp.63-72,78-80,82-83.

considerably, not only ecclesiastically but also politically. One of the most significant popes was Gregory (Gregorius) the Great (approximately 540-604). He used to be the highest civil ruler of the city of Rome (*prefect*), but he abandoned the civil service, and founded a monastery; subsequently he was elected pope. This able church ruler made and executed plans for his *dual* objective, the extension of *Christianity* and of *papal power*. Both sides of this need comment.

a. Extension of Christianity

Gregory the Great contributed much to the Christian mission among the predominantly pagan Germanic and Frankish peoples of North and West Europe. But he simultaneously promoted the spreading of erroneous teachings and practices; first of all by the use of *syncretistic* missionary methods that condoned the remnants of many pagan elements in the new churches. Pagan temples were made into churches, and pagan customs in a 'purified' form were retained, like processions with candles, fires on Easter Day, veneration of holy wells. The Germanic gods, like Wodan, Donar, Frigga, and Saxnot, were officially abolished. But pagan polytheistic notions have never died completely. The same applies for beliefs in spirits, giants, dwarfs, witches, and werewolves.

Pope Gregory I 'the Great', (c.540-604).

Gregory made the bishops more dependent on the pope, although in his propaganda against the Patriarch of Constantinople he called himself *servus servorum Dei* (Latin for: slave of the slaves of God). He pushed the teachings of the church in a *(semi-) pelagian* direction by introducing the doctrine of 'free will'. He also developed the doctrine of purgatory, promoted monasticism, made important changes in the liturgy, fostered the development of liturgical music ('Gregorian') and gave the Roman *schola cantorum* its definite form'. He also propagated the sacrificial character of the mass and masses for the deceased, and he contributed to the veneration of saints by the promotion of miracle stories.

b. Extension of Papal Power

When he became pope, Gregory appointed governors to Italian cities, and established the temporal power of the papacy, i.e. he laid the foundation of the *papal state*. The missionaries he sent out not only had to convert the heathen, they also had to bring existing churches under the authority of the papal see. In this sense the Gregorian mission was directed against the Celtic Church. Both objectives the pope sought to realise by successfully trying to get the assistance of Frankish and Germanic civil rulers.

14.2. Romanising of European Christianity

The new missionary élan of Rome contributed to the *Christianising* of North West Europe, but there was also the *Romanising* of existing churches. The existence of the church outside the Church of Rome was not recognised. In 596 Pope Gregory sent the abbot Augustinus together with forty monks to those parts of Britain (present-day England) that were conquered by pagan Germanic tribes. The Anglo-Saxons allowed him to settle in Canterbury and soon they were converted to Christianity. Roman missionaries even reached Wales, Ireland and Scotland. Their second task was to subjugate the Celtic Church and to take over the results of its missionary work (see chapter 6).

A decision by the Northumbrian King Oswy at a combined synod of Celtic and Roman leaders in Whitby (664) contributed to the victory of Rome. Using *Matthew 16:18*, the Roman party convinced the king that the pope is the successor of the Apostle Peter. After this Roman practice was introduced, although in other regions the Celtic Church remained active for some time. The missionary spirit was kept alive in the romanised British Church. Also, after the *Synod of Whitby* many missionaries, such as Willibrord and Boniface, went to the Continent, but now as representatives of Rome.

Willibrord (658-739) has become famous because of his heroic attempts to convert the pagan Frisians who lived along the coast from Denmark to France. In 690 he, together with eleven companions, landed at the coast of the Low Countries near present-day Katwijk. In 695, after the battle of Dorestad, Western Frisia was occupied by the Franks. In the same year Frankish and papal support for Willibrord was shown when the pope consecrated him *Archbishop of the Frisians*. The Frisians north east of the Rhine, who were still independent, remained very hostile to him. The Frankish king gave him a site for a cathedral just outside Utrecht, on the edge of Frankish political and military influence. Fifty years before, a missionary called Kunibert had built a small chapel on the same site, indicating earlier

Willibrord, 'Apostle of the Frisians' (658-739); an 11th-century picture.

attempts to convert the Frisians. From Rome Willibrord brought relics and rituals, but this did not make Christianising the Frisians any easier. There was fierce resistance. In 714 the Frisian King Radbod occupied Utrecht and destroyed Willibrord's missionary centre. The political situation changed when the Frisians were beaten by the Frankish general Charles Martel in 722 and 733/34. Frisia became dependent on the Franks, but that did not make them Christians. Gradually Willibrord noticed that support by political and military force of the Franks was detrimental to his missionary campaigns. In 698 he therefore removed his centre to Echternach (in Luxemburg), outside Frankish Frisia, where he founded a monastery. Willibrord's work among the Frisians was not very successful, neither was his campaign to Denmark.

Boniface (680-754), in a sense Willibrord's successor, also tried to convert the Frisians, but he became famous because of his work among the Germans. His original name was Wynfrith; like Willibrord he came from Britain. In 712 he went for the first time to Frisia. However the Frisian king did not allow him to preach. After visiting the Pope in 714, who gave him his new name Boniface (Bonifatius: *he who is favoured by fate*), he went to Germany. With the help of Frankish and Germanic rulers he converted many Germans in Hessen and Thüringen. He also contributed much to the systematic subjugation to Rome of churches founded by the Celtic mission. He accused the Irish monks of using syncretistic methods. Bishops of the Celtic Church were discharged by him and replaced by Roman bishops. In 722 he was consecrated bishop by the Pope. On returning to Germany, he cut down a holy Wodan oak at Geismar in Hessen. Then, thousands of pagans wanted to be baptised. Only because of the strong support by the Pope and by the Frankish rulers, especially Charles Martel and his sons, could Boniface succeed in his missionary campaigns and in his reorganisation of the existing Celtic churches to put them under Rome. In 741 the Pope made him archbishop. Boniface decided to resign and return to Frisia. For two years he wandered through Frisia, preaching. But the old hatred against Christianity had not died everywhere. In 754 at Dokkum Boniface was murdered by pagan Frisians. After his death, Utrecht again became a missionary centre, now for training of preachers among the Frisians and among the Saxons. In the 8th century the Frankish Emperor Charlemagne completed the Christianisation of the Frisians.

Boniface (Wynfrith), 'Apostle of Germany' (680-754).

14.3. Christianisation of North Germany and Scandinavia

a. Charlemagne and the Saxons

East of the Frisians lived the Saxons. Although a good number of them were already Christians at the beginning of the 8th century, massive Christianisation took place after they were subjugated by the Frankish ruler Charlemagne. In a series of military campaigns and crushing of rebellions, Charlemagne added the Saxons to his empire. At the same time, he tried to have them completely Christianised. In 777 through a Synod at Paderborn, he introduced *catechetical education*. Willehad and Liudger trained at Utrecht; they belonged to the missionaries among the Saxons. The surrender and baptism of a very influential Saxon leader and rebel, Windekind, led to a breakthrough for Christianity, although there were also new uprisings that were cruelly quenched in blood by Charlemagne.

b. Liudger and Charlemagne

Liudger, or Ludgar (†809) was a Frisian, born near modern Utrecht in The Netherlands. Sources about his life tell us that from an early age he was deeply interested in spiritual questions. He also met with his missionary predecessor Boniface 'when the hair of his (Boniface's) head was white and his body was decrepit with old age'. Liudger studied under Alcuin, the greatest teacher of that age. Physically weak and gentle, he became a missionary to his own people, where his knowledge of their language helped him. Later his gentleness and winning ways converted more Saxons to true Christianity than Charlemagne's forced baptisms ever did. Liudger founded the monastery from which the city of Münster, Germany takes its name. His success was attributed to his great zeal for God, which did not allow him to neglect his devotions. Once the Emperor, desiring to question him for his failure to richly decorate churches (he preferred to use the money for charity), summoned him to appear at court. Liudger kept the Emperor waiting while he finished divine service. When Charlemagne questioned him why it had taken three messengers to get him to report, Liudger replied: 'God is to be preferred to you, O King, and to all men'.[2]

In the period 800-1050 the coastal regions of Europe were hit by pirates from Scandinavia. These *Vikings* plundered and destroyed many churches and monasteries. In addition, they made permanent settlements and colonies in Ireland, Scotland, Wales, South England, France (Normandy) and Italy (on Sicily). Gradually a good number of Vikings converted to Christianity in the countries where they went to, and when returning they preached the Gospel to their fellow Scandinavians. The real Christianisation of the Scandinavian countries, however, was done by missionaries from Saxony and Britain. Anskar (born 801) was a Frankish monk in the Celtic tradition of Columbanus. He first worked among the Saxons. Then, at the invitation of the Danish king, he started working in Denmark and in Sweden. He was not very successful, but in the 10th century Christianity became more and more deeply rooted. The growing church in Denmark and Sweden was sometimes challenged by attempts to reinforce pagan religion and destroy Christianity, e.g. by Kings Gorm and Svend I. In 965 King Harald had himself baptised. This royal conversion also affected Norway, as Harald was king of that country as well. Under Knut (king in 1016), who was conqueror and king of part of England as well, the Christian faith got wide acceptance. Hakon, baptised at the English court, was the first Christian king of Norway (933). Gradually Christianisation progressed through decisions of local governments (the *Thing*). Under Kings Olaf Trygvason and Olaf Haroldson Christianity grew rapidly. The last mentioned invited missionaries from

Bible kept in the monastery of Fulda that was founded by Boniface. According to legend, Boniface used this Bible to ward off the swords of his attackers at Dokkum in 754.

---

[2] From: *Munster Maker*, Christian History Institite, ChiNotes 26-3-2006, www.chinstitute.org

England. In 1030 King Knut of Denmark became king of Norway too, which was in favour of the continuing deployment of the Church.

The Church in Iceland was established by Saxon missionaries, by returning Icelanders who had met Christianity in Norway, and also by Norwegian missionaries like Steven Thorgilson. The final decision to accept Christianity on the island was taken by the government, the *Althing*. The Church in Sweden started with some converts by Anskar and a group of English traders. Olaf Slötkonung was the first Christian king. He invited missionaries from England, and under his son Anund Jakon Christianity grew considerably. After some clashes between representatives of the old religion and Christian leaders, the Christian religion had victory under King Inge. In the end of the 12th century the temple in Uppsala, centre of pagan religion, was destroyed, and on the same site a cathedral was erected.

Eastern European countries like Hungary, Poland, and Bohemia were won for *Western Christianity* by missionaries sent by Rome. Russia was mainly evangelised from Constantinople, i.e. from the centre of *Eastern Christianity*.

15. Church and State in Competition

15.1 The Frankish Holy Roman Empire[1]

a. Merovingians and Carolingians

Before the collapse of Roman hegemony in the West, a period of migration of peoples from East to West had begun. These migrations mark the end of *Antiquity* and the beginning of the *Middle Ages*. In the region of present-day France, the Germanic tribe of the Franks founded a kingdom. Their first dynasty of kings are called the *Merovingians*. The first significant king was Clovis (c.466-511). By political and military means he united the Franks with Romans, Celts, Alemans, Vizigoths (West

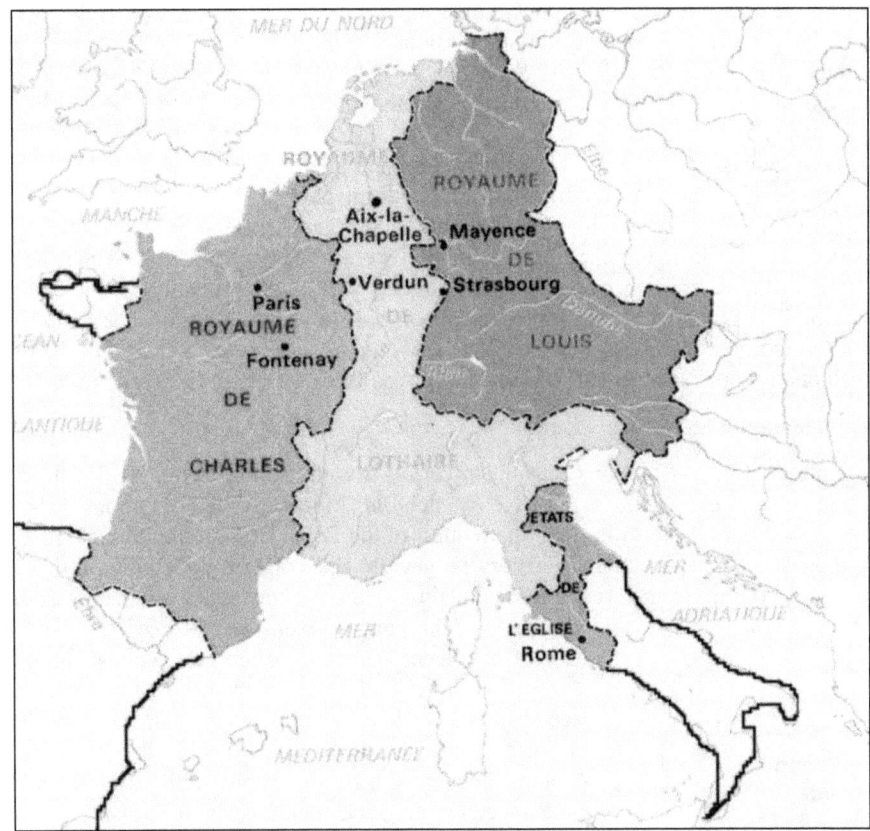

Empire of Charlemagne (Charles the Great), as it was divided among his three sons after his death.

Goths), and Burgundians; he extended his kingdom to the whole of Gaul (*Gallia: present-day France*) and to parts of Germany. The Franks were generally pagans at the time. But after Clovis' conversion to Catholic Christianity and his baptism in 496, the majority of the Frankish people followed their king. Subsequent Merovingian kings

---

[1] See also: Cairns, *Christianity through the Centuries*, pp.176-189; Dowley, pp.238-245; Foster, *Setback and Recovery*, pp.56-63; Renwick/Harman, pp.80-81.

were weaker than their predecessor was. This led to a temporary fragmentation of the Frankish kingdom. It also gave room to the emergence of powerful military functionaries at the royal court. Soon practically all power was in the hands of a dynasty of superior mayors of the palace (in Latin: *maior domus*). They are called the *Carolingians*.

The first Carolingian of European significance is Charles Martel (c. 690-741). In the previous chapter we saw that he beat the Frisians in 722 and in 733/ 734. His victory over the Islamic Saracens at Poitiers in 732 was of decisive importance for the future of Christianity. In his later years he penetrated into Germany and Frisia, where he protected Roman Catholic missionaries like Boniface. His son Pepin III (*the Short One*), 714-768, with the assent of the Pope, and with repeated papal anointments, was elected king by the nobles in 751 instead of the last Merovingian king. Later popes claimed that Pepin had donated to them territories for the papal

Charlemagne, Emperor of the Frankish Empire.

ecclesiastical state, the so called *Patrimony of St. Peter*. Similar claims referring to donations by the Roman Emperor Constantine were already circulating. About 850 a collection of such and other canon law documents was made, probably by one Isodore Mercator. The Lutheran historian Flacius and others investigated these *Pseudo Isidorian Decretals* comprising the so called *Constantinian and Pepinian Donations*. In their church history published in 1559-1574 they proved these papers to be falsifications!

b. Charlemagne Extends his Empire

Charlemagne (c.742-814), or *Charles the Great*, was the son of Pepin III. He became the sole ruler of the Franks in 771. He extended his kingdom in all directions. First he subdued Lombardy (North Italy) at the request of the Pope. He sent the Longobard king to a monastery. The conquered territory he gave to the Pope on the condition that the Pope would refrain from certain political claims. Then, he conducted campaigns against the Saxons. The pagan Saxons were forced to swear an oath of obedience. But they often rose against Frankish authority. Charles had many of them killed and deported (see chapter 14). He also campaigned against the Muslims in Spain; they were pushed back behind the River Ebro. At home he created a strong central administration and he encouraged learning and ecclesiastical reforms.

Alcuin (c.735-804), Charlemagne's adviser; picture in State's Library in Bamberg.

Although the king in his youth had no formal education in reading and writing, he developed a real interest in learning, including theology. With the assistance of the scholar Alcuin he promoted a network of monastery schools in which much of early European civilisation was kept for future generations. Many present-day European universities are located on the sites of these monastery schools.

c. Charlemagne's Church Policy

In his Church policy Charles tried to be independent of the Pope. He prohibited the veneration of statues, and he opposed the abuses of *immorality* and *simony* (the selling of church offices) among clerics. He also propagated the rejection of the heresy of *adoptionism* (i.e. the idea that Christ in His humanity is only the adoptive Son of God), and he materialised the decision (by the Council of Toledo 589) to have the *filioque* (i.e. the Holy Ghost *also* proceeds from the Son) included in the *Nicene Creed*. Charles the Great was much inspired by Augustine's work *De Civitate Dei* (On the City of God). He aspired to the foundation of a *State of God* on earth, a unified community without tribalism, based on political and spiritual unity. Because of the means he used he sometimes was nicknamed *apostolus armatus* (armoured apostle).

Picture of the Emperor Charlemagne (Charles the Great) in a 14th-century manuscript, showing his coronation by Pope Leo III.

The mixture of church and politics is visible in his organisation of the church. He divided his empire into 20 archbishoprics which were subdivided into bishoprics and parishes. This ecclesiastical organisation was part of the political organisation of the empire. Charles often gave civil functions to clerics and the other way round. Bishops sometimes even served as army generals, and often they were the regional rulers in the Frankish political administration. In the *feudal* organisation of medieval society the bishops and other clerics belonged to the vassals (= *feudal tenants*) of the Emperor.

Although Charlemagne succeeded in balancing papal power in his empire, he had to reckon with the growing ecclesiastical and political influence of the Bishop of Rome. Sometimes he bowed to it. In a sense the culmination of his reign was his coronation by Pope Leo III as first *Holy Roman Emperor* on Christmas Day of the year 800.

15.2. The German Holy Roman Empire[2]

a. Emperors and Popes

The Pope and the Emperor were the competing authorities of Europe at this time. Charlemagne successfully resisted most of the papal claims. But the Frankish Empire soon lost much of its greatness and vastness. After Charles' death, his sons divided the territory, so the empire fell into pieces. Moreover, it was weakened by the Norsemen (Vikings) who in the 9th and 10th centuries plundered the European coasts from the Low Lands to Italy.

In this period another power tried to take over the heritage of the Romans: the emerging German Empire, or *Holy Roman Empire of the German Nation*. At first the

---

[2] Cairns, *Christianity through the Centuries*, pp.189-192 (cf. Cairns pp.194-196, 202-210 on *Supremacy of Papacy*); Dowley, p.245, (cf. pp.262-266).

15. Church and State in Competition

German Emperors had an almost absolute power over the church. The *investiture*, i.e. the nomination of bishops, was in their hands. They even appointed some popes.

b. Investiture Controversy

However, this changed after 1073, when Cardinal Hildebrand (c. 1021-1085) was elected to be Pope Gregory VII. Influenced by the ideals of monastery reformation (see chapter 16), the new pope not only worked for reform of immorality and simony in the church, but also for the revival of papal power. In order to check the power of the Emperors he allied himself with the Norsemen and allowed them to have a state in the South of Italy. Gregory demanded that Emperors and kings be anointed by the Pope. He strongly opposed the *lay investiture*, the nomination of clerics by civil authorities. This measure was violently rejected, especially in Germany, France and England. The German king and *Holy Roman Emperor* Henry IV (1050-1106) reacted by having the Pope deposed by a German synod. Subsequently Pope Gregory VII censured Henry with the *interdict*, an ecclesiastical punishment in the Roman Catholic Church excluding the faithful from participation in spiritual things; the main effect is the cessation of the administration of the sacraments, which was very threatening to the medieval mind. The interdict released Henry's subjects from their allegiance to him. Impressed by this, the German nobility and clergy forced Henry to reconcile with the Pope. Henry performed this very humiliating act by going to the Pope, who at the time was staying in the castle of his woman friend in Canossa in 1077. Before accepting Henry's penance, the Pope had him wait for 3 days and night in the snow on the castle's square! After this Henry regained his power and took revenge. He nominated an anti-pope who crowned him *Holy Roman Emperor* in 1084, and then his armies besieged Rome. Gregory was saved by his allies the Norsemen and he died in exile.

Picture of Henry IV (1050-1160), German King and 'Holy Roman Emperor', in a manuscript at Corpus Christi College, Cambridge.

After the acute *investiture controversy* between popes and some European Emperors and kings, a series of compromises were reached in England and France. The final settlement with the

Picture of a Church Council in the 9th century.

German Empire was achieved in the *Concordat*[3] *of Worms* in 1122. Lay rulers were to cease the election of bishops.

c. Summit of Papal Power

The power of papacy came to a climax in Innocent III (1160-1216). He used the *interdict* to subdue France and England. He patronised the new orders of friars: the *Franciscans* and the *Dominicans*. The *Lateran Council* (1215) where decisions were taken on *transubstantiation* and *auricular confession*[4] was the culminating event of his reign. He also propagated the fourth crusade and a crusade by children against Islam. He was co-responsible for the rooting out of the *Albigenses*. Subsequently the extravagant papal power in various European states provoked systematic attempts to be more independent of Rome politically and ecclesiastically. *Gallicanism* (in France), *Josephinism* (in Austria), and *Anglicanism* (in England) belong to these national movements.

---

[3] *Concordat*: An agreement between the Roman Catholic Church and a state.

[4] *Auricular confession* (considered to be one of seven sacraments): private confession of sin to a priest, demanded by the Church as a condition of the absolution.

16. Monastic Reforms[1]

16.1. Degradation of Monasticism

In the transition period of late Antiquity and early Middle Ages monasticism rendered great service to church and civilisation by its missionary and educational activities (see chapter 11). But during the time of the Merovingians the monks lost their zeal and diligence, and many abuses entered the monasteries. The degradation of monasticism contributed to a decrease of the Church's authority, and it diminished the respect by the people towards the clergy.

The Carolingian kings facilitated an improvement of the situation, which enabled Benedict of Aniane (c.750-821) to reintroduce the old *Rules of Benedict of Nursia* with additional stricter rules. Asceticism and isolation were emphasised, as well as prayer and manual labour. There was also an increasing tendency to cut off the monasteries from the jurisdiction of the local bishops and place them directly under the Pope.

By the 10th century the *Benedictine Rule* had relaxed again, and many abuses had re-entered the monasteries. Many monasteries had grown very rich and often the monks led a luxurious and immoral life. This period is characterised by disintegration on the one hand and attempts at reform on the other.

16.2. The Cluniac Reforms

In 909 in Burgundy the monastery of Cluny was founded. It became a centre of reform. The high standard of monastic observance led to the adoption of its customs by many other monasteries, old and new. In the beginning of the 12th-century about 1200 monasteries belonged to the *Congregation of Cluny*. The objects of reform not only included the extended *Benedictine Rule*, but also cultivation of personal spiritual life, stress on the choir office, and the splendour and solemnity of worship generally, with a corresponding reduction in manual labour. Especially in the 11th and 12th centuries, this highly centralised and disciplined order exercised great influence on the life of the Church. The main targets of its external activities were the fight against *simony* and *immorality*. Soon the *Cluniac movement* led to the emergence of parallel movements in countries like England, Germany and Italy.

The Cluniac spirit of reform did not originate from Rome, the centre of Roman Catholicism, but eventually the popes greatly benefited from it. The papacy needed help to restore its authority, because in the late Middle Ages the process of decay had reached its lowest point. At one time there were even three popes who competed in murder, corruption and sexual abuse.[2] Some civil rulers regretted the state of the Church and they tried to introduce reforms. The German Emperors in this period were especially active in this; therefore they favoured the Cluniac movement. At the same time, they tried to replace the Pope as head of the Church. Ironically, their support of the Cluniac movement was counterproductive to their attempts to subdue the popes, for the Cluniac spirit indirectly contributed to a restoration of papal power.

---

[1] Cairns, *Christianity through the Centuries*, pp.217-221; Dowley, pp.260,261,267-275,320-329; Foster, *Setback and Recovery*, pp.143-153.

[2] Cf. Foster, *Setback and Recovery*, pp.130 ff.

16.3. Cluniacs Boost Papal Power

More and more minds were controlled by the principles of *canon law*. They did not recognise any civil authority over spiritual powers. Roman Catholic *canon law* is a body of ecclesiastical rules or laws concerning matters of faith, morals, discipline, and church government, consisting of statements by Church Councils, decrees of influential bishops, and especially letters of popes. About 1140 Gratian collected these texts in his *Decretum*, which was to be used as an important part of Roman Catholic law. In a revised form (1983) this codex is still the most important law book in the Roman Catholic Church. In it the supreme and absolute power of the Pope is stressed, canons 330-335.[3]

The Cluniac reforms facilitated the emergence of a number of very powerful popes, who were able to withdraw from imperial power and sometimes even to temporarily subdue it. The first one was Leo IX (1002-1054). He was influenced by the Cluniacs, and after his election he enforced celibacy on all the clergy. Soon afterwards various Councils promulgated decrees against simony and other abuses. He also was active as a military leader of an unsuccessful campaign against the Norsemen in Southern Italy. In his last year the Eastern Church completely seceded from the Western Church. During the reign of Leo IX and subsequent popes, great influence was exercised by Hildebrand (c.1021-1085) who became Pope himself in 1073. As Pope Gregory VII he worked for the moral reform of the church. He also contributed to final papal victory in the *Investiture Controversy* with the German Emperors and other civil rulers. The controversy between *sacerdotium* and *imperium* culminated in the humiliation of Emperor Henry IV at Canossa (see also chapter 15).

16.4. The Cistercians – Bernard of Clairvaux

A second wave of influential monastic reform began also in France, at Citeaux. There in 1098 the order of the Cistercians was founded. They blamed the Cluniacs for having become complacent, rich and proud. Stricter forms of *Benedictism* were introduced, more primitive than any then existing. The Cistercian life was to be one of secluded communal intercession and adoration. Its churches were to be plain, and manual work was given its primitive prominent position. The constitution was laid down in the *Carta Caritatis*. After Bernard (1090-1153) had entered the monastery of Citeaux in 1112, the Cistercian order developed widely. He established a new monastery at Clairvaux, which soon became the chief centre of the order. A century after this, the Cistercian organisation numbered 671 monasteries. In the 17th century they also spread to other countries. There was a parallel network of houses for Cistercian nuns. The *Trappists* were among the strictest Cistercian monks. Before long Bernard was one of the most

Bernard of Clairvaux (1090-1153).

---

[3] *Codex Iuris Canonici*, Rome: Libreria Editrice Vaticana, 1983.

Abbey of Cluny, founded in 910 (picture from the National Library in Paris).

influential religious forces in Europe. Bernard's significance can be summed up as follows.

a. He contributed to papal power. In the disputed election of 1130 he secured the victory of Innocent II. In 1145 a former pupil of his was elected Pope, Eugenius III. At the same time, he criticised the lust for power and worldly pomp in the church.

b. His authority contributed to the Crusades against Islam. Personally he preached in favour of the second Crusade that started in 1147. Bernard was co-responsible for the foundation of the *Knight's Templars*, one of the orders in which monkshood and knighthood were mixed with the aim of creating an effective military and spiritual force against Islam.

c. He propagated a Biblical kind of mysticism. Conversion to the truth of God has to be experienced in the heart. Famous are his 86 sermons on the Song of Songs in which he deals with the intimate relationship between the believer's soul (the bride) and Christ (the Bridegroom). In his Jesus devotion, Bernard in a way is a forerunner of the 16th-century Reformation of the Church. However, he is not a real Reformer himself. He mixed his mysticism with veneration of the Virgin Mary, and his support of the papacy did not help the Church. Bernard's mysticism was opposed to the development of a philosophical method of *Scholasticism* that gradually tended to give more honour to *human reason* than to Scripture. A representative of this thinking was Peter Abelard (1079-1142). Bernard contributed to his official condemnation by the church.

16.5. Mendicant Orders

The mixture of good and evil in these reform movements is also apparent in the emergence of the mendicant orders, e.g. the *Franciscans* and the *Dominicans*. Members of these orders were forbidden to hold property, either individually or in common. They worked or begged for their living, and they were not bound to one monastery. Their activities, e.g. preaching and hearing confessions, had positive effects for the prestige of the Roman Catholic Church, but also aroused great hostility.

The *Franciscans*, founded by the Italian Francis of Assisi (1182-1226), insisted on complete poverty. He sold his possessions, and with the permission of the Pope he founded an order, called *Ordo Fratrum Minorum* (OFM), the members of which at first went

Francis of Assisi (1181/2-1226), founder of the Franciscan Order.

round as beggars. Therefore, groups like these are called *mendicant orders*. The Franciscans promised to abstain from material possessions, and concentrated on works of mercy and also on the study of theology. They opposed the luxury and wealth of the church, but not the papal structure of the church itself. They devoted themselves to works of charity and later also to scholarly work. In 1212 an order of female Franciscans was founded, the *Claricians*.

Another new *mendicant order* whose members originally lived by begging was the Dominicans (OP = *Ordo Predicatorum*). The order was founded in 1220 by the Spaniard Dominicus Guzman (1170-1221). Like the Franciscans the Dominicans originally practised individual and corporate poverty. They were specifically devoted to preaching and study. The adaptation of Aristotelian philosophy to Christianity was largely the work of Dominicans, e.g. Albertus Magnus and Thomas Aquinas. The popes also used them for preaching in support of the Crusades against Islam. Like the Franciscans they staffed the judicial Courts of *Inquisition* against heretics from 1232 when a full time papal Inquisition was established. Actually, the establishment of the Dominican Order fitted in the plan of Pope Innocent III to convert the sect of the Albigenses. Outside Europe the Dominicans followed the Spanish and Portuguese explorers and conquerors.

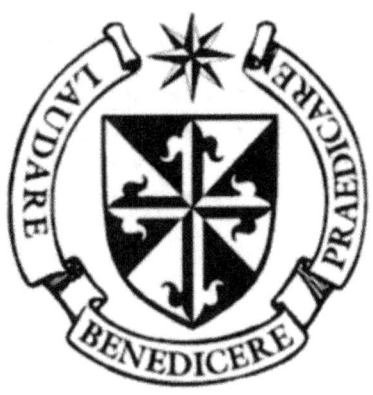

Symbol of the Dominican Order, founded by Dominicus Guzman in 1220/1221.

They also played an important role in the *Counter Reformation*, i.e. the Roman Catholic campaign to crush the Protestant Reformation of the 16th century. Together with the Franciscans they made the *Inquisition* a dangerous opponent of the Reformation. The Counter Reformation was also greatly helped by the order of the *Jesuits*, founded by Ignatius de Loyola in 1534. The Jesuits concentrated on the extinction of the Reformation, as well as on the organisation of education and mission.

Franciscan monastery in Assisi.

There were and there are many more orders. Here are some examples. The *military orders* consisting of persons who were knights and monks at the same time. These orders originated from the period of the *Crusades* against Islam; one of them is the order of the *Carmelites* founded by a Crusader on Mount Carmel in the country of Palestine. A completely different kind is the order of the *Augustinians*, to which once the Reformer Martin Luther belonged.

In the 16th century monasticism vanished in countries that were touched by the *Reformation*, although in some Protestant churches, like the *Anglican Church*, a certain monastic interest remained. After the *French Revolution*, monasticism also declined in Roman Catholic countries. But there was a revival in the midst of the 19th century, followed by a new decline in many countries in the second half of the 20th century. There is also a history of monasticism in the *Eastern Churches* (see chapter 17) and in *Ethiopian Christianity* (see chapter 43.2).

17. Eastern Orthodox Church[1]

17.1. The terms EC and EOC

The term *Eastern Christianity* (EC) is wider than the term *Eastern Orthodox Churches* (EOC). By EC we mean all those forms of Christianity that developed east of the Adriatic Sea, i.e. Greece and eastwards, in countries of South East and North-East of Europe, and in Asia and Africa. We are referring to a great variety of sometimes very different churches. They all are more or less characterised by having their origin in some kind of medieval opposition to the claims of the Western based Roman Catholic Church; and at a later stage they did not find unity with the churches of the Reformation either. So, ironically those African and Asian churches that are derived from missionary activities by Western Roman Catholicism and Protestantism are not to be reckoned as EC.

The most numerous group in EC are the *Eastern Orthodox Churches*. They are a loose federation of churches that are independent in their internal administration. But all share the same faith and are in communion with each other, acknowledging the honorary primacy of the Patriarch of Constantinople.

The other churches in EC are mainly derivations from the Monophysite and Nestorian schisms in 5th and 6th centuries.[2] We mention two churches that are mainly based in Africa, the *Abyssinian Church* of Ethiopia and the *Coptic Church* of Egypt. Then, there are the *Syrian-Jacobite Church* in the Middle East and the *Armenian Church*. Finally, the *Nestorian Churches* are to be mentioned. They had their centre in Persia. By missionary activity Nestorianism spread to Arabia, India (*Thomas Christians*) and China. Today remnants call themselves *Assyrian Christians*.

17.2. Before the Fall of Rome

Icon of Church Father Johannes Chrysostom (c.347-407).

Already before the collapse of the Western part of the Roman Empire there were increasing tensions in the Church between the centres of Rome and Constantinople. This was partly due to the difference between Latin and Greek culture. In the second century a conflict started about the date of Easter. With the developing *hierarchicalism*, especially after 313, the bishops of the main cities began to envy one another's power, which eventually led to a competition between the Pope of Rome and the patriarch of Constantinople. One of the main problems in the East was the absolute power of the State over the Church. The Church Father Johannes Chrysostom

---

[1] Cairns, *Christianity through the Centuries*, pp.196-201; Dowley, pp.316-319; Foster, *Setback and Recovery*, pp.63-70,170-172. In this chapter, we deal with the origin of the EOC only. For some details of other forms of EC that spread outside the Roman Empire, see: J.Foster, *The First Advance*, SPCK, 1994 (2), chapters 7 and 8; J.Foster, *Setback and Recovery*, SPCK, 1991 (9), chapter 4. See also our chapter 6: 'Expansion of Christianity beyond the Roman Empire'.

[2] See chapter 7.

(= *Golden Mouth*), c.347-407, was famous for his preaching and for his courageous protests against the sinful life at the imperial court. His teachings contain the beginning of distinct Eastern Orthodox liturgy which concentrates on *doxology*. By this word we mean the liturgical formula of praise to God (Gr. *doxé* = praise). The word *orthodox* then refers to the right way of praising God (Greek: *orthos* = *right, pure*).

17.3. The Iconoclastic Controversy

After the Fall of Rome, *politically* and *militarily*, the *ecclesiastical* claims by Rome were increasing. In the East papal authority was resisted. There the Byzantine Emperor was the head of the Church, and under him the five main patriarchates of the Greek East with the patriarch of Constantinople in primary position; hence, this system is called *caesaro-papism*. Gradually the East and the West estranged from one another. In the wake of the Monophysite and Nestorian schisms a controversy followed, on the veneration of images

An iconostasis: a screen in Eastern Orthodox churches that separates the sanctuary from the nave. It is covered by icons.

(*icons*), the so called *Iconoclastic Controversy*. Several times Emperors and synods declared the images to be idols and ordered their destruction. Icon-worshippers were persecuted. But in 787 the 7th General Council which met in Nicaea, decided a certain degree of veneration was to be paid to icons, and decreed their restoration throughout the empire. This Council is the last one that is recognised by the EOC, and its date (February 19) is an annual Orthodox feast. In the beginning of the 9th century the conflict ran high again for a short time. But since 843 the veneration of icons has been accepted in the EOC. These images are never statues, but paintings. In the same period in the West the veneration of statues and images was prohibited by the Frankish Emperor Charles the Great, although this measure did not stop the practice.

17.4. Photius, Filioque, Hesychasm, Paulicians

A temporary breach with Rome was brought about by Photius (c. 810-c.895). His appointment as patriarch of Constantinople was rejected by the Pope who deposed him. Photius reacted bitterly. He had a sentence of deposition pronounced against the Pope by a Council at Constantinople in 867. He also had Roman missionaries evicted from Bulgaria.

Photius also exposed his objections against the *filioque* clause in the *Nicene Creed*, which according to him was a bad innovation by Rome. The Latin formula *filioque* (and the Son) expresses the *double procession* of the Holy Spirit. In the West the term was included in the Nicene Creed, first at the Council of Toledo in 589; approximately 800 it became widely familiar throughout the Frankish Empire of Charles the Great. Photius and after him gradually the whole of the EOC have urged that there must be a *single fount* of Divinity in the Godhead; they hold that the Holy Spirit proceeds from the Father only, although *through the Son*. The West is accused of falsely introducing a *dual fount* in the Godhead. Photius, however, tends to attribute to the Son a lower level of Divinity than to the Father (*subordinationism*). It also weakens the oneness of the Son and the Holy Spirit. It suggests that there is a distinctly separate way of salvation by getting unified with the Spirit. In the monasticism of the EOC this leads to a *mystical* practice of meditation and ascesis[3] through which man is supposed to ascend to God *in the way of the Spirit*.

One of the phenomena is the *hesychasm*, associated especially with the monks of Mount Athos. Hesychasm refers to the tradition of inner, mystical prayer, which recommends a particular *bodily posture*, with breathing controlled to keep time with the recitation of the prayer. The aim is that the prayer of the mind becomes prayer of the heart. This leads to the vision of Divine Light, which was supposed to be seen with the material eyes of the body. There is an apparent element of *Gnostic dualism* in this. It explains why in the Eastern Orthodox climate *Gnostic sects* could flourish, though they were often persecuted. We mention the Paulicians, who like the Marcionists denied the reality of Christ's body (= *docetism*) and repudiated the Old Testament.

17.5. The Final Breach, 1054

From the 9th century onwards the tension between Rome and Constantinople intensified. The mistrust as to the West, formulated by Photius, increased. The final breach is dated in the year 1054. Patriarch Cerulanius had repeated the old complaints

Religious situation after the Great Schism that in 1054 separated the Church in the East from the Church in the West.

---

[3] *ascesis* (from Greek *askenein* = exercise): a term used for the exercise of discipline, i.e. 'rigourour self-denial and active self-restraint', especially regarding food and sleep.

of Photius, adding to it that the Westerners had the 'scandalous' practice of using *unleavened bread* in mass. He closed the papal chapel and other Latin churches in Constantinople. A request by the Pope to the Emperor to have Cerulanius deposed, was rejected. Then, the Pope formally condemned and excommunicated the patriarch, whereupon Cerulanius excommunicated the representatives of the Western Church.

The breach has never been healed. The *Crusades* by the West against Islamic power in the Middle East were partly intended to save the Church in the East, but in fact they deepened the alienation between Western and Eastern Christianity. Various attempts were made to reunite East and West, e.g. at the Councils of Lyons (1274) and Florence

Medieval picture of Constantinople the city that in 330 was inaugurated as capital of the Roman Empire by Emperor Constantine the Great.

(1438/1439). In Florence a formal agreement was reached on the main points of controversy, i.e. the *Double Procession* of the Holy Spirit, the use of unleavened bread in the Eucharist, the doctrine of purgatory, and the primacy of the Pope. A *Decree of Union* was signed, but it met with popular resentment in Constantinople, and it never had practical consequences. Fourteen years later (1453) the Islamic Turks captured the city, thus ending the Empire and bringing its Church under Islamic hegemony.

17.6. Moscow, the 'Third Rome'

In the centuries before the Fall of Constantinople the EOC had expanded to the West and North. A missionary advance was inaugurated in the 9th century by Cyril and Methodius. Largely through the efforts of Byzantine missionaries Bulgaria, Serbia and subsequently Russia were converted to Christianity. Constantinople officially remained the main centre of the family of Eastern Orthodox Churches. But in practice the focal point of Orthodoxy was removed from Constantinople, 'the second Rome', to Moscow, 'the third Rome'.

17.7. Different from the West

Teachings and life in the EOC differ from Western Christianity. Here are some examples, in addition to the issues mentioned before.

First, the relationship between Church and State. Contrary to Roman Catholicism that tends to put the Church above the State, and Protestantism that generally wants the Church to be free of the State, Orthodoxism allows the State to be above the Church. This explains why very often Orthodox Churches were tools in the hands of political rulers. At the same time, it must be stressed that many Orthodox Churches managed to survive oppression by hostile regimes, like Islam in the Middle East and Communism in Russia.

Secondly, Eastern piety is characterised by a kind of passivity. Whereas Western Christian thought pertains directly to the practical situations of daily life, in the East religion is withdrawn to the background of daily life, mainly concentrated on prayer and meditation.

The Russian Orthodox Church of St. Peter and St. Paul in Jaroslav.

Thirdly, the centrality of *praise* in the liturgy of the church services. The particular way in which the mystery of the working of the eucharist is presented to the congregation, i.e. the significance of the *iconostasis*; this is a screen bearing icons and separating the sanctuary (altar etc.) from the nave (church attendants). The predominant praise element in liturgy comes to a climax in a kind of *deification* of man, going back on the idea that God became man in order that man would become God. The commemoration of Christ's victory on the cross and his resurrection are particularly emphasised. Whereas *Christmas* is the main Western Feast, in the East it is *Easter*. Unlike the Western churches, the EOC never fixed the exact number of sacraments. The Orthodox vision of the *procession* of the Holy Spirit is reflected in the thought on the sacraments. In baptism the Spirit regenerates man and makes him part of the body of Christ. In the eucharist the Spirit descends and changes bread and wine into body and blood of Christ. Whereas in Rome this *transubstantiation* is said to happen at the words *This is My Body* spoken by the priest, in the EOC it is supposed to take place by the *epiclesis*, i.e. the prayer for the Holy Spirit.

17.8. Lack of Reformation

Except for these differences, Orthodox theology and liturgical practice are rather similar to Roman Catholicism. In both churches there is a hierarchy of priests ('popes', patriarchs) that represent and govern the Church, a semi-pelagian emphasis on merit, anachronistic forms of language in the liturgy, mechanical working of the sacraments, and an important role played by symbols and images. There are some parallels to Protestantism, e.g. lower clergy are allowed to marry, papal power is repudiated, and there is a distinct attention for the work of the Holy Spirit. Yet Orthodox tradition has never been touched by fundamental reorientation on Scriptures of the kind that changed much of Western church life in the 16th-century Reformation.

18. The Crusades[1]

18.1. Pilgrims Threatened

The term refers to a series of military expeditions from Western Europe to the region east of the Mediterranean Sea. These campaigns were designed: (a) to recover the Holy Land from Islam (1095-1204), (b) and then to retain in Christian hands (1204-1291) and (c) later to counteract the expanding power of the Ottoman Empire (1291-1464). The immediate cause was the threatened position of Western Christian pilgrims in the Holy Land.

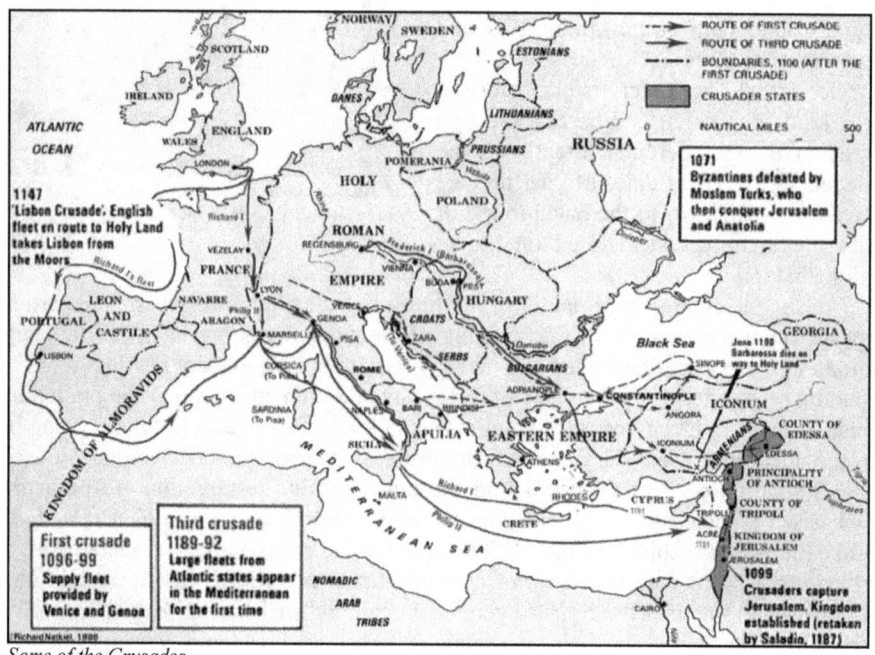

Some of the Crusades.

Constantine the Great's mother Helena had begun the long tradition of pilgrimages to the spots where Christ was born, where He had performed his miracles, where his death, burial and resurrection had taken place. By the end of the millennium the number of pilgrims had increased considerably. Many people felt that the end of the world was nearby and that Christ would return on the Mount of Olives.

The Islamic Arabs had occupied Palestine since the 7th century. Generally, the Arab rulers were rather tolerant towards Christians; they did not hinder pilgrimages from the West. Christian pilgrims were even allowed to build churches. But in the 11th century the Islamic Turks (*Seljuks*) from Central Asia conquered large parts of the Eastern Roman Empire. In 1071 they penetrated deep into Asia Minor, and threatened Constantinople. The Roman Emperor asked the Pope of Rome for help! In 1076 the Turks occupied Palestine. Soon rumours spread in Western Europe about Turkish

---

[1] Cairns, *Christianity through the Centuries*, pp.212-216; Dowley, pp.277-281; Foster, *Setback and Recovery*, pp.73-77.

atrocities against Christian pilgrims, especially those who wanted to visit the Holy Sepulchre. The first plans for the liberation of Palestine were made by Pope Gregory VII. However, because of his conflict with the German Emperor Henry IV he could not put the plans into action. Pope Urban II (c.1042-1099) launched the first Crusade.

18.2. Who Joined and Why?

The crusaders belonged to all layers of medieval society: kings, noblemen, monks, tradesmen, serfs, slaves, adventurers, faithful believers, criminals, and even children. Every group had its own reason for joining. Many factors were involved, religious, social and ideological. Many desired earnestly to liberate the country of Jesus from the Muslims. Many crusaders were motivated because they were granted *indulgences* for secret sins and public crimes, the remission of debts, the status of martyr in the event of death, and free citizenship on their return. Many knights liked the idea of being a clergyman and a warrior at the same time, fighting in the service of the Church. Monks could leave the dullness of a monastery and lead an officially legalised adventurous life.

Urban II (c.1042-1099), Pope from 1088. He launched the First Crusade.

A number of popes, especially Urban II and Innocent III, influenced public opinion in favour of joining the Crusades. They made people believe that these expeditions were carrying out the will of God. This increased their authority. The psychological climate gave them room for planning and approving many other expeditions, for which the same spiritual benefits were promised. They included expeditions against the Muslims in Spain, against heretics like the Albigenses, against Jews, and against the political opponents of papacy. Emperors and kings of e.g. Germany, France, and England had their own reasons for following the papal initiative. They were interested in territorial gains and growth of political influence. Also, the traders, i.e. the merchants of Venice and other harbour cities, profited from the Crusades.

18.3. First Period: Conquests 1095-1204

The 'first' Crusade was a complete failure. Therefore, it is not called the first, but the 'preliminary Crusade'. It was solemnly proclaimed by Pope Urban II at the Council of Clermont in 1095. Peter the Hermit (of Amiens) was one of the most eloquent travelling propagators. Headed by a goat and a goose that were to show the way, and led by Peter, a big and disorderly army marched along Rhine and Danube to Constantinople. On their way in Hungary and Bulgaria they committed many atrocities. When the army had crossed the Bosporus it was met by the Seljuks and annihilated.

18. The Crusades

The *First Crusade* in reality started in 1096. It had a double objective: relieving the pressure of the Shellshock Turks on the Eastern Roman Empire, and securing free access for pilgrims to Jerusalem. The Lotharingian nobleman Godfrey de Bouillon was the leader. His army marched via Constantinople. Although the Crusaders defeated the Seljuks in Asia Minor, the Roman Emperor Alexius felt threatened by them. He feared conquest by the West, especially after the Crusaders founded their own kingdoms in Edessa and Antioch (1098). Finally, 25,000 of the originally half a million Crusaders arrived at Jerusalem. After reinforcements came over sea from Genoa, the army captured the city (1099), and committed many atrocities, e.g. it killed more than 10,000 Muslims who were gathered together in a mosque. Also Jews were murdered in their synagogues. Then, the warriors went bareheaded and barefoot to the Church of the Holy Sepulchre in order to thank the Lord! All this contributes considerably to the bad reputation of Christians among Muslims. But 'the honour' of Western Christianity appeared to be saved. Godfrey of Bouillon got the title of 'Defender of the Holy Sepulchre', and he founded 'the Latin Kingdom of Jerusalem'. On his death in 1100 his brother was crowned king. During the next 20 years a series of Latin states was established in Syria and Palestine, which proved difficult to defend.

Peter the Hermit (1050-1115) preaches the first Crusade. In 1096 Peter the Hermit, a native of Amiens in France, led 20,000 commoners out of Cologne on the Peasants' Crusade. They sacked a number of Christian cities and killed many Jews before they reach Constantinople.

The *Second Crusade (1147-1149)* was provoked by the fall of the Crusaders' kingdom of Edessa in 1144. It was promoted by Bernard of Clairvaux. It was led by the French king, Louis VII, and by the German Emperor, Conrad III. The army never reached Jerusalem. It got stuck at Damascus because it failed to capture the city, owing to lack of support by the Byzantine Emperor. At the instigation of Bernard and others spiritual orders of knighthood were formed, e.g. the *Templars' Order*, the *Order of St. John*, the *German Order*. Members were knights who made the monastic promises of chastity, poverty, and obedience. Originally, they took care of the many sick and wounded Crusaders. But later they became warriors themselves, even the nucleus of the Crusaders' armies. The popes allowed these orders many privileges, which contributed to their subsequent wealth and power.

Crusaders' seal with an image of the Holy Sepulchre.

The *Third Crusade* (1189-1192) was organised because Jerusalem had been recaptured by the Muslims in 1187. Its leaders were a number of European monarchs. King Henry II of England and King Philip (Augustus) II of France took the initiative. The German Emperor Frederick *Barbarossa* who headed an army that marched over land; he was drowned when crossing a river in Asia Minor. In 1189 the English King Henry II died; he was succeeded by the King Richard II, named *Lion's Heart*, who headed a sea borne army.

Richard negotiated with the Muslim Sultan Saladin, the conqueror of Jerusalem. He got free access to some coastal areas in Palestine and to the holy sites in and near Jerusalem. In the 13th century the Crusaders only possessed a narrow territory along the Palestine coast of which Acre was the capital.

The *Fourth Crusade (1202-1204)*, took place at the call of the powerful Pope Innocent III. The crusade was supported by the rich merchants of Venice who delivered the ships. The leaders intended to conquer Egypt. The campaign failed and the crusade was diverted to Constantinople, where a 'Latin Empire' was established from 1204 to 1261.

After this, in 1212, a *Children's Crusade* took place. Headed by a 15-year-old boy, thousands of children, who gathered from France and Western Germany, marched to the Mediterranean seaports with the intention to cross over to Palestine and to recapture Jerusalem. Many did not get as far as embarking. Others were betrayed by traders who shipped them from Marseille to Northern Africa where they were sold on the slave markets.

A crusading nobleman.

18.4. Second Period: Defence 1204-1291

The other Crusades were mainly intended to consolidate and defend the acquired territories in the Middle East.

Frederick I Barbarossa (1122-1190), German King and 'Holy Roman Emperor', as Crusader.

The *Fifth Crusade (1228-1229)*, headed by the German Emperor Frederick II, was successful, especially because the Muslims were weakened by internal conflicts. Frederick recovered Jerusalem by negotiations and the city was in Latin hands from 1229 to 1244. Because he concluded a 10-year-treaty with the Sultan of Egypt, Frederick was excommunicated by Pope Gregory IX.

The next two Crusades were the largest ones. Both were directed against Egypt whose Sultan had recaptured Jerusalem in 1244, both were led by the French King Louis IX, a man of austere and prayerful life, and both campaigns failed.

The *Sixth Crusade* was from 1248 to 1254. The French sailed in 1248 and the following year they captured the Egyptian port of Damietta. In 1250, however, the king and his army were taken prisoner in the Egyptian Nile Delta. He was only released after the payment of a huge amount of money and many of his soldiers had to remain in Egypt as slaves. In 1270 Louis IX launched a new campaign. This was the Seventh Crusade. Again he crossed the Mediterranean with a large army. The city of Tunis was besieged, but the king died of dysentery and the expedition miscarried.

The Crusades failed to take the Holy Land out of Muslim hands, and did not succeed in breaking the power of Islam in the Middle East. At the end of this period, from a Western perspective, Palestine was lost. In 1268 Antioch fell, in 1289 Tripolis, and in 1291 Acre (Acre or Acco), the last Crusaders' possession on the Palestine coast, was recaptured by the Muslims.

18.5. Third Period: Against Turkish Expansion 1291-1464

The expansion of Turkish (Ottoman) power in the East provoked a series of intermittent attempts to organise joint action. The largest of these expeditions was that of 1396, defeated by the Turks at Nicopolis. In 1464 Pope Pius II died after failing to secure European cooperation for further Crusades. In the meantime, in 1453, the capital of the Christian Byzantine Empire, Constantinople, had fallen in the hands of the Turks. The Turks marched on. Consequently, parts of Southern Europe were occupied by them and kept for centuries. The Turkish military momentum was finally stopped before the gates of Vienna in 1683 (see chapter 13.6).

18.6. Consequences of the Crusades

The Crusades have deeply influenced the developments of Church and State in the West and their relationship with the Arab and Turkish Muslim world.

a. Muslim hatred. Although Muslim power was not broken, their expansion in Europe was curtailed. The price of the Crusades is a bad reputation of Christianity in Muslim public opinion.

b. Growing Antisemitism. Very often the Jews were blamed for all misfortunes in the world, especially for the execution of Jesus. On their way to the Holy Land the Crusaders persecuted and murdered many Jews, thinking that this was in accordance with the Crusades' aims. This is the beginning of the cruel tradition of *pogroms*[2] and of the establishing of *ghettos*.[3]

c. Ecclesiastical abuses. The Crusades helped the popes to increase their power of the popes. Crusaders, who lost their lives, often had their possessions bequeathed to the Church, which enormously increased the Church's wealth. The practice of buying *indulgences*[4] was greatly promoted by the Crusades, as was the belief in *relics*[5].

d. Social disorder. The Crusades took a great many lives in Europe and in the Middle East. Many Crusaders returned bodily handicapped and mentally damaged. The influence of years of murdering and robbing had a negative effect on European morals. Many got accustomed to the idea that piety and cruelty could go hand in hand.

---

[2] *pogrom*: organised massacre, especially of Jews.
[3] *ghetto*: quarter of a city outside of which Jews were not allowed to live.
[4] *indulgences:* declarations of forgiveness of sins by the pope.
[5] *relics*: remnants of holy things or holy persons.

e. Emerging of the Third Estate. The Crusades liberated many serfs and slaves. Besides, the estates of nobility and clergy a third estate of free people emerged. This led to the formation of free cities where they lived together and earned money by industry and commerce.

f. Development of commerce. By the Crusades Western Europe made contact with the countries of the East. This led to the development of commerce, which promotes the economies and increases wealth.

g. Development of science. The Crusades facilitated contacts with the Arab culture, which promoted the development of science in the West, e.g. knowledge of Greek philosophy, mathematics, architecture.

h. Desire for Reformation. The abuses and heresies in the Church and the shaking of the foundations of society created with many a longing for a real Reformation. Many Crusaders, when they saw Palestine, realised that the life of Jesus was opposed to the practices of the Church and got to despise the wealth, laziness, misuse of power by the clergy.

19. Medieval Papacy[1]

19.1. Emerging Papalism

The idea of the papacy developed through the ages. The basic offices of church government in the New Testament church are the office of *presbyteros* or *episkopos*, and the office of *deacons*. The presbyters ruled the congregations and some also preached the Word. Gradually the authority of certain presbyters was elevated above other presbyters; some of them took responsibility for more than one congregation. These were called *bishops*. There is no exact knowledge about how this development from *presbyterial* to *episcopal* church government took place. It started in the East and by the second century there were traces of it in the West as well. It was the beginning of *hierarchicalism* in the church.

Soon the bishops of regional capital cities took position above other bishops; they were called *metropolitans*. The next step was that the bishops in the cities where the Apostles founded congregations claimed an even higher status and authority than other bishops.

Gregory VII (Hildebrand), c.1021-1085, Pope from 1073.

These cities were: Rome, Antioch, Jerusalem, Alexandria, Ephesus, and Corinth. Three of them, those of Rome, Alexandria and Antioch were allowed to bear the title *patriarch* by the Council of Nicaea in 325. They were the highest metropolitans. The metropolitan of Constantinople was turned *patriarch* by the Council in this city, in 381. The patriarchs of Rome, however, were not satisfied with this title as they considered themselves higher than the other patriarchs, even higher than the patriarchs of Constantinople who competed with Rome for the chief position in the church. The name *papa* (Gr. papas) got to be used for the Roman patriarchs.

19.2. Growing Power

Siricius (384-395) was the first Pope who in his decretal letters to the Western church claimed universal power. Augustine's saying *Roma locuta, causa finita* (Latin for: When Rome has spoken, the matter is decided) shows that in his time papal claims were widely accepted. Popes Leo 'the Great' (†461) and Gregory 'the Great' (590-615) greatly extended papal influence. Gregory, famous for his organising activity of mission in North West Europe, is called the founder of the worldly power of the popes.

---

[1] Cf. Chapter 14, 'Expansion of Christianity in N.W.Europe' and chapter 15, on *Charlemagne*; Cairns, *Christianity through the Centuries*, pp.192-196 (cf. pp.150-152, 202-211, 159-163); Dowley, pp.118-119, 168, 184, 195-203, 238-239, 242-245, 261-264, 320-321, 330-340; Foster, *Setback and Recovery*, pp.125-140, 161-167.

Consolidation of an ecclesiastical state took place under Pope Nicolas I (†867); he used the *Pseudo* (= falsified) *Isidorian Decretals* (see chapter 15). The Cluniac monastic reform movement supported the spiritual and worldly power of the popes. From their midst came Hildebrand who as Pope Gregory VII (†1085) partly succeeded in counteracting the power of the German Emperors.

19.3. Innocent III and Boniface VIII

In Innocent III (†1216) papal power grew tremendously. In a political sense Innocent III was the most significant Pope. He forced three powerful kings to obedience. In a sense the German Emperor Frederick II (1194-1250) was 'created' by him. Innocent pressed claims to examine as well as to crown the person elected as Emperor. Frederick II was elected on condition that he did homage to the Pope. In France Innocent compelled King Philip Augustus to be reconciled to his queen, Ingeborg of Denmark. The king refused. But then the Pope issued an interdict against the whole French kingdom; all churches closed and ecclesiastical life came to a standstill. This made the king's subjects feel very threatened. So after seven months, the king gave in.

Pope Boniface VIII (c.1230-1303)

The quarrel over the appointment of Cardinal Langton[2] as Archbishop of Canterbury led to the submission of King John of England, who came to recognise Innocent as his feudal overlord. We saw before, that he patronised the new mendicant orders of friars, the *Franciscans* and the *Dominicans,* and invented the *Inquisition.* The Lateran Council of 1215, where teachings such as *trans-substantiation* became doctrine, was the culminating event of his reign.

In defence of universal spiritual and worldly power, Pope Boniface VIII (†1303) issued the bull *Unam Sanctam* which said: 'the worldly sword be submitted to the spiritual one, and the worldly power be submitted to the spiritual one; ... the belief in the absolute power of the Pope is for all men a necessity to salvation'. This idea of *the two swords* he mistakenly derived from *Luke* 22:38. Boniface had published this bull because of a conflict with Philip IV 'the Fair' of France who had taxed the clergy in his country. Finally, the papal claims failed. The king stopped all export of taxation money to Rome and even succeeded in having the Pope arrested. Soon after, Boniface died.

In Gregory VII, Innocent III, and Boniface VIII we see the establishment, the flourishing of, and the decline of the ideal of the papacy as a universal *theocracy*.

19.4. Babylonian Captivity of the Popes (Avignon Period)

Then followed a period in which the papacy was almost completely under the control of the French state. From 1309 to 1377 the popes had no residence in Rome, but in the French city Avignon. The popes of this time, Clement V, John XXII, Benedict XII,

---

[2] Stephen Langton († 1228), Archbishop of Canterbury, is credited with the division of the books of the Bible into chapters.

Clement VI, Innocent VI, and Urban V were Frenchmen and, although some of them had independent influence, they first of all served the French interests. The last mentioned went temporarily back to Rome, but the final resettling of papacy in Rome was achieved by Urban's successor Gregory XI. The Avignon period made the papal organisation more centralised and more effective in its political activities. The attention of the popes to spiritual affairs decreased.

19.5. Popes and Antipopes (Great Schism)

At the same time, the favouring of French political and military interests caused internal divisions in the papacy. Eventually this damaged its unity and caused the *Great Schism in the West*. That is the period of 1378 to 1417 during which the Roman Catholic Church was divided by the creation of anti-popes. In 1378 the election of Urban VI was rejected by some of the cardinals; they elected Clement VII. The first one was supported by Italy and the German Empire and England, the second one by France, Spain, and Scotland. The schism was ended by the Council of Constance in 1417. The prelates restored order by sending all the existing popes packing (there were three at the time!) and by nominating Martin V.

Palace in Avignon that from 1309-1377 was the residence of the Popes.

19.6. Conciliar Movement and Extreme Papal Decay

This act by a Church Council underlined the question as to who is the most superior, the Pope or the council of cardinals and bishops. Advocates and opponents of the subsequent *Conciliar Movement* quarrelled about this for some decades. The question of authority was especially important because of the need of reform of the many abuses in the church. Councils at Pisa (1409), Constance (1414-1418), Basel and Florence (1431-1449) temporarily checked the papacy and tried to take away some abuses, but they did not solve the doctrinal and moral crisis of the Medieval Church. Soon the Councils were neutralised and discarded by the restored papacy.

The popes of the 15th century distanced themselves more and more from the spiritual and moral characteristics that are to be expected from church leaders.[3] The behaviour of the popes contributed to the weakening and perversion of the medieval 'universal church' and to the eventual emerging of 'national' churches. It also contributed to the cry for thorough *Reformation*.

Medieval Ecclesiastical Europe.

---

[3] On the excesses under the Borgia popes, see: Dowley, pp.338-340.

20. Education and Learning[1]

20.1. Schools and Universities

Learning involves the relationship between head and heart, or between reason and faith. The medieval history of schooling and ways of learning in the West was rooted in Antiquity. There were two sources. First, God's Revelation, found in the Bible, and ably expounded and applied by the Church Fathers, especially by Augustine. Secondly, human wisdom found in the ancient Greek philosophers. There was an ongoing interest in the thoughts of Plato, even among Christians. Even Augustine was for some time a follower of Neo-Platonism. Due to the translation work of Boethius (†c.524) the ideas of Aristotle were not completely forgotten.

Formal education for a long time remained limited to few people. Schools mainly originated in the monasteries. The example of the monasteries was followed by bishops in their cathedral schools, or by kings in their palace schools. The later universities, like those of Bologna, Paris, Tübingen, Utrecht and Oxford, grew out of these schools. They often began as a guild of either teachers and students, or of students only. All students had to start with learning the *seven liberal arts*. The basic study consisted of the *trivium* (grammar, rhetoric, and dialectic or logic) and led to a Bachelor's degree. Then, students could continue by studying the *quadrivium* (music, arithmetic, geometry, astronomy), which gave them a Master's degree. Only after that, students could proceed to one of the three faculties of higher education that could lead to a Doctorate: law, theology, or medicine.

20.2. Faith and Reason

Medieval education was interested in unity and harmony. There were many attempts to devise a system of thought in which there was rational understanding of the relationship between the truth from Scripture (*revelation*) and the truth from human wisdom (*nature, philosophy*). Teachers and learners concentrated on two areas: (a) the problem of ultimate reality, and (b) the problem of the relationship between faith and reason.

Anselm, Archbishop of Canterbury (c.1033-1109): 'I believe so that I may understand'.

Plato and Aristotle thought differently on these matters, and so did their followers in the Middle Ages. The discussion on these things came to a head in the period 1050-1350, sometimes called the age of *Scholasticism*. It was triggered by new translations of Aristotle into Latin by William of Moerbeke (1286). Aristotle also reached the West through translations and teachings of the Arabic-Spanish thinker Averroes (†1198) and the Jew Maimonides (†1204). The influence of the new mendicant orders (Dominicans and Franciscans) and of the universities also contributed to the scholastic dispute. The

---

[1] Cf.: Cairns, *Christianity through the Centuries*, pp.226-238; Dowley, pp.152-163, 281-306, 347; Foster, *Setback and Discovery*, pp.155-158, 167-168.

time of the *Church Fathers* had gone, the time of the *teachers* or *doctors* of rational learning had come. Gradually at least three schools of thought formed, which although interested in understanding the relationship between faith and reason, differed considerably. We will look at the schools of *Realism, Conceptualism*, and *Nominalism*.

20.3. Realism

As to the problem of ultimate reality the Realists and the Conceptualists agreed on one point: that ultimate reality consists of thoughts or ideas that are universally valid and true. They are universals (*universalia*), that is: '*abstract concepts* representing the common elements belonging to individuals of the same genus or species'. In other word, they are general truths or ideas. Both Realism and Conceptualism would agree that universals truly exist even apart from contemplating individual things or persons. Yet they differed. In Realism the universals are said to exist *before* the created things ('*universalia ante rem*'), and in Conceptualism they are said to exist *in* the created things ('*universalia in re*'). In both systems of thought universals are things (*res*) in themselves or at least inseparably connected to things. In the idea of Realism this means that man cannot find real significance in himself or in other things. He has to look higher. In Christian thought this would mean that faith goes before reason and forms its basis. Anselm (†1109), in agreement with Augustine (†430), formulated this position as follows: 'I believe so that I may understand' (*Credo ut intelligam*). Later Reformed and Evangelical believers would not find it difficult to endorse these words, which stress the primacy of faith over reason.

Johannes Duns Scotus (c.1265-1308), influential Franciscan scholar who taught the primacy of the will.

20.4. Nominalism

In the 13th century the thinking of Realism collided with a new movement that became known as *Nominalism*. The name Nominalism refers to *nomina* (names). Nominalism says that universals are only names; they are not things. They have a separate existence apart from individual things and persons, as expressed in the words '*universalia post rem*'. Unlike the Realism and the Conceptualism that stress the importance of the group, the Nominalism individualises, emphasising the individual existence of persons and things. As the thoughts on them are just names, the things have no common denominator. Therefore, basically each creature is on its own. In Nominalism we see traditional and new powers at work, i.e. *dualism* and *individualism*. First, in the separating of things from concepts we see an influence of the Greek dualism of matter and spirit, which throughout Antiquity and Middle Ages had maintained itself in heretical movements and sects and as an undercurrent of Catholic piety. Secondly, the individualism of Nominalist thought reflects the breaking through of an interest in each created thing apart from the others, and especially apart from the Creator.

20. Education and Learning

Nominalism is a forerunner of Renaissance and Humanism in the 16th century. More and more the spiritual concepts of the medieval unity and harmony, sought after by Realism and Conceptualism, were cracking. The attention of man, during the Middle Ages directed at heaven, tended to be drawn more to his own bodily and material existence and to the natural things of his environment. The Nominalists are also forerunners of the *Enlightenment* that started in the 17th century, the *Modernism* that began in the 19th century and the *Post Modernism* of today.

Nominalist dualism and individualism does not necessarily deny the authority of the Bible, though in Enlightenment writing it increasingly did so. Basically it relegates faith and reason each to its own domain and its own authority. Natural things are ruled by the authority of reason, whereas faith, church and dogmas find their own separate authority, i.e. in divine revelation. Nominalist individualism, as expressed in the sovereign act of the will, was especially advocated by the new mendicant order of the Franciscans. Duns Scotus (†1308) stressed this *voluntarism* of the individual, 1 but did not join the camp of the Nominalists. William of Ockham (†c. 1349) went further. He loosened faith and dogmas from reason. They cannot be proved by reason, and must be accepted on authority of Scripture.

A medieval Monastery school.

The initial period of struggle between Nominalism and Realism (1050-1150) ended in victory for Realists like Anselm and Bernard of Clairvaux. But the struggle went on, because a third movement, *Conceptualism*, emerged that tried to neutralise both schools of thought by new ideas, and because after 1300 Nominalism re-emerged with greater and ever growing power.

20.5. Conceptualism

Representatives of *Conceptualism*, or *Moderate Realism*, like Abelard (†1142), Albertus Magnus (†1280) and his famous pupil Thomas Aquinas (†1274) tried to build a new system of thought out of elements from both Realism and Nominalism. Like the Realists they stressed that universals are connected to individual things and persons. But they differed from the Realists. They tried to compromise with the Nominalist desire to separate universals and things: things and persons are most real *to our perception*, whereas the universals are most real *in themselves*. At the same time, as opposed to Realism and Nominalism, in Conceptualist thought the universals are *in* the particular things and people. Conceptualism does not separate faith and reason, neither puts faith before reason. Reason is the starting point in Conceptualism, and from there it says to move to faith. Abelard expressed the Conceptualist idea like this: 'I understand in order that I may believe' (*Intelligo ut credam*).

According to Thomas Aquinas, there is not one reality (like in Realism), but there are two distinct realities. They can have many names: things and concepts, nature and grace, material reality and spiritual reality, the domain of creation and the domain of the Creator, nature and supra-nature. Nominalism is not right when it says that the two realms are separate. They are inter-related and need one another. Thomas Aquinas in his *Summa Theologiae* tries to integrate these two realities. (a) Natural things and people harbour the universals, which are vital remnants of *supra-nature* and (b) in its turn *supra-nature* empowers natural things and people by infusing into them the truth of God's revelation. This infusion is performed by the priests of the Church through its sacraments.

Thomas Aquinas' philosophy gives natural man the power to climb up to God, provided his good will cooperates with the Church and its priests. The 16th-century Reformation would oppose this Conceptualist view by denying man and Church these powers and by pointing to faith in Christ, who is the only way of learning reality and of salvation. In its reaction against Roman Catholic teaching, the Reformation sometimes tended to be on the side of the Nominalism. An example of this is Martin Luther's interest in the writings of Ockham. The position of the Reformation, however, is directly related to the medieval school of Realism. Evangelical and Reformed faith continues on the narrow path that on its right and left sides has the ravines of Nominalism and Conceptualism.

Thomas Aquinas (c.1225-1274), called 'Doctor Angelicus', very influential Dominican monk and scholar, whose teaching of Moderate Realism ('I know, so that I may believe'), is still accepted in the Roman Catholic theology.

21. Reform and Dissent[1]

21.1. External dangers

As the Middle Ages went on, the power of the Church of Rome waned. The leaders had to cope with problems outside and inside the Church. Powerful *external* forces competed with the influence of Rome. Here are four examples.

First, the Church of Rome could not spread to the Byzantine Empire, and Russia, because of the Eastern Orthodox Church that had separated itself from Rome since 1054. Under pressure of Islam in the South, *Eastern Orthodoxism* continued to grow in the North (see chapter 17).

Secondly, the papacy at Rome was opposed by heretical movements. One of them was the movement of the *Albigenses* or *Cathari* who in Southern France and in the North of Spain had established a counter church (see chapters 10.4, 15.2.c).

Thirdly, the Church was challenged by the movement of the *Renaissance* that demanded man's attention for non-soul things, like the human body, wisdom, art, and secular life. The Church had pretended to have exclusive power over human existence, but the Renaissance broke this monopoly (see chapter 22.5.).

Fourthly, the unity of European political and ecclesiastical rule that had existed in the Roman, Frankish and German Empires, was weakening by the emergence of *national states, independent regions and cities*, with their own interests. Citizens of England, Spain, Portugal, The Netherlands, France, Saxony, Strasbourg, Bern, Geneva, Utrecht tended to show more loyalty to their own rulers than to the Pope of Rome and his local representatives (see chapter 22.6.).

21.2. Internal causes

Yet *internal* factors were more dangerous causes of the weakening of the Church of the Middle Ages. By 1500 many people realised that the theological and ecclesiastical situation in the Church had become unacceptably bad. The image of the Church had been darkened by many abuses and heresies. Here are five examples.

First, moral abuses among clergy, like the evils of sexual immorality, simony[2] and pluralism.[3]

Secondly, clerical lust for power and riches that led to the ideas of levying papal taxes and selling salvation.

Thirdly, the lack of Bible knowledge, leading to bad preaching or the absence of preaching.

Fourthly, the growth of heretical misconceptions, like semi-pelagianism, the veneration of saints including Mary and of relics, the belief in a purgatory and an ecclesiastical treasure of grace, the belief in the sacraments, especially mass, as channels of grace, the rise of monasticism, the idea of the merit of good works.

---

[1] Cf.: Cairns, *Christianity through the Centuries*, pp.221-224, 239-250, 252-263; Dowley, pp.330-350; Foster, *Setback and Recovery*, pp.155-158, 167-168; Houghton, *Sketches*, pp.62-74.

[2] Simony: The sinful practice of buying or selling church offices, relics or other spiritual benefits. Cf. Simon the sorcerer in Acts 8:9-24.

[3] Pluralism: the medieval practice in the Roman Catholic Church of the holding by a single person of more than one ecclesiastical benefice or office.

Fifthly, the mixing of political and spiritual interests by state and church that were misusing one another.

21.3. Reform Movements

Among many people these things led to dissatisfaction and to the realisation that from top to bottom the Church needed reform. From the 10th century onwards *reform movements* emerged. The first movements mainly criticised the abuses of the clergy and the injustices of the organisation of the Church. Gradually the protests deepened spiritually. At last they also touched aspects of the theological structure of the Church's teaching. This is most apparent in the Forerunners of the Reformation. However, these reform movements and forerunners did not stretch to the width and the depth of the representatives of the 16th-century Reformation who realised that the whole Church needed to be reformed according to Biblical principles, its abuses taken away, and many of its dogmas changed.

First we refer to chapter 16 where we mentioned the attempts for the *reform of monastic life* by the Cluniacs in the 10th century, the Cistercians, the Military Orders and the Mendicant Orders (or Friars) in the 12th century.

The *second* movement of reform involved the *Mystics*, i.e. those who desired union with God. By using meditation, ascesis, and prayer, they attempted to reach ecstatic or emotional union with God. Two lines can be distinguished, the Latin Mystics and the Germanic Mystics. The Latin group, to which the Cistercian leader Bernard of Clairvaux (†1153) belonged, aspired personal emotional experience of *unison* or 'marriage of the soul' with Christ in faith and love. In this unison the believer and Christ remain distinct. Followers of this tradition were Catherine of Siena (†1380), John of the Cross (†1591), Teresa of Avila (†1582). Mystics of the Germanic group try to attain the ecstatic experience of *fusion* of the spirit of the believer and God. In

Jan van Ruysbroeck (1293-1381), leader of a spiritual community near Brussels, within the movement of the Devotio Moderna.

this experience there is no distinction between God and man anymore. One of these mystics, Meister Eckhart (†1327) and his pupil Johann Tauler (†1361), according to Cairns, came close to a kind of *pantheism*, i.e. a pagan idea that man and things can be absorbed by divinity. Tauler was closer to Scripture than his master. He stressed that believers should have an inward experience of God. Later this would attract the Reformer Martin Luther who had one of Tauler's writings edited in German.

Thirdly, there was the *Conciliar Movement* (see chapter 19.6). It arose as a reaction against the failures of the papacy, culminating in the Great Schism (1378-1417). In the Church Councils of Pisa (1409), Constance (1418), Basel, and Ferrara (1431-1449) the collegiate bishops tried to take over the power in the Church and restore order.

Fourthly, the *Biblical Humanists* influenced by the desire to go back on the sources of culture and faith, had re-discovered Scripture. They studied the Bible in its original languages, applied its contents to the situation in State and Church, and in some cases translated it, so that the public of Bible readers widened. One of the foremost Biblical Humanists was Desiderius Erasmus. He sharply criticised the clergy and he reconstructed the Greek text of the New Testament. Erasmus and his friends, however, did

21. Reform and Dissent

not apply their criticism to the doctrinal basis of the Church. This made them different from the *Forerunners of the Reformation* whom we are discussing now.

21.4. Forerunners of the Reformation

The Forerunners of the 16th-century Reformation consciously paved the way for the Church to go back to its Biblical source. They realised that the real problem of the Church consisted of lacking a Biblical foundation for many of its doctrines and teachings.

Girolamo Savonarola (1452-1498), Dominican preacher in Florence, Forerunner of the Reformation.

The *first* example to be mentioned is the Cistercian monk Joachim of Fiore (†1202) and his followers. Joachim protested against the hierarchical Church, its traditions and sacraments. He stressed that salvation is not to be expected from the present Church, but from the approaching new era of the Spirit. He distinguished three stages in the history of the Church: (a) the Age of the Father, characterised by servility to Old Testament law, (b) the Age of the Son or of the New Testament, which would last to the year 1260, and was said to belong to the fleshly Church, (c) the Age of the Spirit, characterised by freedom and love, and of full realisation of spirituality.

Secondly, there were the Waldenses. From the 12th century onwards they had been advocates for Biblical Reformation of the Church. Following their founder Petrus Waldo, a rich merchant in Lyons, they believed that the Bible is the final authority for faith and life and that it should be translated into the vernacular. They preached especially to the poor and uneducated. The Waldenses were considered to be heretics by the Church of Rome. Therefore, Pope Innocent III organised a crusade against them. They were violently persecuted, while the Dominicans were placed at the forefront of preaching against them.

The *third* example was the Italian Dominican Girolamo Savonarola (†1498). He lived in Florence, where he faithfully preached against the sins of the people and their leaders, even against the Pope. In 1497 the Church excommunicated him, and the following year the authorities of Florence had him burnt and hanged.

The *fourth* group were the *Brethren of the Common Life*. They were a fraternity of preachers and teachers who did much to spread Bible knowledge. They founded schools and published Biblical literature.

Fifthly, there was the influence of John Wycliffe (†1384). He was a professor at Oxford who tried to reform the Church, at first only by protesting against the immorality and wealth of its clergy. He was helped and safeguarded by the nobility that wanted to grasp the riches of the Church. After 1379, Wycliffe began to attack the fundamental dogmas of the Church of Rome, e.g.

John Wycliffe (c. 1330-1384), scholar at Oxford, Bible translator, Forerunner of the Reformation.

transubstantiation in mass, and the authority of the Pope. To him the Bible was the only authority. That is why he and his helpers translated Scripture into English. Wycliffe was condemned by the Church. But his followers spread his ideas, and paved the way for the Reformation.

Sixthly, there was the influence of John Huss (†1415). Bohemian students who had studied in Oxford and had been influenced by Wycliffe, in their turn were instrumental in the formation of John Huss' ideas. Huss preached and taught in Prague. His protests against the abuses and heresies of the Church met with hostility of church leaders, including the Pope. The Church Council of Constance, though itself reform-minded, condemned him. When the Emperor Sigismund withdrew his protection, Huss was executed by burning.

John Huss (c.1372-1415), preacher and scholar in Prague, Forerunner of the Reformation.

These witnesses during the last centuries of the Middle Ages are *Forerunners of the Reformation* because of their appeal to the Word of God when they not only wanted correction of external abuses, but also of corrupt doctrine. They differed with the previous reform movements because of a different view of the authority of Scripture.

This is a detail of a page of John Wycliffe's Bible translation: John 1:1.

Bibliography: Middle Ages

Andrea, A.J., *The Medieval Record: Sources of Medieval History*, New York: Cengage Learning, 1997.

Armstrong, Karin, *Muhammad: A Biography of the Prophet*, San Francisco: Harper, 1992.

Armstrong, Karin, *Islam: A Short History*, London: Modern Library, 2002².

Arnold, Th., *Select English Works of John Wycliffe* (2 vols), Oxford: Clarendon, 1871.

Audisio, G., *The Waldensian Dissent: Persecution and Survival c.1170-c.1570*, Cambridge, 1999.

Baillie, J., J.T. McNeill, and H.P. van Dusen (eds.), *The Library of Christian Classics* (26 vols), Philadelphia: Westminster, 1953-1969.

Bartlett, R., *Trial by Fire and Water: The Medieval Judicial Ordeal*, Cambridge UP, 1986.

Barraclough, G., *The Medieval Papacy*, London: Thames and Hudson, 1968.

Bausch, W.J., *Pilgrim Church: A Popular History of Catholic Christianity*, Connecticut, 1989²³.

Bennett, Judith M., *Medieval Europe: A Short History*, New York: McGraw-Hill, 2010¹¹.

Benson, R.L., and G. Constable (eds.), *Renaissance and Renewal in the Twelfth Century*, Oxford UP, 1982 (1985).

Bernard of Clairvaux (selected work), transl. by G.R.Evans, Mahwah: Paulist, 1987.

Bettenson, H., and C. Maunder (eds.), *Documents of the Christian Church*, Oxford U.P., 1999.

Boase, T.S.R., *Boniface VIII*, London: Constable, 1933.

Bossy, J., *Christianity in the West 1400-1700*, Oxford UP, 1985.

Bredero, A.H., 'The Canonization of Saint Bernard'; in: B. Pennington (ed.), *Studies Commemorating the Eighth Century of his Canonization*, Kalamazoo, 1977, pp.63-100.

Bredero, A.H., 'The Announcement of the Coming of the Antichrist and the Medieval Concept of Time', in: M. Wiks (ed.), *Prophecy and Eschatology*, SCH, Subsidia 10, Oxford, 1994, pp.3-13.

Breukelaar, A.H.B., *Historiography and Episcopal Authority in Sixth-century Gaul*, Göttingen: Vandenhoeck & Ruprecht, 1994.

Brockman, N., and U. Pescantini, *A History of the Catholic Church*, Nairobi: Paulines, 1991.

Broek, R. van den, and M.J. Vermaseren (eds.), *Studies in Gnosticism and Hellenistic Religion* (Presented to Gilles Quispel), Leyden: Brill, 1981.

Brooke, Chr., *The Monastic World 1000-1300*, Oxford UP, 1973.

Brooke, Chr., *The Medieval Idea of Marriage*, Oxford UP, 1989.

Brooke, R.B., *Early Franciscan Government*, Cambridge UP, 1959.

Brooke, R.B., *The Coming of the Friars*, London-New York: Allen & Unwin, 1975.

Brooke, R.B., and Chr. Brooke, *Popular religion in the Middle Ages*, London: Thames and Hudson, 1984.

Brown, P., The Cult of Saints: *Its Rise and Function in Latin Christianity*, Chicago UP, 1983.

Burgess, S.M., *The Holy Spirit: Medieval Roman Catholic and Reformation Traditions*, Peabody: Hendrickson, 1997.

Burrell, D., *Aquinas, God and Action*, London: Routledge, 1979.

Cantor, N.F., *Inventing the Middle Ages: The Lives, Works and Ideas of Great Medievalists of the Twentieth Century*, New York: Morrow, 1991.

Cantor, N.F., *The Civilization of the Middle Ages*, New York: Harper Collins, 1993.

Chazan, R., *Daggers of Faith: Thirteenth-century Christian Missionizing and the Jewish Response*, Berkeley: University of California Press, 1980.

Chenu, M.D., *Nature, Man and Society in the Twelfth Century*, Chicago UP, 1968.

Chesterton, G.K., *Saint Thomas Aquinas*, London: Hodder and Stoughton, 1943.

Chibnall, M., *The World of Orderic Vitalis*, Oxford: Clarendon, 1984.

Clanchy, M.T., *From Memory to Written Record: England 1066-1307*, London: Edward Arnold, 1979.

Clanchy, M.T., *Abélard: A Medieval Life*, Oxford: Blackwell, 1997.

Cobban, A.B., *The Medieval Universities: Their Development and Organisation*, London: Methuen, 1975.

Cohen, J.M. (transl.), *The Life of Teresa of Avila,* Harmondsworth: Penguin, 1957.

Comby, J., *How to Read Church History?,* vol.1, London: SCM, 1995.

Copleston, F., *Mediaeval Philosophy: Augustine to Scotus* [2nd volume of: *A History of Philosophy*], London: Penguin, 1950.

Constable, G., *The letters of Peter the Venerable* (2 vols), Cambridge (Mass.): Harvard, 1967.

Constable, G., *Medieval Monasticism: A Select Bibliography*, Toronto UP, 1977.

Constable, G., *The Reformation of the Twelfth Century*, Cambridge (Mass): Harvard, 1996.

Cowdrey, H.E.J., *The Cluniacs and the Gregorian Reform*, Oxford UP, 1970.

Cowdrey, H.E.J., 'The Peace and the Truce of God in the Eleventh Century', in: *Past and Present* no.46 (February 1970), pp.42-67.

Deanesly, D., *A History of the Medieval Church*, London: Routledge, 1969.

Duffy, E., *Saints and Sinners – History of the Popes*, New Haven: Yale U.P., 1997.

Emmerson, R.K., and B. McGinn (eds.), *The Apocalypse in the Middle Ages*, Ithaca-London: Cornell UP, 1992.

Erikson, C., and K. Casey, 'Women in the Middle Ages: A Working Bibliography', in: *Mediaeval Studies* no 37 (1975), pp.340-359.

Esser, C., *Origins of the Franciscan Order*, Chicago: Franciscan Herald Press, 1970.

Fairweather, E. R. (ed.), *A Scholastic Miscellany: Anselm to Ockham,* Philadelphia: Westminster, 1956.

Fatula, M.A., *Catherine of Siena's Way*, Wilmington: Glazier, 1987.

Finucane, R.C., *Miracles and Pilgrims: Popular beliefs in Medieval England*, London: Dent., 1979.

Fletcher, R., *The Conversion of Europe – From Paganism to Christianity 371 – 1386 AD*, London, 1997.

Flint, V.I.J., *The Rise of Magic in Early Medieval Europe*, Princeton UP, 1991.

Foster, J., *Setback and Recovery, AD 500-1500*, London: SPCK, 1974.

Foster, K. (ed.), *The Life of St. Thomas Aquinas: Biographical Documents*, London: Longmans, 1959.

Ganshof, F.L., *Feudalism*, London: Longmans, 1964^3.

Ganshof, F.L., *The Carolingians and the Frankish Monarchy*, London: Longmans, 1971.

Geary, P.J. (ed.), *Readings in Medieval History*, Peterborough/ New York: Broadview, 1991 [first 1989].

Gilby, T., et al., *Thomas Aquinas: Summa Theologiae, Latin Text and English Translation, Introduction, Notes. Appendices and Glossaries* (60 vols), London: Blackfriars, 1964ff.

Gilson, E., *History of Christian Philosophy in the Middle Ages*, London: Sheed and Ward, 1955.

Hamilton B., *The Medieval Inquisition*, London: Historical Association, 1981.

Hillgarth, J.N. (ed.), *Christianity and Paganism 350-750 – The Conversion of Western Europe*, Philadelphia: University of Pennsylvania Press, 1986.

Hinnebusch, W.A., *The History of the Dominican Order*, Staten Island: Alba House, 1966.

Hodges, R., and A. Whitehouse, *Muhammad, Charlemagne and the Origins of Europe*, Oxford UP, 1983.

Hollister, C.W. (ed), *The Twelfth-century Renaissance*, New York/ London: Wiley & Sons, 1969.
Hously, N., *The Avignon Papacy and the Crusades 1305-1378*, Oxford UP, 1986.
Houston, J.M. (ed.), *Bernard of Clairvaux: The Love of God and Spiritual Friendship*, Portland: Multnomah, 1983.
Hurst, D.D. (ed.), *Gregory the Great: Forty Gospel Homilies*, Kalamazoo: Cistercian Publ., 1990.
Huizinga, J., *The Waning of the Middle Ages*, Lonbdon: Penguin, 1955.
James, B. (transl.), *The Letters of St. Bernard of Clairvaux*, Chicago: Henry Regnery, 1953.
Jong de, M.B., *Early Medieval Child Oblation*, Leyden: Brill, 1996.
Jordan, Ch., *Louis IX and the Challenge of the Crusade*, Princeton UP, 1979.
Kavanaugh, K. (ed.), *John of the Cross: Selected Writings*, New York: Paulist, 1987.
Kavanaugh, K. (ed.), *The Collected Works of Teresa of Avila* (2 vols), Washington: Institute of Carmelite Studies, 1976.
Kearns, C. (ed.), *The Life of Catherine of Siena*, Washington: Glazier, 1980.
Keen, M., *The Penguin History of Medieval Europe*, London: Penguin, 1991.
Kelly, J.N.D., *The Oxford Dictionary of the Popes*, Oxford U.P., 1986.
Kieckhefer, R., *On quiet Souls: Fourteenth-century Saints and Their Religious Milieu*, Chicago UP, 1984.
Kirchberger, C. (ed.), *Richard of St. Victor: Selected Writings on Contemplation*, London: Faber & Faber, 1957.
Knowless, D., *The Evolution of Medieval Thought*, London: Longmans, 1965.
Ladner, G.B., 'Homo Viator: Medieval Ideas on Alienation and Order', in: *Speculum* 42, 2 (1967), pp.233-259.
Le Goff, J. (ed.), *The Medieval World* (transl.), London: Parkgate, 1990.
McEvedy, C., *The Penguin Atlas of Medieval History*, Harmondsworth: Penguin, 1979[12].
Lambert, M., *Medieval Heresy: Popular Movements from Bogomil to Hus*, London: Arnold, 1977.
Lawrence, C.W., *Medieval Monasticism: Forms of Religious life in Europe in the Middle Ages*, London, Longmans, 1989[3].
Le Roy Ladurie, E., *Montaillou*, London: Penguin Books, 1980 [translation of: *Montaillou, village Occitan de 1294 à 1324*, Paris, 1975].
Leyser, H., *Hermits and the New Monachism: A Study of Religious Communities in Western Europe 1000-1150*, London: Macmillan, 1984.
Little, L.K., *Religious Poverty and the Profit Economy in Medieval Europe*, London/ New York: Cornell UP: 1978.
Loos, M., *Dualist Heresy in the Middle Ages*, Prague: Academia, 1974.
Lourdaux, W., and A. Verhelst (eds.), *The Concept of Heresy in the Middle Ages*, Leuven/ The Hague: Nijhoff, 1976.
Lourdaux, W., and A. Verhelst (eds.), *The Bible and Medieval Culture*, Leuven UP, 1979.
Lourdaux, W., and A. Verhelst (eds.), *Benedictine Culture 750-1050*, Leuven UP, 1983.
Maalouf, A., *The Crusades Through Arab Eyes*. London: AL Saqi, 1984.
MacKay, A., and D. Ditchburn (eds), *Atlas of Medieval Europe*, London: Routledge, 1997.
Maier, Chr. T., *Preaching the Crusades: Mendicant Friars and the Cross in the Thirteenth Century*, Cambridge UP, 1998[2].
Marcus, J., *The Jew in the Medieval World*, New York: Athenaeum, 1972.
Markus, R.A., *Gregory the Great and His World*, Cambridge UP, 1997.
McCallum, J.R., *Abelard's Christian Theology*, Merrick: Richwood, 1976.

McGinn, B., *Visions of the End: Apocalyptic Traditions in the Middle Ages*, New York: Columbia UP, 1979.

McGinn, B., *The Calabrian Abbot: Joachim of Fiore in the History of Thought*, New York: Macmillan, 1985.

McGinn, B. (ed.), *Meister Eckhart, Teacher and Preacher*, New York: Paulist, 1986.

McKitterick, R., *The Frankish Church and the Carolingian Reform*, London: Royal Historical Society, 1977.

McKitterick, R., *The Carolingians and the Written Word*, Cambridge UP, 1989.

McKitterick, R. (ed.), *Carolingian Culture: Emulation and Innovation*, Cambridge UP, 1994.

McLaughlin, M.M., *Consorting with the Saints – Prayer for the Dead in early Medieval France*, Ithaca/London: Cornell UP, 1994.

Metzger, M., and Th. Metzger, *Jewish Life in the Middle Ages: Illuninated Hebrew Manuscripts from the Thirteenth to the Sixteenth Centuries*, New York, 1982.

Milis, L.J.R., *Angelic Monks and Earthly Men: Monasticism and its Meaning to Medieval Society*, Woodbridge: Boydell, 1992.

Mollat, M., and Ph. Wolff, *The Popular Revolutions of the Late Middle Ages*, London: Allen & Unwin, 1973.

Moore, R.I., *The Birth of Popular Heresy*, London: Edward Arnold, 1973.

Moorman, J.R.H., *The Sources for the Life of St. Francis of Assisi*, Manchester UP, 1940.

Moorman, J.R.H., *A History of the Franciscan Order: From its Origins to the Year 1517*, Chicago UP, 1968.

Morris, C., *Discovery of the Individual 1050-1200*, New York: Harper & Row, 1972.

Morris, C., *The Papal Monarchy: The Western Church from 1050 to 1250*, Oxford UP, 1989.

Murray, A., *Reason and Society in the Middle Ages*, Oxford: Clarendon, 1978.

Oakley, F., *The Western Church in the Later Middle Ages*, Ithaca/London: Cornell UP, 1979.

Oberman, H.A., *The Harvest of Medieval Theology: Gabriel Biel and Late Medieval Nominalism*, Cambridge (Mass.): Harvard, 1963.

Oberman, H.A., *Forerunners of the Reformation*, Philadelphia: Fortress, 1981.

Ozment, S.E., *Homo Spiritualis: A Comparative Study of the Anthropology of Johannes Tauler, Jean Gerson, and Martin Luther in the Context of their Theological Thought*, Leyden: Brill, 1969.

Packard, S.R., *Twelfth-century Europe: An Interpretive Essay*, Amherst: Massachusetts UP, 1973.

Peers, E.A. (ed.), *The Complete Works of Saint John of the Cross*, Wheathampstead: Clarke, 1974.

Pelikan, J., *The Growth of Medieval Theology 600-1300*, Chicago UP, 1978.

Riley-Smith, J., *What were the Crusades?*, Basingstoke 2002[3].

Riley-Smith, J., *The Oxford History of the Crusades*, Oxford UP, 1994.

Robinson, I.S., *Authority and Resistance in the Investiture Contest*, Manchester UP, 1978.

Rosenheim, Barbara M., *A Short History of the Middle Ages*, University of Toronto Press, 2014[4].

Runciman, S., *The Eastern Schism: A Study of the Papacy and the Eastern Churches during the 12th and 13th Centuries*, Oxford UP, 1953.

Runciman, S., *The Fall of Constantinople*, Cambridge UP, 1965.

Runciman, S., *History of the Crusades* (3 vols), Harmondsworth: Penguin, 1971.

Russell, J.C., 'Population in Europe 500-1500', in: C.M. Cipolla (ed.), *The Fontana Economic History of Europe in the Middle Ages*, London/Glasgow: Fontana, 1972.

Saunders, J.J., *A History of Medieval Islam*, London: Henley/ Boston: Routledge, 1965.

Smalley, B., *Historians in the Middle Ages*, London: Thames and Hudson, 1974.

Southern, R.W., *The Making of the Middle Ages*, New Haven: Yale UP, 1965.

Southern, R.W., *St. Anselm and His Biographer*, Cambridge UP, 1963.

Southern, R.W., *Western Society and the Church in the Middle Ages*, Harmondsworth: Penguin, 1970.

Spinka, M., *John Huss at the Council of Constance* (transl.), New York/ London: Columbia UP, 1965.

Steenberghen, van F., *Aristotle in the West: The Origins of Western Aristotelism*, Louvain UP, 1955.

Stroll, M., *The Jewish Pope: Ideology and Politics in the Papal Schism of 1130*, Leyden: Brill, 1987.

Sullivan, R.E., *The Coronation of Charlemagne: What did it signify?*, Boston: Heath, 1959.

Sumption, J., *The Albigensian Crusade*, London/Boston: Faber & Faber, 1978.

Synan, E.A., *The Popes and the Jews in the Middle Ages*, New York: Macmillan, 1965.

Szarmach, P. (ed.), *An Introduction to the Medieval Mystics of Europe*, Albany: New York State UP, 1984.

Tate, G., *The Crusades and the Holy Land*, London: Thames and Hudson, 1996.

Tentler, Th.N., *Sin and Confession on the Eve of the Reformation*, Princeton UP, 1977.

Thomson, J.A., *The Western Church in the Middle Ages*, London/New York: Arnold, 1998.

Tierney, B., *The Crisis of Church and State 1050-1300*, Englewood Cliffs: Prentice Hall, 1964.

Tierney, B., *Foundations of the Conciliar Theory: The Contribution of the Medieval Canonists from Gratian to the Great Schism*, Cambridge UP, 1968[2].

Tierney, B., *Origins of Papal Infallibility*, Leyden: Brill, 1972.

Torpe, L., *Two Lives of Charlemagne*, Harmondsworth: Penguin, 1969.

Trapp, D., 'Augustinian Theology in the Fourteenth Century: Notes on Editions, Marginalia, Opinions and Book-lore', in: *Augustiniana*, 6 (1956), pp.147-265.

Treadgold, W. (ed.), *Renaissances before the Renaissance: Cultural revivals of Late Antiquity and the Middle Ages*, Stanford UP, 1984.

Trevor-Roper, H., *The Rise of Christian Europe*, London: Thames and Hudson, 1965.

Tuchman, B.W., *A Distant Mirror: The Calamitous 14th Century*, New York: Alfred A. Knopf, 1978.

Vasiliev, A.A., *A History of the Byzantine Empire 324-1453*, Wisconsin UP/ Blackwell, 1952.

Wakefield, W.L., and A.P. Evans, *Heresies of the High Middle Ages* (Selected Sources), New York/London, 1969.

Wallace-Hadrill, J.M., *The Barbarian West 400-1000*, London: Hutchinson, 1967[2].

Wallace-Hadrill, J.M. (ed.), *Bede's Ecclesiastical History of the English People*, Oxford: Clarendon: 1993.

Walsh, K.J., and I.M.Edmonds (eds.), *The Works of Bernard of Clairvaux*, 4 vols, Spencer/ Kalamazoo: Cistercian Publ., 1969-1980.

Watkin-Jones, H., *The Holy Spirit in the Medieval Church*, London: Epworth, 1922.

Webb, G., and A. Walker, *St. Bernard of Claivaux*, London: Mowbray, 1960.

Weisheipl, J.A., *Friar Thomas d'Aquino: His Life, Thought and Works*, New York: Doubleday, 1974.

Wieruszowsky, H., *The Medieval University: Masters, Students, Learning*, Princeton: Nostrand, 1966.

Williams, S. (ed.), *The Gregorian Epoch: Reformation, Revolution, Reaction?*, Boston: Heath, 1964.

Wilson, K. (ed.), *Medieval Women Writers*, Manchester UP, 1984.

Winston, R, *Charlemagne from the Hammer to the Cross*, Indianapolis: Bobs-Merrill, 1954.

Wiseman, J.A. (ed.), *John Ruusbroec: The Spiritual Espousals and Other Works*, New York: Paulist, 1985.
Zimmerman, O.J., *Gregory the Great: Dialogues*, New York: Fathers of the Church, 1959.

Websites

Christian History Institute: The Middle Ages, https://www.christianhistoryinstitute.org/study/era/medieval/
Christianity Today: The Middle Ages, http://www.christianitytoday.com/ch/byperiod/middleages
Medieval Full Tekst Sources, http://legacy.fordham.edu/halsall/sbook2.asp
The Hall of Church History: Medieval Churchmen, http://www.spurgeon.org/~phil/medieval.htm

C. Reformation Era 1500-1650

22. An Era of Great Change

22.1. Political Changes

The 15th and 16th centuries are a period of fundamental changes in the Western world and by consequence also in other parts of the world. Therefore, this period is often called the turning point between the *Middle Ages* and the *Modern Times*.[1]

The large empires that were the heirs of the Roman Empire were disintegrating, gradually being replaced by national states, autonomous regions and free cities. In the medieval situation the Empire (area of the Emperor) and the Church (area of the Pope) represented the political and ecclesiastical unity of Europe, in the sense that they competed for hegemony. In this new situation states, regions and cities behaved more independently from the Pope. Their kings and governments considered themselves rulers of state and church. In the 15th century and in the beginning of the 16th century most continued to be loyal to the Pope, but in general this loyalty only was a tool that was to serve their national independence and sovereignty.

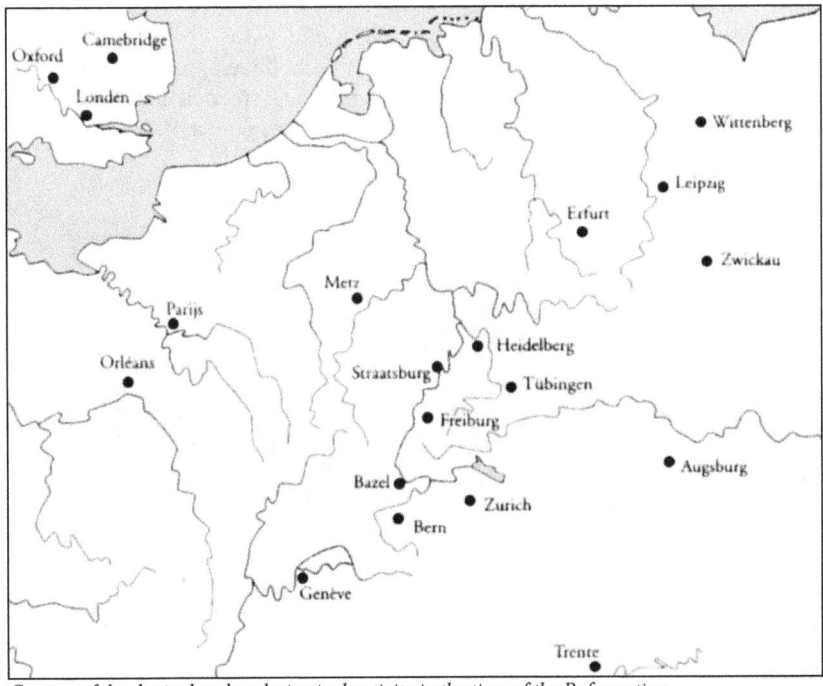

Centres of theological and ecclesiastical activity in the time of the Reformation.

Religious unity of the nation was considered very important, mainly for internal political reasons, but also for external reasons, notably for the need of a united and powerful defence against the Muslim Turks, who had taken Constantinople in 1453 and

---

[1] Cairns, *Christianity through the Centuries*, pp.267-277; Dowley, pp.352-365; Renwick/Harman, pp.97-101; S. Paas, *Chikonzedwe cha Mpingo: Zozintha zazikulu za uzimu 1500-1650*, Blantyre: CLAIM, 2002 (second print), mutu 1.

22. An Era of Great Change

now threatened the heart of Europe. The 'discoveries' on the African coasts, and of America and in the Far East also had political consequences.

22.2. Social Changes

The Crusades marked the beginning of the end of the *feudal system*: a social order in which the population of serfs and slaves was led by the hierarchical systems of the nobility and the clergy, largely on the basis of *loans*. Gradually a *third estate* emerged, a middle class of free citizens who founded cities along the main rivers, and thrived as independent farmers and sailors or in their *guilds* of traders, artisans, artistes. The governments of these free cities to a large degree behaved independently, not only from the state, but also from the church. Very often these cities became centres of learning, which through the invention of book-printing spread to more people than ever before.

22.3. Economic Changes

A money-based capitalist economy with some industrial production had begun, gradually replacing the barter-economy based on the exchange of goods. The free cities became market-centres where commerce and trading was concentrated and where wealth was accumulated. Sea port cities saw the development of shipping and commerce with the newly discovered territories in Asia, America and Africa. Gradually kings and the nobility became dependent on the economic power of the cities.

St. Peter's Church in Rome. The building of this Church in the early 16th century was financed by papal taxes, e.g. the Peter's penny, and money out of the selling of indulgences.

22.4. Psychological Changes

The communal thinking of the Middle Ages was gradually replaced by a more individualistic approach. This worked out economically (man himself is responsible for his upkeep), politically (emphasis on personal rights, freedom and obligations), socially (emphasis on personal man; family is the nucleus of society), religiously (personal responsibility before God; emphasis on personal salvation).

22.5. Cultural changes

There was a longing for fundamental reorientation and change. In this climate there was a rediscovery of the sources of Western culture: classical Greek and Roman society, especially its writings and expressions of art. Arab scholars had played an important role in this by translating the works of Greek philosophers; these works were introduced to Europe through the Crusades and through Spain. An understanding of the present and insight into the future were refreshed by study of the past. The 'ad fontes' (back to the sources) activities expressed themselves in a renewal of Art and Science.

a. Art

This movement is called the Renaissance (lit.: *rebirth*). In the flourishing of painting, sculpture, literature, and architecture, the classical interest in the existence of man and nature was applied to the 15th and 16th centuries in new forms of art. Consequently, artists concentrated less on the religious and metaphysical themes of the Middle Ages.

b. Science

Within the framework of the Renaissance a scientific and scholarly interest in man and nature was born. This movement was called Humanism. First this expressed itself in a change of philosophical orientation. Over the schools of thought like Realism and Conceptualism that emphasised the predominance of faith over reason (e.g. Anselm) or their mutual connection (e.g. Thomas Aquinas), a new school emerged, i.e. Nominalism (e.g. William of Ockham), that separated faith and reason.

William of Ockham c.1280-1347).

The Humanist interest in the 'who and what is man?' greatly extended the scientific and scholarly research of nature both outside man and inside man, gradually disconnecting it from the supra-natural which was said to belong to the realm of faith only. The Laws of Nature and the Laws of God were considered to be different fields that could be studied separately. This meant the dissolution of the medieval unity of thought and the beginning of the development of modern philosophy, science, and technology, growing more and more independent from the Bible. Despite this, Humanists mainly were Christians, and in their own way contributed to the preparations for the 16th-century Reformation of the Church.

22.6. Spiritual Changes

a. Papal Claims Criticised

In medieval thought Empire and Church constituted unity. The Pope considered himself above the rulers of this politico-religious structure (e.g. Boniface VIII, *Unam Sanctam*, 1302: theory of the two swords). He was the Vicar of Christ on earth, carrying out Christ's reign as a Supreme head over political and ecclesiastical matters. This claim was never fully accepted by the Emperors of the Frankish and German Empires. The idea was even less acceptable to the civil rulers of the emerging national states, regions and cities. Absolutist papal power was also opposed by those clergy that favoured the Conciliar Movement.

b. Ecclesiastical Claims Criticised

Church Fathers like Cyprian and Augustine had emphasised that there is no salvation outside the Church (*extra ecclesiam nulla salus est*). But in the Roman structure this expression had been more and more misused to make the 'lay people' dependent on a hierarchy of priests and on the sacraments, manipulated by those priests for their salvation.

Leo X (1475-1521), Pope from 1513. He squandered much of the Church's money, and turned against Luther whom he excommunicated in 1521.

Early attacks by Wycliffe and the *Lollards* on this spiritual dictatorship were followed by Humanist protests.

The realisation that the Church and its priests did not offer secure personal salvation, led to three attitudes: (a) *Individualism*: indifference to the community of the Church, even rejection of (orthodox) Christianity, godlessness. (b) *Reactionalism*: attempts to quench all criticism by defending and strengthening the existing ecclesiastical structures. (c) *Reformism*: trying to reform the Church to a new community that would give room for a more intense piety and longing for salvation.

c. Ethical Abuses of the Church Criticised

The *Carolingian Reforms* in the 9th century and the Monastic Reforms of the 11th and 12th centuries, and the attempts by the *Mystics* came before the growing stream of protests against the ethical abuses by the Church and its clergy in the Late Middle Ages. Except for people like Wycliffe, the critics did not touch the doctrinal position of the Church of Rome before the 16th century.

Some of the abuses to which there was objection were: the extreme power of the Pope, the bishops and other clergy, ignorance of the clergy; pluralism/ non residence, simony, immorality, indulgences, the inquisition. The *Conciliar Movement* tried to remove some of these abuses, but it failed.

d. Doctrinal Heresies Attacked

The basic structure of Roman theology and ecclesiology was fundamentally criticised by the representatives of the 16th-century Reformation. They came to criticise Roman dogmas concerning e.g.: the position of Church and the tradition above Scripture, the position of Roman priesthood, the sacraments, the *semi-Pelagianism*, purgatory (the Church possesses a store of grace), the veneration of saints, the veneration of Mary, the veneration of relics, indulgences, pilgrimages, and the emphasis on monasticism

Forerunners of the 16th-century Reformation like Wycliffe, Huss, Savonarola, the Movement of the *Devotio Moderna* (Geert Grote, Thomas à Kempis), Wessel Gansfort, and his pupil Desiderius Erasmus mainly emphasised ethical reform, although they prepared the way for doctrinal reform.

Thomas à Kempis (c. 1380-1471), writer of Imitation of Christ, representing the spirit of the Brethren of the Common Life.

22.7. The Reformation

The 16th-century Reformation aimed at getting the teachings of the Church and the life of the people in line with the Word of God. The *Humanist* and *Renaissance* movements were originally interested in the Bible, but their main focus was on the Greek and Roman culture of Antiquity. As Humanism developed it weakened its link with the Christian faith. Its interest in man and nature led to the Enlightenment of the 17th century and finally it turned into the kind of Western individualism that has no room for God, the Church, the Bible and faith. Representatives of the 16th- century Reformation, like Luther, Zwingli, Bucer, and Calvin, were interested in Humanism, but were essentially agents of a 'back-to-the-Bible-movement', and therefore had a different orientation.

23. Martin Luther 1483-1546

23.1. His Childhood

Martin Luther was born in 1483 to a poor family in Saxony, which is a region in Germany. First his father, Hans Luther, was a free farmer, but later he bought shares in a copper mine in Mansfeld, which reduced their poverty. Luther was sent to school in Eisenach and after that in Magdeburg, where he was helped by a rich traders' family called Cotta. His father wanted him to study Law. He accepted his father's wish, though he would have preferred to study Theology. Luther thought deeply about the issues of justice and holiness. He soon realised that he could not attain the holiness and justice that God required of man. He tried very hard, but he knew that he could not manage to keep God's laws fully. He also knew that to lawbreakers God was a judge and a punisher. This made him live a fearful life. He expected God's judgment because of the sinfulness of his heart and life.

Martin Luther (1483-1546), German theologian and former Augustinian monk, who became the founder of the 16th-century Reformation of the Church.

23.2. Luther joins the Monastery

In 1501 Martin Luther began to study at the University of Erfurt, but before he had finished the preparatory work for the study in Law, something happened that changed his life totally. One day, as he was walking from Mansfeld to Erfurt, near a place called Stotternheim a thunderstorm rose and the lightning struck a tree that was near to him. In fear of death he cried: 'Holy Anna, if you help me, I will become a monk'.[1] After this, Luther entered an Augustinian monastery in Erfurt, much to the astonishment of his friends and to the disappointment of his father. Monasteries were places where monks thought to please God by isolation, fasting, and other forms of self-punishment, and also by prayer and meditation. The abbot of Luther's monastery was Johann Von Staupitz. He saw how young Luther was in agony because of his sins, and he tried to point him to the work of Christ, and he also advised him to study the Bible. The abbot explained to Luther that only the sacrifice of the blood of Jesus could satisfy God. In 1507 Luther became a priest of the Roman Church. He continued his studies in theology, now at the new university of Wittenberg. In 1510, Luther was sent to Rome the centre of the Medieval Church and of the papacy. During his stay in Rome, Luther was annoyed by the evil behaviour and the lack of spirituality that he saw in the Roman clergy.

---

[1] A *monk* is a male person who has pledged not to marry, and who together with his colleagues lives in seclusion, in a *monastery*.

23.3. His Conversion

In 1512 Luther became a Doctor of Theology. In Wittenberg he studied Biblical subjects, especially exegetics, beginning with the book of Psalms, the letters to the Romans, the Galatians, the Hebrews, and Titus, and after that he continued with other books. Luther did not yet understand the word *righteousness* in the Bible. He even hated that word because he knew that man is unable to satisfy God's demand for righteousness. However, little by little the Holy Spirit showed him that the word righteousness in the Bible is not a demanded righteousness, but a given righteousness that is found in Jesus Christ alone, who gives it as a free gift to anyone who believes in Him.

After this liberating discovery, Luther understood: 'Though Jesus Christ, who was punished because of my unrighteousness and my sin, God grants me the righteousness that Christ obtained for me. In God's eyes a Christian is righteous and holy because of his Saviour'. Luther made his discovery after reading in *Romans* 1:17 that: 'The righteous will live by faith'. He said that at that moment his heart was full of great joy, so that he cried: 'Jesus! You are my righteousness, and I am your sin'. After his conversion, Luther started to study the teachings of Augustine [2] by reading the Church Father's books. He discovered why Augustine opposed

Johann Eck (1486-1543), influential Humanist theologian who opposed Luther in a public debate in 1519.

the teachings of Pelagius[3], and this made him emphasise again that God's grace cannot be earned, but it is given freely. Luther also studied the books of the medieval Mystics (see chapter 21.3.), especially the writings of Johann Tauler[4]. He began to see that man can be saved without the supposedly mediating work of the priests.

23.4. The 95 Theses against Indulgences

Luther became famous because of his opposition to the indulgences[5]. An indulgence was a document signed by the Pope that stated the forgiveness of a certain sin to a certain person. The background was the greed for money of Pope Leo X. He needed it

---

[2] Augustine (354-430) bishop of Hippo Regius in North Africa, see chapter 10.

[3] Pelagius (about 400) taught that a man was born sinless, and that he would be saved if he would be following good examples, that is by his own good works. See chapter 7.2.a.

[4] Johann Tauler, (†1363), a Dominican monk. He emphasised that God lives in the souls of the believers and that believers are united with God in a mystic way through humbleness and total surrender to God. Luther was also very interested in an anonymous mystic writing from the Middle Ages, entitled *Theologia Germanica*, or *Theologia Deutsch*, which he edited in the period 1516-1518 and published.

[5] *Indulgences* in Roman Catholic theology are statements that are supposed to forgive the unrepented sins that have been left, after sacramental forgiveness has been applied.

for the building of St. Peter's Cathedral in Rome. He also needed much money for the extravagant lifestyle of himself and his helpers. In order to raise funds a method of selling forgiveness of sins was devised by allowing some archbishops to appoint men who could sell indulgences to the people.

One of the sellers was a Dominican monk Johann Tetzel. He travelled in some parts of German where he persuaded people to buy indulgences for their own sins and even for the sins of those who had died and were now in purgatory,[6] which was supposed to be a place where dead believers were purified of unrepented sins before entering heaven. Tetzel said that the soul of a beloved relative would enter heaven the very moment the coins for buying an indulgence were put in the money box.

Tetzel's activities roused Luther's indignation. He saw that the practice and the doctrinal background of the indulgences were against Scripture. That is why on 31st October, 1517, he published his 95 theses against indulgences. He also proposed a disputation about his theses with fellow theologians. Luther emphasised that the Pope has no power to forgive sins, and that God will not forgive a sinner who has not repented, also that God will punish all who sell and buy indulgences if they do not repent.

Luther's theses spread rapidly in many regions. Many people agreed with them. The Pope, however, got furious and in 1518 he ordered Luther to appear before his court in Rome to account for his theses. Luther did not go to Rome. The traditional leader of Saxony the elector Fredrick the Wise had become Luther's protector, and he did not allow him to go to the place from where he probably would have never returned. Then, the papal court shifted its venue to the

Johann Tetzel (c.1465-1519), a German Dominican monk who was one of the sellers of indulgences.

German city of Augsburg. There Luther had to appear before the Pope's representative, cardinal Cajetan. This time Luther went. He and Cajetan did not agree on the issues of their disputation, but Luther promised the cardinal that he would obey the decisions taken by a General Council of the whole Church. In 1519 in Leipzig, Luther had a disputation with Johann Eck, a famous scholar and teacher of the Church of Rome. There Luther stated that the papacy is an institution established by men and not by God. Concerning the General Councils of the Church, Luther stressed that these august meetings have sometimes failed.

23.5. His Publications in 1520

Luther published many books. In 1520 he published three important writings. In the first book, entitled *To the Christian Nobility of the German Nation*,[7] he asked the civil population, and especially the members of the nobility, to help in the Reformation of the

---

[6] *Purgatory* (Latin: *purgare* = to purify; *purgo* = I purify) in Roman Catholic thought this is a place where the souls of the believers are purged of sins that have not been confessed and repented.

[7] M. Luther, *An den christlichen Adel deutscher Nation, von des christlichen standes Besserung*, 1520.

Title page of Pope Leo X's Bull against Luther, 1520.

Church. By saying that all believers are priests, he opposed the papal courts and taxations, the papal state, the kissing of the Pope's feet, and pilgrimages to Rome. According to Luther, the papacy is protected by *three walls* which destroyed Christianity. These walls give the Pope power above (a) the civil governments, (b) the Bible and (c) the General Councils of the Church.

In his second book of 1520, in translation from Latin entitled *On the Babylonian Captivity of the Church*,[8] Luther wrote against the order of sacraments of the Church of Rome, which claims that there are seven sacraments: baptism, confirmation, the Lord's Supper, confession of sins, anointing of the sick, anointing priests, and marriage. The Bible mentions only two sacraments. In addition, Scripture does not give to baptism the power of removing original sin, and in the holy communion, the bread and wine do not change into the real body and blood of Jesus Christ. Luther was prepared to give some room for the sacramental character of the confession, the repenting and forgiveness of sin in the auricular confession before a minister of the Church. He stressed that the power of the sacraments depends only on the Word of God that brings man to faith and repentance. Sacraments do not work as a power of their own (*ex opere operato*), nor by a power in the hands of the performing priest, but through faith, which is given by the grace of God. In this book, Luther argued against the thought and practice of Mass (the Lord's Table in Roman Catholicism). In the Roman Mass Luther opposed three things, which he called *three prisons*. The first prison was that the priests did not allow 'lay' persons to touch the cup of wine. Secondly, the mass was a worship of idols, because of the doctrine of *transubstantiation*, which says that the bread and wine are transformed into the real body and blood of Jesus Christ. Luther's own teaching was that in the Holy Communion Christ is bodily present with, in, and under the bread and wine. His view became known as the doctrine of *consubstantiation*. The third prison is that mass is looked upon as a *sacrifice*. Luther finds this thought an abomination. The sacrifice of Jesus Christ cannot take place again, because it happened at Golgotha once, for all times and places.

Charles V (1500-1558), Emperor of the Habsburg Empire, including Germany and other regions of Central Europe, and also King of Spain and its South American colonies, The Netherlands, Naples and the county of Burgundy.

In his third book of 1520 called *About the Freedom of a Christian*,[9] Luther wrote about the liberation and the

---

[8] M. Luther, *De captivitate babylonica ecclesiae praeludium*, 1520.
[9] M. Luther, *Von der Freiheit eines Christenmenschen*, 1520.

justification which a Christian obtains through faith in Christ alone. This is why a Christian is free and also a slave. Luther said that by faith a Christian is free having liberty in all things without being anyone's slave, yet in his deeds he is slave in all things and a servant to all.

23.6. Condemned by Pope (1520) and Empire (1521)

Before long, Luther was condemned by the Pope because of his writings and his deeds. The Pope issued a bull (papal letter) beginning with the words *Exsurge Domine* (Latin for: Stand up, Lord), which described Luther as a wild swine that had entered the vineyard of the Lord, thus destroying the crops of the Church. In response, Luther burnt this letter publicly in Wittenberg together with the book of *canonical law* of the Church of Rome. He also responded by writing a letter against the papal bull, entitled 'Against the Cursed Letter of the Antichrist' (Latin: *Adversus execrabilem Antchristi bullam*). All these things took place in 1520. Consequently, the Pope excommunicated him from the Church. In 1521 the leaders of the Habsburg-German Empire summoned him. Emperor Charles V wanted him to appear before the general assembly (*Diet*) of the political leaders in the city of Worms. Emperor Charles V promised him safety. At the Diet Luther refused to withdraw his books. This led to his condemnation, but he was allowed to leave the city as a free man because of the promise made by the Emperor and also by the protection offered to him by Fredrick the Wise, the elector of Saxony.

Luther at the Imperial Diet in Worms, 1521.

23.7. At the Wartburg

When Luther left Worms, Fredrick the Wise, knowing how Luther's life was in danger, secretly took him to the Wartburg, one of his castles. There Luther stayed for eight months. He changed his name to Jörg. His enemies did not know where he was. During this time Luther began to translate the Bible into German. He finished the translation of the New Testament. The work on the Old Testament was finished much later, and was done with the help of Philip Melanchthon. Luther also published other important writings like those on the doctrine of sin and justification. Luther compared his exile at the Wartburg with John the Apostle's stay on the island of Patmos. Later he also said that at the Wartburg the devil had been trying hard to tempt him and to destroy the work of the Reformation.

The Wartburg, one the Castles of Frederick the Wise. Here Luther was kept in hiding after being condemned by the Diet of Worms in 1521.

23.8. The Prophets of Zwickau

Luther left his refuge at the Wartburg, after he heard of negative developments in Wittenberg. During Luther's absence his representative, Andreas Rudolph Bodenstein, more often known as Karlstadt, wanted to destroy all things in the church buildings that were reminiscent of the Church of Rome, like statues and paintings of Christ, the Apostles and the saints, crucifixes, and other religious objects. Karlstadt befriended the *Zwickau Prophets*. This was a group of very radical people who wanted to draw conclusions from the Reformation that ran against the Bible and against Luther's intentions. In their extremism they believed that the Holy Spirit had placed 'words inside them' which they respected more than the Bible. They abolished infant baptism and undermined the authority of the Church leaders. Unfortunately, these radical prophets had joined the movement of poor farmers who protested against exploitation by the rich nobility. After Luther came back to Wittenberg, he tried to purify the Reformation movement by preaching against extremists and revolutionaries. He felt sorry for the poor farmers who had risen against the nobility because of the oppression they suffered. In the beginning Luther agreed with the farmers' requests and protests. He even admonished the nobility, instructing them to treat their farmers better.

Katherina von Bora (1499-1550), Luther's wife.

But when the farmers' movement became a tool of the Zwickau Prophets and their leader Thomas Müntzer, it turned to extreme violence. Gangs of farmers attacked castles and monasteries, burning them down, and killing many noblemen and clergy. This time Luther changed his mind and condemned the farmers because of the bloodshed. He requested the nobility to cease the bloodshed by crushing the farmers' movement. In 1525, at Frankenhausen the armies of the nobility defeated the farmers. Their leaders, including Müntzer, were executed

During this time, the Humanists, who first had helped the Reformation, began to oppose Luther's work and views, especially his doctrine about sin and grace. Desiderius Erasmus declared that man's will is free to make the good choices for salvation in life. But Luther, in reference to Paul and Augustine, stressed that man after the Fall in Adam out of his own will, does not want salvation. Man's willpower is under the bondage of sin and death.

In 1525, Luther married Katherina von Bora, who was one of the nuns who had abandoned monastery life. Their marriage was of great significance to the Reformation. It demonstrated that the Bible does not reject the marriage of ministers and other clergy, but that marriage is a respectable thing in Christian life.

23.9. The Lord's Table

By this time the Reformation of the Church had spread to other countries. An important centre of the early Reformation was the city of Zürich in Switzerland. Here Huldrych Zwingli became the main Reformer (see chapter 24). The teachings of Luther and Zwingli were very similar, but they disagreed on one aspect of the Lord's Supper. According to Luther's understanding, Christ was bodily present at the Lord's Table, although he denounced the Roman doctrine of *transubstantiation*, which says that in Mass the bread and the wine are transformed into the body and the blood of Jesus Christ. To Luther, Christ's *real presence* and all His saving acts depend on his *bodily presence*, although bread and wine remain the same substance. Zwingli respected Luther very much, but could not accept his emphatic idea of the bodily presence of Christ. In his teaching he stressed that the Lord's Table is just a symbol that reminds us of the breaking of Christ's body and the shedding of Christ's blood. Christ's real body is in heaven[10]. According to Luther, by His words 'this is my body' in *Matthew 26:26* Jesus meant that His body is bodily present in the Lord's Supper, and that to reject this belief is like undermining the work of Christ. He reasoned like this. Every believer knows that Christ was buried in the grave, but he conquered death and rose from the dead. All this was done for my sake, I was buried with him in death, but now I have risen with Him from the dead. Jesus gave me life and his righteousness. Christ is bodily present in the Lord's Supper. Through his bodily presence in the Lord's Supper I know that I have eternal life. According to Luther, the thoughts of Humanism had infected Zwingli and made him deviate from the Biblical view of Christ's bodily presence. In this way – so Luther thought – Zwingli had weakened the power of the Cross and the miracle of the resurrection from the dead.

Philipp Melanchthon (1497-1560), able theologian who helped Luther.

This disagreement brought about disunity among the Reformers. It also weakened the political power and influence of the Reformation. Philip of Hesse, one of the rulers in Germany, and Martin Bucer the Reformer of Strasbourg called for a conference that might solve the problems. In 1529 Luther met with Zwingli and other leaders in Marburg. They agreed on all matters of religion except for the Lord's Supper. In the end Luther disowned Zwingli's party and declared that they were not one because they were of a different spirit. Martin Bucer, Luther's friend Philip Melanchthon and others disagreed with Luther's ideas on this issue.

---

[10] In chapter 26 we will see that Calvin used Luther's and Zwingli's ideas, without accepting every aspect of their thinking. Calvin said that in the Lord's Supper Christ is really present through the Holy Spirit. He agreed that this sacrament is a symbol and added that the Lord's Supper confirms the covenant of grace, and strengthens the faith. Although their views differed somewhat, all Reformers agreed that the Lord's Table helps believers only. They especially agreed in their rejection of the Roman Catholic idea that this sacrament is in some way a re-enacting of Christ's sacrifice.

23.10. The Government of the Church

Many Reformers did not follow Luther's later teachings about the order of the Church. In the beginning Luther emphasised that the Church is the *communion of saints*, and that it is not a sacramental fellowship brought about by the priests of Rome. All believers are priests. The justification through faith not only liberates believers, it also sanctifies them and brings about a real communion of saints. But Luther failed to live up to this principle. Unfortunately, he did not make it foundational to the Lutheran Church. Luther complained that he could not find elders who would be able to lead the Church. He also feared that democracy would destroy peace and order in the churches. This was caused partly by the bloodshed and destruction of the revolutionary movement of farmers and radicals. Therefore, he was not prepared to delegate the power of government in the Church to the collegiate elders or to the congregation. Instead, he asked the nobility and the political leaders to administrate the Church. Thus, in the Lutheran Reformation, the political governments have considerable power and influence over the Church. Here Luther deviated from the Church Father Augustine, who in his book *On the City of God* stressed the difference between the political order of society and the order of the Church. Bucer and Calvin also differed from Luther in this matter.

23.11. Bound Will

In his understanding of the gratuity of grace and the sovereignty of God's electing will, Luther was close to Church Father Augustine, and the other main Reformers followed him in this. He rejected the idea that man has a *free will* that enables him to choose good or evil. In his interpretation of Scripture man's unregenerated will is bound to sin. Hence, Luther spoke of man's *enslaved will*. Man's will is only released through God's election in Christ. By taking this position Luther turned against the old heresy of Pelegianism, but also against the semi-pelagian opinion, found in the Church of Rome, that free will is restored to man through baptism. The famous Humanist Bible scholar Desiderius Erasmus, who had criticised Rome's abuses so much, refused to follow Luther on the way back to a Biblical doctrine of man's will.

Desiderius Erasmus (1469-1536), humanist Bible scholar, who criticised the Medieval Church sharply, but also collided with the Reformation, especially with Luther.

23.12. His Last Years

The work of Luther and his friends transformed religion and politics tremendously. Lutheranism especially spread in Germany, and Scandinavia. Later, through emigration and mission, it developed in many other countries as well. The Bible, which Luther translated into German, the *Creed of Augsburg* (1530), and the two Lutheran Catechisms became important tools of the Reformation. The Lutheran states in Germany and in Scandinavia were a powerful alliance against Roman Catholicism and the Habsburg Empire.

Luther had hoped that the Jews would recognize that he liberated the Church from the bondage of Roman Catholic misinterpretation of the Scriptures and would become followers of his Reformation. However, this did not happen. On the contrary, Jewish leaders turned against him and ridiculed the Reformation. During his last years Luther showed bitter disappointment because of the unwillingness of the Jews to convert to Protestant Christianity. In some writings he severely criticized the religion of Judaism. Unfortunately, in one of them he called for harsh measures against the presence of synagogues and against the Jews themselves and their belongings.[11] Later antisemites including the Hitler-regime of Nazi-Germany have misused Luther's anti-Jewish writings in their propaganda.

Luther died in 1546, after reconciling two Earls of Mansfeld who had quarrelled. The last word, which Luther spoke, was 'yes' when he was asked by his friend whether he had kept the faith in Jesus Christ and the doctrines which he had taught.

Title page of the Luther Bible of 1534.

---

[11] Martin Luther, *On the Jews and their Lies*, in: *Luther's Works*, Philadelphia: Fortress 1971 [translation of: *Von den Juden und ihren Lügen*, 1543, Weimarer Ausgabe 53, S.417-552. Cf. Steven Paas, *Liefde voor Israël nader bekeken: Voor het Evangelie zijn alle volken gelijk*, Kampen: Brevier 2015, p.31-146.

24. Huldrych Zwingli 1484-1531[1]

24.1. His Early Years

The fire of the Reformation that had begun in the German state of Saxony soon spread to other European countries. The country of Switzerland, in the heart of Europe, was reached by the writings of the Humanists and also by the message of Martin Luther. Huldrych Zwingli belonged to those who became deeply influenced by these new thoughts. He was born in the village of Wildhaus in 1484, in the German-speaking North of Switzerland where the work of the German Reformer Martin Luther was easily accepted. The young man appeared to be a gifted student. He was sent to Basel and later to Bern for learning 'the seven liberal arts', with an emphasis on Latin, Dialectics and Music. In Vienna he was schooled in the new approaches of Humanism. This was continued in Basel. There he met the famous Humanist Desiderius Erasmus. There he also studied Scripture and the original biblical languages, Hebrew and Greek. After these theological studies, Zwingli was ordained as a priest of the Church of Rome.

First he became parish priest of Glarus. His feeling of responsibility for the spiritual and bodily welfare of the people made him launch protests against the system of *Reiselaufen*. This German word literally means 'going' or 'walking' (*laufen*) on a journey (*Reise*). It refers to the practice of Swiss young men to hire themselves out as mercenaries to the armies of various states in Europe. They did so out of poverty, as the crowded Swiss valleys could not feed everyone. On the battlefields Swiss soldiers were found on both sides. Many were killed. Others returned home with their bags of money, but physically maimed and psychologically wounded. This undermined the social and spiritual health of Swiss society, and was opposed to the Christian principles of justice and love. It was difficult, however, to stop this practice. Many families lived on the money earned by the mercenaries. The authorities profited from it because they taxed returning soldiers. That is why they did not agree with Zwingli's campaign against the Reiselaufen. Zwingli became persona non grata.

Huldrych Zwingli (1484-1531), founder of the Reformation movement that started in the Swiss city of Zürich.

Eventually he was removed from Glarus. His second posting was Einsiedeln. There he became a curate of the local parish. In this new situation Zwingli met with two problems. Einsiedeln was a centre of Mary devotion. There was a famous statue of Mary, and many pilgrims flocked to it. Of course, the coming of pilgrims was also of

---

[1] Cairns, *Christianity through the Centuries*, pp.293-297; Dowley, pp.378-379; Renwick/Harman, pp.118-125; Paas, *Chikonzedwe*, mutu 3.

24. Huldrych Zwingli 1484-1531

economic significance to Einsiedeln. Zwingli had come to reject the veneration of Mary as intermediary between Christ and believers, and he began to criticise it.

Another heretical practice concerned the monk Samson, who like Tetzel in Germany, traded in indulgences, i.e. written statements that were supposed to forgive sins. Zwingli followed Luther in attacking the selling of indulgences and the theory on which it rested.

24.2. Reformation in Zürich

Zwingli officially turned to the Reformation after he had become priest in the cathedral of Zürich. There he concentrated on preaching. He adopted the method of *lectio continua*, which is following the order of Scripture without skipping parts of it. He started preaching on *Matthew* 1 and then went through the whole New Testament. After that, in the pulpit he worked through the books and chapters of the Old Testament. Zwingli was liked by the people of Zürich, especially after his brave behaviour during an epidemic of *bubonic plague*. He visited many sick and dying. Eventually he became ill himself and nearly died. In the meantime, in his heart Zwingli had decided to reform the church. His marriage with Anna Reinhard underlined his determination to continue into the new direction.

The decision to stop Roman Catholicism in Zürich and to join the Reformation was taken by the city council after a disputation between Roman Catholic and Protestant leaders. At this meeting Zwingli presented a document of 67 theses formulating the necessity of Reformation. In Reformed Zürich Protestantism was the accepted religion.

In 1529 at Marburg, Zwingli and Luther together with some other Reformers, at the instigation of Martin Bucer, met to discuss their teachings, particularly their views on the Lord's Table. Here are the signatures to the Articles on which they agreed.

Zwingli felt united with Luther, and he sought contact with him. Luther, however, could not agree with some of Zwingli's views. Unfortunately, the meeting of both Reformers in Marburg in 1529, organised by Martin Bucer, did not remove Luther's disagreement with Zwingli.

In Zürich there was close cooperation between the leaders of the church and the city. These leaders felt threatened from two sides, first by the Roman Catholic powers in South Switzerland and elsewhere, and secondly by a group of radical Protestants who wanted more change than had been realised. Zwingli clashed with the leaders of this group, who were called Anabaptists. This internal conflict weakened Protestantism.

In the meantime, the Roman Catholic *cantons* (kind of provinces) in the South of Switzerland, encouraged by the Pope and by the Habsburg Empire, of which Switzerland was formally a member, had organised a military campaign in order to wipe out Protestantism in the Northern cantons. In 1531 at Kappel a battle took place between the Protestant and Roman Catholic armies. Zwingli joined the troops of Zürich as an *army chaplain*, and together with many others he was killed on the battlefield.

24.3. Political Climate

Political and religious circumstances influence one another. Note the difference between the political climate of Luther's and Zwingli's Reformation. Luther worked in a region where medieval feudalism was still in existence. In his territory (*Saxony*), which was ruled by one of the principle princes of the German-Habsburg Empire, there was a powerful nobility and a weak 'free citizenship'. Zwingli's Reformation developed in the more 'modern' climate that came first to existence along the big European rivers, especially the Rhine. Switzerland was a loose federation of *cantons*. In name it belonged to the Habsburg Empire, but because of its mountainous situation it remained rather untouched by the central power of the Empire. Three specific political aspects influenced the Zwinglian Reformation:

Medieval city of Zürich in Switzerland, an independent city-state that became the centre of the Reformation led by Huldrych Zwingli and Johann Heinrich Bullinger.

(a) The existence of *free cities with free citizens* (commerce, handcraft, industry) under elected City Councils who used their power to defend the independence of the city-state against the super-powers of the day, i.e. the Habsburg Empire and the Roman Church. There was a tendency to democracy. Because of their political aspirations these Councils (like Zürich's) tended to favour the Reformation.

(b) The emergence of a *nationalistic spirit,* which would eventually lead to the formation of a national Swiss state. Zwingli was not only faithful to the interests of his city-state, but there was in him also a 'modern' love of the Swiss nation, a patriotism that contributes to his resolve to introduce the Reformation in all the *cantons* of Switzerland.

(c) This high respect for the institutions of city and nation influenced Zwingli's *two-kingdoms theory*. In his view, Church and State are very close. The people of Zürich are one religious and political community, a *commonwealth*. The ecclesiastical government is more or less absorbed by the political government. The City Council leads the community. So, the 'two kingdoms' are not much distinguished in Zwingli's thinking. This also explains why he agrees to war against the Roman Catholic *cantons*. He even serves the armies of the Protestant *cantons* as an army chaplain. He desires to introduce the Reformation in the whole of his beloved Switzerland.

24.4. Radical Tendencies

This 'modern' background explains to a certain degree why Zwingli is more radical in his views than Luther. However, this difference should not be over emphasised. Both Reformers valued the supreme authority of Holy Scriptures, and both adhered to the doctrine of justification by faith alone. At the same time, it is true that Zwingli, more than Luther, was influenced by Humanism. His great respect for Greek culture even made him assume that some noble representatives of pagan Greek philosophy were saved, because they saw Christ from afar. His comparatively radical views are also apparent in the following:

a. The Lord's Supper

It is not more than a remembrance. It is not less either! Bread and wine are symbols of the body and blood of Christ. Zwingli adopted the explanation of Christ's words 'This is my Body' by the Dutchman Cornelis Hoen, who read them like this: 'This signifies my Body'. To Luther's ears this explanation sounded like a curse, although in Marburg 1529 he had to acknowledge that many of Zwingli's views were similar to his.

b. Anabaptists

Zwingli accepted the holiness demands by the *Radicals* of his day much more than Luther did. He realised that Christ not only justifies his people, but that He also sanctifies them. But soon Zwingli discovered that the Radicals went much further. By rejecting infant baptism in his church and by segregating state and church the Radicals in Zwingli's view undermined the existence of the Christian 'commonwealth'. Because of their rejection of infant baptism they were nicknamed *Anabaptists* (those who rebaptise), or *Catabaptists* (those who baptise in a wrong way). Zwingli considered this reflective of a revolutionary attitude. Indeed, by being baptised people became members of the Zürich community. So, the doing away of infant baptism was (in the eyes of the Zürich Reformer and of nearly all his contemporaries) a threat to society. As a consequence Zwingli's clash with the Anabaptists was even more violent than Luther's

24.5. Zwinglianism and Calvinism

When Zwingli was killed on the battlefield of Kappel in 1531, he was succeeded by Henry Bullinger, an influential theologian and prolific writer who guided *Zwinglianism* to calmer waters. He modified some of Zwingli's radical views, and he made an agreement with the Genevan Reformer John Calvin, the *Consensus Tigurensis* in 1549, by which Zwinglianism and Calvinism united.

Johann Heinrich Bullinger (1504-1575). He succeeded Zwingli in Zürich, and in 1549 he and Calvin joined their movements in a joint statement, the Consensus Tigurensus.

25. Martin Bucer 1491-1551

25.1. His Early Years[1]

Martin Bucer[2] was born in 1491 in the city of Schlettstadt in the Alsace. This is the German-speaking border region between France and Germany. Through the ages France or Germany alternatively were its owners. These days the Alsace is part of France.

There are some striking parallels between the lives of Bucer and Luther, which exceed the similarity of their first names. Martin Bucer spoke the same language as Martin Luther. Like Luther, in his boyhood Bucer learned at one of the schools of the *Brethren of the Common Life*[3], where the teaching of Scripture was central. Like Luther, Bucer became a monk (1506), and a priest in the Roman Catholic Church. Like Luther, he abandoned Rome (1521), and like him withdrew his vow of celibacy. Both married ex-nuns. Bucer married in 1522, and his wife was Elisabeth Silbereisen.

Martin Bucer (1491-1551), German theologian from the Alsace, former Dominican monk, became leader of Protestant churches in South Germany and Switzerland; he influenced Calvin.

There are also differences. Luther was an Augustinian monk, whereas Bucer was a Dominican monk. This explains another difference between them. Bucer was more influenced by Humanism than Luther. He got this interest from the Dominicans who were generally affected by Humanism, especially by the writings of Desiderius Erasmus. This inclination towards Humanism put him closer to Zwingli.

25.2. Reformation

Bucer met for the first time with Luther in Heidelberg in the year 1518. In this city a disputation (official dispute) took place between Luther and Cardinal Cajetan, a representative of the Pope. Here Luther defended his thought of *theologia crucis*, i.e. to say that the only hope of a person is the cross of Jesus Christ. Luther's words attracted Bucer, and helped to change his life. He left the monastery, married and became a follower of the Reformation.

---

[1] Cairns, *Christianity through the Centuries*, pp.283, 304, 324; Dowley, pp.378, 381, 386; Paas *Chikonzedwe*, mutu 4.

[2] *Bucer* or *Butzer*.

[3] *Brethren of the Common Life*: a religious order in the Late Middle Ages that contributed much to teaching of Biblical subjects and was inspired by the movement of *Modern Devotion*. They are considered as *Forerunners of the Reformation*.

Bucer adopted Luther's teaching of man's justification by faith alone, alongside a humanistically tinged emphasis on sanctification. Little by little he became known. He assisted Christians in the city of Weissenburg in their transit to the Reformation. In 1523 he went to the independent city of Strasbourg where the influence of the Reformation had grown strong.

From 1524 until 1548 Bucer was leader of the Reformation movement in this influential city. Through his work the church of Strasbourg was established, which contributed much to the Reformation in Europe as a whole.

Bucer, preaching.

An important part was played by the foundation of the University of Strasbourg. From 1541 onwards Bucer became leader of all the Protestants in the Southern parts of Germany and in Switzerland.

25.3. Christian Unity

Bucer worked hard for unity of the Church of Jesus Christ. He was deeply impressed by Jesus' command that all God's children be one (*John* 17:21).

First he tried to keep unity in the Reformation movement. That is why he organised a meeting between Luther and Zwingli, which eventually took place in Marburg 1n

View of the city of Regensburg (Latin: Ratisbona) where in 1541, at the initiative of Habsburg Emperor Charles V, the Disputation between Roman Catholic and Protestant theologians took place. The city is located in Bavaria, South East Germany, at the confluence of the rivers Danube and Regen.

1529. He felt pity when Luther adamantly refused to agree with Zwingli on an aspect of the teaching on the Lord's Supper.

Secondly, Bucer attempted to get to an agreement with followers of the Radical Reformation, especially with the Anabaptists. He accepted their challenge that Christians should lead holy lives, and he adapted his idea of church organisation to the principle that the church is the communion of saints.

Thirdly, Bucer contributed to attempts of mediation between the party of the Reformation and the moderates of the Roman Catholic Church. Together with Philipus (Philip) Melanchthon, Luther's famous helper, and other leaders, he diligently partook in various *Conferences on Religion* (Disputations) between representatives of the Reformation and of Rome. These meetings were organised at the initiative of Charles V, Emperor of the empire of Habsburg-Germany. They had some success. In 1541 in Regensburg even a certain agreement on the doctrine of *justification* was reached. However, on the issues of Church, Pope and Sacraments the parties disagreed emphatically. In the end the Pope refused to accept any agreement.

25.4. In England

In 1548 a difficult time began for many followers of the Reformation in the empire of Habsburg-Germany. When Emperor Charles V realised that the disputations on religion could not bring the people of the Reformation back to the Roman Catholic Church, he decided to resort to violent means. With the help of the leaders of the Roman Catholic

Picture of the ancient city of Cambridge, where in 1549 Martin Bucer became a Professor of Divinity.

states of Germany and even one of the leaders of the Protestant states, the armies of the Emperor invaded the Protestant regions and temporarily occupied them. A set of measures, called the *Augsburg Interim*, were pronounced, which led to the banishment of many Protestant leaders. Bucer had to go. In this uneasy situation Bucer and other

Reformers got an invitation to come to England and settle there. The invitation came from the Anglican Archbishop of Canterbury, Thomas Cranmer, on behalf of King Edward VI. In England Bucer became Professor of Theology in Cambridge (1549). And he assisted Cranmer in formulating the Anglican *Book of Common Prayer.* For King Edward VI he wrote his last book, entitled, *On the Kingdom of Christ,* a defence of Christian politics.

In 1551 Bucer died, while in England. When Mary Tudor became Queen of England (1553) she restored Roman Catholicism. During the subsequent wave of persecution the bones of Bucer and other deceased Reformers were exhumed and burnt.

Parts of Germany and Switzerland, including the cities of Strasbourg and Zürich.

25.5. The Communion of Saints

Although Bucer never became famous like some other Reformers, his work was very influential. John Calvin relied on Bucer. When Calvin was banished from Geneva in 1538, he was friendly received in Strasbourg by Bucer. Calvin stayed there until 1541, when he was welcomed back to Geneva. During this period Bucer was his guide and teacher.

Many of Calvin's teachings show the influence of Bucer, for example his thought on the Holy Spirit, on the believer's assurance of justification and sanctification, on the union of love between the Church and Christ, on the importance of marriage and family life.

As to the relationship between Church and State, Bucer (and also Calvin) taught that they should be independent of one another. Church and State both have distinct God given tasks. They serve one another by carrying out these tasks independently from one another. The rulers of the Church should safeguard the Church from interference by civil governments. Rulers of the Church are office bearers. They not only ward off interference by the State, but they also protect the Church against the influences of the Anabaptists and the Epicureans.

The Anabaptists only recognised Christians and churches that in their eyes had reached perfection. Epicureans were pleasure-seekers; they thought that God would not mind what men do with their bodies.

In Bucer's thinking office bearers are elected by the members of the congregation. Office bearers cannot be forced on a congregation from above, because all believing members are priests. He basically saw only one office, that of *presbyters*, although depending on the situation this one office could be sub-divided into many functions. The presbyters are servants of the congregation. In Bucer's view the congregation is the communion of saints. By saints he means believers in Christ, reborn by the Word and the Spirit. This communion is shaped and nursed into one body by diligent pastoral care, which is wider than the work of presbyters only.

25.6. Pastoral Care

In his book *On the true Pastoral Care* (1538)[4] Bucer gives a comprehensive view of pastoral work. It is aimed at the building, or edifying of the entire congregation, thus of the Kingdom of God. It is founded on two principles: (a) the Church has to be organised according to the rules in Scripture and (b) Christ is King and Shepherd in the Church and the world. Only He rules. So, in the Church there is no hierarchical ruling of one office-bearer over the other, of one member over the other. Pastoral care is the responsibility of three classes:

a. The civil authorities

They are also shepherds. They have to create the external conditions for the Church that facilitate the Church in its work in society, but they do not interfere in the internal affairs of the Church.

b. The congregation

The congregation is the communion of saints. All believers are priests and also shepherds. Pastoral care has to be done by every Christian.

c. The office-bearers

In the work of Preaching and Pastorate (including Discipline) Christ works through these officers in the congregation. Their work is aimed at the members, the sheep. They should bear in mind that there are different kinds of sheep: lost sheep, hunted sheep, sick and wounded sheep, weak sheep, healthy and strong sheep. They should safeguard the sheep against the false members that are not real sheep. The false sheep should be identified, isolated and excommunicated. Christ's sheep can be known, because they are obedient to Him.

---

[4] M. Bucer, *Von der wahren Seelsorge*, Strasbourg, 1538.

26. John Calvin 1509-1564[1]

26.1. Initial Period

In 1509 John Calvin was born, in the northern part of France called Picardie. His first name is Jean (English: John); his family name is Cauvin (French), Calvinus (Latin), Calvin (English, German), Calvijn (Dutch). Calvin's father was secretary of the local bishop; which was why he wanted his son to study for the priesthood. Studying in Paris was made possible by the support of a friendly noble family De Hangest.

In Paris Calvin first studied at the Gymnasium *La Marche*. After that, at the *Collège Montaigu*, a very strict college, he studied Latin and the Church Fathers, thus making preparations for theological study. Here one of his teachers, Cordier, informed him about Luther. He befriended the children of the Cop family whose father was a friend of Erasmus and a physician at the Royal Court. In 1528 Calvin suddenly broke off his preparations for the priesthood, at the wish of his father who had quarrelled with his bishop employer.

John Calvin (1509-1564), who from the city of Geneva led a widespread Reformation movement.

Then he turned to the study of law, and in 1532 after periods in Orleans and in Bourges he became a Doctor. Yet apparently the field of law was not his greatest love. He returned to Paris and began a study of Literature. During this time Calvin, though interested in the new ways of religion, was still basically a Humanist scholar. His first book, a comment on Seneca's *De Clementia*, is humanistic in persuasion, and does not show a special interest in the Gospel.

Calvin's signature.

26.2. Wandering Refugee

The exact date and details of Calvin's conversion are not known, although it happened in 1532 or in 1533. According to his own writing, in the preface to his exegesis of the Psalms, it happened 'suddenly'. His conversion is apparent in the text that he wrote in 1533 for a speech that was to be delivered by his friend Nicolas Cop, who had become the new Rector of Sorbonne University. In these words he showed the kind of convictions that were labeled *Lutheran* at the time. Cop's speech kindled the anger of King Francis I, who, after a period of wavering, had just ordered the persecution of all *Lutherans*, i.e. of all people that advocated Reformation of the Church. The king's

---

[1] Cairns, *Christianity through the Centuries*, pp.300-305; Dowley, pp.380-383; Renwick/ Harman, pp.118-125; Paas, *Chikonzedwe*, mutu 5

displeasure turned against Calvin, who had become known as Cop's ghost writer. Calvin avoided arrest by leaving Paris. Some of his friends were arrested and killed.

First he visited some Lutheran and Humanist friends, e.g. the Bible translator Jacques Lefèvre d'Étaples, and (in Ferrara) the sister of King Francis I who had become a Protestant. In this period Calvin wrote his famous *Institution of the Christian Religion*, in short the *Institutes*. The first edition was printed in Basel in 1536. In subsequent editions he enlarged the work; the last one was printed in 1559. The *Institutes* aimed at the edification and instruction of French Protestants. The foreword is a letter to King Francis I, stressing that Protestants are no revolutionary Anabaptists. The contents are organised according to the *Apostolic Creed*: part 1, on God the Father and Creation; part 2, on God the Son and Salvation; part 3, on God the Holy Spirit and Sanctification; part 4, on Church, Sacraments, and Civil Authorities.

The house in Noyon (Picardie, France), where John Calvin was born.

26.3. First Period in Geneva

On his way to Strasbourg, where he wanted to meet Bucer, Calvin had to make a detour in order to avoid the battlefields of warring French and German troops. That's why he landed in Geneva, where he planned to spend a night or two before going on to Strasbourg.

Just before Calvin's arrival the city state of Geneva had replaced the old regime with a Reformation-minded city council. This new council had chased away the Roman Catholic hierarchy, including the bishop. The Reformation was in progress. However, the movement lacked good leaders, despite the fact that the preacher Guillaume Farel did his utmost to provide the needed leadership. There was an unruly, revolutionary, libertine climate that the ministers of the newly established Church could not handle. When Farel heard about Calvin's arrival in the city, he went to him, and by threatening him with God's punishments Farel forced Calvin to stay in Geneva. Farel was not mistaken by assuming that the young and very able scholar would contribute to the ordering of the young Reformed Church and the regulating of its relationship to the city government.

Guillaume Farel (1489-1565), Swiss Reformer, who assisted Calvin in Geneva.

One of Calvin's first activities was the writing of a Church Order, entitled the *Articles for the Organisation of the Church*. After some time, a conflict arose between the ministers of the Church and the members of the city council. The city councillors wanted to decide on the admission of people to the Lord's Supper. When Calvin and other ministers refused to comply with this demand, they were banished from the city.

26.4. Period in Strasbourg

In this German-speaking town, at the time belonging to the Habsburg Empire, Calvin became the minister of a congregation of French refugees who had fled from the persecutions by King Francis I. He married Idelette van Buren, widow of an Anabaptist radical for whom he was an instrument of conversion to the Reformed faith. Helped by Clément Marot, Calvin started putting the Psalms to rhyme.

In chapter 25 we noticed that many of Calvin's teachings show the influence of Bucer, for example his idea of the believer's assurance of justification and sanctification, the union of love between the Church and Christ, and the importance of marriage and family life. We could add that both Reformers tried to fully integrate the work of the Holy Spirit in their theological thought. From the angle of ecclesiastical practice Calvin learnt from Bucer: (a) the value of ecumenical attempts: disputations with Roman Catholics, e.g. Regensburg, 1541, (b) the community character of the congregation, (c) how to deal wisely with Anabaptist radicals, (d) and to have patience.

26.5. Second Period in Geneva

Calvin, preaching in the Church of St. Peter's, Geneva, in his old age.

In 1541 Calvin was called back to Geneva by the city-council. The Genevan leaders felt threatened by Roman Catholic propaganda. They feared that a well written leaflet by Cardinal Jacopo Sadoleto would entice the citizens to change loyalty. These needed an able defender against the Cardinal's popular arguments. The invitation offered Calvin new opportunities to put his ideas to practice. He gave an effective reply to Sadoleto. Then, being re-installed as a minister, he started to organise preaching in the various churches of Geneva. Trying to structure the young Church along Biblical guidelines, he introduced the Church Session, and four classes of office bearers: minister, doctor, elder, deacon. Here he differed with Bucer who only recognised the eldership.

As to church-state relationship, Calvin did not completely succeed in making the Church independent of the State, although he tried to reach this ideal all his time in Geneva. He could not always evade interference by the city council; often city councillors were appointed elders in Church.

Besides, the struggle with the government of the Genevan city state, Calvin met with many problems in his work. There were the movements that went against his attempts for Reformation, e.g. *libertine groups* that refused to accept Biblical ethics, *heretics* like Sebastian Castellio who perverted the exegesis of the Song of Songs, Jerome Bolsec who denied the doctrine of predestination, and Micael Servet who denied the conception of the Trinity.

One of the most important contributions by Calvin was the foundation of an Academy for the training of ministers for countries where the Church of the Reformation was persecuted. Especially for France the *Genevan Academy* continually replenished the many ministers in that country who were arrested and put to death. In 1564, Calvin died. His last words were: 'Let me die, if only I am useful'. Theodorus Beza was his successor.

26.6. Calvin's Theology

a. The Honour of God

When looking at Calvin's theological significance, we should note that Calvin was a second-generation Reformer. He did not imitate his predecessors like Luther, Bucer, and Zwingli, but 'he stood on their shoulders'. This means that he adopted, used, completed, put to practice, and spread much of their original thinking. He did so in a very able and faithful way. But sometimes he emphasised differently.

Luther's central question was: 'How am I saved?' His answer was: Only by faith am I justified before God. Calvin fully agreed with this truth, but he did not use it as the focal point of his theology. In his focal point there is an even more important question: 'How is God to be honoured?' In his answer he stresses that faith not only concerns *justification*, but also *sanctification*. A justified person lives in 'new obedience' to the law of God. The good works that Christ gives in a believer are directed to the highest possible objective, honouring God. So, Calvin's theology is less man-centred and more God-centred than Luther's.

b. The Third Use of the Law

Calvin's thinking is very much related to the Bible; his starting point is the supreme authority of Scripture in all fields of life. In his exegetical method he rejects allegorizing, reasoning, and speculating. The meaning of Bible texts has to be found by comparing Scripture to Scripture. Divine predestination and human responsibility are the two lines he discovers in Scripture. There are three uses of God's Law: (a) it drives man to Christ, (b) it is the rule for civil society (the political use), and (c) obedience to the Law is the way in which saved sinners show their gratefulness.

The formulation of the third use of the Law (*tertius usus*) is an important characteristic of Calvinist theology. It was born as an attempt to meet with the holiness demands by the Radicals.

Michael Servet (1511-1553), physician who denied the doctrine of the Trinity and the true Divinity of Christ. He was first imprisoned by the Roman Catholic Inquisition, but escaped and was then executed in Geneva.

26. John Calvin 1509-1564

c. Presbyterian Church Government

Calvin was not the inventor of Presbyterian Church government (i.e. the government by 'presbyters': elders), but he was the first 16th-century Reformer who succeeded in putting it to practice. He distinguished *elders*, that is ruling elders and ruling elders who also preach, besides *doctors* (teachers) and *deacons*. The Church is not ruled by all (like some of the Radicals advocated), neither by one person at the top (like the Papacy), but by a *Consistory* (Church Session) consisting of elders, who can also meet in *Classes* (Presbyteries) and *Synods*.

d. The Lord's Supper

Means of grace are the administering of the Word, and the administering of the sacraments. Sacraments are not automatic channels of grace by the hands of a priest, neither is the Lord's Supper meant for all nominal Church members (against Rome). Partakers experience the presence of Christ, not bodily but spiritually, which is not less a *presentia realis*, a real presence (against Rome and Luther). The Lord's Supper is not only a symbol, but a seal of the faith, and a strengthening of the faith (against Zwingli). In Communion the hearts of the believers are lifted up to Christ.

Title page of Calvin's Christianae Religionis Institutio (Institutes of the Christian Religion).

e. Aspiring Unity

Calvin tried very much to bring the various strands of the Reformation together. He agreed to the suggestion of the Anglican Archbishop Cranmer for a general council of representatives of all the Protestant churches in Europe. During his Strasbourg period he participated in Bucer's disputations with Roman Catholic theologians and politicians. He also tried to meet with the Anabaptist Radicals.

26.7. Calvin's Political Views

Calvin did not favour absolute power by kings or other rulers; neither was he a democrat or a revolutionary. He favoured certain *oligarchicalism*, i.e. 'the few best are to rule the rest'. He rejected any form of revolution of the people, even against godless and oppressive rulers. But with an eye to the situation in France where the Protestants were cruelly persecuted, he allowed a *limited right to rise*, provided the rising were led by members of the nobility or the magistracy.

26.8. The reception of Calvin's Thought

a. Writings

Calvin wrote many commentaries on books of the Bible (except on Revelation). Many of his sermons were taken down by scribes, of which many are published. They are still influential, like his *Institutes* and other books.

b. Correspondence

Calvin exchanged a great quantity of letters with political and ecclesiastical leaders of Europe. His advice was often sought. These letters are an important source for historical knowledge.

c. The Spread of Calvinism

Theodorus Beza (1519-1605), Calvin's successor in Geneva.

Calvin's thinking produced the churches of the Reformed and Presbyterian tradition, although strands of Calvin's influence are also apparent in sections of the Anglican and Baptist traditions. Calvinism spread to many countries, (a) in the Reformation period to France, Scotland, The Netherlands, Poland, Hungary, parts of Switzerland and Germany; (b) later also to America, Africa, Australia, and Asia.

Medieval city of Geneva in Switzerland, an independent city-state that became the centre of the Reformation led by John Calvin.

27. The Radical Reformers[1]

27.1. The Kingdom

There was much variation in the movement of the 16th-century Reformation. A cluster of groups were more radical in their aspirations than others. In some ways these radical groups were similar to the *Montanists, Novatians,* and *Donatists* of the Early Church. Sometimes these groups are designated as the 'Left Wing of the Reformation'. G.H. Williams in his book *The Radical Reformation* (1962) distinguishes *Magister Reformers* and *Radical Reformers*.

Magister Reformers were Luther, Zwingli, Bucer, Calvin and others. They recognised the civil state and its magistrates, collaborated with them if possible, and also tried to reform them. The *Radical Reformers* were those who in various degrees rejected the contemporary civil state(s). Actually, the Radicals did not aspire to a *reformation* of the present situation of church and state. They hoped for the destruction of all worldly and ecclesiastical structures, which in their view would pave the way for *restitution* of the Kingdom of God. According to the Radicals the *Magister Reformers* had betrayed their originally good principles, shrinking from the radical consequences, and now they collaborated with the powers of world and Satan.

27.2. Kinds

There were different kinds of Radicals. The most orthodox in their teaching were the *Anabaptists* or *Catabaptists*, pejorative terms used by their opponents when pointing at their dissenting view of baptism. Other types were liberal, like the *Spiritualists*, a kind of mystics who degraded the value of Scripture under a supposed amalgamation of the Holy Spirit and their own 'inward spirits' or 'inward lights'. Thy said: 'the letter kills, the spirit gives life'. In their view the written Word, the Bible, was only a less important addition to their inward spirits, a *by-bell*. There were also the *Evangelical Rationalists*. Generally, they replaced the Reformed dogma of justification by faith alone by justification by works. A special group of Rationalists were the sect of the *Socinians*. Like the old Arians and the modern Unitarians and *Jehovah's Witnesses*, they could not live with the dogma of Trinity. According to the prevailing Carolingian Law, denial of the Trinity was a capital offence. To them belonged Michael Servet who lost his life in Geneva.

Although most Radicals were non-violent, they were cruelly persecuted by Roman Catholic and Protestant authorities alike, because in medieval and 16th/17th-century thought they undermined the structures of society and humanity. Some violent episodes in the beginning of Radical tradition contributed to the hatred against them.

27.3. Peasants' Revolts

The Peasants' revolts were a series of risings by farmers in South and Middle Germany who felt oppressed and wronged by the nobility. They wanted social and economic change. An early example was the revolt in 1514 by Poor Konrad (German: *der arme*

---

[1] Cairns, *Christianity through the Centuries*, pp.285, 286, 297-300; Dowley, pp.401-405; Paas, *Chikonzedwe*, mutu 6.

Thomas Müntzer (c.1490-1525), German Anabaptist, leader of the Peasants' revolt that was crushed at Frankenhausen in 1525.

Konrad), also known by its diminutive Poor Kunz. It was a united league of farmers, which rose against Duke Ulrich of Württemberg. They adopted this name because the nobility had used it to mock them.

Much more serious was the rising in the Swiss-German border area by farmers who formed an 'Evangelical Brotherhood' for the liberation of all the oppressed and exploited. They formulated *12 Articles* with demands that were even by Luther recognised as justifiable. Luther then admonished the nobility.

The movement became really violent in 1522 when it was joined by a group of religious radicals, the *'Zwickau Prophets'* who had disturbed Wittenberg and had been sent away by Luther, whereupon they turned very hostile against the Reformer. Their leader Thomas Müntzer mocked Luther's 'sweet Christ'. The farmers accepted this Müntzer as their leader. Attempts by Luther to pacify the farmers failed. And a massive campaign of violence started, including the burning of castles and monasteries and the killing of noblemen, monks and clergy. Then, Luther turned against these riotous farmers. He asked the nobility to crush the movement, which eventually happened in the very bloody battle of Frankenhausen 1525.

27.4. The First Anabaptists

Originally, there was not an immediate connection between the above mentioned violent expression of Radicalism and the Anabaptists. The Anabaptists were first active in Switzerland and in The Netherlands, especially the northern part in Frisia. They believed in the possibility and necessity of personal and ecclesiastical perfection. This *perfectionism* presupposes that the Christians and the Christian congregation have complete victory over sin. They rejected the Magister Reformers' conviction that the Church on earth is necessarily mixed with hypocrites and that regenerated Christians still are sinners, though saved sinners. They meant that man is not a Christian until he shows perfect obedience to the law of Christ. This stance did neither accord with the idea that God deals with man through His covenant, nor to the practice of infant baptism, nor to recognition of a God-given role by the civil state. Although Anabaptists opposed the formulation of Creeds as betrayal to the

Balthasar Hubmaier (1480-1528), a former Roman Catholic priest who became one of the first Anabaptist martyrs.

supreme authority of Scriptures, there is an early Anabaptist formula, the *Schleitheim Confession* (1527).

Almost all the early leaders of the movement were killed because of their conviction. The Swiss leaders Conrad Grebel, Felix Manz, George Blaurock, and the German Balthasar Hubmaier belonged to these martyrs, although they and their followers were peaceful and godly people.

27.5. Violent Anabaptists

Bitterness about the persecutions, and also the activities of men like Thomas Müntzer changed the attitude of many early Anabaptists. They thought that they had to contribute to the crushing of 'satanic' civil and ecclesiastical powers by forcefully establishing the Kingdom of God on earth. Melchior Hoffmann a German of demagogical tendencies who had turned his back on Luther, made many people believe that he was Elijah, that the *Second Coming* was at hand, and that the city of Strasbourg would be the *'new Jerusalem'*, from where the Kingdom of God would conquer the earth. He was arrested and remained in prison in Strasbourg until his death in 1543.

In the meantime, the enthusiastic movement spread to The Netherlands. There John Tripmaker succeeded Hoffmann,. But he was soon arrested and beheaded. His successor Jan Matthijsen led the movement to real violent revolution. He declared the Dutch-German border city of Münster to be the 'new Jerusalem'. His followers flocked to the city, and evicted disagreeing citizens. He introduced a kind of Christian *'communism'*. Those who refused to part with their possessions were put to death. In the meantime, troops of Roman Catholic and Protestant German princes were concentrated around the city. Matthijsen was killed in 1534 when he and others tried to break through the encircling armies. Then, a new 'prophet' stood up, Jan van Leyden. He declared himself king, introduced an Old Testament type of polygamy, terrorised the city, and killed everyone who opposed him. In 1535 the city was captured and bloodshed followed. The leaders were very cruelly tortured and starved to death in a cage hanging from the main church tower of Münster, where it still was to be seen in the mid-20th century.

Jan van Leyden (†1535), last leader of the Anabaptist revolutionaries in Münster.

In the same period there were disturbances in The Netherlands. In Amsterdam Anabaptist enthusiasts walked nude on the streets. There was also the violent occupation by Anabaptist Radicals of a monastery near the Frisian city of Bolsward.

27.6. Mennonites

The tragedy of Munster marked the end of the violent period of Anabaptist history. The *'sword spirits'* gave way to the pacifists. The Frisian ex-priest Menno Simons became the new leader. He abhorred violence and led the movement to peaceful waters. However, he remained faithful to much of the original Anabaptist thinking: a Christian cannot serve the civil government, is not allowed to swear an oath, nor is he to join the army. His theology calls to mind the *Docetism* of the Early Church: Jesus did not take his flesh and blood from the Virgin Mary, but from heaven.

Menno Simons (1496-1561), former Roman Catholic parish priest in Frisia (The Netherlands) who after 1536 became the leader of peaceful Anabaptism.

Mennonites have spread from The Netherlands to North Germany, from there to Eastern Europe, Russia and Siberia. Also, other branches of Anabaptism eventually landed in Russia, like the influential group that was originally founded by Jacob Hutter in Moravia. In the 19th century many of these Russian *Mennonites* and *Hutterites* emigrated or fled to Canada and the United States.

27.7. Reformers and Anabaptists

Luther could not understand the Anabaptists at all. Zwingli, Bucer and Calvin tried to meet their holiness demand, but eventually clashed with them. Perhaps Calvin is the Reformer who gave the best answers to their challenges. In his *'third use of the law'* he stressed the importance of sanctification, although he rejected the Anabaptist anthropology which defines Christians as perfect people. Calvin wrote a book against the Anabaptist dogma of the 'sleeping soul'. In 1544 he discussed the Anabaptist *Confession of Schleitheim* of 1527. In this writing he criticised the Anabaptist views of baptism, discipline, holy communion, pacifism, church offices, and civil authority.[2]

---

[2] Recommended reading: W. Balke, *Calvin and the Anabaptist Radicals*.

28. Reformation in France[1]

28.1. The European Context

The 16th-century Reformation had promising beginnings in nearly all the countries of Europe. According to one estimate, by the 1520's about 90% of Germany favoured Protestantism, and in about 1550 half of France seems to have been on the Protestant side. There were hopeful signs in Spain and Italy as well. However, finally the Reformation was only successful in North, West, and Central Europe, and in parts of Eastern Europe. Scandinavia, part of the Baltic region, and parts of Germany became Lutheran; The Netherlands, parts of Switzerland and Germany, and Scotland became Calvinist. England became Anglican with a Calvinist touch.

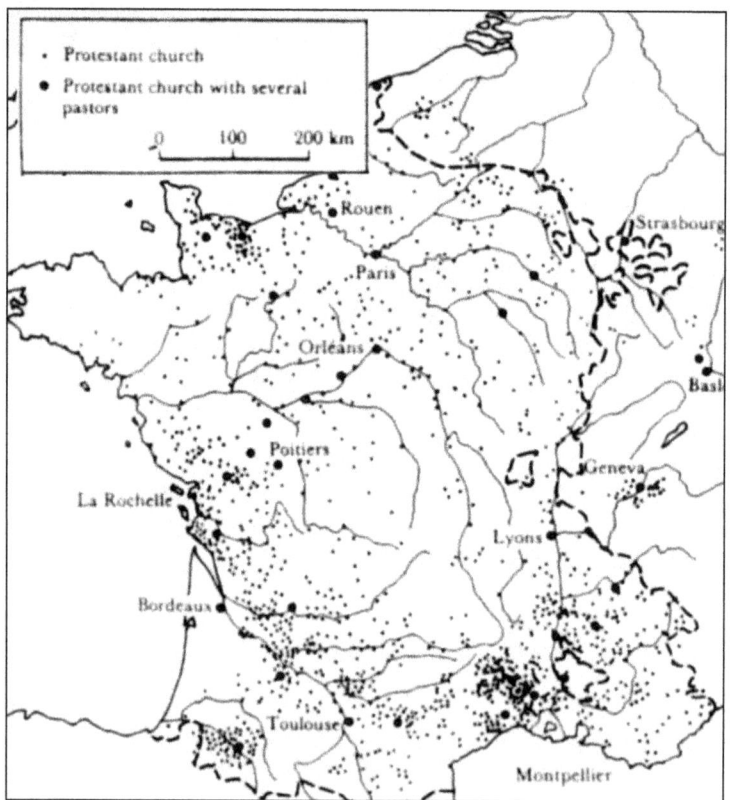

The spread of Reformed churches in France in 1562.

Much depended on the decisions made by the civil governments of autonomous territories, free city states, and emerging national states. Very often the Reformation went side by side with movements for political freedom and independence. Generally, the rulers of the Habsburg Empire did not favour the Reformation, because they feared

---

[1] Cairns, *Christianity through the Centuries*, pp.308-311; Dowley, pp.380, 425-427; Paas, *Chikonzedwe*, mutu 7.

political instability. The Empire combined its efforts with those of the Roman Catholic *Counter Reformation* to root out the Reformation in Spain, Portugal, a number of states in Southern Germany, Belgium, Austria, and parts of Hungary. The Counter Reformation also had the help of secular rulers to extinguish the Reformation in countries like Italy and Poland. For various reasons the southern parts of Ireland, some provinces in The Netherlands and pockets in the Highlands of Scotland remained Roman Catholic. Those peoples of East and South East Europe and Russia that traditionally belonged to the Eastern Orthodox Church were generally not touched by the Reformation. Now we will review the Reformation in some European countries, first France.

28.2. Forerunners

According to some writers, the 12th/13th-century sect of the Albigenses in northern Spain and southern France belonged to the forerunners of the Reformation. However, although we denounce the violent cruelty by which the Albigenses were rooted out by the Dominican *Inquisition Court* in cooperation with the French State, they were more a 'strange' Gnostic sect than a back to the Bible movement.

Elements in the monastic reforms of the 12th and 13th centuries, led by people like Bernard of Clairvaux and Francis of Assisi, were in a way preparatory to the Reformation. But the real forerunners were the Waldenses, an influential Christian missionary movement from the beginning of the 13th century, founded by Petrus Waldo, a rich merchant of Lyons. Although fiercely persecuted, the Waldenses still existed in the 16th century and they linked up with the Calvinist Reformation.

28.3. Spreading

Soon after the publication of his 95 theses in 1517, Luther had followers in France. King Francis I (1515-1547) was influenced by Humanism and he was open to change. In this climate it was even possible to make a translation of the Bible, which was done by Lefèvre d'Etaples. For a long time the royal court wavered between reform and reaction. At first the king condoned Lutheranism, especially because he needed the support of Protestant German princes in his wars against the Habsburg Emperor Charles V. But when overzealous propagators nailed their Lutheran leaflets even on the door of the king's bedchamber, the king took this as a revolutionary action, and immediately retaliated. It was the beginning of harsh persecution. This was the time when Calvin had to leave Paris. But the killings did not prevent *Protestantism* from spreading rapidly, and Calvin contributed much to it by his writings and by the continual replenishment of preachers which he trained at his *Genevan Academy*.

Francis I (1515-1547), who was King of France in the beginning of the Reformation. Calvin addressed his Institutes (1536) to him, yet Francis mistrusted the Reformation and persecuted its followers.

28. Reformation in France

In Paris a secret Synod of the French underground church met in 1559. Its members tried to give guidance to the haunted congregations. Using Calvin's Genevan examples, a Presbyterian system of church government was introduced; a Church Order and a Confession of Faith or a Creed were made.

28.4. Night of St. Bartholomew 1572

About 1560 the name *Huguenots* ('probably a nickname based on a medieval romance about a king Hugo') was applied to the French Protestants. Although the Roman Catholic influence at the royal court remained strong and there was no freedom of religion whatsoever, many members of the nobility became Huguenots. Some did so

The massacre of a large number of Huguenots in the Night of Bartholomew.

because of political reasons; they envied the influence of the Roman Catholic clergy at court. Others had religious motives, e.g. Gaspard de Coligny who became the leader of the Huguenots.

The first period of civil war between the Roman Catholic and the Protestant parties, 1562-1594, was interrupted by the marriage of the Huguenot Prince Henry of Navarre to a sister of the king. This union held great promise for peace. Many Huguenots flocked to Paris to attend the wedding. However, De Coligny and some 30.000 fellow believers were treacherously slaughtered on the *Night of St. Bartholomew*, 23-24 August, 1572. The Pope in Rome organised a mass of thanksgiving and he issued a coin of remembrance.

28.5. Edict of Nantes

The civil war continued until Henry of Navarre succeeded in becoming king of France, after having turned Roman Catholic ('Paris is worth a mass'). Henry did not forget his Huguenot ex-friends, though. In 1593 he issued the *Edict of Nantes*, which gave the

Protestants a number of autonomous regions and cities within the French State. This solution failed to work. Later kings like Louis XIII and especially Louis XIV resumed persecution and civil war. The last Huguenot fortress, La Rochelle, fell in 1628. In 1685 the *Edict of Nantes* was withdrawn.

Many Huguenots were forced to apostatise, many others were executed or perished, because of hard labour in the mines or on the galleys. At least half a million fled abroad, The Huguenot refugees, who were often men skilled in various crafts, wealthy traders, or learned scholars, settled in countries like The Netherlands, England, Ireland, and South Africa. They often founded their own *Wallonian* churches and contributed much to the economic, political and cultural development of these countries.

Admiral Gaspard de Coligny (1519-1572), leader of the French Huguenots, murdered in the Night of Bartholomew

28.6. Huguenots legalised 1802

Losing its best sons and daughters was a bitter experience for France. Only in 1802, after the French Revolution, was the legal standing of the Huguenot Church established. Although there was an increase of numbers in the 19th century, French Protestants remained a small minority. At the moment there are two main denominations, the *Église Réformée de France* and the smaller *Église Réformée Évangélique Indépendente*.

29. Reformation in The Netherlands[1]

29.1. Terms

The historical term The Netherlands (also the 'Low Lands') refers to the region of two present-day national states, the one in the North and the other in the South, situated on the North Sea, opposite England, north of France and west of Germany. The northern part has retained the old name 'The Netherlands'. It has been an independent national state practically since the end of the 16th century, officially since 1648. Actually, it was born out of the Reformation. The English language uses the word *Dutch* as an adjective for its people, language, culture etc. Beyond the Dutch boundaries very often the name *Holland* is applied to the whole country. This is a mistake, because only its seaside provinces South- and North Holland bear this name. The Dutch territory is smaller than the area of Malawi. The southern part of the Low Lands officially seceded from the North in 1648. It was regained by the powers of the *Counter Reformation* and remained to be colonised by Roman Catholic states like Spain, Austria and France, until it was reunited to the North for a short time in the beginning of the 19th century. Its territory is a little smaller than that of the North. In 1830 it became an independent national state, called Belgium. The language of the southern half of Belgium (= Wallonia) is French, whereas in the Northern half (= Flanders) Dutch is spoken, though sometimes called *Flemish*.

King Philip II (1527-1598) of Spain, who did not tolerate Reformation and independence for The Netherlands. Through his marriage in 1554 to Mary Tudor, he also helped the Counter Reformation in England.

29.2. Spanish 'Possession'

The Netherlands was one of the first regions in Europe where medieval feudalism began to disintegrate. Situated on the sea and connected with the European inland by large rivers, especially the Rhine, it was very well equipped for the development of trade and industry. Soon a number of powerful cities with free citizens emerged, and the power of the lower nobility decreased. In the beginning of the 16th century the Low Lands consisted of a number of more or less autonomous duchies (province-states) belonging to the Habsburg Empire. When the Emperor Charles V died in 1555, his son Philip II succeeded to the throne of Spain and its 'possessions'; to which belonged not only vast colonies in South and Central America, but also the Low Lands. The politics of exploitation by the Spanish regime met with wide protests among the higher nobility, from the governments of the provinces, from the city councils, and from the free

---

[1] Cairns, *Christianity through the Centuries*, pp.315-318; Dowley, pp.367, 374, 378, 38-384, 389, 430, 431; Paas, *Chikonzedwe*, mutu 8.

citizens. Spanish taxation was particularly hated. The main centres of early political and economic activity were in the South, i.e. the territory of present-day Belgium.

29.3. Preparation

The incipient conflict with Spain was widened to dimensions beyond repair when the Reformation spread its influence in The Netherlands. From the 14th century Bible education and moral teachings by the *Brothers of the Common Life* had been preparing the grounds. Through their centres of *Modern Devotion* the Brothers had reached influential people like Luther and Erasmus. There was also the influence of Humanism and the Renaissance in the young cities. All this had contributed to the emergence in the North of a national Reformed church-movement, consisting of Humanist scholars, ex-priests, and ordinary people. They resisted the Roman Catholic conception of mass (transubstantiation, sacrifice) by refusing to honour this *'bread god'*. To these *sacramentarians*, as they were called, belonged Cornelis Hoen who influenced Zwingli's symbolic view of the Lord's Supper. The Roman Catholic clergy were alarmed by this group. Assisted by their secular arm, i.e. the Spanish authorities, they tried to crush it. The first martyr in the North died on a stake in Woerden in 1525. His name was Jan de Bakker, an ex-priest.

29.4. Reformation

In the meantime, the South was becoming the main theatre of the spread of the Reformation. The message of Luther reached the Augustinian monastery in Antwerp from where the *'new teachings'* were spread among the people. The authorities soon retaliated. Two Augustinian monks, Hendrik Voes and Johannes van Esschen were the first martyrs in the South (1521). The monastery was demolished, and its prior, Hendrik van Zutfen, was abducted to Germany where he was tortured to death. From about 1540 Calvin's teachings got hold of The Netherlands. Soon the South was won for the Reformation and the North was following. But at the *Council of Trent* the Roman Catholic Church tried to get the situation in hand. As soon as Philip II succeeded to the Spanish throne, his regime together with the Roman Catholic powers of *Inquisition* and *Jesuitism* mobilised a powerful

Jacobus Arminius (1560-1609), Dutch theologian who had studied in Geneva under Beza, but deviated from Calvin's explanation of God's sovereignty and predestination. His followers were called Remonstrants or Arminians.

campaign in order to regain the lost political and spiritual territory. But gradually, organised resistance took shape. Local Calvinist *Church Sessions* played an important role in this. William of Orange, a German prince with territorial rights in The Netherlands, who had turned to Calvinism, became the leader of a national movement of liberation.

29.5. Liberation Struggle

In 1568 a war started against Spain. It would last 80 years! At first the Spanish military force commanded by the Duke of Alva was too strong for the young Republic. In most regions of the South the old regime was quickly reinstalled. An Inquisition Court, which was called the *Blood Council*, condemned a great number of political and ecclesiastical leaders to death. In many cities the population was punished by massive bloodshed. Many believers fled abroad. They constituted congregations of refugees, e.g. in London and in some Lutheran states of Germany. They tried to give guidance and support to the persecuted church at home. The refugee Synods of Wezel (1568) and of Embden (1571) played an important role in this. In 1585 the important city of Antwerp was captured by the Spanish. This meant that the South was lost for the Reformation and for national independence. That is why present-day Belgium has remained a Roman Catholic country.

Stadhouder William I of Orange (†1584), leader of The Netherlands in the war of national independence against Spain.

Also the North, which by the *Union of Utrecht* had concluded a pact that instituted the *Republic of the seven United Netherlands*, was invaded by Alva's army. Although the Spanish deployed their military to all provinces, and captured, plundered and carried out massacres in a number of towns, they could not manage to break the spirit of resistance. The North was greatly helped by thousands of refugees from the South. These refugees strengthened the young nation spiritually, economically and militarily. In a guerrilla war, assisted by French Huguenots, German Lutheran princes and English, the Dutch eventually gained victory. Formal national independence was granted to the Dutch Republic by the *Peace Treaty of Münster* in 1648.

29.6. Education

The Reformed Church in The Netherlands took some of the characteristics of a privileged state church. Nevertheless, the the Dutch people never turned to Calvinism in its entirety. William of Orange recognised the plurality of religious feelings of the Dutch, and he pleaded for freedom of religion and national unity. For various reasons in some provinces Roman Catholicism remained predominant, although not in its political appearance. Moreover, there was a strong Anabaptist minority. The young Reformed Church faced the enormous task of educating the people in the Word of God. The church was greatly helped by the government, which founded universities, including theological faculties for the training of ministers or pastors.

Title page of the first edition of the Heidelberg Catechism in The Netherlands.

The challenge of education produced a number of educational documents, three of which were to be elevated to the level of formal doctrinal creeds, i.e. Confessions of Faith: *The Heidelberg Catechism*, in 1562 compiled by two German theologians, Zacharias Ursinus and Caspar Olevianus. It is a summary of the headlines of Scripture. Many Dutch generations (and others!) were taught from the 129 questions & answers divided into 52 chapters ('Sundays') of this booklet.[2] *The Dutch Confession of Faith* (= Nederlandse Geloofsbelijdenis), in 1561 compiled by the 'Southerner' Guido de Brès who was martyred in 1567. De Brès used Calvin's Genevan Creed when he wrote the 37 Articles of this document, summarising the main doctrines of the Christian faith. *The Canons of Dordt* (Dutch: *Dordtse Leerregels*). This creed was compiled in the years 1618 and 1619 by members of the first and only General Synod of the national Reformed Church of The Netherlands. It is an explanation of the doctrine of *predestination*, and it was formulated as an answer to the heresy of Arminianism.

The creedal documents are called the *Three Forms of Unity*, and as such they have continued to play an important role in churches of the Reformed or Presbyterian family.

Caspar Olevianus, 1536-1587, one of the authors of the Heidelberg Catechism (1562)

Zacharius Ursinus, 1534-1583, one of the authors of the Heidelberg Catechism (1562)

---

[2] In resp. 2003 and 2006 translations were published in Chichewa/ Chinyanja and in Chitumbuka: Zacharias Ursinus ndi Caspar Olevianus, *Katekisma wa/ na Heidelberg*, Zomba: Kachere, Buku la Mvunguti, no. 11 and no. 23 [See website Refo500].

30. Reformation in England[1]

30.1. Spirit of Independence

Although medieval Britain belonged to the European political and ecclesiastical climate, its history is different owing to its insular position. There always has been a spirit of independence from the institutions that ruled the Continent. In the beginning of Christianity the *Celtic Church* came into being independently of Rome. It deployed missionary activities far into the Continent. Only after the conversion of the Anglo-Saxons by the Rome-sent missionary Augustine (597), and after the *Synod of Whitby (664)* did the Celtic churches succumb to papal rule (see chapters 6.3 and 14.2). But a certain spirit of independence remained.

30.2. John Wycliffe

This is shown by the work of John Wycliffe (c 1330-1384), an important forerunner of the Reformation. Like we saw in chapter 21.4 this professor of theology in Oxford became famous because of his heroic early protests against the abuses and doctrinal errors of medieval Roman Catholicism. He maintained that the Bible was the sole criterion of doctrine, that the authority of the Pope was ill-founded in Scripture, and that monastic life had no Biblical foundation. He also attacked the doctrine of transubstantiation as philosophically unsound and as encouraging a superstitious attitude to the Eucharist. Although Wycliffe's followers, the *Lollards*, were fiercely persecuted and nearly rooted out they contributed much to the growing dissatisfaction with Rome among nobility and people.

30.3. Henry VIII's Divorce Problems

Henry VIII (1491-1547), King of England from 1509; his marriage behaviour made him cut with Rome, thus paving the way for the English Reformation.

This dissatisfaction also pertained to the field of economy. Much money, through the Roman Catholic Church, flowed out of the country to Rome. The immediate reason for the break in the relationship between England and Rome was a divorce question. King Henry Tudor VIII (1491-1547) wanted his marriage to the Spanish princess Catherine of Aragon to be dissolved. Catherine was the widow of his brother and she was an aunt of the Habsburg Emperor Charles V. His wife had not given him a son, so he worried about the succession. Moreover, he had a passion for Anne Boleyn whom he wanted to marry. But the Pope did not consent to the divorce, because he feared revenge by Charles V, whose troops were ready to occupy Rome. Then, Henry decided to cut off all links with Rome and with papal power. He

---

[1] Cairns, *Christianity through the Centuries*, pp.320-325; Dowley, pp.386-390; Renwick/Harman, pp.126-139, 150-162; Paas, *Chikonzedwe*, mutu 9.

declared himself to be 'the only supreme head in earth of the Church of England, called *Ecclesia Anglicana'*. The king did not favour the Reformation at all, though. He had some Lutherans killed and even wrote a book against Luther in which he defended the doctrine of *transubstantiation*. Henry wanted a Roman Catholic Church of a national character, without papal authority.

30.4. Reformation and Counter Reformation

But the king's decision had opened up the country for new thought and practice. The newly appointed archbishop of Canterbury, Thomas Cranmer, appeared to be open to Protestant thought, at first for Lutheranism, then for Zwinglianism, and finally he was influenced by Calvin. During the short reign of Edward VI, Henry's successor, the Reformation was allowed to spread widely in England. Cranmer contributed to it by introducing his *Book of Common Prayer*, thus reforming the liturgy of the English Church. The reign of Catherine of Aragon's daughter Mary Tudor (1516-1558) meant for England a temporary return of the old regime. Hundreds of Protestants were killed, among them was Thomas Cranmer, and many fled abroad.

Title page of the Book of Common Prayer, the official service book of the Church of England, compiled by Thomas Cranmer and others. 1549

Thomas Cranmer (1489-1556), the first Protestant Archbishop of Canterbury.

30.5. The Puritan Movement

However, after Mary's half-sister Elizabeth I (1533-1603) came to the throne, Protestantism became the national religion of England, although many old forms, and practices, and some old convictions remained.

To many English the changes were not sufficient. They considered the *Elizabethan Settlement of religion* as kind of 'halfway' reformation which left the essentials untouched. To these *Nonconformists* also belonged representatives of the Anabaptist Radicals, but they were not many in Elizabethan England. English *Nonconformism* consisted mainly of Calvinist Protestants who, unlike the many Calvin oriented *Conformists* in the English state church, wanted to apply the principles of the Reformation not only to matters of personal faith, but also to the *ecclesiology*, i.e. the organisation and offices of the church. They wanted to 'purify' the church of Roman Catholic remnants; hence, they were called *Puritans*. The Puritan movement was very diverse. We mention two main streams.

James I (King of England from 1603), and James VI (King of Scotland from 1567), 1566-1625. In 1611 he authorised a new translation of the Bible.

At first there were the *Presbyterians* (presbyter = elder), originally led by the influential theologian Thomas Cartwright (1535-1603). They accepted the current idea of a State Church under the monarch and worked within it, but they wanted to replace the Anglican system and its government by (arch) bishops with a Presbyterian system of church government which they professed to derive from John Calvin. Instead of the rule by a hierarchy of bishops and priests, they aspired to a hierarchy of Synods (Consistories = Church Sessions – Presbyteries – Regional Synods – General Synod) in which the Reformed ministers were to play the predominant role.

The second group of Calvinist Nonconformists were originally called *Separatists*, because they rejected the principle of a State Church and consequently broke away from the Anglican Church. Robert Browne, Henry Barrowe, John Greenwood, and John Penry were the leaders of these early Separatists.[2] Much more than the Presbyterian opponents of Anglicanism, they were severely punished (prison, executions, banishment) by the Elizabethan regime. They stressed that the congregation is a *community* in which all believers have their priestly office. In their view the church is not governed by a supra structure of ecclesiastical bodies or persons. The congregation and its elders are the highest level of church government. Later the adherents of this principle were called by other names, Congregationalists, Dissenters, or Independents. Many of them took refuge in other countries, like the congregation of John Robinson, which settled first in the Dutch city of Leyden, then in 1620 sailed to America where these *Pilgrim Fathers,* as they were later called, laid the foundation for the United States of America. From some of these groups of English refugees in Holland, the *Baptists* originate, partly as a merger with Dutch Anabaptists.

---

[2] Cf.: S. **Paas**, *De Gemeenschap der Heiligen: Kerk en Gezag bij Presbyteriaanse en Separatistische Engelse Puriteinen 1570-1593*, Zoetermeer: Boekencentrum, 1996: A study of the history of the English Reformation in general, particularly of the early stages (until 1593) of the Movement of Puritanism, especially focusing the early Separatists. Summary in English, pp.385-408.

30.6. Protectorate and Restoration

In the 17th century all of these three main streams of English Protestantism (Anglicanism, Presbyterianism, and Separatism) had their victories and defeats. In the beginning on the surface Anglicanism prevailed, especially because it was favoured by King James Stuart I, who had been King James VI of Scotland, which country he united to England in 1603. James had had bad experiences with Scottish Presbyterians, hated them, and was of the opinion that the church should be ruled by bishops and that the bishops should be ruled by the king ('no bishop, no king').

After his death in 1625, the Presbyterians grew strong, and came very near to the introduction of a Reformed State Church. They succeeded in convening a national synod, the *Westminster Assembly* (1643-1648), which produced e.g. the well-known, *Large and Short Westminster Catechisms*, and a creed, the *Westminster Confession of Faith*. However, English Presbyterianism was never to get permanent roots. In the meantime, a civil war had broken out (1642) in which the Presbyterians sided with the king and the Anglican party. On the other side were the Separatists, now called Independents, whose influence had considerably expanded among the people.

John Bunyan (1628-1688), Puritan (Baptist) preacher, author of Grace Abounding (1666), A Christian's Progress (1678) and other publications

The Independents were led by Oliver Cromwell (1599-1658). Their ultimate victory was followed by the beheading of King Charles I (1649), and an episode of republican rule until 1660. This republic, or *Commonwealth* and *Protectorate* as it was later called, was the outcome of a revolutionary climate in which much radicalism flourished. It was also a time in which the knowledge of the Gospel was deepened and spread. At last the English majority got tired of the Protectorate. In 1660, some time after Oliver Cromwell's death, the Stuarts were called back. After this, *Restoration*, the new king, Charles II, could not resist the temptation of taking revenge for the murder of his father. Violent persecutions ensued which spread into Scotland. More than 2000 ministers were ejected from the Church of England (1662). The prisons were full of Dissenters. To them belonged the influential Baptist preacher and writer John Bunyan (1628-1688), whose books are reprinted and read even today (e.g. *The Pilgrim's Progress, Grace Abounding, The Holy War*).

William III of Orange (Stadhouder of The Netherlands), King of England from 1690, after the Glorious Revolution of 1688.

30.7. The Glorious Revolution

In 1685 James II became king of England. Secretly he had turned to Roman Catholicism. It was thought he wanted to bring the English Church back to Rome. This angered the ecclesiastical and political élite very much, and in 1688 he was dethroned. The Dutch leader '*Stadhouder*' William III of Orange, an able political and military defender of European Protestantism, was invited to become king of England. One of the positive consequences of this *Glorious Revolution* was the introduction of a considerable degree of freedom of religion in Britain.

31. Reformation in Scotland[1]

31.1. Antiquity and Middle Ages

The first Christians in Scotland were of the *Celtic* Church. The congregations were organised around monasteries, which were centres of preparation for missionary work. In the beginning missionaries like Ninian and Columba worked among the Scots, and then they set out for the European continent where they established churches at various places. Their church order differed from that of Rome. Abbots rather than bishops were the leaders of the church, and priests were allowed to marry. After 597 when Roman missionaries had come to Britain, the Celtic Church gradually lost much of its influence. In 664, at the *Synod of Whitby* the Northumbrian King Oswy adopted Catholicism. The Celts were disappointed. Throughout the Middle Ages the Church of Scotland maintained a relative independent attitude to the centre in Rome.

By the end of the Middle Ages, Scotland was still an independent country, ruled by the royal house of the Stuarts. The people had little knowledge of the Bible. Heretical teachings were rampant. Clergy and kings competed with one another for control of power and riches. There was also the movement of the *Lollards,* followers of John Wycliffe (†1384). They opposed the abuses in the Church of Rome, and rejected many of its teachings.

31.2. Patrick Hamilton, the Martyr

From 1520, books of Martin Luther the Church Reformer in Wittenberg, were found in Scotland. Also William Tyndale's Bible translation began to appear. The Stuart kings were not happy about this development. They did not accept any kind of Reformation, and in 1525 a decree was issued that banned Luther's books. Then, the government began to persecute and condemn all Christians who followed Luther's teachings.

Statue of John Knox (c.1513-1572), Reformer of Scotland.

The first to be martyred was Patrick Hamilton. His family belonged to the nobility. In his youth he became the abbot of a monastery. Later he went to Paris for studies, and learned the teachings of Luther. After his return to Scotland, he began to preach. But when he met with much opposition from the authorities he had to leave the country in order to avoid being arrested.

---

[1] Cairns, *Christianity through the Centuries*, pp.312-315; Dowley, 390-392; Renwick/Harman, 140-145; Paas, *Chikonzedwe*, mutu 10.

Hamilton went to Germany. In the city of Wittenberg he was taught by Luther, and there he also wrote a book on Christian doctrines. Because he longed to preach the Word to his own people, he went back to Scotland. Soon Hamilton was arrested. The Archbishop of St. Andrews accused him of preaching the doctrine of justification by faith alone. He was also accused of preaching against the teachings of Rome as to pilgrimages, purgatory, and praying for the dead. Finally, Hamilton was sentenced to death. In 1528, when he was only 24 years old, they burnt him at the stake.

31.3. The Death of George Wishart

The martyrdom of Patrick Hamilton fuelled the opposition against both the Church and the government. And this in its turn hardened the persecution of reform-minded people. King James V deposed Alexander Seton the preacher of the Gospel at his court. The king also ordered the death of David Straton because he had preached against the government. James V married a French woman belonging to the Roman Catholic nobility. This enlarged the power that the French government already had over Scotland. In 1542 when James V died, his daughter Mary Stuart was too young to be able to enforce her father's anti-Protestant policy. The ruling party stopped the heavy persecution of Protestants, and they allowed preaching and teaching the Bible.

But the political and military influence of France brought new persecutions. One of those who were martyred was George Wishart. He had taught Greek to students who were eager to understand the Bible in its original languages. When threatened by arrest, he escaped to England, then to the European continent where he visited cities like Strasbourg, Basel and Zürich. He especially favoured the Zwinglian Reformation. Then, he went back to England where he taught at the university of Cambridge. Finally, he returned to Scotland where he became a famous and beloved preacher. But he was betrayed to the government and arrested. In 1546 Archbishop James Beaton sentenced him to death by being burnt at the stake.

The death of Wishart brought about a spirit of rebellion among many people. Things came to a head when a group of Protestants threatened the palace of the archbishop. The leader of this group, James Melville, was killed, and the group escaped to St. Andrews Cathedral. There they tried to defend themselves against the surrounding royal army. One of the partakers in this rebellion was John Knox. After some weeks, the French army occupied the Cathedral. The rebellious group was deported to France, where they suffered in prisons. Some of them like John Knox became galley slaves for a time, chained to the benches and oars of navy ships having to row. The French government through some harsh laws tried to cut down the influence of the Reformation in Scotland.

31.4. John Knox in England

John Knox was a true and courageous witness of Jesus Christ. After being captured, he stood before the court of the archbishop and he proclaimed that Christ and not man is head of the Church. He also said that the celebration of mass is idolatry. During his time as a galley slave he tried to witness about Christ to fellow slaves. Knox was freed after 19 weeks, but did not go back to Scotland; instead, he went to England, to Berwick on Tweed which was very close to the Scottish border. There he worked as a minister of the Gospel, and there he also got married, to Marjorie Bowes. After that, he became a minister in Newcastle. In 1552 King Edward VI of England and Archbishop Thomas

Cranmer called for him to become *king's chaplain* at the royal court. He was also invited to help Cranmer in writing a new order for worship in the Church of England, the *Book of Common Prayers*. Knox's contribution to this book was the *Black Rubric*[2] a paragraph that dealt with the tradition of kneeling during Mass. Knox said that Mass had become the Lord's Supper now, and that kneeling at the table of the Lord is different from kneeling at Mass, which is idolatry.

31.5. John Knox in Geneva

When Queen Mary Tudor of England began to persecute the Protestants in 1553, John Knox and other leaders fled to Europe. Knox went to Geneva where he worked in cordial collaboration with John Calvin. He became minister of a congregation of people who had fled from England and Scotland. During his time in Geneva John Knox learned much about the ways in which Calvin had worked out the Reformation of the Church. Having in mind to apply his newly acquired insights to the Church at home, he wrote the *Book of Common Order*, also called the *Book of Geneva*, which was a Presbyterian order for church life. In due time the Church of Scotland would accept this book as its order. In 1558 Elizabeth I became queen of England. All refugees were free to return home. Only John Knox was not welcome in England anymore. Elizabeth did not want to have him back because he had written a book against the rule by women.[3] But Elizabeth could not prevent Knox from returning to Scotland. In 1559 he arrived in his home country.

31.6. John Knox, Reformer of the Church of Scotland

During this time members of the Scottish nobility concluded a covenant to defend the preaching of the Word of God against the ruler of the country, Mary of Lotharingen, the widow of King James V. This queen opposed the Reformation and in this she was backed by her home country France. In the meantime, in many cities and villages Reformed churches had been organised. But Mary refused to accept any change, and she continued persecuting the Protestants. The arrival of Knox strengthened the Reformation movement, but also the opposition by the government against it grew stronger. In 1560 soldiers from France conquered Scotland and the new queen, Mary Stuart, wife to King Francis II of France intensified the persecution of the followers of the Reformation. Although it faced strong opposition, the Church of the Reformation continued to grow. It was supported by the Parliament, which endorsed the *Scottish Confession*

John Knox, preaching to a meeting of elders.

---

[2] *Black Rubric*: These words in the *Book of Common Prayer*, which were printed in black letters, were removed after 1800.

[3] John Knox, *The First Blast of the Trumpet Against the Monstrous Regiment of Women*, 1558. The tract was meant to hit Mary of Guise and Mary Tudor.

of Faith, and proclaimed the end of the power of the Church of Rome. Knox was one of the writers of this creed. He also wrote *The Book of Discipline*, which regulates the life of church members and the preaching of the Church.

In 1560 the Protestant Church of Scotland was established. There were many problems. The new establishment was not accepted by Queen Mary Stuart. Knox and Mary were at loggerheads for years. She made treaties with Spain, France and the papacy to fight against the Protestants. Finally, this led to her impeachment by parliament. Then, Mary escaped to England. Soon she was arrested. After some years, she was accused of plotting against the English Queen Elizabeth, who had her executed. In the meantime, the work of organising the Church (Kirk) of Scotland according to the Presbyterianism order continued successfully. In Glasgow a university was established for the training of Reformed ministers. In the whole

John Knox's House, Edinburgh.

country the Church was shaped through the formation of various bodies of elders, *kirk sessions*, *presbyteries*, *regional synods*, and finally a *general assembly*.

31.7. Andrew Melville

In 1572 John Knox died. He was succeeded by Andrew Melville as leader of the Reformation movement. Melville (1545-1612) was an uncle of the early Scottish martyr James Melville (chapter 31.3). He studied and taught in Geneva and in other cities. First he became *Principal* of the University of Glasgow. He also wrote the Second *Book of Discipline* which differed from the First Book of Discipline written by Knox in that it put more emphasis on the power of the ministers and other elders. Melville often was chairman of the General Assembly. He openly opposed the policies of Scotland's new king, James VI, especially in 1584 when that king wanted to take all power over the Church and re-introduce a church government by bishops.

31.8. Kirk versus King

For more than a century the fortunes of Scottish Presbyterianism ebbed and flowed with the determination of the Stuart kings to make the Kirk episcopal. In 1603 the Scottish King James VI became James I of England, thus uniting the two countries. By this the conflict between king and Kirk became even more apparent. The conflict was brought to a head when, in 1637, King Charles I imposed the *Episcopacy* (= rule by bishops) and the *Book of Common Prayer* on the Scots. In 1638 the people concluded a *National Covenant* by which the imposed Episcopacy was swept away. In 1643 the Scots became party in the English Civil War; a *Solemn League and Covenant* was made with the English Presbyterian party who were temporarily influential in the *Long Parliament*. The Solemn League was to impose Presbyterianism throughout the British Isles, if necessary by the help of Scottish military power. This plan was supported by the *Westminster Assembly*. But it was not to happen.

The *Independents* under Cromwell took control of the country. They did away with Presbyterian political influence, and defeated the Scots. After the Restoration of the Stuarts in 1660, there was a period of harsh persecution, and *Episcopacy* was once more imposed. But at the *Glorious Revolution* (1688) and the ascendancy of King William III of Orange, the Scottish Church became Presbyterian again in 1690 and has remained so.

32. The Counter Reformation[1]

32.1. Terms

The term *Counter Reformation* was used for the first time by the German historian Von Ranke in 1843, when he described the Roman Catholic attempts to undo the effects of the 16th-century Reformation. When pointing this out, some also mention the terms *Catholic Reaction* and *Catholic Restoration*. These are negative designations. Other people use the positive term *Catholic Reformation*. They stress the activities for purifying the Roman Catholic Church of ethical abuses; some even observe in it a (re-) emergence of an Evangelical tendency in Rome; though not all adherents of this idea would accept the (Protestant) characteristics of Evangelicalism as such. Anyhow, a kind of revival and reform of the Roman Catholic Church began almost simultaneously with the Lutheran Movement.

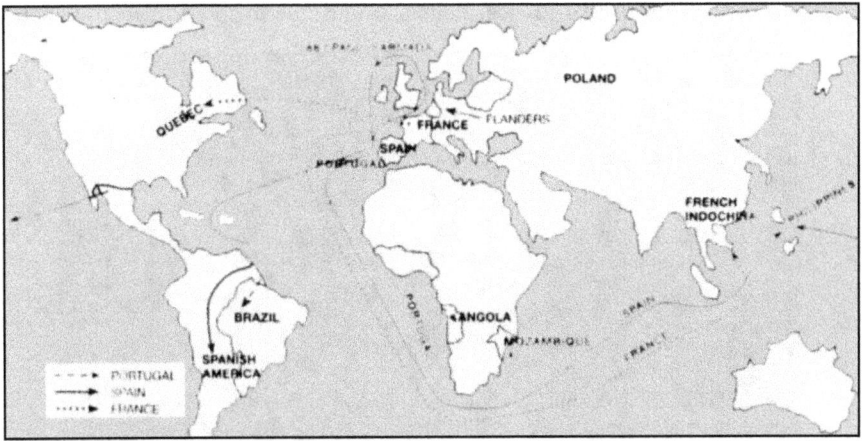

Roman Catholic Expansion in the 16th century.

The *Counter Reformation* can also be understood as part of the wider historical phenomenon of organised action to safeguard Roman Catholic political and religious interests. As such, its history begins far before the 16th-century Reformation era, and has not yet ended. Here we are restricting ourselves to the significance of the *Counter Reformation* in a narrower sense as it extended from the middle of the 16th century to the period of the *Thirty Years' War* (1618-1648), which was concluded by the *Peace Treaty of Westphalia/ Münster* in 1648. The Counter Reformation collaborated with the military and political power of the *Habsburg Empire* and other Roman Catholic states. Within Europe the greatest triumph of the movement was the re-conquest of certain countries and regions that initially had been won for the Reformation, e.g. Poland, Belgium and Southern Germany.

Here we mention some characteristics of the main 16th-century pillars of the Counter Reformation: the *Inquisition*, the *Council of Trent*, and the *Jesuits*.

---

[1] Cairns, *Christianity through the Centuries*, pp.337-349; Dowley, pp.410-428; Renwick/Harman, pp.146-149; Paas, *Chikonzedwe*, mutu 11.

32. The Counter Reformation

32.2. The Inquisition

The word denotes the judicial persecution of *heresy* by special ecclesiastical courts. The so called *Inquisition* came into being in 1232, and was initiated by the Italian Emperor and the Pope. Papal inquisitors were largely chosen from the newly founded orders of the *Dominicans* and *Franciscans*. If those accused of heresy refused to confess, they were tried before an inquisitor who was assisted by a jury of clerics and laymen. Penalties in grave cases were confiscation of goods, imprisonment, and surrender to the secular arm, which meant death at the stake. In 1542 Pope Paul III established the *Holy Office* as the final court of appeal in trials for heresy. In 1965 this court was changed into the *Congregation of the doctrine of the Faith* with the function of promoting and safeguarding Roman Catholic doctrine.

The *Inquisition* soon became notorious because of its cruelties against the Albigenses and the Waldenses. In the 16th century it strangled the incipient Protestantism in countries like Italy, and it contributed much to the rooting out of Protestantism in countries like France, Poland, and S. Germany. A special branch was

Council of Trent called by Pope Paul III; the Council ran from 1545 to 1563 with long breaks in between.

the *Spanish Inquisition*, established with papal approval in 1479. It was originally intended to deal with Spanish Jews and Muslims, later it served against Protestantism, in Spain itself, in The Netherlands, and in other regions. It was finally abolished in 1820.

32.3. Council of Trent

Although the medieval *Conciliar Movement* that wanted to change the ecclesiastical structure by subordinating papal power to a council of bishops had failed to reach its objectives, many Roman Catholic clerics and laymen desired a *General Council* that would introduce moral and administrative reforms in the church of Rome.

Generally, the leaders recognised that there were many abuses. An investigation by some cardinals in 1538 revealed so many shocking details that the *Curia* decided not to publish the report that was made. It incriminated even the Pope, saying that the papacy itself was the source of all abuses. The main challenge that led to the demand for a General Council was the spread of Protestantism. The disputations between Roman Catholics and Protestants, with contributions by members of the *Curia* and Reformers like Bucer and Melanchthon, had created a hope that the Protestants might be led back to Rome if some of their grievances were taken away. Religious unity would be especially in the interest of the Habsburg Emperor Charles V and the French King Francis I who feared political instability. At last Habsburg initiatives convinced the Pope to summon a General Council. It eventually met for the first time at Trent in 1545. There were three session periods between 1545 and 1563. The majority of the members were Italians, and no Protestants took part.

The *first session* upheld the authority of tradition besides Scripture, and the sole authority of the Church (i.e. the clerical hierarchy, and in the last analysis the Pope) to interpret the Bible. Decrees on original sin, justification and merit (*indulgences*) were not to be reconciled with Protestant beliefs.

The *second session* maintained the doctrine of transubstantiation and the mass as a sacrifice, while repudiating Lutheran, Zwinglian and Calvinist eucharistic doctrines.

The *third and last session* affirmed the denial of the Eucharist's vessel to the laity, and defined the sacrificial character of the mass. It also decided that a revision of the Vulgate (Roman Catholic Bible translation in Latin), and the publication of a catechism ought to be made. Trent issued a number of *anathemata* (= curses, derived from *1 Cor. 16:22*) by which the Protestant doctrines on justification, sacraments, church government, etc. were utterly condemned. These condemnations have never been withdrawn. In Trent the Roman Catholic Church reinstalled the order and discipline which it needed to regain part of its lost influence. But at the same time, in Trent the Roman Catholic Church closed the door for real Reformation. The last session of the Council of Trent 'sealed the triumph of the papacy both over those Catholics who wished for conciliation with the Protestants, and over those bishops who had opposed papal claims'.

32.4. The Jesuits

The Society of Jesus (*Societas Jesu* = S.J.) was founded in 1534 (approved by the Pope in 1540) by a Spanish nobleman and army officer Ignatius de Loyola, who got crippled in war and subsequently decided to devote his life and energies to Mary. He studied in Paris at College de Montaigu, shortly after Calvin had been there, and at a number of universities. He gave his order a military organisation form, with himself as the general. This spiritual army had to subordinate itself unconditionally to the Pope. By *spiritual exercises* new members were trained to absolute obedience. The order developed a twofold aim: to counter the Reformation, and to undertake missionary work. Jesuits were educated at high levels

Ignatius de Loyola (1491/5-1556), Spanish nobleman and former military officer, who became founder of the Order of the Jesuits (Societas Jesu).

32. The Counter Reformation

in various fields so that they could be used in key positions, for example as advisers at the royal courts of Europe, or as lecturers at universities. They undertook a variety of tasks arising from the Reformation crisis, for example teaching, conducting catechisms, administering the sacraments. Others deployed missionary activities in countries like India, Malaysia, the Congo, Brazil, Japan, Ethiopia, and China.

In the 17th-century countries like France, Portugal and Spain banished the Jesuits for various reasons; in 1773 the order was even suppressed by the Pope. But in some countries they continued their activities sometimes with and sometimes without the permission of the governments. In 1814 the Pope formally restored the *Societas Jesu*.

Spread of the Confessions by the end of the 16th century.

Bibliography: Reformation

a. General

Adams, H.M. (compiler), *Catalogue of Books Printed on the Continent of Europe 1501-1600* [2 vols], Cambridge UP, 1967.

Anderson, C.S., *Augsburg Historical Atlas of Christianity in the Middle Ages and Reformation*, Minneapolis: Augsburg, 1967.

Bainton, R.H. (ed), *Bibliography of the Continental Reformation*, Hamden: Archon, 1972².

Bainton, R.H., *The Reformation of the Sixteenth Century*, Boston: Beacon, 1953.

Bainton, R.H., *The Age of the Reformation*, Princeton: Nostrand, 1956.

Bainton, R.H., *Women of the Reformation*, 3 vols, Minneapolis: Augsburg, 1971-1977.

Black, A., *Council and Commune: The Conciliar Movement and the 15th-century Heritage*, London: Burns & Oates, 1979.

Bodenkotter, T., *A Concise History of the Catholic Church*, New York, 2005 [first 1979].

Bossy, J., *Christianity in the West 1400-1700*, Oxford UP, 1985.

Bradley, *Handbook of European History 1400-1600*, Leyden: Brill, 1996.

Buck, L.P., and J.W. Zophy (eds), *The Social History of the Reformation*, Columbus: Ohio State UP, 1972.

Cameron, E., *The European Reformation*, Oxford UP, 2012 [first 1991].

Chadwick, O., *The Reformation*, Harmondsworth: Penguin, 1964.

Cheetham, S., *A History of the Christian Church since the Reformation*, London: Macmillan, 1907.

Clark, G.N., *Early Modern Europe from about 1450 to about 1720*, London: Oxford UP, 1957.

Dickens, A.G., *Reformation and Society in Sixteenth-century Europe*, London: Thames and Hudson, 1966.

Dickens, A.G., J.M. Tonkin, and K. Powell, *The Reformation in Historical Thought*, Cambridge (Mass.): Harvard, 1985.

Dobson, R.B. (ed), *Church, Politics, and Patronage in the 15th Century*, Gloucester: Alan Sutton, 1984.

Douglass, E.J.D., *Justification in Late Medieval Preaching: A Study of John Geiler of Keisersberg*, Leyden: Brill, 1966.

Eisenstein, E., *The Printing Press as an Agent of Change*, (2 vols), Cambridge UP, 1979.

Febre, L., and H.J. Martin, *The Coming of the Book:The Impact of Printing, 1450-1800* (transl.), London: New Left Books, 1976.

Elton, G.H. (ed), *The New Cambridge Modern History*, vol. II, Cambridge UP, 1958.

Estep, W.R., *Renaissance and Reformation*, Grand Rapids: Eerdmans, 1986.

Ferguson, W.H., *The Renaissance in Historical Thought: Five Centuries of Interpretation*, Toronto 2006 [first Cambridge (Mass): Riverside, 1948].

Ferm, V.T.A., *Pictorial History of Protestantism: A panoramic view of Western Europe and the United States*, New York: Philosophical Library, 1957.

Fosdick, H.E., *Great Voices of the Reformation*, New York: Random House, 1952.

Gelder H.A.E., van, *The Two Reformations*, The Hague: Nijhoff, 1964.

Green, V.H.H., *Renaissance and Reformation*, London: Edward Arnold 1952.

Greengrass, M., *The European Reformation c. 1500-1618*, London: Longman, 1998.

Greyerz von, K.(ed.), *Religion and Society in Early Modern Europe 1500-1800*, London, 1984.

Grimm, H.J., *The Reformation Era 1500-1650*, New York: Macmillan, 1973².

Heintschel, D.E., *The Medieval Concept of an Ecclesiastical Office*, Washington: Catholic University, 1956.

Hillerbrand, H.J., *The Reformation in its Own Words* [selection from sources], London: SCM, 1964.

Hillerbrand, H.J., *The Protestant Reformation*, New York/ London: Harper and Row, 1968.

Hughes, Ph., *A Popular History of the Reformation* [a Roman Catholic view], New York Garden City: Double Day, 1960.

Hyma, A., *Renaissance to Reformation*, Grand Rapids: Eerdmans, 1951.

Jones, R.T., *The great Reformation: from Wyclif to Knox : two centuries that changed the course of history*, Leicester: Inter-Varsity, 1985.

Kidd, B.J., *Documents Illustrative to the Continental Reformation*, Oxford: Clarendon, 1911.

Kidd, B.J., *The Medieval Doctrine of the Eucharistic Sacrifice*, London: SPCK, 1958.

Kingdon, R.M. (ed), *Transition and Revolution: Problems and Issues of European Renaissance and Reformation*, Minneapolis: Burgess, 1974.

Leonard, E.G., *A History of Protestantism* [transl. from French by J.H.M. Reid and R.M. Bethel; ed. By H.H. Rowley], 2 vols, London, 1965-1967.

Lindsay, Th., *A History of the Reformation* (2 vols), Freeport: Books for Libraries Press, 1972 [first New York 1906-1907].

Lucas, H.S., *The Renaissance and the Reformation*, New York: Harper and Row, 1960^2.

Manschreck, C.L. (ed), *A History of Christianity: Readings in the History of the Church from the Reformation to the Present*, Eagle Wood Cliffs: Prentice Hall, 1964.

McGrath, A.E., *The Intellectual Origins of the European Reformation*, Oxford: Blackwell, 1987.

McGrath, A.E., *Reformation Thought: An Introduction*, Oxford: Blackwell, 1990^2.

McKim, D.K. (ed.), *Encyclopedia of the Reformed Faith*, Louisville: Westminster/ John Knox Press & Edinburgh: T&T Clark, 1992.

Molen de, R.L. (ed), *The Meaning of Renaissance and Reformation*, Boston, 1974.

Latourette, Kenneth Scott, *A History of the Expansion of Christianity*, 7 volumes [vol.III: 1500-1800], New York: Harper 2006 (digital).

Monter, E.W., *Ritual, Myth and Magic in Early Modern Europe*, Brighton: Harvester, 1983.

Norwood, F.A., *The Development of Modern Christianity since 1500*, New York: Abington, 1956.

Oakley, F., *The Western Church in the Later Middle Ages*, New York: Ithaca/ London, 1979.

Oberman, A.A., *The Harvest of Medieval Theology: Gabriel Biel and Late Medieval Nominalism*, Cambridge (Mass.): Harvard, 1963.

Oberman, H.A., *Forerunners of the Reformation: The Shape of Late Medieval Thought, Illustrated by Key Documents*, Philadelphia: Fortress, 1981.

Oberman, H.A. (Ed.), *Masters of the Reformation: The Emergence of a New Intellectual Climate in Europe*, Cambridge UP, 1981.

Ozment, S.E. (ed), *Reformation Europe: A Guide to Research* [Collection of bibliographical essayson Reformation and Reformation society], St. Louis, Mo, 1982.

Ozment, S.E., *The Reformation in the Cities: The Appeal of Protestantism to 16th-century Germany and Switzerland*, New Haven/London: Yale, 1975.

Post, R.R., *The Modern Devotion: Confrontation with Reformation and Humanism*, Leyden: Brill, 1968.

Reardon, B.M.G., *Religious Thought in the Reformation*, London: Longman, 1981.

Roerig, F., *The Medieval Town*, London: Batsford, 1967.

Rupp, E.G., *Patterns of Reformation*, London: Epsworth, 1969.

Schaff, Ph., *The Creeds of Christendom* (3 vols), New York: Harper, 1890^6.

Shaw, I.P., *Nationality and the Western Church before the Reformation*, London: SPCK, 1959.

Smyth, P., *The Age of the Reformation*, New York: Holt, 1920.

Southern, R.W., *Western Society and the Church in the Middle Ages*, Harmondsworth: Penguin, 1970.

Spitz, L.W., *The Renaissance and Reformation Movements*, Chicago: Rand McNally, 1971.

Spitz, L.W., *The Protestant Reformation 1517-1559*, New York: Harper, 1985.

Spitz, L.W., *The Reformation: Basic Interpretation*, Lexington (Mass.): Heath, 1972^2.

Spykman, G.J., *Reformational Theology: A New Paradigm for Doing Dogmatics*, Grand Rapids: Eerdmans, 1992.

Tawney, *Religion and the Rise of Capitalism*, London, 1926 [republished Mentor, 1953 and Peter Smith, 1962].

Taylor, H.O., *Thought and Expression in the Sixteenth Century*, 2 vols, New York: Macmillan, 1920.

Thomson, A., *New Movements: Reform, Rationalism, Revolution 1500-1800*, London: SPCK, 1976.

Thomson, J.A.F., *Popes and Princes 1417-1517: Politics and Piety in the Late Medieval Church*, London: Allen & Unwin, 1980.

Tintler, T.N., *Sin and Confession on the Eve of the Reformation*, Princeton UP (NJ), 1977.

Todd, J.M., *The Reformation*, London: Darton, Longman and Todd, 1972.

Trinkaus, C., and H.A. Oberman (eds), *The Pursuit of Holiness in Late Medieval and Renaissance Religion*, Leyden: Brill, 1974.

Ullmann, K.H., *Reformers before the Reformation* (transl., 2 vols), Edinburgh: T&T Clark, 1855.

Weber, M., *The Protestant Ethic and the Spirit of Capitalism* (transl. T. Parsons, New York: Scribner's, 1958.

Books on Microfilm

Center for Reformation Research, 6477 San Bonita Ave., St. Louis, MO 63105, U.S.A. The Center has about 10, 000 items in microform, including both manuscripts and printed sources, pertaining to the late medieval period and the Reformation, and these are available through interlibrary loan. Besides, the magisterial reformers, the collection includes works of some Catholic theologians and leaders of the Radical Reformation.[1]

General Microfilm Company, 70 Coolidge Hill Road, Watertown, MA 02172, U.S.A. This company has a very large collection of books dated before 1701 that is international in scope', including a collection 'with a focus on Catholic responses to the Protestant Reformation.

Inter Documentation Company, P. O. Box 11205, 2301 EE Leyden, The Netherlands. This is 'one of the world's leading publishers on rare documents in microfiche, with major collections on the Protestant Reformation'

Websites

Bibliography Secondary Sources, http://www.prdl.org/secondary.php

Calvin College Library, http://library.calvin.edu/

Christian History Institute: The Reformation, https://www.christianhistoryinstitute.org/study/era/reformation/

Christianity Today: Early Modern Age, http://www.christianitytoday.com/ch/byperiod/earlymodern

---

[1] J. E., Bradley and R. A. Muller, *Church History: An Introduction to Research, Reference Works, and Methods*, Grand Rapids: Eerdmans, 1995, pp.220-223.

Fire and Ice, www.puritansermons.com/toc.htm
Hall of Church History: The Reformers, http://www.spurgeon.org/~phil/rformers.htm
Johannes a Lasco Bibliothek http://www.jalb.de/7389-0-0-43.html
Refo500 [platform for knowledge, expertise, ideas, products and events, specializing in the 500 year legacy of the Reformation], http://www.refo500.nl/en/pages/212/what-is-refo500.htmlRefo500
(Post-) Reformation Digital Library: http://www.prdl.org/
Reformation Ink, http://truekingdom.org/shanerosenthal/reformationink/classic.htm
Reformation Texts, http://legacy.fordham.edu/halsall/sbook2.asp#ref2
Sixteenth Century Primary Sources, http://www.reformationresearch.org/Links.htm

b. Martin Luther

Primary sources

(Luther Martin) *Luther's Works* [55 vols], ed. by J. Pelikan, J., and H.T. Lehmann, Philadelphia/St.Louis: Concordia, 1955.

(Luther, Martin) in: Baillie, J., J.T. McNeill, and H. P. van Dusen (eds), *The Library of Christian Classics*, Philadelphia: Westminster, 1953-1967, vols 15-18 (works of Luther), vol 19 (works of Melanchthon).

Luther, Martin, *Bondage of the Will: Selections from his Writings*, Dillenberg: Anchor, 1962.

Luther, Martin, *Table Talks*, Philadelphia, 1967.

Secondary Sources

Aland, K., *Martin Luther's 95 Theses*, St. Louis: Concordia, 1994.

Althaus, P., *The Theology of Martin Luther* [transl.], Philadelphia: Fortress, 1966.

Atkinson, J. (ed), *Luther: Early Theological Works*, Philadelphia: Westminster, 1962.

Bainton, R.H., *Here I stand: A Biography of Martin Luther*, Lion Publishing 1983 [first 1950]

Bainton, R.H., *Erasmus of Christendom*, New York: Scribner, 1969.

Bak, J. (ed), *The German Peasant War of 1525*, London: Allen & Unwin, 1979².

Bergendorff, C., *Olaus Petri and the Ecclesiastical Reformation in Sweden*, New York, 1928.

Bigane, J., and K. Hagen, *Annotated Bibliography of Luther Studies 1967-1976*, St. Louis: Center for Reformation Research, 1977.

Boehmer, H., *Martin Luther: Road to Reformation* (transl.), Philadelphia: Muhlenberg, 1946.

Bornkamm G., *Luther in Mid-Career 1521-1530*, London: Darton, Longman & Todd, 1983.

Brecht, Martin. *Martin Luther* [Transl. James L. Schaaf], 3 Volumes. Philadelphia: Fortress, 1985-1993.

Carlson, E., *The Reinterpretation of Luther*, Philadelphia: Westminster, 1948.

Cargyill Thompson, W.D.J., *The Political Thought of Martin Luther*, Brighton: Harvester, 1984.

Davies, R.E., *The Problem of Authority in the Continental Reformers: A study in Luther, Zwingli, and Calvin*, London, 1946.

Dempsey, D.E.J., *Justification in Late Medieval Preaching: A Study of John Geiler of Keisersberg*, Leyden: Brill, 1966.

Dickens, A.G., *The German Nation and Martin Luther*, London: Edward Arnold, 1974.

Dickerson, G.F. (ed.), *Luther and Lutheranism: A Bibliography Selected from ATLA Religion Database*, Chicago, 1982.

Drummond, A.L., *German Protestantism since Luther*, London: Epworth, 1951.

Dunkley, E.H., *The Reformation in Denmark*, London: SPCK, 1948.

Ebeling, G., *Luther, an Introduction to his Thought* (transl.), London: Collins, 1970.
Edwards, M.U., *Luther and the False Brethren*, Stanford UP (Cal.), 1975.
Edwards, M.U., *Luther's Last Battles*, Leyden: Brill, 1983.
Fife, R.H., *The Revolt of Martin Luther*, New Yorkolumbia UP, 1957.
Gerrish, B.A., *Grace and Reason: A Study in the Theology of Luther*, Oxford: Clarendon 1962.
Gerrish, B.A., 'Priesthood and Ministry in the Theology of Luther', in: *Church History* 34 (1965), pp.404-422.
Green, L.C., 'Luther Research in English-Speaking Countries since 1971', in: *Lutherjahrbuch* (Organ der internationalen Lutherforschung), 44 (1977), pp.105-126.
Green, V.H.H., *Luther and the Reformation*, London/ New York: Batsford & Putnam, 1964.
Grossmann, M., *Humanism in Wittenberg 1485-1517*, Nieuwkoop, Der Graaf, 1975.
Hagen, K., and F. Possett, *Annotated Bibliography of Luther Studies 1977-1983*, St. Louis Center for Reformation Research, 1985.
Harran, M.J., *Luther on Conversion: The Early Years*, Ithaca: Cornell UP, 1983.
Kerr, H.Th. (ed.), *A Compendium of Luther's Theology*, Philadelphia: Westminster, 1943.
Lohse, B., *Martin Luther: An Introduction to his Life and Thought*, [transl.], Edinburgh: T & T Clark, 1987.
Lortz, J., *The Reformation in Germany* [transl. by R. Walls], 2 vols, London/ New York: Herder & Herder, 1968.
Manschreck, C.L., *Melanchthon: the Quiet Reformer*, New York: Abingdon, 1958.
Manschreck, C.L. (ed), *Melanchthon on Christian Doctrine: Loci Communes 1555*, New York: Oxford UP, 1965.
Mc Donough, Th. M., *The Law and the Gospel in Luther*, London: Oxford UP, 1963.
McGrath, A.E., *Luther's Theology of the Cross*, London/ Oxford: Blackwell, 1985.
Oberman, H.A., *Luther: Man between God and the Devil*, New Haven: Yale, 1986.
Ozment, S.E., *Homo Spiritualis: A Comparative Study of the Anthropology of Johannes Tauler, Jean Gerson, and Martin Luther 1509-1516 in the Context of their Theological Thought*, Leyden: Brill, 1969.
Pegg, M.A.A., *Catalogue of German Reformation Pamphlets 1516-1546*, Baden-Baden: Koerner, 1973.
Ruff, E.G., and B. Drenz (eds), *Martin Luther* [sources], London, 1970.
Schoenberger, C.G., 'The Development of the Lutheran Theory of Resistance 1523-1530', in: *Sixteenth-century Journal VIII*, 1 (1977), pp.61-76.
Schweibert, E.G., *Luther and his Times:The Reformation from a New Perspective*, St. Louis (Miss.): Concordia, 1950.
Scribner, R.W., *The German Reformation*, London: Macmillan, 1986.
Sider, R.J., *Andreas Bodenstein von Karlstadt: The Development of his Thought 1517-1525*, Leyden: Brill, 1974.
Siggins, I.D.K., *Martin Luther's Doctrine of Christ*, New Haven (Conn.): Yale UP, 1970.
Skarsten, T.R., *The Scandinavian Reformation: A Bibliographical Guide*, St. Louis: Center for Reformation Research, 1985.
Smyth, P., *The Life and Letters of Martin Luther*, New York: Houghton Miflin, 1911.
Steinmetz, D.C., *Luther and Staupitz: An Essay in the Intellectual Origins of the Protestant Reformation*, Durham (DC): Duke UP, 1980.
Straus, G., *Manifestoes of Discontent in Germany on the Eve of the Reformation*, Bloomington: Indiana UP, 1972.
Stupperich, R., *Melanchthon* [transl.], Philadelphia: Westminster, 1966.

Surburg, Raymond, F., 'Luther and the Christology of the Old Testament', Reformation Lectures at Bethany Lutheran Theological Seminary, 28-29 October 1982, Internet [Raymond F. Surburg, 'The Significance of Luther's Hermeneutics for the Protestant Reformation', in: *Concordia Theological Monthly*, 24, p.241-261, April, 1953].

Tillman, W.G., *The World and Men Around Luther*, Minneapolis/Augsburg: Concordia, 1959.

Watson, E.P., *Let God be God: An Interpretation of the Theology of Martin Luther*, London: Epworth, 1947.

Websites

Luther's Works Online, http://www.angelfire.com/ny4/djw/lutherantheology.lutherswritings.html
Luther Online, http://onlinebooks.library.upenn.edu/webbin/book/lookupname?key=Luther%2C%20Martin%2C%201483-1546
Luther: Selected Works, http://www.iclnet.org/pub/resources/text/wittenberg/wittenberg-luther.html
Project Wittenberg, http://www.projectwittenberg.org/
Luther: Sermons, Commentaries etc. http://www.godrules.net/library/luther/luther.htm

c. Huldrych Zwingli

Primary sources

(Zwingli, Huldrych in:) Baillie, J., J.T.McNeill, and H.P. van Dusen (eds), *The Library of Christian Classics*, Philadelphia: Westminster, 1953-1967, [26 vols], vol. 24: works of Zwingli and Bullinger.

Secondary Sources

Courvoisier, J., *Zwingli, a Reformed Theologian*, Richmond: John Knox, 1963.
Farner, O., *Zwingli the Reformer* [transl.by D.G. Sear], London: Archon, 1952.
Gaebler, U., *Huldrych Zwingli: His Life and Work* [transl.], Philadelphia: Fortress, 1986.
Harding, H. (ed.), *The Decades of Henry Bullinger* [transl.], 4 vols, Cambridge UP, 1849-1852.
Jackson, S.M. (et al. eds.), *Huldreich Zwingli*, 3 vols, New York: Putnam, 1912.
Locher, G.W., *Zwingli's Thought: New Perspectives*, Studies in the History of Christian Thought, 25, Leyden: Brill, 1981.
Pipkin, H.W.A., *Zwingli Bibliography*, Pittsburgh UP, 1972.
Potter, G.R., *Zwingli*, Cambridge UP, 1976.
Rilliet, J.H., *Zwingli, Third Man of the Reformation* [transl.], Philadelphia: Westminster, 1964.
Stephens, W.P., *The Theology of Huldrych Zwingli*, Oxfordlarendon, 1986.
Walton, R.C., *Zwingli's Theocracy*, Toronto UP, 1967.

Websites

Huldrych Zwingli: Werke, http://www.irg.uzh.ch/static/zwingli-werke/
Huldrych Zwingli: Selected Works, http://oll.libertyfund.org/titles/1682

d. Martin Bucer

Primary Sources

(Bucer, Martin in:) Baillie, J., J.T. McNeill, and H.P. van Dusen, (eds), *The Library of Christian Classics*, Philadelphia: Westminster, 1953-1967, [26 vols], vol. 19 works of Bucer.

Secondary Sources

Brady, T.A., *Ruling Class, Regime and Reformation at Strassbourg 1520-1555*, Leyden: Brill, 1978.

Chrisman, M.U., *Strassbourg and the Reform, a Study in the Process of Change*, London./ New Haven (Conn), Yale UP, 1967.

Chrisman, M.U., *Lay Culture, Learned Culture: Books and Social Change in Strassbourg 1480-1599*, New Haven (Conn.): Yale UP, 1982.

Chrisman, M.U., *Bibliography of Strassbourg Imprints 1489-1599*, New Haven (Conn.): Yale UP, 1982.

Collinson, P., 'Martin Bucer and an English Bucerian', in: Idem, *Godly People: Essays on English Protestantism and Puritanism*, London: Hambledon, 1983.

Eells, H., 'Martin Bucer and the Conversion of John Calvin', in: *The Princeton Theological Review* 22 (1924), 402-419.

Eells, H., *Martin Bucer*, New Haven/London: Yale UP, 1931.

Harvey, E., *Martin Bucer in England*, Marburg: Bauer, 1906.

Hazlett, I., *The Development of Martin Bucer's Thinking on the Sacrament of the Lord's Supper in its Historical and Theological Context 1523-1534*, Westfälische Wilhelms-Universität zu Münster, 1975.

Hopf, C., *Martin Bucer and the English Reformation*, Oxford: Blackwell, 1946.

Krahn, H.G., 'Martin Bucer's Strategy against Sectarian Dissent in Strassbourg'. In: *Mennonite Quarterly Review* 50 (1976), pp.163-180.

Kroon de, M., 'Martin Bucer and the Problem of Tolerance', in: *Sixteenth-century Journal* 19 (1988), pp.157-168.

Littell, F.H., 'New Light on Butzer's Significance', in: *Reformation Studies in honour of R. H. Bainton*, Richmond, 1962.

Paas, Steven, *A Conflict on the Church and the Sacraments: How Rome and the Reformation Differed at Regensburg in 1541*, Zomba: Kachere, 2006.

Poll, G.J. van de, *Martin Bucer's liturgical ideas*, Assen: Van Gorcum, 1954.

Selderhuis, H.J., *Marriage and Divorce in the Thought of Martin Bucer* [transl. by John Vriend and Lyle Bierma], Sixteenth-century Essays and Studies vol.48, Kirksville Mo: Thomas Jefferson UP, 1999.

Selderhuis, Herman J. and J. Marius J. Lange van Ravenswaay (eds), *Reformed Majorities in Early Modern Europe*, vol.23 of Refo500 Academic Studies Series, Göttingen, Vandenhoeck & Ruprecht, 2015.

Stafford, W.S., *Domesticating the Clergy: The Inception of the Reformation in Strassbourg 1522-1524*, Missoula (Mont.): Scholars Press, 1976.

Spijker van 't, W., *The Ecclesiastical Offices in the Thought of Martin Bucer* (Translated by John Vriend and Lyle D. Bierma), Leyden: Brill, 1996.

Stephens, W.P., *The Role of the Holy Spirit in the Theology of Martin Bucer*, London: Cambridge UP, 1970.

Stalnaker, J.C., Anabaptism, 'Martin Bucer, and the Shaping of the Hessian Protestant Church', in: *The Journal of Modern History* 48 (1976), pp.601-643.

Whitaker, E.C., *Martin Bucer and the Book of Common Prayer*, Great Wakering: Mayhew-McCrimmon, 1974.

Wright, D.F. (ed. and transl.), *Common Places of Martin Bucer*, Abingdon: Sutton Courtenay Press, 1971.

Websites

Martin Bucer on the Internet, https://sites.google.com/site/bucerforfree/
(Post-) Reformation Digital Library: Bucer, http://www.prdl.org/author_view.php?a_id=173
Works by and about Martin Bucer: Internet Archive.

e. John Calvin

Primary Sources

(Calvin, John in:) Baillie, J., J.T. McNeill, and H.P. van Dusen, (eds), *The Library of Christian Classics*, Philadelphia: Westminster, 1953-1967 [26 vols], vols 20-23: transl. works of Calvin.

(Calvin, John in:) Banner of Truth Trust (ed. and transl.), *Letters of John Calvin Selected from the Bonnet Edition*, Edinburgh, 1980.

Calvin, John, *Institutes of the Christian Religion* [transl.], ed. Battles/McNeill, Philadelphia: Westminster, 1960.

Secondary Sources[2]

Battles, F.L., and A.M. Hugo, *Calvin's Commentary on Seneca's De Clementia*, Leyden: Brill, 1969.

Beeke, J.R., *The Quest for full Assurance: The Legacy of Calvin and his Successors*, Edinburgh: The Banner of Truth Trust, 1999.

Bratt, J.H. (ed), *The Heritage of John Calvin*, Grand Rapids: Eerdmans, 1973.

Douglas, R.M., *Jacopo Sadoleto, Humanist and Reformer*, Cambridge: Harvard, 1959.

Duffield, G. (ed), *John Calvin*, Appleford, Abingdon (Berks.): Sutton Courtenay Press. 1966.

Ganoczy, A., *The Young Calvin* [transl. D. Foxgrover and W. Provo], Edinburgh:T&T Clark, 1987.

Graham, W.F., *The Constructive Revolutionary: John Calvin and his Socio-Economic Impact*, Richmond: John Knox, 1971.

Henderson, R.W., *The Teaching Office in the Reformed Tradition: A History of the Doctoral Ministry*, Philadelphia: Heppe, nd.

Hoepfl, H., *The Christian Polity of John Calvin*, Cambridge UP, 1982.

Hughes, Ph. E. (ed), *The Register of the Company of Pastors in Geneva in the Time of Calvin* [transl.], Grand Rapids: Eerdmans, 1966.

Hunt, R. N., *Calvin*, London: Centenary Press, 1933.

Johnson, E. M., *Man of Geneva: The Story of John Calvin*, Edinburgh: The Banner of Truth Trust, 1977.

Kuiper, H., *Calvin on Common Grace*, Goes: Oosterbaan & Le Cointre, 1928.

McGrath, A.E., *Life of John Calvin: A Study of the Shaping of Western Culture*, Oxford: Blackwell, 1996.[4]

McNeill, J.T., *The History and Character of Calvinism*, London: Oxford UP, 1964[2].

Mueller, W.A., *Church and State in Luther and Calvin*, Nashville: Broadman, 1954.

Niesel, Wilhelm., *The Theology of Calvin* [transl. by Harold Knight], Philadelphia: Westminster, 1956.

Parker, T.H.L., *Calvin's Doctrine of the Knowledge of God*, Edinburgh: Oliver and Boyd, 1969.

Parker, T.H.L., *John Calvin, a Biography*, London/Philadelphia: Westminster, 1975.

---

[2] Calvin Bibliography: *Calvin Theological Journal* [published semiannually, in April and November by Calvin Theological Seminary in Grand Rapids] – the bibliography is in no 2 of each year; Kempff, D., *A Bibliography of Calviana 1959-1974*, Leyden: Brill, 1975.

Potter, G.R., and M. Greengrass (eds), *John Calvin* [sources], London: Edward Arnold, 1983.

Reid, W.S. (ed), *John Calvin: His Influence in the Western World:* Contemporary Evangelical Perspectives, Grand Rapids: Zondervan, 1982.

Revesz, J., *Hungarian Protestantism: Its Past, Present and Future*, Budapest: Bethlen Gabor, 1927.

Reyburn, H.Y., *John Calvin: his life, letters and work,* London: Hodder and Stoughton, 1914.

Torrance, T.F., *Calvin's Doctrine of Man*, London: Lutterworth, 1949.

Walker, W., *John Calvin, the Organiser of Reformed Protestantism 1509-1564*, London/ New York: Schocken Books, 1972[2].

Wallace, R. S., *Calvin, Geneva and the Reformation: A Study of Calvin as Social Reformer, Churchman, Pastor and Theologian*, Edinburgh: Scottish Academic Press, 1988.

Wendel, F., *Calvin: The Origins and Development of his Religious Thought* [transl.], Grand Rapids: Eedmans, 1997[4.]

Websites

Christian Classics Ethereal Library: Calvin's Commentaries, http://www.ccel.org/ccel/calvin/commentaries.i.html

Internet Sacred Texts Archive, http://sacred-texts.com/chr/calvin/index.htm

The Complete Works of John Calvin, http://www.godrules.net/library/calvin/calvin.htm

The Hall of Church History: Calvin's Institutes, http://www.spurgeon.org/~phil/calvin/

f. John Knox

Primary Sources

Laing, D. (ed), *Works of John Knox,* 6 vols, Edinburgh: Wodrow Society, 1846-1864.

Secondary Sources

Brown, P.H., *John Knox: A Biography*, 2 vols, London: Black, 1895.

Cowan, H., *John Knox: Hero of the Scottish Reformation*, London/ New York: Putnam, 1905.

Dickinson, W.C. (ed), Knox, John, *History of the Reformation of Scotland*, 2 vols [ed. by W.C. Dickinson] New York: Thomas and Nelson, 1950.

MacGregor, G., *The Thundering Scott: A Portrait of John Knox,* Philadelphia: Westminster, 1957.

Percy, R., *John Knox*, London: Hodder and Stoughton, 1937.

Ridley, J., *John Knox*, Oxford UP, 1968.

Websites

Andrew Lang, *John Knox and the Reformation*, http://www.gutenberg.org/files/14016/14016-h/14016-h.htm

Project Gutenberg, The Works of John Knox, http://www.gutenberg.org/files/21938/21938-h/21938-h.htm

John Knox: Free Online, http://www.sermonaudio.com/new_details3.asp?ID=7807

g. Radical Reformers

Primary Sources

Baillie, J., J.T. McNeill, and H.P. van Dusen, (eds), *The Library of Christian Classics,* Philadelphia: Westminster, *1953-1967*, vol. 26 [works of Spiritualists and Anabaptists].

(Huebmaier, Balthasar in:) Davidson, G.D. (ed.), *The Writings of Balthasar Huebmaier*, 3 vols, Liberty (Mo.): William Jewell College, 1939.

(Muentzer, Thomas in:) Matheson, P. (ed), *The Collected Works of Thomas Muentzer* [transl.], Edinburgh & T Clark, 1988.

(Simons, Menno in:), J. C. Wenger (ed), The Complete Writings of Menno Simons, c. 1496-1561 [transl. Leonard Verduin], Scottdale, PA: Herald.

Secondary Sources

Armour, R.S., *Anabaptist Baptism: A Representative Study*, Scottdale, PA: Herald, 1966.

Baillie, J., J.T. McNeill, and H.P. van Dusen, (eds), *The Library of Christian Classics*, Philadelphia: Westminster, *1953-1967*, vol. 26 [works of Spiritualists and Anabaptists].

Bax, E.B., *The Rise and Fall of the Anabaptists*, New York: Kelley 1970 [reprint 1903 original].

Bender, H.S., *Conrad Grebel c. 1498-1526, the Founder of the Swiss Brethren, sometimes Called Anabaptists*, Goshen: Mennonite Historical Library, 1950.

Bergstren, T., *Balthasar Hubmaier, Anabaptist Theologian and Martyr* [transl.], Valley Forge: Judson, 1978.

Blanke, F., *Brothers in Christ: The History of the Oldest Anabaptist Congregation, Zollikon, near Zurch, Switzerland* [transl.], Scottdale (Pa.): Herald, 1961.

Clasen, C.P., *Anabaptism, a Social History 1525-1618*, London/ Ithaca: Cornell UP, 1972.

Depperman, K., *Melchior Hoffman, Social Unrest and Apocalyptic Visions in the Age of Reformation* [transl.], Edinburgh & T Clark, 1987.

Dyck, C.J. (ed), *An Introduction to Mennonite History*, Scottdale: Herald, 1967.

Estep, W., *The Anabaptist Story*, Nashville: Broadman, 1963.

Friedman, R., *The Theology of Anabaptism*, Scottdale: Herald, 1973.

Garret, J.L, *The Nature of the Church According to the Radical Continental Reformation*, Texas, Forth Worth, 1957.

Gritsch, E., *Reformer without a Church:The Life and Thought of Thomas Muentzer 1488?-1525*, Philadelphia: Fortress, 1976.

Gritsch, E., *Thomas Muentzer:* A *Tragedy of Errors*, Minneapolis: Fortress, 1989.

Gross, T.L., *The Golden Years of the Hutterites: The Witness and Communal Thought of the Communal Moravian Anabaptists during the Walpot Era 1565-1578*, Scottdale: Herald, 1980.

Heriot, D., *Anabaptism in England during the 16th and 17th centuries*, Transactions of the Congregational Historical Society, XII, 1935-1936, XIII, 1937-1939.

Hillerbrand, H.J., *A Bibliography of Anabaptism 1520-1630*, St. Louis: Center for Reformation Research, 1975[2].

Horsch, J., *Menno Simons*, Scottdale (PA.): Herald, 1916.

Horst, I.B., *The Radical Brethren: Anabaptism and the English Reformation to 1558*, Bibliotheca Humanistica & Reformatorica, vol.II, Nieuwkoop: De Graaf, 1972.

Horst, I.B., *Erasmus, the Anabaptists, and the Problem of Religious Unity*, Haarlem: Tjeenk Willink, 1967.

Hosteteler, J.A., *Hutterite Society*, Baltimore: Hopkins UP, 1974.

Keeney, W.E., *The Development of Dutch Anabaptist Thought and Practice 1539-1564*, Nieuwkoop: De Graaf, 1968.

Kot, S., *Socinianism in Poland: The Social and Political Ideas of the Polish Anti-trinitarians* [transl.], Boston: Star King, 1957.

Krahn, C., *Dutch Anabaptism: Origin, Spread, Life and Thought (1450-1600)*, 's-Gravenhage, 1968.

Lienhard, M. (ed), *The Origin and Characteristics of Anabaptism*, The Hague: Nijhoff, 1977.

Littell, F. H., *The Anabaptist View of the Church*: A *Study* in the *Origins* of *Sectarian Protestantism*, Boston: Star King, 1958[2].

Ruth, J.L., *Conrad Grebel:Son of Zurich*, Scottdale: Herald, 1975.

Schulz, S.G., *Caspar Schwenckfeld von Ossig 1489-1561*, Norristown: Schwenckfelder Church, 1946.

Scott, T., *Thomas Muentzer: Theology and Revolution in the German Reformation*, London: Macmillan, 1989.

Stayer, J.M., *Anabaptists and the Sword*, Lawrence (Kan.): Coronado, 1972.

Veder, H.C., *Balthasar Huebmaier*, New York: Putnam, 1905.

Verduin, L., *The Reformers and their Stepchildren*, Grand Rapids: Eerdmans, 1966.

Wenger, J.C. (ed), 'The Schleitheim Confession of Faith'. In: *The Mennonite Quarterly Review XIX (Oct. 1945)*, p.248.

Wilbur, E.M., *A History of Unitarianism: Socinianism and its Antecedents*, Cambridge (Mass.): Harvard UP, 1946.

Williams, G.H., *The Polish Brethren: Documentation of the History and Thought of Unitarianism in the Polish-Lithuanian Commonwealth and in the Diaspora 1601-1685* (2 vols), Missoula: Scholars Press, 1980.

Williams, G.H., *The Radical Reformation*, Sixteenth-century Essays and Studies, no.15, Kirksville, 1992³.

Yoder, J.H. (ed. and transl.), *The Legacy of Michael Sattler*, Scottdale: Herald, 1973.

Zuck, L.H. (ed), *Christianity and Revolution: Radical Christian Testimonies 1520-1650*. Philadelphia: Temple University, 1975.

h. France

Bainton, R.H., *Women of the Reformation in France and England*, Minneapolis: Augsburg, 1973.

Cameron, E., *The Reformation of the Heretics: The Waldenses of the Alps 1480-1580*, Oxford: Clarendon, 1984.

Chambers, B.T., *Bibliography of French Bibles*, Geneva: Droz, 1983.

Greengrass, M., *France in the Age of Henri IV : The Struggle for Stability*, London: Longman, 1984.

Greengrass, M., *The French Reformation*, Oxford: Blackwell, 1987.

Heller, H., *The Conquest of Poverty: The Calvinist Revolt in 16th-century France*, Leyden: Brill, 1985.

Kelley, D.R., *The Beginning of Ideology: Consciousness and Society in the French Reformation*, Cambridge UP, 1982.

Kingdon, R.M., *Geneva and the Coming of the Wars of Religion in France 1555-1563*, Geneva: Droz, 1956.

Knecht, R.J., *Renaissance Warrior and Patron: The Reign of Francis I*, Cambridge UP, 1994.

Muchembled, R., *Popular Culture and Élite Culture in France 1400-1750* [transl.], Baton Rouge: Louisiana State UP, 1985.

Roche, O.J.A., *The Days of the Upright: the story of the Huguenots*, New York: Potter, 1965.

Rothrock, G.A., *The Huguenots Biography of a Minority*, Chicago: Nelson-Hall, 1979.

Salmon, J.H.M., *Society in Crisis: France in the 16th-century*, London: Methuen, 1975.

Sutherland, N.M., *The Massacre of St. Bartholomew and the European Conflict 1559-1572*, London: Macmillan, 1973.

Sutherland, N.M., *The Huguenot Struggle for Recognition*, New Haven (Conn.): Yale UP, 1980.

Materials on Microfilm

Inter Documentation Company, P. O. Box 11205, 2301 EE Leyden, The Netherlands. IDC has a large collection on French Reformed Protestantism

i. The Netherlands

Bangs, C., *Arminius: A Study of the Dutch Reformation*, Nashville: Broadman, 1971.

Crew, P.M., *Calvinist Preaching and Iconoclasm in The Netherlands 1544-1569*, CUP, 1978.

Dosker, J, *The Dutch Anabaptists*, Philadephia: Judson, 1921.

Israel, J.I., *The Dutch Republic: Its Rise, Greatness and Fall 1477-1806*, Oxford: Clarendon, 1998[4], pp.8-220, 361-398, 449-477, 637-676, 1019-1066.

Jong de, P.Y. (ed), *Crisis in the Reformed Churches* [on Synod of Dordt], Grand Rapids: Reformed Fellowship, 1968.

Krahn, C., *Dutch Anabaptism: Origin, Spread, Life, and Thought 1450-1600*, The Hague: Nijhoff, 1968.

Parker, G., *The Dutch Revolt*, London: Allen Lane, 1977.

Schama, S., *The Embarrassment of the Riches: An Interpretation of Dutch Culture in the Golden Age*, New York: Knopf, 1993[3].

Materials on Microfilm

General Microfilm Company, 70 Coolidge Hill Road, Watertown. MA 02172, U.S.A. GMC has many rolls of microfilmed materials on the Reformation History of the Low Countries.

Inter Documentation Company, P. O. Box 11205, 2301 EE Leyden, The Netherlands. They have a vast collection of microfilmed materials of the Dutch Reformation.

j. England

Acheson, R. J., *Radical Puritans in England 1550-1560*, London: Longman, 1990.

Baker, D. (ed.), *The Bibliography of the Reform 1450-1648, relating to the United Kingdom and Ireland for the years 1950-1970*, Oxford: Baker, 1975.

Bettenson, H., *Documents of the Christian Church*, Oxford UP, 1946.

Bindoff, R., *Tudor England*, Harmondsworth: Penguin, 1955[4].

Brachlow, S., *The Communion of Saints: Radical Puritan and Separatist Ecclesiology 1570-1625*, Oxford UP, 1988.

Brightman, F.E., *The English Rite: Being a synopsis of the sources and revisions of the Book of Common Prayer*, 2 vols, London/ Milwaukee: Mowbray/ Young Churchman, 1915.

Bunyan, J., *The Pilgrim's Progress* [ed. J. B. Wharey, revised by R. Sharrock], Oxford: Clarendon, 1960.

Bunyan, J., *Grace Abounding to the Chief of Sinners* [ed. R. Sharrock], Oxford: Clarendon, 1962.

Bunyan, J., *The Holy War and The Life and Death of Mr. Badman* [ed. J. Brown], CUP, 1905.

Burgess, W.H., *The Pastor of the Pilgrims* [on Robinson, Smyth, Helwys, a. o], New York: Cambridge UP, 1987.

Burrage, Ch. (ed), *The Early English Dissenters in the Light of Recent Research*, 2 vols, New York: Cambridge UP, 1967 [first 1912].

Carlson, Leland H. and Albert Peel (ed), *The Elizabethan Nonconformist Texts*, 6 vols, London: Allen & Unwin, 1953-1970.

Carruthers, S.W., *The Everyday Life of the Westminster Assembly*, Philadelphia: The Presbyterian Historical Societies of England and America, 1943.

Clark, H.W., *History of English Nonconformity from Wiclif to the Close of the Nineteenth Century*, 2 vols, New York: Russell and Russell, 1965 [first 1911-1913].

Collinson, P., *The Elizabethan Puritan Movement*, London: Jonathan Cape, 1967.

Collinson, P., 'England and International Calvinism 1558-1640', in: M. Prestwich (ed.), *International Calvinism 1541-1715*, Oxford: Clarendon, 1985.

Collinson, P., *The Religion of Protestants: The Church in English Society 1559-1625*, Oxford: Clarendon, 1982.

Collinson, P., *The Birthpangs of Protestant England: Religious and Cultural Change in the 16th and 17th centuries*, London: Macmillan, 1988.

Cragg, G.R., *From Puritanism to the Age of Reason*, Cambridge UP, 1950.

Cremeans, D., *The Reception of Calvinistic Thought in England*, Urbana: University of Illinois Press, 1949.

Culkin, G., *The English Reformation*, London: Paternoster, 1954.

Dickens, A.G., *The English Reformation*, London: Fontana, 1964.

Dickens, A.G., and D. Carr, (eds), *The Reformation in England to the Accession of Elizabeth I* [documents], London: Edward Arnold, 1967.

Fraser, A.P., *Cromwell, the Lord Protector*, New York: Knopf, 1974.

Edwards, D.L., *Christian England: From the Reformation to the Eighteenth Century*, Grand Rapids: Eerdmans, 1983.

Elton, G.R., *Reform and Reformation in England 1509-1558*, London: Edward Arnold, 1977.

Frere, W.H., and C.E. Douglas, *Puritan Manifestoes*, London: SPCK, 1954.[2]

Gairdner, J., *Lollardy and the Reformation in England*, 4 vols, London: Macmillan, 1908-1913.

Garret, C.H., *The Marian Exiles 1553-1559*, Cambridge UP, 1966[2].

Gee, H., and W.J. Hardy, *Documents Illustrative of English Church History*, London: Macmillan, 1921.

George, T., *John Robinson and the English Separatist Tradition*, Georgia: Mercer UP, 1982.

Hague, D., *Protestantism and the Prayer Book*, London: The Book Room, 1912.

Haigh, C. (ed), *The English Reformation Revised*, Cambridge: James, 1987.

Haller, W., *Elizabeth I and the Puritans*, Ithaca: Cornell UP, 1964.

Haller, W., *The Rise of Puritanism or the way to the New Jerusalem as set forth in pulpit and press from Thomas Cartwright to John Lilburne and John Milton 1570-1643*. New York: Columbia Press, 1938.

Hamilton Thompson, A., *The English Clergy and their Organisation in the Later Middle Ages*, The Ford Lectures for 1933, Oxford, 1947.

Heath, P., *The English Clergy on the Eve of the Reformation*, London, 1969.

Herbert, A.S. et al., *Historical Catalogue of Printed Editions of the English Bible 1525-1961*, London/New York: British & Foreign Bible Society: Br, 1968.

Hill, C., *Society and Puritanism in Pre-Revolutionary England: Ideas during the English Revolution*, London: Hoerger, 1984[3].

Hudson, A., *The Premature Reformation: Wycliffite Texts and Lollard History*, Oxford UP, 1988.

Hughes Ph., *The Reformation in England*, 3 vols, London: Hollis, 1950-1954.

Hutchinson, F.E., *Cranmer and the English Reformation*, London: English UP, 1951.

Jacobus, H.E., *The Lutheran Movement in England during the Reigns of Henry VIII and Edward VI, and its Literary Monument*, Philadelphia: Lutheran Publication Society, 1916.

Johnson, J., *Elizabeth I: A Study in Power and Intellect*, London: Weidenfeld and Nicholson, 1976[2].

Kendall, R.T., *Calvin and English Calvinism to 1549*, London UP, 1979.

Knappen, M.M., *Tudor Puritanism: A Chapter in the History of Idealism*, Chicago UP, 1970.

Lake, P., *Anglicans and Puritans: Presbyterianism and English Conformist Thought from Whitgift to Hooker*, London: Allen & Unwin, 1988.

Mattingly, G., *Catherine of Aragon*, Boston: Little, 1941.

Maynard, Th., *The Life of Thomas Cranmer*, Chicago: Henry Regency, 1956.

McConica, J.K., *English Humanists and Reformation Politics under Henry VIII and Edward VI*, Oxford: Clarendon, 1968.
Moorman J., *A History of the Church in England*, London: Black, 1973³.
Packer, J.I., *A Quest for Godliness: The Puritan Vision of the Christian Life*, Wheaton: Crossway, 1994.
Parker, T.M., *The English Reformation to 1558*, London: Oxford UP, 1950.
Pearson, A., *Thomas Cartwright and Elizabethan Puritanism 1533-1603*, Cambridge UP, 1925.
Pollard, A.F., *Thomas Cranmer and the English Reformation*, New York: Putnam, 1904.
Pollard, A.W., and G.R.A. Redgrave, *Short Title Catalogue of Books Printed in England, Scotland and Ireland, and of English Books printed abroad 1475-1640*, London: Bibliographical Society, 1926.
Porter, H.C., *Puritanism in Tudor England*, Columbia: South Carolina UP, 1971.
Powicke, F.M., *The Reformation in England*, London: Oxford UP, 1941.
Prescott, H.F.M., *The Life of Mary Tudor*, New York: Macmillan, 1962.
Ridley, J., *Thomas Cranmer*, Oxford: Clarendon, 1962.
Robinson, H. (ed), *Original Letters Relative to the English Reformation*, 2 vols, London: Cambridge UP, 1968.²
Rupp, E.G., *Six Makers of English Religion 1500-1700*, London: Hodder and Stoughton, 1984.
Sharrock, R., *John Bunyan*, London: Macmillan, 1968.
Sheils, W.J., *The English Reformation 1530-1570*, London: Longman, 1989.
Smeeton, D.D., *English Religion 1500-1540: A Bibliography*, Macon: Mercer UP, 1988.
Smyth, H.M., *Henry VIII and the Reformation*, London: Macmillan, 1948.
Toon, P., *Puritans and Calvinism*, Swengel (Penn.): Reiner, 1973.
Trinterud, L.J. (ed), *Elizabethan Puritanism*, New York: Oxford UP, 1971.
Wallace, D.D., *Puritans and Predestination: Grace in English Protestant Theology 1525-1695*, Chapel Hill: University of North Carolina Press, 1982.
Wakefield, G., *John Bunyan, the Christian*, London: HarperCollins, 1992.
Warfield, B.B., *The Westminster Assembly and its Work*, New York: Oxford UP, 1931.
Watts, M.R., *The Dissenters*, vol.1. 'From the Reformation to the French Revolution: From the Marian Martyrs to the Pilgrim Fathers'; vol. 2. 'The Expansion of Evangelical Nonconformity 1791-1859', New York: Oxford UP, 1971.
White, R.B., *The English Separatist Tradition from the Marian Martyrs to the Pilgrim Fathers*, London, 1976.

Materials on Microfilm

Early English Books I, 1475-1640, and *Early English Books II, 1641-1700*: these are microfilm collections selected from the Short Title Catalogues of Pollard, Redgrave, Wing, published by University Microfilms International.

k. Scotland

Burleigh, J.H.S., *A Church History of Scotland*, Oxford UP, 1960.
Cameron, E., Patrick Hamilton, *First Scottish Martyr of the Reformation*, Edinburg: Scottish Reformation Society, 1929.
Cameron, J.K., *The First Book of Discipline*, Edinburgh: St. Andrew, 1972.
Cameron, N.M. (ed), *Dictionary of Scottish History and Theology*, Edinburgh: I. V., 1993.
Cowan, I.B., *The Scottish Reformation: Church and Society in 16th-century Scotland*, New York: St. Martin's Press, 1982.

Dickinson, W.C., *A New History of Scotland*, London: Thomas Nelson, 1965².
Dickinson, W.C., et al. (eds), *A Source Book of Scottish History*, Oxford: Clarendon, 1962.
Donaldson, G., *The Scottish Reformation*, Cambridge, 1960.
Donaldson, G., Scotland, *Church and Nation through sixteen centuries*, Edinburgh: Scottish Academic Press, 1972.
Foster, W.F., *The Church of Scotland before the Covenants 1596-1608*, Edinburgh/London, 1975.
Kirk, J., *The Second Book of Discipline*, Edinburgh: St. Andrew, 1980.
Lorimer, P., *Precursors* of *Knox, or Memoirs of Patrick Hamilton, Alexander Alane or Alesius, and Sir David Lindsay of the Mount*, Edinburgh: Constable, 1857.
Renwick, A.M., *The Story of the Scottish Reformation*, Grand Rapids: Eerdmans, 1960.
Rogers, Charles, 'Memoir of George Wishart, the Scottish Martyr', in: *Transactions* of the *Royal* Historical *Society*, 1st ser., 4 (1876)-352.
Wormald, J., *Court, Kirk, and Community: Scotland 1470-1625*, The New History of Scotland, 4, London: Edward Arnold, 1981.
Wyk, J.J., *The Historical Development of the Offices, According to the Presbyterian Tradition of Scotland*, University of Stellenbosch, 1995.

l. Counter Reformation

Allison, A.F., D.M. Rogers, and W. Lottes, *The Contemporary Printed Literature of the English Counter Reformation between 1558 and 1640: An Annotated Catalogue*, Aldershot, 1989.
Bangert, W.H., *A History of the Society of Jesuits*, St. Louis: Institute of Jesuit Sources, 1932.
Boehmer, E., *Bibliotheca Wiffeniana: Spanish Reformers of the Two Centuries from 1520*: *Their Lives and Writings 1874-1904*, 3 vols, Strasbourg and London: Trübner, 1874-1904. [facsimile reprint, New York, 1962].
Brodrick, J., *The Life and Works of bl. R. Bellarminus*, 2 vols, London, 1928.
Brodrick, J., *The Origins of the Jesuits*, London: Longmans, 1941.
Brodrick, J., *The Progress of the Jesuits 1556-1579*, Chicago, 1986 [first London, 1942].
Brodrick, J., *Saint Ignatius de Loyola: The Pilgrim Years*, New York: Farrar, 1956.
Burns, E.M., *The Counter Reformation*, Princeton UP, 1964.
Caraman, Ph., *Ignatius de Loyola*, San Francisco: Harper & Row, 1990.
Corbett, J.A., *The Papacy: A Brief History*, Princeton UP, 1980.
Daniel-Rops, H., *The Catholic Reformation*, New York: Dutton, 1962.
Dickens, A.G., *The Counter Reformation*, New York: Harcourt, 1969.
Dudon, P.P., *Ignacio de Loyola: The Spiritual Exercises*, Westminster Md: Newman Press, 1968.
Dudon, P.P., *Saint Ignatius of Loyola* [transl.], Milwaukee: Young, 1949.
Dyke van, P., *Ignatius Loyola the Founder of the Jesuits*, New York: Scribner, 1926.
Friedrich, Carl. J. *The Rise of Modern Europe*: The *Age* of the *Baroque*. New York: Evanston/London: Harper & Row, 1952.
Evenett, D., *The Spirit of the Counter Reformation*, Cambridge UP, 1968.
Garstein, O., *Rome and the Counter Reformation in Scandinavia until the Establishment of the S. Congregatio de Propaganda Fide in 1622, 1539-1583*, Oslo: Universitetsforlaget, 1963.
Haliczer, S. (ed), *Inquisition and Society in Early Modern Europe*, Londonroom Helm, 1987.
Hammond, L., *Liturgy and Architecture*, London: Barrie and Rockliff, 1960.
Janelle, P., *The Catholic Reformation*, Milwaukee: Pierre Publ., 1949.
Jedin, H., *A History of the Council of Trent* [transl.], London: Thomas Nelson, 1967.

Jedin, H., *Crisis and Closure of the Council of Trent: A Retrospective View from the Second Vatican Council*, London: Burns and Oates, 1967.

Kamen, H., *The Spanish Inquisition*, London: Weidenfeld and Nicolson, 1965.

Kidd, B.J., *The Counter Reformation 1550-1600*, London: SPCK, 1933.

Lea, H.C., *Chapters from the Religious Life of Spain, Connected with the Inquisition*, Philadelphia: Lea Brothers, 1890.

Lea, H.C., *A History of the Inquisition in Spain*, 4 vols, New York: Macmillan, 1906-1908.

Mullett, M., *The Counter-Reformation and the Catholic Reformation in Early Modern Europe*, London: Methuen, 1985.

Olin, J., *The Catholic Reformation: Savonarola to Ignatius Loyola* [documents], New York: Harper & Row, 1969.

O'Malley, J. W., *The First Jesuits*, Cambridge (Mass.): Harvard, 1993.

Peers, E.A., *A Handbook to the Life and Times of St. Teresa and St.John of the Cross*, London: Burns Oates, 1954.

Polisensky, J. V., *The Thirty Years' War* [transl.], Berkeley: University of California Press, 1971.

Redaway, W.F., et al., *The Cambridge History of Poland to 1696*, Cambridge UP, 1950.

Roth, C., *The Spanish Inquisition*, New York: Norton, 1996^3.

Schroeder, H.J. (ed), *Canons and Decrees of the Council of Trent* (original plus transl.), Rockford: Tan Books, 1978^2.

Seward, D., *The Monks of War: The Military Religious Orders*, London: Penguin, 1995^2.

Tedeschi, J.A., *The Literature of the Italian Reformation: An Exhibition Cat.*, Chicago, 1971.

Jourdan, G.V., *The Movement toward Catholic Reform in the early 16th-century*, New York: Dutton, 1914.

Wedgewood, C.V., *The Thirty Years' War*, New Haven: Yale UP, 1939.

Wright, A.D., *The Counter-Reformation*, London: Weidenfeld and Nicolson, 1962.

D. Modern Age 1650 –2000

33. The Enlightenment[1]

33.1. Renaissance and Humanism

The *Peace Treaty of Westphalia/ Münster* of 1648 ended the period of religious wars in Europe. The religious boundaries between areas of Roman Catholic and Protestant influence were more or less fixed. A period of political and ecclesiastical consolidation followed. At the same time, European Christianity as a whole was undermined by a phenomenon that had started before the Reformation. Gradually man had begun to discover his own possibilities and capabilities. The *Renaissance* and *Humanism* had drawn the attention to the antique sources of knowledge and wisdom in Greek and Roman culture. This began a continuous development of physics, medicine, mathematics, law, and technology, which accompanied the discovery of other peoples and cultures.

In itself this deployment of human possibilities did not threaten Christianity. Humanism and Renaissance in their first phases did not turn against the Christian faith, although some of their early representatives, like Nicolaus Copernicus, Johannes Kepler, and Galileo Galilei, came into conflict with the Roman Catholic Church when they discovered some physical laws of the working of the planets in the universe, that were not in accordance with the teaching of the Church. The mathematician Isaac Newton (1642-1722) developed the idea of a basic law that governs all phenomena in the universe. This made people think that the universe is a machine that operates without direct involvement of its Creator. However, many early Humanists, like Erasmus (1469-1536), facilitated the Reformation.

33.2. Enlightenment

But in later phases the adherents of Humanism came to mistrust all authority and tradition in matters of intellectual inquiry, and believed that truth could be obtained only by *reason*, i.e. by the human capabilities to think, observe and experience. Nothing can be accepted that opposes *common sense*. They distanced themselves from the authority of revelation, faith, and Church. This movement of *Rationalism* had its early climax in the 17th century. Still later there was a reaction against the emphasis on reason. Another focal point of human possibilities was stressed then, the emotional aspect, i.e. feeling, conscience, passion, imagination, personality. This movement became known by the name *Romanticism*; it culminated in the 18th century.

Both Rationalism and Romanticism originate in the same root, man's desire for autonomy; they have no use for the authority of the Word of God. In a wider sense they can together be designated by the term *Enlightenment* (Chichewa: *Kuunikira*; German: *Aufklärung*; French: *Illumination*; Dutch: *Verlichting*), although most historians prefer the narrower use of the term, and only apply it to the phenomenon of Rationalism. We look upon Rationalism and Romanticism as respectively the *cold* and the *warm* sides of the Enlightenment. The ideas of the Enlightenment had their rise in the period between the Peace Treaty of Westphalia (1648) and the French Revolution (1795), but their

---

[1] Cairns, *Christianity through the Centuries*, pp.375-388; Dowley, pp.485-499, 504-506; Cragg, pp.9-16, 37-49, 234-255; Thomson, pp.105-109.

consequences are apparent especially today, in the individualism, the materialism, and the secularisation of present-day Western culture.

33.3. Influence on the Church

a. Orthodoxy

The Enlightenment has influenced the character of Church and Christianity in the West. Roman Catholicism with its view of the powers in nature that enable man to climb up to grace could easily accommodate it.

Protestantism was also affected. The liveliness and the renewing force of the 16th-century Reformation was followed by a period of rigid *Orthodoxy* with predominant interest in the schematisation and the consolidation of doctrinal positions, in which to a certain degree medieval *Scholasticism* was revived. This apparent touch by Rationalism even led to the formation of heretical thoughts and sects. Not unlike 16th-century *Socinianism*, some English Presbyterians and Congregationalists from the second half of the 17th century began to weaken the creed of the Godhead of Christ, thus contributing to the emergence of the denomination of the *Unitarians*.

b. Pietism

Long before the culmination of Romanticism in the 18th century, demands for a rightful place for feeling and emotion had already led to the formation of Radical sects to the 'left' side of the Reformation (Anabaptists, Spiritualists, Quakers), and to mystical movements in the Roman Catholic Church (Jesuits, Molinists, Quietists). But there were also movements inside the mainline churches of the Reformation. They were partly a reaction against the 'dead' Orthodoxy that had invaded the churches.

English *Puritanism* is an example, especially in its *pietistic* form, represented by Anglicans like William Perkins (1558-1602) and by Nonconformists like John Bunyan (1628-1688). Parallel movements, mainly in the 17th century, were those of the *Nadere Reformatie* (= Further Reformation) in The Netherlands (e.g. Jean Taffin, 1529-1602; Jacobus Koelman, 1632-1695), and of the *Pietismus* in Germany (e.g. Philip Jacob Spener, 1635-1705; August Hermann Francke, 1663-1727).

In the 18th century they were followed by the *Evangelical Revival* and the *Great Awakening* originating in the Anglo-Saxon culture on both sides of the Atlantic (John Wesley, 1703-1791; George Whitefield, 1714-1770; Jonathan Edwards, 1703-1758) and spreading to other parts of the world. These *pietistic* movements in the 17th and 18th centuries will be dealt with separately. Generally, these movements have rendered great service to the churches of the Reformation. But sometimes they elevated personal religious experience and subjective feelings to a level where it was to be normative for faith and salvation. By their schematising of the religious processes and characteristics in man they were in some way or another linked to the Rationalism of the 17th century and even more to the Romanticism of the 18th century.

33.4. Rationalism as Deism

The general tendency of the philosophical movements of Rationalism and Romanticism was directed against Biblical Christianity. Many leading thinkers assumed a kind of natural religion, a *Deism* (Deus = God), that all men had apart from the Bible. 'God left his creation after He had created it to be governed by natural laws, discoverable by reason'. Many came to propagate universal toleration of all religions. 'They substituted reason and man's senses for revelation as the main avenues to knowledge'.

A number of influential early Rationalist thinkers lived and worked in The Netherlands. Rene Descartes, or Cartesius (1596-1650), took his starting point in 'doubt of everything, except his own consciousness and his ability to think'. He arrived at the conclusion: *I think, therefore I am* (Latin: *cogito ergo sum*). The Jewish philosopher Baruch Spinoza (1630-1693) was a forerunner of Romanticism. He adopted a kind of *pantheism*. He held that the human mind is part of the Divine impersonal intellect. God is a substance, which is the essence of all things. Pierre Bayle (1647-1706), a minister of Divinity, tried to be philosophically a rationalist and religiously a believer by segregating knowledge and faith. Doctrines like *original sin* and *election* can be true religiously and false philosophically.

René Descartes (1596-1650), French philosopher and scientist who wrote his main works on the supremacy of reason in The Netherlands.

England produced a number of very influential Deist thinkers. Francis Bacon (1521-1661) developed the *inductive* method. This method means that the scientist accepts nothing on the basis of authority alone. Only experiments and observation can lead to the formulation of general laws. John Locke (1632-1704) reinforced Bacon's ideas by asserting that true knowledge comes by reflection on sensations. Other English Deists were Edward Herbert (1583-1648), and Lord Shaftesbury (1671-1713), who believed that Christianity can be proved by reason. Deism as a rationalistic structure was attacked by David Hume (1711-1776). According to him, egotism and fear drive man to be religious. In him we see a kind of Enlightenment that has turned its back on the centrality of reason. Now man is going to be oriented on his emotions and feelings. The secret society of the *Freemasons*, founded in 1717, belongs to the consequences of the English 'free thought'.

John Locke (1632-1704), English philosopher who founded the knowledge of God and Christianity on their 'reasonableness', and gave also place to sensation.

The Enlightenment spread from England to France, Germany and America. In France, Montesquieu (1689-1755) published his political and ecclesiastical ideas which were critical towards king and church rulers. Diderot and d'Alembert in the period 1751-1780 published 35 volumes of their *Encyclopédie* in which representatives of the Enlightenment spread their thoughts. There was a growing hostility against church and clergy that culminated in the work of Voltaire (1694-1778).

Gottfried Leibniz (1646-1716) was a forerunner of the Enlightenment in Germany. According to him, Divine revelation has to be proved by reason. His pupil Christian Wolff (1679-1754) even more stressed the position of rational knowledge. Philosophy supplies theology with the methods of mathematics. A group of theologians, the *Neologians*, followed him; all old dogmas of the Church were tested by them according to this rationalist method. Johann Semler (1725-1791) introduced an *accommodation* theory which he applied to Scripture. According to him, the Bible writers accommodated to the primitive level of Antiquity. In modern times we have developed to a level that does not need these primitive accommodations. Gotthold Lessing (1729-1781) followed him. He said that much of Old Testament and New Testament are fantasies; we have to tolerate all religions.

Through immigration the new English colonies in America were exposed to the destructive influences of Rationalism. Among the leaders who promoted Rationalism in America were Thomas Jefferson, George Allen and Thomas Paine.

David Hume (1711-1776), Scottish philosopher who criticised one-sided emphasis on reason, which in his view is a product of experience, and he stressed the importance of imagination, personality, passions, and the will

Gotthold Ephraim Lessing (1729-1781). Stimulated by Reimarus he defined religion as morality and meant to find the truth in all religions; in his play Nathan der Weise (1779) he spread these thoughts

Immanuel Kant (1724-1804), German philosopher. In his extensive system of thought, the rationalism of the Enlightenment is robbed of its central position and is replaced by feeling, intuition, sensation, etc. of man. Like with the rationalists his system is anthroposophical, denying God an independent place.

33.5. Romanticism

Like David Hume in England, Jean Jacques Rousseau (1712-1778) in France turned from reason to feeling and conscience. His book *The Social Contract* is said to have more than any other book ignited the *French Revolution*. The Age of *Romanticism* had arrived. In Germany thinkers and literary men like Friedrich Schleiermacher, Immanuel Kant, Johann Fichte, Georg Hegel, Johann Goethe, and Friedrich Schiller reacted against Rationalism. They demanded room for the feelings and the personality of man. The main line of the Enlightenment, however, was retained: rejection of the Word of God as the highest authority, and deriving final authority from man himself. The *Revivals* and *Awakenings* in the 18th and 19th centuries in the churches of the West tried to answer this challenge, but sometimes they themselves came to be infected by the Enlightenment.

34. Roman Catholicism 1648-1800[1]

34.1. Nationalism

After the *Peace Treaty of Westphalia/Münster* (1648), that more or less settled the religious boundaries in Europe, most Roman Catholic rulers stopped their political and military attempts to bring the Protestant countries back under the influence of the Pope of Rome. This does not mean that these governments allowed freedom to Protestantism.

In Germany the rule of *cuius regio eius religio* (whose is the state, his is the religion) gave the Roman Catholic states, like Bavaria, the right to make life for Protestants impossible.

In France the *Edict of Nantes* (1598), that granted free exercise of religion to the Huguenots, was systematically undermined, and finally revoked by King Louis XIV in 1685. Persecution of Huguenots caused the decrease of French Protestantism to a small minority.

In the southern part of the Low Lands or The Netherlands, Roman Catholicism had been restored. Protestantism in Austria, in parts of Switzerland, and in half of Hungary had been swept away, even more so in Poland.

But after the middle of the 17th century, the performers of these persecutions were more inspired by desire for national consolidation and political imperialism than by subservience to papal aims. The Peace of Westphalia had concluded the devastating religious wars in the Low Lands and in Middle Europe. Its outcome, the recognition of a number of Protestant states, was a severe blow to the political claims of the papacy. The *Counter Reformation* in a narrow sense was ended by it. The comprehensive attack on Protestantism by a combined use of ecclesiastical, political, judicial and military means ground to a halt in Europe, because of lack of support by civil rulers. However, this was far from stopping the movement of *Roman Catholic Restoration* in a wider sense. We mention three factors that favoured this Restoration, the *Conquests*, the *New Orders*, the *Mysticism*, and two movements that checked it, *Gallicanism*, and *Jansenism*.

34.2. Conquests

The conquests and settlement of trading posts outside Europe by Spain, Portugal and France had opened up vast territories where Roman Catholicism could spread through colonial settlements and through the conversion of indigenous peoples. Of course, competitive colonising by the Dutch and the British counteracted this expansion, especially in Southern Africa, North America, and Asia. But in South America, Middle America, Mexico, Quebec, the Philippines, and parts of Africa, Roman Catholic colonial power settled and consolidated. Although the colonising governments consciously ruled church and state independently of the Pope, they often allowed the newly founded missionary orders to work in these vast territories. These new orders deployed activities even in remote areas, like China, Korea, and Japan, where there was no direct cover by the Roman Catholic colonial powers

---

[1] Cairns, *Christianity through the Centuries*, p.388; Dowley, pp.466-475; Thomson, pp.80-89, 127-130, 131-137; Cragg, pp.185-192

34.3. Jesuits and other New Orders

The new orders and congregations are the *second* factor that contributed to the Restoration of Roman Catholicism. They not only organised mission but they also strengthened the inward moral position of the Roman Catholic Church. Already in the Middle Ages orders like the *Cistercians, Franciscans* and *Dominicans* had temporarily strengthened the Roman Catholic Church. Since the 16th century the foundation and deployment of the order of the *Jesuits* had been of great significance to Counter Reformation and Restoration. But now new orders were added to this.

We mention the Lazarists, founded by the Frenchman Vincentius de Paolo (†1660); the Piarists and the Salesians founded by Francis de Sales in 1607/1610. These orders tried to promote the Roman Catholic spirit by obedience to the Pope and by activities for education, nursing of the sick, and social work. The order of the Oratians, founded in 1611, was devoted to scholarly research. So was the congregation of the Maurists, founded in 1621. Its members were well known for their historical and literary work. There were attempts to revive the weakened orders of the past. In 1662 the Trappists were founded in order to lead the old Cistercian order to 'strict observance' of monastic rules.

Of special importance is the order of the *Redemptorists*, founded by Alphonso de Liguori in 1732. It was instituted for mission work among the poor, both in Europe and outside Europe. To a high degree this order imitated the Jesuits. It defended the nucleus of Roman Catholic doctrine and practice, like the veneration of the altar, the veneration of Mary, and absolute obedience to the Pope. It also imitated the so called *Probabilism*, i.e. a system of moral theology, initiated by the Dominicans and further developed by the Jesuits. Probabilism is based on the principle that, if the good or evil of an action is in doubt, it is lawful to follow the opinion that favours the interests of the Roman Catholic Church, even though the opposing opinion might be more probable. This 'jesuitistic' morality was attacked outside and inside the Roman Catholic Church. It was temporarily subdued. But it was rehabilitated when De Liguori expounded his own theories which are founded on Probabilist principles. According to a widely read church historian, this 'is now the most generally accepted system in the Roman Catholic Church'.[2]

Alphonso Maria de Liguari (1696-1778), Italian Bishop and Founder of the Order of the Redemptorists.

34.4. Jesuitism versus Mysticism and Quietism

The *third* phenomenon that helped to restore Roman Catholic influence was the movement of *Mysticism*. This was a revival of tendencies in the Medieval Church (Teresa of Avila, Teresa of Lisieux, John of the Cross) which demanded attention for an immediate knowledge of God attained in this life through personal religious experience. In a state of prayer and meditation man is touched by the Divine and eventually united with God in the so called 'mystic marriage'. It issues an increase of humility, charity, and love of suffering. Although medieval ecclesiastical authorities had generally not

---

[2] E.A. Livingstone, *CDCC*, p.416.

favoured the mystics, and although they found new enemies in the Jesuits, some popes realised that mysticism could be an efficient weapon in the fight against Protestantism.

The Roman Catholic Church owes a revival of mysticism to Francis de Sales, bishop of Geneva, who in 1602 began a campaign of fierce persecution of Protestants in the South of Switzerland. At the same time, he studied medieval Mystics. He propagated the idea that the soul sick of love and yearning for God, climbs up to salvation and bliss in God.

This mysticism of the soul developed further in the movement of *Quietism*. Its representatives, like the Spaniard Michael de Molinos (†1697), taught abandoning to God by complete passivity and annihilation of the will. In their thinking this state was reached by a form of mental prayer in which the soul not only refuses meditation but any distinct act; it only rests in faith in the presence of God.

The Quietists were resisted by the *Jesuits* who had them persecuted, especially by the French clergy under King Louis XIV. The Jesuits stressed the importance of obedience to daily ecclesiastical practice and to the Pope. They confronted the mysticism of the soul by a cult for the veneration of 'the heart of Mary' and the 'most holy heart of Jesus'. Both cults were sanctioned by 17th-century popes. The growing influence of the Jesuits became apparent in their successful defence of certain teachings that eventually were accepted as official doctrine, e.g. the *infallibility of the Pope* (dogma in 1870) and the *immaculate conception of Mary* (dogma in 1854).

They also succeeded in having the Paulinian and Augustinian doctrine of sin and grace, which was already weakened by curses of the Council of Trent, replaced by emphatic *semi-pelagianism*. At this point Roman Catholic theology and practice were definitely influenced into an anti-evangelical direction. Eventually this contributed to the limitation of Roman Catholic influence, because it neutralised the *Jansenist Movement* which could have challenged Protestantism. But, let us look first at another phenomenon that checked papal claims.

34.5. Gallicanism

The term *Gallicanism* in a wider sense denotes a tendency in Roman Catholic countries to be more or less independent of the authority of the papacy (see chapter 15.1). As the phenomenon was most striking in French history, the word *Gallicanism* (the Roman province of Gallia covered more or less the territory of today's France) is used. But in Modern History the same movement also appeared in Roman Catholic countries like Austria, Spain, Portugal, and Italy. The Gallicanists were opposed by the *Ultramontanists* (ultra montanes = beyond the mountains, i.e. beyond the Alps where Rome is situated) who pledged their allegiance to universal papal power.

Gallicanism in France had old roots. In the 14th and 15th centuries the French Church claimed a privileged position in relation to the papacy. In the *Concordat of Bologna* the Pope even conceded the right of French kings to nominate bishops and other church officials. Now, under the absolutist King Louis XIV (1643-1715) these rights were revived and extended. In the *Gallican Articles* of 1682 it was denied that the Pope had dominion over things temporal, and affirmed that kings are not subject to the Church in civil matters. The Articles reaffirmed the authority of a General Council over the Pope. They insisted that the ancient liberties of the French Church were inviolable and asserted that the judgment of the Pope was not irreformable. King Louis XIV, his ministers Richelieu and Mazarin, his court preacher Bossuet and the top of the French clergy quarrelled with Rome about this, even risked a schism, whereas at the same time they tried to strangle Protestantism.

34.6. Jansenism

Gallicanism had political overtones. It counteracted the would-be *supra-national* character of the Roman Catholic Church, i.e. its behaviour as a universal state with the Pope as an absolute monarch. Of course, the Gallican protest also had spiritual aspects. This was also apparent in the Quietists' demand for personal spirituality, and in their defence against Jesuitism.

Spiritual protest against developments in Roman Catholic theology and practice was much more apparent in the movement of *Jansenism*. It started in the Southern part of The Netherlands, where the *Counter Reformation* had rooted out Protestantism. But inside the Roman Catholic Church some influence of Protestant thought was felt. Michel Baius (1513-1589) was a professor at Louvan; he had been one of the representatives at the *Council of Trent*. Although he agreed to the condemnation of the Reformation, he was in favour of

Blaise Pascal (1623-1662), influential French scholar, who in 1654 joined the Jansenist Movement. In his Lettres Provinciales, he ably attacked Jesuit theories of grace and morality, and in his Pensées, he defended basic Christian truths.

reforms. He wanted to lead Roman Catholic theology back to Scriptures. In the line of the Church Father Augustine he taught the doctrines of man's depravity by original sin, the inability of man's will to choose in favour of God, and the unconditionality and the irresistibility of grace. Baius was formally condemned by the Pope, and he made a recantation.

By the influence of the Jesuits and others *semi-pelagian* teachings (= original sin removed by baptism, free will, sacraments enable to make good choices) were to outvote the doctrine of free grace in the Roman Catholic Church. After Baius' death, the Spanish Jesuit Luis de Molina (†1600) tried to combine Augustine's teaching with the *synergism* (= collaboration, i.e. of nature and grace) of Rome. He taught that grace is not founded in God's gift itself, but in the divinely foreknown fact of human cooperation with this gift. The order of the Jesuits followed the ideas of De Molina and this led to a serious controversy with the *Dominicans* who considered them to surpass the boundaries of *semi-pelagian* doctrine. In 1607 Pope Paul V promised to take the final decision on the question, but he never did, neither did his successors!

The controversy revived when Cornelis Jansen (1585-1638), who was born in the Northern part of The Netherlands, continued the defence of Augustinian teachings. Jansen first wanted to become a Jesuit, but he turned into a formidable opponent when he discovered the heresies of Jesuitism. In 1640 he wrote his influential book, *Augustinus*. In it he stated that a man can be saved only through the love of God creating faith. This love becomes effective through conversion, and conversion is dependent on the good pleasure of God. Thus Jansen's teachings on grace implied the doctrine of *predestination*.[3]

Jansen's ideas soon spread to France. The first generation of Jansenists were disciples of Jean de Hauranne the abbot of Saint-Cyran (†1643), Jansen's friend and collaborator. They included the nuns of the convent of *Port Royal* near Paris, where the abbess Jacqueline Arnaud had introduced far reaching reforms. After 1643, Jaqueline's brother Antoine Arnaud became the leader of the Jansenist movement. Soon the Jansenists' position was condemned by the Pope. To their defenders belonged the famous scholar Blaise Pascal (1623-1662). Arnaud's condemnation by the Sorbonne University made Pascal to write the book *Lettres Provinciales,* in which he attacked the Jesuit theories of grace (*Molinism*) and moral theology (*Probabilism*). In 1668 the Jansenists were forced to a certain submission, but the movement continued. Pasquier Quesnel (†1719) revived the movement. This was followed by a formal papal condemnation and persecution of the Jansenists[4]. Port Royal was disbanded. Quisnel was imprisoned, but he escaped to The Netherlands (Holland). There *Jansenism* was free. In 1724 the Jansenists seceded from the Roman Catholic Church and instituted the *Old Catholic Church*.

---

[3] Cragg, pp.25, 26.

[4] Cardinal Lavigerie was an important 19th-century organiser of Roman Catholic mission in Africa and founder of the *White Fathers*. He belonged to the outspoken opponents of the 'protestantising' thoughts of Jansenism, cf. Charles M.A. Lavigerie, *Exposé des erreurs doctrinales du Jansénisme*, Paris; Sorbonne, 1885. See also chapters 49.3; 52.1,5; 57.2.f.

35. Roman Catholicism 1800-1900[1]

35.1. Revolutions

a. The French Revolution of 1789

The epoch of great revolutionary changes in state and church started before 1800 and had its early effects outside Europe in the South American wars of independence against Spain preceded by the North American Revolution (1776 independent from Britain). Especially in Western Europe this led to the crumbling of royal absolutism and the end of the solid connections between the state and the church. The main revolution that changed the whole of Western society was the *French Revolution*. It started in 1789 as a violent protest against oppression and injustice. One of the heralds and prophets of the French Revolution was Jean Jacques Rousseau (1712-1778). In his book *The Social Contract* (1762) he explained some principles that would turn society upside down.

Voltaire (pseudonym of F.M. Arouet), 1694-1778, French philosopher, who criticised the leaders of Church and State, thus paving the way for the French Revolution.

Jean Jacques Rousseau (1712-1778), French author whose writings undermined revealed religion and paved the way for the French Revolution.

'No citizen shall be rich enough to buy another and none so poor as to sell himself'. 'Those who think themselves the masters of others are indeed greater slaves than they. So long as a people is constrained to obey, and it obeys, it does well. But as soon as it can shake off the yoke, and shake it off, it does better'.[2]

Rousseau repudiated the doctrine of divine right, and located sovereignty in the people. In Rousseau and others the *Enlightenment* in a way showed its anti-Christian face. At first the French revolutionist regime was very much opposed to the Roman Catholic

---

[1] Cairns, *Christianity through the Centuries*, pp.23, 99, 242-244, 310-311,392-397; Dowley, pp.508-517; 530-534 (Anglocath.); Vidler, pp.45-55 (Anglocath.), 68-78, 146-156, 157-168, 179-189; Thomson, pp.118-125; Renwick/Harman, pp.186-192, 232-235.
[2] J.J. Rousseau, *Du Contrat Social*, 1762 (Russell, Bertrand, pp.669-671).

Church. In 1801 Napoleon tried to use the Church by concluding a *Concordat* with Rome.

b. The Revolution of 1830

The French Bourbon kings after their Restoration and the Roman Catholic Church depended on one another, although the influence of the papacy declined. King Louis XVIII liked the revolutionary writer Voltaire, but at the same time he sought the support of the Church for his monarchy. King Charles X was a reactionary ruler. He was forced to abdicate in 1830. This July Revolution was an anti-clerical expression of the people. During the new regime under King Louis Philippe (of the House of the Orleans kings) there was intense struggle between Liberal Catholics and the *Ultramontanist Movement.* There were fierce reactions by liberals and anti-clericals against the Roman Catholic Church, and Roman Catholicism lost its status as the state religion in France.

Charles L.J. de Montesquieu (1689-1755), French scholar. He attacked the French government and the Roman Catholic Church, and he defended the idea of the division of

c. The Revolution of 1848

This revolution ended the former regime and introduced the Second Empire under Louis Napoleon, Emperor in 1852, who after the June Revolution by the French proletariat went back to a policy of traditional conservatism. From 1860 this led to anti-clerical attacks against the Church. In 1871 a war with Germany ended this regime. Atheistic communal risings broke out, in direct preparation for the great revolution of 1917 in Russia that would affect the whole of Europe.

d. The Industrial Revolution

The development of science through the Renaissance and the Enlightenment especially in the 19th century led to an outburst of discoveries and inventions. Modern technology was born. It opened doors to new ways of producing goods and trading goods. The societies in Europe that were mainly rural and agricultural changed to urban industrial societies. This had very important consequences for the lives of the people. Many who went to the cities for work in the factories were uprooted and exploited by the captains of industry. At the same time, the fruits of modern technology and education were enjoyed by an increasing number of people. *Capitalism* and *uncontrolled commercialism* opened possibilities for individuals and groups, but also made many poor while amassing wealth for a few. There was an enormous gap between bliss and splendour on the one side and abject poverty and social injustice on the other side.

The enormous changes provoked reactions, either directed against the Church, or reviving the Church. *First* there was the reaction of the movement of *Socialism*, more precisely *Communism*. It is linked with the names of Karl Marx (†1883) and Friedrich Engels (†1895), who in 1848 issued a hard-hitting and fierce pamphlet, entitled *The Manifesto of the Communist Party*. The authors gave an economic interpretation of history. They divided the people into classes of oppressors and oppressed. They advocated a communist revolution in which the oppressed were to raise themselves to the position of ruling class. Subsequently they were to abolish individual property. These thoughts became very influential and led to the formation of internationally linked *Communist Parties* that eventually got to power in Russia and other countries, and to the formation of *socialist parties* all over the West. Communism and socialism in general were strongly opposed to Christianity, and blamed the Church for many of the evils in society. In all European countries, especially in the Roman Catholic South of Europe, millions turned their backs on the Church to become communists or socialists.

Karl Marx (1818-1884), German-Jewish scholar, whose writings contributed to the ideas of 'scientific' materialism and atheism. Especially influential were his Manifesto of the Communist Party (1847) and Das Kapital (1876).

The *second* reaction against negative consequences of the industrial revolution was quite different. Despite criticism by communists and socialists, the Christian Church in most European countries realised the challenges of the time. Movements were unleashed to revive the Evangelical and social spirit of the Church and to reach out to the disprivileged masses. This led to a wide *Christian Social Movement* that particularly became vocal and influential in the *Social Consciousness* of the Evangelicals.[3] In the Roman Catholic Church the revival of social consciousness was later and weaker. That is why it was hit more by the social and political changes of the time than Protestantism.

35.2. Victories and Losses

Generally, the position of the Roman Catholic Church in the 19th century is one of setbacks and gains. Illustrative for this is the disbanding of the *Jesuits* in 1773 by Pope Clement XIV, and the re-instatement of this order in 1814 by Pope Pius VII. The revolutions weakened the influence of the papacy. The Church found it difficult to cope with the waves of liberalism and socialism that attacked the old structures of society. More and more rulers and citizens did not want to be led by the Church. The Roman Catholic Church tried to parry these challenges, first by stressing its doctrines and ecclesiastical structure. This was done for example in 1854 by Pope Pius IX when he declared the *immaculate conception of Mary* to be an official dogma. In 1870 at the

---

[3] Cairns, *Christianity through the Centuries*, pp.269, 384, 398; Dowley, pp.518-521; Vidler, ch. 8.

First Vatican Council Pius IX also stated papal infallibility. This means that papal decisions are supposed to be *infallible*, if they are pronounced 'in cathedra', thus spoken 'ex cathedra', that is 'by virtue of the pope's supreme apostolic authority'.

Pope Leo XIII tried to find answers to the questions of social justice and state-church relationship in his encyclical *Rerum Novarum* (Latin for: Of the New Things) in 1891, after having restored the relations with Germany that during Bismarck's *Kulturkampf* (German for: Culture Struggle) had tried to counteract Roman Catholic influence. He also gave room for *liberal methods* of Bible exegesis, and he encouraged High Anglican attempts for union with Roman Catholicism. Other popes had a much more traditionalist and old-fashioned policy. Pius VI strongly condemned Modernism in Bible exegesis as proposed by scholars like Alfred Loisy and George Tyrrell. Pope Pius XI in his encyclical *Quadragesimo Anno* (Latin for: In the Fortieth Year) went back to the policy of Leo XIII in trying to address social problems.

Pius IX (1792-1878), Pope from 1846. Although he was declared infallible in 1870 his power decreased by the seizure of Rome by Italian nationalists in the same year.

Session of the First Vatican Council (1869-1870). The Council stated the Infallibility of the Pope in cases when he spoke ex cathedra, i.e. defining a doctrine regarding faith and morals.

35.3. Birth of Anglo-Catholicism

Mainly in an indirect way the influence of Roman Catholicism was strengthened by a movement inside Protestantism, namely by the *Oxford Movement* in the Anglican Church (= Church of England). The movement started as an attempt to restore the status of the Anglican Church that was in low esteem. The Church needed reform. The *Evangelical Revivals* had done a lot to improve the situation. Some Anglicans, however, although they wanted an awakening of the Church, did not agree with the Calvinist tendency in the Evangelical Revivals. In their opinion the Revivals supported *Nonconformism*, which is separation. This party of non-evangelical reformists, soon labelled as *Oxford Movement*, were defenders of the Church of England which they believed shared unbroken continuity with the ancient Catholic Church. They became active especially after 1828 when the *Test and Corporation Act* was repealed, so that from then onwards non-Anglicans could also become members of Parliament. In their view this threatened the position of the Anglican Church as the established Church of the country.

John Henry Newman (1801-1890), leader of the Tractarian Movement in the Anglican Church until the last Tract in 1841. In 1845, he became a Roman Catholic and in 1879 he was made a

The earliest representatives of the *Oxford Movement* were a number of Anglican priests: John Henry Newman, R.H. Froude, E.B. Pusey, H.J. Rose, and W.G. Ward. Influenced by attractive descriptions of the Church of the *Middle Ages* these people developed a love for Roman Catholic ideas and practices. To their way of thinking the Anglican Church is a *via media* (middle way) between Roman Catholicism and Protestantism, and the true representative of the Church before the Reformation. They only recognised clergy in the line of the *apostolic succession* of bishops. Newman said: 'We must necessarily consider none to be really ordained, unless ordained by those in apostolic succession'. Also other Roman Catholic ideas, unknown to the Reformed practice of the Anglican Church, were introduced, for example the doctrine of *transubstantiation*. Newman: Clergymen are 'entrusted with the awful and mysterious gifts of making the bread and wine Christ's body and blood'. Pusey defended baptismal regeneration (original sin taken away by baptism). Some openly deplored the Reformation as a break with the Roman Catholic Church and opted for re-union. Frederick Oakely said: 'We are estranged from her [= the Roman Catholic Church] in presence and not in heart: may we never be provoked to forget her'. Ward characterised Protestantism as a 'debased, hollow, inconsistent form of Christianity'.

The Oxford Movement is also called the *Tractarian Movement*. That is because its members propagated their views in a number of widely spread tracts.[4] In tract number 90, in 1839, Newman wrote that the *39 Articles of the Anglican Church* (a Calvinist-oriented creedal statement) 'aim at being Catholic in heart and doctrine'. This made the

---

[4]*tract*: a short essay on religious or political issues.

Anglican leaders turn against the Tractarians. Disappointed, Newman, together with Ward, Faber, Manning and others, left the Anglican Church and joined the *Roman Catholic Church*. Later the Pope nominated Newman as a cardinal. Other followers of the Oxford Movement, originally led by Pusey, continued to realise their aspirations in the Anglican Church. Beside the *Evangelical party* (Low Church) and the *Liberal party* (Broad Church) they formed the *Anglo-Catholic party* (High Church). Although *Anglo-Catholicism* distinguishes itself from Roman Catholicism, it follows part of the Roman Catholic practices and sacramental views, such as mitred bishops who are vested in copes and chasubles, ornamented clergy and churches, images of Mary, candles for Mary, monstrances,[5] mass, masses for the living and the dead, and worship of the Host.[6]

---

[5] *monstrance*: from Latin *monstrare* = to show. A vessel holding the consecrated Host.

[6] *Host*: from Latin *hostia* = sacrifice. In the Roman Catholic mass it is the bread that is handed by the priest to the believers, and which is supposed to have transformed into the body of Christ.

36. European Protestantism 1648–1800

36.1. Expansion outside Europe

In chapter 28.1 we described the expansion of Protestantism in large parts of Europe after the Reformation, in the 16th, 17th and 18th centuries. Soon Protestantism began to spread outside Europe. In the beginning this was mainly due to the seafaring activities, discoveries, and overseas settlements by countries like Britain and The Netherlands. Protestant churches emerged in North America, South Africa and other parts of the growing overseas network of these nations.[1] Until the 19th century the growth outside Europe was mainly caused by European merchants and settlers. In the 19th century Protestant organisations for the first time consciously deployed intensive missionary activities among the native populations, mainly in Asia, and Africa, and thus extended the Church to these continents.

36.2. Enlightenment and Decay

We described how the Rationalist expression of the *Enlightenment*, as a further deployment of 16th-century Humanist appraisal of man's capabilities, influenced the Western churches of the 17th and 18th centuries. This sometimes led to a kind of *Orthodoxism* with much attention to doctrinal structures, inherited to a certain extent from the Scholastic methods of the Middle Ages. The Enlightenment also gradually led to an interest in the sources of Bible manuscripts, and for the history of the compilation of Bible texts. The *historical-critical method* of Bible study emerged.

Although there were some positive fruits, this movement generally degraded the church. In the beginning of the 18th century many Protestant churches in Western Europe and America had come to decay. In the 19th century the Enlightenment, obsessed with attention to man's personality and emotions (*Romanticism*), would produce a spate of *liberal thought* on Scripture and church. This outbreak of *Liberalism* was prepared by the *Arminianism* (condemned by the Dutch National Synod of 1618/1619 in the *Canons of Dordt*), the *Unitarianism* (fostered in English Presbyterianism and Congregationalism by e.g. John Biddle, Joseph Priestley, Theophilus Lindsey), the *Doubting* of the authority of Scripture, the *Deism,* the idea of *Toleration*, etc. This process of degrading was counteracted in the 17th, 18th and 19th centuries by a number of *Revivals* and *Awakenings*.

36.3. Pietist Reactions[2]

a. Streams

We noted that parallel to and following the decay, in many Protestant Churches there was a movement which can be generally designated by the term of *Pietism*. Strains of it are already apparent in the 16th century, in persons like Taffin and the Teelincks in

---

[1] Cairns, *Christianity through the Centuries*, pp.355-371; Dowley, pp.475-484; Thomson, pp.89-91, 92-103, 130, 131; Cragg, pp.174-185.

[2] On the movements of Pietism, Puritanism, Second Reformation, see: Cairns, *Christianity through the Centuries*, pp.376,380-384, 415, 416; Dowley, pp.444-446, 482-483; Cragg, pp.93-106.

Holland, but especially in the early period of *English Puritanism* (William Tyndale, William Perkins).

The revival of Biblical religion is most apparent in further developments of English and Scottish Puritanism, in the *Dutch Nadere Reformatie* (= Further Reformation; Gisbertus Voetius, Jodocus van Lodensteyn, Wilhelmus à Brakel, Jacobus Koelman, Abraham Hellenbroek, Petrus Immens), in the *German Pietismus*, in the *English Methodist Revival*, in the *American Great Awakening*. Its representatives stressed the necessity of sanctification, the work of the Holy Spirit, inward Christian life, the necessity of self-examination, being a Christian in daily practice, the keeping of the Sunday, the maintaining of church discipline, and the freedom of the church towards the state. This series of revivalist movements are cradled in the 17th and 18th centuries, but their effects continue in the 19th and 20th centuries.

b. Extremism

Pietistic reactions against the Enlightenment sometimes derailed into movements of pietistic or even *mystical extremism*, which shows how they were influenced by the *romantic* thought of the time. In The Netherlands some preachers of the Reformed Church, like Wilhelmus Schortinghuis (1700-1750), tended to elevate pious life above doctrinal teaching, feeling above faith. The *Labadists* (followers of Jean de Labadie, 1610-1674) even left the Reformed Church and founded a community on a communist basis with much room for emotionalism. The *Quakers* in the Anglo-Saxon world are another example of Pietistic extremism.[3]

Jean de Labadie (1610-1674), leader of a Pietist sect organised on a communist basis.

Especially in the 18th century groups of spiritual enthusiasts began to arise; for example a movement of deep spiritual agitation in The Netherlands, mainly in the city of Nijkerk, approximately 1749. The labours of diligent Reformed preachers effected deep feelings of guilt, weeping, wailing, moaning and fainting in public, i.e. in the church services and on the streets. Owing to the able and faithful guidance of church session and pastor (Rev. G. Kuypers) much of this movement was channeled into a more balanced direction, so that it finally contributed to the Biblical movement of revival in the Reformed Church. There were parallel phenomena in other countries.

c. Fruits of Puritanism

Many revivals owe much to the *English Puritanism* of the 16th and early 17th centuries. After the *Westminster Assembly* and the Cromwellian period and especially after the *Restoration* of the Stuarts in 1660, Puritanism had lost much of its strength on English soil. But in the previous decades it had contributed to the sowing of seeds for revivalist movements. Puritanism in a way laid the foundations for the above mentioned revivals in The Netherlands. It is also connected to the *Pietismus* in Germany, to the *Evangelical Revival* and the Movement of *Methodism* in the Anglo-Saxon world, and to the *Great Awakening* in North America.

---

[3] See especially: Dowley, pp.500-503.

36.4. German Pietismus

a. Spener

The German Pietismus is a movement in the Lutheran Church started by Philip Jakob Spener (1635-1705). It intended to infuse new life into the official Protestantism of the time. He was a silent and modest person with a deep feeling and understanding of what was lacking in the Orthodoxist chilly climate of the church of his time. Study of Scripture, of the writings of Johan Arndt (an influential *mystic* in 16th-century Lutheranism), of the English Puritans, and the teachings of Calvin (especially the vision of church discipline) made him insist on reforms.

Spener put forward proposals for restoring religion in his *Pia Desideria* (1675): (a) necessity of Bible knowledge, (b) recognition of the priesthood of all believers, (c) stressing of practical consequences of being a Christian, (d) tolerance in religious conflicts, (e) future ministers should be better examined and they should exercise piety and (f) ministers should firstly be edifiers and less rhetoricians and scholars.

He also tried to put his theories to practice by instituting devotional circles (*collegia pietatis*) for prayer and Bible reading. Spener consciously refused to separate from the mainline church. Representatives of Lutheran Orthodoxy accused him of heresy and said that he raised revolt against the offices of the church. But in Spener's conventicles or *ecclesiola in ecclesia* (little church inside the church) many people for the first time in their lives found food for their souls.

Philip Jakob Spener (1635-1705), instigator of Pietismus in the German Lutheran Church, through the organisation of 'collegia pietatis', and his Pia Desideria (1675).

August Hermann Francke (1663-1727). Influenced by Spener he became leader in the Movement of Pietismus in Germany, and was well-known for his educational and social activities.

b. Francke

The movement of Pietismus quickly won support. A clash with the leaders of the church became inevitable when August Hermann Francke (†1727) attacked the theologians of the University of Leipzig. He condemned the University's philosophy, doctrine and homiletics, and he demanded that lectures be turned into devotional meetings. In 1694 Spener, Francke and others founded a new *University at Halle*, which for a time was the centre of the movement of Pietismus. Francke represents the Pietismus in his exemplary social activities, e.g. the foundation of orphanages and schools.

c. Bengel

A special branch of German Pietismus flourished in the state of Württemberg and was much promoted by Johann Albrecht Bengel (b.1687). Generally, the Pietismus was a good counterbalance against the effects of the Enlightenment. Rebirth, conversion, and the struggle of faith (German: *'Busskampf'*) were stressed. But sometimes it emphasised the subjectivity of religious experience too much, at the expense of the objectivity of faith.

d. Von Zinzendorf

This is sometimes apparent in the movement of the *Brudergemeinde* (congregation of brethren) or *Hernhuters*, founded by Nikolaus Ludwig, Count of Zinzendorf (1700-1760). This nobleman was a student of Francke in Halle. There he saw a painting of the crucifixion with the words: 'This I did for you; what are you doing for Me?', which were going to direct his life. In Herrnhut, one of his estates, he received Protestant refugees from Austria (*Moravian Brethrenn*). These refugees formed his first conventicle. Soon he was forced out of the official church. Then began his activity of planting congregations, not only in Germany, but also in Russia, England, America, and The Netherlands. These *Hernhuters* were very active missionaries e.g. among the Eskimos, and among the black slaves in Surinam, a Dutch colony in South America. Von Zinzendorf was opposed to the unbelieving Rationalism and barren Protestant Orthodoxy of his time.

Nikolaus Ludwig Count of Zinzendorf (1700-1760), founder at Herrnhut of a congregation of Moravian Brethren which led to the Herrnhuter mission to many countries.

He proclaimed a 'religion of the heart', based on an intimate fellowship with the Saviour. His emphasis on the place of feeling in religion, profoundly influenced 19th-century German theology, though *not always* in a Biblically balanced sense. Von Zinzendorf rejected the *formalism* of the Pietismus of Francke cum suis. His emphasis on personal experience had little room for the struggle of faith, but more for an enthusiast veneration of the suffering and death of Christ, whereas the work of the Father and the Holy Spirit was not much stressed.

Symbol of the Hernhutters.

36.5. Evangelical and Methodist Revivals after 1700

a. Anglican Decay

In the beginning of the 18th century the English churches were in a process of serious decay. Puritanism was scattered in various groups, weakened by sectarian strife. It was also undermined by *Unitarian* and *hyper-calvinist* heresies, the former denying the Trinity and the latter over-emphasizing the doctrine of predestination. The state church, led by an episcopalian élite, harboured much rationalist tolerance, and gave latitude for moral abuses.

Change was brought about by a powerful *Evangelical Revival*. One of its phenomena was the movement of *Methodism*.[4] Although it was more comprehensive than Methodism, the terms are often used interchangeably.

b. The Wesleys

John Wesley (1703-1791), his brother Charles Wesley (1707-1788), and George Whitefield (1714-1770), were the founders of *Methodism*, and as such important Evangelical Revivalists. Unlike Whitefield's work, the activities of the Wesleys would eventually be narrowed down to the foundation of separate Methodist churches. When a student at Oxford, John Wesley gathered around him a group of devout Christians, who became known as the *Holy Club* or *Methodists*. In 1735, he with his brother Charles and George Whitefield, set out on a missionary journey to North America (Georgia). But the Wesleys alienated the colonists and returned home (1737). Whitefield was to be much more successful in America.

After a visit to Von Zinzendorf in Herrnhut in 1738, John Wesley experienced conversion. He determined to devote his life to evangelistic work. Finding the churches closed to him he began preaching outdoors. His success led him to organise a body of lay preachers to follow up his evangelism. From 1742 he covered the whole of the British Isles, travelling very extensively. In 1744 he held a conference of lay preachers. This became an annual event, for which a legal constitution was provided later. This was the harbinger of the beginning of the *Methodist Church* in England.

John Wesley (1703-1791), revivalist preacher of Arminian persuasion, and founder of the Methodist Movement which after his death would lead to the establishment of a separate Methodist Church.

Methodism was established in America also. From small beginnings in 1760 the Methodist system gradually developed there. The needs for leadership in America induced Wesley to ordain Thomas Cooke (1747-1814) to be superintendent or bishop, and to instruct him to ordain Francis Asbury as his colleague. In this way the foundation was laid for the *Methodist Episcopal Church*. In the course of time break away groups formed a series of other Methodist churches. While Methodism took on separate

---

[4] On *Methodism*, see: Cairns, *Christianity through the Centuries*, pp.376, 381, 382, 384-388, 398-413, 521-525; Dowley, pp.446-457; Thomson, pp.112-116; Renwick/Harman, pp.163-173; Cragg, pp.141-156.

ecclesiastical forms in England as well, Wesley himself wanted the Movement to remain within the *Church of England*. But in reality an increasingly independent system grew up.

The term *methodism* refers to the order or method the revivalist preachers had in mind when proclaiming God's demand of rebirth, and conversion to new life. In Methodist tradition the main aim is the winning of souls. The individual is set apart from his environment and from his former past. There is no attention for God's command to reclaim His fallen creation, i.e. the natural world, and the structures of society to the obedience to the Word of God. The truth of Christian religion is narrowed down to two issues: (a) the effect of the preaching of the Word of God is a sudden experience of guilt and grace, i.e. personal rebirth and conversion, (b) the completely different character of the new life is shown by activity to convert others, abstaining from worldly pleasures, and the realization that perfection is possible in earthly life.

c. Whitefield

Perfectionism was not a general characteristic of early Methodism. It belonged to the Arminian stream in the movement which is mainly attributed to the Wesleys. Their co-founder George Whitefield did not follow the Wesleys in the belief that man's *free will* is decisive for salvation and sanctification. His theology is markedly *Calvinist*, stressing God's sovereignty and His gift of free grace. After returning from his tour with the Wesleys in Georgia, where he founded an orphanage, Whitefield began to hold large open air meetings. His preaching met with remarkable response. Through the help of rich patrons he was able to open a tabernacle in London.

Whitefield is considered to be 'the most striking orator' of the Methodist revival, although after his death the Calvinist strand of Methodism in England was soon overwhelmed by the Arminian mainstream. Inside the Church of England, however, his influence was more lasting.

George Whitefield (1714-1770), influential Methodist preacher of Calvinist persuasion who contributed much to the Evangelical Revival in the Church of England and to the Great Awakening in America.

37. European Protestantism 1800-1900

37.1. Effects of the Revivals

The revivals within the Protestantism of the 18th century continued or resurged in the 19th century, sometimes in different shapes. Generally, they were very wide and influential.[1] They can be characterised as follows.

First, they *slowed down secularisation*. For example, in The Netherlands in 1900 almost all citizens were still baptised.

Secondly, in N.W. Europe they *prevented socialist and communist uprisings*, because of the reforms for social justice they promoted.

Thirdly, they stimulated and gave power to the *Missionary Movement*.

Fourthly, most of them took place *outside the mainline churches*. Here are some examples: The activities of the English Baptist preacher C.H. Spurgeon, the American Congregationalist preachers D.L. Moody and I.D. Sankey, W. Booth who founded the *Salvation Army*, activities of the *Plymouth Brethren* by preachers like J. Darby and G. Müller, the Apostolic Church founded by E. Irving the *Young Men's Christian Association*, founded by G. Williams, the *Keswick meetings*, the *Welsh revivals*, the emergence of the 'old' *Free Church* in Scotland, the revivals of *Reveil* and *Afscheiding* in The Netherlands.

Fifthly, they also either touched or took place in the mainline churches and state churches.

Charles Haddon Spurgeon (1834-1892), influential Baptist revivalist preacher in London where he built a new church, the Metropolitan Tabernacle.

William Booth (1829-1912), founder of the Salvation Army.

John Nelson Darby (1800-1882), left the Church of England of which he had been a priest and joined the Brethren (of J.N. Groves cuss.), who in Plymouth (1845) and Bristol (1847) split into two groups.

The effects of the Revivals can be summarised by pointing out two aspects. They reformed the societies and churches of Western Europe and America. They also ignited the peoples of Western Europe and America to go out for mission in other continents. In the following two paragraphs most examples are taken from Britain. This is not to deny that internal reform and the birth of missionary interest was limited to Britain. The

---

[1] Cairns, *Christianity through the Centuries*, pp.398-416; Dowley, pp.518-540; Vidler, pp.33-44, 45-55, 90-100, 134-145; Renwick/Harman, pp.163-173.

Scandinavian countries, The Netherlands, Germany, Switzerland and other countries were deeply touched by these phenomena as well.

37.2. Reform of Church and Society

The *Evangelical Revival*, stimulated by Whitefield and others, differed from the Methodism of the Wesleys. *First*, it was not Arminian. *Secondly*, it was not limited to a certain denomination only. It deeply influenced Anglicans and others in Britain. Besides, this, it brought revival in existing churches in America. *Calvinistic Methodism*, represented by Whitefield and Selina Hastings, the Countess of Huntingdon, proved to be attractive to many clergymen and other members of the Anglican Church.

An *Evangelical party* in that church emerged which was very influential by the end of the 18th century. Salvation of the individual, and through this the transformation of society, was their aim. Their good works included the care of the weak and destitute, a crusade against slavery, and the promotion of education for the poor. The Evangelicals were very interested in mission and evangelisation. To their early foundations belong the *Church Missionary Society*, the *Religious Tract Society* and the *British and Foreign Bible Society*. Very influential was the *Clapham Sect*, a group of rich and godly leaders, who stimulated social reform and mission.

William Wilberforce (1759-1833), convert of the Evangelical Revival, member of the Clapham Sect, Member of Parliament; he contributed much to the fight against slavery, and it abolition in 1833.

Slavery was successfully resisted by people like William Wilberforce. Lord Shaftesbury won the fight against *child labour* (chimney-sweepers etc.). The *Exeter Hall group* influenced the government to favour reforms. J. Howard was instrumental for the introduction of *prison reforms*. H. Moore and R. Raikes founded the *Sunday School Movement*. Theologically the Evangelical movement competed with the Oxford movement in the Anglican Church. Whereas the Oxford movement aimed at reviving the rites and beliefs of the Medieval Church, the Evangelicals tried to connect to the 16th-century Reformation.

37.3. The Awakening of Mission

Before 1800 Protestantism did not show much conscious effort to expand outside Europe. There were mainly two reasons for this. First the churches of the Reformation were pre-occupied with teaching and evangelising the neglected masses of their own countries. Second, in later stage churches were influenced by the *Enlightenment* with its speculative *deism* and cold *rationalism*, and this was not a good breeding ground for missionary enthusiasm.

Nonetheless, there were early missionary endeavours, aimed at the expansion of international trade together with the settlement of Europeans in other continents. The American Indians were targeted by a corporation established in 1649. John Eliot was

37. European Protestantism 1800-1900

one of its first workers (see chapter 37.3). The British *East India Company* appointed chaplains on its ships and in its trading centres, and as a side effect they spread the Gospel among some of the native people.

The same was done by the Dutch, e.g. in their *United East Indies Company* (VOC: Verenigde Oostindische Compagnie), which was instrumental to the formation of early churches in India, Ceylon, Malaysia and the East Indies. Missionary consciousness never really vanished because of the movements of *Puritanism, Further Reformation*, and *Pietism* that revived and deepened European Protestantism. These movements went before the great *evangelical awakenings* and *revivals* of the 18th and 19th centuries that brought about the birth of modern mission.

The history of modern mission begins with the *Moravian Brethren*. Encouraged by Von Zinzendorf of Herrnhut, these refugees organised themselves as a missionary church in 1732. In the course of time they sent out thousands of missionaries to the remotest and most difficult parts of the world. One of their workers was George Schmidt. He evangelised among the South African Khoikhoi people. The revivalist work of the Wesleys, Whitefield, Edwards and others gave rise to powerful religious and social developments, and it unleashed further missionary energies. For the time being, however, missionary work would be an activity of individuals or associations of individuals, not of the churches.

In 1792 the ex-cobbler and Baptist minister William Carey (†1834), before he went to India as a missionary, founded together with some colleagues the *Baptist Missionary Society* (BMS). To its famous missionaries belonged George Grenfell who made maps of the Congo River, thus contributing to the opening of inland Africa for the Gospel. The BMS was only the first of numerous other missionary organisations.

The Baptist initiative was soon followed by some Presbyterians, Anglicans, and Congregationalists who in 1795 founded the *London Missionary Society* (LMS). The work of the LMS spread to India, China, Africa and the West-Indies. In the beginning they mainly used non-British missionaries. A famous early LMS worker was the Dutchman Johannes van der Kemp. This ex-cavalry officer, medical doctor and theologian together with others founded a society of missionaries in The Netherlands, following the example of the LMS. Then, he was employed by the LMS and he worked among the South African Khoikhoi, connecting with the earlier work done by Moravian missionaries, Schmidt and others. Other famous LMS missionaries were John Philip, John Mackenzie, Robert and Mary Moffat, and their son-in-law David Livingstone.

In 1796 the *General Methodist Society* was formed; it began work in regions like Africa, India, China, Polynesia, and the West Indies.

In 1799 evangelical Anglicans established the *Church Missionary Society* (CMS). It directly resulted from the effects of the Evangelical revival in and outside the Anglican Church and from the activities of the *Clapham Sect* the above mentioned group of influential Anglicans who campaigned for abolishment of slavery and social and religious reform. Soon the CMS was

David Livingstone (1813-1873), missionary pioneer in Central Africa, first for the London Missionary Society. He contributed much to the fight against the Swahili Arab slave trade.

active in India, China, Japan, West Africa, Egypt, Palestine, and Persia. To its missionaries in Uganda belonged George Pilkington and Alfred Tucker. Livingstone's work challenged High Church Anglicans to form the *Universities' Mission to Central Africa* (UMCA) and it also led to missionary initiatives in South and Central Africa, Sierra Leone, India, Jamaica, by members of the Church of Scotland and of the Free Church of Scotland.

Gradually the mainline churches in Europe and America moved from apathy concerning mission to an interest in missionary work. Missionary organisations were taken over by them, or they started missions themselves.

Beside these mainline missions a different type of missionary organisations emerged in the second half of the 19th century. They were called *faith missions* and had a number of special characteristics (see: chapter 55). The first one was the *China Inland Mission*, founded by Hudson Taylor in 1866.[2]

James Hudson Taylor (1832-1905). By founding the China Inland Mission he inspired to a new approach of organising missionary work.

---

[2] Cairns, *Christianity through the Centuries*, 409-313, 529, 530, 534, 509-514; Dowley, 478-484, 557-580; Vidler, 246-256; Renwick/ Harman, 174-181; Fiedler, *Faith Missions*, 11-56; Shaw, *Kingdom*, 127-202

38. North American Protestantism 1600-1900[1]

38.1. Beginnings

By the end of the 16th century Christianity had reached North America with colonisers of the continent. Roman Catholicism as well as Protestantism found its way. The first who came were the Spanish. In 1565 they permanently settled in Florida, thus starting Roman Catholic presence in North America. The French also tried to settle in parts of the continent, e.g. in Florida, and from 1608 onwards in Quebec. Generally, they strengthened Roman Catholicism, although French Protestants arrived later.

Protestantism came with colonisers from North West Europe. British colonisation began with settlements at Newfoundland in 1538 and at the Virginian coast in 1607. An expedition in 1585 miscarried, although it is recorded that a member of the party, Thomas Harriot, made attempts to reach the Indians with the Gospel. The first recorded Indian convert is Pocahontas, the daughter of a chief. She married an English settler, and died after the couple had migrated to England.

The Swedes had a short-lived colony at the mouth of the Delaware River. The Dutch took it from them, and they founded their New Netherlands and New Amsterdam at the place that is now called New York. However, a war with the British ended Dutch rule. By the end of the 17th century much of North America's east-coast had become British territory. Although the colony of Maryland had become a haven for Roman Catholics, most of the early settlers were Protestants. The English were mainly members of the Anglican Church. Only some of them were *Conformists*, i.e. agreeing to the establishment of the Church of England under king and bishops. Most Anglican immigrants were *Non-Conformists*. They had come to America because they disagreed with the establishment, and wanted further Reformation, which they hoped to realise in the new world. Generally, they were called Puritans. The majority of these protesting Anglicans aspired to a Presbyterian type of church government, with elders, ministers, and synods instead of a hierarchy of priests and bishops ruled by the king.

38.2. The Pilgrim Fathers

An influential group of Puritans had decided that the Church of England was a false church which could not be reformed, and consequently had to be left by believers. These Puritans were called Separatists. After 1600 they became known as Congregationalists. They were declared illegal and were persecuted. That is why from the end of the 16th century many of them had fled to the European continent. Puritans who fled to The Netherlands, settled in various cities, and founded congregations there. After some years of exile, the Puritan refugees in the city of Leyden, decided to leave The Netherlands and go to North America.

In 1620 the famous crossing of these *Pilgrim Fathers* took place. In their ship, the *Mayflower*, about 140 persons, after a difficult voyage, reached Cape Cod in the region

---

[1] Cf. S.M. Houghton, *Sketches from Church History: An Illustrated Account of 20 Centuries of Christ's Power*, Edinburgh: The Banner of Truth Trust, 2000[5], pp.165-174,178-185,208-221. Cf.: Cairns, *Christianity through the Centuries*, pp.355-371, 376, 406; Dowley, pp.436-444 and many other pages; Thomson, *New Movements*, pp.92-104.

that would later be called New England. Because of many hardships half of these original settlers soon died. The colony grew rapidly though because thousands of other Puritans joined the Pilgrim Fathers in the following decades. The New England colonists wanted to be independent of control by the government in England. Important persons among these early settlers were John Harvard and John Eliot. Harvard was instrumental in the founding in 1636 of Harvard College (later the University), in Cambridge, Massachusetts. Eliot is the publisher (in 1640) of the first book in New England, a metrical version of the Psalms. Eliot became famous as a missionary and Bible translator among the Indians.

In the 17th century Roman Catholics, Conformist Anglicans, and Puritans, either of Presbyterian or Congregationalist persuasion came to America because at times they were persecuted in their homeland. The same is true for other groups, e.g. the Quakers, once founded by George Fox. Among the Quakers who settled in America was William Penn, the man who contributed much to the foundation of the state of Pennsylvania where any citizen could enjoy religious freedom. Gradually the American population grew in variation, in terms of both ethnical and religious backgrounds. The stream of British immigrants of various denominations continued, but there were also German and Scandinavian Lutherans, Reformed people and Mennonites from The Netherlands,, and after the revocation of the *Edict of Nantes* (1685), Huguenots from France.

38.3. Slavery and Mission

Abraham Lincoln (1809-1865), the 16th President of the United States, whose anti-slavery attitude invoked a War of Secession. In 1863, he proclaimed all slaves to be free, and in 1865, he was murdered.

The 18th century saw the ongoing growth of the slave trade to and in North America. During the 17th century gradually the keeping of African slaves spread over all the southern states. There was never a complete acceptance of slavery though, as can be seen in the condemnation of it by Cotton Mather, a Puritan writer.[2] After 1713, when England took over Spanish monopoly of the slave trade, the trading and keeping of slaves spread in the New England states. Some Americans were against the idea of Christianising the black African slaves, believing blacks had no souls that needed salvation, or fearing that baptism would make them free. Nonetheless, Elias Neau, a French immigrant of Huguenot descent and others worked hard for educating the slaves and converting them to the Christian faith. Mission to the Indians was continued by workers like John Eliot and David Brainerd.

38.4. Awakenings and Revivals

The Methodist revival reached America when the brothers John and Charles Wesley started ministering in the new colony of Georgia, founded in 1733 through the pioneer work of James Oglethorpe.

---

[2] Cotton Mather, *Essays to do Good* (in: Houghton, *Sketches*, p.179).

In America the Wesleyan Methodist revival was soon overwhelmed by a deeper and more lasting spiritual movement, called the *Great Awakening*. There were two waves. The first one was in the years 1734 and 1735. Instrumental to it was the work of an intellectually and spiritually gifted young man, Jonathan Edwards. In his preaching on sin and grace he stressed the 'justification by faith alone' and he avoided Arminian emphasis on works. This led many to repentance and conversion. The second wave of the Great Awakening happened in the years 1740 and 1741. It was greatly influenced by the preaching of George Whitefield. In chapter 36.5.c we indicated Whitefield's significance for the Evangelical revival in the Anglican Church in Britain itself. Perhaps his influence in America was greater than that. Whitefield paid seven visits to North America. He founded an orphanage in Georgia. In his evangelistic campaigns he reached many. He would emphasise that men and women cannot be saved before they have realised that they are lost.

Jonathan Edwards (1703-1758), revivalist preacher of Calvinist conviction, closely related to George Whitefield and the Great Awakening.

The Great Awakening made Christianity grow in numbers and for a time in quality. It was followed by a series of smaller and more local revivals, e.g. in Virginia in 1740. When Jonathan Edwards died in 1758 he was succeeded by Samuel Davies in one of his functions, president of Princeton College. Perhaps Davies' work, stressing the glory of God in pardoning sinners, was instrumental to the revival that occurred later at this college. Many alumni were touched by it. Their influence on society safeguarded a strong Christian undercurrent in the difficult time when the revivals had died down after the American War of Independence (1776-1783). America became largely isolated from Europe, and thus from the ongoing revivals in Britain and elsewhere. The spirit of independence was partly inspired by religious indifference, forms of Deism, or even denial of Christianity. That is why by the end of the 18th century spiritual life declined.

The revival at Princeton and other colleges in the 1780s changed this. The revival was for many in independent America a new beginning of deep religious life. In New England the decades of the end at the 18th century and in the beginning of the 19th century witnessed an almost unbroken series of revivals. An important role was played by Jonathan Edward's grandson Timothy Dwight, who had become a leader at Yale College.

38.5. War and Abolition

The opening up of inland territories like Louisiana and other areas of the great rivers led to new migrations and also to expansion of the Church. Millions of Europeans took part in this new colonisation. To them belonged poor Irish Roman Catholics who left their country because of the famines during the 1840's. Dutch Calvinists settled in Michigan in the 1830's. Many German and Scandinavian Lutherans arrived after the American Civil War (1863-1865). In the meantime, there was a continuation of the mission work among Indians, e.g. by Stephen Riggs who worked among the native American Sioux tribe and made a dictionary of their language.

A heavy burden for American Christianity was the problem of slavery. Although the practice had spread throughout North America, after the War of Independence (1783) the Northern states gradually turned against it. The South, however, stuck to it, mainly for economic reasons. In 1807 the government forbade the importation of new slaves from abroad. Many Christians in North and South disagreed with the complete abolition of slavery. Some even thought abolition to be unscriptural and false. The attempt of Southern states to withdraw from the Union of states led to the American Civil War. This war decided two issues that were interrelated. No state can leave the Union, and slaves have to be set free.

38.6. Other Groups

Beside Presbyterians, Congregationalists, Mennonites, and Roman Catholics, the United States has also attracted other groups, such as the Baptists. Although the Baptists were persecuted originally by the Congregationalist establishment in Massachusetts they grew. In the southern states they even grew to predominance. Heretical groups either came from abroad or formed inside the United States. Followers of the Swede Emanuel Swedenborg could settle freely in America, although they denied the Trinity and other essential dogmas. America is the birthplace of Mormonism, or the Church of the Latter-Day Saints, founded by Joseph Smith and centred in Salt Lake City (Utah). America also gave birth to the Seventh' Day Adventists with their founders William Miller and Ellen G. White.

A very important component of American church history concerns the establishment and the development of the Afro-American or Black churches. Some black congregations belong to predominantly white denominations, others have formed separate and independent denominations, with their own characteristics.[3] Many of them have branches in Africa among the *Africa Instituted Churches* (AIC), for instance the *African Methodist Episcopal Church* (AMEC) and the *Apostolic Faith Mission* (AFM).[4]

38.7. Finney and Hodge

Protestant church life in the 19th century often reflected the theological difference between Arminian and Orthodox-Calvinist approaches of the need for revivals. Charles G. Finney, called by some 'the pioneer of modern mass evangelism', would claim that sinners, instead of praying for a new heart, could make themselves a new heart and spirit and surrender to God. Calvinists stressed that revival depends on God's gift of His Holy Spirit, and not on an act of the human will. C. Hodge and his son A.A. Hodge belong to the most important theologians in the Calvinist tradition in 19th century America. D.L. Moody and I.D. Sankey were perhaps the most well-known evangelists by the end of the century. These theologians and evangelists also played influential roles in Europe. The same is true for A.T. Pierson who became the immediate successor of the famous revivalist C.H. Spurgeon in London. The Atlantic Ocean was not able to divide the Church in the two continents.

---

[3] Some examples: African Methodist Episcopal Church, African Methodist Episcopal Zion Church, National Baptist Convention of America, Church of God in Christ, Apostolic Faith Mission, United Pentecostal Council of the Assemblies of God, United Church of Christ.

[4] Cf. chapters 53.3; 57.4.b, 5; 58.4; 60,2,3.

39. Theological Developments 1800-2000[1]

39.1. Modernism in Theology

As a *reaction* against the secularising spirit of Renaissance, Humanism and Enlightenment (Rationalism, and Romanticism), the Evangelical Revivals in the 18th and 19th centuries generally reasserted the theology of the Reformation. However, the revivalist movements and churches did not just imitate the Reformation. The application of Reformed doctrines in the new context sometimes required other emphases than in the 16th century. In some cases revivalist religion opposed or neglected aspects of the heritage of the Reformation. On the whole, however, the revived and newly established Protestant churches of the 19th century maintained the most central dogma of the church of the ages, the trustworthiness and supreme authority of Scripture.

By 1870 Reformed and Evangelical churches began to be challenged by the successors of 18th-century Enlightenment-Deism, that is to say by the movement of *Modernism*, which can be divided into (1) *Classical Liberalism* (2) *Neo-Orthodoxy*, (3) *Radical Theologies*, finally followed by (4) *Post-Modernism*.

39.2. Classical Liberalism

The ongoing movement of Enlightenment had produced a climate that endangered the Christian faith and the acceptance of the authority of Scripture. Rationalism, romanticism, individualism, revolutions, materialism, and evolutionism contributed to criticism of the Bible. The Bible came to be seen as just a human book that can be subjected to historical research just like any other book. Cairns says: this 'has led many to deny the inspiration of the Bible as a revelation from God through men inspired by the Holy Spirit and to minimise and to deny the deity of Christ and His saving work on the cross of Calvary'. This criticism was born mainly in Germany. A number of *philosophers* prepared the ground for it.

a. Philosophies

Immanuel Kant

He represents the beginning of the movement of *Romanticism* that replaces Rationalism by feelings and idealism. In his view, human reason cannot know God and the soul. Religion does not have its roots in historical facts, but in man's conscience which gives him or her a sense of moral obligations. One's moral nature is the beginning of religion. There is no need for historicity. Man does not need a Redeemer. With his or her free will, following the 'categorical imperative' of God's law, man can develop the 'sparks' of Divinity in oneself.

Friedrich Schleiermacher

In his view, religion starts in one's subjective feelings and emotions. Religion is the feelingsby which one apprehends his absolute dependence on God. Man is neither

---

[1] Cairns, *Christianity through the Centuries*, pp.418-425, 439-440, 459-467; Dowley, pp.548-556, 584-609, 610-627, 628-645; Renwick/Harman, pp.198-202, 203-205; Vidler, chapters 3, 4, 8, 12 [*Modernism*].

dependent on the historical revelation of the will of God, nor on the authority of the Church. Men and women subjectively realise the presence of the Absolute One, and in the same way they may know about Christ, who serves as a Mediator who reconciles with this God. Religion is a variety; its pure expression is *monotheism*, of which Christianity is the purest expression.

Georg Hegel

Pupil of Kant. In his *evolutionary* view of the universe, of law, and of religion, the truth is not a fact or point, but the whole process. This is a *dialectic process* of reconciling *thesis* and *anti-thesis* into a higher *synthesis*. This synthesis then acts as a new thesis that is opposed to a new anti-thesis, just to be reconciled into a new and still higher synthesis. In this way the process goes on. When applied to humans, the process means that man is not a being but a becoming. God is above this process. He uses it in order to manifest Himself.

Albrecht Ritschl

Ritschl was a pupil first of Baur (who was influenced by Hegel), and then of Schleiermacher. He differs from Schleiermacher in that he makes religion start not in feelings of the *individual* dependence, but in the *social* feeling of dependence. The Bible records this community consciousness. The Bible works through the community, not directly through the individual.

Friedrich Schleiermacher (1768-1834), German scholar and preacher. He considered feeling as the basis of religion, and he looked upon religions as bearers of truth of which monotheism is the purest expression, and Christianity the highest level.

Georg Hegel (1770-1831), German philosopher who explained reality as a sequel of evolutionary processes, a becoming.

Albrecht Ritschl (1822-1889), German theologian. He criticised his teacher F.C. Baur, and thought that faith rests on value-judgments, and also that the Gospel is given to a community, not to individuals.

b. 'Higher' Criticism

The common characteristic of these philosophers is that they put man and woman on their own, leaving out the necessity of revealed historical truth given by a divine source outside them. In doing this, they continue the line that had begun in Renaissance,

Rationalism and Enlightenment. Soon these theories began to influence a number of theologians and other church people. It led to a method of exegesis of Scripture that is called 'higher' and 'historical and literary' Bible criticism. Biblical investigation was subjected to the claimed authority of the human mind. It started with the Old Testament. Here are some examples:

Jean Astruc. He invented the idea that the book of Genesis has to be divided into two parts, each coming from different sources documents, the Elohist (E) and the Jehovist (J).

Johann G. Eichorn and *Hermann Hupfeld* extended Astruc's idea to the first six books of the Bible, and also see additional sources, like the Priestly Codex (P).

Karl Graf and *Julius Wellhausen* considered J as the oldest source, and distinguish further D (Deuteronomy) and P. This is worked out in a system that denies the unity of the Pentateuch and their being written by Moses.

Others shifted the chronological order of books, for example Daniel and parts of Isaiah to the post-exilic time, thus taking away the prophetic character of these books. Also, other parts of pre-exilic Scripture were explained as later reflections on history.

New Testament 'higher' criticism started with *Hermann Reimarus*. He feared to air his critical thoughts, so they were published after his death. According to him, the Bible writers were fanatical frauds, writing contradictions. He denied miracles.

Another critic was *Gotthold Lessing*, who thought that religion belonged to the primitive state of mankind that we have overcome now that reason and duty are supposed to be our trustworthy guides.

Ferdinand Baur applied Hegel's thought to the New Testament. Early Christianity is a struggle between various views. The *thesis* we are to see in the writings of Peter which in Baur's view have Judaist tendencies, Paul delivered the *anti-thesis*, and the *synthesis* is to be found in the later Catholic Church, as already reflected by Luke and the Pastoral letters. He arranged New Testament chronology accordingly. Baur also applied this method to the development of doctrine. He denied the historicity of all Pauline epistles as well as of the books of John.

In the 20th century other forms of criticism of the Gospels were added. First, *source criticism*, which focuses on the chronological order of writing. Secondly, *form criticism*. It attempts to discover the origin and trace of particular passages by analogy of their structural forms. When were they transmitted from oral form to written form? What is the earliest history of the written forms, and what is the historical setting that determined them? Thirdly, there is the *redaction criticism* which supposes that Gospel writers, when accounting for Christ's life and work, made additions and changes.

David Strauss said that the Gospels were written in the second century by people who made a legend out of the life of Jesus. The essence of the Gospels is only Jesus' ethical teachings. In his view, Paul spoiled Jesus' simple message by making a difficult redemptive religion of it.

From Germany the thoughts of 'higher criticism' spread throughout Europe and America and also to the mission fields. Scotland was one of the first recipients of this movement of Modernism. In America it was imported by students like *Samuel Driver*, who had studied in Europe. *Walter Rauschenbusch* applied modern liberal thought to social and economic life, thus creating a 'social gospel'. Experience rather than Scripture was emphasised. At colleges many learnt to explain miracles by scientific means and to deny doctrines like original sin and the vicarious atonement by Christ. In education *Horace Bushnell* introduced the idea that a child gradually can grow into grace. University professors of theology like *Charles Briggs* started to teach higher criticism. Inerrancy and inspiration of Scripture were attacked together with the absoluteness of God and the uniqueness of the way of salvation in Christ.

c. The Roman Catholic Church

Classical liberalism also influenced the Roman Catholic Church. The French scholar *Alfred Loisy* accepted Modernism and applied the historical-critical method to the Bible. In his view, Christianity is based, not on the Bible but on the faith of the developed Church as expanded under the guidance of the Holy Spirit. The *First Vatican Council* (1870), convoked by Pope Pius IX, introduced the doctrine of *papal infallibility*. This put the authority of the Pope above the Church and also above Scripture, which could defend either conservative or modernistic views of Scripture. Pius X, who became pope in 1903, resumed a conservative stance. In 1907 he condemned Modernism and in 1910 he demanded an *anti-modernism oath* from the clergy. Before him Pope Leo XIII, in 1902, had encouraged the new methods of Biblical criticism. He founded a Biblical Commission that was to work in the line of Modernism. Pope Pius XII in 1942 in his encyclical *Divino Afflante Spiritu* allowed great freedom for scholars to apply modern thought.

The official Roman Catholic idea that *tradition* is on an equal footing with revelation contributed to acceptance of critical Biblical criticism. The Council of Trent mentions tradition before the Scriptures:

> 'I must steadfastly acknowledge and embrace the apostolic and ecclesiastical traditions, and other observances and constitutions of the same. ... I acknowledge the Holy Scriptures, according to that sense which the holy mother Church has held and holds, to which it belongs to judge of the true sense and interpretation of the Scriptures; neither will I receive and interpret them except according to the unanimous consent of the Fathers'.[2]

Since the Pope had been recognised as infallible in 1870, tradition gets an even stronger emphasis as compared to Scripture. This position, however, does not allow freedom for attacks on the dogmas of the Roman Catholic Church. This was experienced by the English Jesuit *George Tyrrell* (†1901) who was expelled by his order after he denounced scholasticism as 'dead theology', and in 1907 excommunicated. Tyrrell was an evolutionist thinker who questioned the finality of Christianity, and hoped for a universal religion of which Christianity was but the germ.

d. Decline

Classical Liberalism reached its peak in the beginning of the 20th century, but after the end of the First World War (1918) it declined. It broke down because: (a) the horrors of the war and economic depressions had shown the inability of man to rule his own affairs, (b) the theology of *Karl Barth* and the influence of existential theology destroyed the idea of human progress without God and (c) the new movement of neo-orthodoxy reasserted a number of orthodox doctrines.

---

[2] Quoted in: D. Hedegård, *Ecumenism and the Bible*, Edinburgh: Banner of Truth Trust, pp.125,126.

39.3. Neo-Orthodoxy

The Danish theologian *Sören Kierkegaard* developed an existentialist system in which man in the crises of life surrenders to God by a 'leap of faith'. He influenced *Karl Barth* (1886-1968) the father of a new movement that is called either *neo-orthodoxy*, or *theology of crisis*, or *dialectic theology*. To Barth God is the eternally transcendent 'wholly other', whereas man is little, vulnerable, and sinful. Though Barth was a very effective critic of classical liberalism, in his view of Scripture he retained some liberal views, that is to say he retained them in dialectical way. The Bible is not revelation; it is a record, a witness of revelation, a human book that can be researched like any other book. Biblical miracles are true in 'Geschichte' (*holy history*), but not necessarily so in 'Historie' (*secular history*). In a crisis the Bible *becomes* relevant to man, and then it *becomes* an instrument of the Holy Spirit. The Bible is a meeting point, not so much a piece of information. All people are elected in Christ, and it is the Church's task to inform them about this. Barth belonged to the founders of the *World Council of Churches* in 1948, the main representative of the modern Ecumenical Movement. Ecumenical leaders have often appealed to Barth when defending their modernistic views. It remains to be seen whether they have really understood him.

Karl Barth (1886-1968), a Swiss Reformed theologian deeply influenced 20th-century theology.

Barth's influence has been considerable in Reformed and Evangelical churches in Europe and America, and later also in the former mission fields of Asia and Africa. This led to the formation of *Neo-Reformed* theologies. Some of Barth's ideas were criticised by these theologians. *Emil Brunner* (†1966) did not accept Barth's disconnecting of supra-natural holy history and down-to-earth secular history. From creation man retains a limited knowledge of God. There is a 'link', though this connection is not made by the Bible, but by a personal meeting with God. In this he was influenced by the Jewish theologian *Martin Buber* (†1965). *Reinhold Niebuhr* (†1971), after his rejection of classical liberalism, followed Barth to a great extent, but unlike Barth he applied dialectic theology to the social problems of his time. Paul Tillich (†1965) also followed Barth but for him God was a 'ground of being', not necessarily a divine person. Bible and creeds are subjective expressions of human thought. For the Anglican bishop John Robinson (†1983) there is no personal God, 'God is dead'. *Rudolf Bultmann* (†1976) was more on the side of classical liberalism and form criticism than a follower of Barth. His method of *'de-mythologising'* Scripture left people with very little information about Christ; he denied His bodily resurrection and only accepted the crucifixion as a historical fact.

The *Evangelical Movement* also underwent the influence of neo-orthodox liberalism. Harold J. Ockenga invented the term *neo-evangelical*. The mainline was not affected, but in a sub-stream verbal inspiration and inerrancy were questioned. Biblical criticism became accepted by a number of evangelical theologians, as well as evolutionist theories. Neo-evangelicals are open for dialogue with liberal and neo-orthodox ecumenical groups.

Neo-orthodoxy was paralleled by a movement of *Théologie Nouvelle* (new theology) in the Roman Catholic Church.

John A.T. Robinson (1919-1983), Anglican Bishop of Woolwich. In 1963 he wrote a book Honest to God that practically denied the existence of a personal God who has revealed Himself to man: 'God is dead' to his perception

Rudolf Bultmann (1884-1976), German theologian. He radically applied the method of Form Criticism to the Synoptic Gospels, 'demythologising' the New Testament message.

39.4. Radical Theologies and Revivals

In the 1960s in the West a revolution of the mind took place. It had spiritual dimensions. The post-war baby-boomers had become adults, and many of them turned their backs on the traditional churches, or even left the church altogether. The secularisation process that had started in the Enlightenment, and had been fed by *classical liberalism* and *neo-orthodoxy*, developed radically. The background was a general cultural change. Many people protested against the old structures. The revolutionary virus began among students, who turned to protest and violence against traditional society. Riots and even risings spread from the University of Beverley Hills (California) to Amsterdam, Bologna, Copenhagen, and Paris. Many of these students had *Marxist* and *communist* ideas. Hand in hand with this went a more peaceful *hippy-movement* inspired by *occultism* and *eastern mysticism*. Many students as back-packers went to India to find philosophies for a better future. A *flower-power* movement expressed itself in anti-authoritarian behaviour, free sex, and drugs abuse.

This revolution influenced Western Christians too. Theologians and others tried to find its causes, suggesting a combination of things: theological modernism, two world wars, the Auschwitz-syndrome, *decolonisation*, continuing oppression in the Soviet Union and China, oppressing structures in Latin America, the threat of a third world war that could destroy the world, wars in Vietnam, Cambodia, Iraq/Iran, the foundation of the Israeli state and its wars with the Arabs, ecological disasters, individualisation and loneliness especially of the urban population. Generally, the churches were not very much aware of these events and developments. Sometimes they failed to prepare the people for the changes in Western culture. This gave birth to two reactions.

The *first reaction* was the emergence of revolutionary theologies of protest. They also touched the world outside Europe and America. Here are some examples: (a) 'God is dead' theology (J.J. Altizer, H. Cox), (b) Theology of Hope (J.J. Moltmann, W. Pannenberg), (c) Process Theology (P. Teilhard de Chardin), (d) Liberation Theology (G. Gutierrez), expressing itself in various ways, e.g. Feminist Theology, Black Theology (Manas Buthelezi, Desmond Tutu, Allan Boesak) and (e) African Theology (P. Temple, Alexis Kagame, Vincent Mulago, Tharcisse Tshibango, J.B. Danquah, David Smith, John Mbiti, Bengt Sundkler).

The *second reaction* showed how God looks after His Church. The Holy Spirit gave new revivals. The political and social structures of the Western world had become secularised, but at the same time in many churches a new spiritual interest was born. One advantage of secularisation is that nominal Christianity decreases and that spiritual consciousness among the remaining Christians increases. This has given many old churches a new face, and new churches have been established. The revivalist spirit was very much apparent in Africa

Jürgen Moltmann (1926-), representative of a theology of hope, looking upon God's actions as cumulative, i.e. revelation in future is more than revelation in the past.

and Latin America. These continents saw a dramatic growth of Christianity. About 1990 when Russia and other communist countries were liberated, it appeared that after many decades of persecution the church was still very much alive. Even persecutions could not prevent impressive church growth in Communist China.

39.5. Post-Modernism

About 1980 in the West, a climate emerged that gave room to the birth of new religiosity. The world had become a *global village*. The West had been influenced by Eastern religions, creating New Age thinking. The dramatic political change due to the collapse of communism meant the end of the *atheism* as a popular option. Also, the interest in history and historical approaches dwindled. In the thinking of many people the Bible again became a book of some value. It is 'a story that goes'. Classic literary criticism is being criticised these days.[3] That is a positive development. At the same time, there is a negative tendency. Historicity-questions are not asked anymore. This means that to the post-modern mind the historicity of the facts of salvation history have become irrelevant. Whether incarnation, crucifixion, resurrection and ascension really happened is considered as less important than our meeting with an august narrative, an unbreakable piece of literature, which is called the Holy Scripture. In Reformed and Evangelical thought post-modern respect for the Bible is appreciated. Yet unlike in post-modernism, the Bible is recognised as more than just an important piece of literature. Reformed and Evangelical theologians emphatically restate the revelatory character of Scripture and the historicity of God's saving acts in Christ.

---

[3] Stefan Paas, *Creation & Judgment : Creation Texts in Some Eighth-century Prophets*, Leyden: Brill, 2003. In chapter 4 (pp.152-182) the author describes a shift in approach in the work of exegetes, wo have distanced themselves from the classic literary-historical method.

40. Cooperation and Unity

Out of a spirit of *Christian internationalism*, in the 19th century and in the earlier part of the 20th century various movements and organisations emerged that aimed at 'some sort of Christian unity'. We can distinguish two streams, (1) a Reformed-Evangelical movement and (2) an Ecumenical Movement. The *Reformed-Evangelical movement* of Christian cooperation and unity was a product of the Revivals and Awakenings. The *Ecumenical movement* of complete union of churches was generally produced by theological Modernism. [1]

40.1. The Reformed-Evangelical Movement

This movement did not aim at church unity in the first place. It was mainly motivated by *personal-religious* ideas. The revivals had created a sense of solidarity between believers, independent of nationality and denominational connections. Individual Christians united for mutual edification and for common work, e.g. to facilitate mission and further revivals in the interest of the Kingdom of God. Among them there was a desire for unity as a consequence of Christ's admonition to *spiritual* unity.[2] On this *personal-religious* foundation a number of international and national Christian organisations developed.

Among the first there were the World's Evangelical Alliance (England 1846, America 1857), the Young Men's Christian Association (YMCA, 1855), the Young Women's Christian Association (YWCA), the World's Student Christian Federation (WSCF), the American Bible Society (1816), the American Sunday School Union (1824), the Antislavery Society (1833), the Students' Volunteer Movement (1833), the Gideons, Youth for Christ. The constitutions of these organisations show that they were built on the faith of the Christian Church as reflected and re-worded in the 16th-century Reformation and in the evangelical revival movements thereafter. This is illustrated by their constitutions. The YMCA adopted the following doctrinal basis:

> 'The YMCA seek to unite those young men who regarding the Lord Jesus Christ as their God and Saviour according to the Holy Scriptures, desire to be His disciples in their doctrine and in their life, and to associate their efforts for the extension of His Kingdom amongst young men'.[3]

This formula was meant especially as a 'defence against all who denied the Deity of Christ'. It resisted the spirit of Enlightenment and theological Modernism which had led to apostate theology. This is also apparent in the World's Evangelical Alliance. This organisation adopted 9 articles that emphasise the doctrines of the Church of the Reformation: (a) Divine inspiration, authority and sufficiency of the Bible, (b) the right of private interpretation, (c) the Unity and Trinity of God, (d) the total depravity of man, (e) the incarnation of Christ, and His works of atonement, mediation and reign, (f) justification by faith alone, (g) the work of the Holy Spirit in conversion and sanctification, (h) the immortality of the soul, (i) the resurrection of the body, (j) the

---

[1] Cairns, *Christianity through the Centuries*, pp.440-441, 468-504; Dowley, pp.657-659; Renwick/Harman, pp.205-209, 226-232; D. Hedegård, *Ecumenism and the Bible*, London: Banner of Truth, 1964, pp.52-122.
[2] John 17:11, 21.
[3] Quoted in Hedegård, *Ecumenism and the Bible*, p.53.

judgment of the world by Christ to eternal blessedness or eternal punishment, (k) the divine institution of the Christian ministry, and (l) the institution of Baptism and the Lord's Supper.[4]

Evangelical-Reformed attempts at unity go back to Scripture and to plans by Reformers like Luther, Calvin, Bucer, Cranmer, and revivalist leaders like Zinzendorf, Carey, and Huntingdon. Here are some organisations that were formed in the 20th century. The World Christian Fundamentals Association 1919 (against liberalism), the American Council of Churches 1941 (against Federal Council/ National Council, Carl McIntire), the National Association of Evangelicals 1942, the National Black Evangelical Association 1963, the Baptist World Alliance 1905, the World Pentecostal Conference 1947, the International Council of Christian Churches (ICCC) in Amsterdam 1948, the World Evangelical Fellowship 1951.

40.2. The Ecumenical Movement

Beside this personal-religious line there were two other lines of cooperation and unity, (a) the line of *denominational fellowship*, and (b) the line of *practical cooperation*. Both lines deviated from Reformed-Evangelical faith, either from the moment they emerged or at a later stage. They were inspired by theological and practical *Modernism*. As to the first line, in many countries national movements for federative or organic church unity had developed.

Here are some examples of national confederations: the Protestant Federation of France 1905, the Federal Council of Churches of Christ in America 1908, the National Council of the Churches of Christ in America 1950/1951, the British Council of Churches 1942. Also, international organisations emerged, e.g. the Lambeth Conference 1867, the World Presbyterian Alliance 1875, the Lutheran World Federation 1923/1947, and the World Methodist Council 1881/ 1951.

The influence of the Evangelical Alliance can be traced in the beginning of some of these organisations. But after 1910, they became influenced by an international one-church movement that headed into a *liberal* direction. This one-church movement became known as the *Faith and Order Movement* (further: FO). It is this movement that first used the term 'ecumenical'. As to the second line, organisations arose for practical cooperation concerning: (a) peace efforts, (b) social problems, and (c) mission. Threatening developments that would lead to the First World War made Christians form the *World Alliance of Churches for Promoting International Friendship* (Constance 1914). This movement, though short lived, was instrumental after the war to organise cooperation between national movements for social reform in the *Life and Work* (further LW) conference (Stockholm, 1925). International efforts for cooperation concerning mission were combined in the World Missionary Conference in Edinburgh 1910, and in the formation of the *International Missionary Council* (further: IMC) in 1921. After the Second World War FO, LW, and IMC joined together in the *World Council of Churches* (further: WCC).

a. Faith and Order (FO)

In its aim of church unity FO was inspired by developments of cooperation in the mission fields as demonstrated by international missionary conferences, especially the

---

[4] Idem.

one in Edinburgh 1910. At the FO-conference in Lausanne 1927 the Indian Anglican bishop Samuel Azariah of Dornakal said:

> 'Divided Christendom is a source of weakness in the West. In non-Christian lands it is a sin and a stumbling block'.

Before Lausanne the ideal for FO was born in the Anglican and Episcopalian churches in England and America. The goal was an *organic union*, i.e. a 'merging of all churches into a single visible church'. This was more than the cooperation of churches aspired by the already existing Federal Council of the Churches of Christ in America (1908) of which the Episcopalians were not members. The future united church would not be a federation, but it would mean the end of the existence of all joining churches. The initiative for FO was taken by C.H. Brent, an American Episcopalian missionary in the Philippines. This led to a declaration by the American Episcopalian Convention.

> 'to bring about a conference for the consideration of the question that all Christian communions throughout the world which confess our Lord Jesus Christ as God and Saviour be asked to unite'.

Hedegård says that this formula was sincerely meant. At the same time, he points to the fact that the words 'according to the Holy Scriptures' were missing, and that this omission would lead to misunderstandings and misinterpretations.

At the FO-conference in Edinburgh in 1937 the Anglican archbishop W. Temple, who after Brent's death in 1929 had become the leading spirit of FO, condemned every church division as sin, and all who would not take part in the union as unrepentant sinners. In his view, the 16th-century Reformation could have been avoided 'by a more conciliatory temper and a more synthetic habit of mind'. This view of the Reformation implies disregard for the doctrine of justification by faith alone and for the other Reformed doctrines condemned by the Council of Trent. The Reformers understood the words *'Holy Catholic Church'* as the congregation of the saints where the Gospel is rightly taught and the sacraments are rightly administered. Temple and the FO, however, meant a visible united church where the different churches have been united in an organic union. Apparently, such a church should have some sort of supreme government or governor.

In subsequent conferences of FO the *Deity of Christ*, as formulated in its founding formula, was interpreted in such a way that it could even suit Unitarians. Elusive phrases weakened the doctrine of Christ's *eternal pre-existence* and failed to reject modern methods of explaining away the Biblical statements concerning the Deity of Christ.

b. Life and Work (LW)

Movements for social justice were combined in the LW-conference in Stockholm in 1925. The leading person was the Lutheran archbishop of Sweden Nathan Söderblom. The conference wanted to formulate programmes for permanent international peace and social justice. This peace and justice would be more completely realised through Christ *'the fatherhood of God and the brotherhood of all peoples'*. The organisers of the conference asserted that the world's greatest need is the Christian way of life, and that social and ethical problems can be dealt with irrespective of differences concerning faith and order. This view undermines the necessity for the world to accept the Gospel and Jesus Christ as personal Saviour and Redeemer. It takes away the intimate connection between faith and ethics, and promotes the liberal view of 'not doctrine but life'. To a great extent LW was influenced by the so called *'social gospel'* movement. It caricatures classical Christianity as being interested in salvation of the soul only. It suggests that the Church and even the New Testament have been mistaken for 2000 years in believing that the Kingdom of social and political justice cannot be founded on this earth here and now. Some participants of the Stockholm conference objected to the presentation of Jesus as a social reformer, and the idea that the Kingdom of God will reach its perfect development in this age. But particularly in the English-speaking world the *social gospel* and related ideas have remained influential. These ideas became pillar stones of the ecumenical movement.

c. International Missionary Council (IMC)

John Raleigh Mott (1865-1955), chairman of the first international missionary conference, in Edinburgh in 1910, which was followed by the foundation of the International Missionary Council

In the 19th century there already were forms of cooperation between mission organisations as can be concluded from great international conferences where delegates met, e.g. Liverpool 1860, London 1878, London 1888. They discussed practical matters and how the Gospel message could be best propagated. There was no doubt about the contents of the Christian message.

The first world missionary conference in the 20th century, Edinburgh 1910, met in a different situation. In an *optimistic* and *enthusiastic* mood over 1200 delegates from various churches and societies thought the world was open for Christian mission. Only the strategy had to be discussed. Although the majority of the delegates embraced historic Christian faith, there was also a *liberal influence* in the Edinburgh conference. As to heathen religions the conference did not discuss the Christian message as such, but it discussed 'the missionary message in relation to non-Christian religions'.

It was said that 'the missionary should seek for the nobler elements in the non-Christian religions, and use them as steps to higher things – that in their higher forms they plainly manifest the working of the Spirit of God'. The conference of Edinburgh led to the formation of the *International Missionary Council* at Lake Mohonk, New York, in 1921.

Due to crises in the mission fields and the world war the IMC-conference in Jerusalem in 1928 lost optimism. There was a feeling of impotence. A quarter of the 231 delegates were from the younger churches, mainly from China and India. Among the Europeans there were the Anglican archbishop W. Temple and the Swedish archbishop Nathan Söderblom. Influenced by the questions raised by the theology of *Modernism*, the contents of the Christian message was discussed. After 2000 years of mission, a world conference had to investigate what Christianity actually was. Generally, in the contributions the uniqueness of the Christian faith was weakened. Papers on *Hinduism, Confucianism, Buddhism* and *Islam* sought to show the values of these religions to which the Christian message could be linked. Some speakers put Christianity and the heathen religions on the same level, not making distinction between the only true religion and the other religions. Together with these religions Christianity had to combat its main enemy, *secularism*, it was said. Christ was mentioned as leader, teacher, ideal, example, inspirer, unifier 'of those who are seeking eternal life'. It was said that we attain communion with God by living a life exemplified by Jesus. The majority of the delegates were Modernists, among them Chinese, Indian, and Japanese church leaders.

The IMC-conference in Tambaran (South India) in 1938 saw a majority of delegates from the younger churches. Henry van Dusen, who took part in the confession document of the conference, said that the theological position of the delegates in their attitude to fundamental Biblical truths was predominantly liberal. Van Dusen reports:

'The younger Christian churches have grown up largely under the tutelage of missionaries from Britain and North America. Their minds have been schooled in an interpretation of the Christian faith more akin to 'liberalism' than to 'orthodoxy' or neo-orthodoxy'.

However, the leaders of the conference, like Van Dusen himself and the Dutch missiologist Hendrik Kraemer, were not of the *classical liberal* strand of Modernism. At Tambaram they showed Modernism with a *neo-orthodox* or Barthian face. Kraemer in his contribution

Nathan Söderblom (1866-1931), Lutheran Archbishop of Uppsala in Sweden and leader in de movement of Life and Work.

rejected natural religion and heathenism as a stepping stone to the Christian faith, but he also rejected the fight against Modernism by 'fundamentalists' like Arie Kok, a Dutch missionary and diplomat in China. Many delegates objected to Kraemer's view of heathen religions. Liberal theologians like T.C. Chao, A.G. Hogg and W.H. Horton presented:

'the wider view of God's self-disclosure and refused to deny to other religions the presence of the teaching and life-giving activity of God's spirit'.

d. World Council of Churches (WCC)

After an attempt in 1937 (in Utrecht) that failed because of the Second World War, finally, FO and L.W. formed a World Council of Churches (WCC) in Amsterdam in 1948. Delegates from 147 churches in 44 countries representing Protestant and Greek Orthodox Christianity found a common agency. They formulated this constitution:

'The WCC is a fellowship of churches which accept our Lord Jesus Christ as God and Saviour'.

Although this formula looks satisfactorily the words *'according to the Scriptures'* were not included. These words were only added in 1962. Moreover, the interpretation of this basis was said to be 'not a creedal test to judge churches or persons'. In other words, it was left to private opinion how to read the constitution. From the beginning churches and persons that deny or doubt Christ's Deity have been admitted to the WCC. Practically, this gives liberty to reject the nucleus of the Gospel.

The WCC intends to carry on the work of FO and LW. Its goal was the merging of all churches into one united church. This envisaged Church Universal is divided into churches of the Protestant, Roman Catholic, and Eastern Orthodox traditions. The formation of the *International Council of Christian* Churches (ICCC) also took place in Amsterdam in 1948. One of the founders was the above mentioned Arie Kok. The ICCC rejected the Word Council's objective of organisational unity, and for many years has behaved as its vocal opponent. Its ideal was spiritual unity of individual Christians and of churches in accordance to the authoritative position of Scripture. However, many main-line churches went the way of the WCC. In the course of time a number of organic church unions took place. Separate denominations gave up their own existence to unite with others and form new denominations.

Some were of like background, e.g. the Northern and Southern Methodists in the United States (1939), the United Presbyterian Church, the Evangelical Lutheran Church (1988). Also, churches with unlike backgrounds merged. They formed trans-confessional reunions, e.g. the United Church of Canada in 1925 (Presbyterians, Baptists, Methodists, Congregationalists), the Church of South India in 1947 (Episcopalians, Congregationalists, Presbyterians, Methodists).

In 1962 in New Delhi at the Third Assembly of the WCC it was decided that the WCC and the IMC should be integrated. The IMC had agreed to this integration at its Assembly in Ghana in 1957. Also, the Russian Orthodox Church, at the time under communist rule, was admitted as a member church. Here are some other important assemblies or congresses of the WCC: Uppsala 1968, Bangkok 1973, Nairobi 1975, and Vancouver 1983.

The ideas of ecclesiastical ecumenism are not much alive among ordinary church members. The WCC is mainly of interest to modern and post-modern church leaders and theologians. Many of these leaders pushed their churches into the direction of classical liberalism, neo-orthodoxy, radical theologies, and post-modernism. Although these churches have become members of the WCC the grass-root membership are often not aware of the ideas and the influence of (post-)modern theology and organisations.

The first five Presidents of the World Council of Churches, from left to right: Bishop Berggrav (Norwegian, Lutheran), Patriarch Athenagoras of Tyatira (Eastern Orthodox), Rev. Boegner (France, Reformed), Archbishop of Canterbury Fisher (Anglican), Bishop Bromley Oxnam (United States, Methodist).

41. Church and Ideology

41.1. Left and Right

As the influence of the Church numerically decreased due to secularisation in Western Europe, the minds and lives of many Europeans were increasingly occupied by systems of thought that were hostile to religion as such, and especially to the Christian faith. Communism and *National-Socialism* belonged to these systems of thought. They developed into ideologies that claimed universal power over the entire political, economic and social fabric of society. These absolutist movements, at least theoretically, left no room for loyalty to the Church and its King. In practice, however, they had grumblingly to accept the fact that the Church could not be rooted out soon. That is why they tried to use, neutralise and weaken the Church by forcing it to compromising cooperation with the structures of the state. In this way they tried to make the Church a tool of the state in order to reach the objectives of the ideology. In their thought gradually the Church would be confluent with the ideology, then absorbed by it and finally vanish.

The swastika, symbol of National-Socialism.

Communism in the shape of atheistic *Marxism-Leninism* unsuccessfully tried to take power in various Western countries. In 1917 a bloody revolution, led by Vladimir Ilyitsh Ulyanov, called Lenin, made the leaders of the Communist Party the sole rulers of Russia, and of Siberia and territories in Central Asia, that were joined together to form the Union of Soviet Socialist Republics (USSR), in brief the Soviet Union. Through the internationalist socialist movement the communist leaders tried to spread their power to other countries, if possible to the whole world.

National-Socialism took over in Germany after the Germans, disappointed by defeat in the *First World War* and subsequent hardships, had given electoral victory to Adolf Hitler in 1933. The *Nazis* (short for National-Socialists) cooperated with the Fascist party that under the leadership of Benito Mussolini had established dictatorial rule over Italy. Increasingly the axis Berlin-Rome, soon joined by Tokyo, threatened many independent countries in Europe, Africa and Asia.

It should be noted that Communism and National-Socialism acted as enemies of one another. Indeed, they were different in political, social and economic outlook. The one was classified left, and the other right. Yet they derived from the same spirit of 19th-century liberalism in their desire for absolutist power over the mind. They were equally foes to Christianity. Sometimes Christians did not realise the anti-Christian character of the ideologies of communism and national-socialism. Sometimes Christians turned against the one by declaring themselves loyal to the other. This divided the Church deeply, within its denominations and often also between denominations.

The hammer and the sickle, symbol of Marxism-Leninism.

41. Church and Ideology

Jews arrested by the Germans to be transported to concentration camps where they were murdered in gas chambers.

41.2. The Church under Communism

At this point we have to look briefly at the Church in Russia, and pick up the story we left behind in chapter 17.6, 7, 8. Before 1917, the Russian Orthodox Church was the powerful state church under the Tsars. In its messianic consciousness it looked down on Western churches, and considered Moscow as the capital of Christendom (*the third Rome*). The Communists identified the Orthodox Church with capitalist and tsarist oppression, and immediately took away its privileges. Protests of the Church were answered by terror. In the years 1921 and 1922 thousands of bishops, priests, monks, nuns and other Christians were executed, church properties were confiscated, and Patriarch of Moscow Tikhon was arrested.

Confrontation with the state seemed impossible. That is why in 1927 Metropolitan Sergeyi declared the Church to be loyal to the Soviet government. This move broke the unity of the Orthodox Church, and was only followed by even more severe persecutions under the new communist leader Joseph Stalin. In the midst of the extermination of peasants (*kulaks*) and other groups, again many thousands of clergy were killed, almost all monasteries were closed and a very limited number of churches were allowed to be open.

Vladimir Ilyitsh Ulyanov, called Lenin, adapted Marx's ideas for practical application in Russia, where the Bolshevik version of the Communist Party established its rule in 1917.

The Communist state changed its policy in the Second World War when the Soviet Union was

41. Church and Ideology

threatened by the German invasion, and needed the loyalty of all its citizens. The official leadership of the Orthodox Church reacted by giving its support to the Soviet state. After the war there was a period of comparative rest for the Church. However, the persecutions did not end. The absolute powerful Communist Party only allowed the existence of a church that cooperated with the state and accepted the objectives of communism. Orthodox Christians who did not agree to this formed underground churches. They met for worship in secret. Many Russians contributed to the growth of a large network of illegal churches, thus sidelining the official Church. This also happened among the Protestants, who mainly consisted of Baptists and Evangelical Christians. Their churches were the product of western missionary work and as such they were discriminated against by the Orthodox Church and the Tsarist state before 1917. The revolution broke the power of their oppressors.

Joseph Vassilyevitsh Dugashvili, called Stalin, was trained as a priest during his youth in his country Georgia, but as successor of Lenin he became a very cruel persecutor of the Christian Church and of all dissident groups in the Communist-ruled Soviet Union.

Consequently, Protestants at first enjoyed comparatively great freedom. Later the Communist police infiltrated their official churches just like what happened in the Orthodox Church. In the 1960's a great number of Baptists and Evangelical Christians refused any kind of collaboration with the communist authorities. They took the initiative for establishing an *Underground Church*; hence, they were called *Initiativniki*.

After 1945, communist takeovers and revolutions joined all countries of Eastern Europe to the Soviet Union in a communist bloc, under the enforced agreement of the *Warsaw Pact*. These satellite states included Poland, Czechoslovakia, the Baltic countries, Hungary, Romania, Bulgaria, Yugoslavia, Austria, and half of Germany.

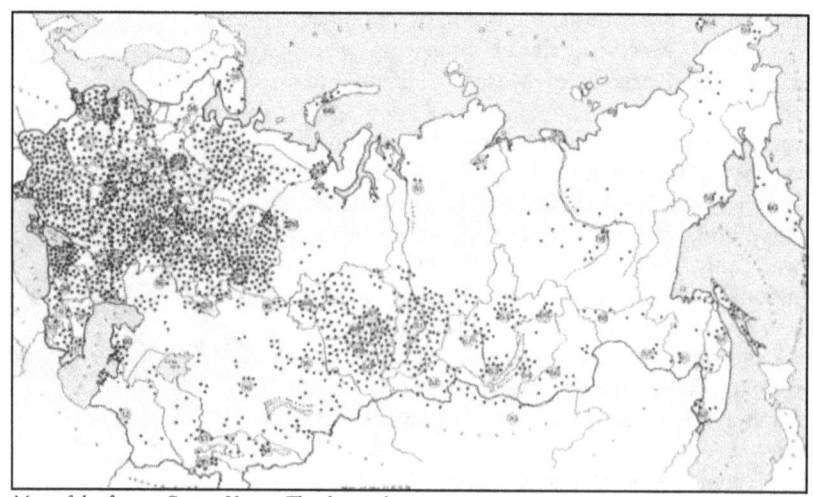

Map of the former Soviet-Union. The dots indicate concentration camps.

They were sealed off from the West by an Iron Curtain. Their governments, acting in line with Moscow, similarly oppressed the Church.

The map of the continent from Berlin to Vladivostok was dotted by concentration camps for the millions of prisoners of the Communist regimes. Many of them were Christians. It was the famous Russian author Alexander Solzhenitsyn who ably mapped out the plight of the victims of this Gulag Archipelago. Others studied the situation in China that since 1948 had been ruled by a Communist Party, and also persecuted the Church.

Oppression in the part of the world controlled by Moscow ended with the Fall of the Soviet Empire in 1991, and the subsequent liberation of Russia and its Asian and European colonies and satellite countries.

41.3. Western Opinion and Persecution

The Cold War and nuclear threat controlled Western public opinion in different ways. Although there was a general rejection of communism as a system of government, people were divided on the answer to give to the situation in the Soviet bloc. This question also divided Christians and Churches. The *Ecumenical Movement* inspired and represented by the *World Council of Churches* had come under Soviet influence as the Russian Orthodox Church and other communist-infiltrated churches had been allowed to become members of the World Council. Through their representatives in the Genevan headquarters of the World Council and at the various world conferences many church leaders came to be influenced by Soviet propaganda. One of the lies that were ably spread was the denial that the Church behind the *Iron Curtain* was persecuted. Representatives from the East systematically denied information on infiltration by the KGB[1], on conviction and deportation of ministers and other Christians to the camps in Siberia, on the destruction of church buildings. This created an ecumenical climate without room for criticism of communism and its behaviour towards the Church. Christians who believed the information on persecution were decried as fanatic anti-communists, cold war mongers, or even neo-Nazis.

Alexander Solzhenitsyn (1918-2008), winner of Nobel prize for literature; especially his Gulag Archipelago (1973) drew the attention of the world to Soviet atrocities to millions of Christians and political prisoners in the numerous concentration camps in Siberia and elsewhere.

In the 1970s the eyes of many people in the West were opened by a spate of undeniable details on persecution in Soviet countries. One of its witnesses was Richard Wurmbrand, a Lutheran pastor who had spent 14 years in Romanian prisons, and had miraculously escaped to the United States. With financial and spiritual help of Western

Richard Wurmbrand, 1909-2001.

---

[1] *KGB*: Komityet Gasudarstvyennoi Besopastnosti = Committee of Governmental Security (name of the secret service of the Soviet Union).

Christians in many countries he founded an organisation for support of the *Underground Church* behind the Iron Curtain, and for informing the general public in the West. After the collapse of communism in 1990, information on persecution could not be hidden anymore, much to the embarrassment of church agencies and leftist political groups that had persisted in denying communist atrocities. This contributed to a decrease of the popularity and the influence of the Geneva led Ecumenical Movement.

One of the reasons of the easy access to Western public opinion that the Soviets found for their propaganda was the comparative popularity of the Soviet Union as an ally in the war against Nazi-Germany.

41.4. The Church and the Nazis

The atrocities of the Nazis in Germany itself and in the many countries that were occupied by their armies have left indelible marks in the European mind. Especially Nazi racism, that considered the Arian (Germanic) race as supreme, led to enormous crimes against humanity. Slavonic people, gypsies, handicapped, sufferers of incurable diseases, and homosexuals, were said to spoil the purity of the German race; hence, they had to be killed. The Nazis particularly hated the Jews, whom they blamed for all the ills of humanity. About six million of them were murdered in camps of destruction. Among the most famous witnesses of the *Holocaust*[2] is Anne Frank, a Jewish girl in Amsterdam who in her *Diary of a Young Girl*[3] depicted the plight of her family and other Jews before they were deported to Germany, and Corrie ten Boom's book *The Hiding Place*,[4] telling about her experiences in Ravensbrück, one of the most dreaded concentration camps.

Martin Niemöller (1892-1984), German U-boat commander in the First World War, Lutheran pastor in the Second World War, together with Barth, Bonhoeffer and others, leader of the Confessing Church, thus of Protestant opposition to National-Socialism.

Dietrich Bonhoeffer (1906-1945), German Lutheran pastor, together with Barth, Niemöller and others leader of the Confessing Church. He was arrested by the Nazis in 1943 and was hanged in 1945.

Yet the churches acted differently towards the regime and its ideology. Except for some discreetly critical remarks by the Pope and some courageous actions by individual Roman Catholics, the Roman Catholic Church remained silent. This was not only true for the Church in Germany, but also for its

---

[2] *Holocaust*: lit.: wholly burnt offering, or wholesale sacrifice/ destruction. The term is used as an indication of the wholesale murder of Jews in the Second World War, although the Jews themselves prefer the indication: *Shoah* (= complete destruction).

[3] Anne Frank, *The Diary of a Young Girl: The Definite Edition*, 1995 (1991), New York: Doubleday [translation by Susan Massothy of Anne Frank's Diary in Dutch edited by Otto H. Frank and Mirjam Pressler, entitled: *Het Achterhuis: Dagboekbrieven van 14 juni 1942-1 augustus 1942* and other material from Anne Frank excluded from an earlier edition].

[4] Corrie ten Boom [co-authors John L. and Elizabeth Sherill], *The Hiding Place*, 1971 [Dutch: *De Schuilplaats*].

universal centre in Rome. The leadership of the German Lutheran Church was either passive or cooperative with the Nazi regime. This example contributed to an uncritical attitude among many Christians.

There were exceptions, e.g. the theologians Martin Niemöller and Dietrich Bonhoeffer. Their courageous attitude led to the foundation of the *'Confessing Church'*. In 1934 at their *Synod at Barmen* this Church accepted the *'Barmer Declaration '*in order to encourage resistance to attempts to make the Church an instrument of Nazi policy. Later many members were arrested or killed, among them Dietrich Bonhoeffer. This pastor was accused of partaking in a conspiracy against Hitler, he was killed in 1945. Christians and their leaders in the occupied countries generally were opposed to the Nazis, for both political and religious reasons. But there was a marked difference between those who played an active role in resisting the German invaders, and those who preferred to be passive. Christians were sometimes divided on issues like hiding Jews, joining armed resistance movements, and deceiving German military and police.

Hitler shaking hands with 'Reichsbischof' Ludwig Müller, leader of the Nazi friendly group of 'German Christians'.

41.5. Church in Crisis

a. Secularisation

During the Second World War the Church flourished. In their distress many secularised people found their way back to the Church. There were hopeful signs that after the war, in liberated Europe, the Church would regain its central place in society. But after a brief period of comparative church growth, the old tendency of secularisation resumed. The dwindling of church attendance was accelerated by processes of industrialisation and urbanisation that undermined and gradually destroyed the rural settings in which the Church had felt at home for centuries. Moreover, religious indifference was promoted by the growth of material wealth. The increase of information and education led many away from the Bible to other spheres of interest. Although communism was not popular, its atheistic propaganda directly or indirectly influenced people, so that many adopted a kind of *agnosticism*[5], or conscious rejection of religion.

b. 'God is dead'

Information on the *Holocaust* created two kinds of post-Auschwitz syndromes. The first one turned against the God of Scripture. Many, who were affected by basic disappointment and pain, did not flee with their hurt feelings to the God of grace and consolation. On the contrary, they reasoned that if God had allowed such horrors to happen, it would not be expedient to believe in Him. On this line of thought others, among them theologians, concluded that 'God is dead'.[6]

c. Extreme Israelism

A different reaction to the horrors of the Holocaust was developed among Christians in the movement of *Israelism*, especially in its extreme form of *Christian Zionism*, which accuses the Church of having been antisemitic since New Testament times and co-responsible for the tradition of pogroms and anti-Jewish terror in Europe. Representatives of the movement demand a complete revision of theology and of the writing of the history of Christianity. The phenomenon is also called *Israelism*, because it includes a completely new view of the position of Israel and the religion of Judaism in the Church, in theology, and in personal faith. Particularly in its appearance of sympathetic Israel-fascination and a literalist approach of Scripture *Christian Zionism* has given today's physical and ethnical Israel a key role in the history and the order of salvation. Consequently, it has decentralized Christ and decreased his uniqueness, thus undermining the Church's foundation and its calling of universally directed mission among Jews and Gentiles. Moreover, it has failed to find a safe sailing route in between the cliffs of antisemitism and philosemitism, despite its claim of combating the former.[7]

Remarkably *Christian Zionism* or *Israelism* almost exclusively occurs within Western Christianity. It is a very varied movement and can be qualified as: (a) a reaction in Western Christianity against the tradition of European antisemitism; (b) a heritage of chiliastic Israel-expectations[8] in the history of *Pietism* (*Further Reformation*), and in some strands in the 19th-century *Awakenings*; (c) an overemphasis on the Jewish identity of Jesus; (d) a claim of extraordinary privileges for the Jews as a restored people, land and religion; and (e) an underestimation of the differences between Christianity and Judaism.[9]

Some orthodox Reformed and Evangelical Christians adhere to milder forms of Israel-expectation. They are opposed to the extreme opinions in Christian Zionism.

---

[5] *agnosticism*: teaching that nothing is known or likely to be known about the existence of God.

[6] Cf. chapter 39.4.

[7] Cf.: Steven Paas, *Christian Zionism Examined: A Review of Ideas on Israel, the Church and the Kingdom*, Nürnberg: Verlag für Theologie und Religionswissenschaft/ Hamburg: Reformatorischer Verlag Beese, 2012. See a bibliography on pp.123-129.

[8] *Chiliastic* Israel-expectations. *Chilia* is Greek for 1,000. In these expectations Rev.20 is used for the theories of *postchiliasm* and *prechiliasm*, i.e. the ideas that respectively before or after Christ's Second Coming during a thousand years He will physically rule the earth together with converted Israel and the other believers.

[9] For a history of Christian Zionism or Israelism, see: Steven Paas, *Israëlvisies in beweging: Gevolgen voor Kerk, geloof en theologie*, Kampen: Brevier 2014, pp.79-226.

However, they think that according to the Scriptures before or after the Second Coming of Christ an extraordinary national conversion of the Jews will take place and a flourishing of the Church.[10]

d. Waves of church leavers

In the early 1960s in the mainline churches an *exodus* began. A kind of revolution took place. It was a cultural revolution with spiritual dimensions. The baby-boomers of the birth wave after the war had become adults. Many of them turned their backs on the church. It started in the Roman Catholic Church. A large number of people left the Church. At the same time, the *Second Vatican Council* was held, with the intention of *aggiornamento*, i.e. to bring the Roman Catholic Church up to date. This attempt to modernise the Church and to adapt it to the taste of modern man did not change the underlying principles of Rome, nor did it stop massive church leaving.

Then the strong waves of church leaving also hit the big Reformed and Lutheran Churches. Decades of liberal or modernist influence had weakened the Christian understanding and church loyalty of many. Now they went, sometimes officially, more often unofficially leaving their names in the registry books of the Church. At the same time, the leadership of those churches spent much energy in the Ecumenical Movement by taking part in the structures of the *World Council of Churches*. Most of their secularised church members had no idea of these activities; even if these members had known about the ecumenical conferences they likely would have still turned their backs on the Church.

41.6. Revivalism and Evangelism

In the 20th century the Church in the West lost much of its central position. This is offset by the fact that the Church elsewhere, in Africa, Asia and Latin America gained a lot of numerical and spiritual growth. This was comforting and strengthening to the remaining Christians in the old Churches of the West. In Europe and America the Church might be decreasing, but the Kingdom of God is marching on. At the same time, in the West there are movements to counteract the influences of secularisation and church leaving.

a. Pentecostalism and the Charismatic Movement

Pentecostalism is an early answer to the challenge of secularisation. It is a distinct variant of Protestantism, born out of the 16th-century Reformation. As such, it is a relatively young phenomenon. Generally, Pentecostal churches are rooted in the Pentecostal revival that began in Azusa Street in the Californian city of Los Angeles in 1906. Soon the movement spread to other parts of the world. In 1908 it arrived in South Africa, where it led to the foundation of the *Apostolic Faith Mission*, at first mainly among the whites. Instrumental in this cross-ocean movement were the South Africans David du Plessis, called 'Mr. Pentecost', and P.L. le Roux. There is also the influence of the radical American-Scottish Pentecostal preacher J.A. Dowie (†1907) of the *Christian*

---

[10] Cf.: Steven Paas, *Liefde voor Israël nader bekeken: Voor het Evangelie zijn alle volken gelijk*, Kampen: Brevier 2015.

Catholic Apostolic Church. He was at the cradle of many Pentecostal churches in Africa, especially in South Africa.[11]

The *Charismatic Movement* as such does not have a direct connection to the Protestant *Reformation* of the 16th century, although like the Pentecostals it is related to some characteristics of the Radical or the Left Wing of the Reformation (see chapter 27). It operates as a spiritual dimension of the ecumenical and post-modern attempts to renew the churches.

The modern *Charismatic Movement* is a loose worldwide 'network' that was begun in California in 1960 by Dennis Bennett. The movement was not affected by missionaries or by a worldwide organisation. Charismatic groups began to emerge in the 1960s as a reaction against secularisation in the Western countries. The Charismatic Movement started in the Protestant, Roman Catholic and Eastern Orthodox mainline churches in America, and then it spread to Europe and the other continents. Generally, it remained a movement inside existing churches, although it also established some 'independent' charismatic churches. The Charismatic Movement is related to *Pentecostalism*, but at the same time it strongly differs from it in terms of origin, social context, and spiritual appeal.

Dennis J. Bennett, an Episcopalian priest in California, who started the Charismatic movement in 1960.

Both Pentecostalism and the Charismatic Movement have not succeeded in bringing the masses of church leavers back to the Church. They operate respectively on the fringe and in the centre of existing Christianity and have not appealed to the multitudes that have lost all contact with the Christian faith. For the phenomena of Pentecostalism and the Charismatic Movement and how they differ in the African context, see chapter 60.

b. Reviving Reformed and Evangelical Churches

Secularisation has pushed Church and faith out of public life. As such, it has destroyed the hold that Biblical conceptions had on the people of Western Europe. Very many have become strangers to the Word of God, although knowledge in secular fields has developed to unknown heights. Western culture has become post-Christian. This means the West has become a mission field for the remaining churches.

Secularisation has had one advantage at least. Together with the waves of church leavers also many of the liberal and modernistic thinkers and practicians left. To the remaining Christians one thing is clear: Liberalism and Modernism have not helped the Church. In a way secularisation has functioned as purification. It has purged the Church of many who consciously undermined the classical Christian principles and dogmas, and they have departed together with their spiritual offspring.

In today's Western world it has become very difficult to call yourself a Christian, and at the same time play around with those values that traditionally have been the basis of the Church. Secularised culture sees through this dishonesty and ridicules it. Post-Christian men and women challenge the Church and the Christians to be true. There is

---

[11] Cf. chapter 45.

hope that this challenge may help to lead many Reformed and Evangelical churches back to their origins. They were born out of the 16th-century Reformation, which was nothing more and nothing less than a back-to-the-Bible movement. By the end of the Middle Ages Europe had not been really Christianised. The Christian faith was a thin veneer only. The Reformation prepared the Church for its missionary task of converting and edifying the masses. Similarly today's churches are called to prepare for that enormous task: evangelising the mission field that is found in their own habitat.[12]

Tim(othy) J. Keller (b.1950), American leading Reformed theologian and revivalist preacher. He is the founder of Redeemer Presbyterian Church in New York City.

Various attempts are being made. For example by the American pastor Tim Keller (b. 1950). He became known as a church planter and apologist in secularised urban environments. His foundation of Redeemer Presbyterian Church in New York was followed by an international network of missionary activities for the establishment of new churches in the large cities of the world.[13]

The new Biblical and therefore promising approach by Keller and others to find the hearts of the modern 'heathen' needs again Reformation and Revival, a thorough re-establishing of the Church in the Word and in the Spirit. Non-Western churches that are living from this spiritual reality, may help their brethren in the West to get ready for this missionary enterprise.

---

[12] Stefan Paas, *Jezus als Heer in een plat land*, Boekencentrum: Zoetermeer, 2001. The author describes a new vision of mission and evangelism in which the countries and cultures of Western Europe (in this book especially the Netherlands) are looked upon as pagan. They have to be missionised like the countries and cultures of Africa and Asia in the previous centuries.

[13] Cf.: Timothy J. Keller, *Center Church: Doing Balanced Gospel-Centered Ministry in Your City*, Grand Rapids: Zondervan 2012.

Bibliography: Modern Age

Ahlstrom, S.F., *A Religious History of the American People*, New Haven: Yale UP, 1972.

Bacon. E.W., *Spurgeon, Heir of the Puritans*, London: Allen and Unwin, 1967.

Bebbington, D., *Evangelicalism in Modern Britain: A History from the 1730s to the 1980s*, London, 1989.

Beeson, Trevor, and Jenny Pearce, *Vision of Hope: the Churches in Latin America*, London: Fount, 1984.

Beeson, Trevor, *Discretion and Valour: Religious Conditions in Russia and Eastern Europe*, London: Fount Books/ Philadelphia: Fortress, 1982.

Belden, A.D., *George Whitefield the Awakener*, New York: Macmillan, 1953.

Best, Geaffrey (ed. and intr.), *The Oxford Movement*, Chicago UP, 1970.

Boom, Corrie ten [co-authors John L. and Elizabeth Sherill], *The Hiding Place*, Guideposts Associates, 1971 [Dutch: *De Schuilplaats*].

Brauer, J.C. *Protestantism in America* (revised edition), Philadelphia: Westminster, 1965.

Bromily, G.W., *An Introduction to the Theology of Karl Barth*, Grand Rapids: Eerdmans, 1979.

Brooke, J., *Science and Religion: Some Historical Perspectives*, Cambridge UP, 1991.

Brown, B.W., *Lewis Tappan and the Evangelical War Against Slavery*, Cleveland: Western UP, 1969.

Burgess, S.M. and G.B. McGee (eds), *Dictionary of Pentecostal and Charismatic Movements*, Grand Rapids; Zondervan, 1988.

Busch, E., *Karl Barth: His Life from Letters and Autobiographical Texts* [transl.], London: SCM, 1976.

Butler, C., *The Vatican Council 1869-1870*, London: Fontana, 1962.

Brauer, J.C., *Protestantism in America*, London: SCM and Philadelphia: Westminster, 1966.

Carwardine, R., *Trans-Atlantic Revivalism: Popular Evangelicalism in Britain and America 1790-1865*, Westport CT: Greenwood, 1978.

Chadwick, Owen, *The Secularization of the European Mind in the Nineteenth Century*, Cambridge UP, 1990 [first 1978].

Chadwick, Owen, *The Victorian Church : An Ecclesiastical History of England*, 2 vols, London: A. & C. Black, 1969-1972.

Chadwick, Owen, *The Popes and European Revolution*, Oxford: Clarendon, 1981.

Chadwick, Owen, *The Christian Church in the Cold War*, London: Penguin, 1992.

Coad, F.R., *A History of the Brethren Movement*, Grand Rapids: Eerdmans, 1968.

Cochrane, A.C., *The Church's Confession under Hitler*, Philadelphia: Westminster, 1962.

Coen, C.C., *Revivalism and Separatism in New England, 1740-1800*, New Haven: Yale UP, 1962.

Coleman, J.A., *The Evolution of Dutch Catholicism 1958-1974*, University of California Press, 1979.

Conkin, P.K., *The Uneasy Center: Reformed Christianity in Antebellum America*, Chapel Hill: University of North Carolina Press, 1995.

Conway, John S., *The Nazi Persecution of the Churches 1933-1945*, London: Weidenfeld and Nicholson, 1986.

Cragg, G.R., *The Church and the Age of Reason 1648-1789*, Harmondsworth: Penguin, 1990^4.

Crumb, L., *The Oxford Movement and Its Leaders: A Bibliography of Secondary and Lesser Primary Sources*, Metuchen NJ: Scarecrow, 1993.

Curtiss, J.S., The *Russian Church and Soviet State 1917-1950*, Boston: Little, 1953.

Delumeau, J., *Catholicism from Luther to Voltaire: A New View of the Counter-Reformation*, London: Burns and Oates, 1976.

Devlin, J., *The Superstitious Mind: French Peasants and the Supernatural in the Nineteenth-century France*, New Haven: Yale, 1983.

Ervine, St. John, *God's Soldier: General William Booth*, 2 vols, New York: Macmillan, 1935.

Faber, G., *Oxford Apostles: A Character Study of the Oxford Movement*, London: Faber, 1974².

Fey, H.E. (ed.), *A History of the Ecumenical Movement 1948-1968*, Geneva: World Council of Churches, 1986².

Ford, D.F., *The Modern Theologians*, 2 vols, Oxford: Blackwell, 1997².

Frank, Anne, *The Diary of a Young Girl: The Definite Edition*, 1995 (1991), New York: Doubleday [translation by Susan Massothy of Anne Frank's Diary in Dutch edited by Otto H. Frank and Mirjam Pressler, entitled: *Het Achterhuis: Dagboekbrieven van 14 juni 1942-1 augustus 1942* and other material from Anne Frank excluded from an earlier edition].

Gay, P., *The Enlightenment: An Interpretation*, 2 vols, Harmondsworth, 1968.

Gill, Frederick C., *Charles Wesley the First Methodist*, New York: Abingdon, 1964.

Glover, R., *The Progress of Worldwide Missions* (revised by Herbert Kane), New York: Harper, 1960.

Grant, J.W., *A History of the Christian Church in Canada*, 3 vols, Toronto: McGraw-Hill, Ryerson, 1966-1972.

Hampson, N., *The Enlightenment*, Pelican History of European Thought, Volume 4, Harmondsworth: Penguin Books, 1968.

Handy, R.T., *A History of the Churches in the United States and Canada*, New York: Oxford UP, 1976.

Hebblethwaite, P., *The Christian-Marxist Dialogue: Beginnings, Present Status and Beyond*, London: Darton: Longman & Todd, 1977.

Hedegård, D., *Ecumenism and the Bible*, London: Banner of Truth, 1964.

Hempton, D., *The Religion of the People: Methodism and Popular Religion c.1750-1900*, London: Routledge, 1996.

Holmes, J.D., *More Roman than Rome: English Catholicism in the Nineteenth Century*, London: Burns and Oates, 1981.

Howse, E., *Saints in Politics: The 'Clapham Sect' and the Growth of Freedom*, Toronto U.P, 1952/ London: Allen and Unwin, 1971.

Hunter, L.S. (ed.), *Scandinavian Churches: A Picture of the Development of the Life of the Churches of Denmark, Finland, Iceland, Norway and Sweden*, London: Faber & Faber, 1965.

Hutchison, W., *Errand to the World: American Protestant Thought and Foreign Missions*, Chicago UP, 1987.

Keith, R. Thomas, *Religion and the Decline of the Magic: Studies in Popular Beliefs in Sixteenth- and Seventeenth-Century England*, Harmondsworth, 1973.

Keller, Timothy J., *Center Church: Doing Balanced Gospel-Centered Ministry in Your City*, Grand Rapids: Zondervan 2012.

Kent, J., *Holding the Fort: Studies in Victorian Revivalism*, London: Epworth, 1978.

Klingberg, F., *The Anti-Slavery Movement in England*, Hamden: Archon, 1968.

Kolarz, W., *Religion in the Soviet Union*, London: Macmillan, 1967.

Latourette, K.S., *A History of the Expansion of Christianity*, 7 vols, New York: Harper, 1937-1945.

Latourette, K.S., *Christianity in a Revolutionary Age: a History of Christianity in the 19th and 20th Centuries,* London: Eyre and Spottisood, 1963.

Latourette, Kenneth Scott, *Christianity in a Revolutionary Age*, 5 volumes, Exeter: Paternoster/ Grand Rapids:

Zondervan/ New York: Harper and Row, 1970 [first 1955-1965].

Lincoln, C.E. and L.H. Mamiya, *The Black Church in the African-American Experience,* Durham NC: Duke UP, 1990.

Littell, F.H., and H.G. Locke (eds), *The German Church Struggle and the Holocaust*, Detroit: Wayne State UP, 1974.

Marsden, G.M., *Fundamentalism and American Culture: The Shaping of Twentieth-century Evangelicalism 1875-1925*, Oxford UP, 1980.

May, H.F., The *Enlightenment in America*, London: Oxford UP, 1976.

McDonnell, *The World Council of Churches and the Catholic Church*, Toronto Studies no.2, Toronto: Mellen, 1985.

McGrath, A., *The Making of Modern German Christology 1750-1990,* Grand Rapids: Zondervan, 1994².

McGrath, A., *Christian Theology: An Introduction*, Oxford: Blackwell. 1994.

McLeod, H., *Religion and the People of Western Europe 1789-1970*, Oxford UP, 1981.

McManners, J., *The French Revolution and the Church*, London: SPCK, 1969.

Mode, P.G., *Source Book and Biographical Guide for American Church History*, Menasha Wis.: Banta, 1921.

Murray, I.H., *Jonathan Edwards*, Edinburgh: Banner of Truth Trust, 1987.

Nash, H.S., *The History of Higher Criticism of the New Testament*, New York: Macmillan, 1906.

Neill, S., *Christianity and Colonialism*, New York: McGraw-Hill, 1966.

Neill, S., *History of Christianity in India*, Cambridge UP, 1984-1985.

Neill, S., *A History of Christian Missions*, New York: Bantam, 1986².

Noll, M.A., *A History of Christianity in the United States and Canada*, Grand Rapids: Eerdmans, 1992.

O'Connor, Daniel (et al.), *Three Centuries of Mission: The United Society for the Propagation of the Gospel 1701-2000*, London/ New York: Continuum, 2000.

Oldroyd, D., *Darwinian Impacts: An Introduction to the Darwinian Revolution*, Milton Keynes: Open UP, 1980.

Oppenheim, J., *The Other World: Spiritualism and Psychical Research in England 1850-1914*, Cambridge UP, 1985.

Orr, J.E., *The Flaming Tongue: impact of twentieth-century revivals* [on the revivals of 1901-1910], Chicago: Moody, 1973.

Paas, Steven, 'Reformation and Pietism', in: Idem, *Johannes Rebmann: A Servant of God in Africa Before the Rise of Western Colonialism*, Nürnberg: VTR, 2011, pp.19-31.

Paas, Steven, *Christian Zionism Examined: A Review of Ideas on Israel, the Church and the Kingdom*, Nürnberg: VTR, 2012.

Patterson, G.N., *Christianity in Communist China*, Waco Tex.: Word, 1969.

Poland, B.C., *French Protestantism and the French Revolution: A Study in Church and State, Thought and Religion, 1685-1815*, Princeton UP, 1957.

Pollard, J., *The Vatican and Italian Fascism 1929-1932: A Study in Conflict*, Cambridge UP, 1985.

Porter, R., *The Enlightenment: Britain and the creation of the modern world*,London: Allen Lane, 2000.

Reardon, B., *Liberal Protestantism*, Stanford UP, 1968.

Reardon, B., *Religion in the Age of Romanticism*, Cambridge UP, 1985.

Ricard, R., *The Spiritual Conquest of Mexico*, Berkeley: University of California Press, 1966.

Rouse, R. and S. S. Neill, *A History of the Ecumenical Movement 1517-1948*, Philadelphia: Westminster, 1964².

Rupp, G., *Religion in England 1688-1791*, Oxford: Russell, 1995².

Schweizer, A., *The Quest of the Historical Jesus: a Critical Study of this Progress from Reimarus to Wrede* [transl.: W. Montgomery], London: Black, 1954³.

Stock, E., *The History of the Church Missionary Society: Its Environment, its Men, its Work*, 4 vols, London: CMS 1899.

Stott, J., *Christian Mission in the Modern World*, London: Falcon, 1975.

Strickwerda, *A House Divided: Catholics, Socialists, and Flemish Nationalists in Nineteenth-Century Belgium*, Lanham: Rowman & Littlefield, 1997.

Sweet, L.I. (ed.), *The Evangelical Tradition in America*, Macon: Mercer UP, 1984.

Sykes, N., *Church and State in England in the Eighteenth Century*, Cambridge UP, 1934.

Synan, V., *The Holiness-Pentecostal Movement in the United States*, Grand Rapids: Eerdmans, 1971.

Temu, A.J., *British Protestant Missions*, London: Longman, 1972.

Thomson, A., *New Movements: Reform, Rationalism, Revolution 1500-1800*, London: SPCK, 1990¹⁰.

Vidler, A.R., *The Church in an Age of Revolution, 1789 to the Present-day*, Harmondsworth: Penguin, 1974³.

Wagner, P.C. (ed.), *The Third Wave of the Holy Spirit: Encountering the Power of Signs and Wonders Today*, Ann Arbor: Servant Publications Vine Books, 1988.

Walvin, J., *Black Ivory: A History of British Slavery*, London: Fontana, 1993.

Ward, W.P., *The Life of John Henry Cardinal Newman 1801-1890*, [2 vols], New York: Longman, 1912.

White, R.C. jr., and C.H. Hopkins, *The Social Gospel: Religion and Reform in Changing America*, Philadelphia: Temple UP, 1976.

Wintle, M., *Pillars of Piety: Religion in The Netherlands in the Nineteenth Century 1813-1901*, Hull UP, 1987.

Young, E.J., *An Introduction to the Old Testament*, Grand Rapids: Eerdmans, 1949 [on the history of criticism].

Websites

Christian History Institute: Post Reformation,
https://www.christianhistoryinstitute.org/study/era/post-reformation/
Christianity Today: Modern Age, http://www.christianitytoday.com/ch/byperiod/modern
Post- Reformation Digital Library: http://www.prdl.org/

Part II

The Faith Moves South

E. Africa in General

42. Africa on the Eve of Change

42.1. Earliest Regions of Christianity in Africa[1]

Christianity first expanded in the regions around the *Mediterranean Sea*. There were two important centres or schools of thought of early Christianity, those of Antioch in Syria and Alexandria in Egypt. The earliest Christian regions in Africa were Egypt and North Africa. In Egypt the Greek and the Coptic cultures were dominant, and in North Africa the Latin and the Berber cultures dominated.

a. Egypt

For the sake of expediency, let us repeat in this section chapter 3.3.c. where we noticed that in Egypt Christianity developed first in the context of the Greek culture that was predominant in the eastern part of the Roman Empire, beginning among the many Hellenised Jews living there, subsequently also among other Greek-speaking people. Alexandria became an influential centre of Christianity, often in opposition to the Antiochene School of thinking. Clement of Alexandria (†215), Origen (†254), and Athanasius (†373) were among the early Church Fathers who laid the foundation of Christian theology in the Hellenist world.

A Coptic Church in Aswan, Egypt

At an early stage also many non-Hellenised people in the Egyptian countryside also turned to Christianity. They were called *Copts*, and the Bible was translated into the Coptic language. The Copts, after the *Council of Chalcedon* in 451, stuck to the *Monophysite* position in Christology. They were separated from and replaced the official Greek (Melkite) church, using their own Coptic language. The Coptic Church survived first persecutions by pagan Roman Emperors, then conflicts with the Catholic Church, and finally oppression under Islamic rule.[2]

b. North Africa

Another region of early Christian history is North Africa, like Egypt then a province of the Roman Empire. In part I of this book we noticed its importance for the development of the European Church.[3] Here we look at it from an African perspective of course. First, for the sake of expediency, let us connect to and overlap with the introductionary subsection of chapter 3.3.c. The name *'Africa'* referred to the coastal area with the city of Carthage as the centre, and also to the highlands of Numidia and the more remote Mauritania. The Roman province of North Africa covered more or less the territories of

---

[1] For a more extensive account of North Africa's Christian Era, see: P. Brown, *Augustine of Hippo: A Biography*, London: Faber & Faber, 1967; P. Brown, *Religion and Society in the Age of Augustine*, London, 1972.

[2] For an effective overview of early Egyptian Christianity, see: Kenneth Sawyer and Youhana Youssef, 'Early Christianity in North Africa', in: Kalu (ed.), *African Christianity,* pp.45-66.

[3] Cf. chapters 8.4 [Tertullian], 9 [Cyprian], 10 [Augustine], 12.5 [Africa and Europe].

present-day Tunisia, Algeria, and Morocco. Unlike Egypt, North Africa was influenced by the western part of the Roman Empire, where Latin gradually became the most important vehicle of culture. Latin Roman names and Latinised African names appear in reports of persecution and condemnation of Christians of the period before 313. The theological school of Carthage became influential. Tertullian (†c.[4] 225) and Cyprian (†258) were at the cradle of the development of theology in the Latin language. Much more important, however, was Augustine (†430), whom Baur even calls 'the culminating point of the whole Western theology', which means that Africa was also deeply influenced by his theology.[5]

It is true that the Western church owes much to Africa. That is why the ancient

Church Father Aurelius Augustine (†430) of Hippo, North Africa.

Church of North Africa still captures the imagination of many modern people. We wonder about its rapid original growth, we also wonder about the internal quarrels and schisms that contributed to its complete eradication. The liberation of Christianity in 313 was followed by a hundred years of internal quarrels that damaged the church of North Africa. These *Donatist* upheavals[6] were followed, just after Augustine's death, by a hundred years of occupation by the Germanic Vandals, who persecuted the African Christians forcing them to accept the heresy of *Arianism*.[7] In the meantime, in the West the Roman Empire had collapsed (476). This historic event had significant consequences for the relationship between Africa and Europe. After the invasion by Arab Muslims in the 7th century, North African Christianity faded out.[8] Baur refers to Arab writers who 'mention a few Christian villages still existing in 1400 and a solitary Christian community in Tunis, the New Carthage, in 1500'.[9] Sawyer and Youssef are inclined to be more optimistic. They combine details from Stark and Jenkins[10] and think that the number of North African Christians decreased from 8 million by 500 to 5 million by the year 1000, to 2.5 million by the year 1200, to 1.5 million by the year 1500. They say that the decline accelerated during and after the Crusades.[11] Anyway, in the early history of Christianity in North Africa the traditions of Europe and Africa meet one another.

---

[4] c. = circa or approximately.

[5] John Baur, *2000 Years of Christianity in Africa: An African History 62-1992*, Nairobi: Paulines, 1994², p.28.

[6] Cf. Steven Paas, *A Conflict on Authority in the Early African Church: Augustine and the Donatists*, Zomba: Kachere, 2005².

[7] Arianism: The principal heresy which denied the true Divinity of Christ, so called after its author Arius († c.336), maintaining that the Son of God was not eternal but was created.

[8] W.C.H. Frend, *The Donatist Church: A Movement of Protest in Roman Northern Africa*, Oxford University Press, 1985²; P. Hincliff, *Cyprian of Carthage*, London: Chapman, 1974; N.B. McLynn, *Ambrose of Milan: Church and Court in a Christian Capital*, Berkeley/Los Angeles, 1994.

[9] Baur, *2000 Years*, p.29.

[10] Rodney Stark, *The Rise of Christianity*, Princeton University Press, 1996; Philip Jenkins, *The Next Christendom*, Oxford University Press, 2000.

[11] Sawyer and Youssef, 'Early Christianity in North Africa', in: Kalu (ed.), *African Christianity*, pp.72, 73.

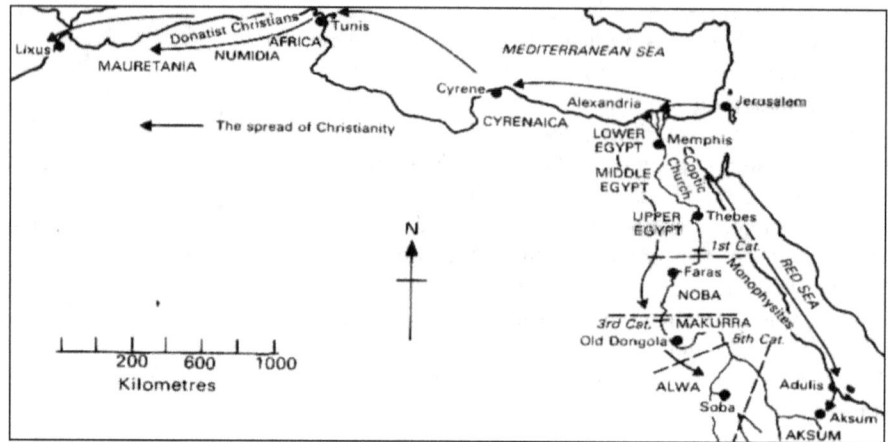

Map of the Spread of Christianity in North Africa from the 1st to the 6th century (from: Shillington, History of Africa, p.67).

42.2. A New Era of Contact

During the European Middle Ages Christianity did not penetrate further into the African continent than North Africa, Egypt, Nubia and Ethiopia. In the 7th century both Egypt and North Africa were conquered by the Arab armies and were included in the Islamic Empire. Both Egyptian and North African Christianity had to compete with Islam, the one survived and the other vanished. The same is true for Christianity in Nubia and Ethiopia, the former vanished and the latter continued to be a factor of significance. Islam remained the great competitor in the history of the church in much of the rest of Africa. Together with the *Saharan Desert*, Islam had created a barrier between Europe and the large sub-Saharan part of the African continent. Africans and Europeans did not know much about one another. Especially to sub-Saharan Africa no early conceptions about Europe were known. In the Middle Ages Europe's interest in Africa did not go beyond vague imagination, which linked India to Africa, and in which a legendary Christian king played a role: *Prester John*, who was supposed to rule a powerful kingdom in the midst of Muslims and pagans, perhaps in the interior of Africa.[12]

The European church was at first preoccupied with the evangelisation of pagan European peoples, and then with its own inward affairs. Francis of Assisi belonged to the very few early medieval Christians who were conscious of the church's missionary task for the peoples beyond Europe; he tried to make peace between Muslims and Crusaders.[13] Raymond Lull (†c. 1315), a follower of Sir Henry Bartle Frere (1815-1884), Francis was not very rather successful in his seeking support for plans to evangelise Muslims and Jews.[14]

---

[12] Baur, 2000 Years, 42, 43ff.

[13] *Franciscan Mission among the Muslims: Occasion of the 8th Centenary of Francis' Birth*, A Friar Paper, Assissi, Italy, 1982.

[14] Raymond Lull, or Raimundus Lull(i)us was a Franciscan. He promoted the teaching of Arabic and on Islam to future missionaries, and he was martyred in Ceuta in North Africa (Morocco) in 1315 where he worked as a missionary among Muslims. Cf.: J. van Amersfoort and W.J. van Asselt, *Liever Turks dan Paaps?*, Zoetermeer: Boekencentrum, p.115. For the Portuguese attempts to evangelise Africa (on the way to India),

In the 15th and 16th centuries there was an important change of focus. Attention to the outside world was born out of the movements of the *Renaissance* and the *Reformation*. Profound changes in religion, learning, economy and social life meant the beginning of a *New Era*. Africa and Europe would rediscover each other!

42.3. The Situation of Traditional Religions

What was the religious situation in Africa when the *New Era* witnessed the encounter between Europeans and Africans? Although *Christianity* had maintained itself in Egypt and Ethiopia, *Islam* was advancing in North, West and East Africa, and *Traditional Religions* were the major force in most of the continent.[15]

Unlike Northern Africa where Islam barred any Christianisation attempt, sub-Saharan Africa opened up to Christianity quickly, especially in the 19th century. Sundkler says that four categories of people were the gates through which the Christian faith entered Africa: (1) *kings*, (2) *young men*, (3) *freed slaves and refugees*, and (4) *women*.

First, the *king* was the door through which missionaries had to pass. Using any other way often led to suffering and failure. The centrality of kings was also true for the lower chiefs who ruled villages and regions with no large scale political structures. Many Africans lived in such units. It was much more true for the kings or chiefs of the bigger African kingdoms with their capital cities that already existed in the Middle Ages. Similar to the Nubian kings and the Egyptian pharaohs, these African traditional rulers were more than secular functionaries, they were sacred kings. Sometimes they even were looked upon as *divine*. They then functioned as *mediator* between heaven and earth, bridging the gap with the ancestors and providing the necessities of life, like rain, or victory in war.

The *kingship* in African traditional religion is closely related to *kinship*. Together *kingship* and *kinship* are at the foundation of traditional religion. This kinship means that the individual is part of the whole; he or she cannot exist alone, only corporately. One's identity is found in community. This corporateness includes the *ancestors*. God is seen as the *Great Ancestor*, though conceptions and names of God vary. Kinship ties are hierarchical and generational. Therefore, dead ancestors, believed to have continuing impact from the spirit world, are venerated as leaders. This means that the living need contact with the world of the spirits of the ancestors. This explains the necessity of *mediators* who bridge the gap, medicine men and women, diviners, and especially the *sacred kings*. In their priestly function kings were a link between human rule and spiritual government; only they could be heard by the *ancestral spirits*. As such, they were 'guardians of the land' or guardians of 'rain-making' shrines. As in pharaonic Egypt, some kings were regarded as *semi-divine beings*, superhuman figures. They were the hope of the people, the guarantee of peace and prosperity, the power that can destroy the evils of enemy attacks, diseases, drought and famine.

In certain *cults* there was a kind of competition between the king and the priestly figure at the shrines. The territorial cults of *Mwari* and *Mhondoro* in Zimbabwe were

---

see especially chapter 44.

[15] For this chapter, also see: Shaw, *The Kingdom of God in Africa*, pp.75-90; Hastings, *The Church in Africa*, pp.46-53, 188-193, 306-337; K. Shillington, *History of Africa*, London: Macmillan, 1995², pp.62-225; Sundkler and Steed, *A History of the Church in Africa*, pp.81-96.

related to what was seen as God, and also to the veneration of human beings that were thought to be divine.[16] The *Mbona* cult in Malawi centres on a prophet-rainmaker who was killed by a king, while being innocent, and who revealed himself supernaturally.[17] These cults and those who administered the rites checked the power of the kings.[18]

Secondly, the African Church was primarily a movement of the *youth*, both for the missionaries and their converts. Many missionaries spent their youth, and often their old age as well, in Africa. They preached the Gospel to the heathen, many of whom were young. The African masses were reached largely by the work of young African converts themselves. These young *catechists* and *evangelists* were especially able to preach to Africans of their own age.

Thirdly, *uprooted people* were the first to accept the Christian message. *Freed slaves* who were on the run from their masters, and other categories of *refugees* found certainty and comfort in the Gospel of Jesus Christ.

Fourthly, *women* were perhaps the most marginalised category in African society. The Church gave them a position that they had never had before, religiously, in the family, and even in society.

These factors prepared and facilitated the spread of Christianity. However, *African Traditional Religions* harboured strong powers that were ready to counteract the Gospel and the kingdom of God. Deeply rooted conceptions of a distant and unapproachable *Supreme Being* and of the nearly divine role of ancestral spirits as *living dead* left no room for God's immanence in Jesus Christ. In addition to this, all over the continent the powers of *witchcraft* and *magic* had deeply invaded the inner being of society and of individuals. Having victory over these powers would take more than the initial meeting with Christianity.

42.4. The Situation of Islam

a. Two Gateways

Mark Shaw has characterised Africa as a 'continent with a triple heritage', referring to the long histories of Traditional Religions, Christianity, and Islam.[19] Islam reached Africa through two gateways, from the east and from the north.[20] From both directions the carriers of Islam navigated across vast empty spaces, the waters of the Indian Ocean and the sands of the Sahara desert. The *Sahara Desert* and the *Red Sea* and *Indian Ocean* were not great barriers to the spread of Islam. Arabs had lived, travelled and traded in desert conditions for centuries before the founding of Islam. Moreover, since the Arabian Peninsula is bordered on three sides by water, Arabs were experienced sea traders. The regions where Islam first successfully spread are Egypt, North Africa, and

---

[16] J.M. Schoffeleers, *Guardians of the Land*, Gweru: Mambo Press/ Kachere Text, 1999², pp.235-310.

[17] J.M. Schoffeleers, *River of Blood: The Genesis of a Martyr Cult in Southern Malawi, c. A.D. 1600*, Madison: University of Wisconsin Press, 1992; Schoffeleers, *Guardians*, pp.131-234.

[18] J.M. Schoffeleers, *Religion and the Dramatisation of Life*, Blantyre: CLAIM\ Kachere/ Bonn: Culture and Science Publ, 1996, pp.34-65.

[19] Shaw, *The Kingdom of God in Africa*, p.75.

[20] A condensed survey of early expansion of Islam in Sub-Saharan Africa is offered by: Ioan M. Lewis, [Islamic Frontiers in] 'Africa South of the Sahara', in: Joseph Schacht with C.E. Bosworth (eds), *The Legacy of Islam*, Oxford: Clarendon, 1974², pp.105-115.

North-East Africa; in later stages these regions were followed by sub-Saharan Africa in the West, in the East, and in some Southern and Central parts.[21]

b. The Islamisation of Egypt

Egypt was the first African country to come under the influence of Islam. At the time of the arrival of the first Muslim traders Egypt was predominantly Christian. Indeed, Christianity had become the main religion in Egypt hundreds of years earlier, soon after the formation of Christianity.

After the collapse of the Roman Empire in the West, Egypt became part of the Eastern Roman Empire, ruled from Constantinople. The Coptic population found Byzantine rule to be corrupt and oppressive. Therefore, they did not resist occupation by the Muslim Arabs in the 640s. The Arabs moved the capital from Alexandria in the north to Cairo in the centre of the country, where they were relatively close to the Coptic peasant population. There was a process of Islamisation, generally not through violence, but through indirect means, such as extra taxation of Christians, education in Arabic, and immigration of Arab peasants. By the end of the 10th century Arab rule was pushed aside by an essentially North African Berber movement, the *Fatimids*, who were a kind of *Shi'ites*, claiming descent from Mohammed's daughter Fatima. The greatest Fatimid Caliph was Saladin He warded off a Christian Crusade army in the 1160s, and recaptured Jerusalem for Islam in 1187, which provoked European leaders to organise the third Crusade. The Fatimids were succeeded by the *Ayyubid* dynasty who returned the Egyptians to the *Sunni* main branch of Islam. In the meantime, the process of Arabisation of Egypt continued, especially in the period 950-1350, when large numbers of Arab Bedouin peacefully invaded the country.

Saladin (1137/1138-1193), a Kurdish Muslim general who founded the Ayyubid dynasty in Egypt and Syria. This picture with the words 'Saladin, king of Egypt' is from a 15th-century manuscript. The globe in his left hand is a European symbol of kingly power.

Fatimids and Ayyubids both imported Turkish slaves to serve in their armies. These Turks were called *Mamluks*. Gradually they developed into a new military and landed aristocracy that eventually, in 1250, took over the rule of the country. The *Mamluk* military dictatorship extended Egyptian rule to Western Asia, including Medina and Mecca, and defeated the fourth Crusade. Harsh taxation of the Egyptian peasants, among them many Christians, finally weakened the Mamluk regime.

In 1517 the *Ottoman Turks* conquered Egypt. In 1453 the Ottomans had taken Constantinople, ending the Eastern Roman Empire. Egypt was added to their vast Ottoman Empire. Now it was ruled from Istanbul, the new name of Constantinople. The Ottomans extended the Egyptian boundary southwards into Nubia in the 1550s, and even Massawa on the Red Sea was occupied. This barred Portuguese soldiers, traders and missionaries from entering the Red Sea and Ethiopia. Egypt became an important gateway through which Islam spread to other parts of Africa.

---

[21] Cf.: Akitunde E. Akinade, 'Islamic Challenges in African Christianity', in: Ogbu U. Kalu (ed.), *African Christianity: An African Story*, Universtity of Pretoria, 2005, pp.117-138; A.Rahman I. Doi, *The Planting and Diffusion of Islam in Africa, South of the Sahara*, 1971 [Internet].

42. Africa on the Eve of Change

c. The Islamisation of North Africa

From Egypt the Arab armies conquered the regions to the West, calling this vast North African territory *al-Maghrib* (the West). In the 690s, Carthage and the former Roman territories in Africa were conquered. These were called *Ifriqiya* by the Arabs. In the beginning the Berber population of the interior resisted, but gradually the Muslims pushed on. In 711 they reached the Atlantic coast of Morocco. Berber society soon abandoned Christianity, and many of them formed part of the Islamic army. Arab and Berber intermarriages contributed to the formation of the North African Muslim peoples.

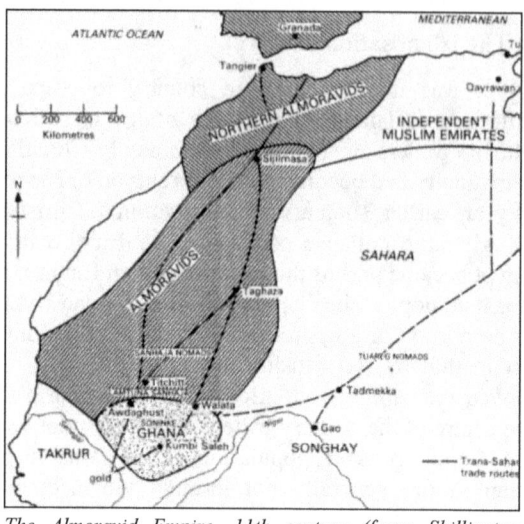

The Almoravid Empire, 11th century (from: Shillington, History of Africa, p.91)

After the 7th century, Islam became divided into conflicting movements. The main division was between the *Sunnite* majority and the *Shi'ite* minority. Power over the Sunnite majority was soon seized by representatives of the *Ummayad* dynasty, who moved the Muslim capital from Madinah to Damascus. The *Abbasid* dynasty took over and they made Baghdad the capital.[22] North African Muslims asserted independence from the Ummayad and Abbasid *caliphs*. They formed the *Kharijite Movement*, which was related to the Shi'ites, and according to Shillington reminiscent of the Berber *Donatists* of the Christian era.[23] The Kharijites were considered heretical by the Sunnite majority of Islam. Kharijite independence gave rise to the *Fatimid dynasty*, mentioned in the previous section, which took control over most of the Maghrib. They tried to take over power from the Abbasids in the whole Muslim world. In 969 they conquered Egypt.

Raymond Lull (from: Jorn Barger, 2002).

In the 10th century a revival among Sanhanja Berber converts beyond the Sahara on the Atlantic side led to the emergence of a strict Islamic movement, the Almoravids. Parts of Western Sub-Sahara, Mauritania and Morocco belonged to the *Almoravid Empire*. By the middle of the 11th century the empire had split into a southern part that conquered or deeply influenced the Ghana kingdom of the Soninke people, and a northern part that invaded Spain. In 1040 the northern Almoravids were overthrown by more strict Muslim Berbers from the

---

[22] Karen Armstrong, *Islam: A Short History*, chapter 2.
[23] Shillington, *History of Africa*, p.77.

south, who founded the Almohad Empire. In the 12th century the whole of the Maghrib was united in this state, which was, with Muslim Spain, together successful in spreading and strengthening the intellectual achievements of Islam, like in the fields of mathematics, science, physics, astronomy, and chemistry.[24] The Almohad unity in the Maghrib collapsed in the 13th century. At the same time, however, the Spanish and Portuguese started to throw the Muslims out of the Iberian Peninsula. In 1492 the Muslims lost Granada, their last foothold in Spain.

The Almoravid and Almohad states contributed much to contacts between peoples in North Africa and south of the Sahara. Especially they played a role in the trade of gold from sub-Saharan to North Africa and to Europe.

In the meantime, the process of Arabisation of the Maghrib intensified. Many Arab Bedouin moved from Arabia into North Africa, spreading Arabic language, culture and their specific type of Islam. Large numbers of Berbers were absorbed by the Arabs, although the Berber language survived in the interior.

In the 16th century the Ottoman Turkish Empire on the one side and the Spanish and Portuguese on the other struggled for control of the Maghrib, mainly of the sea ports. The Turks lost dominance of the Mediterranean when they were defeated at Malta in 1565 and at Lepanto in 1571. But Tripoli, Tunis and Algiers became Turkish ports and the interior became the territory of the Turkish Empire. The Turks supported trans-Saharan contacts.

Morocco was not absorbed by the Turks, nor was it conquered by the Iberians. Under King Ahmad al-Mansur (†1603) a Portuguese invasion was warded off (1578 at the battle of al-Ksar Kebir), and Morocco extended its territory beyond the Sahara into Western 'Sudan'[25] by occupying the Songhay country, thus acquiring control of the trade in gold and slaves.

42.5. The Fullness of Time

God is the ruler of history. His hand has prepared the world for receiving the Gospel of Jesus Christ. This has been so in a special way since the beginning of the history of the Christian Church. The 'fullness of time' had come.[26] Missionaries who went out after the outpouring of the Holy Spirit at Pentecost penetrated into societies that were disappointed or bored by their pasts, which made them ready for change. God had worked in the hearts and in the circumstances of many people to make them open for receiving the message of salvation through Jesus Christ. For sub-Saharan Africa, the 'fullness of time' became visible many centuries later. In the Modern Era, after 1500,

---

[24] Christian Western Europe learned many skills from the Arabs and Berbers in Spain and North Africa, like paper making, Hebrew grammar, the decimal system, modern medicine, and above all Aristotle's philosophy, which Thomas Aquinas made the foundation of his *Thomistic Theology*, and which still is officially recognised in the Roman Catholic Church. Cf.: Joseph Schacht with C.E. Bosworth (eds.), *The Legacy of Islam*, Oxford: Clarendon, 1974², pp.244-505: the influence of Islam culture on the West for: Art and Architecture (Oleg Grabar and Richard Ettinghausen), Literature (Franz Rosenthal), Philosophy, Theology and Mysticism (George C. Anawati), Science (Martin Plessner and Juan Vernet), Music (O. Wright).

[25] The name *Sudan* in a wider sense applies to the territory South of the Sahara desert, stretching from West to East. It is derived from the Arab name for the whole continent of Africa, *Bilad al-Sudan*, which means *land of the black people* (cf. Akitune E. Akinade, 'Islamic challenges', in: Kalu (ed.), *African Christianity* (p.118). In a narrower sense *Sudan* is the name of a national state in the East of Africa.

[26] *Galatians* 4:4: 'When the time had fully come, God sent forth his Son'.

changes became increasingly apparent, socially, economically and politically. In the next sections we will see emerging and collapsing kingdoms, movements of migrating peoples, wars feeding disruption and slavery, and the opening of trading routes. *Kings, youth, slaves, refugees* and *women* were the categories that were most affected by these changes. They were the ones through whom, according to Sundkler, the Christian faith would invade sub-Saharan Africa. The modern missionary enterprise in Africa started in the 19th century. However, Mission and Church had to compete, not only with *African Traditional Religions*, but also with *Islam*.

The occupation by Islam of Egypt, North Africa and Nubia was followed by the Islamic conquest of the Sahara. Then, the Eastern and Western coastal areas of sub-Saharan Africa were penetrated, Niger, East Sudan, West Sudan. This happened hundreds of years before the arrival of the missionaries. The Hausa belonged to the first sub-Saharan peoples that were converted to Islam. From about 1750 the Fulani people, voluntarily joined by the Hausa, in a violent way founded a large and powerful Islamic state.[27] Gradually during the 18th and 19th centuries Islam spread southwards, sometimes using violent, sometimes peaceful methods.[28] In West Africa this expansion could not continue to the South of the continent. But, in the coastal areas of East Africa the influence of Arabic Islam reached the very South, leading to the foundation of Muslim island and city states. Swahili Arabs and allied tribes were active as hunters and traders of slaves. In the East and the South of Africa Islam not only spread from Arabia, but also by means of the migration of workers from India to Africa.

Christian Mission did not enter a religious vacuum. The older Missions before 1800 and the modern missions of the 19th century had to struggle with the continuing impact of *African Traditional Religions*. Missions and Churches also met with the increasingly powerful presence of Islam in many places.[29] Now, in this chapter, let us look separately at each of the sub-Saharan regions.

42.6. The Situation in Sub-Saharan Africa

a. West Africa

Generally, it took many years for West African leaders to be fully convinced of the virtues of Islam and to convert. It was not until the leaders of a kingdom or state had converted that an effort was made, usually with the full support of the leader, to convert ordinary citizens. It often took several generations before the majority of the people in a particular kingdom or societies were practicing Muslims. This gradual process resulted in a situation where people would adopt some Islamic practices and beliefs while maintaining some of their indigenous beliefs and practices. Gradually, Islamic practice

---

[27] K. Shillington, *History of Africa*, London: Macmillan, 1995, discusses on pp.90-106 the early spread of Islam in the Sudanic states of West Africa.

[28] Cf. J.S. Trimingham, *Islam in West Africa*, London, 1959; *Islam in the Sudan*, London 1949², repr. 1965; *Islam in East Africa*, London: Oxford University Press, 1964; *The Influence of Islam on Africa*, 1968; J. and L. Kritzeck (ed.), *Islam in Africa*, 1969; E.C. Mwandivenga, *Islam in Zimbabwe*, Gweru: Mambo Press, 1983; D.S. Bone (ed.), *Malawi's Muslims: Historical Perspectives*, Blantyre: CLAIM, 2000 [with an annotated bibliography].

[29] For a case-study of the life of Mission and Church within a powerful Islamic context, see: Martha Frederiks, *We have toiled all Night: Christianity in The Gambia 1456-2000*, Zoetermeer: Boekencentrum, 2005.

became more predominant, but often elements of indigenous belief and practice would continue.

Many sub-Saharan societies remained loosely organised in villages, joined together in chiefdoms. However, in many other cases, cities played an important role in African society. In the West 'Sudan' they were called *kafu* and were often walled. These cities were the beginning of early kingdoms, with a much more tightly knit organisation. Here are some examples.

The *Soninke kingdom of Ghana* (900-1100). It was actually situated hundreds of kilometres northwest of modern Ghana. Its inhabitants were mainly the Soninke people. The Soninke state was renowned for its gold trade. It was situated halfway between the Sahara and the gold fields in Senegal. The Soninke traders sold Saharan salt from the north in exchange for gold from the south. Through Berber contacts, especially the Almoravids, either peacefully or violently, the Soninke became Muslims by the middle of the 11th century. One of their kings was Tenkaminen who held court in his capital city of Kumbi. The king controlled both political and religious life.

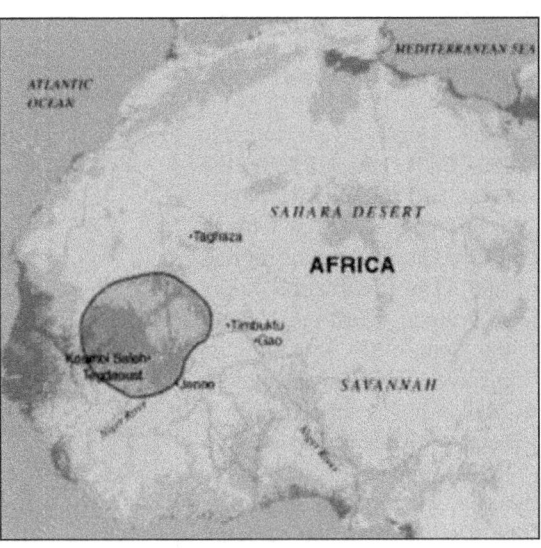

The Soninke kingdom of Ghana, located in what now is southeastern Mauretania, and part of Mali, in its largest extent, about mid 11th century.

The *kingdom of Mali* (1200-1400). It was begun by a Soninke chief of Sosso (or Kaniaga) who conquered most of the Ghana kingdom, and also the homeland of the Malinke to the south. The Sosso-empire was built on violence. This provoked resistance from the Malinke, who under king Sundiata took control of the whole Soninke and Malinke territory. Sundiata extended his empire southwards to Bure on the Niger where gold was found. Traditionally the Malinke people believed that contact with the ancestor spirits secured peace and prosperity. The chiefs, or *mansa*, were considered mediators with the ancestors. All political and religious power was in their hands. King Sundiata took over all *mansa*-titles of lower chiefs; consequently he was treated with extreme respect. Most kings after Sundiata were Muslims, but they never completely rejected traditional religion. Under kings Musa and Sulayman in the 14th century the Mali Empire reached the summit of its glory and wealth. King Musa's free spending of gold in Cairo, when he was on his way to Mecca, even unsettled prices at the Egyptian gold market. Major Mali cities Timbuktu and Jenne were filled with libraries, and schools of law and theology. In the 15th century the empire declined, because outer

A 14th-century lithograph of Mansa Musa, celebrating his power on his Hajj to Mecca.

provinces grasped independence; the most important of them was Songhay.

The kingdom of Songhay (1400-1600) consisted of the area around the middle Niger. The first capital was at Kukiya and then Gao. By the beginning of the 11th century the rulers had become Muslims. Under King Sonni Ali (†1492) the Songhay absorbed the kingdom of Mali. Ali was succeeded by a general, Muhammad Ture (†1528), founder of the Askiya dynasty, who became known as the *Caliph of the Sudan*. Timbuktu again was a centre of Islamic learning. A Moroccan visitor, Leo Africanus, visited the town, and observed 'many doctors, judges, priests and

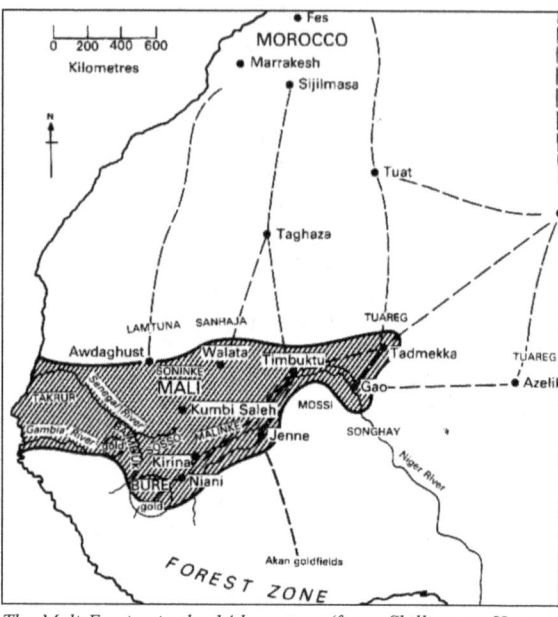

The Mali Empire in the 14th century (from: Shillington, History of Africa, p.95).

other learned men, who are well maintained at the King's cost'. He also saw 'various manuscripts and written books ... sold for more money than other merchandise'.[30] The Songhay kingdom broke down in 1591, when a Moroccan army took the rulers by surprise. Until 1660 the Moroccan sultan was formally in authority in this sub-Saharan territory on the river Niger.

Some other West African states were the *Takrur* in the Senegal valley, who adopted Islam already in the 11th century, and were allies of the Almoravids, and the kingdom of *Kanem-Borno* in the central 'Sudan', shaped by King Idris Alooma in the 16th century as a federation of three Hausa kingdoms, whose capital was Kano.

The Yoruba-speaking people also formed states of their own. Most important were the kingdoms of *Ife, Benin, Oyo,* and *Dahomey*. All these states at times cooperated with the slave trade and profited from it, although the Dahomeian King Agaja (†1740) tried to stop the transport of African slaves across the ocean and have Europeans establish plantations in Africa where slaves could be put to work.[31]

A 16th-century Mosque in Agadez, Niger (from: website, exploringafrica)

Let me conclude this survey with a few words on the Akan states, of which the Ashanti kingdom was the most important. The traditional trade route for Akan gold was

---

[30] Shillington, *History of Africa*, p.105.
[31] Shillington, *History of Africa*, p.193.

through the Sahara desert. Slaves were working in the gold mines. But in the 1480s the Akan started trading their gold and their surplus of slaves to the Portuguese, who first reached the West African coast in the 1470s. The Akan formed a number of states that in the 1670s joined together to the Ashanti state under King Osei Tutu. Under his successor Opuku Ware (†1750) the Ashanti kingdom covered most of present-day Ghana. The gold trade amassed an enormous wealth for the Ashanti kings.

When the Portuguese ships for the first time touched the West African coast, this signalled the beginning of a new era for life in villages, chiefdoms, kingdoms and empires.

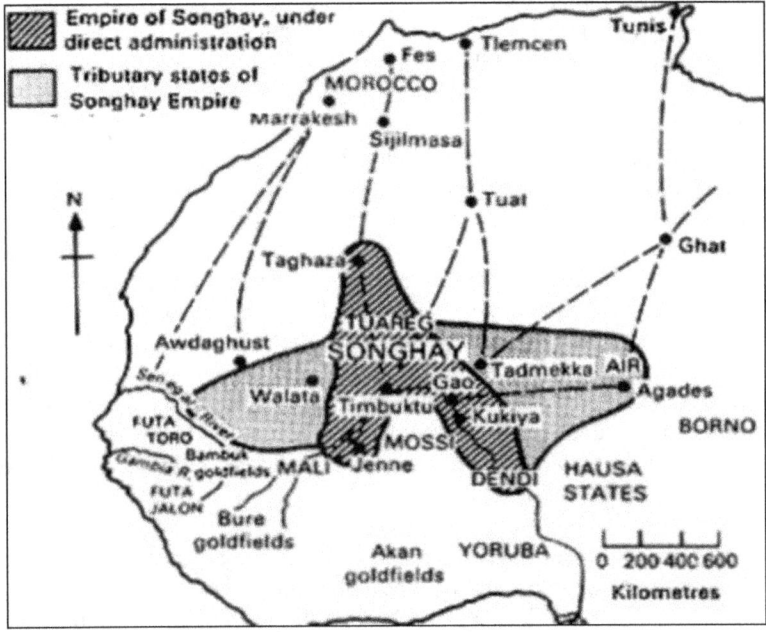

The Songhay Empire in the early 16th century (from: Shillington, History of Africa, p.102)

b. East Africa

Apart from Ethiopia and Swahili-Arab settlements in the coastal regions, there is very little written evidence of East Africa's history before 1500. Yet much historical information can be derived from oral sources, archaeological findings and the study of languages. Historians agree that Bantu-speaking peoples entered the East African interior south of Ethiopia in the early centuries AD. They increasingly relied on cattle. In the period 1400-1700 people speaking Nilotic languages from the North also invaded East Africa, also keeping cattle. There was much blending of these two main groups. Political and religious developments in the interior were heavily influenced by what happened at the coast. Greek and Roman traders used to refer to the East African coast as *Anzania*. The Anzanian people were probably Bantu-speaking fishermen and farmers, at least in the 5th century.

In Arab literature the East African coast and its off-shore islands are called *Zanj*, which means 'land of blacks'. There was an increasing Arab presence in this region, caused by the spread of Islam in the 7th and 8th centuries. The Arabs, who often intermarried with Africans, were conscious of their mission, but they were also sailors and traders. Gold, slaves, leopard skins, and ivory were traded. Their ships connected the African coast and the Islamic world of West Asia and India. They established market-towns along the coast, often on the off-shore islands, like Mogadishu, Pate, Mombasa, Malindi, the Lamu Islands, Pemba, Zanzibar, Mafia, Kilwa, the Comoro Islands, Mozambique Island, Sofala, all together some forty towns. In these cities and coastal regions developed the *Swahili culture*. Ki-swahili means 'language of the people of the coast'. It is a Bantu language with Arab additions. The Swahili-Arabs were Islamic in religion and African in language. These merchant city-states were ruled by a council of *wazee* (Swahili: elders) and a kind of king, a *sheikh*. An example is Zanzibar, in the 16th century ruled by a *Mwinyi Mkuu* (Great Master), who was surrounded by the sanctity of a divine chief. Swahili traders depended on inland African tribes for the delivery of goods. Until the arrival of the Portuguese in 1498 there was relative peace in the Swahili *land of Zanj*

In the interlake regions of present-day Kenya, Uganda, Rwanda, Burundi and Tanzania also a number of states emerged. The most important one is *Buganda*. It rose in the 17th century after having asserted itself against the Bunyoro cattle-raiders, who in their turn had taken over from the Chwezi state in the 16th century. The Buganda kings were called *Kabaka*. In the 18th century Kabaka Mawanda founded a strong centralised kingship. To the south, in Rwanda and Burundi, gradually two states took shape in which the Tutsi people dominated. East of Lake Victoria the Maasai entered, being of Cushite stock, probably related to the Oromo of Ethiopia. They settled under various names (e.g. Karamojong, Teso, Turkana, and Samburu) in present-day Uganda, Kenya and Tanzania. They traded and partially mixed with Bantu peoples they met, for example with the Kikuyu of central Kenya, and the Chagga of the Tanzanian plateau.

c. South-Central Africa

In the South East of present-day Congo chiefs of the Luba people joined together in a kingdom under the Ncongolo dynasty. The Luba kings were given great *mystical and religious authority*. In the 1450s the royal house split, and a rival kingdom was founded, the Lunda. Ideas of centralised religion facilitated later territorial expansion. In the 17th and 18th centuries the Lunda grew to great power. They even founded a new state to the South East in the copper area of present-day Zambia, founded by the *Kazembe dynasty*. The Kazembe kingdom traded with ports on both the Atlantic and the Indian Ocean. Another break-away from the Lunda were the *Kinguri kings*, who founded a raiding state in central Angola, and later were called the Imba-ngala people. In Angola by 1500 the Ndongo people joined together under Ngola, the main guardian of the rainmaking shrine.

In the south west of today's Congo the chiefs of the BaCongo people were united in a single kingdom by 1400. The kings of this *Congo Kingdom* were called ManiCongo. Their authority rested much on the guardians of the rain-making shrines.

The *Maravi Kingdoms* of central and southern Malawi originated from a wider tradition, the Luangwa, that stretched to halfway through Zambia, including Chewa, Bisa and Bemba peoples. The Maravi people consisted of the Nyanja just south of Lake Malawi, the Mang'anja further south in the Shire Valley, and the Chewa to the West. They were ruled by respectively the Kalonga dynasty, which was started about the year 1400 by a joining together of the Banda and Phiri clans, and its off-shoots, the Lundu and Undi dynasties. Their religious rituals for rain and soil fertility connected to the position of the king probably originate the Luba tradition. The Maravi peoples traded in ivory and iron. In the 16th century they resisted Portuguese imperialism. Kalonga Masula (†1650) welded the Maravi peoples together into one empire that stretched from the Zambezi to Mozambique Island. He even invaded the Mutapa Empire in Zimbabwe. However, due to lack of administration and leadership the Maravi Empire declined. The Yao people took over the Maravi trading routes to the Swahili ports.

South of the Zambezi there were the *Toutswe* communities of eastern Botswana. In western Zimbabwe there were the communities of the *Leopard Kopje culture*, especially the Mapungubwe people. They were cattle breeders and traders. This community of Shona people was the beginning of the rise of the state of *Great Zimbabwe*. They built and extended big stone enclosures (*zimbabwe* comes from *dzimba dzamambwe* = stone buildings) for cattle, for they were able masons. From Great Zimbabwe the Swahili coast, especially Kilwa, was supplied with gold and ivory. But in about 1450 the site was abandoned, leaving the mysteries of the history of Great Zimbabwe unsolved. It was followed by the foundation of the *Torwa State*, which continued the tradition of building stone enclosures. By the end of the 17th century the Torwa rulers were defeated by cattle-raiders called *Rozvi* (meaning: destroyers), led by one Dombo, who was known by the title *changamire*. Dombo even expelled the Portuguese from the collapsing Mutapa territory, thus forming his own *Rozvi Empire*.

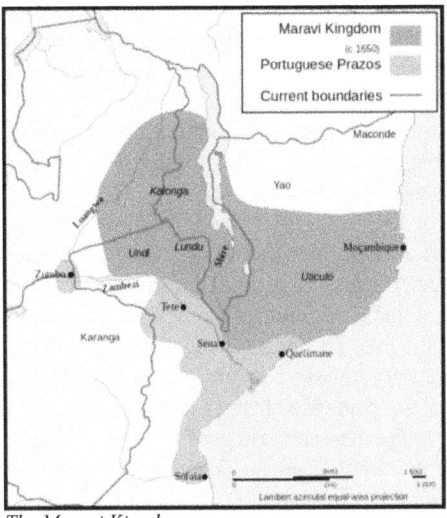
The Maravi Kingdom

The *Mutapa Empire* had started in about 1420 when one Mutota segregated himself from the Great Zimbabwe state. Together with his son, Matope, he formed an alternative state in the Northern Shona region at Dande. They and their successors adopted the title of *Mwene Mutapa* (= conqueror). In the 16th century the Mutapa empire succesfully resisted Portuguese attempts to check it, thus keeping control of trade to the Swahili coast. In the 17th century, however, the Portuguese military influence increased, making the Mutapa Empire crumble, only to be saved by invading Rozvi cattle-raiders, who expelled the Portuguese.

d. South Africa

The Khoikhoi and the San are the oldest peoples of South Africa. By 1600 Khoikhoi and San clans lived in southern Namibia and the South West Cape. The Bantu also claim ancient rights. Sotho-Tswana presence south of the Limpopo and Vaal Rivers can be traced back to before 1400. South east of Drakensberg another Bantu sub-group, the Nguni-speaking peoples, had settled, the southernmost of them being the Xhosa.

By the 19th century they had developed *Zulu kingdoms* under kings such as Shaka, Dingane, and Mpande. Their wars created an *mfecane*, that is a diaspora of numerous

42. Africa on the Eve of Change

movements of refugees, which as Sundkler stresses,[32] would indirectly contribute greatly to the acceptance and the spread of Christianity. But first, in the 17th century all these peoples were to meet Dutch (see chapter 54) and somewhat later English settlers (see chapter 55).

Islam came to South Africa quite recently. The demand for cheap labour was responsible for the introduction of Islam into this region. Muslims mainly came to South Africa in two waves.

The first group was brought in by Dutch colonial settlers who in 1652 had arrived at what today is Cape Town. The Dutch settler-farmers needed cheap labour to work on their farms. In response to this demand, the Dutch began to import slaves from Dutch colonies in South East Asia (Malaysia and Indonesia). Most of these slaves were Muslim. Throughout the years of slavery and after emancipation in the early 19th century, the descendants of these slaves maintained their strong religious affiliation with Islam. Today, a strong minority of Muslims are living in the area around Cape Town.

The second group of Muslims came to South Africa in the 19th century. At this time, British settler-farmers had developed huge sugar plantations in the province of Natal. Slavery had been abolished, but these farmers were able to recruit inexpensive labour from India. Today, there are more than one million people of Indian heritage living in South Africa. Many of them belong to the Islamic faith.[33]

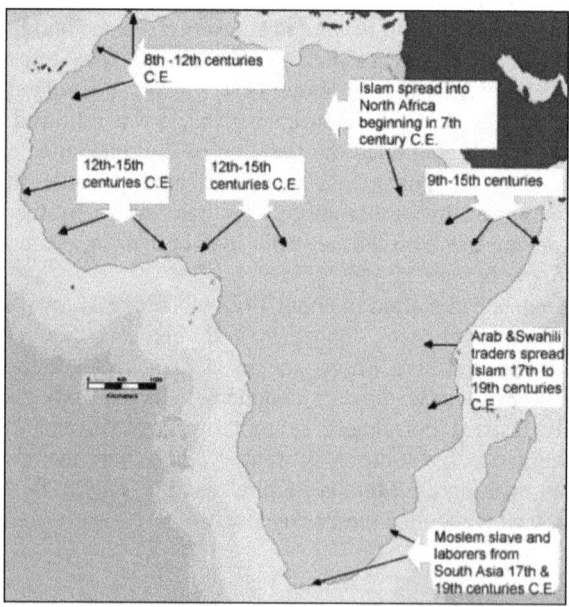

The spread of Islam in Africa through the centuries.

---

[32] Sundkler and Steed, *A History of the Church in Africa*, pp.82,83.

[33] Akinade, 'Islamic Challenges', in: Kalu (ed.), *African Christianity*, p.135, quotes the 1993 census which says that half a million South Africans are Muslims, almost half of them Indians, also almost half are Coloureds. The other few are Blacks and Whites.

43. Nubian and Ethiopian Christianity

43.1. Nubia excavated[1]

a. Archaeological Findings

The history of Christian Nubia was hidden and almost forgotten for a very long time. This changed in the period 1959-1969 when a series of 59 archaeological expeditions, coordinated by UNESCO, uncovered important testimonies of early Christian presence in the region. Here are some of the findings. The reference in *Acts* 8:26-39 to Candace the Queen of the Ethiopians, whose treasurer was baptised by Philip, does not actually point to present-day Ethiopia but to *Kush*,[2] later Meroe, in present-day Northern Sudan, where Queens with the title Candace ruled. In the third century the kingdom of Meroe was overrun, probably by Ethiopian warriors. Later, from the ruins of Meroe, the three kingdoms of Nubia were shaped, Nobatia in the North with its capital Faras, Makuria in the Centre with its capital Dongola and Alodia in the South with its capital Soba.[3]

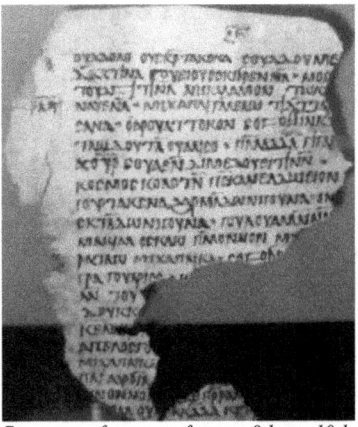
Remnant of a page from a 9th or 10th-century translation in Old Nubian of a book on the Archangel Michael, found at Qasr Ibrim (British Museum).

Excavations have uncovered the city of Faras which revealed remnants of Christian churches dating from the early fifth century. These findings agree with reports in Rufinus' *Church History* (approximately 400) who said that Coptic monks from Egypt, travelling southwards on the river Nile, had penetrated Nubia by that time.

b. Monophysitism

In surveys of the history of Nubian Christianity we are reminded of intensive missionary activity supported by Byzantine Emperors in the 6th century. Perhaps the year 543 can be looked upon as the official beginning of Nubian Church History. In that year the Coptic priest Julian reached Nubia. He was sent by the Byzantine Empress Theodora. Julian baptised a Nobatian king and his nobles, nominated a bishop, and he converted a pagan temple into a church. At the same time, he tried to propagate the

---

[1] For a more extensive survey of the history of the Nubian Church, see: R. Werner, W. B. Anderson, and A. Wheeler, *Day of Devastation, Day of Contentment: The History of the Sudanese Church Across 2000 Years*, Nairobi: Paulines Publ., 2000, William B. Anderson and Ogbu U. Kalu (ed.), 'Christianity in Sudan and Ethiopia', in: Kalu (ed.) *African Christianity*, pp.75-104; M. R. Shaw, *The Kingdom of God in Africa: A Short History of African Christianity*, Baker Books, 1996, pp.65-72, 92-98; J. Baur, *2000 Years of Christianity in Africa: An African History 62-1992*, Paulines Publ., 1994, pp.31-34; B.Sundkler and C.Steed, *A History of the Church in Africa*, Cambridge UP, 2001[2], pp.30-34; K. Shillington, *History of Africa*, London: Macmillan, pp.68,73,163,164.

[2] The Hebrew word *Kush* appears in Scripture, e.g. as the name of one of Noah's sons. Later *Kush* became the name for *Ethiopia* of which it is the Greek translation. Literally the word means 'black man'. (Cf. Anderson and Kalu, 'Christianity in Sudan and Ethiopia', in: Kalu et al. (eds), *African Christianity*, pp.75, 76).

[3] Nobatia, Makuria and Alodia are Greek names. Anderson and Kalu, *African Christianity*, p.77, use the Arab names: Nuba, Maqurra and Alwa.

ideas of Empress Theodora on the two natures of Christ. She advocated the *Monophysite* view of a union of Christ's divine nature and His human nature, as if the divine nature had absorbed the human nature at the incarnation. This belief deviated from the official stance of the Church as formulated at the *Council of Chalcedon*, in which not only the bond between the two natures was stressed, but also their being distinct.

So Nubia became another battleground in the conflict between *Monophysitism* and *Chalcedonian* conceptions of Christology. Julian was followed by another Monophysite missionary, Longinus. He established the Monophysite form of Christianity also in the most southern Nubian kingdom, Alwa. The kingdom of Makuria, however, received Orthodox (Melkite) missionaries and accepted Christianity in its Chalcedonian version. Orthodox ideas seem to have gradually triumphed in the whole of Nubia.

Empress Theodora (c.500-548) of the Byzantine or Eastern Roman Empire, wife of Emperor Justinian I, depicted on a mosaic. She sent the Monophysite missionary Julian to Nubia.

c. Royal Power

After the Arab conquest of Egypt in the 640s, the Muslim armies pushed southwards. The extension of Arab rule and of Islam isolated Nubia from the Christian culture around the Mediterranean Sea. Yet for a long time Nubia maintained its independence. In 642 a large Nubian army halted the Arabs at Dongola, the capital of Makuria, and confined them north of the cataracts of the Nile. About 700 a peace treaty, the *Baqt*, secured the Nubians' independence, provided they delivered slaves and goods to the Arab regime in Egypt, respected the presence of a mosque in their capital.

Soon after the *Baqt* treaty, the three kingdoms united with Dongola as capital. United Nubia maintained itself for some centuries as a counterbalance to Muslim power. Nubia had influence in Egypt and defended the interests of Egyptian Christians. King Georgios II received official recognition from the Caliph in Baghdad. The Fatimid rulers who seized power in Egypt in 969 were tolerant towards the Christians and friendly with Nubia.

As in Byzantium (and in Ethiopia) the Nubian Church was headed by the king. Under the king state and church were bound together in a kind of theocracy. Kings even played the role of priests. Impressive church buildings and other Christian monuments were there, but this may not have made Nubian Christianity to become much more than a court religion, only superficially understood by the masses. The largest church building unearthed is a

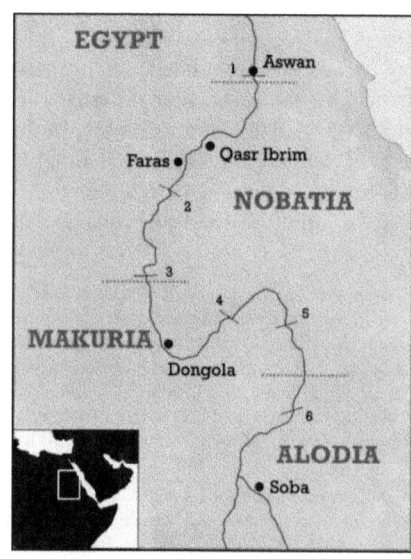

Christian Nubia consisting of three kingdoms, Nobatia, Makuria and Alodia.

cathedral in the Nobatian capital Faras, built by king Merkurios (697-707) and bishop Paulos. Paintings and writings on the walls show names and faces of bishops, at least some of whom were black. Faras cathedral was hit by a fire in 926, partly destroyed in 1170, and after that it was gradually covered by the sand of the desert.

The Church in this Northern kingdom of Nobatia, especially in the period of kings Georgios I (†920) and Georgios II, seems to have played a role in supporting and defending the Coptic patriarch of Alexandria and in sending clergy to the ailing Church in Ethiopia. This was not the first missionary challenge. In the beginning of Nubian Christianity Nobatia had been asked by the Southern kingdom of Alodia to send missionaries. In the Christianising of Southern Nubia traders from Axum (Ethiopia) were also active. At Soba the remnants of a cathedral were dug out, which indicates a strong presence of Christianity. Even much farther to the West, at Darfur, halfway from the Nile to the Niger, Christian symbols originating from Nubia were uncovered.

The Church in Nubia grew from the 6th to the 8th centuries, and it flourished in the period from the 8th to the 11th centuries.

d. Decline

From the 12th century onwards, owing to Muslim influence and pressure, the Nubian Church declined almost to extinction. In Egypt the Ayyubids ended Fatimid rule and thereafter in 1260 the Turkish *Mamluks* took over. The *Crusades* had made them extra hostile towards Christians. In 1276 a Nubian claimant to the throne, Shekanda, had himself crowned king under Mamluk protection. Under Muslim pressure Shekanda allowed Arab Bedouin to enter the country. This was the beginning of the end. In 1315 Nubia got a Muslim king, Abdallah Marshambo. In 1317 the main church of Dongola was converted into a Mosque. For some centuries a Nubian kingdom continued to exist in further southward in Alwa, but by the beginning of the 16th century it could no longer resist the invading Arab nomads, and the territory was militarily conquered by Islam from the south, by the Islamised Funji people.

Shaw and Sundkler mention the following reasons for Christianity's demise in Nubia: (a) lack of evangelism, (b) isolation from the rest of Christianity, especially because of the surrounding Islamic forces, (c) influences from and intermarriages with Muslim nomads who had been allowed to enter, (d) lack of locally trained leaders, (e) clericalism, in that the church could not function without bishops or priests, (f) the church was bound and used by the state, especially by the king, (f) the fact that Christianity was mainly a court religion, which points to a shallowness of faith, (g) the fact that the Nubians got socially uprooted when they changed from agricultural life to a nomadic mode of existence. Anderson and Kalu are of the opinion that the Nubian Church was strong, but that it could not adjust to radical change, like the interference by Muslim Egypt becoming more intense by the *Crusades*, and the imposition of religious taxation (*jizya*) on the Christians after the conquest by Egypt.

Ancient Nubia comprised the north east of present-day Sudan, the largest country in Africa. Sudan gained its independence from Britain in 1956.The Sudan was declared an Islamic Republic in 1983. Muslims form 70 percent of the population, with Sunni Islam in dominance. Almost the entire indigenous northern population is Muslim. There are several powerful Sufi orders, of which the largest is the Ansar, followers of the Mahdi. Christians comprise 19 percent, most of whom live in the South, in the Nubian mountains, and in Khartoum's southern section. Traditional religions comprise 9.9 percent of the population.[4]

43.2. Ethiopia[5]

a. Ethiopia until 1100

Ethiopia is said to be *'the oldest continuing Christian country not only in Africa but in the world'*. The beginning of Christianity in Ethiopia is recorded by Rufinus (c.345-410). Whereas Christianity came to Nubia through the river Nile, it came to Ethiopia through the Red Sea. It began in the northern kingdom of Axum (or Aksum) in the 4th century.

Coptic icon of Church Father Athanasius (289-373), Archbishop of Alexandria.

The first seeds were sown by two young men from Tyre (present-day Lebanon), Frumentius and Aedesius. On their way to India, their ship was intercepted and captured on the Axumite coast, present-day Eritrea. The ship's crew was killed; the passengers were captured and their lives were spared. They were taken to king Ella-Amida of Axum, who gave them the important positions of steward and cup-bearer. On the king's death Frumentius was even made administrator for successor Ezana who was still under age. Frumentius and Aedesius used their influential positions for allowing Christian traders who arrived through the Red Sea to spread the Gospel. They also encouraged the establishment of churches. When given leave to return home, Frumentius went to Alexandria to meet patriarch Athanasius. Frumentius was ordained bishop and in 334 he was sent back to Ethiopia in the official capacity of a missionary and Abba Selama, that is Archbishop of Ethiopia.[6] This was the direct preparation for the formation of the Ethiopian Church, and also of its subordination to Alexandria for 1600 years. After Frumentius' return, King Ezana, who in the meantime had enlarged his kingdom, became a Christian. He and his successors created a close connection between the Christian Church and the Ethiopian royal court.

Until the 5th century Christianity was largely confined to the royal court. Missionary work among the ordinary people began to develop by the activities of a group of Syrian monks, the *Nine Saints*. They translated Scripture into the Ge'ez language. They also

---

[4] George W. Braswell, Jr., *Islam Its Prophet, Peoples, Politics and Power*, pp.192-193.

[5] For a fuller account of Ethiopian Church History, see: Sundkler and Steed, *A History of the Church in Africa*, pp.35-41, 73-80, 150-168, 694-699, 927-930; Foster, *First Advance*, pp.110-112; Shaw, *Kingdom*, pp.62-65, 71-72, 118-119, 183-187, 273-275; Baur, *2000 years*, pp.34-39, 43-44, 50-54, 153-170, 399-402; Hastings, The *Church in Africa*, pp.3-45, 130-172, 194-196, 222-241, 611-613; A. Hastings, *A History of African Christianity 1950-1975*, Cambridge, 1979, pp.35-38, 219-221; K. Ward, 'Africa', in: A. Hastings (ed), *A World History of Christianity*, London, 1999, pp.197-200; Shillington, *History of Africa*, pp.68-71, 107-115, 164-167, 284-288, 364-366.

[6] Cf. Anderson and Kalu, 'Christianity in Sudan and Ethiopia', in: Kalu et al. (eds), *African Christianity*, p.106.

made a compilation in Ge'ez of Patristic texts, entitled *Qerilos*, which would become fundamental to Ethiopian theological thought. The *Nine Saints* gave Ethiopian Christianity its specific monastic character (*Abba Aregawi*). They built churches and monasteries on almost inaccessible mountain tops. The oldest existing monastery is *Debre Damo*. They took the Christian message to the illiterate masses. But their missionary methods were superficial. There was not much teaching and not many preachers were trained. This led to *syncretism*, and real Christian commitment was rarely to be found. The Nine Saints were *Monophysites* (of *Unionite* persuasion); As such, they were deviating from Christianity as defined by the great Church councils. Yet the Christian Church was established among the nobles and the peasants of Ethiopia. Its leading bishop was the *Abun*, nominated by the patriarch of Alexandria. But the most central position was that of the king. Christian political responsibility was shown by King Kaleb (†558) who invaded Zafar and Najram in South Arabia to revenge for the massacre of Christians in that region. He established Ethiopian churches there. Perhaps the legend of Ethiopia's link with Old Testament Israel and the house of King Solomon – told in the ancient document *Kebra Nagast* – was born in this time.[7]

In the early Middle Ages there were important changes. The first change was that Christianity had to compete with Islam, the new world religion that emerged in Arabia and rapidly spread from mid 7th century. Shaw opposes the 'popular belief that Christianity in Africa was extinguished by the rise and spread of Islam'.[8] Ethiopian Christianity survived, although not much is known about the 7th through the 9th centuries. Shaw assumes that Ethiopian Christianity in that period developed quite peacefully; its Islamic neighbours to the north did not cut off communications with the patriarchate in Egypt, and pilgrimages to Jerusalem went on. One can wonder about Shaw's picture of a peaceful relationship between Islam and the Church in early Ethiopia when taking into account that the power of Islam had been undermining Ethiopian Christianity in a very apparent way. Sundkler stresses that by 1300 half of Ethiopia was under Islam. In the beginning of the 16th century Muslim military violence nearly swept away the whole of Ethiopian Christianity.

The second change in the position of medieval Ethiopian Christianity was that in the 8th century the Ethiopian Church's centre moved from Axum to the central highlands of Ethiopia, taking with it the Ge'ez language, its liturgy and its Unionite views. This defensive move contributed to its isolation from the outside world.

In the 10th century Ethiopia was threatened from the south by the pagan Agau people who caused a serious decline of Christian rule. The Ethiopian kingdom had become very weak. The Church blamed this decline on unfaithfulness to Ethiopia's calling as the newly chosen people of Israel. The Church also reproached the kings for having severed the ties with the patriarch of Alexandria, so that for a long time no *Abun* had been sent.

b. The Zagwe Kings

A new dynasty of kings, the Zagwe, tried to meet with this criticism. Like the kings in the Axum line they claimed to be descendants of Solomon. Whereas the Queen of Sheba was said to have given birth to Menelik I, who became the first Axumite king,

---

[7] The story says that Ethiopian queen Medaka visited King Solomon and that out of this a son was born, Ebria Hakim, who as King Menelik I established a Judaistic religion in Ethiopia.

[8] Shaw, *Kingdom*, p.75f.

the kings of the Zagwe dynasty said that they were descendants of Solomon and the Queen of Sheba's handmaid. They swept aside the old house of the Axum kings, killing all its members, except for one, as the story goes. The Zagwe moved the capital from Axum in Tigray (or: Tigre) southwards to Wollo. They expanded Ethiopian territory, and revived Christian literature and art.

The most important Zagwe king is Lalibela (1190-1225), also known by his throne name Gare Maskal (*Servant of the Cross*). There are many legends about him. During a near death experience in his youth, he is said to have been carried by an angel to heaven. Returned once more to earth he withdrew into the wilderness then took a wife upon God's command with the name of Maskal Kebra (*Exalted Cross*) and flew with an angel to Jerusalem. As a mystic he lived in Jerusalem for a long time. He viewed himself as king and priest, and as such he reported that a revelation had come to him to build the *New Jerusalem*. There was a theological and a political side to this project. The *New Jerusalem* is a New Testament image, signifying the Second Coming of Jesus Christ.[9] Therefore, by the foundation of the city Lalibela had in mind to express honour to Jesus Christ. With this idea he stressed that he was different from the old Axum kings who derived their symbols of power mainly from the Old Testament. He also broke the Axum tradition of building churches on mountain tops. Lalibela commissioned churches to be carved out of the rock, based on the vision he had.[10] These churches of his *New Jerusalem* were situated near holy and healing waters, accessible to the people. There are twelve churches and chapels, including various shrines. Four churches are monolithic in the strict sense; the others are excavated churches in different degrees of separation from the rock. The walls of the trenches and courtyards contain cavities and chambers sometimes filled with the mummies of pious monks and pilgrims. Legend says that the churches were built with the help of angels within 24 years. One of the churches is called *Bet Abba Libanos*. According to legend, Lalibela's wife, Maskal Kebra, with the help of angels, created this Church in one night. It is dedicated to one of the most famous monastic saints of the Ethiopian Church, Abba Libanos.

St. George's Church, one of the rock cut churches of King Lalibela, built mid 12th century. This cruciform-shaped Church is the most magnificent of the 11 churches.

Despite their achievements the Zagwe kings were not popular. They did not fit into the idea of the sacred calling of Ethiopia as the continuation of Old Testament Israel. The above mentioned national myth of the Queen of Sheba (1 *Kings* 10: 1-13) is related in the *Kebre-Nagast* document. Her son Menelik I, as the first king in the *Solomonide dynasty*, is said to have brought the *Ark of the Covenant* with him from Jerusalem where he visited his father. The document is not friendly to the Zagwe kings. It suggests that they are usurpers. Had they not moved the capital and destroyed the real Solomonic

---

[9] Rev.21.

[10] Anderson and Kalu, 'Christianity in Sudan and Ethiopia', in: Kalu et al. (eds), *African Christianity*, pp.109,110.

line? Yet they did not succeed in completely rooting out the supposedly Ethiopian branch of the house of Solomon. The only survivor was hiding in the *Debre Libanos* monastery. In 1270 the leader of this monastery, Tekle Haymanot, helped to restore the ancient line of Axum kings by handing over power to the hidden survivor, Yekunno-Amlak, who agreed to the claim that he was a descendant of King Solomon. Yekunno-Amlak contributed much to the creation of a problem that in later ages would harm the Ethiopian Church tremendously. Out of gratitude he gave the Church one third of Ethiopia's land, making it a big landlord. Later, as a consequence of this the Church would be classified with the exploiters of the landless and the poor. Yekunno-Amlak and his successors expanded the kingdom, at the expense of the Muslims. Under King (by now also called Emperor) Amde-Zion (†1344) there were massive conversions to Christianity.

The Solomonide kings also facilitated a religious revival. The central figure in it was Tekle Haymanot. He had grown up in the southern region of Shoa where Christians suffered from pagan attacks. After a period of personal spiritual crisis and experiences in a monastic community in Tigray in the north, he started a new monastic order (*Dabra Asbo*) that worked successfully among the pagans of Shoa. After Tekle Haymanot's death, the revivalist and missionary activities were strengthened by the new *Abun* Yaqob and by new military conquests. A conflict between church and state, mainly of Abbot Fillippos and Abun Yaqob versus Emperor Amde-Zion gave the church more influence in society. *Monasticism* united the country, but at times it was also a dividing power, for instance when, in opposition to Tekle Haymanot's community, the order of *Ewostatewos* arose. A bone of contention was the question of whether Saturday or Sunday should be kept as the *Sabbath* for Christians.

The conflict was resolved at a Church Council convened by Emperor Zar'a-Ya'qob[11] (†1468). The new Emperor tried to reform and reunite the Church. He wanted to make new contacts with Rome and the West. Under his rule, although it was harsh and ruthless at times, the Ethiopian church flourished. Around 1430 opposition against Zar'a-Ya'qob's theocratic rule came from the newly founded monastic order of the *Estifanites*. They aimed at a spiritual kingdom of the heart and rejected the Emperor's cult of the cross and of Mary.

c. Decline and Survival

After Emperor Zar'a-Ya'qob's death in 1468, Ethiopia came under rapidly increasing pressure of Islam. In the beginning of the 16th century Muslims occupied more Ethiopian territory than Christians, although many Muslim settlements were not connected, and were ruled by Christian overlords. Yet through slave trade and pilgrimages Ethiopian Muslims communicated with the Arab and Turkish branches of the *ummah*.[12] Anti-Christian sentiments led to a widespread Muslim rising, led by a liberated slave, Imam Ahmad (†1543). People saw him as the Imam of Judgment Day who had returned to lead Islam to final victory. The Turks provided him with modern weapons. In 1529 at Shimbra-Kure the Ethiopian army was crushed by the forces of Imam Ahmad. Much Christian culture was destroyed during the 12 years of his campaigns, including many churches and monasteries. The situation was aggravated by

---

[11] Seed of Jacob; cf. Anderson and Kalu, 'Christianity in Sudan and Ethiopia', in: Kalu et al. (eds), *African Christianity*, p.110.

[12] *Ummah* (Arabic): nation or community, used to designate the community of all Muslim nations.

a revolutionary movement of the pagan Oromo in the South, directed against both Christianity and Islam.

In the meantime, resulting from the Portuguese campaigns of discovery, conquest and mission, a Portuguese embassy had opened in Ethiopia (the *Alvarez Embassy*, 1520-1526). In despair Zar'a-Ya'qob's great-grandson, King Lebna Dengel (†1540) appealed to the Portuguese for assistance. The Portuguese sent a fleet to Massawa with Vasco da Gama's son Christoph as the admiral. Under King Galawdewos (†1559), the Ethiopians and the Portuguese defeated and killed Imam Ahmad in 1543. Christian rule was reinstated. But church and state had become weaker and more vulnerable. The great vision of the New Israel and the New Solomon was darkened. Many had lapsed to Islam. A book of penitence, *Mesihafe Qedir*, was to teach the way back to the church.

d. Jesuit Attempt Fails

By appealing to the Portuguese a new competitor had been given entrance to the country, the Roman Catholic Church with its universal claims of authority. Some of Christoph da Gama's soldiers remained in the country, and soon they had a bishop of their own, Andrew de Oviedo. Portuguese Roman Catholic activity in Ethiopia was coloured by the European situation where the Roman Catholic *Counter Reformation* tried to root out heretics, including followers of the Protestant Reformation. In the eyes of Rome the Ethiopian Orthodox Church was heretical, and had to be brought under the wings of the Pope. In 1557 Jesuits came to Ethiopia, with the intention of changing the Ethiopian church and of uniting it with Rome. Of course, this challenged the independence of the Ethiopian Church and also the position of the patriarch of Alexandria who nominated the *Abun*. King Galawdewos resisted the attempts of the Jesuits to introduce Latin rites and Roman Christology.

In the 17th century the independence of Ethiopian Christianity was again felt to be threatened by Western Jesuits. Pedro Paez, a Spanish Jesuit, entered the country in 1603. He was meant to become the patriarch of a transformed Ethiopian Church under Rome. Paez succeeded in winning the hearts of Kings Za-Dingil and Susenyos. He even convinced them of the christological error of Unionism. In 1622 King Susenyos decided to become a Roman Catholic. In 1626 the union of the Ethiopian church and the Roman Church was officially proclaimed. But in the meantime, Paez had died. He was succeeded by Alfonso Mendez, an authoritarian Spanish prelate, who demanded re-baptism of all and re-ordination of the clergy. Mendez also demanded the abolition of Ethiopian rites and customs. This led to a rebellion and much bloodshed, so that King Susenyos in 1632 stopped the campaign of Romanisation by a public proclamation that restored the *Ethiopian Coptic Church*. Subsequently Susenyos abdicated. His son Fasilidas (†1667) withdrew to Gondar where a new capital was established. He chased away the Jesuit missionaries, and cut off relations with the Portuguese. As a reaction to this disappointment with foreigners a period of isolation followed. For two centuries the Ethiopian Church would mainly concern itself with internal affairs.

e. Conflicts and Disintegration

In this period of isolation the church tried to remedy some of its weaknesses. In the south Christianity was definitely weaker than in the North. The Church in the south lacked leadership and communication. They were surrounded by the pagan Oromo people. Two migratory movements supported the Church. Migrants from the North settled in the south and helped the Church in its missionary activity. Many Oromo people migrating to the North were influenced by the Church and became Christians.

Unfortunately, this positive development did not stop processes of decline and division in church and state. In Gondar, people quarreled about issues like the right day for the Sabbath, leadership in the Church, and the role of Alexandria. More serious were the controversies on the two natures of Christ. They had split the church into at least four sections, the *Unionites*, the *Unctionists*, the *Unionists*, and the Sost Ledat, that is the *Three Births party*. The Unionites (*tewahido*) were classical *Monophysites*. They claimed that the uniting force of Incarnation had brought about one unique divine-human nature. In practice, however,

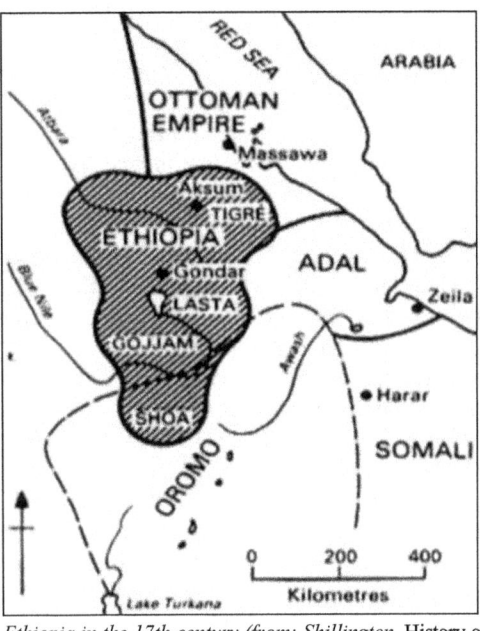

Ethiopia in the 17th century (from: Shillington, History of Africa, *p.166)*

they only stressed Christ's divine nature. According to the Unctionists, the Holy Spirit through His unction (*qibat*) has united Christ's divine and human natures. Thus they were open to the heresy of *Subordinationism*, putting the Son under the Spirit. The Son-of-Grace party (*ye-siga-lij*) were a kind of *Adoptionists*. They distinguished Christ's eternal sonship by the Father, his temporal sonship by Mary, and his redemptive sonship by the Holy Spirit. By union of his temporal and his redemptive sonship He is adopted as the eternal Son of God. By the end of the 18th century a variant of the Son-of-Grace-party would emerge, the Sost Ledat party, claiming that as a consequence Christ was born three times.

The parties in the controversies on Christology were regionally divided and weakened church and state. Royal policies aggravated the situation. In 1654 King Fasilidas supported the Unctionists, only to provoke rebellion among the Unionists. Yohannes I (†1682) also favoured the Unctionists. His son Isayu I (†1706), however, forced the Unctionists to accept the Unionist position.

These quarrels divided society very deeply along the lines of the Alexandrian patriarchate, the monastic movement of Tekle Haymanot, and the monastic movement of Ewostatewos. The *Abun* represented the Alexandrian party, which made him unacceptable to others. The *Echege* who was sent to Gondar was just a representative of the Tekle Haymanot party. Even Echege Filpos appeared to be powerless. Ethiopian Christianity seemed to be at the verge of total collapse.

In the 18th century the quarrels led to political chaos. The central power of the kings at Gondar ceased to be effective. The power vacuum was filled by local rulers, called *ras*, who were ruling their own mini-states. Attempts by regional chiefs to grasp royal power failed. One of them, Wibe of Simien, was beaten by Muslim Oromo at Debre Tabor in 1842. A Christian group among the Oromo, the Yeju, managed to take control of the royal house at Gondar, but they could not make their power effective in other parts of the country. In the midst of this the theological disputes went on. Islam was greatly helped by this chaos. Many people were confused and became Muslims.

This period of great instability and disorder is called the *Era of the Princes*, or the Era of the Judges (*Zamena mesa fint*). It would last until 1855 when one of the local chiefs fought his way to the top, and became 'king of kings'. His name was Tewodros II and he lived from 1818 to 1868.[13] The new king, or Emperor, ended the chaos and proclaimed a new era of justice, peace and order. His qualities are summed up by Anderson and Kalu: He told the clergy to forget about disputes on Christology, and just stick to the classical *Monophysite* faith of Alexandria. He attempted to unify the nation, to reform the church, to introduce social programmes for the masses, to redistribute the land, and to have the Bible translated in the Amharic language.[14] Besides, Tewodros adopted the claims of his Solomonic predecessors by calling himself 'Son of David'. He behaved independently towards the Patriarch of Alexandria by not accepting him to act as an envoy of Egyptian Muslim rulers. It was only when the patriarch sent Selama (†1867) as the new *Abun* that the Emperor started to show his favour. Selama was educated at a school of the *Church Missionary Society* (CMS) in Cairo. There he was trained in a Protestant Evangelical way, which made him favour Protestantism. Selama was liked by the Emperor, which enhanced his influence. Unfortunately, later they clashed. Selama was sent to prison where he died. Despite this Tewodros remained interested in the Protestants.

f. The First Protestant Missionaries in Ethiopia

Protestant missionaries had already arrived in Ethiopia before the reign of Tewodros started. In the previous section we noticed that Ethiopian Christianity seemed to be collapsing because of divisions and controversies. In this critical period, for the first time Protestant missionaries came to the country. They were Samuel Gobat, Johann Ludwig Krapf, Martin Flad, H.A. Stern and others (1830). They all belonged to the *Church Missionary Society* (CMS), an organisation born out of the Evangelical revival in the Anglican Church. The CMS did not intend to establish new churches. They wanted to purify and strengthen the Ethiopian church and use it as a bridge for evangelisation of eastern and central Africa. The French and German names of these missionaries demonstrate the inability of the CMS to recruit Englishmen for their first enterprises. It also shows the international character of the 19th-century missionary movement. Gobat started with the distribution of Bibles and tracts. His influence grew rapidly, e.g. with *Echege* Filpos, and he was even invited to become *Abun*. Later he became Anglican bishop of Jerusalem, and kept contact with Ethiopia through visiting pilgrims. Krapf was especially interested in converting the pagan Oromo or Galla in the South. In his vision converted Oromo would be missionaries to the central regions of Africa. He made a grammar of the Galla language and translated the Gospels into it. Flad and Stern worked among the Falashas, 'the black Jews of Ethiopia', and led a number of them to the Ethiopian Church.

However, the Ethiopians soon noticed that the CMS-missionaries opposed *monasticism*, the prayers to Mary, and the veneration of images. Moreover, they felt that

---

[13] Tewodros = Gift of God.

[14] Anderson and Kalu, 'Christianity in Sudan and Ethiopia', in: Kalu et.als (eds), *African Christianity*, pp.113,114.

their presence might prelude British colonialist attempts. Krapf favoured a British presence in Ethiopia to ward off Roman Catholic missionary attempts. These factors made the Ethiopian *ras* suspicious. That is why these first Protestant missionaries were expelled in 1842 and 1843.

Protestant missionaries showed a keen interest in the work of Bible translation. By the mid 19th century the Scriptures had been translated into the Amharic language. When Protestants began working on this, there were already other translations. There was an old translation of the Gospels made by Peter Heyling in the 17th century. In the 18th century an Ethiopian monk, helped by a French diplomat in Cairo, made a completely new translation of the whole Bible, which was ready in 1840.

Krapf started to improve this translation of the Bible. He continued this work even after his banishment and published his translation in 1870. Orthodox clergy, especially in Tseazega, put this Bible in place of the ancient Ge'ez version and used it for Bible study. In the meantime, Krapf had gone to Zanzibar, and Mombasa in Kenya; from there he again tried to approach the Oromo people.

g. Another Roman Catholic Attempt Fails

The period just before the rise of Emperor Tewodros also witnessed the arrival of Roman Catholic missionaries. This was the first time since the failure of Jesuit attempts in the 16th and 17th centuries. The coming of Justin de Jacobis to Ethiopia (1839) signalled new Roman Catholic attempts to bring Ethiopian Christianity under Rome. The climate seemed favourable. Many Ethiopians were tired of the chaos and disorder that had been brought about in the Era of the Princes. They longed for the order and authority that Rome could give. Moreover, it was thought Rome could end the disputes on Christology, as at least two of the parties, the Unctionists and the Unionists, seemed to be close to Roman Catholic theology.

De Jacobis was an Italian Lazarist. He cooperated with bishop Massaja, a Capuchin, who consecrated him to be bishop. They kept this consecration secret, so as not to arouse suspicions from the Ethiopian clergy, who certainly would disagree with their vision of having Ethiopia united with Rome. They started seminaries, converted people, and managed to win the favour of the *echege* and of Wibe, the local *ras* of Tigray. The latter entrusted De Jacobis with headship of a group that was to ask the patriarch of Alexandria for a new *Abun*. Ironically this journey led to the nomination of Abun Selama, who was a friend of Protestantism. In 1841 Selama became the new Abun of Ethiopia, thus restoring the contacts with the Coptic patriarchate of Alexandria after a long time. He disliked Roman Catholicism, and especially after 1855 when his protector Tewodros became Emperor, he opposed the work of Roman Catholic missionaries.

De Jacobis tried to establish an indigenised Roman Catholic Church in the North. Massaja started in 1846. He first worked together with De Jacobis, and then he went to the pagan Oromo in the South. And finally until 1879, he worked for the establishment of a Roman Catholic Church in the central Shewa province. In all three places he was expelled, and in the last one even banished from the country.

h. New Protestant Missions

Emperor Tewodros was interested in the technological products of Western Protestant culture, so he re-opened the doors for Protestants. Through the help of Gobat and Krapf able artisans were recruited from Chrischona, a Pietist Lutheran centre near Basle in

Switzerland. The first group arrived in 1856. Some of them married Ethiopian wives and never returned to Europe. The country was opened for Protestant missionaries again. After the restoration of Ethiopian unity by Emperor Tewodros, Selama emphatically turned against Roman Catholics, forcing De Jacobis into hiding and expelling Massaja from the South.

Eventually Selama got into conflict with the capricious Emperor, and he ended his life in prison in 1867. The Emperor too ended his life tragically. Because of the levying of land taxations and the confiscations of church land, he estranged himself from the Church. His desire to be accepted on equal terms by Western powers was not fulfilled. Soon the Emperor collided with the British government, who did not comply with his wishes for military support against rival leaders. He put all English missionaries in prison. However, instead of giving in, the English sent an expeditionary navy force. In 1868 his army was crushed by the English, and he committed suicide.

i. Ethiopia Maintains its Independence

Tewodros was succeeded by Yohannes IV (†1889). The new Emperor strengthened the unity of state and church. He also ended the public controversies as to Christology, by calling all parties to the *Council of Boru Meda* in 1878, and forcing them to conform to the classical *Monophysite* position of the *Unionites*. Not only Christians, but also pagans and Muslims were forced to concede to the decision of the Council. In this way the Emperor started a successful campaign of forcing non-Christians into Christianity. He also extended Ethiopian territory by building garrison towns (*katema*) at the frontiers of his empire. In these cities the army and the church were actively represented. Many Muslims were brought under Christian rule, and eventually became Christians, especially among the southern Oromo.

Yohannes IV tried to resist the powers of imperialism that threatened Ethiopian independence. He defeated the Egyptians in 1875 and 1876, but he could not prevent the Italians from occupying the coastal town of Massawa. He attacked a new messianic Muslim movement under *Mahdi* Muhammad Ahmed, but in the battle of Qallabat in 1880 he was mortally wounded.

During the reign of his successor, Menelik II (†1913), Ethiopia was threatened by Italy, which in 1885 occupied Eritrea, seeking to establish a colonial empire in Africa. However, the Ethiopians defeated the Italian army in the *Battle of Adowa* in 1896. This feat contributed much to the movement of *'Ethiopianism'* that soon would spread among the Christians of colonial Africa, and inspire black imagination all over the world. Menelik II built a new capital, Addis Ababa, welcomed Western artisans and missionaries, and had his cousin's son Ras Tafari Makonnen, later Emperor Haile Selassie I, educated in Europe. In line with his predecessor he tried to turn as many pagans as

Menelik II (1844-1913), Emperor of Ethiopia, whose army under General Ras Makonnen beat the Italians in the Battle of Adowa in 1896.

possible to the Orthodox Church, to be baptised after an absolute minimum of instruction.

In the meantime, the Evangelical movement continued to spread. Contacts between Evangelical missionaries from Sweden and Orthodox clergy in Hamasen encouraged the study of the Bible in Amharic. This encounter with Scripture led many to the discovery that there is no salvation but through faith in Christ. Persecution by local rulers made a group of Hamasen Christians flee to Egypt and later to Eritrea, at that time occupied by the Italians. Later they returned to form an indigenous Protestant church in the Hamasen highlands. Among the Oromo an Evangelical church took shape, aided by a new Bible translation in the Oromo language by a liberated slave Onesimus and Aster Ganno, which was completed in 1899.

In 1916 Ras Tafari Makonnen became regent over Ethiopia, and in 1930 he became Emperor Haile Selassie. In 1936 Ethiopia was conquered by Italy. The Pope congratulated the Italian army, and Roman Catholic missionaries began to pour into the country, while many Protestant missionaries were expelled.[15] Emperor Haile Selassie started a guerilla war from neighbouring countries, in which many Ethiopians had taken refuge. Many refugees in Kenya met with Anton Jönsson, a Swedish teacher and preacher, and came into contact with Evangelical faith. The Italian occupation lasted until 1941. The Ethiopian Church was forced by the Italians to break ties with the Coptic Church in Egypt. After the occupation, the Ethiopian Church became completely independent, not by force but voluntarily. A series of conferences with the patriarchate of Alexandria led to an agreement in 1959.

Mengistu Haile Mariam, leader of the Marxist-Leninist revolution in Ethiopia in 1977, who persecuted the Church.

In 1944 the government declared a large part of the country a 'no-go-area' for foreign missionaries, who did not cooperate with the Ethiopian Church. This confirmed the policy of some Protestant organisations that cooperated with the Ethiopian Church. Other foreign missions were only allowed to work in pagan Oromo-land in the South. Yet a number of independent Evangelical denominations arose, like the *Word of Life Evangelical Church* (Sudan Interior Mission – SIM) and the *Ethiopian Evangelical Church Mekane Yesus*.[16] The *Mekane Yesus Church* (the name means: the place where Jesus lives) was founded in 1959 with about 20,000 members, as a result of various Lutheran Missions, e.g. the *Bauern Mission* from Hermannsburg. According to the Mission's website, the church has more than 3 million members now.

After the end of the Italian occupation, the Roman Catholic Church at first experienced a backlash of Ethiopian revenge, but it soon regained and strengthened its position.

---

[15] Cf. Hildebrandt, *History of the Church in Africa*, p.235.
[16] EECMY, for further information consult their website: http://www.eecmy.org/CO/index.shtml

In 1974 Emperor Haile Selassie was overthrown by an army council, the Derg. In 1977 a Communist revolution led by Colonel Mengistu Haile Mariam brought Ethiopia under *Marxist-Leninist* rule, which lasted for a decade. Christianity was suppressed, and the population suffered immensely from the cruelties of this regime. The suffering was intensified by the Ethiopian-Eritrean war. Mengistu especially persecuted the Protestant churches. Buildings were confiscated, organisations were infiltrated by communist agents, many leaders were imprisoned and some murdered. Later the Orthodox Church was hit by waves of persecution. After the end of Mengistu's regime, it became clear the churches had survived, either publicly or underground. The Evangelical churches, which had suffered most, had seen a tremendous growth of membership. In the Orthodox Church the leadership by non-clergy had grown stronger, and so had the interest in personal and communal Bible study.

44. Africa and Early Portuguese Missions

44.1. Henry the Navigator

The defeat of Islam and the establishment of Christian rule was the dream of Prince Henry of Portugal (†1460), which he not only sought to realise in his own country, but also in other parts of the world, not least in Africa. He is known as Henry the *Navigator*, because of his nautical plans and activities. Henry aimed at the discovery of territories beyond the seas that thus far had been largely unknown to the Europeans. Early world maps show that before 1500 Europeans were greatly ignorant about the geography of sub-Saharan Africa.[1]

From Henry the Navigator onwards this situation of ignorance was going to change. Bypassing the Arabs and getting direct access to the gold fields of West Africa was an important motive of the Portuguese seafarers. The ultimate goal was reaching India with its opportunities for the very rewarding trade in spices. Henry's plan to enter Africa to defeat Islam and establish Christianity met with approval by Popes Martin V (1418) and Nicolas V (1452). Henry even got papal blessing for trading in African slaves. The exploration and the conquest of foreign lands were to be aimed at evangelising the pagans. Therefore, Henry's explorations were not only the work of sailors and soldiers, but also of missionary priests. In a special arrangement the Pope allowed these priests to work in the system of *padroado*,[2] which made them directly responsible to the Portuguese government.

Infante Dom Henrique, Prince of Portugal, known in English as Henry the Navigator (1394-1460), contributed much to the development of Portugal as a seafaring nation and to plans for Portuguese expansion.

In 1441 Portuguese ships landed in Mauritania. In the 1470s the Fante coast, connected to the Akan gold fields, was reached. Soon the trade routes of gold, which used to run through Songhay and the Sahara desert, were diverted to the Portuguese and other European trading forts on the Atlantic coast. Contacts between Portuguese and the kingdom of Benin (from 1472) provided the Portuguese with Benin slaves whom they used as commodities in exchange for Akan gold. In 1485 the Congo was reached, and in 1486 the Cape of Good Hope, by Bartholomew Diaz. In 1494 in the *Treaty of Tordesillas*, Spain and Portugal divided the newly discovered world on either side

Martin V, originally Oddone Colonna (1368-1431), one of the Popes who approved of Portuguese plans to beat Islam and extend Christianity.

---

[1] Peter Whitfield, *The Image of the World: Twenty Centuries of World Maps*, San Francisco: Pomegranate Artbooks, 1994, pp.20-26.

[2] *Padroado* (Portuguese: patronage): arrangement or treaty between the the Pope and the Portuguese state, by which he delegated to the Portuguese Kings the administration of the local Roman Catholic Church.

of the Atlantic Ocean, thus granting Portugal the right to colonise Africa. This move was sanctioned by Pope Julius II in 1506.

In 1498 Vasco da Gama rounded the Cape and discovered the Zambezi, Mozambique Island, and other Swahili city states. The Portuguese discoveries and conquests were immediately followed by missionary efforts. Here is a general survey of early Portuguese missionary work. [3]

44.2. Islands and the West Coast

Franciscan monks had worked on the *Canary Islands* since the beginning of the 15th century alongside commercial activities. By 1500 the bishop of Madeira was overseeing the mission work in Cape Verde, São Tomé and the Azores. In the meantime, in 1462, Alfonso de Balano, also a Franciscan, was appointed to oversee the missionary work at the *Guinea Coast*.

Cape Verde. This archipelago off the North Western coast of Africa became a base for slaves. It also became a base for the recruitment of African priests who were to be sent to Lisbon for training before they would enter the African continent as missionaries.

São Tomé and Principe Islands. On these uninhabited islands Portuguese settlers developed sugar plantations. Slave labour was used, first from southern Russia,[4] and then from the African mainland. Here is the beginning of the slave trade that for centuries would dominate relations between Europe and Africa, and which was extended to a 'triangular trade' that included America. *São Tomé* became the main transit point for slaves being transported by the Portuguese to Brazil. A church was established among the settlers, so African slaves were touched by Christianity.

Mali and *Ghana*. Diogo Gomez converted a vassal king of Mali in 1457. In 1482 Diogo da Azambuja unsuccessfully tried to convert a local king in Ghana, and the church he founded became a symbol of hostile foreign presence. In 1503 another local king embraced Christianity, but later lapsed. Initial successes by Augustinians, Capuchins and Dominicans all ended in failure. Ghana or the Gold Coast was reached in 1482. The Portuguese sailors landed in Elmina. There a Fort was established. Missionary attempts by Jesuits, Dominicans, Franciscans, Augustinians and Capuchins achieved some initial success, until the Fort of Elmina was captured by the

View of Fort Elmina, St. George's castle was built in 1482-6 by the Portuguese, who were the first European builders in West Africa. It is the largest of the fortified buildings on the coast. In 1637 the Dutch took Fort Elmina from the Portuguese (from: Friere, 1546).

---

[3] On the early Portuguese involvement in Africa, see: Shaw, *Kingdom*, pp.107-119; Baur, *2000 Years*, pp.43-99; Foster, *Setback and Recovery*, pp.180-183; Thomson, *New Movements*, pp.80-81; Hastings, *African Church*, pp.71-129; Ward, 'Africa', in: Hastings (ed), *World History*, pp.200-203; Shillington, *History of Africa*, pp.170-173, 198-201

[4] Shillington, *History of Africa*, p.171.

Dutch in 1637.

Benin. During the decades around 1500, the Portuguese received war captives from the Benin kings. These captives they sold as slaves to Akan in exchange for gold. Spanish Jesuits, who in 1655 baptised the Benin king, were ordered by Portuguese soldiers to leave.

Early Roman Catholic Mission in West Africa had 'considerably limited success'. Kpobi says that by the end of the 17th century, the mission was, for all practical purposes, 'over'. Except for some relics, mission had practically died out, because it was dominated by trade, and effectively resisted by African culture and religion, while the mass baptisms by Roman Catholic missionaries made 'converts' easily lapse into their former religion. Perhaps the greatest drawback to mission was the slave trade. Roman Catholic Portuguese got involved in the purchase and shipment of African slaves. For almost four centuries the Atlantic slave trade affected Africa, not only the

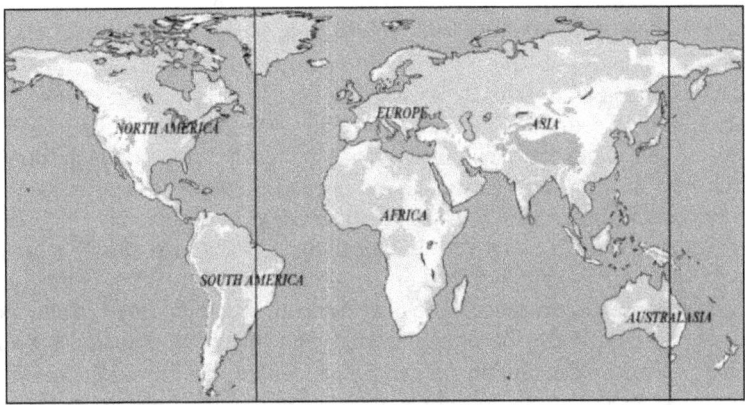

The Treaty of Tordesillas of 1494 divided the world outside of Europe between Portugal and Spain along a north-south meridian west of the Cape Verde Islands (46° 37' W). The lands to the east would belong to Portugal and the lands to the west to Spain.

West Coast, but also the territories to the south of it, the Congo and Angola. Christian mission 'in such circumstances was most difficult, if not impossible'.[5]

44.3. The Congo

In 1491 the first group of Portuguese missionaries arrived at Mbanza Congo.[6] In 1493 many Africans were baptised, among them Prince Mvemba Nzinga; he changed his name to Alfonso I (†1543). After ascending the throne in 1506, pushing aside his brother who was the rightful heir, he destroyed the pagan temple and capital, and built a new capital, São Salvador, with a cathedral. He invited many Portuguese missionaries, and sent his sons and grandsons to Lisbon for theological training. In 1531 his son Henrique was ordained bishop.[7] The church was planted throughout the kingdom.

---

[5] N.A. Kpobi, 'African Chaplains in Seventeenth-century West Africa', in Ogbu U. Kalu (ed.), *African Christianity: An African Story*, University of Pretoria, 2005, pp.144-148.

[6] Mbanza Congo (formerly: São Salvador do Congo) is situated in the North-West of present-day Angola.

[7] H. Gundani, 'Iberians and African Clergy in Southern Africa', in Ogbu U. Kalu (ed.), *African Christianity: An African Story*, University of Pretoria, 2005, pp.176-178.

However, many Portuguese missionaries were sexually immoral, and also joined the slave trade. In 1516 the Benin kings stopped selling slaves. Then, the trade shifted southwards to the Congo kingdom. King Alfonso had become very dependent on the Portuguese. His wars of conquest produced many captives whom the Portuguese could use as a trade commodity and in their plantations on São Tomé.

An invasion by the Jaga people in 1568/1569 would have ended the authority of the Congo kings, if the Portuguese army had not saved and re-installed them. In the 17th century the kingdom disintegrated, and its regional factions increasingly built their economies on the trade in slaves.

In the meantime, at the request of King Alfonso's successors, at last more zealous Christian missionaries were sent. The Jesuits' presence was strengthened, and they constructed a college, headed by M. Cardoso, who in 1524 translated a catechism into KiKongo. In 1645 the Capuchins[8] arrived. This religious order would remain in the Congo for 190 years. They baptised many people and started numerous schools in the Congo capital São Salvador, and also in Mbanza in the coastal province of Soyo. They successfully resisted Protestant missionary attempts in the period 1641-1648 when the Dutch ruled the Congo. However, the missionary methods of the Capuchins excluded a real understanding of traditional African beliefs and sometimes raised hostility. Moreover, Rome forced them to use superficial methods, allowing baptism of those who were 'in the faith of the church' (*in fide ecclesiae*), although they did not understand the Christian faith as such. This opened the door to *syncretism*. Gradually Christianity became mixed with *fetishism* and *superstitions*.

When King Antonio I went to war against the Portuguese the Congo Kingdom developed a very serious crisis. In the battle of Ambuila (1665) a Portuguese army from Angola almost ended its existence. The provinces, among them Soyo, made themselves independent. São Salvador became deserted and many missionaries withdrew to Angola. In the chaotic situation the church in the Congo/ São Salvador almost vanished. According to Baur, 'only in the province of Soyo remained a truly flourishing church'.[9] Gray thinks that Soyo Christianity at least for some decades was a 'vigorous and expanding' power.[10]

These positive qualifications of Soyo Christianity cannot hide the fact that the number of missionaries further decreased when in 1759 the anticlerical Portuguese government, led by the Marquis of Pombal,[11] prohibited missionary work by the Jesuits and in 1834 forbade mission by all religious orders. That is why also the last Capuchins had to leave, in 1835.

The phasing out of missionaries contributed to the 'dying out of Christianity'[12] in the Congo Kingdom, and also to a revival of *African Traditional Religion*. The Christian faith had never been able to take the place of traditional beliefs and customs, such as veneration of ancestors and spirits. This once again opened the door to *syncretism*. Gradually Christianity mixed with *fetishism* and *superstitions*.

---

[8] The *Order of Friars Minor Capuchin* (OFM Cap) is an order of friars in the Roman Catholic Church, the chief and only permanent offshoot from the Franciscans.

[9] Baur, *2000 Years*, p.65.

[10] Richard Gray, *Black Christians and White Missionaries*, New Haven: Yale UP, 1990.

[11] Sebastião José de Carvalho e Melo: 1st Marquis of Pombal (1699-1782).

[12] Baur, *2000 Years*, p.70.

Prophetess Kimpa Vita, or Dona Beatrice (1684-1706) in the Congo.

This is the context of the movement of prophetesses Maffuta and her successor Dona Beatrice or Kimpa Vita. Influenced by Roman Catholic Mariology, Maffuta had visions of Mary informing the leaders of church and state of Christ's dissatisfaction with them, especially because they had removed the centre from São Salvador to Kibangu. Dona Beatrice also criticised this change of capital. She foretold a glorious future for São Salvador in terms of the New Jerusalem. She had a consort, Barro, who was called St. John. Donna Beatrice herself used the name of St. Anthony, the Capuchins' patron saint. She ordered the people to burn their fetishes and even crucifixes. All this challenged the king, his council and the Capuchins. They agreed to consider her as a rebel. That is why she was condemned and, together with Barro, eventually burnt as a witch in 1706.

In the province of Soyo, Christianity mixed with traditional rites to the fertility snake Mumba. Traditional offerings of the fertility spirit for healing, rain and blessing had been replaced in Mpinda by offerings to a wooden statue of Mary, the Mama Nzambi i.e. Mother God. Christianity decayed and finally almost vanished. Baur indicates that when the *Holy Ghost Fathers* arrived in the Congo in 1865, they found relics of the church, and also a Christian community still in existence.[13]

44.4. Angola

Since 1519 the Portuguese had been active in Angola. In 1526 the Ngola[14] of the Ndongo people was converted to Christianity, and by 1570 the Portuguese began to conquer the whole country. In 1575 they settled a colony in Luanda, the capital of the kingdom of Ndongo. The Jesuits also settled there. From the king, the Ngola, the Portuguese bought slaves to be transported to *São Tomé* and from there to Brazil. As a result, the Ngola kingdom grew militarily and economically at the expense of its enemies in the interior. By the middle of the 18th century Luanda alone was exporting more than ten thousand captives a year.[15] The Imbangala in the interior cooperated with the Ngola of the Ndongo in the slave trade, and later took over direct contacts with the Portuguese.

The Jesuits in Luanda founded a church among settlers and slaves, and they tried to establish African Christian communities, using the village model. They were not very successful. The invasion by the Dutch (1641-1647) stopped their work all together. Later some Africans from Angola were

Ngola Ann Nzinga Mbande (c.1583-1663) was one of the most famous monarchs in pre-colonial Angola. She ruled over the Ndongo and the Matamba people, and successfully resisted Portuguese colonial expansion during the time of her life.

---

[13] Baur, *2000 Years*, pp.70-73.

[14] *Ngola* means King. The name Angola is derived from it.

[15] Shillington, *History of Africa*, p.201.

trained for the priesthood on *São Tomé*. One of them, called Francisco Necessitades, belonged to the few African priests who continued the work after 1840, when all white missionaries left Angola. The invasion by the Dutch (1641-1647) stopped this work.[16] David Livingstone, when he visited Angola in 1854, found little evidence of Christianity.

44.5. Southern and Eastern Africa

The first Portuguese naval captain to touch Southern Africa was Bartholomew Diaz. He rounded the Cape in 1488 and he erected a cross at False Island (Kwaaihoek), west of the Bushmans River mouth.[17] After him, in 1498 Vasco da Gama sailed past the Cape of Good Hope on his way to discover a sea route to India. He saw a beautiful strip of coast that he called Terra de Natal. The Portuguese established bases along the Pacific Ocean coast. They succeeded in capturing most of the Muslim-Swahili city-states, especially Sofala, Mozambique Island, Kilwa, Zanzibar, Mombasa, Malindi, and Lamu.

Fort Jesus, a Portuguese stronghold, built in 1593, on Mombasa Island, Kenya.

The first missionary to work in the region of Sofala was Gonçalo da Silveira, a Jesuit. Victory over Muslim resistance and domination of the Indian Ocean was achieved by a naval victory in 1509. The Portuguese gradually put stone fortresses in these coastal cities. Fort Jesus in Mombasa (completed 1599) for a long time was the centre of Portuguese power in eastern Africa. In this way the Portuguese began to control the trade by these city-states with the African interior. Missionary work followed, in and around the fortified settlements, and also in the interior.

Vasco da Gama, Portuguese seafarer, who was the first to go beyond the Cape of Good Hope, and along the east coast of Africa to Mombasa in 1497-1498.

As in other African territories, the Portuguese in Mozambique 'made minimal contact with the interior' until the end of the 19th century. Colonial administrators, missionaries, and soldiers rarely crossed the line from Sofala to Quelimane. The Dominicans established a station on the Island of Mozambique in 1577. In 1559 the Jesuits arrived, and opened stations along the Zambezi River. But their work was not permanent. The Dominicans trained a few African priests, among them Luiz de Esprito Santo, who mixed his missionary work with political and military involvement in Portuguese actions against Kaparidze, the Emperor of the Mutapa Empire. He was killed by the latter in 1631.[18]

Sometimes the Portuguese pressed on to the interior of East Africa, searching for the legendary Empire of *Prester*

---

[16] Gundani, 'Iberians and African Clergy in Southern Africa', in: Kalu (ed.), *African Christianity*, pp.185, 186.
[17] Cf.: Pillay and Hofmeyr, *Perspectives on Church History*, p.233.
[18] Gundani, 'Iberians and African Clergy in Southern Africa', in: Kalu (ed.), *African Christianity*, pp.182-185.

John. At one time they thought they had found it in Christian Ethiopia (see chapter 43.2). At another time they imagined it might exist along the Zambezi River. An army was sent to establish contacts and also to seize control of it and of the trade between Sofala and the Zambezi interior. Instead of finding this great Christian ruler, in 1560 missionary Gonçalo da Silveira met with Emperor Mwene Mutapa (or Munhumutapa), who resided in Zimbabwe. The Jesuit succeeded in baptising the Emperor. His Zimbabwean empire seemed to be open for Christianity. However, Muslim traders convinced the Mwene Mutapa that Silveira was a sorcerer and a spy. This changed the Emperor's ideas, and he had the missionary executed. Portuguese attempts at military conquest of the Mutapa state in 1571 and 1574 were not successful.

Still, a kind of Portuguese overlordship was established. Up to the 18th century the Mwene Mutapa had Portuguese names and considered themselves Christians, though there was not much of a church in Zimbabwe. Some Shona were trained as Dominican friars in Goa, but they did not return to Africa.[19] There was a greater presence of Christianity in the Zambezi Valley with Tete as its centre, but when the *Enlightenment* began in Europe, and the Portuguese

Swahili city states on Africa's east coast in the 15th and 16th centuries (from: Shillington, History of Africa, p.133).

government became hostile to the Roman Catholic Church, no more missionaries could come, and the Zambezi and Zimbabwe missions became extinct. When the *Enlightenment* came to an end, there were only a few Roman Catholic priests in the whole of Africa, most of them serving the white settlers on the offshore islands and in a few coastal settlements like Lorenço Marques and Luanda.[20] Gundani says that the shortage of missionary priests, beside the 'vitality of traditional culture', was a main

---

[19] Gundani, op. cit. pp.179-182.

[20] Cf. Hildebrandt, *History of the Church in Africa*, pp.64,65, who says that 'by the end of the 18th century the Portuguese church seems to have completely died out in the interior', and that 'by the beginning of the 19th century there were no Roman Catholics left along the coast, except for some foreign traders'.

reason for the 'limited impact' of Christianity in the early stages of Roman Catholic mission in the Portuguese territories of Southern and Eastern Africa. He refers to some factors that were behind this: the concept of *padroado* was beyond the capacity of Portugal's resources, entering the unsafe and disease-ridden interior of Africa deterred the clergy, and the Portuguese government and Rome were at loggerheads concerning the recruitment of missionaries.[21] Hildebrandt mentions more reasons why the Portuguese failed to establish a lasting Church: the desire for trade and wealth including the slave trade, lack of understanding for the African culture, and superficial methods of missionaries like the practice of mass baptisms.[22]

Although the Portuguese presence was impressively demonstrated by military constructions like Fort Jesus in Mombasa, the missionary efforts in the city-states along the East coast eventually were not successful. There was a hopeful change when the Augustinian Hermits came to Mombasa. They baptised many people, sometimes providing rice to the new Christians as a reward, in a vast region stretching from the Lamu archipelago to Zanzibar. Missionary success seemed assured when in 1625 the Sultan of Mombasa, Yusuf bin Hasan, was converted. But after a conflict with the Portuguese military, the Sultan turned against Christianity and started to persecute the Christians, having 300 of them killed. The Portuguese restored their power, but further attempts at Christianisation failed.

Also in Ethiopia, Portuguese and Roman Catholic missionary attempts failed. In chapter 43.2.c and 44.5 we described the *Alvarez Embassy* (1520-1526), Portuguese assistance to ward off Muslim invasions, the Jesuit mission in Ethiopia, the official reunion of the Coptic and the Roman churches (1622), the failure to implement this reunion, and in 1632 the cutting off by Ethiopia of ties with Rome and Portugal.

---

[21] Gundani, op. cit. pp.173,174.
[22] Hildebrandt, *History of the Church in Africa*, p.68.

45. Africa and the Dutch until 1800

45.1. Gold Coast, the Congo, Angola[1]

The Dutch presence in Southern Africa is very well known. Yet it should be noted that they touched and influenced other regions in Africa as well. The motive was predominantly commercial, yet there were also some missionary attempts. Portuguese sea power was increasingly challenged by the Dutch. Born out of the Reformation and out of a successful war of independence against Spain, *The Republic of the Seven United Netherlands* developed as a mighty naval force, mainly directed at trade. This force was not under the direct responsibility of the Republic's government, but under the rule of a number of private trading companies.

Gold Coast (Ghana). By 1593 a Dutch trader, Barent Ericzoon and his company were among the first to settle on the Guinea coast. At Moree they built Fort Nassau, near the Portuguese fort at Elmina, which they captured from the Portuguese in 1637. For many years the Dutch remained the most powerful nation on the African West Coast.

The Dutch, and also Danish, Swedish and Prussian traders continued to compete with the Portuguese military presence and with Portuguese attempts to spread Roman Catholicism. In this way the *Dutch West Indies Company* helped to neutralise Portuguese influence in West Africa. People in Ghana were exposed by the Protestant Dutch to Calvinist teachings. This continued until the 18th century when Dutch influence began to dwindle.[2] In 1871 the Dutch Gold Coast settlements were sold to Britain and incorporated into the Gold Coast.

Of some impact was the training and ordination of 'sick-comforters' and ministers who served on the ships and also in the permanent settlements on the African Coast. They contributed in a very modest way to missionary work. Among these pastors were some African converts. For example, Jacobus Capitein, a Fante tribesman, was taken to Holland as a boy. He entered Leyden University in 1737. Five years later, he wrote his *Doctoral Dissertation* in which he put forward the Biblical defence of slavery.[3] He was ordained in Amsterdam and returned to minister in Africa. He established a school, and he did much to promote the writing of the Fante language, e.g. by translating the *Lord's Prayer*, the *Twelve Articles of Faith* and the *Ten Commandments*, which were published in a booklet that was printed in Holland. Capitein also met with many difficulties that frustrated his work. He died at Fort Elmina in 1747 at the age of 30.[4]

---

[1] On the early Dutch involvement in Africa, in the framework of local developments, see: Shaw, *Kingdom*, pp.119-124; Hastings, *Church in Africa*, pp.197-198; Shillington, *History of Africa*, pp.212-225, 258-266; G.J. Pillay and J.W. Hofmeyr (eds), *Perspectives on Church History: An Introduction for South African Readers*, Pretoria: De Jager-HAUM, pp.232-247.

[2] Du Plessis. *Evangelization*. pp.109,110.

[3] Jacobus Eliza Joannes Capitein, *Dissertatio Politica-Theologica de Servitute, Libertati Christianae non contraria* (Politico-Theological Dissertation on Slavery as not being Contrary to Christian Liberty). The Latin text was translated into Dutch in the same year and saw at least four prints: Jacobus Elisa Joannes Capitein, *Staatkundig: Godgeleerd Onderzoekschrift over de Slavernij, als niet Strijdig tegen de Christelyke Vryheid*, Leyden: Philippus Bonk/ Amsterdam: Gerrit de Groot, 1742.

[4] For a condensed survey of Capitein's life and significance, see: Kpobi, 'African Chaplains', in: *African Christianity*, pp.156-159; A. Eekhof, *De Negerpredikant Jacobus Elisa Joannes Capitein*, Leiden: Bredee, 1917.

Another African who worked as a minister in Dutch missionary work was Christian Jacob Protten (1715-1769). He was a mulatto, the son of a Danish merchant, based at Christiansborg, and an African mother. Together with another mulatto boy, Frederik Pederson Svane, he was taken to Copenhagen. There they studied theology. After his studies, Protten went to the Moravian headquarters at Herrnhut. As a missionary of the *Moravian Movement* he went back to Africa. First he was based in the Dutch Fort Elmina, and then in the Danish Fort Christiansborg. Protten worked on reducing the Ga language to writing, and produced translations of Biblical material. He is also reported to have written a Fante grammar book. Frederik Pederson Svane joined the Pietists during his studies. He married a Danish wife. He worked at Christiansborg as a missionary, and returned to Denmark in 1746.[5]

Jacobus Eliza Capitein (1717-1747), was taken to The Netherlands, graduated at the University of Leiden, and became a minister in the Gold Coast.

These West Africans reflected the Protestant taste for putting the Scriptures into the language of the local people. This should be positively appreciated as a practical consequence from the Protestant Reformed theology of *sola scriptura*.[6] The Roman Catholic writer Adrian Hastings is less positive about this. He describes the African chaplain-missionaries as failures. He blames them for not fully maintaining their African identity by marrying white wives, or in the case of Jacobus Capitein not marrying at all, as his intention to wed an African woman was rejected in Holland as 'dangerous'. Often these African evangelists lived in tiny slaving communities, consisting mainly of whites, close to the Fort, working only among the coloured minority of mulattos.[7]

The Congo. The earliest Dutch contact with the African coast was at Soyo. Trade with the Dutch was considered of such importance that the Soyo ruler Garcia III made a successful revolt against the Portuguese and the Congo monarchy. The coming of the Dutch to the northern coastal kingdom of the Congo in 1641 boosted Soyo's fortunes. The Dutch traded in guns and ammunition in exchange for copper and slaves. There were earlier victories against the Congolese monarch in 1665 and 1669. With the Dutch firepower, Soyo's army successfully defeated the Portuguese at Kitombo in 1670.

Between 1641 and 1648 the Dutch were powerful in the Congo. Some attempts were made to spread Protestantism among the Congolese people. Despite the cordial relationship existing between the Dutch and the Congolese, the former were unable to make tangible inroads with their Calvinistic theology among the Soyo population. The Roman Catholics, through members of the Capuchin order, were much more successful. This is because King Garcia II favoured the Dutch in commerce, but in religion he favoured Roman Catholicism, thus diminishing Dutch Protestant influence. King Garcia II wanted to make clear it that they did not really depend on the Dutch, and that their

---

[5] Kpobi, 'African Chaplains', in: Kalu (ed.), *African Christianity*, 163-166.

[6] *sola scriptura*: Latin for: only the Scriptures.

[7] Hastings, *Church in Africa*, pp.178,179.

agreement with them was only concerning trade. This thwarted the Dutch hopes of propagating Calvinistic teachings while the Capuchins gained much ground.

No wonder then that after the Portuguese had retained their position in the Congo in 1648 Protestant literature spread by the Dutch was collected and made into a bonfire.[8] Hence, the Dutch were unable to make any missionary gains in the Congo.

Angola. By 1640 the Dutch had started to conquer some coastal regions of Angola. In 1641 a fleet of 20 ships and 3000 sailors belonging to the Dutch *West Indies Company* (WIC) attacked Luanda and drove the Portuguese out of their trading posts in Angola.[9] Just as the Portuguese Roman Catholics had been barring missionary attempts by people of other faiths, the Dutch were equally anxious to check Portuguese and Roman Catholic progress in Angola.

A Ship of the Dutch East Indies Company anchoring at the Cape of Good Hope.

Jan van Riebeeck (1618/1619-1677), Governor of the Cape 1652-1662 for the Dutch East Indies Company.

By 1780 African Protestant Christianity in Angola and other coastal regions was a reality. Yet progress was slow. As we have seen above, the Dutch, English and Danish forts along the slave coasts had had chaplains since the late 17th century. But due to high white mortality rates and other frustrations their work did not develop much. The activities of these chaplains mainly consisted of baptism, worship services on Sundays, and small scale educational work. Dutch and English chaplains did their missionary work under the gloomy cloud of slavery. In some way they were involved in the purchase of fellow human beings and forcibly detaining them before shipping them in overcrowded ships across the oceans to America where their compatriots had opened up newly discovered land, farms and mines in need of intensive cheap labour.[10]

45.2. Boers and Khoikhoi

The Dutch also competed with the Portuguese in East Asia. The *United East Indies Company* (Verenigde Oostindische Compagnie – VOC) was the main trading organisation. This powerful organisation developed an interest in the southern tip of Africa. For their ships, heading for the East Indies, they needed a refreshment station, for replenishment with fresh food. Therefore, in 1652, Jan van Riebeeck and other VOC

---

[8] Richard Gray, *Black Christians and White Missionaries*, London: Yale UP 1990, pp.37,38,41; J. du Plessis, *The Evangelisation of Pagan Africa*, Cape Town: Juta, 1929, p.26.

[9] Cf.: S. Paas, *Het Protestantisme in Angola: Tussen Wereldraad en Concordaat*, Amsterdam: ICCC, 1973, p.6.

[10] Hastings. *Church in Africa*, pp.95,197.

employees established a lasting and growing settlement at the Cape. They grew fruits and vegetables for their ships and built a hospital for sick sailors. The Dutch bought fresh meat from the local population, the Khoikhoi and the San.

However, the farms and the Khoikhoi cattle were at first not sufficient to supply the VOC settlement and the passing ships. That is why more people were brought in, who settled as farmers. In Dutch the word farmer is *boer*; hence, the name *Boers* by which the South African Dutch are known. Slaves from Madagascar, Mozambique, and Indonesia were imported to work on these farms. The spread of these Boer settlements conflicted with the Khoikhoi and San peoples,[11] who saw their grazing grounds diminished. When the Boers started penetrating deeper into the territory, this led to a series of Khoikhoi-Boer wars. After a period of military resistance, most of the Khoikhoi either escaped Boer influence by withdrawing into the interior, or they were forced to work for the Boers. Gradually they adopted much of Dutch culture, including the Dutch language.

45.3. Nguni and Tswana

In the 18th century, Boer penetration into the Eastern interior led to contacts with the Xhosa people. They were the southern fringe of Nguni-speaking peoples. At first the contacts were rather peaceful, but in the second half of the century serious conflicts arose between Boers and Xhosa cattle-keepers over the use of grazing lands. During a war in 1799 the Boers were defeated, which temporarily slowed down the white 'trek' northward. In the West there were other peoples who gradually came into contact with the expanding Boer population. The Herero and Ovambo had moved in from the North, into Namibia. East of the Kalahari the Sotho-Tswana had established their kingdoms (*morafe*), in a political structure that included religious functions for their kings (*kgosi*). There was much blending between Nguni-Xhosa and Soto-Tswana and Khoisan.

King Moshoeshoe (1786-1870)

By the end of the 18th century the Nguni peoples in the North had developed three distinct kingdoms. One of them, the Mthedwa kingdom, included the Zulu people. In the beginning of the 19th century, the Zulu leader Shaka seized power. His regiments soon subdued the armies of fellow Nguni kings. He established a large empire that would clash with the Boers, especially after Shaka's death in 1828. External and internal Nguni conflicts, including the wars of the Shaka Empire, brought about much disruption and chaos. Many peoples were uprooted and scattered. That is why the Soto-

Shaka, or Chaka (ca. 1781-1828), Emperor of the Zulu.

---

[11] The *Khoikhoi* and *San* became also known as Hottentots and Bushmen.

Tswana called this period the *Difaqane*, 'the scattering'. The Nguni word for it shows a different angle, *Mfecane*, which means 'the crushing'. Out of the movements of refugees from the Shaka terror new states arose, for example the Sotho State established by Moshoeshoe, and the Ndebele state led by Mzilikazi. In 1835 Nguni groups under Zwangendaba, fleeing from Shaka's successor Dingane, crossed the Zambezi River. After Zwangendaba's death in 1848, they broke apart in various groups that settled in Malawi, Zambia, Mozambique, and Tanzania.[12]

In the meantime, at the Cape the British had taken over control from the Boers. They complicated the relationship between whites and blacks by mixing the interests of the British Empire into the pattern of Xhosa, Zulu, and Boer aspirations. All these moving and migrating parties were challenged by fundamental changes that created fear and uncertainty concerning the basics of life. That is why the Gospel of peace and new life was found to give hope to many, first among the new arrivals from Europe and then also among the Africans.

45.4. Planting of the Dutch Reformed Church

The Dutch settlers at the Cape imported their religion into Africa. They established *Dutch Reformed* church life. Jan van Riebeeck's group did not include ordained ministers. Pastoral work was mainly done by 'sick-comforters'. Willem Wylant was the first one. Sacraments were administered by visiting ministers. The *Dutch Reformed Church* founded its first congregation there in 1665 with the arrival of Johan van Arckel (†1666), the first minister to settle in South Africa. It was decided that baptised slaves were to have the same rights as any other Christians. Initially mixed marriages of whites and baptised blacks and coloureds were not prohibited. At the Lord's Table all believers joined together.

The second congregation was established at Stellenbosch in 1687, after groups of 'free burghers' had settled there. At first sick-comforter Sybrand Mankadan had served them, and then after the establishment of the congregation, the ordained ministers Abraham Overney and Gerard van Andel came to work there. Soon there was a network of churches. From 1688 the Dutch were joined by *Huguenot*-refugees. They were Protestants who had fled from France when, in 1685, King Louis XIV revoked the *Edict of Nantes*, thus taking away their religious freedom.[13] The Huguenots brought a minister with them to the Cape, Pierre Simond (†1713). Later also Lutherans (from Germany) blended with the *Boers* and their Reformed Church. After much struggle and tension, in 1778 the VOC-councillors also allowed Lutheran immigrants to have their own Lutheran Church, the first Lutheran minister being Andreas Kolver (†1799).

45.5. Early Mission Work

Among the early Dutch settlers there was some recognition of the task of spreading the Gospel to the local population. Perhaps the first convert was the Khoikhoi woman Krotoa, named Eva by the Dutch. She was the niece of a Khoikhoi chief and proved to be such an excellent learner of languages that she was soon able to serve the Van

---

[12] See: D.D. Phiri, *From Nguni to Ngoni: A History of the Ngoni Exodus from Zululand and Swaziland to Malawi, Tanzania and Zambia*, Limbe: Popular Publ., 1982.

[13] Cf. chapter 28; also: Paas, *Chikonzedwe cha Mpingo*, pp.75,76.

Riebeeck family and others as a translator from the Khoikhoi language into Dutch and Portuguese and the other way round. In 1662 she was baptised into the Dutch Reformed Church and she married a junior Dutch surgeon, Pieter van Meerhof.[14]

Sick-comforter Willem Wylant was the first Christian to do regular evangelism work among the Khoikhoi people. After him, a minister, Petrus Kalden (†1739), took up the work. In 1689 Huguenot minister Pierre Simond tried to pave the way for a separate mission to the Khoikhoi.[15] There were also some attempts by German and Danish missionaries. In a way these attempts challenged the Dutch Reformed home church in Amsterdam. As the church leadership did not react, some members addressed Count von Zinzendorf and the congregation of *Moravian Brethren* at Herrnhut.[16] The Herrnhuters responded by offering to the Council of the Lords Seventeen[17] to send the Moravian refugee George Schmidt (†1785). In 1737 Schmidt arrived at the Cape. The following year he moved on and settled among the Khoikhoi people at a place that later became known as Genadendal (Valley of Grace). Schmidt gathered a flock of followers. He helped the Khoikhoi with their farming, planting vegetables and fruit trees. He baptised a few people, although he was not ordained. This caused confusion with the Dutch clergy. Soon the Dutch Reformed Church began to mistrust him, among other things because of some of the teachings of the Moravian leader Von Zinzendorf, who had criticised Reformed doctrine on predestination. In the meantime, Von Zinzendorf had ordained Schmidt, but the Dutch found it impossible to accept his ordination. Neither did they recognise baptisms done by Schmidt.

Title page of a book on the Khoikhoi woman Krotoa, who was probably the first convert of early Dutch Reformed Mission at the Cape (Trudie Bloem, Krotoa-Eva: The Woman from Robben Island, Stormberg, 1999).

Though he was not expelled, the nagging treatment by his fellow whites in and around Genadendal (later called Baviaan Kloof) caused him to return to Europe in 1744 only two years after his arrival to South Africa. Officially, he left for The Netherlands in order to sort out problems in Amsterdam. But he never came back.[18]

Mission work at the Cape was not started again until the arrival in 1786 of Helperus Ritzema van Lier, a Dutch Reformed minister who became an instigator of the *South African Missionary Society*, founded in 1799. In 1792 he and others welcomed Moravian missionaries Hendrik Maarsveld, Johann Schwinn and Johann Kühnel, who re-opened the mission station at Genadendal (Baviaans Kloof). They met an 80-year-old Christian, Lena, who had been baptised by Schmidt fifty years earlier. She had been his cook and she showed how she valued contacts with Schmidt by displaying a much

---

[14] Harriet Deacon, *The Island: A History of Robben Island 1488-1990*. Unfortunately, Krotoa's husband was soon killed, whereupon she allegedly fell into the habit of beer drinking and irregular behaviour, and she died as a prisoner on Robben Island in 1674.

[15] Hildebrandt, *History of the Church in Africa*, p.70, says that 'the early efforts by pastors of the Dutch Reformed Church to win these people [Khoikhoi] to Christ, did not succeed'. This statement cannot be completely true, as there were at least some early Khokhoi conversions.

[16] On the Moravians see: chapters 36.4.d and 37.3.

[17] *Lords Seventeen*: The VOC-Board consisted of 17 members, the 'Heeren Zeventien'.

[18] Pillay and Hofmeyr, *Perspectives on Church History*, pp.242,243; Hastings, *The Church in Africa*, p.197.

treasured New Testament wrapped in a sheepskin that Schmidt himself had given her. The three baptised many people. Among them were the descendants of men and women who had been baptised by George Schmidt half a century earlier.

The Moravian spirit was different from that of the Dutch Reformed Church, which at the Cape functioned as a state church. Although in 1792 this Moravian group was warmly welcomed, it was also opposed by some white farmers who saw the Moravians as a threat to their labour and social structure.

By 1798 through marriage and immigration the white community of Moravians had grown considerably. They were devout and practical people helping and teaching their black brethren. The white wives taught the Khoikhoi and coloured women and girls many skills. Together with the black people they numbered 1200 persons. The place was renamed Genadendal like in George Schmidt's times. Prayer, worship and manual labour were the main activities. Soon the local people saw Genadendal as a haven from the oppressive white masters where they could find 'dignity, stability, a modest degree of prosperity and the opportunity to learn'. The Moravians, being somewhat Lutheran in outlook, did not bother to fight against the injustices being perpetrated on the Khoikhoi and coloured people by the white masters, but they assumed a quietist attitude. Their main emphasis was on conversion, rather than on addressing the social evils.[19] In 1808 this thriving Khoikhoi and Moravian Christian community was extended to a new settlement in Mamre (Groene Kloof).

Finally, in 1806, the rule of the Cape by the *Council of the Lords Seventeen* and the *Batavian Republic*[20] ended. The British took over the Cape.

---

[19] Adrian Hastings. *Church in Africa*, pp.198,201,216,218; cf. Martin Malikebu, 'Dutch Missionaries in Africa in the Period 1650-1950', an unpublished thesis for Zomba Theological College, 2004.

[20] As a result of the *French Revolution* and the subsequent French occupation of large parts of Europe, the Netherlands had temporarily become a French puppet state which had adopted the name *Batavian Republic*.

46. Africa and the British until 1885

46.1. The Empire extends to Africa

a. Competition

Originally, commercial interests, rather than territorial ambition, dictated the growth of the early British Empire. England in the 16th century was a poor country, lacking the wealth of Portugal and Spain. Unlike the Spaniards and Portuguese, the English originally were less motivated by mission or colonisation. In the 17th century the English began to realise the huge commercial potential of overseas acquisitions, starting with the lucrative exploitation of sugar and other produce from the West Indies. The union of England with Scotland as Great Britain, in 1707, added to the power for expansion overseas.

The British successfully competed with other seafaring nations that had started to expand overseas trade and territorial acquisitions earlier. The Portuguese were first. They had deployed mainly to the South and the East of the globe. In the West they had to share territory with the Spaniards. These Iberian nations had been attacked in their overseas trading posts and incipient colonies by the Dutch. Also, the French had begun to establish their stations overseas. Now it was time for all to experience the expansion of British sea power. Beside Africa, almost the whole world including South and North America, India, Ceylon, Indonesia and Australia were the places where the struggle of beginning colonial expansion and competition took place. Here we only look at the aspects that directly concern Africa.

William Hawkins of Plymouth was probably the first English trader who settled on the West Coast. Soon other English traders joined him. In 1618 they formed a trading company, and in the meantime they had built forts in the Gold Coast and in the Gambia. Like the Scandinavians and the Dutch, the English made use of chaplains for pastoral work in and around their forts. One of them was Thomas Thompson, a missionary of the *Society for the Propagation of the Gospel* (SPG). He first worked among the native American Indians. In 1750 he was sent to the West African Cape Coast or Gold Coast. He worked not only among the whites in the forts, but also among the local Africans. Thompson helped to send Africans for study to England. One of them was Philip Quaicoo (1741-1816). After completion of his studies, Quaicoo was the first African to become a priest in the Anglican Church. He married an English woman, and in 1766 he returned to the Gold Coast as a missionary, where he worked for fifty years.[1]

b. Triangular Trade

In North America, the Thirteen Colonies along the Atlantic seaboard between French Canada and Spanish Florida were firmly established by 1733. The English colonists had begun to plant cotton in the 17th century, and this plantation crop was grown on a very large scale by the late 18th century. This combined with a scattering of forts and trading settlements in West Africa and the trade from the West Indies created the *Triangular Trade*: (a) British ships took manufactured goods and spirits to West Africa. (b) They exchanged them for slaves whom they landed in the West Indies and the southernmost

---

[1] Kpobi, 'African Chaplains', in: Kalu (ed.), *African Christianity*, pp.160-163; Hildebrandt, *History of the Church in Africa*, pp.71-74. In his account Quaicoo is called Quaque.

of the Thirteen Colonies. (c) The ships then returned to Britain with cargoes of cotton, rum, sugar, and tobacco, produced mainly by the labour of the slaves. Britain's prosperity was bound up with the slave trade, until it became illegal in 1807, by which time the Empire had ceased to be dependent upon the slave trade as other forms of commerce had become more profitable and Britain was starting to emerge as the leading industrial nation, inevitably reducing the economic demand for slave labour.

c. Southern Africa

William Carey (1761-1834), founding father of the Missionary Movement, inspired to the foundation of the Baptist Missionary Society in 1792.

After the slave trade was ended by Britain in 1807, the British continued to show interest in Africa. Already before the scramble for territory of the 1880s, various forts, controlling ports, were kept in West Africa, where gold and ivory kept their importance.

An early example was the colony of Sierra Leone founded in 1788 with the taking of a strip of land to provide a home for liberated slaves; a protectorate was established over the hinterland in 1896.

Another early example was South Africa. The Cape of Good Hope was occupied by two English captains in 1620, but initially neither the government nor the British *East India Company* was interested in developing this early settlement into a colony. The Dutch occupied it in 1650, and Cape Town remained a port of call for their *United East Indies Company* until 1795, when, after French revolutionary armies had occupied the Dutch Republic, the British seized it to keep it from the French. Under the *Treaty of Paris* in 1814, the United Kingdom bought Cape Town from the new kingdom of The Netherlands for $6 million. British settlement began in 1824 on the coast of Natal, which was proclaimed a British colony in 1843.[2]

In the previous chapter we noticed that British colonisation of the Cape was emphatically rejected by the Dutch settlers. The need to find new farmland and establish independence from British rule led a body of Boers (Dutch: *farmers*) from the Cape to make the *Great Trek* northeast in 1836, to found Transvaal and the Orange Free State. The conflict between the British government and the Boers eventually led to war, as we will see in chapter 50.2.b.

46.2. Effects of the Great Awakening

a. Rediscovery of the Centrality of Christ

British colonialism aimed at the extension of economic and political power. The slave trade soon became its main pillar. In their colonies in South, Central, and North America the Europeans were lacking labour; therefore slaves were imported from Africa. The Portuguese began this trade in the 16th century, the Dutch played an

---

[2] Cf.: Hutchinson, *New Century Encyclopedia*; Shillington, *History of Africa*.

important part, but in the 18th century Britain dominated the slave trade. It had become the backbone of the economy in these countries.

The selfishness and cruelty of colonialism began to be ameliorated by important developments in the field of religion. Though legal and widely accepted, slavery and the slave trade began to be resisted. In Britain and North America the faith which had been rediscovered in the Reformation, but had grown cold and weak through the effects of *Enlightenment* and *Orthodoxism*, revived and awakened in the 1730s and 1740s. In England, Scotland and Wales, the preaching of George Whitefield and John and Charles Wesley brought about a profound evangelical revival inside and outside the Anglican Church. It comprised 'Evangelicals within the Church of England, Methodism, Calvinistic Methodism, and Dissenters or Nonconformists'.

Especially influential was the so called *Clapham Sect*, a group of high-ranking Evangelical lay people. The revival led by George Whitefield, Jonathan Edwards, the brothers Gilbert, John, and William Tennent and others did the same in North America.[3] Collectively these revivals on both sides of the Atlantic Ocean are called *The Great Awakening*.[4] It was characterised by 'three powerful convictions':

> (a) the centrality of the death of Christ for salvation, (b) the necessity of a new birth and (c) the certainty of the Second Coming of Christ and his kingdom of righteousness.[5]

b. Missionary Movement

The revivals not only prepared the ground for the rejection and *abolition* of slavery, but were also a strong incentive for a declaration of war against the evil of injustice in society, and for the birth of the modern missionary movement. William Carey (1761-1834) belonged to the foremost who opened their eyes of many for the responsibility of mission. Walls mentions some factors that helped the emergence of movements for mission and social justice: (a) the realisation that there is a 'human solidarity in depravity ... a spiritual parity of the unregenerate of Christendom and the heathen abroad', (b) a logistic network, creating the interregional, interdenominational and international contacts that formed the backbone of missionary societies, and (c) the staffing of missionary organisations by evangelicals.[6]

Olaudah Equiano, an ex-slave from Nigeria who in 1789 published an influential book against the slave trade.

Walls says that evangelicalism not only addressed the unbelieving world, but was also a 'religious protest against a Christian society that is not Christian enough'.

---

[3] On this revival and awakening, read: Cairns, *Christianity through the Centuries*, pp.383-416, 428-434; T. Dowley (ed.), *The History of Christianity*, Lion Publ., 1990[7], pp.436-457, 518-540.

[4] Cf. Jehu Hanciles, 'Back to Africa: White Abolitionists and Black Missionaries', in: Ogbu U. Kalu (ed.), *African Christianity: An African Story*, University of Pretoria, 2005, p.194.

[5] Shaw, *Kingdom*, pp.129-132, where he explains these three convictions.

[6] A.F.Walls, *The Missionary Movement in Christian History: Studies in the Transmission of Faith*, New York/ Edinburgh, 1996, pp.79-85.

Evangelicalism accepted the idea of a Christian nation with *national righteousness* (therefore no slave trade) and *social righteousness* (therefore a no to children's labour). In the first place, however, there is the necessity of *personal holiness*, which is a personal knowledge of the radical nature of sin, personal trust in Christ's finished work, and a godly personal life. According to Walls, the evangelical revivals were 'perhaps the most successful of all reformulations of Christianity in the context of changing Western culture'. They 'contextualised the Gospel for the Northern Protestant world'. They also tried to translate the Gospel overseas. More than elsewhere this enterprise was successful in Africa. The effects of evangelicalism in its anti-slavery movement and in its missionary movement were felt very much in Africa.

c. Anti-Slavery Movement

The anti-slavery movement or abolition movement started with the activities of Granville Sharp and Lord Mansfield, who campaigned for making slavery illegal in Britain. In 1787 three important events enlarged the scope of the movement:

> (a) the establishing of a colony of freed slaves in Sierra Leone, (b) the founding of the *Society for the Abolition of the Slave Trade*, with Sharp as chairman and Wilberforce as one of the members, (c) the publication of a book by the Ghanaian ex-slave Ottobah Cugoano (c.1757-after 1791)[7] about his life as a slave, which made great impact on the general public.

Henry Morton Stanley (1841-1904), American journalist and explorer who contributed to preparations for the work by missionary organisations.

Members of the *Clapham Sect* continually tried to destroy the legal position of slavery. Gradually public opinion began to favour abolitionism. Helpful was the autobiography of an ex-slave from Nigeria, Olaudah Equiano, who showed that abolition would promote legitimate commerce.[8] The work of William Wilberforce in particular, was instrumental in making Parliament accept a bill prohibiting the slave trade in 1807 and finally the *Abolition of Slavery Bill* in 1833.

The year 1871 marked the beginning of Britain's campaign to end the slave trade in East Africa itself and Christianise the people. In 1871 Dr. Livingstone was found in Africa by the journalist Henry Morton Stanley. Stanley travelled along with Livingstone, who had been living in Africa for almost 30 years, and began writing stories about Livingstone's life and aspirations to end slavery and spread Christianity. When Stanley published his stories about Livingstone, it aroused a great deal of support among the British people, and it strengthened Britain's movement to abolish the slave trade *de facto*. In 1875 with the strong urging of the British Government, Zanzibar ended its slave-trading Empire.

---

[7] Ottobah Cugoano, *Narrative of the Enslavement of a Native of Africa*, 1787.
[8] Olaudah Equiano, *The Interesting Narrative of Olaudah Equiano, or Gustavus Vassa, the African*, New York: Dove Publications, 1999 [original edition 1789].

d. The Classical Missions

In the meantime, evangelicalism had continued to give shape to the beginning of a missionary movement. A number of missionary organisations had been formed, first the *Baptist Missionary Society* (1792), then the *London Missionary Society* (1795), and the *Church Missionary Society* (1799). This movement would lead to rapid spread of missions in 19th-century Africa, and to the real emergence of Christianity in sub-Saharan Africa. The most important theological innovation for foreign mission work was the idea of the *Mission Society*, which would work with and for the Church, but keep its independence in terms of rules and regulations, leadership personnel, the necessary training, and finances. Such *Mission Societies* could work beyond the natural boundaries of their churches, and it was the *Mission Societies*, not the churches that effectively evangelised Africa.[9]

The success of the anti-slavery movement and the missionary movement was not only fed by a revival of evangelical-Biblical faith, but sometimes also by a great optimism with regard to the good potential of Western civilisation, imperialism, and capitalism. Perhaps Shaw is right when he says that in this optimistic activism 18th and 19th-century Western evangelicalism 'became an unconscious ally'[10] of the movement it wanted to resist most, the *Enlightenment* with its expectations from man's autonomous rational power.[11]

---

[9] Cf. Klaus Fiedler, *The Story of Faith Missions: From Hudson Taylor to Present-day Africa*, Oxford: Regnum Books, 1994, pp.20-23;

[10] Shaw, *Kingdom*, pp.132,138,140.

[11] Also: Shaw, *Kingdom*, pp.127-138; Baur, *2000 Years*, pp.105-106, 109; Walls, *Missionary Movement*, pp.79-84; Hastings, *Church in Africa*, pp.173-188.

47. Western Africa 1800-1900

47.1. Sierra Leone

Kpobi distinguishes three periods in the era of Mission and Church planting in sub-Saharan Africa. *First* there was the period of the European 'discovery' of the western coast of Africa, starting from about the middle of the 15th century. Kpobi says that during this period 'the church was no more than an appendage to the commercial enterprise and therefore had very little attraction for the African population'.

The *second period* of mission in Africa started from the middle of the 18th century 'when attempts were made at evangelisation alongside the slave trade'. Again this was a comparatively 'unfruitful period', as Kpobi maintains. However, it contributed to the preparation of the ground.[1] That became apparent in the late 18th century or in the beginning of the 19th century, when the *third period* of mission began, which was its real beginning of the Christianisation of sub-Saharan Africa.

One may wonder why Protestantism waited so long before really starting mission in other continents. At first Protestantism was a weak and persecuted minority. When it had become numerous, free and well established, it had a tremendous task of evangelising the European and American masses who, like Hildebrandt stresses, 'had never heard of salvation through the atoning blood of Jesus Christ'.[2] The major thrust of missionary activity came through the *Great Evangelical Awakenings* in the Protestant churches of Europe and North America in the 18th and 19th centuries.

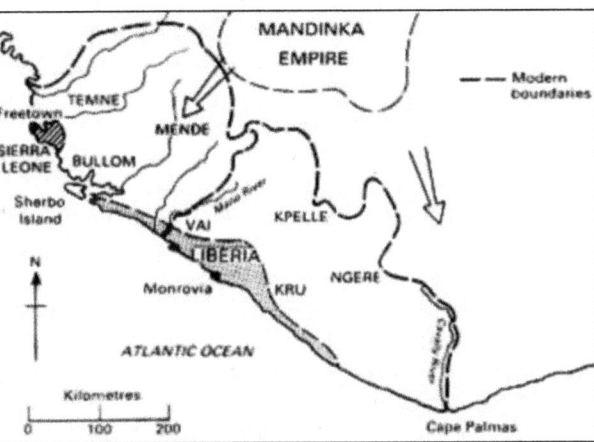

The Coasts of Sierra Leone and Liberia in c.1880 (from: Shillington: History of Africa, p.240).

Yet modern African Christianity is not in the first place the result of missionary activity from the North. Walls stresses that African Christianity 'has been principally sustained by Africans, and is to a surprising extent the result of African initiatives'.[3] Much of modern mission started in West Africa.[4] The first attempt in West Africa was a joint enterprise by whites and blacks, the settlement of a Christian community in Sierra Leone. Under the protection of the British government, Granville Sharp and the *Clapham Sect* in 1787 had settled 411 freed slaves of the 'Black Poor', yet including 70

---

[1] Kpobi, 'African Chaplains', in: Kalu (ed.), *African Christianity*, pp.140,141.
[2] Hildebrandt, *History of the Church in Africa*, pp.67,68.
[3] Walls, *Missionary Movement*, p.86.
[4] Also: Shaw, *Kingdom*, pp.139-158; Baur, *2000 Years*, pp.103-152; Hastings, *Church in Africa*, pp.177-188, 338-358; Ward, 'Africa', in: Hastings (ed), *World History*, pp.203-209.

white prostitutes,[5] from London in Sierra Leone on the West African coast. This settlement, enthusiastically called *Province of Freedom*, soon appeared to be a failure. Many settlers died, others became slaves again. Then, a *Sierra Leone Company* was formed, which facilitated in 1792 the coming of almost 1200 black British ex-soldiers from Nova Scotia in Canada to Sierra Leone. Many of these black settlers were Baptists. They built a city, Freetown, and organised Christian life according to Puritan principles. Some of these black 'founding fathers' like David George and Thomas Peters established Baptist churches. Methodism was represented by Moses Wilkinson, and there was also the work of Anglican chaplains. Soon missionary initiatives were taken. Hanciles stresses that modern Church and Mission 'began not with white missionary agency, but as the initiative of ex-African slaves'.[6] In 1800 more than five hundred ex-slaves from Jamaica, *Maroons* as they were called, were added to the community. In 1808 Sierra Leone became an official British colony. Agriculture and especially trade began to flourish. Schools were founded, among them in 1827 by the Anglican CMS *Fourah Bay College*, for the training of ministers, teachers, catechists, and missionaries.

After the banning of the slave trade by Britain in 1807, the British navy, intercepting slave ships, brought in thousands of 'recaptives'. These freed slaves were Muslims or African traditionalists. Most of the latter category became Christians, but many Muslims resisted conversion to the Christian faith. The Sierra Leonean immigrants built their own culture (Creole), a mixture of African and Western traditions, and they shaped their own language (*Krio*) with English vocabulary and African syntax.

This new Christian community developed missionary activities far beyond Sierra Leone, supplying 'African missionaries for the rest of West Africa' and elsewhere, even in Kenya.[7] They were helped by Western missionaries. The Methodists sent out pioneers such as Samuel Brown, George Warren, and Richard Davies. The Quaker missionary Hannah Kilham did language work and started a school for girls. The first CMS missionaries partly failed, but from 1804 with men such as M. Renner, P. Hartfeld, J.G. Prasse, L. Butscher, and M. Nyländer the work progressed. However, at the beginning of the 19th century Western missionary activity was not yet the numerous and powerful movement that it would be by the end of the century. The actual outreach in missionary work was done by Africans, in the case of Sierra Leone by the Creoles.

The most famous indigenous missionary was Samuel Ajayi Crowther (†1891), a Yoruba domestic slave from the Nigerian village of Abeokuta, who was sold to a slaver bound for Brazil, but was freed by the British navy and taken to Freetown in 1822. He was the first students of *Fourah Bay College*. After his training, he served a period as teacher and partaker of an expedition in the Niger area, then he went to London, where he was ordained priest in 1843. In 1864 he became the first African bishop of the Anglican Church.

47.2. The Niger Mission

Inspired by the success of Freetown, ex-slaves established other Christian communities along the West African coast. Started by two Hausa ex-slaves from Trinidad a

---

[5] Hastings, *Church in Africa*, pp, 179,180.
[6] Jehu Hanciles, 'Back to Africa: White Abolitionists and Black Missionaries', in: Kalu (ed.), *African Christianity*, p.204.
[7] Walls, *Missionary Movement*, pp.86,67.

settlement was made at Badagry in Nigeria. The Methodist Thomas Birch Freeman, himself an ex-slave, helped to organise a church among the receptives and to start Christianisation of nearby areas. The chief of Abeokuta allowed ex-slaves to return to his region. 'By 1851 there were already some 3000 returned emigrants in Abeokuta alone'. Among the returned exiles was Samuel Crowther, who was reunited with his mother and sisters, who were subsequently baptised. Initial persecutions hindered the Christians at Abeokuta, but after the conversion of some leading diviners (*babalawo*), Christianity was widely accepted.

In the same period Christianity spread to Calabar, Bonny, Lagos and many places along the Niger. The African initiative continued to play an important role. At the same time, there was an increase of expatriate missionary efforts. The *Baptist Missionary Society* (BMS), the *London Missionary Society* (LMS), and the *Church Missionary Society* (CMS), were followed by the *American Board for Foreign Missions* (1810), the *Wesleyan Methodists' Mission* (1813), the *Basel Mission Society* (1814), and soon many others sent out their missionaries. These first missionaries in West Africa worked independently from government control, often had little formal education, and were rarely ordained. Many of them worked in the area of language and translation, CMS-missionary S.W. Koelle and his *Polyglotta Africana* being a notable example.

Samuel Ajayi Crowther (c.1807-1891), the first African who became an Anglican Bishop, leader of the Niger Mission.

Samuel Crowther and other homecoming Sierra Leoneans were ready to contribute to the conversion of the inland of Africa. Many of them belonged to the Yoruba people and had not forgotten their language and culture. Crowther and other Yoruba were trained at *Fourah Bay College* in Freetown, and in 1843 he was the first to be ordained as an Anglican minister. The missionary work in the Sierra Leone, and later also in the Badagry and Abeokuta areas, mainly developed under the responsibility of Anglican Evangelicals of the *Church Missionary Society* (CMS). Soon Crowther was given an important role to play in the activities of the CMS in West African Inland, along the Niger River, at least in the plans of Henry Venn (†1873), who from 1841 was Secretary of the CMS. Venn propagated the 'three selves': the necessity of a self-supporting, self-propagating, and self-governing African church. Also, he worked out the idea of cooperation between Christianity and commerce, implying that African economic independence was an important instrument for the shaping of an African church. He developed the idea that the indigenisation of native churches ought to become a national institution that would supersede denominational distinctions.

Venn was instrumental in making Crowther a bishop of the Anglican Church. Then, he placed Crowther at the head of an organisation that was to evangelise a vast area along the Niger. Hanciles calls this 'a bold experiment in African leadership and initiative'.[8] Unfortunately, Crowther as a Yoruba was a relative stranger to the Niger

---

[8] Hanciles, 'Back to Africa: White Abolitionists and Black Missionaries', in: Kalu (ed.), *African Christianity*, p.206.

area, where many other peoples lived, e.g. Igbo, Nupe and Hausa. He had to cope with a variety of languages and cultures, enormous distances between a series of stations along the River Niger, and stiff resistance by Islamicised tribes. The CMS gave him a steamer, which made communications easier, but made him also dependent on traders whose goods he transported for money that he needed for the mission. This dependence was undermining the integrity of the mission, as missionaries were sometimes identified with the ruthless capitalist practices and the immorality of many traders. Besides, some members of Crowther's own group were guilty of misbehaviour, like manslaughter and misappropriation of funds.[9] These were considerable hindrances to the work. However, the Niger mission did not become a failure. Crowther's qualities as a scholar, pastor and faithful missionary contributed to its relative success. In Onitsha a missionary centre was established, and among the Brass people of the Niger Delta Christianity found acceptance, at least temporarily.[10]

By the end of the century the character of mission changed. There was an increase of missionaries from Europe. Colonial powers had started their 'scramble for Africa'. This decreased the room for Venn's Africanisation programme. In 1890 a CMS committee consisting of young newly arrived missionaries decided to discharge almost the entire staff of Crowther. Crowther was humiliated and after his death he was replaced by a white missionary. Hastings underlines that this event 'damaged black-white Church relations for many years'.[11] These days Crowther's significance is widely recognised. Hildebrandt says: 'There is little doubt that he was one of the greatest African church leaders of the nineteenth century'.[12]

Mary Slessor (1848-1915) was a Scottish missionary for the United Presbyterian Church to Calabar, south-eastern Nigeria She was commonly called 'Ma' Slessor.

Although the CMS now had less room for the idea of an independent native pastorate, the ideal of Africanisation was kept alive. It was defended by the Afro-American missionary and Liberian statesman Edward W. Blyden (1832-1912). It was also propagated by the Sierra Leonean pastor James Johnson (c.1836-1917), because of his exemplary lifestyle often called 'Holy' Johnson. Johnson was born in Sierra Leone to Yoruba parents who were freed slaves. After his study at *Fourah Bay College*, he was ordained and became a missionary worker for the CMS. In 1874 the CMS sent him to the Lagos area in Nigeria. Although Johnson promoted a church under African leadership, he never abandoned the Anglican Church. However, members of his CMS founded church separated and formed an independent 'Ethiopian' church. This led to a break between Johnson and his former associate Garrick Braide (see chapter 53.4). In

---

[9] Shaw, *Kingdom*, pp.155,156.
[10] Hastings, *Church in Africa*, pp.339-349.
[11] Hastings, *Church in Africa*, pp.392.
[12] Hildebrandt, *History of the Church in Africa*, p.103. Cf. Gerdien Verstraelen-Gilhuis, "Bishop Crowther and the 'Young Purifiers': A Search into the Background of the Conflict of the Niger Mission via an Analysis of the Action of the 'Sudan Party'", Amsterdam: Free University, 1969 [unpublished MTh Thesis in Dutch].

1900, ten years after Crowther had left, Johnson became assistant bishop of the Niger Mission.[13]

In south-eastern Nigeria a notable work of the Scottish Presbyterians started in the Calabar area in 1847. A Bible translation in the Efik language was completed in 1868. Four years later Esien Ukpabio, the first baptised convert, was ordained as a minister of the Nigerian Presbyterian Church.[14] Mary Slessor worked as a single missionary lady in the area from 1888 to her death in 1915. She also opened mission stations further to the north in Iboland.[15]

Sierra Leone and the Niger area also witnessed the return of Roman Catholic Mission to Africa. The *Holy Ghost Fathers* or *Spiritans*, led from Algiers by François Libermann, were the first. They also spread to other countries in West Africa and in East Africa (see chapter 52.1).

47.3. Liberia

Following the example of Britain in Sierra Leone, the United States of America shaped a place for freed slaves on the African West Coast. In 1816 the *American Colonization Society* was formed. This was followed by the founding of Liberia as a home for free blacks in 1821. The first leaders of Liberia, and its main settlement Monrovia, were Jehudi Ashmun and Lott Carey. The latter served the colony as missionary, doctor, governor and soldier. By 1866 the colony had about 18,000 inhabitants. In the late 1870s black emigration to Liberia grew substantially. In the Liberian Constitution (1847) more rights were given to the 'homecoming' emigrants than to the indigenous people, which was the cause of increasing tensions.

Successively missionary work among indigenous Africans was started by black Methodists, Baptists, Roman Catholics, Episcopalians and Presbyterians. Before 1880 almost all black missionaries were sent and financed by white churches and mission boards. To them belonged Joseph and Mary Gomer, Alexander Crummel, and Edward W. Blyden. Other black missionaries were sent by black denominations. Generally, they did not work among the indigenous people, but among the settlers who had come from America, and together with them they had 'extremely negative views of African cultures'. In time, however, the interest in *Africanness* was strengthened. Blyden contributed much to the Africanisation of politics and mission. He was a significant missionary and statesman. His book *Christianity, Islam and the Negro Race* (1880) encouraged respect for African

Edward Wilmot Blyden (1832-1912), Liberian educator and statesman.

---

[13] Cf.: Norbert C. Brockman's DACB-article [DACB-website].

[14] Hildebrandt, *History of the Church in Africa*, p.105.

[15] Hildebrandt, *History of the Church in Africa*, pp.158,159.

languages, cultures and customs. As such, he was a father of African *nationalism* and of the movement of *Ethiopianism*.[16]

47.4. Ghana, Cameroon, Senegal, Gabon, Zaire

a. Ghana and Cameroon

In the Gold Coast (present-day Ghana), work was started by German and Swiss missionaries of the *Bremen Mission*, and the *Basel Evangelical Missionary Society*. Missionaries such as Johann Zimmerman and Johann Christaller did much work in the Twi language.

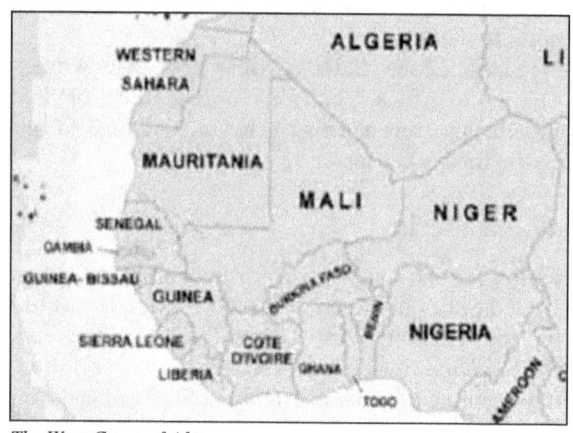

The West Coast of Africa.

The *Basel Mission* began on their own in 1828, after first having sent missionaries through other organisations, like the CMS. They faced a lot of hardship and almost all died. An interesting example of early African missionary initiative concerns two Africans, Joseph Smyth and William de Graft. The former was leader of a British school for colonial administration and the latter a student in that school. They were sincere Christians who organised the spreading of Bibles and Bible study. Later their work was absorbed by the Wesleyan Methodist Mission that came to Cape Coast in 1834.[17] The Methodists had great impact, especially through the work of the West Indian Thomas Birch Freeman (1809-1890), a missionary of Anglo-African descent, who arrived in Ghana in 1838 and worked there for fifty years. He contributed much to the Christian awakening in West Africa.

In *Cameroon* missionary work started around 1850 among freed slaves on the island of Fernando Po. The mission was started by the *Baptist Missionary Society* with Jamaican missionaries, Alfred Saker and others, many of whom were liberated slaves who were very motivated to bring the Gospel back to Africa.

b. Senegal, Gabon and Zaire

The original Protestant mission in Gabon, started by Americans of the *Board of Commissioners for Foreign Mission*, was resisted by the French colonial authorities and was handed over to missionaries of the American Presbyterian Church who began work in Gabon in 1861. Roman Catholic attempts in Gabon and Senegal were eventually successful, mainly through the work of the *Holy Ghost Fathers*, founded by the French (ex-) Jew François Libermann in 1841. Among the workers were Edward Barron, John

---

[16] Hanciles, 'Back to Africa: White Abolitionists and Black Missionaries', in: Kalu (ed.), *African Christianity*, pp.211-214.
[17] Hildebrandt, *History of the Church in Africa*, pp.92,93.

Kelly, and Jean Bessieux, who founded St. Mary of Gabon, the first modern Roman Catholic mission station in Africa. Through the *Paris Mission Society*, the famous German physician Albert Schweitzer worked in Gabon, at Lambarene, for fifty years. He did a commendable medical work, although his liberal teachings on Scripture weakened his missionary contribution.[18]

In the 1890s missionaries of the *Sacred Heart of Jesus* and *Jesuits* entered the Congo River area where Roman Catholic Christianity had completely collapsed after the death of Congo King Garcia V in 1830, and after the departure of the last Capuchins, who were under pressure from an anti-clerical government in Portugal. They were soon followed by missionaries of many other Roman Catholic orders.

In 1878 Protestant missionaries were welcomed. Thomas Comber and George Grenfell of the interdenominational *Livingstone Inland Mission* began work there.[19] They were actually members of the *Baptist Missionary Society* from Britain. The *Livingstone Inland Mission*, originally led by Fanny Guinness, was the first Faith Mission to start work in Africa. They wanted to establish a chain of mission stations from the coast to the interior. In 1983 they had 10 stations, the first and the last 800 kilometres apart. In 1884 the work was handed over to American Baptists, but the Swedish LIM members continued their work as a Faith Mission, also entering Congo-Brazzaville.[20] In 1910 another Faith Mission entered the Congo in 1912, the *Africa Inland Mission* (AIM), by now led by C.E. Hurlbert, joining together in 1913 with the *Heart of Africa Mission* and its missionary C.T. Studd (See chapter 55.6.b).

47.5. Angola

a. Comparative Roman Catholic Weakness

Roman Catholic Mission had been favoured by the Portuguese colonial authorities since their arrival in the 15th century. However, by the beginning of the 18th century a serious recession of Roman Catholic mission work began. This period of missionary weakness would last till the beginning of the 20th century. It gave an opportunity for mission by Protestant Churches and organisations. Here are some of the reasons why Roman Catholic Mission grew weak and Protestant mission could penetrate the country: (a) Until the end of the 19th century Portuguese colonial rule was limited mainly to the coastal regions, leaving the interior to other

Map of Angola.

---

[18] Cf.: Hildebrandt, *History of the Church in Africa*, p.165.
[19] Hastings, *The Church in Africa*, pp.257,318,319,385,435; Cf.: Fiedler, *The Story of Faith Missions*, pp.169-183.
[20] Fiedler, *Story of Faith Missions*, pp.37-39.

influences. (b) There was a rather strong tradition of anti-clericalism among the Portuguese which also affected the overseas territories. (c) There were internal disputes between Portuguese and Spanish Church leaders and the Vatican. (d) Colonial rulers realised that the Portuguese colonial empire needed good relationships with Great Britain. (e) The *Berlin Conference* of 1884/1885, which allowed European states to colonialise Africa, demanded freedom of religion.

By 1850 in almost all parts of the country, except for the South, Roman Catholic mission activity had ended.[21] The *Capuchins* had been active in the South since the 1830s when they were authorised by the Pope to work in this area, but the work gradually declined.[22] In 1866 the French *Holy Ghost Fathers* entered the region. Their main problem was that they were hindered by the Portuguese authorities because of their nationality. That is why their leader Charles Du Pirquet started a seminary for the training of Portuguese missionaries. Later they were reinforced by clergy from the Portuguese enclave Goa in India. In the eyes of the authorities the presence of Portuguese clergy safeguarded Portuguese culture and theology. Within a decade the *Holy Ghost Fathers* had taken full control of the coastal region of Southern Angola. Many of their missionaries died, however.[23]

b. Opportunities for Protestant Mission

The comparative weakness of Roman Catholic Mission and Portuguese colonial rule in the interior of Angola provided opportunities for Protestant Mission. Let us look at some of the Churches and organisations which started work in Angola.

(a) *Baptist Missionary Society*. The arrival of English Baptist missionaries in 1878 made them the first Protestants in Angola. From their headquarters in Sao Salvador they opened many stations in the northern part of Angola.[24]

(b) *Methodists*. They came from America and their leader was William Taylor, who was consecrated 'bishop of Africa' in 1884. Taylor arrived in Angola in 1885. He was a famous preacher and also a missionary strategist. He had made a plan of establishing a chain of mission stations from the Atlantic Ocean to the Indian Ocean. Taylor defended the idea of self-supportive missions, which in his view was what the Apostle Paul had meant. Between 1885 and 1896 not less than 186 missionaries were sent out. By the 19th Century the mission had opened stations at Luanda, Quingwa Pingo-Sundango, Quessna, and Malanje.

(c) *Canadian Congregationalists*. These missionaries arrived in Angola in 1880 and settled in the Ovimbundu highlands near Lobito. Among their leaders were W.T. Currie, Gladwyn M. Childs, and John T. Tucker. They established good contacts with the traditional African kings. [25] They built their headquarters and schools at Dondi.[26] In 1911 followed the establishment of a school for the training of native evangelists and teachers.[27] In addition, an extensive network of primary schools was organised with thousands of pupils and native teachers. Although the Portuguese didn't want things be

---

[21] Hildebrandt, *History of the Church in Africa*, p.135.
[22] K.S.Latourette, *A History of the Expansion of Christianity* vol. 5, p 398.
[23] Hildebrandt, *History of the Church in Africa*, pp.170,399
[24] Latourette, *Expansion* (vol.5), p.399; Hildbrandt, *History of the Church in Africa*, p.170
[25] Baur, *2000 Years*, pp.99,221
[26] Cf. Lawrence W. Henderson, *A Igreja Em Angola: Um Rio Com Várias Correntes*, Lisboa: Al
[27] Hildebrandt, *History*, pp.215,243.

done in the native languages, the Canadians tried hard to make sure that the vernacular language was used. Soon many portions of the Bible were translated into the vernacular.[28]

(d) *American Board of Commissioners for Foreign Mission*. Du Plessis describes their early attempts, problems and growth. The first party of this mission included American blacks such as Samuel T. Miller, who was educated at Hampton Institute, W.W. Bagster, and W.H. Sanders. They landed at Benguela in 1880. In 1882 the group was attacked by fever, and in 1884 the unfriendly Chief Ekwikwi chased away the missionaries. But with the support from the governor, they were allowed back for their work, and two stations were formed inland.[29] However, in the same year they were betrayed by hostile traders. Because of the problems the mission had to withdraw to Benguela on the coast. All this slowed down progress. In 1889 the mission re-established itself, and especially in the interior. Rapid growth of the church returned after 1914.

(e) *Angola Evangelical Mission*. This non-denominational mission was founded by M.Z. Stober and was mainly supported from people in Britain. It started work in Northern Angola among Congo-speaking people in 1898. Its headquarters was in Kabinda.

(f) *Plymouth Brethren* (Garanganze Mission – Christian Mission in Many Lands). They arrived in 1889 and worked in partnership with the Canadian Congregationalists. Their leader was F.S. Arnot, who in his youth was inspired by Livingstone.[30] In 1884 he arrived at Benguela. Here he met Msidi (or Kathanga), the chief of the Luba-speaking Garanganze, who asked him to settle at his capital Bukenya, in 1886. In 1891 Belgium occupied Katanga. They wanted Msidi's submission, but he refused and was shot dead. Armot was replaced by Swam Faulkner. He wrote a book called *Garanganze* describing his 'seven years of pioneer missionary work in Central Africa'. Later he returned to Angola and made great contributions in language work. Finally, because Msidi's Empire had collapsed, the Garanganze Mission dispersed. Arnot died in Johannesburg in 1914.

(g) *Andrew Murray Memorial Mission*. This mission worked in the South East of Angola. It started under the leadership of A.W. Baily in 1889,[31] and was named after Andrew Murray, the famous South African instigator of Mission. After some decades of successful work, especially leading to Christian education, the mission clashed with the Portuguese authorities. In 1922 they decreed that all schools were to be closed. Local Christians were not allowed to preach unless accompanied by a white missionary. Faithful Christians were imprisoned.[32] In practice Christians were barred from worshipping God.

(h) *Philafrican Mission*. This mission was a by-product of Bishop Taylor's Methodist mission. His missionary approach aroused an interest among a number of Swiss people, some of them Swiss immigrants in America.[33] In 1887 the mission became independent.

---

[28] Du Plessis, *Evangelisation* (Central Africa), pp.230-237
[29] Du Plessis, Evangelisation (Central Africa), pp.234-6.
[30] Du Plessis, *Evangelisation* (Central Africa), p.235.
[31] Du Plessis, *Evangelisation* (Central Africa), pp.239-400.
[32] Latourette, *Expansion* (vol.5), pp.398-399.
[33] Du Plessis, *Evangelisation* (Central Africa), p.234.

Although there was a hardening of resistance against Protestant mission, in 1924 the number of missions in Angola was extended by the arrival of the *South Africa General Mission* and the *Mission of the Seventh Day Adventists*.[34]

Protestant Mission was successful, yet the majority of Angolans became connected to the Roman Catholic Church. Estimates of the number of Roman Catholics after the end of Portuguese colonialism (1975) varied from 55 percent (1985) to 68 percent (1987). The proportion of Protestants in the Angolan population was estimated at 10 percent (1960s) to 20 percent in the late 1980s. The Angolan government recognised eleven Protestant denominations: the *Assemblies of God*, the *Baptist Convention of Angola*, the *Baptist Evangelical Church of Angola*, the *Congregational Evangelical Church of Angola*, the *Evangelical Church of Angola*, the *Evangelical Church of South-West Angola*, the *Our Lord Jesus Christ Church in the World* (Kimbanguist), the *Reformed Evangelical Church of Angola*, the *Seventh-Day Adventist Church*, the *Union of Evangelical Churches of Angola*, and the *United Methodist Church*.[35]

---

[34] For a more recent survey of pre-independence Protestant presence in Angola, see: Paas, *Het Protestantisme in Angola*, pp.56-62.

[35] These data were derived from: *Library of Congress Country Studies*, February 1989.

48. Southern Africa 1800-1900

48.1. The Dutch-Speaking Settlers

In original missionary work in West Africa a crucial role was played by Africans educated in Europe or America. Before 1880 there was room for African initiative as the number of expatriates was relatively small. Unlike in West Africa, however, in South Africa the power of *white settler Christianity* and *white missionary presence* was much more substantial. The African scene was influenced by Dutch-speaking settlers, and later also by an English-speaking community.[1]

During the Napoleonic wars the British had begun to occupy the Cape, and in 1815 it was declared a British colony. Immigrants from Britain began to pour in, expanding the white community. They established branches of their own Anglo-Saxon churches. British missionary organisations, already active in West Africa, began to take an interest in South Africa. The new situation was increasingly unacceptable to the Boer population for various reasons.

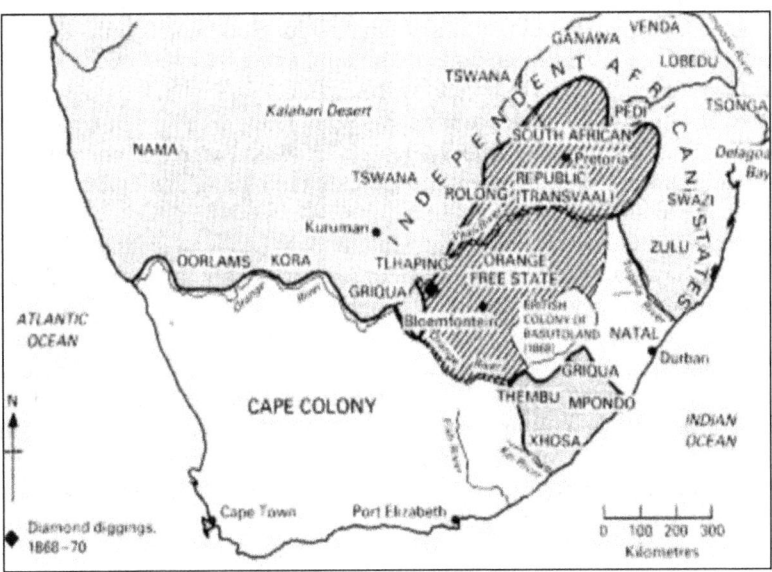

Map of Southern Africa, about 1870 (from: Shillington, History of Africa, p.274).

First, the thinking of the Dutch at the Cape were remained in line with opinions in their original homeland The Netherlands, where there was a general mistrust against the British, who had been competitors at sea and even enemies in a number of sea-battles. *Secondly*, the new arrivals created a growing need for more land. *Thirdly*, the newcomers criticised the way the Boers dealt with coloured and black Africans, treating them as slaves. *Fourthly*, the Boers had developed a feeling of nationhood, a sense of being preserved as the 'Afrikaner Volk' (Dutch: *volk = people*).

---

[1] For this section also: Shaw, *Kingdom*, pp.159-180; Baur, *2000 Years*, pp.188-214, 412-440; Hastings, *Church in Africa*, pp.250-252, 358-371; Ward, 'Africa', in: Hastings (ed), *World History*, pp.209-214.

Many Boers decided to withdraw from British rule. In their *'Great Trek'* they migrated across the Orange river and into the interior beyond the Vaal river, where they established independent states. In this way they intended to defend their identity against British intrusion. The spirit of defence, often characterised as *'laager-mentality'*, was also strengthened at the Blood river in 1838 where a small number of Boers, after having pledged a *'Vow of the Covenant'*, defeated a large Zulu army under Shaka's successor Dingane.

The majority of the Boers were members of the *Nederduitsch Gereformeerde Kerk* (NGK) originating from the main Protestant church in The Netherlands. In English literature this Church is often referred to as the *Dutch Reformed Church* (DRC). Not all NGK church members at the Cape shared the sentiments of the Trekkers, which caused differences within the NGK. Other differences were caused by the movements of the *Great Awakening* that did not fail to have their impact on the settlers in South Africa. Scottish Evangelicalism, revivalist secessions in Holland, and by the end of the century the Dutch neo-Calvinism of Abraham Kuijper, contributed to dissension in the NGK, and to the formation of separate churches among the Boers, the *Nederduitsch Hervormde Kerk* (NHK) and the *Gereformeerde Kerk* (GK), also named *Dopper church*. The Coloured people, being from mixed Boer and African stock, were considered as part of Afrikaner national and religious identity, though later, when *apartheid* took shape, they formed their own churches.

Prior to 1843 the NGK church was not very active in mission. Pauw mentions some reasons. First, up to that date the NGK church was under the control of foreign ecclesiastical and political powers, first the Dutch until 1806, and then the British. The latter did not encourage mission work by the Boer churches. Secondly, there was a chronic shortage of ministers some of whom were liberals. Thirdly, the Boers felt threatened by the attitude of certain foreign missionaries, especially those of the *London Missionary Society*, who were critical of slavery.[2]

The arrival of a number of Scottish ministers and teachers did not lead to the intended anglicising of the Dutch, but Dutch-Scottish familiarity strengthened the opposition against *liberalism*, and it encouraged missionary efforts. Most of the Scots belonged to the evangelicals in the *Church of Scotland* or to the *Free Church of Scotland*. Father and son Andrew Murray took the lead in the missionary enterprise. Decisions at the NGK synod of 1857 signalled the beginning of missionary work among the blacks of Africa. Mission stations were opened in Northern Transvaal (1863), Western Transvaal (1864), Botswana (1877), Malawi (1888), Zimbabwe (1891), Zambia 1899, Mozambique (1908), Nigeria (1911), and Kenya (1944). In many respects Andrew Murray Jr. (†1917) was the initiator of mission by the NGK. He also took the initiative for mission in Malawi. His nephew Andrew Charles Murray became the first NGK missionary to Malawi, and in the period 1886-1916 some fifteen other Murrays went to foreign mission fields, most of them to Malawi. Missionaries were also deployed in Lesotho, Swaziland, Zimbabwe, and Namibia. This missionary work has led to the creation of a Dutch Reformed family of autonomous churches spread over all of Southern Africa and elsewhere.[3]

---

[2] Christoph Martin Pauw, *Mission and Church in Malawi: The History of the Nkhoma Synod of the Church of Central Africa Presbyterian, 1889-1962*, University of Stellenbosch, 1980, pp.44,45.

[3] Pauw, *Mission and Church in Malawi*, pp.45-49.

48.2. The English-speaking Missions

For English-speaking settlers the way to South Africa was paved by the British Empire which firmly established its rule in this part of the world. The first attempt was made in 1795 as a measure against France that had occupied large parts of Europe, including the fatherland of the Dutch-speaking settlers. The British counteracted French aggression by seizing as many French colonies as they could. As The Netherlands had been adopted into the French Empire, therefore the British also tried to take Dutch colonies and settlements. In 1795 they conquered and occupied the Cape. However, when Britain at Amiens in 1802 concluded a peace treaty with France, the Cape Colony was given to the *Batavian Republic*, a puppet regime, that was dependent on Napoleon. Four years later the British recaptured the Cape Colony, and during the *Congress of Vienna* (1814-1815) the Cape and its dependent regions was 'given' to Great Britain. British rule remained until the *Anglo-Boer Wars* at the end of the century, and the establishment of the *Union of South Africa* in 1910, which gave the country an autonomous dominion status in the British Empire.

In the first section of this chapter we noticed that British rule was not accepted by many of the Dutch-speaking Afrikaners or Boers. They withdrew to the north and established their own republics that for the time being were left untouched by the British. First the British subjugated the Zulu and Swazi peoples, and eventually they also destroyed the independence of the Boers. In the meantime, from about 1820 immigrants from England and Scotland began to enter the new colony. With the exception of the Scottish evangelicals mentioned in the previous paragraph, the British settlers that came to South Africa as a result of British colonisation established their own churches, mainly Anglican, Methodist, Congregationalist, Presbyterian, and Roman Catholic. Generally, these churches had already formed missionary agencies. That is why their contribution dominated mission in Southern Africa during the larger part of the 19th century. In 1792 the *Moravian Brethren* resumed their work among the Khoikhoi by re-opening the old settlement at Genadendal. A more important early contribution to mission, however, was made by the *London Missionary Society*, especially by Johannes van der Kemp, John Philip, Robert Moffat, and David Livingstone.

Johannes van der Kemp (†1811) will be discussed in section 4 of this chapter. He was followed by others.

John Philip (†1851), a Scottish pastor, was sent to the Cape to be Van der Kemp's successor. He advocated the equality of blacks and whites, concentrating on the protection of Khoikhoi and Xhosa, wrote an influential book on these matters, *Researches in South Africa* (1828), and he supported the idea of tribal autonomy under British law.

Robert Moffat (†1883). For more than fifty years he worked among the Khoikhoi and the Tswana, operating from his station at Kuruman at the southern edge of the Kalahari Desert. He had strong relations with the local Tswana king, and translated the Bible into Tswana. At Kuruman for the

Robert Moffat (1795-1883) was a Scottish pioneer missionary to South Africa, for the London Missionary Society. He arrived in Cape Town in 1817. He and his wife settled at Kuruman in Bechuanaland and established a mission there. He translated the Bible into the language of the Bechuanas. Their oldest daughter Mary, married David Livingstone.

first time the whole Bible was printed in Africa.[4]

David Livingstone (†1873). He was a son-in-law of Moffat. He was less successful as a missionary than as a discoverer who paved the way for others to do missionary work. In 1840 he joined the LMS and established stations at Mobatsa, Chonuane and Kolobeng. His only convert was Sechele, king of the Bakuena. His greatest fame was acquired when searching for the sources of the Nile. He journeyed across Africa in 1852-1856, which enabled him to give a first-hand report on the extent of the slave trade. In his view, this 'open wound' could be removed by introducing mission, trade, and commerce. In 1857 during a stay in England, Livingstone left the LMS and devoted the rest of his life to the work of exploration and documenting the slave trade and of useful waterways, propagating the combination of Christianity and commerce.

Livingstone inspired many missionary enterprises. He personally led the unsuccessful Makololo missionary attempt through the Kalahari. The LMS and the Roman Catholics followed his path to Zimbabwe's Matabele. Moreover, the LMS penetrated into Zambia, where also the *Brethren* (Frederick Stanley Arnot), the *Paris Mission* (François and Christine Coillard) and the *Primitive Methodists* went. Livingstone's appeal to the senate of Cambridge University in 1857 led to the formation by the Anglicans of the *Universities' Mission to Central Africa*. The news of Livingstone's death in 1873 'sent a wave of missionary zeal throughout Britain', and influenced the Church of Scotland and the Free Church of Scotland to take up missionary work in Malawi.[5]

The *Methodist Mission* was more successful, mainly through the work of William Shaw (†1854) at the Western Cape, where he established a settlement for freed slaves. Shaw was a missionary strategist. He developed a vision of founding stations throughout South Africa through which a general growth of the Methodist Church was assured.

Presbyterian Missions. William Govan of the *Glasgow Missionary Society* made an important early contribution to the training of black and white evangelists and catechists with the opening of *Lovedale College* in 1841. One of its principals, James Stewart, in 1816 helped found *Fort Hare University*, a breeding ground for African leadership. James Stewart was instrumental in making the Free Church of Scotland begin work in Malawi, and in 1875/1876, together with Laws, he was to lead the initial search by the Livingstonia mission for a site on the shore of Lake Malawi.[6] Stewart also played a positive role in promoting cooperation between the Scottish Presbyterians and the NGK of the Boers.[7] Later he worked as a missionary in Kenya.[8]

---

[4] Cf.: Bruce Ritchie, *The Missionary Theology of Robert Moffat*, Kachere: Zomba, 2006; John Smith Moffat, *The Lives of Robert and Mary Moffat by their son John Smith Moffat,* New York: Armstrong & Son, 1888; E.W. Smith, *Robert Moffat: One of God's Gardeners*, London: SCM, 1925; Cecil Northcott, Robert Moffat: *Pioneer in Africa*, London: Lutterworth, 1961; William Walters, *Life and Labours of Robert Moffat*, London: Walter Scott, 1882.

[5] There are many biographies of Livingstone, among them those by: J. Simmons (1955, repr. 1962), G. Martelli (1970), T. Jeal (1973), and O. Ransford (1978). See also the recent study by Andrew C. Ross, *David Livingstone: Mission and Empire*, London: Hambledon & London, 2002. A brief but helpful survey is given by: Hildebrandt, *History of the Church in Africa*, pp.111-119.

[6] Pauw, *Nkhoma Synod*, pp.22,23.

[7] Pauw, *Nkhoma Synod*, pp.55,56.

[8] On Stewart, see chapters 49.2, and 57.3.b.

Anglicanism in South Africa had steadily grown since the beginning of British colonisation. In 1848 Robert Gray became bishop of Cape Town. He felt that his administration of the Anglican dioceses was undermined by John W. Colenso (†1883), who in 1853 was appointed the first Anglican bishop of Natal, and missionary bishop to the Zulus. As an adherent of *Broad Church* principles Colenso propagated liberal ideas on ethical and doctrinal questions. In a study of Paul's letter to the Romans he rejected the doctrines of both substitutionary atonement and everlasting punishment. He also wrote a study on the Pentateuch and Joshua, in which he applied 'historical critical' methods to the text and challenged the historical reliability of Scripture. When Gray and other bishops wanted him to recant, Colenso refused. Then, Gray excommunicated him. Another bishop was nominated in Natal, yet Colenso stuck to his rights and officially could not be deposed. By the end of his life Colenso became an able advocate of the interests of the Zulus, especially when the British started a war against them in the years 1878 and 1879.[9]

Cartoon of John William Colenso (1814-1883), the first Anglican Bishop of Natal.

Lutheran presence in South Africa was strengthened by the arrival of the *Berlin Mission* in 1834, the *Norwegian Missionary Society* in 1843, the *Bauern Mission* from Hermannsburg in 1854, and the *Swedish Church Mission* in 1876. Together with the *American Lutheran Mission*, which arrived in 1927, these Missions are the origins of the churches that in 1975 established the *Evangelical Lutheran Church in Southern Africa*

Roman Catholicism at first was not welcome in South Africa, but in 1820 the colony was officially opened to Roman Catholics, and in 1837 a Vicariate Apostolic was established by the Dominicans. From 1852 there were missionary attempts among the Zulu, Sotho and the Indian immigrants. Prominent work was done from the missionary monastery of Mariannhil in Natal. Today the Roman Catholic Church has 27 Dioceses in South Africa with 3 million members.[10]

Throughout the 19th century the relationship between the Dutch-speaking community and the English-speaking community was bad. This harmed the Church and its mission to the unreached masses of Africans. Fortunately, in both communities there were Christians whose visions and activities went beyond the boundaries of language and race. They contributed to the reconciliation between Boers and British. They were the founding fathers of mission in and from South Africa, and as such they were of great significance for the relationship between Whites and Blacks.

---

[9] Cf.: Gerald Parsons, 'The Theology of Bishop J.W. Colenso', Open University Text.
[10] http://www.catholic-hierarchy.org/country/scza1.html

48.3. Andrew Murray

a. Scottish-Dutch descent

Andrew Murray jr. (1828-1917) belonged to the Afrikaans-Dutch community in South Africa.[11] Through his father and namesake, he was of Scottish descent, and through his mother he was of Afrikaans-German descent. The Murrays were incorporated in the Afrikaans-Dutch community. Their national loyalty was on the side of the Boers. This played an important role during the *Anglo-Boer Wars*. After the Jameson raid that in 1881 led to the first war, Murray published a protest against the politics of imperialism. He addressed the English people pleading for peace and stressed that the Boers have just as much right as the British to freedom, national independence, and use of their own language.

His loyalty did not prevent Murray from cooperating with ministers of the English churches in working and praying for peace. Murray realised that in due course the Boers and the English would have to become reconciled.

b. Missionary Strategist

Murray's influence was nationwide. His work affected the Dutch-speaking community, but also the people of British descent. Through his efforts both communities became more conscious of their responsibilities towards the Blacks and Coloureds. This is particularly true for his missionary endeavours. In a time when mission did not seem a matter of course to the NG Kerk, Andrew Murray passionately tried to prepare South African Christians for missionary work in various ways. He tried to achieve his objective, from 1859 onwards, as a member of the Church's Committee for Mission. But after some time, he concluded that the NG Kerk was too slow to finance the sending out of missionaries.

Andrew Murray (1828-1917), influential writer and preacher in the Dutch Reformed Church of South Africa, who inspired to mission.

That is why he took a personal initiative of organising a *Society of Ministers for Mission*. The Society was established at Cradock in 1886. Members pledged personal financial support to the mission. The Society, chaired by Andrew Murray himself, especially aimed at building up missionary work in Malawi. The Nyasa mission was started by the Chairman's nephew Andrew Charles Murray together with Teunis Vlok. Missionaries of the *Church of Scotland* and of the *Free Church of Scotland* had come to Nyasaland earlier, but they were unable to cover the whole region. That is why the Free Church had offered to the NGK (DRC) Church a wide mission field in the central part of Malawi. Encouraged and facilitated by Andrew Murray and his Society, the Murray family got increasingly involved in the work in Malawi; quite a number of them worked physically in the region, among them Andrew Murray's son Charles. In 1891 seven NGK Church missionaries were in

---

[11] Cf.: Ben Conradie, *Andrew Murray na Honderd Jaar*, Stellenbosch: Christen Studenten Verenigingmaatskappij, 1951; For an extended biography: J. du Plessis, *From The Life of Andrew Murray of South Africa*, Marshall Morgan and Scott, 1919.

Malawi, and in 1899 the number had grown to fourteen. In spite of the *Anglo-Boer War* of 1899-1902, missionary activities developed further. In 1903 there were 28 workers in the Malawian mission field. In the same year the NGK Synod absorbed the Society and put the Nyasaland mission under its *General Committee for Mission* of which Andrew Murray became Chairman.

The scope of Murray's missionary vision was wider than the NGK (DRC) Church and the Dutch-speaking community. He also affected English speakers, e.g. through his involvement in the *South Africa General Mission* (SAGM). Murray invited Spencer Walton to start organised mission in South Africa. In 1889 the *Cape General Mission* (CGM) was established. Its two-fold objective was mission among the neglected and backsliding masses of South Africa and foreign mission. The CGM cooperated with the yearly held Keswick conferences. Murray had copied these meetings from the movement of the *Keswick Convention* in England. They contributed to reviving church people and attracting outsiders. Foreign work started in 1890 with the establishment of a mission station in Swaziland, soon followed by stations in and outside South Africa, i.e. South East Africa, Zululand, Tembuland, Pondoland, Bomvanaland, Natal, Gazaland, Nyasaland and North Rhodesia.

Missionary consciousness was also promoted by the work of South African branch of the *Students' Volunteer Movement* (SVM), founded in 1890. Members promised to be 'ready and eager on God's will to become a missionary among the heathen'. The movement was soon re-shaped to the *Christian Students' Society of South Africa*. Donald Fraser and Luther Wishard were involved in its foundation. Murray remained the Society's guide until the end of his life.

In 1900 in New York a *World Mission Conference* took place. Andrew Murray was one of the invited speakers. Because of the *Anglo-Boer War* he could not go. Yet Murray made an important contribution to missiological thought after he received an account of the conference's dealings, by writing *Key to the Missionary Problem*. In this book he described the problem of mission as a personal matter:

> 'The Lord Jesus Christ is the Author and Leader of Missions. Whoever stands right with Him, and abides in Him, will be ready to know and do his will. It is simply a matter of being near enough to Him to hear his voice, and so devoted to Him and his love as to be ready to do all his will. ... He needs me for his service, and in love I gladly yield myself to Him'.[12]

This call contributed to growing missionary consciousness. An impressive example was given by ex-prisoners of war. The British victors in the *Anglo-Boer War* had put these people in camps in Ceylon. There a revival took place and some 150 pledged to give their lives to Christ and back in South Africa they were trained to spread the Kingdom of God in Africa. In the meantime, the number of missionary organisations was growing. In a booklet, published in 1906, Murray described the work of 31 missionary societies in South Africa. In 1911 he published *The State of the Church*, in reaction to the *World Mission Conference* in Edinburgh in 1910. In this book Murray showed how the impotence of the churches in the face of the unfinished task of world missions is the sign of common spiritual poverty and proof of the unrevived state of their members. He pleaded for more prayer and more sanctification.[13]

---

[12] Andrew Murray, *Key to the Missionary Problem*, Fort Washington: Christian Literature Crusade, 1979 [first edition 1901], p.134.

[13] Andrew Murray, *The State of the Church*, Kempton Park: The Andrew Murray Consultation on Prayer for

c. Writings

Andrew Murray's influence was not limited to South Africa. He received leading foreign evangelists and missionaries like Henry Varley, George Grubb, Donald Fraser and John Mott. His name was especially known in the Anglo-Saxon world, e.g. by his involvement in the *Keswick Convention* in England, he attended the one of 1883, and he personally addressed the one of 1895.

The main reason for Murray's lasting significance and fame in and outside Africa is the books he produced. They were spread widely, e.g. of *The Spirit of Christ* 53,000 copies were sold in the period 1882-1888. Apart from articles, brochures and letters, Murray published about 250 titles. Later some 25 or 30 of them were published in one volume, *Collected Works*. Most of his writings were focused on sanctification and edification of believers. Originally, Murray wrote in Dutch, but later he also wrote books in English. His first published book was *Jezus de Kindervriend* (1858), later translated as *Life of Christ*. It dealt with the training of children, and was designed to assist the Christian mothers. For that matter, all his Dutch writings were translated, mostly into English. We mention some examples using the English titles only: *Abide in Christ* (1992), *Like Christ, The New Life* (1885),[14] *With Christ in the School of Prayer* (1886), *The Holiest of All* (1895). In 1906 Andrew Murray retired, one year after the death of his wife. After this, he intensified his work as a writer. From 1897 his daughter Annie helped him as a secretary.[15] In 1917 he died.

d. Theological Significance

In Conradie's view Murray's theology had three important aspects, which can be summarised in these words: prayer, holiness, evangelism.[16]

Prayer. Murray was convinced that 'prayer is the indispensable condition for anything that God wants to perform on earth'. This he preached, and this he practised personally. He lived and died in prayer. He was called 'the Church's most prolific writer on the subject of prayer and deeper life'.[17]

Holiness. He stressed that Christians should live holy lives. Sanctification shows justification. A person who is saved by the blood of Christ lives a life of obedience to God. The Cross of Christ is the centre of this. Believers, who have progressed far on the way of sanctification, always are deeply conscious of their sin for which Christ had to give his life. Murray could perhaps be classified as a leading exponent of the European *Holiness Movement*, sometimes called *Third Awakening* that was, in a way, channelled by the movement of the *Keswick Convention*.

Evangelism/Mission. This aspect is a consequence of the previous one. Obedient Christians necessarily are preachers of the Gospel to others. God wants more and more people to be converted to Him. That is why the Gospel has to be proclaimed. Make known to all: Become reconciled with God through Christ.

Revival and Mission, 1985 [first edition 1911].

[14] Murray's *The New Life*, was originally written in Dutch as *Het Nieuwe Leven* (1885). In 2002 it was published by Searchlight/ Christian Resource Ministries (Blantyre) in Chichewa, mistakenly entitled *Kubadwa Kwatsopano*, and in 2005 by Kachere (Zomba) as *Moyo Watsopano: Mawu a Mulungu kwa Ophunzira Ongoyamba a Yesu Khristu* [editor: Steven Paas].

[15] For Murray's writings, see: Du Plessis, *The Life of Andrew Murray*, pp.460ff.

[16] Conradie, *Andrew Murray*, pp.14-150.

[17] Smithers, *Andrew Murray*, p.5.

48.4. Johannes van der Kemp

a. With the London Missionary Society

Because he was a Dutchman, Johannes Th. van der Kemp (†1811), should be classified with the Dutch-speaking settlers.[18] While the *Moravian Brethren* before with Dutch help had made their contributions to the native evangelisation of South Africa, there came on the South African scene in 1799 a different kind of Dutchman. He differed from other Dutch settlers, first because he worked for an English mission, the *London Missionary Society* (LMS), and secondly because of his different social and political outlook. Both factors helped him to look wider and further than ethnic boundaries.

Van der Kemp was one of the Dutch pioneer missionaries; he was also the most remarkable of all. In 1792 he had been at the cradle of the first Dutch mission organisation in The Netherlands,[19] which was shaped after the example of the *London Missionary Society*. This happened after the history of his life has taken some sharp turnings. As a young man, Van der Kemp was a cavalry officer and womaniser. But soon after marriage, he quit the army and studied philosophy and medicine at Edinburgh, publishing works of originality in both fields. In 1791 he lost his wife and daughter in a sailing tragedy. This brought him to conversion to Christianity. After meeting the Moravians in 1792, his mind was set on becoming a missionary. From the Moravians he learned about the establishment of the *London Missionary Society*. As the *Dutch Society of Missionaries* was not yet ready to send people, Johannes Van der Kemp joined the *London Missionary Society* who employed him for work in the Cape Colony.

Johannes T. van der Kemp (1747-1811), missionary among the Xhosa, the San, and the Khoikhoi.

b. Work among Khoikhoi, San and Xhosa

In 1799, at the age of fifty, Van der Kemp arrived at the Cape and somewhat later he started work among the Khoikhoi (Hottentots), identifying himself with them. His living together with the Khoikhoi and his preaching of conversion and justice was not warmly greeted by the Boer settlers; it led to a growing hostility.[20]

Van der Kemp also worked among the San (Bushmen) and Xhosa tribes, though because of the language barrier this work miscarried. His subsequent idea to achieve conversion of the Xhosa through war and force was resisted by the Khoi Khoi and by white settlers who had gathered round Xhosa king Ngika. Later he started learning the

---

[18] For his life, see: L.H. Enklaar, *Life and Work of Dr. J.Th. van der Kemp 1741-1811: Missionary Pioneer and Protagonist of Racial Equality in South Africa*, Capetown-Rotterdam, 1988.
[19] *Nederlandsch Zendelingen Genootschap* [transl.: Dutch Society of Missionaries], founded in 1797.
[20] L.A. Loetscher *A Brief History of Presbyterians*, Philadelphia: Westminster Press, 1978³, p.34.

Xhosa language; he wrote an elementary grammar and word list entitled *Specimen and vocabulary of the Kafree language*, which he classified into 21 classes. Though his missionary attempts seemed to end in a failure, Johannes Van der Kemp made lasting impressions on King Ngika and the Xhosa. Among the Xhosa he was known by the name Yankanna or Nyengana. Later generations of converts were given this name as their identity. They were commonly called *amaYankanna* or *people of Johannes Van der Kemp*.

Hastings lists four characteristics that in his view set Van der Kemp apart among his contemporaries: *First*, he was seen as a man of God, a man full of prayer, a spiritually powerful man, and a rainmaker. *Secondly*, he was a man of poverty. He went about walking bareheaded and barefooted unlike his fellow whites who often put on a hat and shoes. He fed on anything given to him and was contented to live under these poor conditions. *Thirdly*, he was a very intelligent person. For example, he endeavoured to know the Xhosa language and was anxious to explain the role of electricity in lightning to Xhosa King Ngika. *Fourthly*, Van der Kemp was noted for his sense of equality, behaving in a friendly, familiar manner to everyone in every way. Differences of colour, race, material level, culture and living conditions he did not recognise as divisive realities. That is why 'he touched more hearts than was immediately evident', so Hastings concludes.

Drawing of Khoikhoi people worshipping the moon.

The authorities gave him Betheldorp, a model community that he ruled as a missionary settlement. Due to bad conditions of the land, he found it increasingly difficult to realise his plans. Van der Kemp married a slave girl from Malagasy whom he had freed by buying her together with her parents. In 1807 slave trade at the Cape was abolished altogether, much to the relief of Van der Kemp. In general, he disagreed with his fellow whites on matters of the treatment of the non-whites and slaves.

His influence among the Khoikhoi was considerable. He spread his missionary message to them, using the Dutch language too, teaching them some elementary Dutch, at the same time finding a written mode for the Hottentot language. The consequence of this was that most Khoikhoi after some generations could hardly speak their native language. Apart from being Christianised, they spoke Dutch, and had Dutch names.

At a later stage many Khoikhoi became missionaries themselves, and they infiltrated the Gospel in non-Christian societies of South Africa. Some went outside South Africa; in most cases they helped European missionaries who worked in the interior of Africa. Some Khoikhoi missionaries were Andries Waterboer, Jager Afrikaaner, Jan Stoffels, Klaas Stuurman, and Jan Tshatshu. Besides, Van der Kemp influenced such very important religious figures in South Africa as Ntsikana.[21]

---

[21] Malikebu, 'Dutch Missionaries in Africa in the Period 1650-1950'; John De Cruchy, *The Church struggle in South Africa*. pp.12,13; Gray, *Black Christians, white Missionaries*. p.87.

49. Eastern Africa 1800-1900

49.1. Swahili-Arab rule

Let us revisit the eastern part of Africa now.[1] The term East Africa is often used for the region of mainly today's states Kenya, Uganda, Tanzania, Mozambique, and Madagascar. According to Ward, in Eastern Africa 'the figure of the missionary took on a greater importance' than it did in West Africa and Southern Africa. Whereas in the West and the South missionary work soon led to 'an actual African Christian Church', in the East for a long time the scene remained dominated by 'the missionary as explorer, as visionary of radical social transformation, as strategist'.[2]

Missionary activity in East Africa preceded the rise of Western colonialism by the end of the 19th century. Since 1528 Fort Jesus had proudly towered over the Isle of Mombasa off the East African Coast. It was a reminder of the period of military subjugation by the Portuguese and of the early attempts by the Roman Catholic Church to Christianise the region. Soon Christian perception of Jesus symbolised by the Mombasa fortress had been replaced by Muslim ideas on Prophet Isa that were spread by the imams of the Sultan of Oman and Muscat. This Arab dynasty ruled the African east coast from Somalia to Mozambique, including Zanzibar and many other islands, for almost three hundred years. Sultan Sayyid Said ruled from 1804 to 1856. In 1837 he asked the assistance of Shaikh Isa bin Tarif in conquering the town of Mombasa. Fort Jesus was renamed Fort of Isa, after the victorious Shaikh.

In this long stretched out coastal area Arab and African influences met and mixed into a Swahili-Arab culture. The Sultans developed their thriving economy through slavery and the slave trade. From Africa's east coast the Swahili-Arabs penetrated into the interior, and with the help of tribes that they converted to Islam, they dragged numerous Africans from their villages, killing those that they deemed not useful, to the island of Zanzibar, where they were sold to slave-buyers in Muslim-ruled East Africa, the Arab world, Persia and India. From the early 19th century also people of Lake Nyasa had been targeted by Swahili-Arab slave-traders and their e.g. Kamba, Yao or sometimes Chewa helpers. From the whole East African interior tens of thousands of e.g. Jagga, Samba, Nika, Bemba, Chewa, Mang'anja and Tumbuka were cruelly captured, assembled and transported to the coast of the Indian Ocean, finally to places where the Sultans of Oman and Zanzibar had extended their power.

49.2. Rebmann and Krapf[3]

In this 19th-century context of Arab power and Muslim religion God chose to start His Church. The first missionaries were Lutheran Germans, sent by the Anglican Church, most importantly Johannes Rebmann (1820-1876). He was shaped by the 19th-century

---

[1] This section connects to chapter 44.5. Cf.: Shaw, *Kingdom*, pp.139-158; Baur, *2000 Years*, pp.103-152; Hastings, *Church in Africa*, pp.177-188, 338-358; Ward, 'Africa', in: Hastings (ed), *World History*, pp.203-209.

[2] Hastings (ed.), *World History*, p.209.

[3] Cf.: Steven Paas, *Johannes Rebmann: A Servant of God in Africa Before the Rise of Western Colonialism*, Nürnberg: Verlag für Theologie und Religionswissenschaft/ Bonn: Verlag für Kultur und Wissenschaft, 2011 [edition afem – mission academics]; Marjorie Oludhe Macgoye, *Rabmann: A Novel*, Scarith, 2014.

Awakening Movement, in the line of German Pietism and the Reformation. He was trained to be a missionary in Basel (Switzerland), and he joined the English Church Missionary Society (CMS), which in 1846 sent him and Jakob J. Erhardt to Muslim-ruled East Africa. There he stayed for 29 years, before returning to his German hometown Gerlingen in Württemberg, blind and sick, soon to die. Rebmann was a faithful servant of God, who used his spiritual and linguistic gifts for the extension of the Kingdom. When Rebmann arrived he met with his fellow missionary and compatriot Johann Ludwig Krapf,[4] who had been sent by the CMS to Mombasa a few years earlier, after the Ethiopian government had blocked the continuation of his work in the Shoa Province. Together with his wife Krapf had established the first Protestant mission station in Kenya at Mombasa in 1544. The death of his wife very soon after this event was a hard blow for Krapf. First, Krapf, Rebmann and Erhardt together tried to establish mission stations in the interior. Krapf wanted to develop a far-reaching plan of counteracting the ever continuing penetration of Islam in Africa, by a chain of mission stations from the Indian Ocean along the Sahara to the Atlantic Ocean. Dreaming of chain of mission stations across the African continent, they made journeys as far as Kilimanjaro and Mount Kenya. Krapf's main contribution is his book, *Travels, Researches and Missionary Labours* (1853) and his work in the Swahili language.[5] Krapf's approach proved impractical in comparison to Rebmann's idea of staying in the coastal region and adapting to the local situation, thus gradually finding access to the hearts of the people. Krapf stayed there together with Rebmann during seven years. They kept contact even after Krapf had left Africa. When Johannes Rebmann, in 1875 near the end of his life, came home to Württemberg, Krapf was there to assist him. After 1885, other CMS workers tried to put some of Krapf's plans into practice, although they modified them from a chain of mission stations across Kenya to Uganda.

Johannes Rebmann, back in Germany in 1875, almost blind, and his friend Isaac Nyondo, who guided him on the journey home. Basler Mission Archive: QS-30.003.0178.01.

Both missionaries got deeply involved in the Swahili world of the coastal region of East Africa. However, their vision pertained to more than that region. Krapf's main focus was the Galla of Abyssinia. Rebmann felt called to pave the way for missionaries to the people of Central Africa, where at that time a large interior lake was supposed to be. Like many contemporaries Rebmann and Krapf were touched by the enthusiasm of David Livingstone, born in 1812, who travelled to the interior of Africa, opening it up to 'Christianity and commerce', hoping to heal the 'open wound' of slavery and slave-trafficking, and to find the enigmatic sources of the Nile. At a time when Africans were in the shackles of slavery, traditional religions, and Islam, Rebmann believed in God's

---

[4] Jochen Eber, *Johann Ludwig Krapf: Ein schwäbischer Pionier in Ostafrika*, Riehen: Arte Media/ Lahr: Johannis, 2006.

[5] Cf.: Paas, *Johannes Rebmann*, pp.43-67, 207-214; Hildebrandt, *History of the Church in Africa*, pp.122-126.

plan for Africa. God's plan, not only for the Swahili, Nika, and Jagga people of Mombasa and its opposite mainland, among whom he worked, but also for the people of Lake Nyasa, more than 2000 kilometres from his Mombasa area. Rebmann was convinced that God had promised to use him as an instrument for initiating Christianity on the eastern coast and in the interior of Africa. By the end of his work in Africa, when he had become very weak, he continued to believe in God's faithfulness. *Gott ist getreu* (German for: God is faithful), that he wanted to proclaim at all places (*an allen Orten*).

Rebmann was not only a faithful witness of Christ, but he was also a gifted linguist. Together with Krapf he made the Swahili and Nika languages available in writing. This affected a language that is probably the largest in sub-Saharan Africa. Reading and writing Swahili had enormous positive consequences for the communication of the Word of God and for multifaceted development of the Swahili-speaking peoples. Perhaps just as important is Rebmann's significance for the language of the people of Lake Nyasa. He was one of the first to reduce this language to writing, and the first to compile a dictionary of it into English. Since a few decades before Rebmann's arrival in Africa also the people of Lake Nyasa had been targeted by Swahili-Arab slave-traders and their Yao or Chewa helpers. From the 1840's the Jumbe dynasty had ruled over a Swahili-Arab kingdom at Nkhotakota. Also, south and north of Nkhotakota slave-traders settled.[6] Many Chewa, Mang'anja and Tumbuka were cruelly captured, assembled and transported across the Lake to the coast of the Indian Ocean, mostly to the slave-markets at Zanzibar and other places where the Sultans of Oman and Zanzibar had stretched their power, and from there even often sold beyond the Indian Ocean. Mombasa, at almost 250 km from Zanzibar, was a place where slaves were used, also slaves originating from the regions of present-day Malawi. In Rebmann's contact with these people the Dictionary of the Kiniassa language (now Chichewa or Chinyanja) was born.[7] His informant was Salimini, a slave from central Nyasaland (Malawi). Probably notes from of this tool of communication helped some people in the settlement of freed ex-slaves that was established in Mombasa about the time of Rebmann's return home. Also, the first missionaries to Malawi used a hand-written copy. To some extent it was for them an instrument for mastering the language and spreading the Gospel. Indirectly Rebmann's linguistic and missionary work strengthened those religious and political influences from overseas that put a definite end to the shame and misery of slavery and slave trade in East Africa.

49.3. Kenya

Rebmann's departure in 1875 marked the beginning of a new period of mission in East Africa. First, the harvest, which he had expected for such a long time, began to show its fruits. After he left, the small young Church continued to experience the wonderful work of the Holy Spirit. In 1878 at the new CMS mission centre in Frere Town – a British-ruled settlement for freed slaves near Mombasa – 45 catechumens were

---

[6] Steven Paas, 'History of Islam in Malawi', in: Paas, *Beliefs and Practices of Muslims: The Religion of our Neighbours*, Good Messenger Publications, Zomba: 2006, pp.125-133.

[7] Steven Paas, 'A History of Chichewa Lexicography', in: Idem, *Dictionary/ Mtanthauziramawu: Chichewa/ Chinyanja - English and English - Chichewa/ Chinyanja*, 4th edition, Blantyre/ Veenendaal: Foundation Heart for Malawi/ Christian Literature in Action in Malawi, 2013. See: Interner

confirmed by the Anglican bishop of Mauritius.[8] Before that more Giriama people had begun to go to missionary W.S. Price to be baptised. Price sent a teacher, who found some 30 people who the whole day were meditating on the Word and praying for forgiveness of sins.[9] Conversions and baptisms continued to take place. The young Giriama Church was exposed to persecution and suffering. Their leader Abe Sidi was considered a rebel by the Muslim rulers of Mombasa. In 1883 Fuladayo was obliterated by a Swahili-Arab attack, and 'Abe Sidi was killed, becoming a Christian martyr'. The British at Frere Town did not help, as they depended on friendly relations with the Governor of Mombasa.[10]

When Rebmann left, informally the CMS had already started its new strategy for East Africa, concentrating on Frere Town, the establishment of liberated slaves on the coast, and on preparations for penetration into the interior. More successful than Krapf's idea of a 'chain of mission stations'[11] was the missionary concept of establishing cities for freed slaves (*othawa kwao*). The first one was opened in 1874 on the initiative of Bartle Frere, British emissary at the court of the Sultan of Zanzibar. Hence, it was called Freretown. In these *'cities of refuge'* a strong Christianity developed, often referred to as *'kitoro'* (= refugee) Christianity, which produced Kenya's first Christian martyr David Koi, beheaded by the Arabs in 1883,[12] and other influential Christians, such as William Jones.

Henry Bartle Frere (1815-1884), British diplomat who was sent to Zanzibar to negotiate a treaty with the sultan for the suppression of the slave traffic, and contributed to the establishment of refuges for ex-slaves.

After 1885, the policy of Western mission organisations changed. The emphasis in the activities of their missionaries shifted from being dependent on much desired contributions of Africans to activities by Western missionaries who operated independently from African contributions or initiative. The presence of many missionaries, colonial civil servants and soldiers made missionaries feel less dependent on cooperation with the representatives of African culture and traditional religion than Rebmann was.

Also cooperation between English and German missions became more difficult. The colonial border between German Tanganyika and British Kenya and Uganda frustrated interdenominational mission and international cooperation. The German Lutheran Rebmann, trained in a non-denominational institution in Switzerland, employed by the English Church in pre-colonial Africa, belonged to a different era. That's why the influence of Rebmann and contemporary missionaries on missionary approach and method declined after 1885. By the end of the century the number of missionary organisations in Kenya and Uganda had grown considerably. One example was the

---

[8] Scheffbuch, *Große Entdecker*, p.91.
[9] Jehle, *Der Entdecker*, p.15,16.
[10] Sundkler and Steed, *A History of the Church in Africa*, p.556.
[11] Cf.: Fiedler, *Story of Faith Missions*, pp.73-84.
[12] Cf.: Hildebrandt, *History of the Church in Africa*, p.183.

Church of Scotland Mission (CSM), pioneering in the interior of Kenya. They worked hand-in-hand with the Anglicans of the CMS.

By the end of the century the number of missionary organisations in Kenya had grown considerably. Again we meet James Stewart of Lovedale (see previous chapter), now as a missionary of the *Church of Scotland Mission* (CSM), pioneering in the interior of Kenya. These Scottish Presbyterians arrived in the Nairobi region in 1898, and they worked hand-in-hand with the Anglicans of the CMS. They were followed by the *Methodists,* who moved from the coast into the interior in 1910, the *Neukirchener Mission* and others. Also, a series of Faith Missions started work in Kenya; first was the *Africa Inland Mission* of Cameron Scott (1895). [13]

On the Roman Catholic side the *Holy Ghost Fathers* came to Kenya. They arrived in 1889, temporarily withdrew, and started work among the Agikuyu in 1899. They were followed by the *Consolata Fathers* in 1902 and then *Mill Hill Fathers* in 1903. The completion of the Uganda railroad in 1901 made it much easier for missionaries to enter the interior. In 1894 Kenya became a protectorate of Britain.[14]

49.4. Tanzania

The routes of the slave trade and the traffic in ivory to Zanzibar ran through Tanzania. It was the Anglican UMCA, founded at Livingstone's appeal in 1857, that in 1861 under Bishop Charles Mackenzie in Malawi had collided with the Yao slave-traders.[15] This early attempt miscarried and under Bishop William Tozer the UMCA withdrew to Zanzibar in 1864, where they established St. Andrew's College and a cathedral. In 1875 the UMCA moved to mainland Tanzania, establishing centres for freed slaves at Magila (1868), Masasi (1876) and Newala (1878).[16] The UMCA became one of the largest missionary organisations in that country. The Evangelical Anglican *Church Missionary Society,* located mainly in Uganda, also entered Tanzania. In 1888 they opened a station in Nassa, on the east coast of Lake Victoria. But as it was difficult to administer this work from Uganda, the CMS transferred it to the *Africa Inland Mission,* in 1909.[17]

Also the *Holy Ghost Fathers* made a refuge for freed slaves, at Bagamoyo, a former collecting point of slaves on the Tanzanian coast, opposite Zanzibar. Schooling, manual work and rigorous discipline made the settlement self-supporting, but also led to a lack of freedom and protests by the inhabitants. The *Holy Ghost Fathers* were more successful in their new missionary stations along the coast and around Kilimanjaro. Christian communities of ex-slaves and others were also established by the *White Fathers* of Cardinal Charles Lavigerie, who arrived at Lake Tanganyika in 1879.

The Germans followed the example of Britain and other colonizers. Otto von Bismarck felt that colonisation in Africa would give the recently unified German state due respect in the world. German colonial presence concerned territories in South, West and East Africa. One week after the *Berlin Conference* ended, on 26 February 1885,

---

[13] Cf.: W.B. Anderson, *The Church in East Africa 1840-1974*, Nairobi/ Dodoma/ Kampala, UZIMU/ CTP/ CPH, 1981 [first 1977]; R. Oliver, *The Missionary Factor in East Africa*, London: Longmans, 1965².

[14] Baur, *2000 Years,* pp.257,258.

[15] Hastings, *Church in Africa*, pp.268,286,293.

[16] Hastings, *Church in Africa*, p.257.

[17] Cf.: Hildebrandt, *History of the Church in Africa*, p.181.

Germany took possession of Tanganyika, the land south of Kilimanjaro, henceforth called *German East Africa*, present-day Tanzania. Before German rule in Tanganyika began, the CMS, through Rebmann, Krapf and others, had been working in Zanzibar and on the coast south of Mombasa since 1844. The Roman

Mount Kilimanjaro in North West Tanzania, its highest point is Uhuru peak (5,895 metres).

Catholics were already at Bagamoyo, opposite Zanzibar; the *Holy Ghost Fathers* made a refuge there for freed slaves. They also established missionary stations along the coast and around Kilimanjaro. The establishment of German colonial rule was followed by the arrival of German missionary organisations.

Before the First World War German missionaries were already active for each of the four classical German Protestant missions in various parts of Tanzania. In 1885 the CMS started to work among the Jagga in the Kilimanjaro region. First it seemed that the English could continue their work in German Tanganyika. There at the foot of the mountain, in Moshi, CMS Bishop James Hannington appointed a missionary.[18] However, the German Governor closed the CMS station in 1892, and in 1893 the work was taken over by the *Leipzig Evangelical Mission*, which had come to Tanzania in 1991. In 1886, stimulated by the example of Krapf and Rebmann, the Bavarian pastor Max Ittameier founded the Protestant-Lutheran *Hersbrucker Mission* in the Kilimanjaro region.[19] On their arrival in 1891 the *Leipzig Mission* took over the work of the Bavarians. In the north Bruno Gutmann worked for the *Leipzig Mission* among the Jagga from 1902 to 1938, interrupted only by five years of exclusion (1920-1925) from the territory due to the Versailles Peace Treaty. The *Berlin Mission* was represented by Klamroth and Hermann Neuberg, working in the coastal areas. Ernst Johanssen was active for the *Bethel Mission*. There were also missionaries of the *Moravian Mission*, e.g. Traugott Bachmann, who worked among the Nyakyusa and the Nyiha.[20] The *Neukirchener Mission* had started work among the Kamba people in Ukambani, which came under British jurisdiction. In Usambara and further to the South the *Bielefelder Mission* and the *Berliner Mission* deployed.

49.5. Uganda

From the 15th century there had existed the kingdom of Buganda, ruled by its sacred kings, the *Kabaka*, who were most central figures in the traditional *balubaala* cult. The religious situation changed when Kabaka Mutesa I (d. 1884) and his court turned to

---

[18] *AMZ*, 1894, pp.139,509.

[19] Cf.: Eber, *Krapf*, p.240.

[20] Klaus Fiedler, *Christianity and Culture: Conservative German Protestant Missionaries in Tanzania 1900-1940*, Blantyre: Kachere/ CLAIM, 1999 [first published by Brill in Leiden, in 1996]; cf. Hildebrandt, *History of the Church in Africa*, pp.181-183.

Islam. However, Stanley, during his visit in 1875, explained to the king the advantages of Christianity, which made the king change again. Protests by Muslims at court were quenched in blood.

In witnessing the Gospel Stanley was ably assisted by one of his African employees, Dallington Muftaa.[21] When Stanley left Buganda Muftaa remained and continued to teach the people. His work prepared the way for the evangelical Anglican CMS. They began to send missionaries in 1877. Alexander Mackay was the most successful. He began to translate the Scriptures into Luganda, and preached a Christian revival leading to the rule of Christ over individual, social, and national life.

In 1879 the Roman Catholic *White Fathers* entered Uganda. They rejected the suggestion of going to new mission fields, and started work near the Protestant stations. Competition between Protestants and Roman Catholics confused King Mutesa. He returned to the traditional *balubaala* cult. The ban on preaching and teaching was lifted in 1880. While Protestantism and Roman Catholicism grew, the new *Kabaka*, Mwanga, who demanded freedom for his *homosexual* practices, became very hostile against Christianity. After having newly appointed Bishop James Hannington murdered, he ordered the death of three African CMS Christians in 1885. In 1886 he burnt 31 Roman Catholics and Protestants in the capital, and had many others killed in other parts of the country.[22] This cruel act against the *Ugandan Martyrs* was followed by three revolutions: the first one brought the Muslims to power, the second one gave power to the Christians in general, and the third one, the Protestants. In 1894 Uganda became a British protectorate.

49.6. Mozambique

In chapters 44.2.d,g and 47.5 we referred to the comparative weakness of the early stage of Roman Catholic Mission in Africa. This also applies to Mozambique. Until the beginning of the 20th century the Portuguese administration and the Portuguese missionaries proved unable to establish lasting influence in the interior. Apart from the negative influence of their involvement in the slave trade, even until the end of the 19th century, the Portuguese had not much impact in the interior. This negatively affected the growth of the Roman Catholic Church and mainly limited it to the coastal regions. Another factor that hindered Roman Catholic progress was Portuguese paternalism and the lack of medical services and schools. Besides, the political situation in the European homeland sometimes turned against the missionaries, as was experienced by the Jesuits who worked in the Zambezi delta, but were driven out of the country as a result of an anti-clerical revolution in Portugal. Around 1850 the Portuguese had expelled all Roman Catholic missionaries for some time. In 1914 some Jesuits re-entered the country. Roman Catholic Mission in Mozambique was greatly stimulated in 1940 when Portugal's government under Salazar introduced a new mission policy.

The relative weakness of Roman Catholic Mission made it easier for Protestant missions to make progress in Mozambique.[23] African initiative is apparent in the establishment of a church in Southern Mozambique by an African evangelist who had

---

[21] Hildebrandt, *History of the Church in Africa*, pp.128,129.

[22] Louise Pirouet, *The Witness of the Ugandan Martyrs*, Kampala: Church of Uganda Literature Centre, 1969; cf. Hildebrandt, *History of the Church in Africa*, pp.187-189.

[23] Sundkler and Steed, *A History of the Church in Africa*, pp.482,487.

been trained at a Swiss mission station in Transvaal. This is another example of the importance of the refugee factor. The Dutch Reformed missionary F. Hofmeyer at Goedgedacht worked among the Thonga, who had adopted a positive attitude to the Transvaal government. In 1879 the *American Board of Commissioners for Foreign Missions* sent a missionary to Mozambique, but because of bad climate a permanent mission was not built until 1883.[24] Methodist, Pentecostals, Presbyterians, Anglicans, Episcopalians, Baptists, and African Independents followed and established churches.

The Boer wars in general created serious problems in South Africa, but indirectly they were a blessing in Mozambique because amongst the returning miners there were many Christians who helped to spread Christianity in their home villages. [25] Africans greatly contributed to the mission work. This is not to deny that 19th-century Christian mission in Mozambique failed to reach many places.

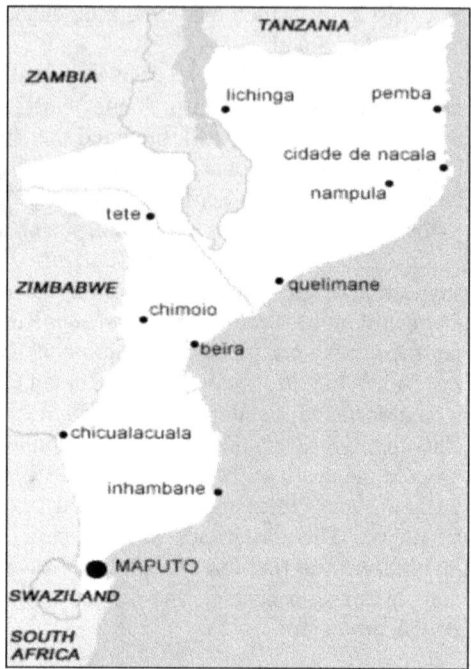

Map of Mozambique.

49.7. Madagascar

a. First Roman Catholic Attempts

The island of Madagascar is populated by Bantu in the coastal regions mainly in the south, probably taken there as slaves by the Arabs from the 7th century onwards. The Arabs also started making notes on the island and this can be considered as the beginning of written history of the island. The highlands in the centre are the homeland of the Hova (Merina and Betsileo peoples). They are of Malayan or Indonesian descent, and they immigrated from the 1st century onwards. This means that Madagascar's population is of mixed Asian and African origin. Its main vernacular language is Malagasy.

The first missionary efforts in Madagascar were made by the Roman Catholics in the 16th century. European contact began after Diego Dias sighted the Island in 1506. Efforts by Portuguese Jesuits in the 17th century had no lasting fruits.

Also in the 17th century the *French East Indies Company* established trading posts along the East coast, e.g. Fort Dauphin. In the period 1642-1674 they attempted to make these posts the basis of a French colony on the island. Members of the orders of the

---

[24] Cf.: Hildebrandt, *History of the Church in Africa*, p.176.
[25] Sundkler and Steed, *A History of the Church in Africa*, p.487.

Carmelites and the Lazarists tried to start missionary work. They left in 1674 after many of them were murdered by local people. In the 18th century new attempts were made by French Lazarists, 'but the French Revolution put to an end all such work'.[26] About 1800 all traces of the early Roman Catholic efforts had vanished, leaving the Madagascar coast for some decades as a favourite hiding place for pirate ships.

b. Start of Protestant Mission

In the meantime, the Merina rulers had started to establish power over almost the entire island, 'imposing on it a political as well as a linguistic unity'.[27] They looked for support from the British. In 1817 in a Treaty with Great Britain the Merina king promised to abolish slavery in exchange for British protection. British influence opened the island for Protestant missions.

The first Protestant missionaries were sent by the *London Missionary Society* (LMS). On 18th August 1818 David Jones and Thomas Bevan arrived in Toamasina, the harbour on the east coast of Madagascar. They enjoyed the protection of King Radama I (1810-1828). They opened a school and succeeded in attracting many young people from noble Malagasy families. In subsequent years many more schools were opened. Though all missionaries, with the exception of Jones, died soon after their arrival, the work went on. Until the death of King Radama I other LMS missionaries were allowed to come to the island. One of their important achievements was reducing the Malagasy language into Latin script; the first translation of the Bible was published in Antananarivo in 1835. In the meantime, starting with the Merina court, hundreds of Malagasy people had converted to Christianity.

c. Persecution

Under Radama's widow and successor Ranavalona I (1828-1861) a period of brutal persecution began. In 1835, the same year as the Bible was published, the missionaries were forced to leave the country and many Malagasy converts suffered martyrdom. The Queen was put on the throne by a conspiracy of people who did not favour the modernisations brought by the missionaries. The Queen was led to maintain the royal protection of the missionaries, but exercised stricter control over their activities because she was afraid of seeing Christianity become the focus of opposition. To obtain popular support and to make people forget the doubtful origins of her power, the Queen relied on the soothsayers and restored old institutions of monarchical power. Eventually she forbade missionaries to preach, and then banned the baptism of soldiers and children.

Finally, in March 1835 the Queen decreed that anyone would be put to death 'who practises the new religion'.

In 1836 the missionaries left the kingdom and took refuge on the East coast, at Tamatave. They left behind them a small group of about fifty dedicated Christians. Because these Christians kept in contact with the missionaries by letter, today this correspondence gives us direct evidence of this first wave of persecution and the way in which it was experienced. The correspondence shows the central place occupied in the community by the Bible and after that by Bunyan's *Pilgrim's Progress*. During the persecutions the number of Christians grew to almost 3000. Some went into exile

---

[26] S. Neill, *A History of Christian Missions*, London: Watson and Vinely, 1964, p.199.
[27] Neill, *Christian Missions*, p.318.

beyond Madagascar when the threat became too strong, like Mary Rafaravary, daughter of a court dignitary, the first to organise prayer meetings in her home. Arrested in July 1836 and condemned to death, she escaped execution thanks to a providential fire which caused panic among the soldiers and allowed her to get to Tamatave. There she took a ship for Mauritius with a group of Christians. The whole adventure was immediately likened to the adventures of the 'pilgrim' in Bunyan's book with whom Mary is identified. She thought of Christians crossing the valley of the shadow of death, but recalled that it is through numerous tribulations they must enter the kingdom of heaven. During the same year, 1837, the martyrdom of another woman, Rafavavy Rasalana, became the symbol of answering and edifying determination.

It was in 1849 that the persecution reached its height. After being interrogated, a group of Christians were condemned, some to fines and the confiscation of their goods, others to be flogged, and eighteen to be put to death, four to be burnt and fourteen to be hurled from a great rock and then burnt to ashes. Tertullian's adage 'The blood of the Martyrs is a seed' came true in Madagascar, as it could be observed that the faithful attitude of Christians convinced others. At the end of the persecutions their number had grown to 3000 Christians and eleven years later to 27,000.

Ranavalona I (1778-1861), Queen of Merina, Madagascar. After succeeding her husband, Radama I in 1828, she was also known as Ranavalo-Manjka I.

The memory of this dark period plays a significant role in the life of the churches in Madagascar.[28]

d. Freedom Restored

Under the short reign of Ranavalona's son Radama II the situation changed again. He freed the imprisoned Christians, favoured mission, and sought to modernise the country. Neill cited how this wonderful experience was greeted by the persecuted Christians. Out of the recesses of the forests there came men and women who had been wanderers and outcasts for years. They re-appeared as if risen from the dead. Their brethren from the city went out to meet them and to help them and as they saw their old city again, they sang the pilgrim song. 'When the Lord turned again the captivity of Zion, we were like them in our dream'.[29]

After the beginning of the new freedom, the *London Missionary Society* returned in the island, soon to be joined by Anglicans, Norwegians, Lutherans, Quakers, and Roman Catholics.

Again there was a brief period of danger for the Christians. An epidemic broke out, and some non-Christians misinterpreted it as revenge by the ancestral spirits. In 1863 King Radama II was overthrown and put to death. His wife Rasolerina became Queen.

---

[28] Cf.: A.P. John, 'The Martyrs of Madagascar (1835-1861)', in F.J.Balasundaram (ed.), *Martyrs in the History of Christianity* [Internet]; Chenu Bruno et al., *The Book of Christian Martyrs*, London: SCM, 1990, p.143; E. Isichei, *A History of Christianity in Africa from Antiquity to the Present*, University of Canterbury, 1995, p.151.

[29] Neill, *Christian Missions*, p.319

She supported those spirit-worshippers who had threatened the Christians. She died in 1868. Her successor, Ranavalona II, was a daughter of the notorious Ranavalona I, but she did not follow her mother's and Rasolerina's examples. She was rumoured to have been a secret adherent of the Reformed faith, even while her mother was in power. She built a church alongside the palace and in 1869 she was baptised. Large numbers of the upper class followed her example.

e. French Colony

In 1883 the French started to colonise Madagascar. In 1885, the year of the *Berlin Conference* and the subsequent 'scramble for Africa', the British accepted the imposition of French influence in return for eventual control over Zanzibar as part of an agreement on spheres of influence in East Africa and the Western Pacific. In the same year the French urged Queen Ranavalona III to conclude a Pact with them. In 1895 they occupied the capital Antananarivo and forced the queen to sign another Pact that made Madagascar first a *French Protectorate*, and then in the following year a French Colony. In 1897 the French exiled the queen of Madagascar.

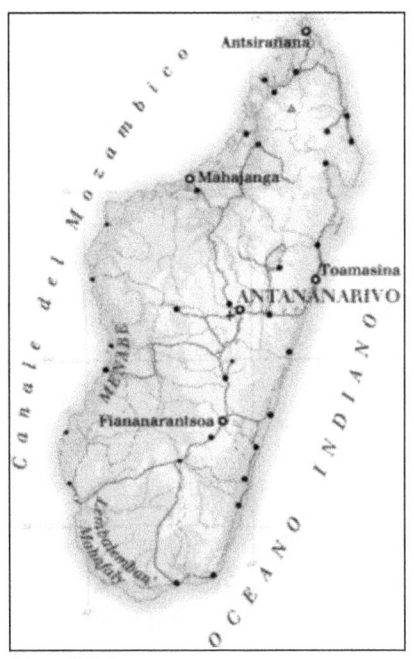

The growing influence of France gave ample opportunities for Roman Catholic mission. As a result of its more favoured position Roman Catholicism spread rapidly, especially among the Bantu people in the coastal regions. This led to tensions between Roman Catholics and Protestants. To strengthen their work, the Protestant mission asked for the support of the *Paris Evangelical Missionary Society* in 1895. Throughout the colonial period the rivalry between Roman Catholicism and Protestantism continued. Although the official separation of Church and State in France demanded equality of both denominations, French tradition made it difficult for the colonial authorities to treat them equally.

Map of Madagascar

A nationalist revolution in 1947 was the beginning of the end of French colonialism in Madagascar. In October 1958 Madagascar became an autonomous republic within the *French Commonwealth*, adopting the name Malagasy, and in June 1960 it declared itself fully independent. Especially the Protestant churches had supported the movement that led to independence.

f. Independence

At the present time about half of the Madagascar people are members of Christian churches, divided almost evenly between Roman Catholicism and Protestantism. The *Malagasy Council of Christian Churches* (FFKM) comprises four denominations, the *Reformed Protestant Church of Jesus Christ in Madagascar* (FJKM), the *Lutheran*

Church, the *Anglican Church*, and the *Roman Catholic Church*. The other half of the Malagasy are Muslims (less than 10%) or they still belong to traditional religions with much emphasis on cults of the dead, i.e. the custom of *famadihana*, or 'turning over the dead'. 'In this ritual relatives' remains are removed from the family tomb, re-wrapped in new silk shrouds, and returned to the tomb following festive ceremonies in their honour'.

The influence of traditional religious perceptions and customs has remained strong in the Churches and in the lives of many Christians. This together with the influence of liberal theologies seems to have diminished the once fervent spiritual life. Today, many who attend church seem to have little understanding of their faith and their churches make the impression of being spiritually dead. This challenges Christians to pray and work for revival within and without the mainline churches. *Africa Inland Mission* belongs to those who have consciously responded to this challenge by taking the initiative of evangelistic work amongst nominal Christians, students, and non-Christians.

50. Africa's Old Colonisers after 1885

50.1. The Scramble[1]

During most of the 19th century the majority of the missionaries in sub-Saharan Africa were the guests of African rulers,[2] except for those who worked under British rule at the Cape and some other places, and those who worked near the Portuguese colonial centres. However, this rapidly changed. Economic and other interests enticed countries like France, Germany and Belgium, preceded by Britain, to colonise the whole of Africa.

In the 1870s King Leopold II of Belgium had already claimed the Congo, while Portugal had strengthened its grip on Angola and Mozambique. In 1882 Britain occupied Egypt. The *Berlin Conference* of 1885 made a plan of partition; this initiated the *Scramble for Africa*. Before 1880 only 10% of Africa was controlled by European Powers. The European-controlled areas consisted of colonies dotted along the coast of West Africa from the defunct slave trade, settlements in southern Africa by Dutch, English, and Portuguese, and Algeria in the north, conquered by the French.

Berlin Conference of 1884-1885 of the foreign ministers of 14 Western states, to divide Africa. This meeting was held at the Berlin residence of Chancellor Otto von Bismarck in 1884 (from: The Horizon: History of Africa, American Heritage Publishing Co., New York, 1971, page 452).

Other African territories were taken by the Italians (Libya, Eritrea, and part of Somaliland), and by Spain (part of Morocco, part of the Western Sahara: Equatorial Guinea). By 1902 only Ethiopia and Liberia had remained free of European control. By this point in history, even the Dutch *Afrikaner Republics* in South Africa were conquered by the English in the infamous *Boer War*. A history of 75 years of Western colonial rule over Africa had begun.

In the period 1885-1960 the number of Christians grew remarkably, from 4 million in 1900 to 34 million in the 1950s, being then about 20% of the population.[3] The

---

[1] Cf.: Thomas Pakenham, *The Scramble for Africa 1876-1912*, London: Abacus, 1991.

[2] Cf.: Ward, 'Africa', in: Hastings (ed) *World History*, pp.216f.

[3] Cf.: Shaw, *Kingdom*, p.207, who quoted: R.Oliver, *The African Experience*, San Francisco: Harper/Collins, p.207, and with: K.Fiedler, 'Christian Missions and Western Colonialism: Soulmates or Antagonists?' in:

missionary movement aimed at the conversion of Africans to Christianity emerged together with imperialism, followed by colonialism, but they were not necessarily partners. In the chapter 52 we will look at the relationship between mission and colonialism. But first we need to see how the events of the *Scramble for Africa* profoundly changed the political situation in the continent.

Map of Africa about 1880, at the time when the Scramble was about to start.

50.2. The British

Britain's imperialistic activities in Africa were aimed at finding new markets and raw materials, attaining world prestige, and spreading the English style of orderly government. They also wanted to safeguard their interests by protecting their overseas territories from German or French invasions.

a. Egypt and the Sudan

After the French completed the Suez Canal in 1869 the British began to take notice of Egypt. Britain realised that the Suez Canal would make travel to India faster and less expensive. The only problem the British had with the Suez Canal was that it was controlled by the French. After defeating Arabs and Egyptians who had risen against foreign intrusion, the British became the most powerful force in Egypt and France lost her claim for not helping put down the rebellion.

In 1885 British troops pushing south from Egypt encountered resistance from a large Muslim Sudanese army which defeated the army of General Charles Gordon, killing the General himself in a massacre at Khartoum. In 1898 the reconquest of the Anglo-

---

K.R.Ross, ed., *Faith at the Frontiers of Knowledge*, Blantyre: CLAIM, 1998 [Kachere Series no.6], p.224, who quoted: D. Barrett, *World Christian Encyclopedia: A Comparative Survey of Churches and Religions in the Modern World AD 1900-2000*, Nairobi/Oxford/New York, 1982.

Egyptian Sudan under General Horatio Kitchener ended with the Omdurman massacre. Later Kitchener's army at Fashoda almost clashed with a French force in the regions of the Upper Nile, one of the few unclaimed areas left by then. This almost led to a European war until the French pulled out.[4]

To secure the sea routes to India and the Far East the British considered it necessary to colonise Somalia. The first treaty was signed in 1827, and in the 1880's Somali tribes formed a British Protectorate. There were wars against Muslim fundamentalist Muhammad bin Abdullah, called the 'mad mullah' in the years before the *First World War*, and during the *Second World War* against Italian invaders. For their military campaigns the British not only used troops from Europe but also from the colonies. An example is the *King's African Rifles*,[5] recruited from Nyasaland (Malawi), Kenya, Tanganyika, Uganda and British Somaliland, an army unit that from 1902-1966 was active in Somaliland, Kenya, Tanganyika, Ethiopia, and other parts of the British Empire.

Charles Gordon (1833-1885), commander of the British army defeated and killed in the Battle of Khartoum.

b. South Africa

After the *Berlin Conference*, British colonialism in Southern Africa intensified. The conflict between the British government, which claimed sovereignty over those areas, and the Boers culminated, after the discovery of gold in the Boer territories, in the *South African War* or the *Boer War* 1899-1902, which brought Transvaal and Orange Free State under British rule. Given self-government in 1907, they were formed, with Cape Colony and Natal, into the *Union of South Africa* in 1910. A very important role in British colonialism in Southern Africa was played by Cecil John Rhodes (1853-1902). He was a financier, statesman, and philosopher of mystical imperialism. Rhodes dreamed of a railway from the Cape to Cairo. His ideal was that the whole of Africa eventually would be under British control. He went to Africa in 1870, became a diamond miner, and in 1888 he started a very successful mining company, called the *De Beers*, that by 1891 owned ninety percent of the world's diamond mines. Once he was elected to the Cape Parliament, and in 1890 as Prime Minister, he began to pursue his territorial dreams. However, resistance by the Boers and interference by German colonialism made it impossible for him to reach his objectives. In chapters 57, 58 and 59 we will see that, facilitated by the plans of Rhodes and of other empire builders, Botswana, Southern Rhodesia (later Zimbabwe), Northern Rhodesia (later Zambia), and Nyasaland (later Malawi) were added to the British Empire.

---

[4] N.R.Norman, *Africa and Europe: From Roman Times to National Independence*, Holmes and Meier, 1984[2]; P.Bohannan and P. Curtin, *African and Africans*, Waveland Press, 1995[4]; P. Curtin (ed.), *African History: From Earliest Times to Independence*, Addison Wesley, 1995[2].

[5] Clement A.D. Namangale, *A Brief History of the Origins of the Malawi Rifles to Mark the Centenary of the Formation of the King's African Rifles, 1902-2002*, Lilongwe: Malawi Defence Force, 2002; Cf. Colin Baker, *A Fine Chest of Medals: The Life of Jack Archer*, Cardiff: Mpemba Books, 2003; For an extensive study of the K.A.R, see: H.Moyse-Bartlett, *The King's African Rifles: A Study in the Military History of East and Central Africa, 1890-1945*, 2 volumes, Ridgewood: Naval & Military Press, nd.

c. Sierra Leone

In chapter 47.1 we saw how Sierra Leone had become a free haven for returning slaves. In 1794 the French plundered the colony. In 1807 the private rights of the Sierra Leonean company were transferred to the British government, the same year that the British Parliament declared the slave trade illegal. British warships that captured slave ships brought the freed slaves to the colony and thus the population grew. Internal exploration continued and an agreement with the French delineating the frontier was signed in 1895, shutting out Sierra Leone from its natural hinterland. In 1896 it became a *British Protectorate*, which remained separate from the colony of Freetown until 1951.

British Colonial Africa by 1915 (from: Hildebrandt, History, p.141)

d. Ghana

The West African 'Gold Coast' (later Ghana) since the late 15th century had been the stage of Portuguese, Dutch, Danish, and English activity. Trade in gold and slaves was the main interest. The slave trade was fed by the taking of prisoners of war, because of the continual conflict between the Ashanti and the Fante tribes. With the abolition of the slave trade in 1807 control passed from the merchants to the British government. British control gradually predominated on the coast and was recognised by the Ashanti. In 1824 after inciting the Fante to rise against the Ashanti, the British occupied the interior. In 1826 the Ashanti were defeated. Eventually treaties were worked out between the Fante and Ashanti. The Ashanti war of 1873-74 resulted in the extension of British influence. Further exploration north of Ashanti with various treaties secured the Northern Territories of the Gold Coast in 1897.

e. Nigeria

British influence in Nigeria began through the activities of the *National Africa Company* (the *Royal Niger Company* from 1886), which bought Lagos from an African chief 1861 and steadily extended its hold over the Niger Valley until it surrendered its charter in 1899; in 1903 the two protectorates of North and South Nigeria were proclaimed, and in 1914 they were merged to become Britain's largest African colony.

f. East Africa

In chapter 49.2 we noticed that through the CMS-missionaries Krapf and Erhardt and particularly through Rebmann Protestant Christianity had entered East Africa before the rise of Western colonialism. Because of its climate, East Africa was far more suitable for settlement by white colonists than the colonies in the west. Once again, private companies under charter from the British government pioneered the way, establishing their control over Kenya in 1888 and Uganda in 1890.

From the 8th century Arabs and Persians had made settlements along the coast gaining some political supremacy and leading to the formation of the so called *Zanj Empire*. The Masai pastoral people came into the area in the 18th century from the north and during the 19th century the agricultural Kikuyu steadily advanced from the south. In chapter 44.5 we saw that Portuguese traders operated in the region during the 16th and 17th centuries and that Roman Catholic mission had made an early attempt. However, control of the coastal towns was still under the Sultan of Zanzibar, until concessions were made to the British and Germans in the 19th century. British coastal trade began in the 1840s. In 1887 a trading company secured the lease of a coastal strip from the Sultan of Zanzibar. The Germans also courted concessions and soon agreements between Britain and Germany ratified British claims to the districts inland from Mombasa. With more concessions and agreements with the Germans, the company's lands spread from the coast up to Ethiopia in the north and Lake Victoria in the west. In 1895 the territories became a *British Protectorate* and in 1920 Kenya became a Colony. From 1896 until 1903 the railway from Mombasa to Lake Victoria was built, thus linking Kenya with Uganda.

Edward Mutesa II, King of Buganda from 1924 to 1969 and President of Uganda from 1963 to 1966.

With regard to Uganda we here connect to chapter 49.4, which described the importance of the Kingdom of Buganda that dominated the lands of Lake Victoria in the 18th and 19th centuries. Mutesa I, the Kabaka or King of Buganda, welcomed English explorers hoping for protection against Arab slave and ivory traders. Anglican and French Roman Catholic missionaries entered the country, as well as Muslim missionaries sent by the Arabs. Following Mutesa's death in 1884 tensions developed between his successor, Mwanga, and the Anglicans, Catholics and Muslims culminating in successively the killing of a number of Christians, and factional fighting. In an Anglo-German treaty of 1890 Uganda was assigned to Britain. The British *East Africa Company* placed Buganda and the western states Ankole and Toro under its protection, and in 1894 these territories became a British Protectorate. After the Second World War, the last Kabaka, Mutesa II backed the protectorate government in suppressing Buganda nationalist risings in 1945 and 1949. In 1953 he tried to secede his Kingdom from the protectorate but that was denied by the Ugandan High Court and he was deported, only to return in 1955 as constitutional monarch.

Tanganyika (later Tanzania) became German East Africa (see also chapter 49.4). In 1890 Germany, which had already relinquished its interests in Uganda, ceded her interests in Zanzibar to Britain in exchange for Heligoland, an island off the German coast. The *First World War* ousted Germany from the African continent (see chapter 51.3).

g. Decolonisation

Among the British African colonies Egypt was the first to become independent, in 1951. The Sudan followed in 1956. Then, the Gold Coast, renamed Ghana, followed in 1957. Then came Nigeria (1960), Sierra Leone (1961), British Cameroons (1961), later to be divided into independent Cameroon and Nigeria, Tanganyika (1961), later to become Tanzania, Uganda (1962), Kenya (1963), Zambia (1964), Nyasaland (1964), later to become Malawi, The Gambia (1965), Botswana (1966), Swaziland (1968), and, after a period of unilateral independence and guerrilla warfare (1980) Rhodesia, later to become Zimbabwe.

50.3. The Portuguese

a. Extension

After 1885, the Portuguese increased their efforts to extend effective rule to the remote parts of the vast regions that they had claimed. In Southern Africa their aspirations even stretched beyond the boundaries of Angola and Mozambique (see also: chapter 47.5). Whereas the British wanted to occupy an uninterrupted territory that would link the Cape and Cairo, the Portuguese wanted to connect their colonies in the West and in the East of Africa. That is why the Portuguese attempted to include the South of Nyasaland (present Malawi) and Northern Rhodesia (present Zambia) in their colonial empire. Portuguese intentions for Nyasaland were much disliked by Protestant missionaries, and finally they clashed with the British colonial Empire.

In Angola and Mozambique the extension of Portuguese administration also brought about a confrontation with the interests of Protestant mission. Nationalistic cultural pride (*Lusitanianism*) and a traditional preference for Roman Catholicism were the two important factors that hardened intrinsic anti-Protestant tendencies. In the early 20th century this began to make life difficult for Protestant missionaries and the churches they had established.

b. Lusitanianism

Portuguese cultural nationalism could not tolerate the Protestant way of using African vernacular languages in education and mission work. The use of the Portuguese language was demanded, especially for schools. In 1921 the colonial government decreed that all schools should teach only in the Portuguese language. They forbade teaching or printing of books in the African languages. Everything was to be communicated in Portuguese. This measure especially hindered Protestant missionary and educational work.[6] Protestant missionaries worked at learning the local languages, in part to communicate better with the people in

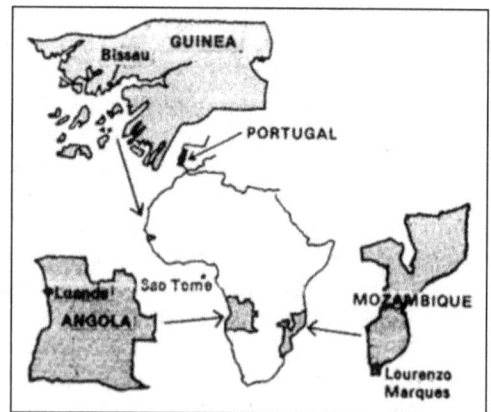

Map of Portuguese Africa by 1914 (from: Hildebrandt, History).

---

[6] Decree 77 of 17th December 1921, issued by the High Commission of the Portuguese Republic. For a translation of the text, see: Paas, *Het Protestantisme in Angola*, pp.53-56; cf. Hildebrandt, *History of the Church in Africa*, p.135.

the field, particularly to translate the Bible into the African tongues. The decree was followed by the *Colonial Act* of 1930 which advanced the view that Portuguese Roman Catholic missions overseas were 'instruments of civilisation and national influence.'

c. Between Concordat and World Council of Churches

The tendency of favouring Roman Catholicism, was emphatically confirmed by a *Concordat* concluded between the Portuguese State and the Roman Catholic Church on 7th May 1940. In this Pact the Portuguese State pledged to teach the Roman Catholic religion in state schools. It also included a missionary agreement that promised public money and other facilities to Roman Catholic missions in the overseas provinces. Protestant Missions were permitted to engage in educational activities, but without subsidy and on condition that Portuguese be the language of instruction.

The Portuguese colonial empire had started earlier and was disbanded later than other European colonial empires. Whereas the other powers, except for the Soviet Union, gave up their colonies around 1960, Portuguese overseas rule remained until 1974. In the meantime, protests against Portuguese colonial presence grew stronger, not only inside Africa, but also in Europe and America. The *World Council of Churches* (WCC), founded in 1948, contributed much to an almost universal outcry against Portugal. The WCC to a certain extent was motivated by the desire to defend classical Protestantism that suffered under Portuguese nationalism and Romanism. In general, however, the WCC supported religious liberalism and subsequently a kind of ecumenism that was less motivated by Scripture than by modern ideology.

d. Wars and Independence

This situation created room for the Portuguese to continue maintaining their colonial presence in and outside Africa. The Soviet Union tried to win influence in the 'third world' at the expense of the West by giving military support to liberation movements that had risen against oppressive regimes. The Portuguese in their propaganda of defending their colonial empire pretended to defend the interests of the West as a whole. Yet the Portuguese increasingly clashed with public opinion in the West which coincided with growing resistance of Africans in the Portuguese colonies. Wars of liberation were started by Africans. The Portuguese reacted by military and political action. In 1971, through issuing a special Law, they changed their religious policy. Full religious freedom was proclaimed. However, the law did not take away the main conditions of the old 'missionary agreement' that favoured Roman Catholicism.[7] Eventually

Jonas Savimbi (†2002), leader of the UNITA liberation movement which later became a rebel army in independent Angola.

Portuguese rule in Africa collapsed as a result of the combined effect of Western public opinion and African resistance. The Portuguese handed over power a decade later than most of the other colonisers. In 1975 Angola, Mozambique, Guinea Bissau, Cape Verde, São Tomé and Principe became independent.

---

[7] State Law no 4/71 of 21st August 1971 on religious freedom; for a translation, see: Paas, *Het Protestantisme in Angola*, pp.48-52.

A new era started. Yet the newly won political and religious freedom was seriously undermined by the continuation of war. African liberation movements were deeply divided along the front between Western interests and Soviet-communist interests. That is why the ex-Portuguese countries became a stage where the competing world powers tried their weaponry. The Soviet Union and the United States each supported opposing parties in a series of devastating and cruel civil wars that continued for decades. In Angola the MPLA[8] and the UNITA,[9] and in Mozambique the FRELIMO[10] and the RENAMO[11] were the parties that tried to destroy one another. Some leaders of these former liberation movements continued fighting long after they had lost in the competition for power. A notable example was Jonas Savimbi. As founder and leader of UNITA he once was a promising factor in Angola's struggle for political and religious freedom.[12] But gradually he became deranged and got entangled in a cruel and useless struggle for personal victory and glory, until he was murdered in 2002.

In the early 1990s the situation changed as a result of the collapse of the Soviet Union and of international communism. As power patterns in the world had become different, the opposing parties in the Angolan and Mozambican civil wars lost their allies. Gradually peace was restored under new governments. In the new era there were chances for development and freedom. The churches have profited from this. The Roman Catholic Church has been liberated from its very close ties with the State. It has made an effort to reorganise and to make clear that the Church does not operate anymore on the side of the oppressor. These attempts have improved its image. Numerically the Roman Catholic Church in both countries is still the largest one. But Protestant Churches are growing now that they have acquired freedom for evangelism and mission. Old and new foreign missions are free to enter Angola and Mozambique.

---

[8] Movimento Popular de Libertação de Angola.
[9] União Nacional para a Independência Total de Angola.
[10] Frente de Libertação de Moçambique.
[11] Resistência Nacional Moçambicana.
[12] Cf.: Fred Bridgland, *Jonas Savimbi: A Key to Africa*, Edinburgh: Mainstream Publ., 1986; Sousa Jamba, *Patriots*, London: Penguin/ Viking, 1990.

51. Africa's New Colonisers after 1885

51.1. The Belgians

a. Congo Free State

The *Congo Free State* was a private kingdom owned by Leopold II of Belgium between about 1877 and 1908. It included the area now known as the Democratic Republic of the Congo. The kingdom was the scene of exploitation, greed, and mass killings and maimings of those who opposed Leopold's rule or who did not work hard enough as forced labourers in rubber plantations or other profit-making ventures.

Leopold II (1835-1909), King of Belgium, until 1908 private ruler over the Congo Free State.

At the *Berlin Conference* in 1885, King Leopold gained international support for his creation of the Congo Free State through proposals to end slavery in the Congo, protect the rights of the natives, and guarantee free trade. In the popular media he was often portrayed as a philanthropist who was selflessly devoting his efforts to rescue and civilise the peoples of Central Africa.

Soon, however, reports from missionaries and merchants began to filter to Europe and the United States about slave labour, mutilations, and other forms of torture used to increase the collection of ivory, rubber, and other products. Most of the missions were Protestant, mainly British and American Baptist and Presbyterian and Swedish Lutheran. The first one to start work in the Congo was the *Livingstone Inland Mission*, led by Fanny Guinness. It started work in the Congo in 1878.[1] Fiedler says that the first agitation against the atrocities was connected to the Guinness family, and that the first missionary to make them public was J.B. Murphy of the *American Baptist Missionary Union*.[2]

Leopold did not give preference to any religion, but he wanted Belgian missionaries in the first place, which practically excluded Protestants. To this end he even made an agreement with the Vatican, which gave way to the newly founded *Society of Scheut* and to Belgian Jesuits. However, the Belgian Roman Catholics were unable to fulfil the need for missionaries and the rapid spread of Protestant missions could not be stopped.[3] In general, the early relations of Protestant missionaries with the Belgian rulers were not warm. During the existence of the *Congo Free State* often Protestant missionaries witnessed and publicised abuses against the population. Reports of atrocities were systematically countered by Leopold's sophisticated public relations efforts.

In 1893, a young writer, inspired to adventure by the celebrated travels of Henry M. Stanley and believing the glowing reports of Leopold's rule, got a job on a steamer heading up the Congo River. Joseph Conrad turned his Congo experiences into the novel *Heart of Darkness*, published in 1899, describing in fiction the horrors he saw.

---

[1] Fiedler,*Story of Faith Missions*, pp.37-39,72.
[2] Fiedler, *Story of Faith Missions*, pp.227,228.
[3] Hastings, *Church in Africa*, p.416.

51. Africa's New Colonisers after 1885

Efforts to bring widespread public attention to atrocities in the Congo were largely unsuccessful until Edmund Dene Morel formed the *Congo Reform Association* in 1904. Morel's interest in the subject grew from hearing accounts of the Congo from merchants with whom he had contact as a clerk for a Liverpool shipping company. Born in France and speaking French fluently, he was often sent to Belgium on company business. He resigned from his job with the shipping company in 1901 to work full-time as a journalist, to highlight conditions in the Congo more directly. Morel was an able journalist being careful to provide documentation that would stand despite Leopold's denials. He was also able to organise a trans-Atlantic movement for reform in the Congo that included some of the leading political and cultural figures in Britain and the United States.

Joseph Conrad (1857-1924), whose original name was Joseph Korzeniowski, was a famous writer of short stories and novels. In Heart of Darkness (1902) he contributed to revealing the atrocities in the Congo Free State.

In September 1904, six months after he had founded the *Congo Reform Association*, Morel left for the United States to represent the Association at the *International Peace Conference* held in Boston. During the trip, Morel lobbied the American government, presenting a memorandum on the Congo to President Theodore Roosevelt, and helped to solidify the organisation of an American branch of the *Congo Reform Association* based in Boston.

Both branches gained support from leading political and cultural figures in both countries, including Arthur Conan Doyle in England, and Mark Twain and Booker T. Washington in America. Reports of slave labour, mutilations and other forms of torture employed to increase the collection of ivory and rubber were highlighted by this Association in efforts to end Leopold's rule of the Congo.

In 1908 King Leopold II formally relinquished personal control of the Congo Free State and the renamed Belgian Congo came under the administration of the Belgian Parliament.

Prisoners in the Congo Free State. This vast territory, which was the private domain of King Leopold II of Belgium until 1908, experienced excesses of colonialism. Millions of people died as a result of pacification, forced labour, portage, indiscriminate slaughter, and slavery-like conditions.

b. Congo Colony

The Belgian administration can be characterised as paternalistic colonialism favouring Roman Catholicism, though not excluding Protestant missions. The ruling élite consisted of the 'colonial trinity' of State, Roman Catholic Church, and the agro-industrial companies. Protestant missions did not belong to these institutions. That is why they did not enjoy the same degree of official confidence as was given to their Roman Catholic counterparts. For example, until after the end of the *Second World War* state subsidies for hospitals and schools, were reserved for Roman Catholic institutions. In the period between the world wars the number of Protestant missions more than doubled with the arrival of among them the Norwegian Baptists (1919), the American Mennonites (1920), the Seventh Day Adventists (1921), the Belgian Protestants (1921), the Swedish Evangelical Free Church (1921), the Assemblies of God (1921), the Ubangi Evangelical Mission (1923), and the Anglican Mission from Uganda (1926). Nevertheless, the number of Roman Catholic missionaries remained the largest force, and they continued to receive money and advice from the Belgian government. In 1926 the Belgian government and the Vatican agreed that all subsidies for education should be given to Roman Catholic Missions. It was only in 1948 that the law was changed 'to allow some Protestant Missions to receive government money'.[4]

The colonial government divided up the colony into spiritual franchises, giving each approved mission its own territory. Political administration fell under the total and direct control of the mother country; there were no democratic institutions. Native curfews and other restrictions were not unusual. Following the *Second World War* some democratic reforms began to be introduced, but these were complicated by ethnic rivalries among the African population.[5]

Protestant teaching was mistrusted, especially when it prepared for leadership by Africans. For this reason Simon Kimbangu, a successful Baptist preacher, was put in prison, where he stayed until his death in 1951. Yet his followers formed a very big Church, which was not allowed to exist by the authorities. The *Kimbanguist Movement* was instrumental in preparing the Congo for independence. Kimbangu inspired nationalist leaders like Joseph Kasavubu.[6]

c. Independence

The Belgian Congo became independent in 1960, later was renamed Zaire, and after that the Democratic Republic of Congo. The Belgian colonies Rwanda and Burundi became independent in 1961.

At independence in 1960 some forty-six Protestant missions were at work in the Congo, the majority of them North American, British, or Scandinavian in origin. The missions established a committee to maintain contact and minimise competition among them. This body evolved into a union called the *Church of Christ in the Congo* (l'Eglise du Christ au Congo). This united Protestant Church was established in 1935 by ten missions. In 1972 the government of Zaire decreed that all Protestant churches should either join the union or disband. The *Church of Christ* developed rules that permitted

---

[4] Hildebrandt, *History of the Church in Africa*, pp.212-217.
[5] This section leans on: J. Zwick: *Reforming the Heart of Darkness: The Congo Reform Movement in England and the United States*; Wikipedia Encyclopedia, *Scramble for Africa*, and *Congo Free State*.
[6] A. Hastings, *A History of African Christianity 1950-1975*, Cambridge UP, 1979, pp.84,85,124,131.

members of one evangelical congregation to move to and be accepted by another. This organisation of Protestant Churches is one of the four mainstreams of Christianity in the Congo, beside the Roman Catholics, the Greek Orthodox and the Kimbanguists.

51.2. The French

a. Before Berlin 1885

To some extent France belonged to the old colonisers of Africa. At least two countries of Africa had met with French colonial power before the *Berlin Conference* of 1884/1885, Madagascar and Algeria.

With the French conquest of Algiers in 1830, the Ottoman rule ended, and Algeria became French. They occupied the North African nation and relentlessly pursued the objective of extending French sovereignty to Algeria. The French liked to consider Algeria as an ordinary province of France. That is why many French from Europe migrated to this region of North Africa. However, many Algerian Muslims expressed disagreement, either by armed and unarmed resistance, or by emigration to a Muslim territory. One of the results was a bloody guerrilla war waged by the Algerian people and the forced extirpation of French colonialism from Algeria in the late 1950s.

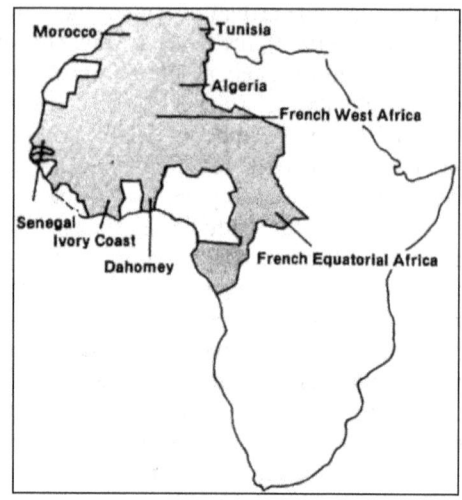

French Colonial Africa by 1915 (from: Hildebrandt, History, p.140).

France's attempts to get a foothold on the island of Madagascar date from the 17th century. They were interrupted by the *French Revolution*, and resumed in the second half of the 19th century. Some years before the *Berlin Conference* the French began to rule the island as their colony. In 1960 Madagascar became an independent country. In chapter 49.7 Madagascar's history as a French colony, including the position of Mission and Church, is briefly described.

b. From Berlin 1885

In France's colonial history in the rest of North Africa and in sub-Saharan Africa a tradition of much military and political violence is continued. By the time of the *Berlin Conference* (1884/1885) the French had already claimed Senegal, Gabon, and North Congo, and from Senegal they penetrated inland to the Niger River. They actually sought to expand their influence in the whole of North Africa and from West Africa to Eastern Sudan. They negotiated treaties with African leaders from a powerful military position. France focused on the military direction of the expansion, by going from fort to fort and taking over control. The French were harsh in their administration and in their attempts to increase economic footholds. They used forced labour and imprisonment of Africans to maintain and expand their interests. By 1900 France had occupied large territories of North West and Central Africa.

In the North the French extended their rule to the Muslim territories of Morocco and Tunisia. In West Africa they added to their empire Dahomey, French Guinea, French Sudan, the Ivory Coast, Mauritania, Niger, Senegal, and Upper Volta. These eight overseas territories were joined together in a Federation in 1895. The capital was Dakar. In Western Central Africa in 1910 they joined together four territories as the federation of *French Equatorial Africa*. It consisted of Gabon, Middle Congo, Chad, and Ubangi-Shari. The capital was Brazzaville.

We conclude this sub-section with a few remarks on mission in the French colonies of Africa, focusing on West and Western Central Africa. The French colonial authorities favoured Roman Catholic missions, and in general they wanted missionaries who were French citizens. In Senegal Roman Catholic mission had already started before French colonial rule. However, the favour of the colonial government did not include help in making converts among the Muslim majority with their history of almost 800 years. In the Ivory Coast Roman Catholic Mission started in 1895. After the missionary campaign of Harris in 1914, the Wesleyan Methodists were allowed to enter and do some limited work, 'trying to consolidate people who had responded to Harris's message'. In Dahomey, present-day Benin, the colonial government encouraged the Roman Catholic Society of African Missions, which about 1914 had become very large, and also permitted some work by the Wesleyan Methodists. In Gabon the Roman Catholic Church was much helped by the government with money and guidance, so that it grew more rapidly than the small number of Protestant missions that were allowed to enter. This was in line with what happened in the whole of *French Equatorial Africa*. The Pope had assigned this region to the French *Holy Ghost Fathers* making it to a special Vicariate, heavily supported by French financial assistance.

c. Decolonisation

Of the French North African colonies, Morocco and Tunisia were the first to receive independence, in 1956. Algeria had to wait until 1962. In 1958 the territories of the West African Federation became autonomous republics in the French Community, except for French Guinea, which became independent and withdrew from the French Community. The Federation was dissolved in 1959. In 1960 the other territories became fully independent within the French Community, Dahomey became Benin, French Sudan became Mali, Upper Volta became Burkina Faso; the others, the Ivory Coast, Mauritania, Niger, and Senegal did not change their names.

Also in 1960 the four territories of *French Equatorial Africa* became fully independent within the French Community: Gabon, the Congo, later to become Republic of the Congo, Chad, and Ubangi-Shari, later to become Central African Republic. This was followed by the independence of Cameroon (1960), Togo (1960), Madagascar (1960), Seychelles (1967), Mauritius (1968), Equatorial Guinea (1968).

51.3. The Germans

a. The German Scramble

Germany joined the Scramble for Africa quite late (cf. chapters 49.4 and 50.2.g). The Germans followed the example of France and Britain, knowing that these powerful nations would not waste their time, resources, and energy on something that was not profitable. Otto Von Bismarck and the rest of Germany felt that colonisation in Africa would help Germany and force others to reckon with them.

The German colonial presence in Africa basically concerned four territories. It began in 1884, just before the opening of the *Berlin Conference*, by taking control of the Cameroons. One week after the Conference ended, in 1885, Germany took possession of Tanganyika, hence called German East Africa, present-day Tanzania. Then, it claimed Togoland, a small strip between Dahomey and the Gold Coast. Finally, Germany colonised South West Africa, present-day Namibia. There were also periods of German colonial rule in Burundi, Rwanda, and Zanzibar.

b. The Cameroons and Togo

In the Cameroons the strict Germanification programme made life difficult for the English *Baptist Mission*, started by Alfred Saker, in the Duala area (see chapter 47.4.a). In 1886 they handed over the work to the *Basel Mission*, a Swiss organisation with Swiss and German personnel. The *Basel Mission* was followed by a German Baptist Mission in 1890. In the same year German Roman Catholics and American Presbyterians were welcomed by the German colonial rulers. Missionaries were not allowed to work in strong Muslim areas.

In the *First World War* France and Britain divided the Cameroons; a small portion in the north-west became British and the larger part became a French colony. The French wanted all German missionaries permanently out. Protestant work was taken over by the *Paris Missionary Society* and Roman Catholic work by the French *Holy Ghost Fathers*.[7]

In Togo the arrival of the North German *Bremen Mission* preceded German colonial rule. They started work in the 1850s. After the establishment of colonial rule, the *Basel Mission* arrived; they left in 1902, only to return in 1912. The Roman Catholics started work in Togo in 1890. During the First World War the French and the British ended German rule over Togo, and in 1916 German missionaries were forced to leave. The work of the *Basel Mission* was taken over by the *United Free Church of Scotland*. The work of the *Bremen Mission* was handed over to African pastors, one of them was R.D. Baeta. In 1924 the British allowed the German missions to return to British colonies, including the territories taken over from German colonial rule. Subsequently German and Scottish missionaries in Togo and the Gold Coast cooperated for the establishment of one African Reformed Church.[8]

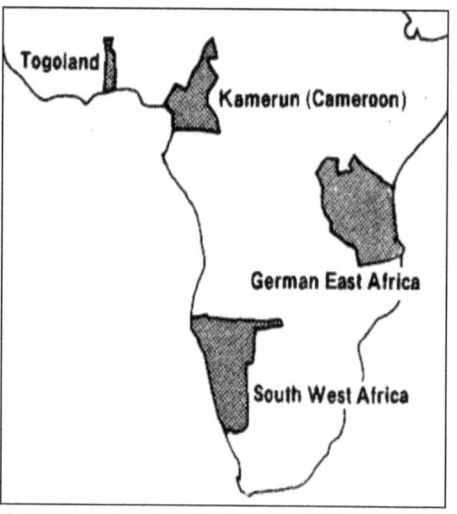

German Colonial Africa by 1914 (from: Hildebrandt, *History*, p.143).

---

[7] Hildebrandt, *History of the Church in Africa*, pp.162-664,211,212.
[8] Hildebrandt, *History of the Church in Africa*, pp.157,200-202.

c. German East Africa

When German rule in Tanzania began, the *Roman Catholics*, the *Church Missionary Society*, the *London Missionary Society* and the *Universities Mission* had already established mission stations in the country. In chapter 49.4 we noticed that German colonial rule was followed by the arrival of German missionary organisations. Now German organisations were added, *Berlin III* (1887), the *Berlin Missionary Society* (1891), the *Moravian Mission* (1891), the *Leipzig Missionary Society*, and the *Bethel Mission* 1893 the CMS withdrew to Kenya, handing over its work to the Leipzig Mission. Missionary work was weakened by the First World War. It took the Allied Forces four years to defeat the German army and its able commander Paul von Lettow-Vorbeck. German missionaries had to leave. The young Church was severely hit by this, although from Kenya the *Church Missionary Society*, and from Malawi the *Universities Mission* and the *Scottish Missions* tried to help out. In 1925 the German missionary societies began to return to their former regions.[9]

d. South-West Africa

In Namibia, or South West Africa, German presence had begun in the 1870s, before the colonial annexation, with the arrival of German missionaries. In 1842 the *Rhenish Missionary Society* started work beyond the Orange River. Later the *Finnish Missionary Society* entered the North. After 1907, also the Roman Catholics made progress in Namibia.[10]

Adrian Dietrich Lothar von Trotha (1848-1920), German military commander in Tanganyika, Rwanda, Burundi, and Namibia.

The establishment of colonial rule was followed by an increase of white immigrants, many of them Germans. These settlers moved inland, occupying land. They clashed with the local Herero people in the North and the Nama people in the South, who refused to give up their land. This led to a brutal attack by German troops under the command of General Lothar von Trotha, notorious for his cruelties in Tanzania (Tanganyika), Rwanda and Burundi. In the period 1904-1907 his army butchery exterminated at least 65,000 Herero, that is about 80% of them, and about 10,000 Nama.[11] Church and Mission had tried to protect the Herero and Nama. Yet the colonial war made it much more difficult to lead African people to Christ.

e. Defeat

The Germans were the first European power to abandon their colonies. This was not an example of decolonisation, but a change of colonial ruler. After their defeat in the *First World War*, the Germans were forced to relinquish their colonies. Although a long and tough war was required to defeat them in Tanganyika (Tanzania), they were easily displaced from the Cameroons, Togo and South-West Africa. In 1921-1922 under the

---

[9] Hildebrandt, *History of the Church in Africa*, pp.226,227.
[10] Hildebrandt, *History of the Church in Africa*, pp.172,173.
[11] Cf.: Philip Ngunjiri, 'Germany Refuses to Apologize for Herero Holocaust' [Internet]; 'Herero and Namaqua Genocide [Internet].

Treaty of Versailles the *League of Nations* gave temporary supervision of these territories to other countries. Tanganyika became a British mandate. Burundi and Rwanda were mandated to Belgium. Togoland was divided between the British and the French. The British joined their part to the Gold Coast. The Cameroons were divided among the British and the French. Later, the French part became the independent state of Cameroon together with the Southern section of British Cameroon. Northern British Cameroon was added to Nigeria (1972). South-West Africa was mandated to the *Union of South Africa* and became the independent state of Namibia in 1990.

52. Missions and Colonialism 1885-1960

52.1. Protestant and Roman Catholic Missions

In the previous chapter we surveyed the way most of Africa was colonised by European powers after 1885. By this the question of the relationship between Missions and Colonialism arose.[1] We noted that Christian institutions from Europe had already started to send missionaries to Africa before that date. In general, missionary presence preceded colonialist presence. Colonialist rule and Christian mission originated from different agencies at different times. Most European missionaries came from those countries that took part in the 'scramble for Africa', although quite a number of them did not work in regions ruled by their own people. In general, they were motivated by the revivals and awakenings that had taken place since the early 18th century.

Here are the names of some of the missionary societies that started activities in Africa from about 1800. In 1792 the *Baptist Missionary Society* (BMS) was founded by William Carey. In 1795 the *London Missionary Society* (LMS) started as an interdenominational organisation (Anglicans, Methodists, Presbyterians, and Congregationalists). In 1796 the *Edinburgh Missionary Society* (EMS) and the *Glasgow Missionary Society* (GMS) followed. Then, in 1797, the *Netherlands' Society of Missionaries* was organized by Van der Kemp and others. The *Church Missionary Society* (Evangelical Anglican) followed in 1799. In 1858 a society called the *Oxford and Cambridge Mission to Central Africa* was founded. The name was later changed to *Universities' Mission to Central Africa* (UMCA) and it first deployed activities in Malawi. In the 1870s the Free Church of Scotland and the Church of Scotland started organisations that were to work in Malawi as well.

In 1810 in the USA the *American Board of Commissioners for Foreign Missions* started to raise money for mission. The Baptist Foreign Mission Society (BFMS) followed in 1814, the *American Bible Society* in 1816, and the *General Missionary Society* (GMS) in 1818, the FMB of the Methodist Episcopalian Church, the FMS of the Protestant Episcopalian Church (1820), the FMB of the Presbyterian Church (1837).

The Germans began to work in Africa in 1822 with various organisations: the *Rhenish Missionary Society* (1818), the *Berlin Missionary Society* (1824), the *Leipzig* and the *Bremen Missionary Societies* (1836), the *Bauern Mission*, and the *Hermannsburger Mission* (1853). The French started with the *Paris Missionary Society* (1824), the Swedish started in Africa in 1835, and the Norwegians in 1842.

The above mentioned missionary societies represent the majority of Protestant missions that started work in Africa before the *Berlin Conference* and the ensuing *Scramble for Africa*. These organisations were related to the mainline Protestant churches in Europe and America, and as such they could be named *Classical Missions*. Towards the end of the 19th century the classical missions slowed down in reaching out to new mission fields for reasons that we will see in chapters 55 and 56. However, other Protestant bodies took over the initiative of sending missionaries. In general, they were private organisations, independent of denominational structures and clergy. As such, they were sometimes called *Post-Classical Missions* or more often *Faith Missions*.[2] The

---

[1] For this chapter, also: Shaw, *Kingdom*, pp.139-158; Baur, *2000 Years*, pp.103-152; Hastings, *Church in Africa*, pp.177-188,338-358; Ward, 'Africa', in: Hastings (ed), *World History*, pp.203-209.

[2] Cf.: Klaus Fiedler, *The Story of Faith Missions: From Hudson Taylor to Present-day Africa*, Oxford:

first one to arrive in Africa (1878) was the *Livingstone Inland Mission*, founded by Fanny Guinness.

In the 20th century some classical denominations resumed the initiative by founding new missionary societies. Among them were some Dutch Missions, e.g. the *Reformed Mission League*, who started work in Kenya in the 1960s and later in Malawi and other parts of Southern Africa, the *Christian Reformed Mission*, who work in Mozambique, and South Africa, and the *Mission of the Reformed Congregations*, who work in Nigeria.

The modern Roman Catholic Missions entered Africa later than most of the Protestant organisations. Actually, there had been a lot of Roman Catholic missionary activity in the 16th and 17th centuries. But it had either come to an end, or slowed down. Restoration of Roman Catholic influence in 19th century Europe eventually also affected Africa. Roman Catholic missions experienced a revival in the 1840s. To the old religious orders of the Benedictines, Dominicans, Franciscans, Jesuits, Augustinians, etc., a series of new orders and congregations were added. In the 19th century the *Holy Ghost Fathers* and the *White Fathers* were the first ones.

François Libermann (1802-1852), who revived the Congregation of the Holy Ghost (Holy Ghost Fathers), which opened the new beginning of Roman Catholic mission in Africa.

*The Congregation of the Holy Ghost.*³ This Congregation was originally founded in 1703 for the purpose of preparing missionaries. Since 1765 the Pope had entrusted it with direct care of mission in the French colonies. It suffered much from the French Revolution, and was threatened with extinction. In 1848 the dying Congregation was saved by François Libermann (1802-1852). Libermann was born in a Jewish family, but converted to Roman Catholicism in 1825. He opened a novitiate for the *Society of the Immaculate Heart of Mary* to send priests abroad, with a special interest in France's colonies. His order and the *Holy Ghost Fathers* merged. Libermann became superior general of the united Societies. The agreement included supervision of a seminary to train clergy for the French colonies, among them African black clergy. They started work on Africa's West Coast, and gradually spread to Angola, Senegal, Gambia, Sierra Leone, Gabon, the Congo, Nigeria, Guinea, and Spanish West Africa. They also started work on the East Coast, in Madagascar, Bagamoyo, and Kenya. Since the eventual downfall of Roman Catholic Mission in the 16th, 17th and 18th centuries, the *Holy Ghost Fathers* were practically the first Roman Catholic missionaries of the new era to arrive in Africa.

Charles Martial Allemand-Lavigerie (1825-1892), founder of the Missionaries of Our Lady of Africa (White Fathers), which started mission in various parts of Africa.

Secondly, the *White Fathers*. Charles Lavigerie (1825-1892), who was appointed by Pope Pius IX as the Archbishop of Algiers in 1867, used that position as a stepping stone to found the *Missionaries of our Lady of*

Regnum, 1994.

³ This religious order is also known as the *Spiritans*, or as the *Holy Ghost Fathers*.

Africa of Algeria, more popularly known as the White Fathers, since they dressed in flowing white Arab robes. Lavigerie's see included all of the Sahara and French Sudan; that is, all the nations bordering the Sahara, from the Atlantic Ocean eastward. In 1874 the work began to expand further south, to Equatorial Africa, the Congo, Tanganyika, and Nyasaland.

Other orders followed, including the *Congregation of the Mission* (Lazarists), the *Oblates of Mary Immaculate*, the *Society of Mary*, the *Oratorians and Oblates of St. Francis de Sales*, the *Redemptorists*, the *Paulists*, the *Congregation of the Sacred Hearts of Jesus and Mary*, and the *Priests of the Foreign Missions* (Missions Etrangères). Among the Colleges of the regular orders for the training of missionaries may be mentioned the College of St. Fidelis (Capuchin), the College of St. Anthony (Franciscan), the College of St. Isidore (Irish Franciscan), the College of the Irish Augustinians at Rome, the Seminary of Scheut, near Brussels (Congregation of the Immaculate Heart of Mary), and the Veronese Institute and the Colleges of the Society of the Divine Word.[4]

52.2. Competing Missionary Movements

Since the 16th century Protestantism and Roman Catholicism had been trying to counteract each other along the lines of Reformation and Counter Reformation. This religious struggle was continued in the African mission fields. It was also an important aspect of the relationship between the Colonialist State and the Mission organisations. In general, Roman Catholic colonising countries favoured Roman Catholic Mission. Some of them even prohibited Protestant missions to enter. On the other hand, the culture of Protestant colonial powers would be more compatible with Protestant missions. Yet on both sides there were exceptions.

In the interest of their Lusitanian nationalism and because of deeply rooted anti-clericalism the Portuguese often rejected interference by the Vatican and by other Roman Catholic nations. In some Portuguese colonies, especially Angola, but to a lesser extent in Mozambique, this created room for relatively relaxed relationships with the Anglo-Saxon world and for allowing missionaries from Protestant Europe and America.

King Leopold of Belgium deliberately prohibited non-Belgian Roman Catholic missionaries from entering the *Congo Free State*, though he permitted several Protestant missionaries to work there. The number of Belgian Roman Catholic missionaries increased steadily after Belgium took over administration of the Congo in 1908, and their relationship with the Belgian administration was as close.

French colonial rule before 1900 prohibited Protestant Missions to enter, and was exclusively allowing Roman Catholic missionaries to work. In French West Africa the colonial administrators arrived in the interior before the missionaries, all of whom were French Roman Catholics. Most of these were White Fathers, supported by the French government in order to ensure their compliance in the work of colonial pacification. At the turn of the century the French government turned anti-clerical, ended diplomatic relations with the Vatican, and ended subsidies to the missionaries in the colonies. The missionaries were nevertheless permitted to remain.

Roman Catholic missionaries in Africa were loyal to the cult of Mary and more interested in obedience to the Church's teachings and authority than in literacy or access

---

[4] *The Catholic Encyclopedia*, Volume X, Online Edition 2000.

to the Bible, which they believed could easily be misunderstood without proper filtering and interpretation by the church. Missionaries rarely addressed political or social issues out of that understanding.[5]

On the Protestant side there were many more exceptions. Protestant colonising powers did not make it impossible for Roman Catholic Missions to enter their territories. While generally the Protestant churches suffered in the French, Portuguese and Belgian colonies 'because of opposition and lack of support, the Roman Catholic Church in British Africa got the same subsidies as the Protestants'.[6]

At a later stage the position of Roman Catholicism further improved. Protestant Missions became critical of their own colonial governments as evidenced in their sympathy and support for African movements for independence. That is why colonial rulers began to mistrust Protestant missions. At the same time, the rulers started to become friendlier towards Roman Catholic missionary activities that seemed more in line with colonial paternalism and autocracy. Moreover, governments of the Protestant countries of Europe and America have never prohibited their own Roman Catholic minorities from sending missionaries overseas, or from receiving them in their colonies. Here are some examples of Roman Catholic institutions organised in or from traditionally Protestant countries that trained missionaries for Africa: English, Irish, Scotch, American, and Canadian Colleges at Rome, Josephinum College at Columbus on Ohio, United States, American College at Louvain in Belgium, English Colleges at Valladolid in Spain and Lisbon in Portugal, Scotch College at Valladolid in Spain, St. Joseph's Seminary of the *Mill Hill Fathers* at London in Britain; and St. Joseph's College at Rozendaal in The Netherlands.

The histories of Roman Catholicism and Protestantism in Africa contain many instances of mutual mistrust and a spirit of competition. The Colonial States often used this situation to their own political benefit. This pattern of negative relationship changed to a certain extent when, in the 1960s the colonial states were disbanded and replaced by African governmental systems. For Roman Catholicism the decolonisation process in Africa coincided with the *Second Vatican Council* (1962-65). Vatican II introduced a programme of *aggiornamento*, i.e. adaptation to the modern age. As a result of this the Roman Catholic Church in the Western homelands and in the former mission fields made a number of changes in its practical attitude towards Protestants. The Council opened the door to co-operation with Protestant Churches. The use of the vernacular, rather than Latin, in worship was prescribed. They also permitted, and even encouraged African Roman Catholics to read Protestant vernacular translations of the Bible, and strongly cooperated in joint Bible translation efforts.[7]

The scene has become much more African. By the early 1970s the European missionary priests and bishops began to leave Africa, voluntarily relinquishing their leadership positions to African churchmen. By the time of the *African Synod* of 1994 ninety percent of the hierarchy was African.[8] The changes at least led to greater

---

[5] Cf.: Hastings, *Church in Africa*; Hastings, *African Catholicism: Essays in Discovery*, London: SCM Press, 1989, passim; Isichei, *A History of Christianity*. Bauer, *2000 Years of Christianity*, passim;

[6] Hildebrand, *History of the Church in Africa*, p.227.

[7] A product of such joint work is the new translation of the Bible into Chichewa, *Buku Loyera*, published by the Bible Society of Malawi in 1998.

[8] Cf.: Thomas J. Reese (S.J.), *The Synod on the Church in Africa* (part 1), *The African Synod: You had to be there* (Part 2), America Press 1994.

openness between Roman Catholics and Protestants. But Africanness and openness do not necessarily take away the fundamental differences in theology and ecclesiology. Sometimes Africans themselves contributed to reappearance of the old problems. As the missionaries left the African bishops often became more conservative than their white predecessors, and began to undo some of the reforms initiated by the missionary priests and bishops. This coincided with a political shift to an increasingly repressive series of regimes in the 1970s. In the 1990s a number of the more repressive African regimes were overthrown and a greater openness became possible again. Partly as a result of this, the African Roman Catholic Church gathered in a great and important Synod, held in Rome, in 1994. This *African Synod* tried to list and solve some of the old and new problems that had risen. The Synod stressed the need to inculturate Christianity in the areas of liturgy, marriage, and reverence for ancestors.[9]

In general, the Colonial States of the 19th and 20th centuries, either originating from Protestant Europe or from Roman Catholic Europe, were not very much interested in religion. They were very much the products of the *Enlightenment* and of *Secularism*, and as such they did not have much use for the Church and for orthodox Christian beliefs. Christian Mission was not their first priority. The main focus was on an equilibrium of power and a maximum of economic profit. This they tried to reach through systems of *Indirect Rule* (the British), aiming at creating distance between the colonial rulers and the Africans, or *Direct Rule* (the French and the Portuguese), aiming at assimilation of the Africans. Christian Mission could disturb the equilibrium and diminish the profits. That is why British and French colonial officials often actively discouraged Christian mission work in Muslim areas. As a result of this Islam was able to consolidate its hold in certain African colonies. In this concern modern African political leaders do not seem to be much different from their colonial predecessors. Will the Church be able to challenge the State by redefining its Biblical call of mission to the Muslim masses?

Now we will have a closer look at this period in African history, especially highlighting the relationship or interaction between colonialism and mission.

52.3. Accusations

The unprecedented success of Christian missions in colonial Africa has been severely criticised in some quarters. Shaw mentions four major criticisms: (a) *collaboration* with the government, (b) cultural and religious *imperialism*, (c) *paternalism* in the church, and (d) *indoctrination* in education.[10]

The *first charge* is that 'missionary and colonial powers were allies in oppression ... partners in the crime of imperialism'. Missionaries and colonialists are seen as *soulmates*. Here Fiedler refers to the Marxist concept that reduces religion to 'just a reaction to material deprivation'. In the Marxist view Christianity was successful in Africa, because it was 'part and parcel of the colonial machinery of oppression', and the missionaries were collaborators in that machinery just as much as the explorers, traders, and soldiers. Missionaries 'had the important task of keeping the engine of colonialism

---

[9] Hastings, *African Catholicism: Essays in Discovery*, pp.128,129; Aylward Shorter, 'The Roman Catholic Church in Africa Today', in: C. Fyfe et al. (eds) *Christianity in Africa in the 1990s*, Edinburgh: Centre of African Studies, University of Edinburgh, 1996, pp.22-38.
[10] Shaw, *Kingdom*, pp.207-210.

from overheating and thereby destroying itself'. Not only did they lubricate the system by preserving its social relations, they also sweetened and softened the harsh impact of colonialism to the taste of the Africans, so that the Africans would be obedient subjects and useful workers. According to Marxist theory, African Christianity would collapse at the end of colonialism. When the Marxists observed that their prediction did not come true, they labelled the period after 1960 as *neo-colonialism*, which enabled them to continue applying their theories to the growth of Christianity in Africa and elsewhere in the Third World.[11] The other accusations are closely related to this first one.

According to the *second charge*, the missionaries were religious imperialists. They were intolerant of African culture and religion; to them there was nothing valuable in it.

The *third charge* is that missionaries demanded total control of the heart and the mind of the Africans. They ruled the church, even when Africans were capable of leadership. Paternalistically they addressed the African as if he or she were a child.

The *fourth of the charges* mentioned by Shaw is that the missionaries indoctrinated the Africans in a narrow pietistic way, emphasising spiritual and inward aspects, and neglecting political and social aspects.

52.4. Neither Soulmates nor Antagonists

Answering the main accusation, of *collaboration*, Fiedler says missions and colonialism cannot have been just soulmates, because of three indisputable facts. *First*, missions are older than colonialism. Christianity from its earliest beginning has been a missionary religion. As for Africa, missionaries reached 'a number of areas before any colonialist cast a coveting eye on them'. *Secondly*, the relationship between missions and colonial rulers was characterised by both cooperation and conflict. *Thirdly*, after the end of colonialism, neither church nor mission died. Church membership even grew considerably after the colonial period, to about 48% of the population by the end of the second millennium.

Fiedler admits that missionaries sometimes 'put the colonial system to their own use', profited from it, and cooperated with it. At the same time, however, missionaries resisted the cruelties and injustices of colonial rulers. Fiedler concludes that missionaries were neither soulmates nor antagonists of colonialism. Like the colonialists they were children of their times, but their agenda was older than and different from the agenda of colonialism. It was 'the agenda of the *Kingdom of Christ*, a kingdom not of this world, but with quite some effects on it'.[12]

Hanciles offers a more critical view. Regarding the charge of *cooperation* of missionaries with colonialists, he says that the abolition movement in a sense paved the way for colonialism, which he calls 'another more subtle and enduring form' of slavery. This leads him to the conclusion that 'Western missionaries, to a large extent, were conscious or unconscious agents' of colonialism.[13] Njoku adopts this idea and lists various ways in which he thinks colonial governments have acted as a 'protective shield' or source of help for the missionaries.[14]

---

[11] Fiedler, 'Soulmates', in: Ross (ed), *Faith*, pp.218-221.

[12] Fiedler, 'Soulmates', in: Ross: *Faith*, pp.221-234.

[13] Hanciles, 'Back to Africa', in: Kalu (ed.), *African Christianity*, p.215.

[14] Njoku, 'The Missionary Factor in African Christianity 1884-1914', in: Kalu (ed.), *African Christianity: An African Story*, pp.246-252.

Shaw like Fiedler distinguishes two sides. He emphasises that colonialism was a mixed blessing for missions. Sometimes the 'colonial principle' distorted and undermined the Gospel message. Many missionaries realised the disadvantages, and though they cooperated, they also 'relished their role as leading critics of colonialism'. This 'double-mindedness' was often rooted in the conviction of God's sovereign will that directs the nations, but also makes them morally and spiritually responsible.

Reacting to the accusation of *cultural and religious imperialism*, Shaw makes three observations: *First*, missionaries often functioned as a bridge between Western culture and African tradition, making the collision between the two less damaging. *Further*, Africans became Christians voluntarily, and not as a result of some force of religious imperialism. Also, generally missionaries and not colonialists were the ones whose language work has helped African culture a lot. *Thirdly*, the strong conviction of the uniqueness and the saving power of Christ did not bar missionaries from studying the traditional worldview of *African Traditional Religion*.

Regarding the accusation of colonialist *paternalism* Shaw admits that the policy of partnership by CMS's Venn and others was replaced by a *new paternalism* in the late 19th and early 20th centuries. But authoritarian patterns contributed to the fostering and empowerment of African leadership. Real understanding of their own discipleship gradually forced the missionaries to abandon paternalism. Anyhow, missionaries have always been dependent on African evangelistic zeal and expertise. As to the accusation of narrow pietistic indoctrination, Shaw admits that missionaries often equated modern thought with Christianity, as if Western technology and culture were Christian products. At the same time, however, he points to the fact that the mission schools produced the first leaders of African independence. Mission education implied the conviction that the coming Kingdom of Christ is more important than any Western colonial or African traditional power. This led to a conscious feeling for righteousness, both spiritually and also in the earthly structures. In agreement with Fiedler's view, Shaw concludes that missionaries were neither 'heroic angels', nor 'imperialistic devils'. Many were just 'fools of Christ', who worked paradoxically in this world, using 'foolish things to confound the wise'. Shaw is led to this conclusion by tracing developments in the history of colonialism and mission.

The era can be divided into three periods: 1885-1918, 1918-1945, and 1945-1960.

52.5. The 'Heyday of Missions' 1885-1918

After 1885, African Christianity changed. Missionary activities reached their climax, and the African church emerged. Shaw distinguishes three features: (a) new *growth*, (b) a new kind of *cooperation*, (c) a new *aggressiveness*.

a. Growth

The number of converts grew enormously in the period after the *Berlin Conference* and the beginning of the scramble for Africa. Did Africans turn to Christianity because in many places, they perceived the colonial power 'to exercise effective and beneficial control', or was it out of self-preservation, fearing the consequences of not being part of the new status quo? Probably Africans were not motivated by either of these two options. Colonialism as such was not perceived as a positive factor, and it cannot be seen as the cause of growth. Yet Njoku thinks that the *Berlin Conference* indirectly contributed to growth, because 'it paved the way for stability and order in the missionary enterprise'. He says that 'the controlling and moderating presence of the colonial powers prevented' mission from becoming 'unduly disruptive and even explosive'.[15] Besides, the relative peace and order resulting from the *Pax Britannica* facilitated safe travel and communication by missionaries and catechists. This helped the extension of religions. It supported the spread of the Gospel and the growth of the Church. Even Islam grew most under colonial rule.

Dramatic growth was seen: in Nigeria after 1888 in all places where the British colonial impact was strong; in Ghana after a British victory over the Ashanti in 1896; in South Africa after the *Union* of 1910 had brought Cape Colony, Transvaal and Orange Free State together; in Nyasaland after British rule was extended over the whole country in 1891; in Uganda after the British established a protectorate in 1894. Because of the apparent growth of Christianity, this period of early colonialism between 1885 (*Berlin Conference*) and 1918 (end of *World War I*) is sometimes indicated as the *'hey-day of missions'*.

b. Cooperation

There was a kind of unofficial partnership between the missionaries and the colonialists, which benefited both, although their causes and aims differed. Roland Oliver calls this 'a happy accident'.[16] Mission was not just an extension of colonialism, but it profited from the 'law and order' brought by it. In most cases the Africans did not blame the missionaries for this. According to Ward, for most Africans the colonial takeover belonged to a series of crises and changes that incorporated Africa into a global enlargement of scale, impinging on all aspects of life. The missionaries seemed to 'offer resources to cope with these radical changes'. Christianity, being the religion of the colonial powers, was 'equated with the modern, and modernisation was seen as essential for Africa, in material as well as intellectual and even spiritual terms'.[17] So, the colonial rulers and the missionaries were often enthusiastically welcomed.

George Grenfell (1849-1906), an English Baptist missionary, who worked in Africa for thirty-two years, the first three years in the Cameroons and then in the Congo.

As far as the imperialistic pride, the atrocities and the injustices of colonialism go, the attitude of missionaries had two sides. First, there are the historical facts of *missionary co-responsibility* for the beginning of colonial rule. The Scottish missions in Nyasaland campaigned for the British government to colonise the country before the Portuguese would occupy the Shire Highlands. The British started to protect the Makololo in 1889, and finally, in 1891 the British Protectorate was proclaimed. The CMS asked Britain to take over Uganda because of disorder in the country and the threat by Germany. BMS-missionary George Grenfell in the Congo advocated the advent of Belgian colonial rule because of

---

[15] Chukwudi A. Njoku, 'The Missionary Factor in African Christianity 1884-1914', in: Ogbu U. Kalu (ed.), *African Christianity*, p.220.

[16] Roland Oliver, *The Missionary Factor in East Africa*, London: Longmans, 1965².

[17] Ward, 'Africa', in: Hastings (ed), *World History*, p.218.

the 'chaotic sway' of local chiefs. Cardinal Lavigerie of the White Fathers lobbied European powers to combat slavery by taking over political power in East Africa. Ndebele king Lobengula lost his land to Cecil Rhodes because LMS-missionary Charles Helm in 1888 on purpose wrongly translated a contract.

On the other side missions were *opponents* of aspects of colonialism. Ward says, they 'were predisposed to outspoken criticism of the perceived shortcomings or injustices of colonial rule'.[18] Missionaries disclosed the atrocities in the rubber plantation economy of the 'Congo Free State'.[19] In East Africa they protested against forced labour. CMS missionary Miller was co-responsible for the foundation of an organisation for political freedom in Northern Nigeria. In the German and Portuguese territories missionaries protested against administrative policies and mistreatment of people.

c. Aggressiveness

The early colonial period produced changes in the character of the missionaries and in the Africans who adopted the Christian faith. A different consciousness and attitude emerged, according to Shaw characterised by a 'new aggressivenes', intensifying the struggle for leadership between missionaries and African converts. Unlike the older missionaries like Henry Venn who had tried to *Africanise* church leadership, the new missionaries wanted to keep leadership in their own hands.

The new attitude was inspired by various ideas: (a) the thought that a superior Western Christian civilisation was called to put the world under the Kingdom of God, (b) the belief that Christ's Second Coming was to be drawn near by the evangelisation of the world, (c) concentration on salvation of the individual. The consequences were that the shaping of Africanised churches became less emphasised.

Most of the new missionaries were younger and less educated than the older type. Yet their contribution to language work, converting and schooling Africans was considerable. The spirit of new self-consciousness also touched the African Christians. Most of them were converted through the work of fellow African catechists, teachers and evangelists. This is how they met with Christianity in their own vernacular languages. This is generally true for the classical 'mainline' churches, it is even more true for those churches that broke away from the missionary bodies and went on independently.

The 'new aggressiveness' sometimes led to outspoken protests against colonialism, and against white domination in the church and in the state. In Nigeria the Anglican assistant bishop James Johnson ('Holy Johnson') propagated an African version of Christianity. Charles Domingo in Nyasaland, after his clash with the *Livingstonia Mission*, came under the influence of Joseph Booth and Ethiopianism. He was convinced that European 'Christendom' had betrayed the Christian faith.[20] Much more radical was John Chilembwe, another pupil of Booth. In 1915 he initiated an armed rising against the British rulers in Nyasaland, thus becoming an early symbol of African

---

[18] Ward, 'Africa', in: Hastings (ed.), *World History*, p.217; Hildebrandt, *History of the Church in Africa*, p.228.
[19] Cf. Hastings, *The Church in Africa*, pp.434-437.
[20] Cf. Harry W.Langworthy (ed.), *Letters of Charles Domingo*, University of Malawi, Sources for the Study of Religion in Malawi No. 9, 1983.

nationalism.[21] The new consciousness of independence was encouraged during the *First World War* when many Western missionaries left missionary work and church, leaving the leadership practically in the hands of Africans.[22]

52.6. Strained Partnership 1918-1945

Although the First World War had left much of mission and church in African hands, after 1918 the returning whites, even more than before, took over the responsibilities. Shaw says, 'the control in Africa by colonist and missionary grew in size and scope'. Europeans took all the important initiatives. Yet inwardly the structures of imperialism and colonialism weakened, as did the idea of the superiority of Western civilisation. Liberal thinking undermined the fundamental stance of classical churches. Gradually the European majority at international mission conferences gave way to the presence of non-Europeans. Missionaries began to question the validity of classical colonialism. In the meantime, African Christianity and missionary presence continued to grow.

A new vision of colonialism led the colonial rulers to pay greater attention to *education*. In a process of education Africans had to be taught how to exist in the modern world, and how to govern themselves independently. Until reaching that point the African would be under colonial rule. With this educational aim in mind the *Phelps-Stokes Commission*, a missionary-inspired and privately financed group, travelled about Africa in the early 1920s. One of its members was the Ghanaian educationalist and Ethiopianist church leader J.E.K. Aggrey.[23] The Commission saw many mission schools, but generally considered them insufficient. Yet in 1924 the Commission 'called for partnership between missions and government, not separate development'. They advised the colonial governments to make use of the existing network of mission schools. In order to make them meet the educational requirements, the governments should subsidise, inspect and improve these schools.[24] Soon many mission schools worked under the new regulations. Generally, the work of the Commission elevated and affirmed the 'school in the bush' and it underlined the importance of cooperation between black and white.[25] The advantage was great progress of education, stimulating new missionary initiatives.

However, for the missions and the churches there were also disadvantages: (a) The energy of mission and church sometimes was more directed at education than at the spreading of the Gospel. (b) Mission schools could easily become an extension of the colonial structure. (c) Government control could weaken the ties between church and schools and secularise the schools.

---

[21] G.Shepperson, and Th. Price, *Independent African: John Chilembwe and the Origins, Setting and Significance of the Nyasaland Rising of 1915*, Edinburgh UP, 1958, re-edited: Blantyre: CLAIM, 2000; Patrick Makondesa, *The Church History of Providence Industrial Mission 1900-1940*, Zomba: Kachere, 2006.

[22] For the effects of the First World War on the Livingstonia Mission, see: J. McCracken, *Politics and Christianity in Malawi 1875-1940: The Impact of the Livingstonia Mission in the Northern Province*, Cambridge UP, 1977, pp.266-276.

[23] Cf.: Hildebrandt, *History of the Church in Africa*, p.203.

[24] The *Phelps-Stokes Commission Report* of 1924 was followed by a Colonial Office Memorandum of 1925, entitled, *Education Policy in British Tropical Africa*, in which these regulations were described. See also: Verstraelen Gilhuis, *A New Look at Christianity in Africa*, pp.39-61 ['African Education as seen from Le Zoute 1926'], especially pp.46-50.

[25] Ward, 'Africa', in: Hastings (ed), *World History*, pp.218,219.

West Africa especially became the scene of widespread mission initiatives in education. In Nigerian Igboland the Irish missionary Joseph Shanahan established many schools. In Ghana and Cameroon Christianisation programs through schooling were very successful, although there were problems when the German *Basel Mission* had to leave temporarily in 1916, and the work had to be taken over by British Baptists. In Togo the Presbyterians continued schoolwork that was started by the *Basel Mission*, after the latter's departure due to the *First World War*. The Liberian 'American Negro Bureaucracy' limited education to themselves, excluding the interior tribes. In the Congo the Belgian government favoured Roman Catholic schools to the disadvantage of Protestant education.

In South Africa, Christianity flourished. Although the British colonial rule had practically ended by the establishment of the Union in 1910, colonial thinking was still alive in racialist legislation. Training of black leaders continued by e.g. the work of the *Paris Evangelical Mission Society* and by the University of Fort Hare, founded in 1916.

Especially in Kenya the tension between missions and the colonial government intensified. The bone of contention was the increasing number of white settlers occupying African land. There was tension between missionaries and Africans, for instance in the Kikuyu girls' circumcision crisis of 1929.[26] Missionary actions against this practice caused anger of the Kikuyu traditionalists and eventually resulted in the formation of African Independent Churches.[27] After the *Africa Inland Mission*, other missions too started moving into the interior of Kenya, e.g. the *Church of Scotland Mission* and the *CMS*, and the *Seventh Day Adventists*. In 1890 the Roman Catholic *Holy Ghost Fathers* entered Kenya, first at Mombasa, by 1899 they had reached Limuru. Beside the white missionaries, there were also early black missionaries, e.g. Shadrack Mliwa who worked for the CMS among the Kikuyu, and Yohana Mbila, one of the first *Church of God* workers at Kima.[28]

52.7. Final Period 1945-1960

The defeat of Germany and the liberation of Europe contributed to a global desire for freedom. Africans saw the white man's divisions, and realised that whites could be defeated. In Africa winds of independence began to blow, even leading to the formation of liberation movements. Charles de Gaulle's plan of 1958 for autonomous African states within a federal French community never became a reality, but in 1960 it changed to a plan for full independence which France's colonies received in the 1960s.[29] In 1957 colonial Gold Coast became the independent nation of Ghana. Its first leader Kwame Nkrumah promoted a pan-African movement of liberation. In 1962, after the Mau-Mau rebellion of the mid-1950s, Kenya became independent.

The *négritude* movement of Léopold Sédar Senghor was one of the African expressions of culture and literature that stimulated independence. The rediscovery of

---

[26] On this topic and related issues, see Klaus Fiedler, 'Bishop Lucas' Christianization of Tradtional Rites, the Kikuyu Female Circumcision Controversy, and the Cultural Approach of Conservative German Missionaries', in: Noel O. King, and Klaus Fiedler (eds), Robin Lamburn, *From a Missionary Notebook, The Yao of Tunduru and other Essays*, Saarbrücken: Breitenbach, 1991.

[27] Hildebrandt, *History of the Church in Africa*, pp.231,232.

[28] Cf.: Hildebrandt, *History of the Church in Africa*, p.186.

[29] Hastings, *History of African Christianity*, p.132.

African culture had been anticipated in Tempel's book *Bantu Philosophy* (1945). The desire for a real African Christianity was gradually emerging, although most missionaries were not yet conscious of the necessity of indigenisation of faith and doctrine.

In the meantime, the number of Christians kept on growing, for instance through the *East Africa Revival* climaxing in the 1950s. In this decade before political independence many mission-founded churches became autonomous in part or completely. Both missionaries and African Christians agreed to the training of leaders aimed at the transition from mission to autonomous church. Theological departments and colleges were shaped to that end. It was widely realised among whites and blacks that only in this way African Christianity could escape from secularism and syncretisism. Examples in East Africa are the *Presbyterian Church* which became completely independent in 1961, John Gatu becoming its first General Secretary, the *Anglican Churches* in Kenya and Uganda, the *Africa Inland Church*, and the *Lutheran Chuches* in Tanzania. In general, the churches progressed, although Christianity was hindered by Mau Mau violence in Kenya and Muslim violence in Sudan. By 1960 mission and church in the colonial era had ended, because – as we have seen in chapters 50 and 51 – the majority of the African states had begun their history of independence.

53. African Instituted Churches

53.1. Two Traditions

The term *African Instituted Churches* (AIC)[1] generally means 'churches founded in Africa, by Africans and for Africans'. There are alternative terms, such as *African Independent Churches*, *African Initiated Churches*, *African Indigenous Churches*, and *African International Churches*,[2] all maintaining the same abbreviation: AIC.[3] They refer to churches that emerged outside and independent from churches instituted as a result of the work by 'classical missions'. *'Classical missions'* then are the missionary organisations of 'mainline churches' from Europe and North America. The term *'mainline churches'* is often used for the Roman Catholic Church, and for the churches coming from the main-stream of the 16th-century Reformation, excluding the offspring of the more radical wings of the Reformation. These terms have relative significance, because often they can only partly define the real situation, which is rather more complex.[4] We make four observations.

First, all African churches, including the mainline churches, have become independent, at least autonomous, in the second half of the 20th century; they do not necessarily behave like the Western 'mother' churches. Besides, after the 1960s, Africans have instituted churches similar to the established classical type, although classical missions were not instrumental in their foundation.

Secondly, Western missions of Mennonites, Baptists, Pentecostals, Adventists and others, derived from the more radical wings of the Reformation, though dubbed as independent, generally did not behave differently from the missions of the established mainline churches. The most essential difference (although not in all cases) was that the former started mission work in Africa later. Although less than the classical missions, they too gave rise to African independency outside their 'daughter'-churches.

Thirdly, Protestant mainline churches in Africa are not necessarily more faithful to the principles of Reformation Orthodoxy than African instituted churches. Neither being mainline classicist nor being African instituted guarantees that a church is more pure or true.

Fourthly, right from the beginning of classical missions in Africa, there was the powerful factor of African initiative. Therefore, it is impossible to separate the history of African instituted churches after 1890, from early features of independency inside the main mission founded churches.

Ward stresses that 'it would be wrong to think too much of rigid contrasts between two conflicting traditions'.[5] Both the mainline mission founded churches and the *African Instituted Churches* are very diverse. Both demonstrate a wide spectrum of

---

[1] For this section, also: Shaw, *Kingdom*, pp.239-257; Baur, *200 Years*, pp.349-359; Hastings, *Church in Africa*, pp.437-539; Ward, 'Africa', in: *World History*, pp.221-226; Walls, *Missionary Movement*, pp.85-89,92-93,111-118.
[2] Afe Adogame and Lizo Jafta, 'Zionist, Aladura and Roho: African Instituted Churches', in: Kalu et al. (eds) *African Christianity*, pp.310-313.
[3] The abbreviation AIC can be confusing, as it is also used for the churches established by the *Africa Inland Mission*, which do not belong to the African Instituted Churches.
[4] Cf.: Walls, *Missionary Movement*, p.114.
[5] Ward, 'Africa', in: Hastings (ed), *World History*, p.223.

judgments about doctrine, church organisation, ethical behaviour, and the relation to African tradition. Walls comes to the same conclusion. He says the whole of African Christianity is likely to be a 'new religious movement' reworking old and newly found aspects of the Christian faith. Therefore, the distinction between 'independent' and 'older' churches is of decreasing value, as both are 'new' manifestations of Christianity.[6]

53.2. Early African Initiatives

Apart from North Africa, Egypt, Nubia and Ethiopia, where African churches founded by Africans emerged and partly vanished, there is not much to tell about African Christian initiative prior to the end of the 18th century. Independent contributions were made by King Alfonso I in the Congo and his successors, by the prophetess Beatrice (Kimpa Vita), who met her unhappy death in 1706, by Mother Lena who independently preserved and continued the work of the Moravian missionary George Schmidt, and by the ex-slave Ottobah Cugoano whose book was instrumental to the emergence of the anti-slavery movement, and others.

Yet as Walls says, African Christianity 'is to a surprising extent the result of African initiatives'. The Evangelical Revivals of the 18th and 19th centuries not only put Europeans on the track of mission, they also directly ignited many Africans. The Sierra Leonean Church, founded by ex-slaves, was not a missionary creation. The settlers brought their own preachers with them, and in the course of years 'they supplied African missionaries in quantities for the rest of West Africa' and elsewhere. In Sierra Leone the *Church Missionary Society* alone 'over a 60-year period produced a hundred ordained men, in addition to countless catechists, teachers, and other mission workers'. Walls also points to the 'vital importance' of African evangelists and catechists in countries like Uganda and Nigeria. At a later stage there was the emergence of dynamic and influential preachers, whose effectiveness was recognised by the mission churches, although they did not easily fit into the organisational structures of those churches. Examples are William W. Harris in the Ivory Coast, Sampson Oppong in Ghana, Joseph Babalola in Nigeria, Walter Mattita in Lesotho. Their work led to a 'massive expansion' of existent mission-led churches.[7]

Before the era of colonialism (1885-1960) the Christianisation of sub-Saharan Africa, though in many aspects dependent on African initiative, was led by Western missions. Subsequently these missions, partly because of pressure by Africans, took the initiative of founding African churches under missionary tutelage. By the end of the colonial period missionary supervision ended.

Since about 1890, Africans had begun to institute churches, completely independent from the mission-led churches. The feature of *separatism* in the history of Protestantism may have been one of the causes, and also the dislike of missionary *authoritarianism* and the desire to keep something of African tradition. Shaw thinks that behind this there is a deeper cause. He points to the problem of evil and deliverance from evil. Westerners tend to look at it *philosophically*, whereas to Africans evil first of all is a functional problem. Africans saw evil in how the missionaries dealt with them, and they

---

[6] Walls, *Missionary Movement*, pp.112,113.
[7] Walls, *Missionary Movement*, pp.85-88.

reacted to it. Successively this evil appeared to the Africans with different faces. That is why the reactions also were different.

In the movement of church independency before 1960, we can discern three phases, (a) the Ethiopianist reaction, (b) the emergence of *Prophet-Healing churches*, (c) the East and West African Revivals. These three phases were followed by a period of explosive growth of all kinds of *independency*. In the following sections we will look at these phases or waves.

53.3. The Rise of Ethiopianism 1890-1910

The first wave of independency was a reaction against the evil of *'humiliation and shame'* caused by missionaries' disrespect or contempt. This reaction led to the movement of *Ethiopianism*, the separation of churches from the missionary churches.[8] The separations were motivated by the desire for having the leadership in African hands, and not so much by questions of doctrine and worship practice. Ethiopianism, triggered by the Ethiopian victory over Italian invaders in 1896, looked for an all-African theocracy of racial justice and hope, anticipating – in Shaw's view – the *Black Theology* movement in the 1960s.

Ethiopianism was fed by Biblical notions or perceptions referring to connections between Africa and the Old and New Testament histories, like the stretched out hand of Ethiopia, or rather Kush, in *Psalm* 68:3, the Queen of Sheba's visit to Solomon and the 'Solomonic' dynasty of Ethiopian kings, the story of the Falasha linkage with ancient Israel, the flight of Jesus to Egypt, the African who carried Jesus' cross, the journey to and from Jerusalem by the Treasurer to the Queen Mother (Candace) of Meroe. Afro-American returnees motivated by anti-slavery values were especially interested in searching for heroic roots of black Africa's past, and the heroic destiny of the Negro Race.

Hanciles characterises *Ethiopianism* as 'the most potent African Christian reaction', which 'epitomized anti-slavery, sowed the seeds of African nationalism, and enshrined alternative visions of African Christianity that found full expression in African independent church movements'.[9] Kalu seems to position the beginnings of *Ethiopianism* in West Africa, and thinks it started in about 1860. He views it 'as an example of African response to colonial Christianity'.[10] In the descriptions by Barrett[11] and Sundkler[12] *Ethiopianism* started in South Africa, a bit later. Let us now look at some phenomena of *Ethiopianism* in South, South-Central, and West Africa respectively.

In *South Africa* the Ethiopianist movement began in 1884, when Nehemiah Tile (†1891) left the white-controlled Wesleyan Methodist Church in Tembuland, and founded the *Thembu National Church*.[13] This was followed by separations from

---

[8] Cf.: Hastings, *History of African Christianity*, pp.35-38,219-221.
[9] Hanciles, 'Back to Africa: White Abolitionists and Black Missionaries', in: Kalu (ed.), *African Christianity*, p.215.
[10] Ogbu U. Kalu, 'Ethiopianism in African Christianity', in: Kalu et al. (eds) *African Christianity*, p.262.
[11] David B. Barrett, *Schism and Renewal in Africa: An Analysis of Six Thousand Contemporary Religious Movements*, Nairobi: OUP, 1968.
[12] Bengt Sundkler, *Bantu Prophets in South Africa*, London: Oxford UP, 1948.
[13] J.A. Millard, 'Tile, Nehemia, d. 1891: Thembu National Church, South Africa' [DACB website].

Methodist, Presbyterian and Congregationalist churches. An important role was played by the Afro-American *African Methodist Episcopal Church* (AMEC) that had entered Africa. Wesleyan Methodist Mangena M. Mokone (†1936), in protest against racial segregation, first founded his *Ethiopian Church* in Pretoria.[14] This united with the AMEC of Bishop Henry M. Turner, who visited South Africa in 1898, and contributed to the spirit of Ethiopianism. Turner befriended Mokone's assistant James M. Dwane (†1915), who had fiercely reacted against white church leadership. The famous song 'Bless, o Lord, our Land of Africa',[15] is a product of the Ethiopian movement, through its composer Enoch Mankayi Sontonga (†1905), who had studied at mission-controlled *Lovedale Institution*, but had become a member the African Presbyterian Church, founded by Pambani J. Mzimba who had similarly abandoned the Presbyterians of Lovedale.[16]

Enoch Mankayi Sontonga (1873-1905), a Xhosa from the Eastern Cape, who wrote the hymn Nkosi Sikelel'i Afrika.

In *South-Central Africa*, the initiative to independency was taken by a white missionary. In Nyasaland (Malawi) the Australian missionary Joseph Booth (†1932) inspired the foundation of various independent churches. His book, *Africa for the African* (1897),[17] is also a straightforward protest against colonialism. His pupil John Chilembwe (†1915) was also directly influenced by Afro-American Baptists. Chilembwe's rising against British colonial power in 1915 belongs to the very rare cases of the Ethiopianists resorting to violence.[18]

Ethiopianism in *West Africa* started with the missionary activities of Afro-American returnees in Sierra Leone and with CMS secretary Henry Venn's vision of African leadership. From Sierra Leone it spread to Liberia, the Gold Coast, and Nigeria. Leading figures in the movement were James Johnson (†1917), often named 'Holy' Johnson of Freetown and later of the CMS mission among the Yoruba in Nigeria; the Methodist layman J.E. Casely Hayford (†1930), who adopted the African name Ekra-Agiman, and contributed to the emergence of an African literature. Then, there was the Yoruba preacher David Brown Vincent (†1917) who also advocated a non-missionary version of African Christianity; he took on his original African name Mojola Agbebi, and in 1888 he seceded from the Baptist missionary work to found the *Native Baptist Church*. In 1913 Agbebi became the first president of the *African Communion of Independent Churches*.[19] In the field of Africanisation of education, contributions were made by Henry Carr, and especially by the Ghanaian J.E.K. Aggrey (†1927). Trained as

---

[14] Cf.: Hildebrandt, *History of the Church in Africa*, p.175.

[15] M.E. Sontonga, *Nkosi Sikelel'i-Afrika*; in Chichewa: *Mbuye dalitsani Afrika* (Nyimbo za Mulungu/ Hymns for Malawi, no.375).

[16] Kalu, 'Ethiopianism', in: Kalu et al. (eds), *African Christianity*, pp.274,275.

[17] Joseph Booth, *Africa for the African*, 1897 [re-edited by Laura Perry and re-published as Kachere text no.6, Blantyre: CLAIM/ Kachere, 1996].

[18] See chapter 55.

[19] Robert C. Brockman, 'Agbebi, Mojola (David Brown Vincent) 1860 to 1917: Native Baptist Church, Nigeria' [DACB Website].

a minister of the AME Zion Church in America, Aggrey also was a leader of Ghana's model school at Achimota, established in 1924.[20]

Generally, Ethiopianists remained within the boundaries of orthodox Christianity, but some adopted deviating ideas, like E.M. Lijadu (†1926), who preached that the Yoruba deity Orunmila was a pre-figuration of Jesus'.[21] Many Ethiopianists felt inspired by the Afro-American Liberian missionary and statesman Edward Wilmot Blyden (†1912), who 'foresaw the coming shift in the centre of the gravity of Christianity from the north to the south Atlantic, and its import for African Christianity'.[22]

J.E.K. Aggrey (†1927), a Ghanaian educaltionalist and Ethioianist church leader.

After 1910, the Ethiopian movement became Africa-wide. It also became more political, as can be seen in the activities of Reuben Spartas, in *Uganda*, who not only founded the *African Greek Orthodox Church* but also tried to realise nationalist and pan-African ideas. In *Kenya* there was a wave of independency, for example the 'Luo-schisms' resulting in the *Nomiya Luo Mission* cutting its ties with the Anglican Church in 1914. The *Mario Legio of Africa* split from Roman Catholicism.[23] By becoming political the Ethiopian movement lost its specific ecclesiastical characteristics and became part of a general movement for African independence from colonial rule. Kalu described the 'swan song' of Ethiopianism by summing up some reasons for its demise. In the period between the World Wars it was absorbed by the emergence of a wider pan-African ideology and a shift from cultural to political nationalism.[24]

53.4. The Rise of Prophet-Healing Churches

The *Prophet-Healing Churches* not only addressed the evil of foreign leadership, they also reacted against the evil that 'destroys life', such as 'illness, infertility, pestilence, famine and sudden or inexplicable death'. According to *African Traditional Religion*, these evils were caused by ancestral and demonic spirits and brought about by sorcery and witchcraft. Traditional healers had been unable to have victory over these powers, but the Christian prophets could, because their power originated in Christ.

For that reason, religious leaders from the traditional context, like the Xhosa Nxele and Ntsikana, and the Igbo Dede Ekeke Lolo shifted by adopting some aspects of Christianity in the expectation of thus becoming successful healers. In general, the new prophets emerged from the newly established Christian churches. An example is the revivalist preacher and wandering Liberian prophet William Wadé Harris (†1929).

---

[20] Hildebrandt, *History of the Church in Africa*, p.203.
[21] Kalu, 'Ethiopianism', in: Kalu et al. (eds), *African Christianity*, p.271.
[22] Kalu, 'Ethiopianism', in: Kalu et al. (eds), *African Christianity*, p.272.
[23] Adogame and Jafta, 'Zionists, Aladura, and Roho: African Instituted Churches', in: Kalu et al. (eds), *African Christianity*, p.315.
[24] Ogbu U. Kalu, African Christianity: From the World Wars to Decolonization', in Kalu et al. (eds), *African Christianity*, pp.333-341.

Sundkler calls him the instigator of 'the greatest Christian mass movement on the West Coast'.²⁵ Harris preached 'the bringing of all nations under the political, peaceful rule on the earth of the Messiah Jesus of Nazareth'. His eschatological message was sometimes understood as politically subversive. He was accused of taking part in the rising of the Grebo people and was thrown into jail, where according to his own witness, he was called as a prophet in a vision by the Archangel Gabriel. After being released, he travelled around the Gold Coast and the Ivory Coast, preaching and healing. He preached about the imminent *Parousia*, and called people to immediate conversion to God in Christ, to destroy fetishes, to reject idols, to conquer traditional spirits, and to accept the authority of the Bible.²⁶ Perhaps between 60,000 and 100,000 people who had repented were baptised by him.

William Wadé Harris, an influential prophetic preacher in West Africa (from: Waterville, A History of Christianity in Ghana, in: Hildebrandt op.cit.).

In the Gold Coast he stayed only for three months, yet his preaching led to the growth of existing churches, like the Methodists and the Roman Catholics, and also in the Nzima district to the springing up of four indigenous independent churches. In 1914 Harris was arrested in the Ivory Coast, a country which at that time had not been touched by the Gospel except for some work by Roman Catholics since 1895. Harris was accused of revolutionising the people. Later Harris told how the French administrators who interrogated him mocked his prophetic ministry and the Bible. He was extradited to his homeland Liberia, where he was kept under house arrest until his death. Harris did not aim at starting new churches, but his work led to the growth of mission churches in the region, among others the Methodist Church. Later, however, after 1923, with the help of the Methodist missionary Platt,²⁷ Harrist independent congregations arose where there were no established churches, for example in the *Church of the Twelve Apostles* in the Gold Coast. Hildebrandt calls Harris 'another one of the outstanding figures of African Church History'. He went where God directed him, without asking for gifts or building a personality cult. In this way he 'was able to point thousands of people to Christ'.²⁸

Another prophet of the faith-healing movement is Garrick Sokari Daketima Braide (†1918). He was of Igbo-Kalabari birth, originating from south-eastern Nigeria. After his conversion, in an Anglican church in New Calabar, he gradually started a very successful prophetic preaching, accompanied by healing, dreams and visions. He declared himself to be Elijah II. In 1916 he left the Anglican Church together with many followers, because he did not find sufficient recognition for his ministry. Suspicious of his popularity, the authorities arrested Braide. In 1918 he died in jail. His followers founded *Christ Army Church*, an Ethiopianist type of church that 'still continues to this day'.²⁹

---

²⁵ Sundkler and Steed, *A History of the Church in Africa*, p.780.
²⁶ Graham Duncan and Ogbu U. Kalu, 'Bakuzufu: Revival Movements and Indigenous Appropriation in African Christianity', in: Kalu et al. (eds), *African Christianity*, pp.285,286.
²⁷ Hastings, *Church in Africa*, pp.505-507.
²⁸ Hildebrandt, *History of the Church in Africa*, pp.153-155,202.
²⁹ Duncan and Kalu, 'Bakuzufu: Revival Movements', in: Kalu et al. (eds), *African Christianity*, pp.288,289; Hildebrandt, *History of the Church in Africa*, p.204.

Nigeria was also the cradle of the *Aladura-movement* (*aladura* = praying people).[30] The earliest group was the *Cherubim and Seraphim* (C&S). Originally, this was an interdenominational society of men and women of prayer against magic, witchcraft and idols, but in 1925, as a reaction against 'intolerance by mission churches' an independent church was established. The wandering preacher Moses Tunolase Orimolade (†1933),[31] together with a young woman, Christiana Abiodun Emmanuel, née Akinsowon (†1994),[32] became the nucleus of the network of faith-healing communities of the C&S. The *Christ Apostolic Church* (CAC) originated in an Anglican prayer group by three Nigerians: Joseph Babalola, Isaac Akinyele, and David Odubanjo. In the 1930s especially the revivalist preaching of Joseph Babalola did much to spread the Aladura-movement in Nigeria.[33] The *Church of the Lord-Aladura* (CLA) was founded in 1930 by Josiah Ositelu, after the Anglican Church suspended him as a catechist. Another Aladura church is the *Celestial Church of Christ* (CCC), founded in 1947 by Samuel Bilewu Oschoffa (†1985).[34]

In East Africa it was the *Arathi* and the *Abarohi* (= people of the Holy Spirit) that expressed the prophet-healing movement. Like in the Aladura there is an element of Pentecostalism in these movements (see chapter 60.5).

In the *Congo* Simon Kimbangu (†1951) was the prophetic figure of independency. As a lay evangelist of the Baptist Church his preaching and healing had been very successful. But the Belgian colonial government and the Roman Catholic Church saw him as a threat. In 1921 he was condemned to 120 lashes and death. The Belgian king Albert commuted the punishment to life imprisonment. In Lubumbashi (Elizabethville) he remained a prisoner until his death. However, his influence continued, and eventually led to the establishment of the flourishing *Church of Jesus Christ on Earth through the prophet Simon Kimbangu*, probably 'the biggest independent Church in Africa'. In 1971/1972, along with the Roman Catholics, the Protestants and the Greek Orthodox, the Kimbanguists were allowed by President Mobutu to be one of the only four denominations in the Congo. The Kimbanguist Church is one of the few African Independent Churches that are members of the *World Council of Churches*.[35] Kimbangu's successors and followers allowed the members of the Kimbanguist Church to keep many tradional beliefs, trying at the same time to keep up 'the appearance of being a type of Christianity'.[36]

Simon Kimbangu (c.1889-1951) founded a church, with many members, although he himself spent most of his life in prison.

---

[30] Adogame and Jafta, 'Zionists, Aladura and Roho', in: Kalu et al. (eds) *African Christianity*, pp.316-318.

[31] Cf. 'Orimolade Tunolase, Moses 1879 to 1933: United Church of Cherubim and Seraphim, Nigeria' [DACB Website].

[32] Cf. Ebeye Boniface, 'Christiana Abiodun Emmanuel 1907 to 1994: Cherubim and Seraphim Society, Nigeria' [DACB Website].

[33] Hastings, *Church in Africa*, pp.513-518.

[34] Cf.: Elijah Olu Akinwumi, 'Oschoffa Samuel Bilewu 1909-1985: Celestial Church of Christ (Aladura), Nigeria' [DACB Website].

[35] Sundkler and Steed, *A History of the Church in Africa*, p.967.

[36] Cf.: Hildebrandt, *History of the Church in Africa*, p.214.

In *South Africa* Zulu Zionism was an expression of the prophet-healing movement. Zionism was inspired by the American Pentecostal J.A. Dowie of Chicago and the South African NGK missionary Le Roux, who promised complete spiritual and bodily healing in a newly established Jerusalem on the earth, before the speedy coming of the Messiah. Thousands of black Zion churches emerged, with a membership of 4 million (1990). One of the 'Zulu prophets' was Isaiah Shembe (†1935). He was very influential and controversial as well. In 1911 he founded the *amaNazaretha Church* and later the centres of Ekuphakameni near Durban as the New Jerusalem, and mountain top Inhlangakazi, calling himself the 'Promised One'. Stress was put on leadership, worship, and hymns. There is a difference with the Zion movement in that the focus was on Jehovah of the Old Testament, and on the leader himself. His son Johannes Galilee Shembe (†1967) and grandson Londa Shembe (†1988) succeeded him as leaders of the church.[37] In chapter 60, under the heading of Pentecostalism, the account of Zionism will be continued.

Independent Churches among the Shona of *Zimbabwe* are described in detail by M.L. Daneel. In three volumes he deals with their history, and with the kind of 'messianic' leadership and the fissions that he observes in Independency, especially in the prophet-healing churches. Daneel looks positively at these characteristics. He understands independent 'messianic' leadership as a 'translation and interpretation of the work of Christ' and within the processes of fragmentation and fission of independent church groups he sees seeds for Christian unity. In 1972 Daneel founded the *Conference of Shona Independent Churches*, popularly referred to as *Fambidzano*.[38]

Prophet-healing churches have a mythical understanding of Biblical Zion, believed to have come from heaven in their own Zion mountain-top centres. They show no interest in the Ethiopianists' idea of 'Africa for the Africans', being non-political in principle.

In this section we have seen that the prophet-healing movement led to a wave of *African Instituted Churches* all over sub-Saharan Africa. They were sometimes very different from one another. Walls tried to describe some general characteristiscs. All of them were characterised by two urgent quests: (a) a desire for the demonstrable presence of the Holy Spirit, (b) a desire to directly address the problems and frustrations of modern African urban life. The prophet-healing churches in West-Africa arose from a revival prayer group after World War One that wanted to demonstrate God's power amid human misery. The movement came 'from an indigenous reading of Scripture and a lively apprehension of the priorities of many anxious people'. Church life is characterised by prophecy, healing, divination, and revelation. They have a strict and precise church order, with a detailed code of regulations, exhortations, and prohibitions, often under a charismatic leader and with much congregational participation. Members may wear uniforms, and there is much fasting and prayer. Combating witchcraft and sorcery, identifying witches, and curing witches are among the activities.[39]

---

[37] Sundkler and Steed, *A History of the Church in Africa*, pp.840,841.

[38] M.L. Daneel, *Old and New Southern Shona Independent Churches*, volume 1: 'Background and Rise of the Major Movements', The Hague, 1971 (a), volume 2: 'Church Growth: Causative Factors and Recruitment Techniques', The Hague, 1974, volume 3: Leadership and Fission Dynamics, Gweru: Mambo Press, 1988.

[39] Walls, *Missionary Movement*, p.92.

53.5. The East Africa Revival

The *East Africa Revival* or *Balokole* (= saved ones)[40] is an example of a movement within the missionary church, seeking to transform the spiritual situation. It was an answer to lack of spirituality, decay, and deadness in the churches. Shaw calls this an answer to the evil of being alienated from the power of God 'by attitudes like spiritual coldness and deadness'. The shedding of blood is necessary to do away with this evil. This makes the blood of Christ and His sacrificial death the central symbol of this new awakening. Through the movement many nominal Christians who had become church members without real conversion for the first time in their lives were led to confession of sin and personal saving knowledge of Christ.

The revival started in Rwanda, at an Anglican mission station. The leading figure was Simeoni Nsibambi, of the Baganda people. After a deep religious experience, he began to preach repentance and renewal. The CMS missionary Joe Church found himself in agreement with Nsibambi. He and Nsibambi together with Nsibambi's brother Blasio Kigozi went out to preach total surrender to Jesus Christ. In 1933/1934 Nsibambi and Church preached at Gahini, which the Holy Spirit used for a mass revival that spread widely with many converts (*abaka* = *those on fire*) which made sleeping churches awake (*zukuka* = *awake*). Meanwhile, Kigozi and others spread the message to Uganda, and after Kigozi's death in 1936, also to Kenya, Sudan and Tanganyika. William Nagenda became Kigozi's successor as leader of the revival movement, soon called Balokole. In line with traditional Protestant revivals and perhaps influenced by the *Keswick Convention*, the Balokole preachers proclaimed salvation through faith in Christ and also 'spiritual renewal, commitment, uncompromising truthfulness and moral integrity'.

William Nagenda (1912-1973) and his family. In a brief biography he was called 'Lover of Jesus'. This Ugandan preacher and teacher was a leader and a powerful witness in the East African Revival.

The movement especially helped the work of the *Church Missionary Society* in eastern Africa. It spread from Rwanda to Uganda, then southwards to the CMS areas of Tanzania, north to Sudan and eastwards to Kenya. In Uganda the Anglican Bishop C.E. Stuart was very sympathetic to the Balokole. That was not always a matter of course, because there were also criticisms, mainly because of emphases on *second blessing* and potential *perfection* in the awakening movement. A break-away-group even thought they could be free of sexual lust. The mainstream, however, rejected this doctrine of striving (*okufuba*), which implies that Christians through a second blessing can get to a state of near sinlessness. Mainstream leaders stressed that the greatest blessing is the cross of Christ, and being washed in the blood

---

[40] The Luganda word *bakuzufu*, meaning being re-awakened, renewed, resurrected, was used as a description for the English word *revival*, according to Duncan and Kalu, 'Revival Movements', in: Kalu et al. (eds), *African Christianity*, p.278; the movement was also referred to as Rwandaism or Wandugu (Hildebrandt, *History of the Church in Africa*, p.233).

of Him, by faith alone. They also stressed that in this life Christians will never reach perfection.

In 1941 the Balokole movement led to a conflict at Tucker Theological College at Mukono in Uganda. A group of students, led by William Nagenda, resisted the warden's prohibition of their revivalist prayer group. The prayer group had emerged as a reaction against theft, immorality, theological liberalism, and High Church worship in this college. In the students' view the modernist spirit at Mukono 'minimizes sin, and the substitutionary death of Christ on the Cross, and mocks at the ideal of separation from the world to a holy and victorious life'. The revivalist students were dismissed. This almost led to a split. Eventually Bishop Stuart reconciled the Balokole with the college and the church by issuing guidelines for unity.[41] Waves of revival continued after the *Second World War*.

The movement harboured Ethiopianist elements, because it supported the principles of self-propagating, self-supporting and self-governing, and opened the way for recovery of African responsibility and leadership.[42] Some of the first African bishops in the Anglican Church belonged to the Bakolole, e.g. Erica Sabiti who was the first Anglican Archbishop in Uganda.[43]

There were also secessions. In 1948 Ishmael Noo formed his own church. In 1958 the revivalist Matthew Ajuoga and his *Johera* (= people of love) founded the *Churches of Christ of Africa*, breaking away from Anglicanism in western Kenya.[44]

53.6. The Golden Age of Independency

The age preceding political independence witnessed a rapid growth of the movements of ecclesiastical independency. *Ethiopianist* churches, *prophet-healing* churches, *revivalist* churches reached their height during the 1950s and early 1960s. All of them spread throughout Africa; independency was internationalising. Hastings says that the 1950s probably were 'the greatest decade for ecclesiastical independency in Africa'.[45] It was an age of expansion, consolidation, increasing self-confidence, and of expectations. Colonialism was weakening. There was an increasing tension between missionary church structures on the one hand and African initiative and ambition on the other hand. The foundation of independent churches was an important outlet for these feelings of tension. The movements of independency were not united. Ethiopianism aimed at combating inequality and racism; it saw nationalism as a means to reach this. The prophetic and revivalist movements stressed the spiritual side of evil and aimed at spiritual solutions.

Sometimes nationalist and spiritual interests clashed. New prophetic movements led by women prophets like Alice Lenshina in Zambia, Gaudencio Aoko in Kenya, Mai Chaza in Zimbabwe, Miriam Ragot, Ma Nku, and Ma Mbele in South Africa sometimes were even persecuted by African nationalists. Alice Lenshina (†1978) founded the independent Lumpa Church like a theocratic state with herself as queen. Her home village, the new Zion, was the centre of many other Lumpa-villages where her followers

---

[41] Hastings, *Church in Africa*, pp.597,598.
[42] Duncan and Kalu, 'Bakuzufu: Revival Movements', in: Kalu et al. (eds), *African Christianity*, pp.289-293.
[43] Cf.: Hastings, *Church in Africa*, pp.598,608, 609.
[44] Cf.: Hastings, *Church in Africa*, p.523.
[45] Hastings, *African Christianity*, pp.121-130.

were gathered under her rule. Zambia's first president Kaunda banned this Church, had the villages destroyed, killed some 700 of her followers, and had Lenshina imprisoned.[46] In Kenya the Balokole movement collided with the *Mau Mau* nationalists. Revivalists refused to take the Mau Mau oath that implied the repudiation of Christianity, and many paid with their lives. In Uganda Balokole followers clashed with dictator Idi Amin, which cost the lives of Archbishop Janani Luwum and other martyrs. In other cases, however, nationalist and spiritual expressions of independency were able to cooperate, like in Ghana and Swaziland.

53.7. Continuing Independency after 1960

In the 1960s Africa received political independence and ecclesiastical autonomy. In the meantime, the mission-instituted churches had generally become independent as well. They also tended to be partners of the new regimes, more or less similar to what the mission churches had been to the colonial governments. Some of the older independent churches, again in their diversity, gradually came to resemble the mission-founded mainline churches. Thus, in many cases the differences have faded out, but the old problem of evil has not died. After the era of colonial mission, Africans took over, giving way to new forms of misuse of power, mismanagement and corruption. Also, now there is the need of integrating the Gospel into the African mode of being, so that salvation can really protect people against the dangers that threaten life.

There is also the ongoing desire to react against spiritual coldness and deadness, and against *theological liberalism*. Very often the old evils have returned with new faces, but the old independency is often found to be unable to give answers to the challenges. Critics of church government policies, advocates of Africanisation, and revival groups often feel strangers in their own churches. That is why movements of separatism and independency have continued.

However, we prefer not to classify all these newer movements by the historical term *African-Instituted Churches*. Walls points to the new radical *charismatic churches*. Like the old prophetic-healing churches they derive from prayer and revivalist groups in the older churches. They also proclaim divine deliverance from diseases and demonic afflictions. But unlike the older independent churches their style of preaching and worship resembles the practice in American Charismatic and Pentecostal churches. Yet they are very African in origin, leadership and finance. In their church services there are no African drums and uniforms, but there are the keyboards and the guitars, while the preachers wear business suits and the choir wear ties. It is the Charismatic Movement in an African way. A more aggressive type of charismatic churches was derived from Christian students' groups. They seek discipleship while protesting against the complacency, compromise and spiritual weakness of the established churches. They introduced a new African asceticism with emphasis on 'prayer, fasting and readiness to suffer'.[47] Many of these young Christians met in the *Scripture Union*. Charismatic revivalism is also found in the *Students' Christian Organisation of Malawi* (SCOM). It stimulated the emergence of the *Born Again Movement* in the established churches, and it also led to the formation of independent churches. Yet the characteristics of the *Charismatic Movement*, and of the earlier *Pentecostal Movement*, are not the same as

---

[46] Hastings, *Church in Africa*, pp.524, 525.
[47] Walls, *Missionary Movement*, pp.92, 93.

those of the Ethiopianist churches, the prophet-healing churches, and the revivalist movements mentioned in the sections above. Pentecostalism and the Charismatic Movement were motivated by other theological challenges, often in a different political context. That is why we will deal with these movements separately, in chapter 60.

When evaluating the Christian witness of the movements for African Instituted Churches, and in a wider sense for African Independency, distinguishes three categories. The *first* group contradicted the Gospel of the Kingdom of Christ. This group, e.g. followers of Shembe and Kimbangu, obscured Christ by focusing mainly on the leader of the movement and by mixing the Christian witness with man-centred religion. Walls refers to the *'Hebraists'* who made a clear and conscious break with Christianity; in their schemes they took Christ away from the central place; a few like the Bayudaya of Uganda developed to a form of Judaism. The *second* category is characterised by a longing for and witness to the coming world order of Christ, of justice and righteousness. The *third* category points to the nature of the churches' spiritual warfare. The second and the third categories are indispensable for a church, provided they submit to the unique authority of Scripture. Much of the Harrist, Aladura and Balokole movements reflect this desire for re-orientation on the Bible. That is why they helped the Church in its quest for Reformation, that is for renewal or adjustment, and for reformulation of the Christian faith in African terms.[48]

---

[48] Cf.: Walls, *Missionary Movement*, p.113.

54. Church and Mission in Independent Africa

54.1. The Joy and the Pain of Change

The decolonisation process that started about 1960 rapidly brought national independence to most African countries. It also brought a sense of African internationalism demonstrated in the formation of the *Organisation of African Unity* in 1963. Decolonisation also paved the way for a renaissance of African culture. All this contributed to the restoration of the dignity and respect of the African.

However, the hopeful enthusiasm of the first years of independence soon was put to the test. The new ruling élites often resorted to repression and messianic nationalism. Often this resulted in revolutions and military dictatorships. Africans suffered under ruthless African authenticity campaigns, under communism, and under Muslim oppression. It was only in later years that in many countries civil freedom was restored. Africa's attempt to establish democracy had begun. The position of the church during these stages of political independence varied from being persecuted to being an ally of the government, sometimes even co-responsible for the violence.[1]

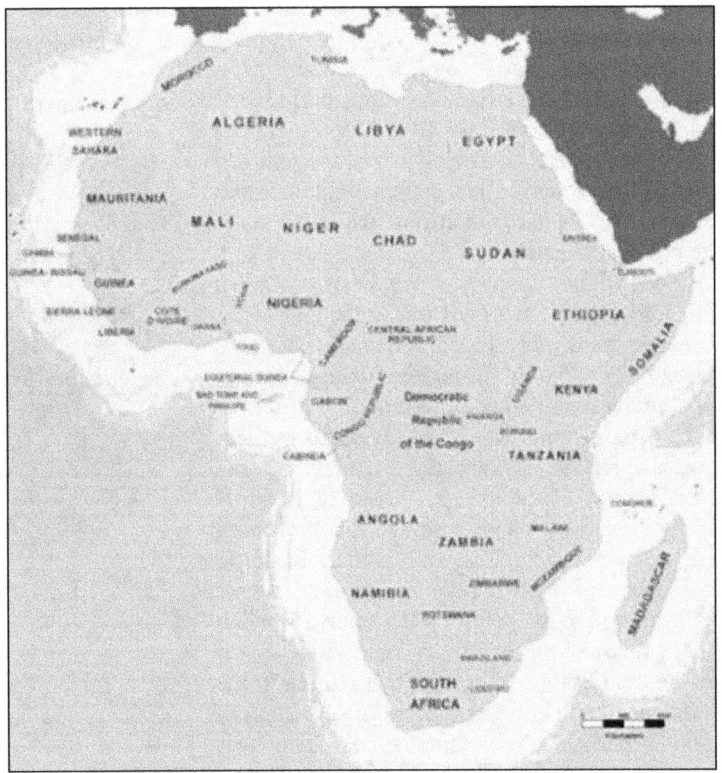

Map of Africa after regaining political independence.

---

[1] For this chapter also: Shaw, *Kingdom*, pp.259-282; Hastings, *African Christianity*, pp.131-274; Ward, 'Africa', in: Hastings (ed), *World History*, pp.226-233.

54.2. Churches Responding to Independence

In the new political situation the relationship between Church and State had shifted, which initially led to many problems. Here are some examples of Africa's first stages of political independence, and the Church's response to it.

Angola, Mozambique, and *Guinea-Bissau* continued to be under Portuguese rule until the 1970s. Especially the Protestant churches suffered because of this situation.

In southern *Sudan* the Arabs continued to persecute the Christians. Many fled to neighbouring countries. In *Somalia* the Muslim government expelled missionaries and forced the Church underground.

In *Liberia*, the patronising rule of W.Tubman was followed by the rule of W. Tolbert, and then power was seized by S.K. Doe in 1980.[2] Doe and his supporters killed Tolbert and almost the whole Liberian government. His regime was characterised by tyranny, manipulation and misrule. Some church leaders protested, but generally the church left politics alone, not crying out against injustice. After Doe was assassinated in 1990, a civil war broke out and the country collapsed. Again the churches did not protest. Although they grew in the midst of chaos, according to Shaw, the churches only tried to ameliorate the suffering.

In *Zaire* many Christians were killed during the rebellions of 1961 and 1964. Mobutu seized power in 1965. He established a one-party state. He presented himself as kind of messiah, and introduced *'mobutuism'* as a replacement of other religions. In this period the churches adopted a low profile. By 1980 Mobutu backed away from his messianism, but after 1990 chaos returned and increased. Although the churches sometimes collaborated with the regime, there were also attempts to improve the political situation.

Alice Auma in 1986 proclaimed herself under the orders of a Christian spirit named Lakwena. She raised an army in Northern Uganda, called the 'Holy Spirit Mobile Forces'. With it she waged a war against the Ugandan government and against internal enemies in the form of 'impure' soldiers, witches, and sorcerers.

Nigeria is one of the countries where *messianic Islam* clashed with Christianity. In a civil war at the end of the 1960s many Christians were killed and many churches were destroyed. The Northern region, mainly Hausa, tended to be aggressively Muslim, although there were Protestant Christian minorities. The Western region, mainly Yoruba, and the Eastern region, mainly Igbo, were predominantly Christian. In 1966 Igbo army officers led by General Ojukwu rose against the central government and declared the Eastern region of Biafra to be an independent non-Muslim state 'in a raging Islamic sea'. During the ensuing civil war, many western churches and missionaries tried to help Biafra, for instance by the organisation of relief flights. In 1970 the Biafran rising ended and a rather successful campaign of reconciliation began. At the same time, there was growing tension between Christians and Muslims, and an increasing pressure to bring Nigeria under Muslim law

---

[2] For a brief case study of church and state in Liberia in the period 1975-2000, see: J.W. Hofmeyr, 'Mainline Churches in the Public Space 1975-2000', in: Kalu et al. (eds), *African Christianity*, pp.367-372.

(*sharia*).

Also in *Uganda* the church faced aggressive Islam. In 1971 the dictatorship of Obote was replaced by the very cruel dictatorship of Idi Amin. Islam was promoted and churches were suppressed; some church leaders, among them the Anglican Archbishop Luwum, and many other Christians were killed. In 1979 Amin was violently overthrown by Obote, who in his turn was overthrown, and in 1986 succeeded by Museveni. Suffering and bloodshed seemed to have ended, except for the activities of the *Holy Spirit Rebels* of prophetess Alice Lakwena (or: Lekwana) who violently tried to establish a Christian kingdom on Ugandan soil. This *Army of the Lord* was defeated by Museveni's troops, but a section of it, the *Lord's Resistance Army*, remained active after 1995.

C.F. Beyers Naudé (1915-2004), minister in the Dutch Reformed Church in South Africa, who started a protest and reform movement, the Christian Institute, against the system of apartheid.

In *South Africa* the massacre of many participants in a protest demonstration at Sharpville in 1960, the prohibition of black political parties, and the banning of black leaders, led to an increasing consciousness of *apartheid* being against the Word of God. C.F. Beyers Naudé of the *Christian Institute*, Desmond Tutu leader of the *South African Council of Churches*, Allan Boesak and others in 1985 contributed to the *Kairos Document* that condemned apartheid. In 1990 Nelson Mandela was released from Robben Island. After De Klerk's government had dismantled apartheid, the elections of 1994 brought Mandela and the ANC to power.[3]

Zambia is one of the countries where the introduction of socialism was attempted. Kenneth Kaunda adopted this ideology, notwithstanding his professed personal faith in Christ, and when he became president he tried to make his country a socialist state. However, the attempt became a failure. In 1991, in multi-party elections, Kaunda was replaced by Frederick Chiluba, a professed Protestant Christian as well, who had to answer accusations of massive corruption during his regime, made by his successor President Levy Mwanawasa.

Julius Nyerere (1922 – 1999) known as Mwalimu or teacher, was President of Tanzania.

In *Tanzania* President Nyerere, a Roman Catholic, tried to introduce his version of socialism (*ujamaa*), but also here it failed, at least economically. The challenge of Islam was increasingly felt after Zanzibar joined the *Islamic Conference Organisation*.

In *Ethiopia* the Marxist-Leninist version of socialism began to be forced on the people after Mengistu seized power in 1977. In 1991 he was overthrown after having brought intense suffering to the church and to many individual Christians.

Generally, the initial criticism of Christianity during the decolonisation process was soon followed by powerful currents which served to reinforce Christianity. These currents especially helped the mission-founded churches.

---

[3] For a brief case study of church and state in South Africa in the period 1975-2000, see: J.W. Hofmeyr, 'Mainline Churches in the Public Space 1975-2000', in: Kalu et al. (eds), *African Christianity*, pp.378-385.

Like of old in the colonial era – so Ward indicates – the majority of Africans expected more from churches coming from the West than from African Instituted Churches.[4] On the whole the growing churches contributed to (a) the *consolidation* of independence, (b) in some cases there was a *brave witness* against tyranny or barbarism, (c) and eventually churches helped the movements towards *democratisation*.

54.3. Theology Responding to Independence

In theology the church formulates and defends its position and message in response to the challenges from outside and inside the church. In the historical mainstream, Roman Catholic theology and Reformed theology, as well as the more modern theologies of *Liberalism* and *Ecumenism*, have had universal significance, though they have been coloured by their Western setting. In a way missionaries exported their theological convictions and differences to the mission fields outside Europe and America. At the same time, missionary Christianity developed its own colours, theological tendencies and even theological differences. We can distinguish various expressions of theology in Africa after the beginning of independence.

a. African Theology

The term *African Theology* gives a face to a movement that attempts to indigenise and inculturate theology in Africa. Generally, this movement 'has sought to demonstrate the value of the African religious heritage and to build bridges between that heritage and the Christian faith'.

In the *Roman Catholic* context, it began with Placide Tempel's book *Bantu Philosophy* (French: 1945, English: 1955) who said that *life-force* is the essence of African thought. In the wake of this a conference in Ghana in 1955 'defended the continuity between African culture and Christianity', exhorting the church to 'use African culture as the only language to proclaim the Gospel in Africa'. This inspired a 'generation of francophone Catholic scholars' such as Alexis Kagame (in Rwanda) and Vincent Mulago and Tharcisse Tshibangu (in the Congo). Kagame and Mulago belonged to a group of African students who, during their study in Rome, rethought the problem of 'African fundamental theology'. Tshibangu claimed that the seeds of authentic African Christian theology can be provided by African religion and philosophy. Alfred Vanneste criticised Tshibangu's thought by insisting that theology should be transcultural and international. Generally, the ideas of inculturation and indigenisation prepared the ground for wider acceptance of the reforms initiated by the *Second Vatican Council* in the 1960s. Expatriate missionaries still governed the church to a great extent, although the number of African priests rapidly grew, especially in the area of pastoral theology. Yet the expatriates, not the locals, were the ones who pushed through the transformations suggested by Vatican II.[5]

On the *Protestant side* a milestone was the book *The Akan Doctrine of God* (1944) by the Ghanaian Joseph Danquah. He presented African traditional religion 'as basically monotheistic' and 'compatible with the Christian view of God'. More emphatic in this line is the Methodist missionary Edwin Smith who advocated 'a synthesis of African views of God and shaped it as a coherent, unified theology'. Following the same line

---

[4] Ward, 'Africa', in: Hastings (ed), *World History*, pp.229,230.
[5] Ward, 'Africa', in: Hastings (ed), *World History*, p.231.

was John Mbiti's book *African Religions and Philosophy* (1969). Another initiative was taken by the Swedish Lutheran missionary Bengt Sundkler in his book *Christian ministry in Africa* (1960) which in 1966 led to a theological consultation in Nigeria of theologians such as Kwesi Dickson, John Mbiti, and Harry Sawyer, who published their findings in *Biblical Revelation and African Beliefs*. Some theologians believed traditional African culture and religion – similar to what Christianity was said to have – has a *'liberating dimension'*, which had to be rediscovered because colonialism had buried it.[6] Later, when it was experienced that African independence could threaten the church, the original ideas of African theology began to be criticised. People like the Ugandan writer and anthropologist Okot p'Bitek (1931-1982) began to reject the idea that traditional African society is saturated with a kind of religion that is 'basically consonant with Christianity'.[7]

Steven Bantu Biko was one of the founders of the Black Consciousness Movement in South Africa in the late 1960s. He was arrested and died in a prison cell in 1977.

b. Liberation Theology

In the 1970s a new emphasis was added to the emphasis on traditional religion and culture. Racial, political, economic and social justice came to be stressed as the starting point and as the aim of theology. Meetings by the *World Council of Churches* in Nairobi (1975) and by the *Third World Theologians* in Dar es Salaam (1976), strongly advocating the combat of *racism* and a just world order, contributed to the birth of the movement of *Liberation Theology* which professed to begin with the need of the poor and the oppressed, and to give them the hope of the coming kingdom. African theology was influenced by Liberation Theology and by some of its sub-movements.

Feminist theology is a strand of Liberation Theology; it has affected the thinking of many male and female theologians in Africa.[8]

Another influential strand is the movement of *Black Theology*.[9] It originates from Afro-American writers like James Cone, and it developed particularly in the South African struggle for racial equality with representatives such as Allen Boesak, Manas Buthelezi, and Desmond Tutu; it directly influenced the *Black Consciousness Movement* and Steve Biko's *South African Students' Organisation*. The *Kairos Document* of 1985, drawn up by black and white South African theologians, is seen as its major expression of protest against the apartheid regime.

Desmond Mpilo Tutu (born 1931), Anglican Archbishop, leader of the South African Council of Churches, and an influential figure in the struggle against apartheid.

---

[6] Cf.: Tinyiko Sam Maluleke, 'Half a Century of African Christian Theologies: Elements Emerging Agenda for the Twenty-First Century', in: Kalu et al. (eds), *African Christianity*. pp.469-485.

[7] Cf.: Ward, 'Africa', in: Hastings (ed), *World History*, p.232.

[8] Cf.: Tinyiko Sam Maluleke, 'Half a Century of African Christian Theologies: Elements Emerging Agenda for the Twenty-First Century', in: Kalu et al. (eds), *African Christianity*. pp.489-491.

[9] See ththe survey in: Verstraelen-Gilhuis, *A New Look at Christianity in Africa*, pp.25-33.

c. Evangelical and Reformed Theology

Evangelicalism aims at re-assertion of the final authority of Scripture as the only source of the central truths of the Christian faith. *Evangelical Theology*,[10] is rooted in the *Evangelical revivals* and *awakenings* of the 18th and 19th centuries. In a wider sense – as meant here – it does not differ from classical *Reformed Theology*. Unfortunately, to some the term *Reformed Theology* has been tainted negatively by a connotation with the South African Dutch Reformed churches which supported the apartheid system. Basically, however, *Reformed Theology* is a movement that emphasises the continuous importance of going back to the sources, i.e. to Scripture.[11] It recognises much in the Evangelical revivals and awakenings, in that they were a reiteration of the theology of the great Reformers of the 16th century. That is why, especially in the Anglo-Saxon world, the words 'evangelical' and 'reformed' basically cover the same tradition of thought and practice. The term *Presbyterian theology* is an alternative name for Reformed theology, although it reflects more of its ecclesiastical side.

Byang Kato (1936-1975) Evangelical theologian from Nigeria, co-founder of the AEAM.

Reformed, Presbyterian, and Evangelical theological thought has put a lot of emphasis on the importance of the Christian Congregation, and as such it could be called *Congregational Theology*.

The 20th century, however, saw the beginning and growth of movements of Neo-Reformed and Neo-Evangelical thinking that consciously deviated from the theology of the Reformation. This means that one can be confused by literature that refers to modern evangelical and reformed thought, without qualifying it in comparison to the theological heritage of the Reformation. Shaw for instance, does not define in this respect what he means by *Evangelical Theology* when he represents *African Evangelicalism* as one of the faces of African Christian Theology. Making the usual claim that Africa has many evangelicals, he mentions a number of theologians who, in his view, were formative for African Evangelical Theology: Byang Kato, Osadolor Imasogie, Cornelius Olowala, Tokunboh Adeyemo, all from Nigeria, Bediako (Ghana), and Tite Tiénou (Burkina Faso). Some Evangelical theologians, like Byang Kato, emphatically rejected the optimistic idea that bridges could be built between African Traditional Religion and Christianity. In 1966 in Limuru, Kenya, they founded the *Association of Evangelicals of Africa and Madagascar*, AEAM, now AEA. In 1982 they started a magazine, *Africa Journal of Evangelical Theology*. In the AEA the various national associations of Evangelicals are represented.

---

[10] Cf.: Maluleke, 'Half a Century of African Christian Theologies', in: Kalu et al. (eds), *African Christianity*. pp.487,488.

[11] Cf.: Steven Paas, 'Some Principles of Reformed Theology', paper at Workshop by Reformed Mission League, in Liwonde, Malawi, June 2004.

Shaw has called Byang Kato (1936-1975) 'the founding father of modern African Evangelical Theology'.[12] In his doctoral thesis, *Theological Pitfalls in Africa*,[13] Kato was ready to contextualise the Gospel for Africans in the specific African cultures. At the same time, Kato emphasised the Bible as the unique Word of God, 'the ultimate source and authority for all legitimate theological expression, including African'. Though appreciating the riches and inherent values of African traditions and cultures, Kato was of the opinion that *at their most fundamental level* they include a 'meaning and purpose of life' that is essentially incompatible with Christian faith. That is why he stressed the discontinuity between the Gospel and any traditional, non-Christian religion. There had to be a radical break with traditional beliefs, including *African Traditional Religions*. This view he also applied to Western cultures and all other cultures, stressing that the Gospel ultimately transcends and challenges all cultures. Kato was not a-cultural let alone anti-cultural. In his thought the preachers of the Gospel should engage seriously with traditional culture. Domestication of the Gospel reveals and vitiates the essential integrity of African cultures. Kato responded to the universalism and syncretism which he observed in African churches and theologies, by the influence of liberal theologians like John Mbiti and Bolaji Idowu, and of the ecumenical movement, and also of the growth of politically inspired movements of opposition to the church in some post-colonial African states. Kato denounced all liberal theology and philosophy that deviated from the authority of the Bible as the Word of God. His adage was: 'Let African Christians be Christian Africans!'[14]

Shaw, although he appreciates the work of Kato and others, would have liked African Evangelical theologians to have achieved more, whether academically or in 'interaction with current African issues'. It is true that perhaps more could have been done, but African Christianity has maintained a strong classical Protestant, Evangelical tendency. By the end of the 20th century this tendency was still strong in Africa, and it showed signs of renewal. Shaw admits this, and he thinks that contributions to new life were made by international Evangelical revivals in the wake of the *Lausanne Covenant*, formulated at the *Lausanne Conference* in 1974, where many Africans were present. He observes positive developments in *African Evangelical Theology*: (a) the formation of *Evangelical National Fellowships* in Zambia, Kenya, Nigeria and other African countries which stressed the uniqueness of Christ for salvation, thus counteracting the rampant ideas of religious pluralism that degraded Christianity to just one way of truth; (b) a new understanding of the positive relationship between Gospel and Culture; (c) the re-assertion of a Christ-centred view of the Kingdom of God at the end of time, 'that refused to be identified with human ideologies or programs' for a new political, social and economic world order.

In Shaw's words, African Evangelical theologians are challenged to re-discover 'the lordship of the risen and returning Christ of Orthodoxy', who is the hope of the world. This re-discovery signifies the failure of: (a) theological liberalism; (b) escapist mainline traditionalism; (c) overspiritual charismatic expression; and of (d) the overrealised eschatology in the *Charismatic Movement* and in the various branches of

---

[12] Shaw, *The Kingdom of God*, p.278.

[13] Byang Kato, *Theological Pitfalls in Africa*, Kisumu: Evangelical Publishing House, 1975.

[14] This paragraph is a summary of: Keith Ferdinando's well documented DACB article on Byang Kato [DACB Website].

liberation theology. In other word, African evangelicals are different from liberals, traditionalists and charismatics.

d. Other Theologies

Besides, these schools of theology in Africa, there are others. Maluleke mentions some of them. *Theologies of the AIC's* concentrate on the exposure of the significance of African Instituted Churches for African Christianity and Theology. Christian Baeta, David Barrett, Martinus Daneel, and Harold Turner are the leading theologians. *Translation Theologies*, with theologians such as Lamin Sanneh and Kwame Bediako, study the way the Gospel should be made to speak to the African situation. *Theologies of Reconstruction* reject the old approaches of African Theology, Liberation Theology etc. Their theologians like Jesse Mugambi and Charles Villa-Vicencio want to improve the quality of African life by engaging into dialogue with politics and economics.[15]

54.4. Africa and Mainstream Theologies

Discussion will continue about the interaction between African Christianity and the mainstream theologies that came to Africa in and after the missionary era, e.g.: Reformed/Evangelical theology, Roman Catholic theology (classical and post Second Vatican Council), Liberal theology (theological Modernism), Neo-reformed/ Neo-evangelical theology, Ecumenical theology, and Post Modern theology. These lines of theological thought may have originated in the West, yet they belong to global Christianity. Now they are in the process of being inculturated in Africa. All continue to be challenged by Scripture, which is the touchstone of any theology whether global, Western or African.

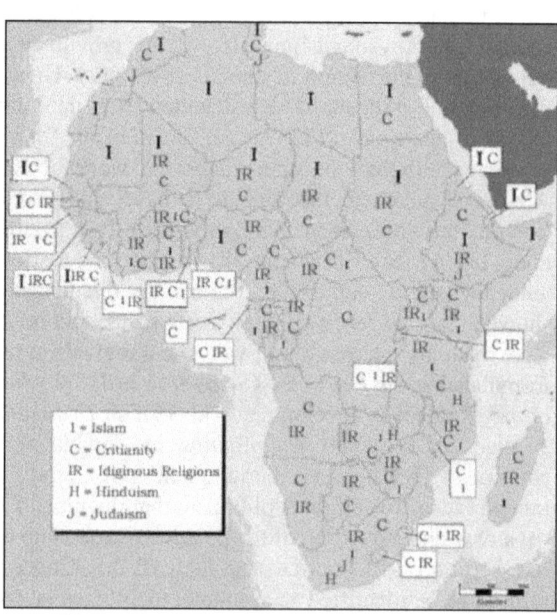

Map of the main religions in Africa.

---

[15] Maluleke, 'Half a Century of African Christian Theologies', in: Kalu et al. (eds), *African Christianity*. pp.485-487, 488-489, 491-492.

55. Faith Missions

55.1. Pre-Classical Missions

Missions are as old as the Church; there is nothing new and strange in that. But in the first centuries after the Reformation the Protestants only concentrated on evangelising their own peoples. They did not do much mission overseas. The only major exception perhaps is the mission by the *Moravian Brethren*. For reasons that will be shown below, the *Moravian Mission* is called (by Fiedler[1]) a *Pre-Classical Mission*.

55.2. Classical Missions

Protestants became active in mission overseas by the end of the 18th century. According to Kenneth Scott Latourette, this Protestant Missionary Movement comes to a climax in 'the great century of mission', 1792-1914, when it spread over the whole world. It is spiritually related to the *Great Awakening*, with people like Jonathan Edwards. The Methodists were among its exponents, with people like Charles and John Wesley. John Wesley declared: 'The world is my parish'. They strongly influenced the Anglo-Saxon area and prepared the ground for the Missionary Movement.

In 1792 William Carey was the first to reshape the *Great Awakening* to a *Missionary Movement*. In 1793, after publishing his famous book *Enquiry*,[2] he started modern mission to India. With this aim he founded the *Baptist Missionary Society* (BMS). Carey's initiative was fed by the idea that missionary societies instead of the churches themselves would be the agencies of mission. This is how *Classical Missions* started. The movement of Classical Missions was very successful. Through it Africa became Christian. It led to the foundation of Classical Churches, like the Church of Central Africa Presbyterian (CCAP), the Anglican Church, the Congregationalists, the Lutheran Churches, and the Roman Catholic Church. They achieved a lot, but not enough. The *Classical Missionary Movement* did not reach everywhere, but stuck mainly to the coast. In general, the interior was not reached. This was so in China and also in Africa. By 1880 inner Africa, e.g. the Sudan Belt and the Congo, had still not been touched by Christianity. Even Roman Catholic efforts in Angola, and the Congo, that started in the 16th century, had stuck to the coast and had not progressed much further by 1880. Other initiatives were needed to reach the interior. The *Classical Missionary Movement* could not fill the gap because their hands and money were bound by the new churches that they had to nurture.

55.3. Revival Ferment

In view of the need of mission to unreached lands, so Latourette says, the Holy Spirit pushed the Church forward through revivals that led to ever new organisations. Around 1800 some of the fervour of the *Great Awakening* had subsided, and the next great revival (the *Second Evangelical Revival* or the *Holiness Revival*) was still two

---

[1] Klaus Fiedler, *The Story of Faith Missions: From Hudson Taylor to Present-day Africa,* Oxford: Regnum, 1994², pp.32-111.
[2] William Carey, *An Enquiry into the Obligation of Christians to Use Means for the Conversion of the Heathen,* Leicester, 1792.

generations ahead in time. In the early decades a new revival broke out, which may be called the *Restorationist Revival*, which had the aim of restoring the Primitive Church once more before the end of the world.[3]

a. Brethren Movement

Of the movements brought about by the *Restorationist Revival*, the *Brethren* (also called 'Christian Brethren') became important for mission. They loved the Bible and discovered from it that there is no need for any clergy. All are Brethren and all share the missionary obligation, at home and worldwide. The Brethren never became many, but with the exception of the Moravians a century earlier, no denomination ever was as mission-minded as they were.

The *Brethren* missionaries mostly work under the name *Christian Mission in Many Lands*, and they contributed greatly to the evangelisation of Africa, in Northern Angola, Northern Zambia, and the Eastern Congo from the Copperbelt to the north. Many Brethren also joined the Faith Missions, and Brethren played an important role for the early *China Inland Mission*. For a large part of Evangelical Christianity the *Brethren* were instrumental in changing the eschatology of Christ's Second Coming from amillennial (as in general Christian tradition) or postmillennial (as in *Pietism* and the *Great Awakening*) to premillennial.[4]

b. Prophetic Movement

Part of the revival ferment of those days was the *Prophetic Movement*. In it the Brethren were central, but it encompassed much of Evangelical Christianity. The *Prophetic Movement* stressed that the Scriptures, especially Daniel and Revelation, give a picture of the future of the Church in the end time. There was much concentration on and longing for the Second Coming of the Lord that was expected to happen soon. However, according to *Matthew 24:14*, there is a pre-condition, the Lord will not return until the Gospel has been preached to all nations. Therefore they wanted to do their utmost to fulfil this pre-condition, until the last tribe will be reached.

One of the leading teachers of the *Prophetic Movement* was Grattan Guinness (†1910), whose wife Fanny started the *Livingstone Inland Mission* (1879), the first Faith Mission in Africa. In 1873 both together started the *East London Training Institute for Home and Foreign Missions*, which became the first of many Bible Schools training Evangelical missionaries. The most famous of these is perhaps the Moody Bible Institute in Chicago. One of its students for some time was Daniel Malikebu, who later

---

[3] Klaus Fiedler, 'A Revival Disregarded and Disliked', in: *Festschrift Käser*, Bonn: VKW, 2004. He characterizes the various churches in the *Restoration Revival* movement. Since the New Testament does not provide a clear and unified picture of how the primitive church was organised, the resulting 'restored' churches differed greatly: the *Brethren* emphasised the breaking of bread in Biblical simplicity, the *Apostolic Movement* around Edward Irving emphasised the Apostles and the spiritual gifts, the *Adventist Movement* emphasised the preparation for the coming of the Lord, and the *Churches of Christ* emphasised the independence of each local congregation.

[4] See my *Christian Zionism Examined*, pp.43-65, 120-122 for an explanation of the tenets of Millennialism or Chiliasm. *Amillennialism*: The view that the 1,000 years of Christ's reign on earth, referred to in *Revelation* 20, are figurative and pertain to the present era, not to the future only. *Postmillennialism*: The theory that before the return of Christ there will be a 1,000 years of peace and righteousness. *Premillennialism*: The theory that after the return of Christ there will be a 1,000 years in which Christ physically reigns on the earth.

became successor to John Chilembwe as leader of the *Providence Industrial Mission* in Nyasaland.

c. Holiness Movement

The third element in the revival ferment of the first half of the 19th century was the *Holiness Movement*. It started with Phoebe Palmer in 1835. The aim was the promotion of sanctification in the lives of believers. This included great dedication and commitment, strengthening the power to serve, not in the least in mission, at home and abroad.

55.4. Faith Missions

On the strength of the spiritual energies of these three movements, and fuelled by the next major revival, the *Second Great Awakening* (or the *Holiness Revival* as Fiedler puts it), new missionary organisations emerged. The Second Great Awakening spread throughout the Anglo-Saxon world and the European Continent. Personal holiness and the power to serve were emphasised. In this movement the churches played no important role. The Faith Missions started with James Hudson Taylor. Deeply influenced by this holiness revival he more or less personified the movement's disinterest in church affiliations. Hudson Taylor began as a Methodist, then he moved to the *Free Methodists*, then he joined the Brethren, subsequently he became a member of a Mission Hall Church, and he ended his life as a Baptist. This shifting of churches does not mean, however, that Taylor and his brethren were shaky in their beliefs. To them church affiliation was a matter of expediency. Moving freely from one church to another was typical for the whole movement.

Phoebe Palmer (1807-1874) was a very influential Methodist in America. She was at the cradle of the American Holiness Movement, from which eventually emerged Pentecostal denominations, social reforms and also missions.

Taylor's desire was to be a missionary in China, and he went there with the help of the *Brethren Movement*. He had a significant relationship with George Müller, founder of an orphanage, who had been a disciple of Anthony Norris Groves, a onetime missionary to Baghdad (1828) and India. Groves taught that there is no need for ordination, as the Bible does not mention it. God will supply the missionary with the necessary means. He must not beg or ask for money (except in prayer to God), and must not incur debts either. Müller followed this principle, and he transferred it to Taylor. When the *Brethren* forgot about him and left him in China without support, this principle became very important to Taylor. He became an independent missionary, who relied on God's help as the answer to private prayer. Often support came from George Müller, whom he had met only once before going to China.

James Hudson Taylor (1832-1905), founder of the China Inland Mission, which was an example for others to establish Faith Missions for Africa.

After working years as a pioneer not far from the coast, Taylor became sick, and in 1861 he returned to England. But he continued to be consumed by the desire to spread the Gospel in Inland China. He travelled all over Britain trying to enlist support from various missionary organisations, but he had very little response. The *Classical Missions* had been so successful that they were unable to accept any other commitments. Their approach did not leave them extra capacity. In order to become a missionary you had to study theology first and be accepted and ordained as a minister. Not many other people were allowed to be sent out by the classical missionary organisations, so that much missionary capacity remained unused.

A.B. Simpson was the first to call for the use of *'neglected forces'* (non-clergy, women) and so reach the unreached at new places, and go to the last tribe. This led to the emergence of an innovative movement that encouraged the use of new forces, new types of missionaries, and new missionary ideas. The new (post-classical) organisations were not asking for money. They employed mostly missionaries that would not have been accepted according to traditional opinion. Being called was the most important thing that counted.

In 1865 the first organisation of the new type was formed, the *China Inland Mission*. The founders were James Hudson Taylor and his wife Maria. After Maria's death, Taylor married Jennie Faulding who also played an important role in the CIM.[5]

55.5. Special Characteristics of Faith Missions

The *China Inland Mission* and the other *Faith Missions* that followed its example differed in a number of ways from the *Classical Missions*. These different principles were not looked upon as a law for all missionary organisations, but as indicating how God had led this particular Faith Mission.

The *Faith Missions* accepted missionaries from all Protestant denominations. This was done on an individual basis. The aim being not corporal (denominational) unity, but individual unity in the common faith. Apart from perhaps a reference from the local pastor, the churches where the candidates came from were not asked for permission or support. Most candidates for ordinary mission posts came from *Presbyterian, Baptist,* and *Anglican Churches*, whereas the leaders often came from *Free Churches*. In many cases candidates came from the *Brethren*, or they had been influenced by them. Many missionaries in their careers once or more often changed denominations.

People from different churches with different church orders and ecclesiological views could only cooperate if they considered the ecclesiological order to be of secondary importance. In some cases missionaries of a certain church were given their own field where they were allowed to establish a church of their own denomination, e.g. Anglicans working for the *Africa Inland Mission* in the West Nile Province of Northern Uganda were allowed to found an Anglican Church there.[6] In this way contradictions could be made acceptable.

The majority of the missionaries, however, did not much care for definite rules of church order. They did not consider different views of church order as dividing. In general, this question was worked out *pragmatically* in the field. In most cases this resulted in the formation of churches that mixed a kind of *Presbyterian order* with the

---

[5] Cf.: Howard Taylor (and his wife), *Biography of James Hudson Taylor*, London: China Inland Mission Overseas Missionary Fellowship, 1965; Peter Hammond, *The Greatest Century of Missions*, Howard Place: Christian Liberty books, n.d., pp.101-109.

[6] Fiedler, *Story of Faith Missions*, p.83.

Baptists' believer's baptism, although the majority of the missionaries came from churches with *infant baptism*.

The *Classical Missions* were voluntary associations of people who contributed. Their missionaries were not members but employees, who were paid salaries according to a scale that allowed for differences in payment. Faith missions, however, were not based on (fixed) contributions. Their missionaries were *members*. They were the owners of the organisation, and as such they did not get salaries. Instead of salaries they got support, based on needs and situations, not based on juniority, seniority, or education.

Classical and Post-Classical missionaries both lived and worked by faith. Post-Classical missions are called *Faith Missions*, not only because the missionaries were not paid salaries, but also because they did not ask for gifts or collections. Faith was to be the only guarantee that money would come in. Taylor's principle was never to take up a collection. He felt God did not allow him to do this. His adage was: *'God's work, done in God's way, will never lack God's supply'*. At the same time, *Faith Missions* did not allow getting into debts and lending or borrowing money. If no money would come in for a certain project, then it was concluded that the project did not have God's blessing and should be stopped. In Taylor's thinking, which was adopted by many others, the faith principle of funding was to be understood as a communal faith. This meant that God would supply *'us all'*, so that everything that came in would be *shared* in the field by all workers. In later times others have changed this communal faith principle into a principle of *individual faith*. The individual missionary would supply his or her own support. This change often made income rise considerably.

Spirituality, not intellectual training, is decisive. God will enlist people from any class and with all kinds of qualifications. In order to prepare this great variety of workers for the mission field, in 1873 the first *Bible School*, the *East London Training Institute*,[7] was founded by Fanny and Grattan Guinness. The project was strongly recommended by Taylor. The term 'Bible School' was adopted, because the students did not know Greek and Hebrew, and used the Bible in the English vernacular. Taylor and other leaders of Faith Missions did not object to the ordination of ministers or of candidates for the mission, but he did not consider it necessary. In principle God ordains you.

In the *Faith Missions* the wives of missionaries were accepted as full missionaries in their own right. In the Classical Missions a wife was just the wife to the missionary. The Faith Mission's rule was that if one was accepted single, and wanted to marry later, then also the wife had to qualify before she would be accepted.

Especially the *Holiness Movement* paved the way for single women to various functions in the mission field. Many single women in their own right became evangelists, even heads of mission stations. The choice of women was not a matter of expediency because of the lack of male candidates, but Taylor wanted to use new people, new ideas, for new places. He could have found at least a few men for all missionary areas, but he consciously wanted to give a place to women too.

Faith missionaries were to live the life of the local people, using their language and accepting their living conditions. CIM-missionaries wore Chinese dress. Identification also meant not leaning on your foreign power and privileges. Some missionaries, who went far in the acculturation, were subjected to suffering, even to death, as was the case

---

[7] Perry, L. (ed.), *Joseph Booth: Africa for the African* (1st ed. 1897), Blantyre: CLAIM, 1997, pp.73,77,105: Joseph Booth's son Edward attended this school before coming to Malawi, where he died soon after.

55. Faith Missions

with the missionary martyrs in China around 1900. There is no direct link between their acculturation and death, though. Acculturation made it possible for them to live in the interior, but they were killed as foreigners, and they would even have been killed if not acculturated.

Other characteristics are acceptance of sacrifice and suffering, the principle that evangelism precedes the institution, stress on itineration of the missionary, acceptance

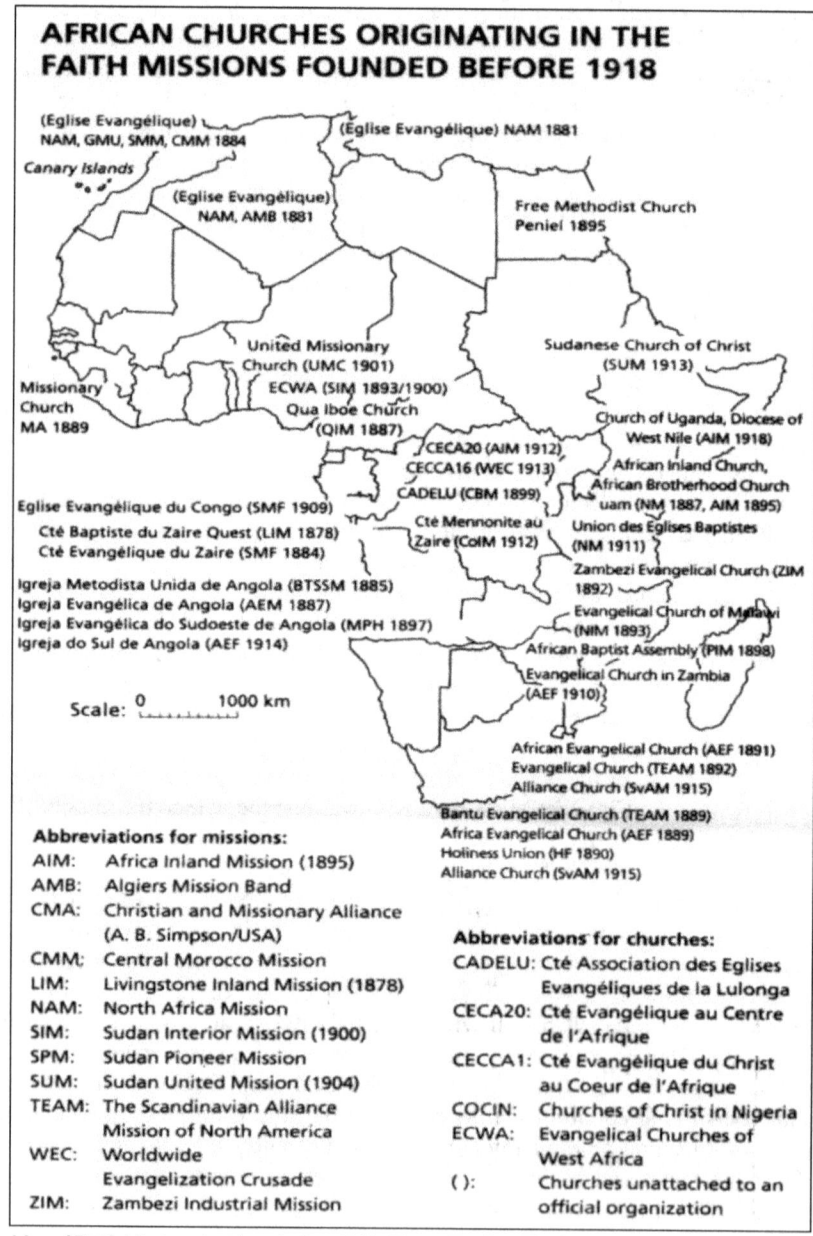

Map of Faith Missions in Africa before 1918 (From: Fiedler, The Story of Faith Missions, p.82).

of the international character of mission organisations, and the principle that leadership of a mission is centralistic and field-based.

55.6. Faith Missions in Africa

A map in Fiedler's handbook on the *Faith Missions*[8] shows the unreached areas in Africa and some of the Faith Mission organisations that filled up the inland gap. The Classical Missions had covered regions like South Africa, Madagascar, part of Ethiopia, Egypt, and southern Nigeria. But the advance had stopped because of the following reasons: (a) consolidation of their successes, (b) decline of the classical revival movement, (c) loss of spiritual power, (d) lack of cash, (e) lack of personnel. Therefore, the Classical Missions had little power to go into the interior. But the Post-Classical Missions provided new forces, personnel, spirituality, ideas, and money for the missionary enterprise in inland Africa. We mention the following *Faith Missions* in Africa.

a. Livingstone Inland Mission

The *Livingstone Inland Mission*, originally led by Fanny Guinness, was the first Faith Mission. They started their work from the mouth of the Congo River. In 1884 the work was handed over to American Baptists, but the Swedish LIM-members continued their work as a Faith Mission, entering also Congo-Brazzaville.[9]

b. Africa Inland Mission

Peter Cameron Scott was at the cradle of the AIM. He was born in Glasgow, but his family emigrated to America. At first he was a missionary of the *Christian and Missionary Alliance* (CMA) which was founded by A.B. Simpson. Simpson had been a minister of the Presbyterian Church in Canada and in the USA. He was dismissed because he accepted believers' baptism, and was privately 're-baptised', although he never became a Baptist. Then, Simpson started his own church and in 1889, influenced by 'power for service' adage of the *Holiness Movement*, began the *Christian and Missionary Alliance* (CMA). This evangelical and innovative mission organisation touched Africa in only a few places, like the Congo and Sierra Leone.

Peter Cameron Scott (1867-1896), founder of the Africa Inland Mission.

In 1891 Simpson ordained Peter Cameron Scott who was sent to the west coast of the Congo (in the border area of present Congo and Cabinda) to be a missionary there. Scott's idea was to establish a *chain of mission stations* across Africa, first from the West (Congo) to the East (Kenya – Mombasa), and when this did not work out, from the East to the West, or even from both sides at the same time. However, Scott's preliminary attempts were not successful during his lifetime. After three years, he fell ill and had to return. Moreover, Simpson decided against his plans.

---

[8] Fiedler, *Faith Missions*, p.53, cf. pp.77,83.
[9] Fiedler, *Story of Faith Missions*, pp.37-39.

55. Faith Missions

A.B. Simpson (1843-1919), founder of the Christian and Missionary Alliance.

Then, in 1895, in line with the individualistic spirit of many faith missionaries, Scott quit the CMA, and started his own mission, the *Africa Inland Mission*, to work in inland Kenya. Scott's death at Kangundo in 1896 caused a serious crisis in the AIM, but the *Philadelphia Missionary Council* took over full responsibility, and the Principal of their Bible School, C.E. Hurlbert, accompanied by his wife and five children and some other workers, went to Mombasa, to become missionaries. The missionaries experienced many difficulties, but Scott's work survived. At Kijabe the AIM centre in Kenya was established. The AIM work in Kenya grew into a big church, the *Africa Inland Church*, with more than a million members. It is a Baptist-type church, with somewhat Presbyterian structures. The work of the AIM was extended to Tanzania where also a Baptist-type church was established, and to North West Uganda where under the AIM flag, an Anglican church came into being. With the intention of creating a 'chain of mission stations across Africa', beginning in Mombasa, the AIM headed for North East Congo, and in the direction of Lake Chad.[10]

c. Sudan Missions

The founder of the *Sudan Interior Mission* was Roland V. Bingham. He was converted under the influence of the *Salvation Army*, which he joined. After his emigration to Canada, he met with the leader of the CMA in that country, and became a pastor in the CMA. Like many faith missionaries, Roland Bingham made several changes of denomination.

He was influenced by the Brethren as well, and later he became a Baptist. In 1893, as independent missionaries, Roland Bingham together with others went to the interior of Sudan, trying to reach Lake Chad. All except Bingham died due to problems of malaria and lack of equipment.

A second attempt was made in 1900, by which time Bingham had formed his own society, the *Sudan Interior Mission*. The SIM was successful in regions like Northern Nigeria, Niger, Southern Ethiopia, Sudan, Liberia, Somalia, and Ghana. The work led to the foundation of *Evangelical Churches of West-Africa* (ECWA), which now has two or three million members and its own missionary society with about a thousand missionaries.[11] The success of SIM in Nigeria and other countries after the *Second World War* was partly due to its literature and radio work.[12]

Hospital of the Sudan Interior Mission in Galmi, Niger.

In 1904 the *Sudan United Mission* was founded by Lucy Kumm, the daughter of Grattan Guiness, and her husband Karl Kumm. The mission began in Nigeria and from

---

[10] Fiedler, *Faith Missions*, p.49,53,74,75,83; Hastings, *Church in Africa*, pp.424,455; Hildebrandt, *History of the Church in Africa*, p.169.

[11] Fiedler, *Faith Missions*, p.50;

[12] Cf.: Hildebrandt, *History of the Church in Africa*, pp.208,209.

there it penetrated further into the Sudan belt. The results were a church with millions of members,[13] which later in several regions became heavily persecuted by Muslim regimes.[14]

In the north of the Sudan belt SIM and SUM worked in a border situation with Islam. They aimed at converting the remaining pagan tribes of Northern Nigeria before they would turn to Islam. Unfortunately, many of the northern border tribes converted to Islam.[15] However, Kumm's vision of getting to tribes before the Muslims partially

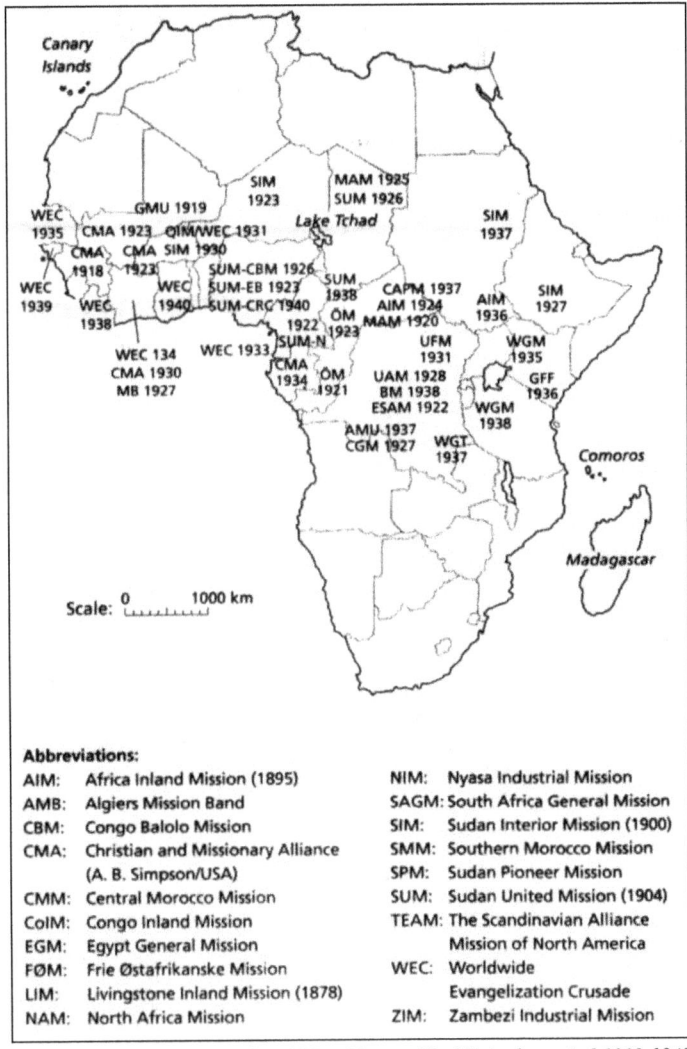

Map of Faith Missions in Africa("New Mission Work") in the period 1918-1940 (From: Fiedler: The Story of Faith, p.85).

---

[13] Hildebrandt, *History of the Church in Africa*, p.205, describes a doubling of church attendance in SUM areas in Nigeria and other places of West Africa between 1935 and 1940.

[14] Cf.: Hastings, *Church in Africa*, p.552.

[15] Cf.: Hildebrandt, *History of the Church in Africa*, pp.159,160.

succeeded. Half or more than half of the traditionalist tribes in Nigeria were converted to Christianity.[16] Those that fell to Islam are still being evangelised and the church is still growing in northern Nigeria, though at places heavily persecuted.

---

[16] Operation World [Internet] 2015: with 81 million members, Christianity is the largest religion of Nigeria.

56. Unity and Cooperation

56.1. What is Unity?

a. Diversity and Truth

The issue of unity and cooperation has attracted the attention of many people, especially the church leaders.[1] Unity, according to Scripture, is characterised by *diversity* and by *truth*. This applies to God and also to His creation.

A Family: Unity in Truth and Diversity (from: website: syr.edu/).

First, in unity there is *diversity*. God is One. *Deuteronomy* 6:4 (KJV) says: 'Hear o Israel, the Lord our God is one God'. In *Mark* 12:29,32, *Romans* 3:30, and *James* 2:19 this is repeated. But our God is also diverse. 'There are three that bear record in heaven, the Father, the Word, and the Holy Ghost, and these three are one' (1 *John* 5:7 KJV). God's diversity is an essential aspect of His character. It reflects His Tri-Unity, the Father who creates, the Son who recreates, and the Holy Ghost who quickens to life. Together the three are in all the works of our one God. Diversity in unity is a main characteristic of the created things, including man. In 1 *Corinthians* 12:12ff. we are reminded of the human body's diversity. Yet in its diversity the body is cohesive. The members of the body and the senses and functions of the mind are different, but there is no schism, for they are cooperating harmoniously, thus constituting the oneness and strength of the human being.

Secondly, in unity there is *truth*. Being one, having unity is being true. This again is first of all shown in God. 'He is a God of truth, and without iniquity'.[2] And Jesus Christ, through whom we know God in his oneness, says: 'I am the way, the truth, and the life'.[3] And again this is reflected in the created things. True unity, however varied it may be, is strong, healthy, and trustworthy. The bodily members and the spiritual functions of the human being can be trusted to cooperate in truth and faithfulness. The whole of nature is a composition of endless variety that is composed to a faithfully working oneness of beauty and strength. In the true harmony of its parts the whole of nature gets its magnificence and glory. We see it also in marriage and family life. Husband and wife, their children, may be very different in character, but in their togetherness they are a strong and attractive unity, even reflecting the relationship between Christ and the congregation of believers (cf. *Eph*.5:22ff). Thus, Scripture shows that there is unity in God and also unity in the things created by Him.

---

[1] For this chapter, also: Shaw, *The Kingdom*, pp.282-288; Sundkler and Steed, *History of the Church in Africa*, pp.1018-1035; Hastings, *African Christianity*, pp.159-162, 169, 292, and other pages; cf. Cairns, *Christianity through the Centuries*, pp.468-500.

[2] Dt.32:4.

[3] John 14:6.

b. Analogy Qualified by Scripture

There is an analogy between the unity of God and the unity of the created things. According to Thomas Aquinas (†1274), this analogy is an *analogy-of-being* (Latin: *analogia entis*). This opinion is a result of Thomas's view of the way in which the universal reality exists. He says that the structure of nature is similar to the structure of supra-nature. In principle there is comparability. Being in the eternal reality can be compared to being in the finite reality. This analogy enables natural reason to penetrate into the supra-natural knowledge of God, although with the help of God's grace. In Thomas' view the possibility of salvation for man depends on this. Salvation is only possible within the framework of *analogical togetherness* of human nature and divine grace. And this *analogical togetherness* leads to the possibility and the necessity of *cooperation* between human reason and divine revelation. 'Natural reason ascends from below above the knowledge of created things to God. And God descends from above meeting man'. In various ways Thomas tried to defend this idea which gives nature an upward power that can penetrate into the supra-natural. In his view, the lower things support the higher ones; they even absorb part of them, which enables them to climb higher.[4]

Depiction of Thomas Aquinas (from: The Demidoff Altarpiece by Carlo Crivelli).

But the analogy between Creator and created things cannot be explained in these terms of Thomist philosophy. Creatures do not harbour such a positive upward quality, because of the reality of *sin* and *death*. God is perfect, but God's creation has lost its perfection. According to some, the fact of God's unity necessarily means that the diversity in nature is truly one in the same way. But this view denies the difference that is there between God and his creation. God is then supposed to be in everything, all things in nature would be divine; hence, they would be one. This view also denies the awesome reality of the brokenness of created things by *sin*. Creation has fallen into sin. That is why the splendid unity in diversity and truth has been damaged utterly.

c. Restoration through Salvation by Christ

Restoration of the real unity in the God given diversity and truth cannot be achieved by men or women. The way to the regeneration of unity is the way of the Cross where Jesus Christ through his suffering and death restored unity by defeating the powers of Satan, death and sin. Only in Him is unity to be found. Through faith in Him humans can go the way of the true and diverse unity that God has meant for His people. Faith in Christ comprises the acceptance of the Word of God as the highest and authoritative rule for all aspects of life. This applies to individuals and also to churches. Unity without being in Christ and without being obedient to the Word of God is no real unity. It can be even the *opposite* of it. Satan also pretends to seek unity. But this unity,

---

[4] The analogy-of-being Thomas developed in the first part of his *Summa Theologiae* (I,q.45a.7, and I,q.47a.1); we used a survey in: H. Meyer, *Thomas von Aquin: sein System un seine geistesgeschichtliche Stellung*, Bonn: Hannstein, 1938, pp.152-167.

however attractive it sometimes may seem, is a damaging unity that has no future but leads to eternal loss.

It is good to realise these things when we are discussing the pursuits for unity in the world in general, and in the churches in particular. Throughout history man has attempted to make his own unity in a way that distorted Christ and the Word, or even swept Christ and the Word aside. Real Christian unity is a spiritual and theological unity that is rooted in the Scripture, which through the Holy Spirit gives 'truth in love'.[5] However, attempts at unity that were labelled truly Christian, without being guided by the authoritative voices of the Word and the Spirit, have been no exception.

56.2. Syncretism

When Christian scholars and ministers lose confidence in the absolute divine authority of the Bible, they readily mix and combine elements which are contradictory in nature. Compromise is made in order to accommodate contemporary teachings and traditions. This has been done in Western theology by the liberal movements of Modernism and Post-Modernism. In an African context, liberalism also plays a role.

In some quarters of older African mainline churches Western liberalism has invaded. This has produced a mentality that it does not really matter what you believe, as long as there is some superficial connection to the Bible. This attitude in the African context paved the way for another consequence of liberal thought, syncretism, i.e. for the joining together of opposite beliefs of African Traditional Religions and Christianity.[6] Early examples of syncretism are the cults of the Nyau Societies and the Mbona shrine in Malawi. After the missionaries arrived, members of these cults tried to combine their religious views with elements from Christianity.

Syncretism often operates under the disguise of *African Christian Theology*. By the end of the colonial era efforts were intensified to relate Christian theology to the African context. Although this process was started by white theologians, at a later stage it connected to the opinion of many Africans that the theology of the missionaries was too much a presentation of Western issues, and that it had failed to answer the important questions in African culture. Serious attempts were made to create a genuinely *African Christian Theology*. As such, inculturation or incarnation of Christian teaching in Africa cannot be opposed by any Christian. But by mixing religious concepts the uniqueness and the absolute authority of the Word of God gets lost. Like the Israelites in the Old Testament who worshipped YHWH and also other Gods, African syncretists mix their vision of God with the traditional idea of the Supreme Being.[7] They fail to realise that God will not tolerate the worship of Himself to be joined with the practices of non-Christian religions as He is the jealous God. Many traditional rituals are related to non-Christian religions.[8]

It is not difficult to understand why Africans tend to practise syncretism. People want to rediscover their African cultural past. Since culture and religion are so closely related, this has led to a return to traditional religious practices. Another important cause

---

[5] Eph.4:11,15.
[6] Wilbur O'Donovan, *Biblical Christianity in Africa Perspective*, Carlisle: Paternoster Press, 1992, p.258.
[7] R.J. Gehman, *African Traditional Religion in Biblical Perspective*, Nairobi: East African Educational Publishers, 1993³, p.274.
[8] O'Donovan, *Biblical Christianity*, p.257.

was emotional concern for the spiritual welfare of relatives who died before the Gospel came. Besides, many Christians have not distanced themselves from the traditional African perspective that God is distant and unapproachable. That is why they remain attached to a closely related pre-Christian perception of the nearness of lesser spirits and divinities, who are said to help in the ordinary problems of life. Traditional African people find it difficult to address Christ directly. They are used to the idea of the ancestral spirits that play an intermediary role.[9] These are some of the reasons and backgrounds many people, including some leading theologians, try to justify pre-Christian traditional religions.

Many Africans think they are following Jesus Christ, without actually recognising Him as their only Saviour in all circumstances of life. In crisis situations they tend to go back to ancestral spirits or to mystical and magical powers. Then, they resort to syncretistic practices by visiting the witchdoctor for assistance, or by indulging in the use of fetishes, magic, charms, divination and even sorcery.[10]

56.3. Examples in Malawi

African history – just as European history – shows that Christianity took a long time to ban *Traditional Religions* and in quite some cases has never fully succeeded in doing that until today. Bregje de Kok studied the situation in Malawi. She noted that many Christians in Malawi 'are said to continue performing indigenous religious practices like funeral rites, birth rituals, and initiation ceremonies', and that 'many Malawians did not leave behind their traditional beliefs like witchcraft and ancestral spirits'. De Kok looked into the backgrounds of 'devoted Christians' who at the same time can 'be involved in *African Traditional Religion* (ATR)', against the pronounced will of their churches.[11] 'ATR is to a large extent alive for different people from different strata of the population'. Yet Christianity is the central religion of the country, and those who turn to ATR do mainly so at *crisis-moments*, when death and sickness strike. Therefore, De Kok thinks that ATR and Christianity 'co-exist in the lives of many Malawians' in such a way that they separate the two, and 'consider the two as not obstructing each other'. In her opinion this situation does not reflect the mixing or fusion of religions that is generally meant by the concept *syncretism*, and as such 'has obtained negative connotations'. She thinks that Malawian Christians lead their dualistic lives 'in a skilful and unproblematic way'.[12]

Much of De Kok's interesting analysis of the religious situation in Malawi is likely to be true, but her conclusion is certainly not. The Christian faith cannot go side by side with other faiths in the lives of Christians. At all moments and especially face to face with death their allegiance is to Christ only. How can there be a living relationship with Christ as Saviour when at decisive moments one resorts to witchcraft and magic?

---

[9] O'Donovan, *Biblical Christianity*, p.262.
[10] Maxford Blessings Chilindeni, 'Development of Syncretism in African Churches', Zomba Theological College, 2004 [unpubl. Paper]; M.F. Salanjira, *The North-Eastern Chewa: Response and Conversion to Christianity*, Zomba: Chancellor College nd [c. 1987].
[11] Bregje de Kok, *Christianity and African Traditional Religion: Two Realities of a Different Kind*, Zomba: Kachere Series, 2004, pp.4-6,20.
[12] De Kok, *Christianity and African Traditional Religion*, p.57.

Another example of syncretism concerns education. For a long time Mission and Church were the main organisers of education. However, after the *Second World War* 'the period in which the Church had been the most important contributor in education was drawing to a close',[13] first in West Africa and then also in other parts of Africa. The colonial governments and after them the national independent governments tightened their hold on education. In some countries officially room was given for anti-Christian feelings in schools, in other countries a policy of religious neutrality was developed.

Still others tried to operate from a position of religious plurality, offering pupils and students the idea of a general religious approach in which all religions to an extent would be taken together on the basis of equality. Of course, this approach is apt to transgress the boundaries of faithfulness to Christ and Scripture. An example of it is to be found in the new syllabus of *'Religious and Moral Education'* developed for Malawian Government Schools, issued in 1998 by the *Malawi Institute of Education* under the responsibility of the Ministry of Education, Sports and Culture.[14] Technical and financial support was given by the *World Bank* and by some NGOs. The new syllabus says it is aimed at the addressing of certain problems, such as overpopulation, gender, pollution of the environment, AIDS, violence, drug abuse. It is thought that these problems could be addressed with the support of Malawi's three main religions, Christianity, Islam and African Traditional Religion. According to official opinion, the problems could be tackled through *multi-faith instruction* in secondary schools. During three teaching periods a week, over 30 weeks in a year, certain religious themes are discussed from the angles of the three religions. Proselytising in favour of one of the religions is not allowed. There is the suggestion in this that one religion is as good as any other. Of course, the elements in a religion that exclude the other religions cannot be included in the syllabus. Only those elements that the religions are supposed to share are highlighted. Everything that could annoy or anger the other is left out or played down. In the end comparisons between the three religions make them look like one another. For instance, when the syllabus deals with the causes of death, the three positions are almost similar. It is striking though, that the Christian view of sin acknowledging it to be the origin of death, is conveniently not discussed. The approach of the new syllabus inevitably leads to a denial of the main principles of the Christian faith.

56.4. Ecumenism and Christian Cooperation

There has always been a desire for Christian unity, as a consequence of Christ's admonition to *spiritual unity* in *John* 17:11,21. This desire is reflected in the *Apostolic Confession of Faith,* referring to the most basic characteristics of the Church, its *catholicity,* its *holiness,* and its *unity.* In these characteristics the Church expresses that it belongs to Christ. The Church is catholic, holy and one because it is the communion of people that are bound to Christ in faith. In a special way this is experienced by

---

[13] Cf.: Hildebrandt, *History of the Church in Africa,* p.207.
[14] The new syllabus is widely discussed, for instance by: Jessica Olausson, *Christianity, Islam, Malawian Traditional Religion and the Malawian Culture: Possible Implications of the New Primary School Syllabus in Religious Education in Malawi,* Linköping University, 1996; S.W. Breton, 'Religious and Moral Education Syllabus', in *The Lamp,* Sept./Oct. 2000, no.25, p.17;

56. Unity and Cooperation

Christians when they recognise one another in Christ, beyond the boundaries of churches and denominations. They discover their *spiritual unity*.

Many considered spiritual unity as a preparation for *organisational unity*. Reformers in the 16th century like Luther, Zwingli, Calvin, Bucer, and Cranmer tried hard to safeguard the organisational unity of the Church. Impressive attempts started in the 19th century as a consequence of the *Evangelical Revivals* and *Awakenings*, especially because of the desire to facilitate mission. People like Von Zinzendorf, Carey and Huntingdon led the way. Sometimes this led to *complete fusion* of old denominations into new ones. Even churches of unlike backgrounds fused, like the Presbyterians, Baptists, Congregationalists, and Methodists who fused into the *United Church of Canada* in 1925.

Nicholas Ludwig, Count von Zinzendorf (1700-1760), founder of the Moravian Mission at Herrnhut.

But earlier and more often it led to all kinds of *cooperation* between churches and denominations. The first organisation of cooperation was the *Evangelical Alliance* (London 1848, America 1867), which linked individuals rather than churches. In its wake other national and international bodies took shape mainly as a reaction against the emerging *liberalism* and *modernism*. Examples of this kind are: *World Christian Fundamentals Association* 1919, *American Council of Churches* 1941 (Carl McIntire)[15], *International Council of Christian Churches* 1948, *World Evangelical Fellowship* 1951.

The 20th-century 'ecumenical movement' aspired to organisational unity, even at the expense of spiritual unity. The term *'ecumenical'* was used first by the *Faith and Order Movement* at its conference in 1936. This *Faith and Order Movement*, and the *Work and Life Movement* joined together into an entirely new organisation the *World Council of Churches* (WCC) in 1948. In 1961 the *International Missionary Council* was added to the pillars of this WCC during its World Assembly in New Delhi. The word 'ecumenical' coined by the WCC is derived from the Greek word *'oikoumene'* which was in use during the time of the Roman Empire as a secular reference to the inhabited world. Since 1948 in many countries *National Councils of Christian Churches* were formed with most of the mainline churches and often also the *Roman Catholic Church* as members. The majority of these national councils and mainline churches are affiliated to the WCC. The *Roman Catholic Church*, however, although having the status of observer, never joined the WCC. After the *Second Vatican Council* in the 1960s, the Roman Catholic Church gave way to a more ecumenical attitude. Since then they have cooperated with the 'separated brethren' mainly in Bible translation and ethical issues. In 1961 in New Delhi many of the *Eastern Orthodox Churches* joined the WCC. Besides, international Protestant bodies representing churches with similar backgrounds, like the *Lutheran World Federation* (LWF) and the *World Alliance of Reformed Churches* (WARC), became affiliated to the WCC.

But still a large number of churches and international church alliances have not joined because of the *liberal* and *(neo-) modernistic* tendencies in the ecumenical

---

[15] The *American Council of Churches* should not be confused with its liberal counterpart the *Federal* or *National Council of Churches*.

movement of the WCC. Since the fall of *communism* and the Soviet Empire WCC-membership in the West has become less popular, because many realised that this liberal branch of ecumenism had done little to protect and defend the persecuted Christians in the former communist countries. Reformed and Presbyterian Churches have several national and international organisations of cooperation, like the *Reformed Ecumenical Synod* (based in Grand Rapids, USA), the *International Conference of Reformed Churches* (presently based in Surrey, Canada), and since 2010 the *World Communion of Reformed Churches* (Grand Rapids), which has united WARC and REC.

56.5. The Situation in Africa

In Africa various forms of cooperation, union and fusion took shape, some under the umbrella of the WCC ecumenical movement, and others as a reaction against it or just as an expression of unity of churches with like background. Like in the West, in most African countries *National Councils of Christian Churches* have been formed, sometimes with combined Protestant and Roman Catholic membership. They originated in the thought that missionary societies could cooperate more. Early examples are the *Gold Coast Christian Council* and the *Christian Council of Nigeria* (1929). 'In Kenya the movement toward a joint missionary council was preceded by an attempt to form a single Protestant Church which would be built up by Protestant Missions'.[16] In 1913 a constitution was signed by representatives of the Africa Inland Mission, the Church Missionary Society, and the United Methodist Mission. However, immediately after that, Anglicans of the CMS began to oppose the process of full unification, and also the AIM showed hesitations. A schism in the Anglican community on the issue of *Theological Modernism* complicated the relationship with other Missions and Churches. Attempts for a united Church in the period 1961-1967 failed too. Like other countries Kenya got its *National Christian Council*, in 1944. Later these *National Christian Councils* became *National Church Councils*. They were originally meant to promote evangelism and church growth. After the *Second World War*, they often became politicised, when liberal leaders tried to push them into the ecumenical movement.[17]

As for international bodies, most of the above mentioned universal organisations play roles in Africa. In addition, there are African international bodies. The pioneer international body of the general ecumenical movement is the *All Africa Conference of Churches* (AACC), founded in Kampala in 1963. Its Headquarters is in Nairobi. The first leader was Canon Burgess Carr of Liberia. In collaboration with the *World Council of Churches*, and financially supported by this ecumenical organisation, the AACC developed various political, social and educational programmes. In the course of time it dealt with issues like reconciliation of warring peoples, and African self-hood. A controversial issue was Burgess Carr's call at AACC's General Assembly in Lusaka 1974 for a *moratorium* on foreign mission that is, on 'external assistance in money and personnel'. The call was earlier aired by John Gatu, president of the *Presbyterian Church in Kenya* and by the Anglican bishop of Nairobi, Henry Okullo.[18] Some Western churches subsequently reduced their assistance. But the Roman Catholic

---

[16] Hildebrandt, *History of the Church in Africa*, pp.229-231.
[17] Cf.: Hildebrandt, *History of the Church in Africa*, pp.205,206.
[18] Cf.: Ogbu U. Kalu, African Christianity: From the World Wars to Decolonization', in: Kalu et al. (eds), *African Christianity*, pp.359,360.

Church and the Evangelicals rejected the proposal. Continuing full strength Roman Catholic missionary presence, urbanisation, and the resurgence of Islam revived missionary interest in some Western churches and movements, and other challenges made the moratorium programme fail, and this also led to a new increase of mission agencies in Africa, and to the establishment of new *partnership structures* between Western and African churches.

On the Evangelical side in various countries *Evangelical Fellowships* were formed. Sometimes cooperation at a regional level led to the formation of new churches. An example is the establishing in 1954 of the *Association of Evangelical Churches of West Africa*, resulting from the work by SIM. The Association has its own *African Missionary Society*.[19] From 1967 to 1973 its Secretary General was the Byang Kato (see chapter 54.3.c).

In 1966 these fellowships founded the *Association of Evangelicals in Africa and Madagascar*, AEAM, later AEA, also based in Nairobi. The second Secretary General and the first African to hold that position, was Byang Kato. Unfortunately, this promising theologian died in 1975, at the age of 39. The danger of emerging liberalism in theology and church life was one of the reasons for the establishment of the AEA. The constitution says that the Association is meant to 'alert Christians to trends and spiritual dangers which would undermine the Scriptural foundation of the Gospel testimony'.[20] The assemblies of the AEA have mainly dealt with issues like evangelism and witness. Evangelical parachurch organisations have opened new ways for cooperation. An example is the *Accrediting Council for Theological Education* (ACTEA), which works on upgrading the standards of theological training and providing new ways for church unity. Other organisations are *World Vision, World Relief, Tear Fund*, and *MAF*.

Theologically and ecclesiastically related to Evangelical orthodoxy are the organisations in which the more classically Reformed and Presbyterian Churches cooperate. An example is the *Reformed Ecumenical Synod* with members among the Reformed family of churches in South Africa and in regions where this family spread to, e.g. the *Reformed Church of East Africa* in Kenya and the *Nkhoma Synod* of the Malawian Presbyterians. Cooperation of Orthodox Evangelicals, Presbyterians and Reformed churches in the *International Council of Christian Churches* (ICCC) has spread to Africa. In 1975 the Ninth World Congress of the ICCC took place in Nairobi's Jomo Kenyatta Conference Centre, some months before its liberal competitor and counterpart, the *World Council of Churches*, convened for its Ninth General Assembly at exactly the same place. Another important example of cooperation is NetACT, which is a network of theological institutions in the Presbyterian and Reformed tradition in sub-Saharan Africa. In NetACT the Faculty of Theology of the University of Stellenbosch cooperates with sister theological institutions in sub-Saharan Africa. It aims at promoting 'Congregational theology as practised in the Christian Congregation as the body of Christ, discerning the will of God, in the process of interpreting the Scriptures and its own specific context, empowering the Congregation to address multiple problems, challenges and sufferings'.[21]

---

[19] Hildebrandt, *History of the Church in Africa*, p.209.

[20] In: Hildebrandt, *History of the Church in Africa*, p.245.

[21] See: http://academic.sun.ac.za/theology/netact.html

Independent churches also have their cooperative organisations. Some, like the Kimbanguists, are members of the WCC, others are not. Sometimes Independent churches profited from cooperation with Independents overseas, for example with Mennonite missionaries, who supported them in the field of theological education. In 1963 the *African Independent Churches Association* (AICA) was formed, arranging an 'ambitious educational programme' for leaders and other members. Expert Western volunteers gave their support. Unfortunately, the organisation collapsed because of financial troubles. Other independent churches cooperate in the Organisation of African Instituted Churches (OAIC). The OAIC had its origins in the work of Bishop Markos of the *Coptic Orthodox Church* of Egypt with individual AICs in Nairobi, 1976. In 1978 Pope Shenouda III invited leaders of AICs from various countries for a conference in Cairo where the OAIC was founded. The basic aims of the organisation were teaching and training.

A Session of the African Synod of the Roman Catholic Church in Rome in 1994.

The *Roman Catholic Church* in Africa has become more open to cooperation because of the influence of the *Second Vatican Council*, and also because of a strong desire to be African. In 1994 a special Synod of African bishops was held in Rome, which was considered as recognition of African Roman Catholic self-hood. The mainline type of Roman Catholicism in many parishes in Africa is also generally more traditional than in the West.

Small Christian Communities (SCC) have emerged. These groups function at the levels of prayer and Bible study, pastoral activities, social action, and also in ecumenical activities. Through the *Charismatic Movement* there is an interaction between these groups and charismatic groups in the Protestant churches.

Bibliography: Africa

a. Various countries

Adams, W.Y, *Nubia: Corridor to Africa*, Princeton UP, 1977.

Adedibu, Babatunde, 'Mission from Africa: A Call to Re-imagine Mission in African-led Pentecostal Churches in Britain', in: *Missio Africanus Journal of African Missiology*, vol. 1, issue 1, April 2015.

Adeyemo, Tokunboh (ed.), *A Christian Mind in a Changing Africa*, Nairobi: The Association of Evangelicals in Africa and Madagascar (AEAM), 1993.

Adeyemo, Tokunboh, and A. Scott Moreau (eds), *Deliver us From Evil: An Uneasy Frontier in Christian Mission*, Nairobi, 2002.

Adeyemo, Tokunboh, *Is Africa Cursed?*, Nairobi: Christian learning materials Center, 1997 (CLMC), 1997.

Adeyemo, Tokunboh, *Salvation in African Tradition,* Nairobi: Evangel Publ., 1997 (first 1979).

Adeyemo, Tokunboh, *The Making of a Servant of God*, Nairobi: Christian Learning Materials Centre (CLMC), 1993.

Ajayi, F.F.A., 'Henry Venn and the Policy of Development', in: O. Kalu (ed.), *The History of Christianity in West Africa*, London: Longman, 1980.

Ajayi, J.F.A., *Christian Missions in Nigeria 1841-1891*, London: Longmans, 1965.

Anderson A., and O.S. Tumelo, *The Faith of African Pentecostals in South Africa*, Pretoria: Unisa, 1993.

Anderson, D., *We felt like Grasshoppers: The Story of Africa Inland Mission*, Nottingham: Crossway, 1994.

Anderson, W.B., *The Church in East Africa 1840-1974*, Nairobi/ Dodoma/ Kampala: UZIMA/ CTP/ CPH, 1981 [first 1977].

Asante, Molefi Kete (b. Arthur Lee Smith), *The History of Africa: The Quest for Eternal Harmony*, London: Routledge, 2007.

Ayandele, E.A., *The Mission Impact on Modern Nigeria 1842-1924: A Political Analysis*, London: Longmans, 1966.

Baëta, C.G. (ed.), *Christianity in Tropical Africa*, Oxford UP, 1968.

Bane, M.J., *The Popes and Western Africa: An Outline of Mission History 1460-1960s*, New York: Alba House, 1968.

Barrett, David B., *World Christian Encyclopedia: A Comparative Survey of Churches ad Religions in the Modern World AD 1900-2000*, Nairobi/ New York: Oxford UP, 1982.

Barrett, David B., *Schism and Renewal in Africa: An Analysis of 6000 Contemporary Religious Movements*, Nairobi: Oxford UP, 1968.

Barrett, David B., 'AD 2000: 350 million Christians in Africa', in: *International Review of Mission*, 59 (1970).

Barrett, David B., *Schism and Renewal in Africa: An Analysis of Six Thousand Contemporary Religious Movements*, Nairobi: Oxford UP, 1968.

Baur, J., *2000 Years of Christianity in Africa: An African History 62-1992*, Nairobi: Paulines, 1994.

Beachley, R.W., *A History of East Africa 1592-1902*, London: Tauris, 1995.

Becken, H.J. (ed.), *Relevant Theology for Africa*, Durban: Lutheran Publ., 1973.

Bediako, Kwame, *Jesus and the Gospel in Africa: History and Experience*, Orbis Books 2004.

Bediako, Kwame, *Christianity in Africa: The Renewal of a Non-Western Religion*, Edinburgh: Orbis, 1995.

Bediako, Kwame, *Jesus in African Culture: A Ghanaian Perspective*, Accra: Asempa Publ., 1990.

Bediako, Kwame, *Theology and Identity: The Impact of Culture upon Christian Thought in the Second Century and Modern Africa*, Oxford: Regnum Books, 1992.

Beidelman, T.O., *Colonial Evangelism*, Bloomington: University of Indiana Press, 1982.

Beinart, William, *Twentieth-century South Africa*, Oxford UP, 1994.

Birmingham, David, *The Decolonization of Africa*, London: University College of London Press, 1996.

Blyden, E.W., *Christianity, Islam and the Negro Race*, Edinburgh UP, 1967 [reprint of 1988].

Boahen, A.Adu (ed.), *Africa under Colonial Denomination*, vol. 7, *General History of Africa*, Paris: UNESCO, 1990.

Boahen, A.Adu, *African Perspectives on Colonialism*, Hopkins UP 1989.

Boesak, A., *Farewell to Innocence: A Socioethical Study on Black Theology and Power*, Maryknoll: Orbis, 1977.

Bowers, P., 'Nubian Christianity: The Neglected Heritage', in: *East Africa Journal of Evangelical Theology* 4, no 1 (1985), pp.3-23.

Breman, Christina M., 'A Portriat of Dr. Byang Kato', in: *Africa Journal of Evangelical Theology* 15, no.2 (1996), pp.135-151.

Breman, Christina M., *The Association of Evangelicals in Africa: Its History, Organization, Members, Projects, External Relations and Message*, Zoetermeer: Boekencentrum, 1996.

Brown, P., *Augustine of Hippo: A Biography*, London: Faber & Faber, 1967.

Brown, P., *Religion and Society in the Age of Augustine*, London, Faber & Faber, 1972.

Bujo, B., *African Theology in Its Social Context*, Maryknoll: Orbis, 1992.

Burton, Keith Augustus, *The Blessings of Africa: The Bible and African Christianity*, IVP Acadenic, 2007.

Carey, William, *An Enquiry into the Obligation of Christians to use Means for the Conversion of the Heathen*, facsimile edition of the original of 1792 edited by Ernest A. Payne, London, 1961.

Chirenje, J.M., *Ethiopianism and Afro-Americans in Southern Africa 1883-1916*, Baton Rouge: Louisiana State UP, 1987.

Church, J., *Quest for the Highest: An Autobiographical Account of the East Africa Revival*, Exeter: Paternoster, 1981.

Danquah, J.B., *The Akan Doctrine of God*, London: Lutterworth, 1944.

Davidson, Basil, *Africa in Modern History: A Search for a New Society*, London: Penguin, 1978.

Davidson, Basil, *Old Africa Rediscovered: The Story of Africa's Forgotten Past*, London: Victor Gollancz, 1959.

Davidson, Basil, *The African Past: Chronicles from Antiquity to Modern Times*, Boston: Brown, 1964.

Davidson, Basil *The Black Man's Burden: Africa and the Curse of the Nation-State*, Westminster: Three Rivers Press, April 27, 1993 [first London: Currey,1992].

De Gruchy, J.W., 'From Cairo to the Cape: the significance of Coptic Orthodoxy for African Christianity', in: *Journal of Theology for Southern Africa*, no 99 (November 1997), pp.24-39.

De la Haye, S., *Byang Kato: Ambassador for Christ*, Ghana: Africa Christian Press, 1986.

Dickson, K., *Theology in Africa*, London: Darton, 1984.

Donovan, V., *Christianity Rediscovered: An Epistle from the Masai*, New York: Orbis, 1978.

Eber, Jochen, *Johann Ludwig Krapf: Ein schwäbischer Pionier in Ostafrika*, Riehen: Arte Media/ Lahr: Johannis, 2006.

Ejofodomi, L.,'The Missionary Career of Alexander Crummell in Liberia 1853-1873'; unpublished PhD thesis, Boston University, 1988.

Elphick, R., *KhoiKhoi and the Founding of White South Africa*, Johannesburg: Ravan, 1985.

Evangelicals of Africa and Madagascar (AEAM), 1993.

Fage, J.D., *A History of Africa*, London: Hutchinson, 1988².

Fage, J.D., and R.Oliver (eds), *The Cambridge History of Africa*, 8 vols, Cambridge UP, 1975-1986.

Falk, P., *The Growth of the Church in Africa*, Grand Rapids: Zondervan, 1979.

Faupel, J.F., *African Holocaust: The Story of the Uganda Martyrs*, New York: Garland, 1990.

Fiedler, K., 'Christian Missions and Western Colonialism: Soulmates or Antagonists?', in: K.R. Ross (ed.), *Faith at the Frontiers of Knowledge*, Blantyre: CLAIM, 1998, pp.218-234.

Fiedler, K., *Christianity and African Culture: Conservative German Protestant Missionaries in Tanzania 1900-1940*, Blantyre: CLAIM/ Kachere, 1999².

Fiedler, K., P. Gundani, Hilary Mijoga (eds), *Theology Cooked in an African Pot*, Association of Theological Institutions in Southern and Central Africa (ATISCA) Bulletin, no 5/6, Zomba, 2000².

Fiedler, Klaus, *Christianity and African Culture: Conservative German Protestant Missionaries in Tanzania 1900-1940*, Blantyre: CLAIM, 1999².

Fiedler, Klaus, *The Story of Faith Missions From Hudson Taylor to Present-day Africa*, Oxford: Regnum International, 1998.

Fitts, L., *Lott Carey: First Black Missionary to Africa*, Valley Forge: Judson, 1978.

Frederiks, Martha, *We have Toiled all Night: Christianity in The Gambia 1456-2000*, Zoetermeer: Boekencentrum, 2003.

Frend, W.C.H., *The Donatist Church: A Movement of Protest in Roman Northern Africa*, Oxford UP, 1985².

Gehman, R., *African Traditional Religion in Biblical Perspective*, Nairobi: East African Educational Publishers, 1993³.

Gilbert, Erik T., and Jonathan T. Reynolds, *Africa in World History: From the Pre-history to the Present*, Pearson Education, 2011³.

Glover, R., *The Progress of Worldwide Missions* (revised by Herbert Kane), New York: Harper, 1960.

Goedhals, Mandy M., "'Ethopia shall soon stratch out her hands to God': the Order of Ethiopia and the Church of the Province of Southern Africa 1899-1999", in: Daniel O'Connor (et al.), *Three Centuries of Mission: The United Society for the Propagation of the Gospel 1701-2000*, London/ New York: Continuum, 2000, pp.382-394.

Gray, R., *Black Christians and White Missionaries*, New Haven: Yale UP, 1990.

Groves, C.P., *The Planting of Christianity in Africa*, 4 volumes, London: Lutterworth Press, 1948-1964.

Gschwandtner, Walter, 'The Church in East Africa Encounters the Challenge of Islam: A Historical Perspective', in: Thomas Schirrmacher und Christoph Sauer(Hg.), *Mission verändert – Mission verändert sich-Mission Transforms –Mission is Transformed: Festschrift für Klaus Fiedler*, edition afem mission academics 16, Nürnberg: Verlag für Theologie und Religionswissenschaft (VTR), 2005, pp.193-210.

Habarurema, Viateur, *Christian Generosity according to 2 Cor.8-9: Its Exegesis, Reception, and Interpretation Today in Dialogue with the Prosperity Gospel in Sub-Saharan Africa*, Protestantse Theologische Universiteit, Groningen, 2015.

Hadfield, P., *Traits of Divine Kingship in Africa*, London: Watts, 1949.

Haliburton, G., *The Prophet Harris*, New York: Oxford UP, 1973.

Hamilton, J. Taylor, *Twenty Years of Pioneer Missions in Nyasaland: A History of the Moravian Missions in German East Africa*, Bethlehem (Pa): SPG, 1912.

Hargreaves, J.D., *Decolonization in Africa*, London: Longman, 1988.
Harrison, C., *France and Islam in West Africa 1860-1960*, Cambridge UP, 1988.
Hastings, Adrian (ed.), *A World History of Christianity*, London: Cassel, 1999.
Hastings, Adrian, *A History of African Christianity 1950-1975*, Cambridge UP 1979.
Hastings, Adrian, *African Catholicism: Essays in Discovery*, London: SCM, 1989.
Hastings, Adrian, *African Christianity: An Essay in Interpretation*, London: Chapman, 1976.
Hastings, Adrian, and Godwin Tasie, *Christianity in Independent Africa*, Bloomington: Indiana UP, 1978.
Hastings, Adrian, *The Church in Africa: 1450-1950*, Oxford: Clarendon, 1994.
Hildebrandt, J., *History of the Church in Africa: A Survey*, Achimota (Ghana): African Christian Press, 1990 [first: 1981].
Hilton, A., *Kingdom of Kongo*, Oxford: Clarendon, 1985.
Hincliff, P., *Cyprian of Carthage and the unity of the Christian Church*, London: Chapman, 1974.
Idowu, E.B., *African Traditional Religion*, London: SCM, 1973.
Idowu, E.B., *Toward an Indigenous Church*, London: Oxford UP, 1965.
Isichei, Elizabeth, 'African Neo-Traditional Reigions', in: Christopher H. Partridge, New Religions: *A Guide: New Religious Movements, Sects and Alternative Spiritualities*, New York Oxford UP 2004.
Isichei, Elizabeth, *A History of Christianity in Africa From Antiquity to the Past*, London: SPCK, 1995.
Jahn, J., *Muntu: An outline of Neo-African culture*, London: Faber & Faber, 1961.
Jenkins, P., 'The Roots of African Church History: Some Polemic Thoughts' in: *International Bulletin of Missionary Research*, vol. 10, no 2, April 1986, pp.67-71.
July, R., *The Origins of Modern African Thought: Its Development in West Africa during the 19th and 20th Centuries*, London: Faber & Faber, 1968.
Kairos Document, *Challenge to the Church: A Theological Comment on the Political Crisis in South Africa*, Braamfontein: The Kairos Theologians, and London: CIIR/BBC, 1985.
Kalem'Imana, J.B., 'Christianity and Socialism in Tanzania', Drew University, 1986 [unpubl. PhD thesis].
Kalu, O.U. (ed.), *African Christianity: An African Story*, University of Pretoria, 2005.
Kalu, O.U. (ed.), *African Church Historiography: An Ecumenical Perspective*, Bern: Evangelische Arbeitsstelle Oekumene Schweiz, 1968.
Kalu, O.U., *History of Christianity in West Africa*, London: Longman, 1980.
Kamill, J., *Coptic Egypt: History and a Guide*, Cairo: American UP, 1987.
Kanya-Forstner, A.S., *Conquest of the Western Sudan*, Cambridge UP, 1969.
Kaplan, S., *Monastic Holy Man and the Christianization of Early Solomonic Ethiopia*, Wiesbaden: Steiner, 1984.
Kato, Byang H., *A Critique of Incipient Universality in Tropical Africa*, Doctoral Dissertation, Dallas Theological Seminary, 1974.
Kato, Byang H., *African Cultural Revolution and the Christian Faith*, Jos: Challenge Publ., 1976.
Kato, Byang H., *Biblical Christianity in Africa*, Achimota: Africa Christian Press, 1985.
Kato, Byang H., *Limitations of Natural Revelation*, Master's Thesis, Dallas Theological Seminary, 1971.
Kato, Byang, *Theological Pitfalls in Africa*, Kisumu: Evangelical Publ. House, 1975.
Kessel van, Ineke, *Merchants, Missionaries & Migrants: 300 years of Dutch-Ghanaian relations*, KIT, Amsterdam/ Sub-Saharan Publ. 2002.

Killingray, David, and R.Rathbone (eds), *Africa and the Second World War*, London: Macmillan, 1986.

Klingberg, F., *The Anti-Slavery Movement in England*, Hamden: Archon, 1968.

Kpobi, David Nii Anum, *Mission in chains: The Life, Theology and Ministry of the Ex-slave Jacobus E.J. Capitein (1717-1747) with a translation of his major publications*, Zoetermeer: Boekencentrum, 1993.

Krapf, J.L., *Travels, Researches and Missionary Labours During an Eighteen Years' Residence in Eastern Africa*, London: Frank Cass, 1968 [1st edition 1860].

Kwabena Asamoah-Gyadu, J., 'Born of Water and the Spirit: Pentecostal/ Charismatic Christianity in Africa', in: Kalu et al. (eds), *African Christianity*, pp.403-406.

Kwiyani, Harvey C., 'Missio Dei: An African Appropriation', in: *Missio Africanus Journal of African Missiology*, vol. 1, issue 1, April 2015.

Kwiyani, Harvey C., *Sent Forth: African Missionary Work in the West, American Society of Missiology*, book 51, Orbis Books, 2014.

Kwiyani, Harvey C. "The Mission of God Belongs to Africa Too: The Emerging Story of the African Missionary Movement', in: *Journal of Contemporary Christian Studies* 1, no. 1 (2014).

Lagerwerf, L., *They Pray for You: Independent Churches and Women in Botswana*, Leiden: IMO, 1982.

Langat, R., 'Western Evangelical Missionary Influence on East African Culture', unpubl. PhD thesis, Denver: Iliff School of Theology, 1991.

Latourette, Kenneth Scott, *Christianity in a Revolutionary Age*, 5 volumes, Exeter: Paternoster/ Grand Rapids: Zondervan/ New York: Harper and Row, 1970 [first 1955-1965; on Africa: parts of vols 3 and 5].

Latourette, Kenneth Scott, *A History of the Expansion of* Christianity, vol.5: *The Great Century: The Americas, Australia and Africa*; vol.6, *The Great Century: North Africa*, Grand Rapids: Zondervan 1970.

Law, Robin, *The Oyo Empire, c.1600-c.1836*, Oxford UP, 1977.

Lipschutz, Mark and R. Kent Rasmussen, *Dictionary of African Historical Biography*, Berkeley: University of California, 1989.

Lovejoy, Paul, E., *Transformation in Slavery: A History of Slavery in Africa*, Cambridge UP, 2000^2.

Lutterodt, Philip, 'Leadership Traits and Practices: Insights from African Christologies', in: *Missio Africanus Journal of African Missiology*, vol. 1, issue 1, April 2015.

MacGoye (Oludhe), Marjorie, *Rebmann: A Novel*, Scarith, 2014

Manning, Patrick, *Francophone Sub-Saharan Africa, 1880-1985*, Cambridge UP, 1988.

Manning, Patrick, *Slavery and African Life: Occidental, Oriental, and African Slave Trades*, Cambridge UP, 1990.

Manus, U.C., *Christ is the African King*, Frankfurt: Lang, 1993.

Mbiti, J., *African Religions and Philosophy*, London: Heinemann, 1969.

Mbiti, J., *Bible and Theology in African Christianity*, Nairobi: Oxford UP, 1986.

McLynn, N.B., *Ambrose of Milan: Church and Court in a Christian Capital*, Berkeley/Los Angeles/ London, 1994.

Miers, Suzanne, and Richard Roberts (eds), *The End of Slavery in Africa*, Madison: Wisconsin UP, 1989.

Molyneux, G., *African Christian Theology: The Quest for Selfhood*, San Francisco: Mellen UP, 1993.

Murray, Andrew, *Key to the Missionary Problem*, Washington: Christian Literature Crusade, 1979 [first 1901].

Murray, Andrew, *The State of the Church*, Kempton Park: Andrew Murray Consultation, 1985 [first 1911].

Neill, Stephen, *Christianity and Colonialism*, New York: McGraw-Hill, 1966.

Neill. Stephen, *A History of Christian Missions* (revised edition by O. Chadwick), Harmondsworth: Penguin, 1986 [1964].

Newitt, Malyn, *A History of Mozambique*, Bloomington: Indiana UP, 1993.

Ngimbi, Kibutu, *Les Nouvelles Eglises Indépendantes Africaines (NAIC):* Un phénomène ecclesial observe au Congo/ Kinshasa et auprès de ses extensions en Europe occidentale: Approche historico-missiologique, Heverlee (Louvain/ Leuven): Faculté de Théologie Evangélique (Evangelical Theological Faculty), 2000.

Njeri Mwaura, Philomena, 'Gender and Power in African Christianity: African Instituted Churches and Pentecostal Churches', in: Kalu et al. (eds), *African Christianity*, pp.410-445.

Northcott, Cecil, *Christianity in Africa*, London: SCM, 1963.

Noshy, I., *The Coptic Church: Christianity in Egypt*, Washington: Sloan, 1955.

Nwulia, Moses D.E., *Britain and Slavery in East Africa*, Washington DC: Three Continents Press, 1975.

Nyamiti, C., *Christ as our Ancestor: Christology from an African Perspective*, Gweru: Mambo Press, 1984.

O'Donovan, Wilbur, *Biblical Christianity in African Perspective*, Carlisle: Paternoster Press, 1992.

Oden, Thomas C., *How Africa Shaped the Christian Mind: Rediscovering the African Seedbed of Western Christianity*, IVP Academic, 2010.

Ofori, P.E., *Christianity in Tropical Africa: A Selective Annotated Bibliography*, Nedel: KTO Press, 1977.

Ojo, Matthew A., 'The Charismatic Movement in Nigeria Today', in: *International Bulletin of Missionary Research*, July, 1995.

Okot p'Bitek, *African Religions in Western Scholarship*, Kampala: East African Literature Bureau, 1970.

Oliver, R., and G.Matthew (eds), *A History of East Africa*, New York: Oxford UP, 1963.

Oliver, R., *The African Experience*, San Francisco: Harper/Collins, 1991.

Oliver, R., *The Missionary Factor in East Africa*, London: Longmans, 1965².

Olofinjana, Israel, 'Celebrating the Life and Legacy of Bishop Ajayi Crowther', in: *Missio Africanus Journal of African Missiology*, vol. 1, issue 1, April 2015.

Oosthuizen, G.C., *The Healer-Prophet in Afro-Christian Churches*, Leiden: Brill, 1992.

Paas Steven, *Christian Zionism Examined: A Review of Ideas on Israel, the Church and the Kingdom*, Nürnberg: Verlag für Theologie und Religionswissenschaft (VTR)/ Hamburg: Reformatorischer Verlag Beese (RVB), 2012.

Paas, Steven, *A Conflict on Authority in the Early African Church: Augustine of Hippo and the Donatists*, Zomba: Kachere, 2005².

Paas, Steven, *Johannes Rebmann: A Servant of God in Africa Before the Rise of Western Colonialism*, Nürnberg: Verlag für Theologie und Religionswissenschaft/ Bonn: Verlag für Kultur und Wissenschaft, 2011 [edition afem – mission academics].

Paas, Stefan, 'Mission from Anywhere to Europe: Americans, Africans, and Australians Coming to Amsterdam', in: Brill, *Mission Studies* 32 (2015).

Page, J., *The Black Bishop: Samuel Ajayi Crowther*, London: Hodder and Stoughton, 1908.

Pakenham, Thomas, *The Scramble for Africa 1876-1912*, London: Abacus, 1991.

Parrat, J., *A Reader in Africann Theology*, London: SPCK, 1987.

Parrat, J., *Reinventing Christianity: African Christian Theology Today*, Grand Rapids: Eerdmans, 1995.

Parrinder, G., *African Traditional Religion*, London: Sheldon, 1962².

Pearson, B., 'Earliest Christianity in Egypt', in: Pearson and Goering (eds), *The Roots of Egyptian Christianity*, Philadelphia: Fortress, 1986.

Phiri, I.A., D.B. Govinden, and S.Nadar, *Her-Stories: Hidden Histories of Women of Faith in Africa*, Pietermaritzburg: Cluster Publ., 2002.

Pillay, G.J. and J.W. Hofmeyr (eds), *Perspectives on Church History: An Introduction for South African Readers*, Pretoria: De Jager-HUM, 1991.

Pirouet, Louise, *The Spread of Christianity in Uganda 1891-1914*, London: Rex Collings, 1978.

Pirouet, Louise, *The Witness of the Uganda Martyrs*, Kampala: Church of Uganda Literature Centre, 1969.

Pobee, John S., 'The Anglican Church in Ghana and the SPG', in: Daniel O'Connor (et al.), *Three Centuries of Mission: The United Society for the Propagation of the Gospel 1701-2000*, London/ New York: Continuum, 2000, pp.409-422.

Pobee, John S., *Toward an African Theology*, Nashville: Abingdon, 1979.

Présence Africaine [two volume account of early African writers/artists] in: *Le Monde Noir*, special issue of nos 8-9, Paris, 1950; see also: *Des Prêtres Noires s'interrogent*, Paris: Du Cerf, 1956.

Rapozoh, I.B. and Malemu Bambo Dirkx, *Ulendo Wathu monga Mbumba ya Mulungu*, Limbe: Popular Publ., 1992.

Reader, John, *Africa: A Biography of the Continent*, New York: Vintage, 1999.

Roberts, C., *Manuscript, Society, and Belief in Early Christian Egypt*, London: Oxford UP, 1979.

Robertson, Claire C., and Martin Klein (eds), *Women and Slavery in Africa*, Madison: Wisconsin UP, 1983.

Rooms, Nigel, 'Loving the British for the Sake of Mission', in: *Missio Africanus Journal of African Missiology*, vol. 1, issue 1, April 2015.

Sanneh, Lamin, *Whose Religion is Christianity?: The Gospel Beyond the West*, Grand Rapids: Eerdmans, 2003.

Shank, D., 'A Prophet for Modern Times: The Thought of William Wadé Harris, West African Precursor of the Reign of Christ', 3 vols, unpublished PhD thesis, University of Aberdeen, 1980.

Shaw, Mark, *The Kingdom of God in Africa: A Short History of African Christianity*, Grand Rapids: Baker, 1996.

Shelburne, G.B., *Mbiri ya Mpingo*, Thondwe: Namikango Bible School, 1994².

Shenk, D.W., *Peace and Reconciliation in Africa*, Nairobi: Uzima, 1983.

Shenk, Calvin, E., 'The Demise of the Church in North Africa and Nubia: Its Survival in Egypt and Ethiopoia: A Question of Cointextualization?', in: *Missiology: An International Review*, Vol. XXI, No.2, April 1993 [Internet].

Shillington, K., *History of Africa*, London: Palgrave Macmillan, 2005³.

Smith, E. (ed), *African Ideas of God: A Symposium*, London: Edinburgh House, 1959.

Smith, Robert S., *Warfare and Diplomacy in Pre-Colonial West Africa*, Madison: Wisconsin UP, 1989².

Stott, John, *Christian Mission in the Modern World*, London: Falcon, 1975.

Sundkler, B., and C. Steed, *A History of the Church in Africa*, Cambridge UP, 2000.

Sundkler, B., *The Christian Ministry in Africa*, London: SCM, 1962².

Tamrat, T., *Church and State in Ethiopia 1270-1527*, Oxford: Clarendon, 1972.

Tasie, G.O.M., *Christian Missionary Enterprise in the Niger Delta 1864-1918*, Leiden: Brill, 1978.

Taylor, J.V., *Christianity and Politics in Africa*, London: Penguin, 1957.
Taylor, J.V., *The Growth of the Church in Buganda,* London: SCM, 1958.
Taylor, J.V., *The Primal Vision: Christian Presence amid African Religion*, London: SCM, 1963.
Tempels, Placide, Fr, *La Philosophie Bantoue,* Elizabethville: Lovania, 1945.
Temu, A.J., *British Protestant Missions*, London: Longman, 1972.
Trimingham, J. Spencer, *The influence of Islam upon Africa*, London and Harlow: Longmans, 1968.
Turner, H.W., *African Independent Church*, 2 vols, Oxford UP, 1967.
Vantini, G., *Christianity in the Sudan*, Bologna: EMI, 1981.
Walker, S., *The Religious Revolution in the Ivory Coast: The Prophet Harris and the Harrist Church*, Chapel Hill: University of N. Carolina Press, 1983.
Walls, A.F., 'The Gospel as a Prisoner and Liberator of Culture', in: *Faith and Thought*, vol. 108, 1981.
Walls, A.F., *The Missionary Movement in Christian History*, Edinburgh: Clark/ New York: Orbis, 1996.
Walls, A.F.,*The Significance of Christianity in Africa*, Edinburgh: Church of Scotland Centre, 1989.
Walvin, J., Black *Ivory: A History of British Slavery*, London: Fontana, 1993.
Ward, K., 'Tukutendereza Yesu: The Balokole Revival Movement in Uganda', in: Zablon Nthamburi (ed.), *A Handbook of Christianity in East Africa*, Nairobi: Uzima, 1991.
Worden, N., and C.Crais, *Breaking the Chains: Slavery and its Legacy in the 19th-century Cape Colony*, Wit Watersrand UP, 1994.
Wright, Marcia, *German Mission in Tanganyika 1891-1941: Lutherans and Moravians in the Southern Highlands*, Oxford: Clarendon, 1971.
Wyse, Akintola, *The Krio of Sierra Leone: An Interpretive History*, Madison: Wisconsin UP, 1989.

Websites

Africa by country, http://www.dmoz.org/Regional/Africa/
African Church [Wikipedia], http://en.wikipedia.org/wiki/The_African_Church
Anglicans Online: Africa, http://anglicansonline.org/world/africa.html
Christian Africa, http://www.africanchristian.org/
Christianisation of Nubia, http://www.ancientsudan.org/history_13_christianization.htm
Dictionary of African Christian Biography, http://www.dacb.org/
Modern Evangelical African Theologians, http://www.neednotfret.com/content/view/211/47/
Short Story of Africa [Standford], http://aero-comlab.stanford.edu/jameson/world_history/A_Short_History_of_Africa.pdf
Story of Africa (BBC), http://www.bbc.co.uk/worldservice/africa/features/storyofafrica/index_section8.shtml

b. South Africa

Anderson A., Bazalwane, *African Pentecostals in South Africa*, Pretoria: Unisa, 1992.
Anderson, A., *Zion and Pentecost: The Spirituality and Experience of Pentecostal and Zionist/ Apostolic Churches in South Africa*, Pretoria: Unisa, 2000.
Brain, J.B., *Catholic Beginnings in Natal and Beyond*, Durban: Griggs, 1975.

Colenso, J.W., 'A Sermon Preached in the Cathedral Church of St. Peter, Pietermaritzburg', Pietermaritzburg: Yale Divinity School Archives, 1879.
Conradie, Ben, *Andrew Murray na Honderd Jaar*, Stellenbosch: Christen Studenten Verenigingmaatskappij, 1951 [an extended biography].
Dachs, A.J. (ed.), *Christianity South of the Zambezi*, Gweru: Mambo, 1973.
De Gruchy, J.W., *The Church Struggle in South Africa*, Grand Rapids: Eerdmans, 1979.
Denis, Ph., *Orality, Memory and the Past: Listening to the Voices of Black Clergy under Colonialism and Apartheid*, Pietermaritzburg: Cluster Publ., 2000.
Du Plessis, J., *From The Life of Andrew Murray of South Africa*, Marshall Morgan and Scott, 1919.
Duminy, Andrew, and Charles Ballard (eds), *The Anglo-Zulu War: New Perspectives*, Pietermaritzburg: University of Natal Press, 1981.
Enklaar, L.H., *Life and Work of Dr. J.Th. van der Kemp 1741-1811: Missionary Pioneer and Protagonist of Racial Equality in South Africa*, Capetown-Rotterdam, 1988.
Guy, Jeff, *The Destruction of the Zulu Kingdom: The Civil War in Zululand 1879-1884*, London: Longman, 1979.
Hamilton, Carolyn, *Terrific Majesty: the Powers of Shaka Zulu and the Limits of Historical Invention*, Cambridge (Mass.): Harvard UP, 1998.
Hincliff, P., *The Church in South Africa*, London: SPCK, 1968.
Hofmeyr, J.W., and J. Pillay (eds), *A History of Christianity in South Africa*, Pretoria: Haum Tertiary, 1994.
Le May, G.H.L., *The Afrikaners: an Historical Interpretation*, Oxford: Blackwell, 1994.
Moffat, John Smith, *The Lives of Robert and Mary Moffat by their son John Smith Moffat*, New York Edition: Armstrong & Son, 1888.
Murray, Andrew, *The Key to the Missionary Problem*, Fort Washington: Christian Literature Crusade, 1983 [first London: Nisbet, 1901].
Murray, Andrew, *The State of the Church*, Kempton Park: The Andrew Murray Consultation and Prayer for Revival and Mission, 1985 [first 1911].
Northcott, Cecil, *Robert Moffat: Pioneer in Africa*, London: Lutterworth, 1961.
Oosthuizen, G.C., *The Birth of Christian Zionism in South Africa*, KwaDlangezwa: University of Zululand, 1987.
Pauw, B.A., *Christianity and Xhosa Tradition*, Cape Town: Oxford UP, 1975.
Ritchie, Bruce, *The Missionary Theology of Robert Moffat*, Zomba: Kachere, 2006 [PhD Thesis].
Smith, E.W., *Robert Moffat: One of God's Gardeners*, London: SCM, 1925.
Sundkler, B., *Bantu Prophets in South Africa*, London: Oxford UP, 1948.
Sundkler, B., *Zulu Zion and Some Swazi Zionists*, London: Oxford UP, 1976.
Thompson, Leonard M., *A History of South Africa*, New Haven: Yale UP, 1985.
Walters, W., *Life and Labours of Robert Moffat*, London: Walter Scott, 1882.

Websites

South Africa, http://en.wikipedia.org/wiki/Religion_in_South_Africa
South African History: The Missionaries, http://www.sahistory.org.za/missionaries
Stanford, http://web.stanford.edu/dept/SUL/library/prod//depts/ssrg/africa/history/hisreligion.html
The Story of Southern Africa (BBC), http://www.bbc.co.uk/worldservice/africa/features/storyofafrica/index_section12.shtml

F. South-Central Africa

57. The Church in Malawi

57.1. David Livingstone

The history of missionary developments that led to the foundation of the Church in Malawi[1] starts with the initiative and the work of David Livingstone. This Scottish missionary and explorer visited Malawi in 1856. In 1841 he had arrived in Cape Town as a worker of the *London Missionary Society* (LMS). This society was in principle non-denominational, but in practice congregational. Livingstone's first mission was among the Makololo, but later he travelled northward and then across Africa, from Luanda on the Angolan Atlantic coast to Quelimane on the Mozambican Pacific coast, seeing the Victoria Falls on the way. On completing this journey he visited England in 1856 where he caused a great enthusiasm for the missionary enterprise. Livingstone expressed his own missionary aims as follows:

David Livingstone (1813-1873), through his travels contributed much to the preparations for Mission in Africa.

> 'Sending the Gospel to the heathen must include much more than is implied in the usual picture of the missionary, namely a man going about with a Bible under his arm. The promotion of commerce must be attended to, as this more especially than anything else, demolishes that sense of isolation which heathenism engenders, and makes tribes feel themselves mutually dependent on, and mutually beneficial to each other'.

In 1856 Livingstone addressed the Senate House of Cambridge University, appealing to the Church of England, represented by her two universities, Oxford and Cambridge, to start mission work as well as commerce in Malawi. He finished his speech with these words:

> 'I go back to Africa to try to make an open path for commerce and Christianity. Do you carry on the work I have begun? I leave it with you'.

---

[1] For the History of the Church in Malawi, also: Christoph Martin Pauw, *Mission and Church in Malawi: The History of the Nkhoma Synod of the Church of Central Africa Presbyterian, 1889-1962*, University of Stellenbosch, 1980; John McCracken, *Politics and Christianity in Malawi 1875-1940: The Impact of the Livingstonia Mission in the Northern Province*, Cambridge UP, 1977 [reprinted by Kachere/ CLAIM in 2000]; Andrew C. Ross, *Blantyre Mission and the Making of Modern Malawi*, Blantyre: CLAIM, 1996; D.D. Phiri, *History of Malawi From the Earliest Times to the Year 1915*, Blantyre: CLAIM, 2004, pp.111-199; Sundkler and Steed, *A History of the Church in Africa*, pp.118,415-416,448,457,467-482, 646,652,795-799,975,978-981; Baur, *2000 Years Christianity*, pp.428-431; Hastings, *The Church in Africa*, pp.210,212-213,257,276,406,410,411,418,422-423,425,427-229,432-433,455,457,475,487-480,483-484,486-488,504-505,522,528,532,543-544,549,557,580,584,590-593,603; M.S. Daneels, *Mbiri ya C.C.A.P. Sinodi ya Harare 1912-1982*, Harare: CCAP, nd, pp.11,12,18,19,47;

As a consequence, in 1858 a society called the Oxford and Cambridge Mission to Central Africa was founded. The name was later changed to Universities' Mission to Central Africa (UMCA), including also the Universities of Durham and Dublin. Before his return to Africa in 1858, Livingstone resigned from the LMS and was appointed royal consul for 'Exploration in East and Central Africa'. His work led to the beginning of missionary activities by mainline churches from Britain and elsewhere in Central Africa. These missions sometimes are called *'classical'*, in order to distinguish them from later missions by younger denominations using different methods, called *'post classical'*.

Swahili Arab ruler Mlozi and his slave-raiders, Karonga, Lake Malawi 1890 (from: Shillington: History of Africa, p.256).

57.2. Classical Missions

a. Universities' Mission to Central Africa[2]

The *Universities' Mission to Central Africa* (UMCA), from which the present Anglican Church in Malawi grew, was the first classical mission to work in Malawi. The first UMCA-party left England for Malawi in 1860. It was led by Bishop Charles Frederick Mackenzie. They were helped by Livingstone whom they met at the mouth of the Zambezi River. They found a suitable mission site in the Shire Highlands, at a place called Magomero, north-east of Blantyre, situated on a slave-trading route. When seeing the plight of the slaves in a passing slave caravan, the missionaries decided to liberate them. Soon the mission site became a kind of refugee camp and the missionaries got entangled in an armed campaign against the slave-traders and mixed up in inter-tribal

---

[2] Also: A.E.M. Anderson-Morshead, *The History of the Universities Mission to Central Africa*, vol. I 1859-1909, London: UMCA, 1953; A.G. Blood, *The History of the Universities Mission to Central Africa*, vol. II 1907-1932, London: UMCA, 1957; R.G. Stuart, *Christianity and the Chewa: the Anglican Case 1885-1950*, University of London, 1974.

disputes. This made their position very difficult. Moreover, Mackenzie got ill and died. Abashed by the setbacks the group withdrew, first to Chibisa (now Chikwawa), and then under the new Bishop, William Tozer, through Morambala to Zanzibar, where they arrived in 1864.

Yao slave-trader in southern Malawi, c. 1860 (from: Shillington: History of Africa, p.248).

Many years later the Anglicans returned to their first love. After some soundings in Malawi by Edward Steere, it was William Percival Johnson who actually re-started the work in Malawi.[3] He arrived at the lake in 1881, and laboured in the area until his death in 1928. In 1885 a site on Likoma Island was given to the mission, and the steamer *Charles Janson* was launched. Likoma became the new headquarters. For some time the mission conducted its activities into the mainland from there. Chauncy Maples took charge of the work on the island practically founding a mission there, while Johnson worked on the mainland from the steamer. Johnson built schools and churches at many places along the shore, each one put under a teacher. Priests who visited these places by steamer could be left to work at villages along the coast. Also should be mentioned the work Johnson did in translating the Anglican prayerbook and the Bible into Chinyanja, in the Likoma dialect. The former is available on the internet, dated 1909.

On Likoma Island, schools were started for boys and girls. Most of them formed the core of the new Anglican Church, though not all in the same way. One of the pupils was John George Philips. At baptism he got the name of a local missionary. Philips became known as a faithful evangelist among migrant workers to South Africa. Finally, he left the Anglican Church and established the independent *Christian Catholic Apostolic Church in Zion*, of which he himself became bishop.

In 1897 the Diocese of Likoma was separated from Zanzibar. In recognition of his work Chauncy Maples was consecrated Bishop of the island in 1895. He drowned, however, on the way back to Likoma after consecration in England.

b. Livingstonia Mission[4]

Livingstonia Mission was the second classical mission to set foot in Malawi. The beginning of this mission is linked with the history of the missionary-explorer David Livingstone, who had died at Chitambo village in Zambia on the 1st of May 1873. His servants, Chuma (Juma) and Suze (Susi), buried his heart there, but his embalmed corpse was brought to the coast, taken to Britain, and buried in Westminster Abbey in April 1874. After Livingstone's funeral, James Stewart, a missionary of Lovedale in

---

[3] For his life, see: Beryl Brough, *St. Johnson of Lake Malawi*, Zomba: Kachere 2004.
[4] John McCracken, *Politics and Christianity in Malawi 1875-1940: The Impact of the Livingstonia Mission in the Northern Province*, Cambridge UP, 1977 [reprinted by Kachere/ CLAIM in 2000]; Kenneth R. Ross (ed.), *Christianity in Malawi: A Source Book*, Gweru: Mambo/ Kachere, 1996, pp.13-80; Bill Jackson, *Send Us Friends*, CLAIM, nd, pp.3-258.

South Africa, proposed to the General Assembly of the Free Church of Scotland that a mission should be established at Lake Malawi. He said:

> 'I would humbly suggest as the truest memorial of Livingstone, the establishment by this Church, or several churches together, of an institution at once industrial and educational, to teach the truths of the Gospel and the arts of civilised life to the natives of the country, and which shall be placed in a carefully selected and commanding spot in Central Africa, where from its position and capabilities it might grow into a town, and afterwards into a city, and become a great centre of commerce, civilisation, and Christianity. And this I would call Livingstonia.'

Stewart appealed to rich businessmen, mostly in Glasgow, for financial support. His request elicited immediate response. On 21st May 1875 the first group of missionaries set off for Malawi, under the leadership of E.D. Young, a naval officer, who had previously visited Lake Malawi during the Livingstone search expedition in 1867. Robert Laws, a medical missionary, who was later to become the leading figure of the mission, was the only ordained minister of the six men who comprised this party.[5] At Cape Town the party added four Malawians to its number. Among them were Tom Bokwito and Sam Sambani whom Livingstone had freed from the Arab slave-traders at Mbame village in 1861, and had eventually been sent to Lovedale for studies. These men proved to be very useful since they acted as interpreters.

Robert Laws (1851-1934), missionary of the Free Church of Scotland to Malawi.

On the 12th of October the party arrived in Malawi in the Mangochi area of chief Mponda, who allowed them to settle anywhere on his land. The party chose Cape Maclear as a suitable site because it had a good harbour, was sheltered from wind, and appeared to be a healthy place. On Sunday 17th October 1875 they opened the first station of the Livingstonia Mission.

The following year James Stewart brought four Xhosa missionaries from Lovedale: Isaac William Ntusane Koyi, Mapas Ntintili, Shadreck Ngunana, and Isaac Wauchope.[6] They played an important role in the development of the Livingstonia Mission. In 1876 Young returned to Scotland, and James Stewart took charge for fifteen months, until the end of 1877, when Robert Laws took over as head of the mission, a position which he held for fifty years.

Work at Cape Maclear

The missionaries used the method of establishing a 'Christian village'. They encouraged Africans to come and live at the mission, and by 1880 there were 590 of them, mostly refugees fleeing from slave-traders, but also Makololo sent there from Lower Shire for schooling. In terms of conversions, the work at Cape Maclear was not very fruitful. For

---

[5] Hamish McIntosh, *Robert Laws: Servant of Africa*, Carberry: Handsel Press, 1993.
[6] T. Jack Thompson, *Touching the Heart: Xhosa Missionaries to Malawi 1876-1888*; McCracken, *Politics and Christianity in Malawi 1875-1940*, pp.68,79,232f; George H. Campbell, *The Lonely Warrior*, Blantyre: CLAIM, 1975 [A short biography of William Koyi].

the five years during which the mission laboured there, they had only one baptised convert, Albert Namalambe, baptised on the 27th of March 1881. Furthermore, by the end of the five years, five missionaries, including Shadreck Ngunana from Lovedale, had died at Cape Maclear. The site thus proved to be unhealthy, therefore Laws decided to transfer the mission to Bandawe, which happened in 1881. Albert Namalambe was left in charge of the old mission station.

Mission work was indirectly facilitated by the *Livingstonia Central Africa Company*, set up for industrial and commercial purposes, under the management of John and Alfred Moir. Later the name was changed to *African Lakes Company*, popularly known as *Mandala*.

Work at Bandawe

Isaac William Ntusane Koyi, Xhosa missionary to the Ngoni people.

At Bandawe, on the lakeshore about 20 miles south of Nkhata Bay, the missionaries were welcomed by the Tonga, a tribe of some 60,000 people, who had been raided by the Ngoni. Their fortified villages were not safe enough. That is why they wanted the protection of the missionaries. Discussions in 1887 by Laws with the Ngoni chief Mbelwa prevented the subjugation of the Tonga.[7]

Laws decided that no civil jurisdiction should be exercised by the mission. Consequently, the 'Christian village' approach was abandoned and replaced by evangelisation and schooling in the Tonga villages. The Tonga were eager to take advantage of the educational opportunities provided by the mission. By 1894 there were 18 schools in Tongaland with over 1000 pupils; in 1906 the number of schools had increased to 107 with over 3000 pupils.[8] These people valued the mission because it gave them the techniques which were needed for dealing with the new western-oriented world. But for a long time there were no converts. The growth of the number of converts was not similar to the educational response. Traditional Tonga religion kept its hold for a long time. The first Tonga baptism took place in 1889, and in the 1890s the number of baptisms increased.

Mission to the Ngoni

Although the Ngoni were political and military conquerors over the Tonga and others, they soon followed the Tonga in their turn to Christianity. In 1882 William Koyi and William Sutherland went to the Ngoni and set up a mission at Njuyu. Walter Elmslie joined the work in 1885. The mission had some influence through evangelistic services and through employing labour. Chief Mbelwa at first did not fully welcome the missionaries, but William Koyi, having a Zulu background and being able to speak the language of the Ngoni chief, opened communications. In 1886 Mbelwa wanted missions in all the divisions of the Ngoni area. This was impossible, but Laws promised a station

---

[7] McCracken, *Politics and Christianity in Malawi 1875-1940*, pp.16-112.
[8] McCracken, *Politics and Christianity in Malawi 1875-1940*, pp.113,114.

as soon as possible at Mount Walos, where the mission station Ekwendeni was founded in 1889. Later Njuyu became a sub-station of Ekwendeni.

Laws and Elmslie especially tried to convert the higher ranks, reaching first the patriarchal and aristocratic structure of Ngoni society. This elitist approach changed with the arrival of Donald Fraser.[9] In 1889 another station was opened at Hora which was moved to Loudon in 1902, and was called Embangweni. Donald Fraser was in charge of this station. Fraser had been inspired by the English *Holiness Movement* of Keswick. Right from the beginning of his work among the Ngoni (and the Tonga) he showed an interest in the conversion of the masses. From 1898

Mission station at Livingstonia, Northern Malawi.

he led a series of mass meetings in Ngoni country for Baptism and the Lord's Supper. At these meetings thousands confessed sin and guilt, turned to Christ, and accepted forgiveness and peace. In the wake of these meetings many were sent as missionaries to Northern Zambia,[10] and other revivalist campaigns were organised giving room for the continuation of the work of the Holy Spirit. These were instances of religious excitement that were uncommon in Presbyterianism. The new religious climate opened up to African forms. Fraser encouraged the composers of vernacular hymns. Among the best known of these composers of hymns were Mawelera Tembo, Charles Chinula and Peter Thole.[11]

Khondowe

Bandawe was not to be the permanent site of the Livingstonia headquarters. In 1894 the mission moved to Khondowe, and there it settled permanently under the name of *Livingstonia Mission Station*.

As a consequence of the great educational response from the Tonga, Tumbuka[12] and Ngoni, Laws set up the *Overtoun Institution* for the training of artisans and clerks, teachers, evangelists, and pastors. There was an industrial department that gave training to apprentices in such skills as carpentry, building, engineering and printing. The

---

[9] T. Jack Thompson, *Christianity in Northern Malawi: Donald Fraser's Missionary Methods and Ngoni Culture*, Leiden: Brill, 1995.

[10] The best known of these missionaries was David Kaunda; he was the father of Kenneth Kaunda, who became President of Zambia (cf. Sundkler and Steed, A *History of the Church in Africa*, pp.473, 974).

[11] For the hymns, see: Kenneth R. Ross (ed.), *Christianity in Malawi: A Source Book*, Gweru: Mambo/ Kachere, pp.49-67 ('Hymns of Early Christian Converts').

[12] Tumbuka general and religious history is described in: Silas S. Ncozana, *The Spirit Dimension in African Christianity: A Pastoral Study among the Tumbuka People of Northern Malawi*, Blantyre: Kachere/ CLAIM, 2002, pp.43-110; For a brief but helpful survey of Tumbuka history, see: D.D. Phiri, *History of the Tumbuka*, Blantyre: Dzuka, 2000.

Central School taught regular schooling and trained certified teachers. Above this there was a one-year theology course. Later were added four more post-primary courses, one for evangelists, one for store and office workers, one for dispensary and hospital assistants, and one in arts. Law's vision that the Institution would one day develop into a University, was curbed towards the end of his career, and has only recently been taken up again.

c. Blantyre Mission[13]

This was the third mission to arrive in Malawi. It was started by the Established Church of Scotland, and was called Blantyre Mission after David Livingstone's birthplace in Scotland.

Its first worker, Henry Henderson, entered the country as a member of the first Livingstonia party. Henderson, accompanied by Tom Bokwito, set out from Cape Maclear and travelled to the Shire Highlands in the southern region to look for a suitable site. Chief Kapeni gave Nyambadwe Hill, between Ndirande and Soche Mountains, as a place for the establishment of the mission. Around the site, eventually the city of Blantyre emerged. The first party of missionaries arrived in the country in 1876. They opened Blantyre Mission Station on 23rd October 1876. The site seemed so suitable because the population was numerous and of a friendly disposition. Henderson received instruction to act as the general director and as a Christian magistrate of the settlement. The aim of the mission was stated as follows:

> 'The mission is industrial and evangelical, designed to be a nucleus of advancing centuries of Christian life and civilisation to the Nyasa and the surrounding region'.

St. Michael's and All Angels, CCAP church in Blantyre, designed by David Clement Scott, and built by Africans.

---

[13] Andrew C. Ross, *Blantyre Mission and the Making of Modern Malawi*, Blantyre: CLAIM/ Kachere, 1996.

In July 1878 Duff Macdonald arrived to take charge of the mission. He had to carry out the Home Board's intention to create 'mission villages', that is, settlements with missionaries exercising civil jurisdiction. In this Yao-dominated area slaves and refugees would seek shelter in the mission village. There they were safe from slavery and persecution. At the same time, they were withdrawn from traditional African law and rule. Not well acquainted with African tradition, the missionaries soon encountered conflicts with the people they had come to Christianise. In 1878 this even led to severe disciplinary action and the death of a black offender. When the situation was noted, the Home Board sent a special commission of inquiry. Duff Macdonald was charged with mismanagement, and in March 1881 he and the first staff were withdrawn.

A new start took place when David Clement Scott (1853-1907) was sent to take charge of the mission in October 1881.[14] Scott set himself the goal of concentrating more on promoting religious work. He defined his aim as follows:

> 'Our purpose we lay down as the foundation of our work, that we are building the African Church, not Scottish or English, but African'.

Harry Apika Mtuwa (†1949), one of David Clement Scott's pupils who were trained and encouraged by him to be pastors and leaders of the young African Church. Mtuwa became a minister of the CCAP church in Zomba in 1916 (cf. Zomba CCAP Congregation, Then and Now: A Centenary Booklet, Zomba, 1998, pp.7-10), and the picture has a place in its vestry.

Scott laid great emphasis on local leadership and responsibility in the church. He encouraged people like Joseph Bismarck,[15] Harry Matecheta,[16] John Gray Kufa, and Harry Mtuwa. Scott's Africanisation programme earned him mistrust by the colonial government. Long after his departure, the investigators of the rising of John Chilembwe in 1915, would try to blame him. Scott also developed a school system. This led to the establishment of the *Henry Henderson Institute* offering training in various areas. Another achievement was the publication of the *Cyclopaedic Dictionary of the Mang'anja language*, produced initially in 1892.

His 'excellence as linguist and cultural specialist' enabled him to initiate and contribute to the translation of Scripture into the vernacular language. Wendland says that 'the four Gospels appeared in print by 1893 and a number of Pauline epistles were added the following year'.[17] In Blantyre, Scott is best remembered as the architect of the church of *St. Michael's and All Angels*, built in a combination of Western and Eastern styles. Alexander Hetherwick joined him in 1883,[18] and the two did much to restore and promote the good name of the mission. By the

---

[14] For an assessment of his life and work, see: Andrew C. Ross, 'Wokondedwa Wathu: The Mzungu who Mattered', in: *Religion in Malawi* 7:3-8 (1997).

[15] Joseph Bismarck, 'A Brief History of Joseph Bismarck', Occasional Papers of the Department of Antiquities, no. 7, Zomba 1968, pp.49-54.

[16] Harry K. Macheta, *Blantyre Mission: Nkhani ya Ciyambi Cake*, Blantyre, Hetherwick Press, 1951.

[17] Ernst R. Wendland, *Buku Loyera: An Introduction to the New Chichewa Bible Translation*, Blantyre, CLAIM/ Kachere, 1998, pp.20-23. He apparently makes a writing error when he says that the 'entire New Testament [in Mang'anja] was published in 1886'; he probably meant: in 1896.

[18] For his memoirs, see: Alexander Hetherwick, *The Romance of Blantyre: How Livingstone's Dream Came True*, London: James Clarke, nd [1931].

time Scott left for Kenya in 1897, and was succeeded by Hetherwick, the mission was running well. More stations such as Domasi, Zomba and Mulanje had been opened. Hetherwick was head of the mission until his retirement in 1928. In 1929 he published a revision of Scott's Dictionary, entitled *Dictionary of the Nyanja Language*,[19] and he also made a comprehensive *grammar book of the Nyanja language*.

d. Dutch Reformed Church Mission[20]

The *Dutch Reformed Church Mission* (DRCM) or *Nederduitsch Gereformeerde Kerk Sending* (NGKS) from South Africa was the fourth mission to join in the evangelisation of Malawi. In 1886 the Synod of the Cape Province of the *Dutch Reformed Church* was looking for a new field for missionary work. Andrew Charles Murray, a nephew of Andrew Murray, the instigator and leader of South African mission work (see chapter 48.3), then a student of theology, made contact with Robert Laws through James Stewart of Lovedale.

Consequently, Andrew Charles Murray became the first missionary of the South African *NGK Mission* in Malawi. He arrived in the country in July 1888, and was welcomed at Bandawe by Laws. On a visit to an Nkhonde chief at the north of the Lake, Murray suffered from sunstroke. He went to Njuyu to recover. While he was there Elmslie explained to him the policy and the experiences of the Livingstonia Mission. Since the Livingstonia Mission was operating in the north and the Blantyre Mission in the south, it appeared appropriate for the Dutch Reformed mission to operate in the centre.

In 1889 Murray together with Theunis C. Botha Vlok, who joined him that year, explored Ngoniland in Central Malawi, and decided to settle in the area of Chief Chiwere. They opened their first mission station at Mvera, situated midway between Salima and Lilongwe, on 28th November 1889. Murray saw two particular needs. One was a good translation of the Bible, and the other was an institute for the training of teachers and evangelists. As soon as the work had started, in 1890 a school and medical services were opened at Mvera. The school was run by Tomani whom Murray had fetched from Cape Maclear.

During its early days the mission was regarded as part of the *Livingstonia Mission*. In 1894 a division was made between the area of the Livingstonia Mission and the area of the *Dutch Reformed Mission*. The dividing line was a little north of Kasungu. Shortly afterwards, more workers came from South Africa, including William Hoppe Murray, who remained in Malawi until 1937. W.H. Murray took over as head of the mission when A.C. Murray returned to South Africa in 1901. W.H. Murray's ideal was to expand the mission by means of outposts, schools and mission stations. By 1899 the number of missionaries had increased to eighteen, and by 1903 there were stations at Mvera, Kongwe, Livulezi, and Nkhoma. A network of schools was established, with Albert Namalambe as the first African inspector. In 1904 a Normal School was opened

---

[19] David Clement Scott and Alexander Hetherwick, *Dictionary of the Nyanja Language*: Being the Encyclopaedic Dictionary of the Mang'anja Language, London: Lutterworth Press, 612 pages, 1929 [reprints in 1951 and 1957].

[20] Christoph Martin Pauw, *Mission and Church in Malawi: The History of the Nkhoma Synod of the Church of Central Africa Presbyterian*, 1889-1962, University of Stellenbosch, 1980; A.L. Hofmeyr, *Het Land langs het Meer*, Stellenbosch, 1910; K.J. Mgawi, *CCAP Nkhoma Synod: Mbiri ya Mpingo ndi Mudzi wa Nkhoma 1896 mpaka 1996*, Nkhoma: Nkhoma Synod nd.

at Mvera for the training of teachers. By 1914 there were 2000 African helpers, preaching to 60,000 people in 200 villages. J.L. Pretorius wrote that the Dutch Reformed mission made its greatest contribution at the village level. Its aim was always to establish a local church which would be self-supporting, self-governing, and which would expand from its own inner strength. The other emphasis of the mission was rural development. The mission stressed the need to set up village industries, and to promote agriculture. Until 1909 they issued their own money, a coin punched with two holes and stamped 'MM' (Mvera Mission).

The priority of the Dutch Reformed Church Mission was always the ingathering of souls for the Kingdom of God, followed by the building of the local church, schooling, and improving the medical and material conditions of the people. The Mission stressed the Bible as the highest authority for the life and the teaching of the Church and of individual Christians. It was strongly opposed to the Roman Catholic Church that was supposed to put the authority of Tradition and Church higher than the Bible.

Another notable aspect of the mission was the emphasis it placed on working with women and girls. Boarding homes for girls were opened at most of its stations. These girls were instructed in Christian matters, including various practical subjects which would help them to be good wives in their future marriages. Further the mission introduced pastoral or advisory activities among the girls, called *Chilangizo*, in order to impress upon them a more Christian life. At a later stage a Women's Guild (*Amayi a Chigwirizano*) was formed to coordinate all the activities of women's work.[21]

One of the most valuable contributions of the mission was the great role it played in translating the Bible into Chichewa, especially by the efforts of W.H. Murray. Together with Hetherwick and two African teachers, Murray worked on the New Testament and they published a new translation in 1906. The translation of the Old Testament by Murray and a team of African and European assistants took much longer. Eventually, in 1922, with the help of the *Scottish Bible Society* and the *British and Foreign Bible Society* the full Bible was published, entitled *Buku Lopatulika* (Holy Book).[22]

e. Church of Central Africa Presbyterian

Many of the early Scottish missionaries had been intent on the founding of a local church. Laws was of the opinion that the mission church should not merely be a presbytery of the Home Church. He wanted to 'work towards a Central African Presbyterian Church which should include Blantyre and the Dutch'.

In 1899 the Livingstonia Presbytery was founded. This was seen as the first step towards a *Church of Central Africa Presbyterian* (CCAP). In 1902 the Blantyre Presbytery was set up as a Presbytery of the Church of Scotland. A meeting took place in 1904 with a view to uniting Blantyre and Livingstonia in a single church. It was decided not to use any existing confession of faith from the home churches as the doctrinal basis of the union, but to draw up a simple statement of Christian faith, and to have the *Apostles' Creed* as the sufficient confession of faith for the church.

In 1910 a *General Missionary Conference* was held at Mvera between representatives of Blantyre and Livingstonia. Dutch Reformed missionaries L. Hofmeyr and William H. Murray were present as observers on behalf of their mission. They were

---

[21] Isabel Apawo Phiri, *Women, Presbyterianism and Patriarchy: Religious Experience of Chewa Women in Central Malawi*, Blantyre: CLAIM/ Kachere, 2000², pp.73-93, and many other pages.

[22] Wendland, *Buku Loyera*, pp.23-25.

hesitant to join, because they feared that modernistic teaching would be brought into the CCAP by certain missionaries from Scotland, as some of their missionaries, working in South Africa, were accused of denying the Atonement and various other doctrines.

On the 27th of September 1924 the two Presbyteries of Blantyre and Livingstonia held a united session. The motion to unite in one common Synod was unanimously approved, and Robert Laws was unanimously elected the first moderator. Thus came into being a united indigenous African Church. The next step was for the *Dutch Reformed Mission Church* with their centre at Nkhoma to join. Nkhoma joined in 1926 after being satisfied that the conditions and safeguards the *Dutch Reformed Mission Church* desired were included in the constitution.

CCAP church at Nkhudzi Bay

f. The Roman Catholic Mission

Portuguese claims

The penetration of Central Africa by the Roman Catholic missions was started through the efforts of Charles Lavigerie (see chapter 52.1), founder of the order of the *White Fathers*, who in 1887 became Archbishop of Algiers. Apart from the White Fathers, an important role was played by the *Montfort Missionaries*.

In the beginning Lavigerie in his campaign in Central Africa cooperated with the Portuguese. In 1888 a Portuguese official, Antonio Cardobo, contacted chiefs in the area south of Lake Malawi about the possibility of starting a Roman Catholic Mission to counteract the Scots. He made treaties with several chiefs, including Mponda and Matipwiri. Meanwhile two explorers, Serpa Pinto and Henry de Macedo, approached

Lavigerie, because the Portuguese had no missionary orders of their own to occupy the area. Lavigerie would have liked the mission to be under his control, but the Portuguese claimed that the ecclesiastical jurisdiction in that part of Africa had been given to them by the Pope in the early 16th century.[23] Lavigerie was in no position to argue. The mission was to teach in the Portuguese language. The mission stations were to be Portuguese property, and spiritual authority was to be exercised by the Bishop of Mozambique. The Portuguese promised financial assistance to the mission until it should be self-supporting. The Portuguese wanted it to be a national mission. However, it was agreed that any Portuguese priest who joined the mission should undergo training with the White Fathers.

The White Fathers and the Montfort Fathers

In June 1889 Lavigerie sent *White Fathers* from Algiers to Malawi. This was part of Lavigerie's plan for sub-Saharan Africa. The *White Fathers* everywhere were to establish a series of mission stations. Lavigerie laid down detailed instructions for the community life of the *White Fathers* in each one of these stations, and for their missionary work. Each station must have at least three members. Their life was to be centred on prayer, meditation, and spiritual reading. They had to study and record details of religious, political and economic life of the people amongst whom they lived. The *White Fathers* placed great emphasis on religious instruction of the people. New converts had to undergo a four-year preparation for baptism, and the examinations were taken very seriously. They tended to concentrate on the intensive cultivation of a limited area rather than on rapid expansion. The funds of the mission were limited, and so it was necessary for them to become, as far as possible, self-supporting. Vegetable gardens were planted at the stations, cash crops were developed and herds of cattle were started. The missionaries were practical men; many of them had been brought up as farmers.

The three lonely missionaries who stayed in Malawi for two years were not very successful. From 1889 to 1891 these *White Fathers* were at Mponda, south of Lake Malawi. Political difficulties arising between Great Britain and Portugal on the question of demarcation of colonial territories contributed to the failure of this first attempt.[24]

Permanent settlement of the Roman Catholic missions dates from 1901 and 1902, when successively the *Montfort Fathers* and again the *White Fathers* started their work.[25] The *Montfort Fathers* were of French and Dutch background.[26] In 1901 they sent their first missionaries including Pierre Bourget, who was leader of the group, Antoine Winnen, and Auguste Prezeau. These men started work among the Ngoni. Sundkler says that they 'understood the authoritarianism of the Ngoni more readily than the Chewa system which had more indeterminate authority'.[27] On 25th July 1901 the

---

[23] Under the *Padroado Agreement* between the Pope and the Portuguese, missionary priests in Portuguese colonies were directly responsible to the Portuguese Government.

[24] Cf.: Ian Linden, *Mponda Mission Diary 1889-1891*, Lilongwe: White Fathers, 1989. Extracts in: K.R. Ross (ed.), *Christianity in Malawi: A Source Book*, pp.15-22.

[25] Cf.: Roland Vezeau, *The Apostolic Vicariate of Nyasa: Origins and First Developments 1889-1935*, Rome: Archives, Missionari d'Africa, 1989 [re-edited by Kachere, 2006];

[26] Hubert Reijnaerts, Ann Nielsen, and Matthew Schoffeleers, *Montfortians in Malawi: Their Spirituality and Pastoral Approach*, Blantyre: Kachere/ CLAIM, 1997. A note on p.137 says that the *Montfort Fathers* are often confused with the *Marist Brothers*, who also work in Malawi.

[27] Sundkler and Steed, *A History of the Church in Africa*, p.479.

party reached the area of Njobvuyalema, a sub-chief of the Maseko Ngoni paramount chief Gomani. Without much preparation a number of Ngoni were baptised.[28] The Montfortian missionaries in the first four years are said to have baptised seventy-six people.[29] The *Montfort Fathers* also associated with the Lomwe people, a weak and vulnerable group, who had arrived in southern Malawi as refugees from Mozambique. Through the work of the *Montfortians*, the Roman Catholic Church in the south has a strong Lomwe majority.[30]

Edel Mary Quinn (1907-1944) planted the work of the Legion of Mary in Malawi and in other countries of East and Central Africa.

In June 1902 *White Fathers* under the leadership of Guyard and Perrot opened their first mission at Chiwamba. In September a second station was opened at Mua near the southern Lake shore, and a year later Kachebere was founded. In 1912 the *White Fathers* opened a seminary at Mua, which was transferred to Kasina in 1927. In 1939 the seminary was moved to Kachebere. The *White Fathers* also started a leprosarium at Mua, in 1927. In 1932 they opened a printing press at Bembeke, and shifted it to Likuni in 1949.

The founder of the *Legion of Mary* in Malawi was Edel Quinn. The Legion of Mary was an organisation for lay apostolate originating from *Catholic Action*. Edel Quinn was based in Nairobi from 1936 until her death in 1944. She visited Malawi in 1940-1941, and recruited the first organisers of the Legion of Mary.[31]

Roman Catholic secondary school teaching was helped by the arrival of the *Teaching Brothers*, the *Marists*.

Conflict with the Nyau Societies

There was a continual struggle between the Roman Catholic missions and the *Nyau societies*. The missionaries especially objected to certain dances and ritual practices and the introduction of new masks.[32] The Nyau sometimes used masks that distorted the Christian message by representing Mary, Joseph and Peter. They presented themselves as the guardians of traditional society that was said to be disrupted by the missionaries.[33] In order to combat mission influence the Nyau rules were changed, so that children of school age were able to join. Thus the *Nyau Societies* were a powerful force in reducing school attendance.

---

[28] Reijnaerts, et al., *Montfortians in Malawi*, pp.32-34.
[29] Reijnaerts, et al., *Montfortians in Malawi*, p.123.
[30] Cf.: Sundkler and Steed, *A History of the Church in Africa*, p.797.
[31] Cf.: Reijnaerts, et al., *Montfortians in Malawi*, pp.238,239,247.
[32] Cf.: Claude Boucher, *When Animals Sing and Spirits Dance: Gule Wamkulu, the Great Dance of the Chewa People of Malawi*, Kungoni Centre of Culture and Art, 2012. The introduction offers information on the conflict between Nyau and the Roman Catholic Church.
[33] Cf.: Orison Chaponda, *Gule Wamkulu in the Catholic Church, Lilongwe Rural: A Cultural Phenomenon and a Pastoral Problem*, Zomba: University of Malawi, 1998 [unpublished MA module].

57.3. Post-Classical Missions

In 1891 Malawi became a British Protectorate. In the new colonial situation the classical missions had to re-orientate themselves as to the state-church relationship. At the same time, colonial rule gave room for a type of missions that deviated from the classical ones. Some of the characteristics of these Post-Classical Missions or Faith Missions are mentioned in chapter 55.

a. Joseph Booth and the Industrial Missions

Unlike the Faith Missions in general, those in Malawi did not come to an unreached area. By 1890 there were missionaries in all regions of Malawi. Yet many people of Nyasaland had never heard the Gospel.

Joseph Booth was the main founder of several Post-Classical Missions in Malawi.[34] He was also one of the first missionaries to plead for the rule of Church and Society by Africans themselves.[35] Booth was a British man, but he had worked in Auckland (New Zealand) and Melbourne (Australia) as a businessman, selling milk products for ten years. After a dream by his wife Mary Jane, in which she saw a Chinese person calling them to become missionaries, the couple applied with organisations like the *China Inland Mission* and the *Baptist Missionary Society*. But being considered too old, they were not accepted. Mary Jane Booth died three weeks before departure. In the meantime, they had

Elliot Kamwana (second from the left) and Joseph Booth, 1909 (from: Chakanza, Voices, p.28).

founded their own organisation. Booth came to Malawi in 1892 to establish missions that would be interdenominational, and whose missionaries should earn their living by their industry.

The idea of industrial missions was new to *Faith Missions*, although it had been applied by *Classical Missions* like Livingstonia, Blantyre, and Nkhoma. However, there was a difference. Whereas these Classical Missions used the idea for training people in industrial skills like agriculture, carpentry, or laundry, for Booth industry was the means for the missionaries to support themselves, independently from any overseas donor. He would accept money from donors, but basically the missionaries were to live on their own industry. That is why he started to grow cash crops, mainly coffee. As he needed the vicinity of people and markets where he could sell the goods, he settled near the *Blantyre Mission*. Allegedly he 'stole' John Chilembwe from Blantyre Mission. Chilembwe had been to school there, but was not yet baptised.

---

[34] H. Langworthy, *Africa for the Africans: The Life of Joseph Booth*, Blantyre: CLAIM, 1996;

[35] Cf.: Joseph Booth, *Africa for the Africans*, 1897 [edited by Laura Perry, reprinted by CLAIM/ Kachere in 1996]; Kenneth Ross, *Christianity in Malawi*, pp.181-194; Hildebrandt, *History of the Church in Africa*, p.219, misunderstands Booth's defence of African selfhood, by accusing him of teaching 'racial intolerance' towards the whites;

In 1892 Booth opened the *Zambezi Industrial Mission* (ZIM) at Mitsidi near Blantyre. ZIM is now called *Zambezi Evangelical Church* (ZEC). It is a kind of Baptist church, although its organisation is similar to that of the Presbyterians.

In 1893 Booth founded the *Nyasa Industrial Mission* at Likhubula, now *Evangelical Church of Malawi* with its centre at Ntambanyama.

Elements of Booth's varied message were taken over by others, who followed ways that were not necessarily Booth's own. Examples are Elliot Kamwana and Charles Domingo, alumni of Livingstonia's *Overtoun Institution*. Kamwana turned to Booth when he was at the Cape in 1907. He was especially attracted by Booth's fascination for the Watchtower message.[36] The movement of *Jehovah's Witnesses* started with the thousands that were baptised by Kamwana.[37] Charles Domingo was one of the foremost of Livingstonia's students and teachers and also was at Lovedale in the Eastern Cape. Between 1907 and 1910 Domingo broke with Livingstonia, to set up his own independent African *Seventh Day Baptist Church*.[38]

In 1895 Booth began the Scottish *Baptist Industrial Mission* at Gowa in Ntcheu, since 1929 *Churches of Christ*.[39]

Another branch of Baptism in Malawi was founded by Booth's disciple John Chilembwe, under the name *Providence Industrial Mission* (PIM). Although PIM indirectly is one of Booth's churches, we will deal with it separately in the next section.

In 1901 the *Seventh Day Baptists* sold *Plainfield Mission* to the *Seventh Day Adventists* (SDA) from America, who renamed it Malamulo (appr. 40 km. south of Blantyre). The first missionary was Joseph Booth together with the Branch

John Chilembwe (†1915) and his Family.

---

[36] George Shepperson and Thomas Price, *Independent African: John Chilembwe and the Origin, Setting and Significance of the Nyasaland Native Rising of 1915*, Blantyre: CLAIM/ Kachere, 2000, pp.153-159.

[37] Cf.: J.C. Chakanza, *Voices of Preachers in Protest: The Ministry of two Malawian Prophets, Elliot Kamwana and Wilfred Gudu*, part 1 'From Preacher to Prophet: Elliot Kenan Kamwana and the Watchtower Movement in Malawi 1908-1956', CLAIM/ Kachere, 1998, pp.12-54.

[38] Shepperson and Price, *Independent African*, pp.159-164; Cf.: Kenneth Ross, *Christianity in Malawi*, pp.131-144.

[39] Literature on the Churches of Christ in different denominational groups, includes: Ernest Gray, 'The History of the Churches of Christ Missionary Work in Nyasaland, Central Africa 1907-1930', in: *Churches of Christ Historical Society Occasional Paper*, no. 1, Cambridge, 1981; Anne Thiessen, *The Warm Heart of Africa*, Winona: Choate Publ., 1998; C.B. Shelburne, 'History of the Church of Christ in Malawi' np, nd [A brief factual account of the history of the Church of Christ in southern Malawi].

family, black Americans. The daughter, Mable Branch, founded and taught at the first school at Malamulo. Booth did not stay long. In 1907 they were replaced by Cyril Rogers. Mark Chakachadza started the SDA church at Matandani (about 30 km west of Zomba). Rogers gave the permission and bought the mission plot in 1908, and the Koenigmachers built it up.[40] Also beginnings were made of the development of medical services at Malamulo and Matandani.[41] Today the SDA Church has become the third largest denomination in Malawi.

But these Missions do not have the specific characteristics of *Faith Missions*, as they are denominational.

b. Africa Evangelical Church of Malawi

The *South Africa General Mission*, whose headquarters was in London with a regional office in Cape Town, came to the Lower Shire at Nsanje in 1898, and later moved its centre to Chididi. At Luriwe Mission a school for the blind was established. In 1996 the name of the mission was changed to *Africa Evangelical Fellowship* (AEF),[42] and later joined SIM-International.[43] The church that resulted from its work is the *Africa Evangelical Church of Malawi*.[44]

c. Providence Industrial Mission[45]

The *Providence Industrial Mission* was started by a Malawian, John Chilembwe. He was a Yao, born in Chiradzulu, who went to a Scottish mission school in Blantyre for his early education. In 1892 Chilembwe joined the work of Joseph Booth. In 1897 Booth took him along to the United States. There he studied at a black Baptist institution, *Virginia Theological Seminary* in Lynchburg. In 1900 Chilembwe returned to Malawi. Supported by the *National Baptist Convention Inc.* in America, now in Malawi known as *African Baptist Assembly*, Chilembwe started his own mission, called *Providence Industrial Mission*, at Mbombwe, in his home district Chiradzulu.

Chilembwe aimed at running his mission by involvement in industrial enterprise. His policy was not to depend on whites but upon his own people, whom he encouraged to take up farming and other industries. Chilembwe himself started farms of coffee and cotton. By 1910 he is said to have organised 'a well-dressed and drilled community'.[46]

The mission had a serious setback when an uprising broke out in January 1915. The rebellion started as a revolt against the bad and cruel treatment of African labourers by white planters, traders and other settlers during the period of famine in 1912-1914. People also resented the hut tax and forced participation of Africans in the *First World War*. After failing to obtain satisfaction by stating his grievances peacefully, Chilembwe

---

[40] Mvula and Lwesya, *Flames of Fire*, p.66f; cf. Stefan Höschele, *From the Ends of the World to the Ends of the Earth: The Development of Seventh Day Adventist Missiology*, Zomba: Kachere, 2004.

[41] Cf. Yonah Hisbon Matemba, *Matandani: The Second Adventist Mission in Malawi*, Zomba: Kachere, 2003.

[42] Cf.: Hildebrandt, *History of the Church in Africa*, p.175.

[43] SIM = *Society of International Missions* (now: *Scriptures in Mission*), the former *Sudan Interior Mission*.

[44] Mvula and Lwesya, *Flames of Fire*, p.66.

[45] Patrick Makondesa, *The Church History of Providence Industrial Mission 1900-1940*, Zomba: Kachere, 2006; Shepperson and Price, *Independent African*, pp.165 ff, etc.; D.D. Phiri, *Let us Die for Africa: An African Perspective on the Life and Death of John Chilembwe of Nyasaland/ Malawi*, Blantyre: Central Africana, 1999; Kenneth Ross, *Christianity in Malawi*, pp.145-154.

[46] Shepperson and Price, *Independent African*, pp.142-147.

and his followers decided 'to strike a blow and die'. Thus on the evening of 23rd January 1915 the uprising started, between Chilembwe and his followers on the one side and the planters and the government on the other side. Chilembwe was captured and shot dead on the third of February 1915.[47]

But the mission did not die on account of the loss of its founder. Chilembwe's leadership was taken over by Daniel Malikebu (c.1890-1978).[48] In 1905 Malikebu had gone to the United States to study, invited by Emma De Lany, one of the early American missionaries with the PIM. In 1917 he qualified as a medical doctor, and after that he continued to study theology with a hope of serving the Church as a medical missionary. In 1926 Malikebu returned to Malawi in. He found that the PIM church had been reopened with government permission in 1924. Then, Malikebu was allowed to reopen and reorganise the mission Chilembwe had founded. He led it for almost 30 years. In 1971 he was succeeded by Leonard Muocha who was PIM-chairman until 1987.[49]

The present PIM church in Chiradzulu.

57.4. From Mission to Church[50]

a. Forms of Cooperation

The uniting of three strands of Presbyterianism in 1926 was influential to further forms of cooperation between Missions and Churches in Malawi. The CCAP partly resulted from a wider form of cooperation that had started earlier. From 1900 to 1949 a series of

---

[47] Hildebrandt, *History of the Church in Africa*, p.220, misrepresents or at least oversimplifies the *Chilembwe Rising* by reducing Chilembwe's motivations to hatred against enemies.
[48] Shepperson and Price, *Independent African*, pp.391,412,440,455,509.
[49] Patrick Makondesa, *Moyo ndi Utumiki wa Mbusa ndi Mai Muocha wa Providence Industrial Mission*, Blantyre: CLAIM/ Mvunguti, 2000.
[50] Pauw, *Mission and Church in Malawi*, pp.37-43.

six *General Missionary Conferences* took place, which aimed at bringing Protestant Missions together to discuss and plan matters like recognition of one another's membership, education, Bible translation, and issues concerning the relationship with the government. Except for the Anglican UMCA, the PIM, and the *Seventh Day Adventists*, all Protestant Missions were represented at these conferences.

In 1910 during their Conference at Mvera, representatives of almost the whole of Malawian Protestantism decided to establish a Consultative Board of Federated Missions and Churches. Eventually six Missions joined: the *Livingstonia Mission*, the *Dutch Reformed Church Mission*, the *Blantyre Mission*, the *Zambezi Industrial Mission*, the *Nyasa Industrial Mission*, and the *South Africa General Mission*. These Missions pledged to recognise one another's membership and discipline, promised to devise a common standard of religious instruction and knowledge required for (full) members, and agreed to respect one another's sphere of work. The *Consultative Board* further functioned as a mouthpiece to the government, and it paved the way for the formation of an indigenous African Church in Malawi. In it there was close cooperation in matters such as Bible translation and the composition of a hymn book (*Nyimbo za Mulungu*). In 1949 the Board agreed on full African membership. In 1962 it adapted its name to be a Fellowship of Churches. In 1967 the *Consultative Board* was disbanded.

In the meantime, since 1939, a wider and more general body of ecclesiastical cooperation had emerged, the *Nyasaland Christian Council*. All Missions and Churches, including the UMCA, the Seventh Day Adventists and the Roman Catholics were invited to join, of which the latter two declined. Since independence it has operated under the name *Christian Council of Malawi*. As such, it continues to coordinate aspects of the work of different Churches in the country.

b. Matchona churches

Throughout the 20th century many Malawians went to Tanzania, Zambia, Zimbabwe and South Africa as migrant workers.[51] Sometimes, where they went, they founded Malawian churches, like the PIM in Soweto, and the CCAP Harare Synod. Others joined existing churches at the places where they went, and when they returned home, brought these churches with them. They were called the Matchona churches, the Migrants' churches. Examples of such migrants were John George Philips, who brought the *Catholic Apostolic Church in Zion*,[52] Robert Chinguwo who brought the *Apostolic Faith Mission* (1933),[53] Moses Phiri who brought the *Free Methodist Church*,[54] and John Wesley Dingswayo who brought the *Zion Church*.[55]

---

[51] *Matchona* (singular: *mtchona*) is the Chichewa word for *migrant labourers*. For an account of such migration, read: Masiye Tembo, *Touched by His Grace: A Ngoni Story of Tragedy and Triumph*, Zomba: Kachere, 2005.

[52] Cf: Shepperson and Price, *Independent African*, p.412, who quote Sundkler.

[53] Ulf Strohbehn, *Pentecostalism in Malawi: A History of the Apostolic Faith Mission 1931-1994*, Zomba: Kachere, 2005, pp.44-52; Kwiyani, Harvey C., 'Coming of Age: Pentecostalism and Umunthu in Malawi', in: Vinson Synan, Amos Yong and J. Kwabena Asamoah-Gyadu, *Global Renewal Christianity: Spirit-Empowered Movements Past, Present, and Future*, Vol. Iii of *Africa and Diaspora*, Lake Mary, FL: Charisma House Publishers, expected 2016 [version of Kwiyani's article on Internet, pp.4,5].

[54] Henry Church, *Theological Education that Makes a Difference*, Blantyre: CLAIM/ Kachere, 2001.

[55] Cf.: Smart Y.J., Msinkhu, 'Zionism in Malawi: The History and Theology of 'Zion City Church' in Ntcheu District' [University of Malawi, 2005].

An example connected to Malawi's first President Hastings Kamuzu Banda concerns his uncle Hanock Msokera Phiri, who brought the *African Methodist Episcopal Church* (AMEC) to Nyasaland.[56] In 1915-1916, Phiri, who had been a teacher at the Livingstonia Mission School, together with his nephew left on foot for Southern Rhodesia (now Zimbabwe). In 1917, they left on foot for Johannesburg in South Africa, where they worked at the Witwatersrand. During this time, they met Bishop W.T. Vernon of the African Methodist Episcopal Church (AMEC). Vernon helped Kamuzu to get to the United States for further study. Hanock Phiri became a faithful AMEC member, who after his return planted the church in Nyasaland.[57]

The *Evangelical Lutheran Church* was brought from Tanzania to Malawi.[58] Another branch of Lutheranism, the *Lutheran Church of Central Africa* (LCCA) was brought to Malawi from Zambia by Richard Mueller and Raymond G. Cox, and started among Malawian workers returning from the Copperbelt.[59] The *Evangelical Brethren Church* was brought in from South Africa by Joshua Monjeza.[60] Some of these Matchona churches later also attracted Western missionaries, like the *Apostolic Faith Mission*, and the *Assemblies of God*. They will be further discussed in chapter 60, together with other Pentecostal Churches.

57.5. Independent Malawi

a. Church and State

In 1964 Malawi changed from colonial rule to independence.[61] The new government led by Hastings Kamuzu Banda soon turned the country into a dictatorial one-party state. In the new situation the relationship between the state and the various denominations changed.

This was most apparent in the state's attitude towards Roman Catholicism and Protestantism. Because of the *Chilembwe Rising* in 1915 the British colonial government generally had come to mistrust the educational success of the Protestant churches, as it aimed at the Africanisation of leadership. The Roman Catholic Church with its training of obedience to the leading hierarchy of priests was found more fitting to the colonial system. Baur says: 'Soon the marked difference between Catholics and Protestants was that between the critical and the obedient mind'. The Presbyterians in particular had produced an élite of leaders. Some of them later underwent radical influences, and became independent activists, like Elliot Kamwana, Charles Domingo,

---

[56] Cf.: Devlin Chirwa, 'The History of the African Methodist Episcopal Church in Malawi, The Karonga Branch (1943-2000)'.

[57] Roderick J. Macdonald, 'Reverend Hanock Msokera Phiri and the Establishment in Nyasaland of the African Methodist Episcopal Church', in: *African Historical Studies*, Vol. 3, No. 1 (1970), pp. 75-87.

[58] Cf.: H.Z. Mwimba, 'The Establishing of the Evangelical Lutheran Church in Malawi', Tanzania, Makumira, 1992 [unpublished B.Div. paper of Makumira Lutheran Theological College].

[59] This Church is born out of the mission work by the Wisconsin Evangelical Lutheran Church in the United States. Cf.: Harold R. Johne, and Ernst H. Wendland, *To Every Nation, Tribe, Language and People: A Century of WELS World Missions*, Milwaukee: Northwestern Publ. House, 1993², pp.206-221; Ernst H. Wendland, *A History of the Christian Church in Central Africa: The Lutheran Church of Central Africa 1953-1978*, Wisconsin: Mequon, 1980.

[60] Joshua Monjeza, 'Distinctives and Polity of the Evangelical Brethren Church in Malawi, including Church History', nd [about 1995].

[61] For a missionary witness, see: Jackson, *Send Us Friends*, pp.233-396.

and John Chilembwe. Emerging African nationalism looked upon Roman Catholicism as a supporter of the status quo. That is why Chilembwe not only attacked the colonialist establishment, but also the Roman Catholic Church, destroying the church at Nguludi. This made the Roman Catholic Church more respectable in the eyes of the colonial rulers than the Protestant churches.

For the independent government after 1964, however, this was reason to trust the Protestants more than the Roman Catholics. The movement towards independence was a Protestant affair till the last moment. Native Associations and the Malawian African Congress were Presbyterian enterprises. President Kamuzu Banda (†1997) liked to present himself as a Presbyterian elder, and his first cabinets mainly consisted of Presbyterians. That is how Malawian independence took away the Roman Catholic Church's position as much trusted partner of the government. Protestant churches took over this favoured place.

Hastings Kamuzu Banda, President of Malawi from 1964 to 1994.

However, the pattern of state-church loyalties would change again by the end of the Banda regime.[62] The publication of the *Lenten Pastoral Letter* by the Roman Catholic bishops in 1992[63] was instrumental in the downfall of the one-party government and the transition to a multi-party democracy in 1994. Whereas the CCAP, especially the Nkhoma Synod, was looked upon as the Banda-government-comrades-in-prayer,[64] the new government led by Bakili Muluzi cherished its contacts with the Roman Catholic Church. Whether the new situation has led to a growth of Roman Catholicism in Malawi is uncertain.[65] The CCAP Livingstonia and Blantyre Synods cooperated with Roman Catholic and Muslim groups, the Law Society and the Chamber of Commerce in the Public Affairs Committee (PAC), which in 1995 was established for the promotion of good governance and human rights. In this way they tried to bring about the desired

---

[62] Cf.: Matthew Schoffeleers, *In Search of Truth and Justice: Confrontations between the Church and the State in Malawi: 1960-1994*, Blantyre: Kachere/ CLAIM, 1999, pp.121-354; Kenneth R. Ross (ed.), *God, People and Power in Malawi: Democratisation in Theological Perspective*, Blantyre: Kachere/ CLAIM, 1996; Matembo S. Nzunda and Kenneth R. Ross, *Church, Law and Political Transition in Malawi 1992-1994*, Gweru: Mambo/ Kachere, 1997²; Kenneth Ross, *Christianity in Malawi*, pp.203-236.

[63] *Living our Faith* [Pastoral Letter of the Catholic Bishops of Malawi to be read in every Catholic Church on 8 March 1992]; later reprinted in: Kenneth R. Ross (ed.), *Christianity in Malawi*, pp.203-216. For much detail, see: Matthew Schoffeleers, *In Search of Truth*, pp.116ff,181ff.

[64] The Blantyre and Livingstonia Synods joined the struggle against Kamuzu not long after the Lenten Letter, and they were supported by the WARC.

[65] In line with publications on spectacular growth numbers of Roman Catholicism in Africa as a whole it is suggested that the relative popularity of Roman Catholicism after the *Lenten Letter* could have led to recent increase of the number of converts in Malawi, although no local evidence is found (cf. Bryan T. Froehle and Mary L. Gautier, *Global Catholicism: Portrait of a World Church*, Maryknoll: Orbis Books, p.5; Baur, *2000 Years*, p.431).

change. In spite of their support for the new dispensation, the churches have grown increasingly worried about corruptive and dictatorial tendencies in the new administration.

Roman Catholicism and Protestantism have differed as to the degree and the pace of Africanisation. In 1966 there were only 75 Malawian priests in the Roman Catholic Church. The Africanisation of the hierarchy began with Cornelio Chitsulo, who later became a bishop. He was succeeded by James Chiwona in 1956, who became Archbishop of Blantyre in 1967. The third was Patrick Kalilombe, who in 1972 became bishop of Lilongwe.[66] In the Presbyterian churches the Africanisation had largely taken place before the beginning of independence in 1964.[67] Developments in the Anglican Church were slower. The first Malawian bishop, Josiah Mtekateka (1903-1996), was ordained in 1965.[68]

Anglicans and Presbyterians decided to cooperate in training, by establishing a joint institution at Chilema in 1974, and joint theological training in *Zomba Theological College* (ZTC) in 1976. However, in 2006 the Anglicans withdrew from ZTC and the established Zomba their own *Leonard Kamungu Theological College* (LKTC). In the *Christian Council of Malawi*, churches cooperate in the *Christian Hospitals Association of Malawi* (CHAM).

Banda's regime clashed with the *Jehovah's Witnesses*. The *Watchtower Movement* had been banned in Zambia and Malawi at an early stage in its history after the *First World War*. They would not cooperate with the governments. Many considered Jehovah's Witnesses not to be Christians, as they do not believe in the divinity of Jesus.[69] After independence, the *Jehovah's Witnesses* refused to become members of the omnipotent *Malawi Congress Party*. They were exposed to very harsh treatment, including killing, burning, captivity in concentration camps, and banishment. Many were chased away to Zambia, only to be chased back to Malawi and then deported to Mozambique to new persecution and suffering.[70]

b. New Missions after the 'End of Missions'

When around the time of independence the mainline churches received Malawian leaders, the missions supporting them stepped aside, so to speak, and the daughter churches now became sister churches. While this marked the end of established missiological strategy, many Malawians happily welcomed new missions. Several *Pentecostal Churches* enriched Malawi's Christian diversity.[71] The *Baptist Convention* was set up in 1960 by American Southern Baptists from Zimbabwe.[72] The *Lutheran*

---

[66] Baur, *2000 Years*, p.430,431.

[67] For an example, see: Silas Ncozana, *Sangaya: A Leader in the Synod of Blantyre Church of Central Africa Presbyterian*, Blantyre: CLAIM/ Kachere, 1999, pp.19-21.

[68] Cf.: Henry Mbaya, *Josiah Mtekateka* [DACB Website].

[69] Cf.: Hildebrandt, *History of the Church in Africa*, p.222, who mistakenly says that *Jehohah's Witnesses* 'do not believe that Jesus is the Son of God'.

[70] K. Fiedler, 'Power at the Receiving End: The Jehovah's Witnesses' Experience in One-Party Malawi', in: K.R. Ross (ed.), *God, People and Power in Malawi: Democratization in Theological Perspective*, Blantyre: CLAIM/ Kachere, 1996, pp.149-176.

[71] Ulf Strohbehn, in his PhD Module for the University of Malawi, 1998, found that in Blantyre there are more than 120 denominations of Pentecostal and Charismatic character.

[72] Cf.: Judy Garner, *History of the Baptist Mission in Malawi: A Rambling Remembrance of Some People and*

Church of Central Africa[73] came from Zambia; Moses Phiri brought the *Free Methodists* from Zimbabwe.[74]

The *Reformed Presbyterian Church* (RPC) of Malawi was born out of a Bible study group in Ndirande consisting of Ephraim Tembo and Edward Mwase, Justin Gonakumoto later also Wyson Chitsulo Phiri. These people from Baptist, SDA, and Nazarene backgrounds had developed a special interest in the *Westminster Catechism and Confession of Faith*, and had an informal relationship with the Free Presbyterian Church (FP Church) of Scotland, especially its extension in Zimbabwe. Contacts grew, and in 1988 the FP Church sent a missionary, Dick Vermeulen, a Dutch immigrant in New Zealand. The FP Church Mission withdrew in 1995, but a Dutch interest in the RPC remained, first mainly through the *Stephanos Foundation*,[75] but later especially through the denomination *Herstelde Hervormde Kerk* (HHK), born out of a schism among Reformed Christians in The Netherlands in 2004.[76]

c. Revival

While the decade of transition to independence may have seen some slackening of religious interest, the 1970s and the 1980s were decades of revival, centred in the cities, especially Blantyre, and with much influence among middle and upper class and among the educated. Whereas the 1970s revival mainly strengthened the evangelical element in the church,[77] the 1980s revival gave strength to the *Charismatic Movement*, which may now comprise more than 5% of all Malawian Christians,[78] with the *Living Waters Church*, led by Apostle Stanley Ndovi being the biggest church.

d. Women's Organisations

In all churches in Malawi women outnumber men, and often women provide much of the strength of a local church. In addition, almost every church has its own women's group, often distinguished by a specific uniform and a specific name, like *Mvano* (CCAP Blantyre Synod, PIM), *Chigwirizano* (CCAP Nkhoma Synod),[79] *Umanyano* (CCAP Livingstonia Synod), *Mpingo wa Azimayi* (Anglicans), *Umodzi* (Baptists),

---

Events in the History of the Baptist Mission in Malawi, Lilongwe: Baptist Publications, 1998; Rachel Nyagondwe Fiedler, *Women of Bible and Culture: Baptist Convention Women in Southern Malawi*, Zomba: Kachere, 2005; D.L. Saunders, *A History of Baptists in East and Central Africa*, Southern Baptist Seminary 1973 [unpublished PhD thesis]; Harry Longwe, 'The History of BACOMA', Zomba: Kachere [2006].

[73] Ernst H. Wendland, *A History of the Christian Church in Central Africa*, op. cit.

[74] Henry Church, *Theological Education that Makes a Difference: Church Growth in the Free Methodist Church in Malawi and Zimbabwe*, Zomba: Kachere, 2002, pp.44-46.

[75] Cf. Ephraim Tembo, 'History of the *Reformed Presbyterian Church of Malawi*', np, nd.

[76] The *Hersteld Hervormde Kerk* (HHK) (Restored Reformed Church) was formed in opposition to a merger of two large Protestant denominations, the Gereformeerde Kerk in Nederland (GKN) and the Nederlandse Hervormde Kerk (NHK) into the Protestantse Kerk in Nederland (PKN). Reformed Dutch missionary interest for Malawi within the PKN continues to be channelled through the Gereformeerde Zendings Bond (GZB), a Reformed missionary league that supports projects in the CCAP. In cooperation with the Malawian branch of Scripture in Mission (SIM) the GZB has developed missionary activity among Muslims, especially through the organiation *Mthenga Wabino* (Good Messenger).

[77] Cf. J.C. Selfridge, *Jack of All Trades Mastered by One*, Fearn: Christian Focus, 1989.

[78] For an overview see: Klaus Fiedler, 'The Charismatic and Pentecostal Movements in Malawi in Cultural Perspective', in: *Religion in Malawi*, 9 (1999). In all the country there are about 150 different Pentecostal and Charismatic denominations.

[79] Phiri, *Women*, pp.71-90 and other pages.

Amayi a Dorika (SDA), *Otumikira mwa Chikondi* (Assemblies of God), and *Chiyanjano cha Azimayi* (Churches of Christ). On the Roman Catholic side, in addition to the *Amayi a Chifundo*, *Amayi a Tereza*, and the *Legio Maria*, there are the Religious Orders of the Malawian Sisters, like the *Daughters of the Blessed Virgin Mary*[80] and the *Sisters of our Lady of Africa*.[81]

---

[80] Nelly Michongwe, *Meet the Daughters of the Blessed Virgin Mary in Malawi Africa*, Zomba: Kachere, 2005².

[81] Reijnaerts, et al., *Montfortians in Malawi*, refers to the *Sisters of our Lady of Africa* (p.65), and also to the *Daughters of Wisdom* (pp.65,314), and to others.

58. The Church in Zambia

58.1. East Zambia

Our survey of Zambia[1] starts in the East. In Eastern Zambia the *Dutch Reformed Church Mission* (DRCM) of South Africa was active. Reformed missionaries entered Northern Rhodesia (present-day Zambia) from two directions. One group came from the central region of Malawi where the Western Cape Synod of the DRC had established many stations and congregations.

The other group came directly from South Africa, and was sent by the Orange Free State Synod of the DRC. Reformed missionary influence also came from the north of Malawi, where the Livingstonia Mission of the *Free Church of Scotland* worked among the Tonga, Tumbuka and Ngoni. A mass movement among the Tonga led to mission campaigns beyond the Malawian boundaries. Scottish Free Church missionaries even went to the Bemba people in the north of Northern Rhodesia, and also to the centre. One of these workers was John Afwenge Banda. Another early Tonga evangelist in Northern Rhodesia was David Kaunda, father of Kenneth Kaunda, who became the first President of independent Zambia. In their turn the Bemba spread the Gospel to neighbouring tribes. Zambian Christians adopted the Livingstonia idea of 'welfare organisations' and Zambian churches had their leaders trained at Malawi's *Overtoun Institution*.

58.2. South Zambia

By the end of the 19th century the south and the west had been invaded by two foreign powers. The first was the *Chartered Company* of Cecil Rhodes that eventually would secure British hegemony over Zambia. The presence of a European power was a challenge to the loyalty of European missionaries. Generally, African leaders offered various degrees of resistance, except for King Lewanika and his Lozi people, who adjusted to the situation. Lewanika represented the other invasion, namely by the Kololo, some members of a Sotho-tribe, who had subjugated and enslaved various other tribes, thus establishing in Barotseland the kingdom of the Lozi. King Lewanika of the Lozi only allowed missionaries who would accept and honour his supremacy. Initially this led to problems with Evangelical, Methodist, Baptist and Jesuit missions.

We follow the attempts by the evangelical *Paris Mission* in Barotseland, which was led by François Coillard. Coillard had worked in Lesotho and assumed that knowledge of the Sotho language might give him an easy entry among the Sotho- speaking élite of the Lozi kingdom. However, the king got angry because in his view the *Paris Mission* had entered his kingdom through a wrong route. Consequently, Coillard and his Sotho co-workers had to leave, only to be received and accepted seven years later. In 1889 the first convert was baptised, Nguana Ngombe, a slave boy. In 1894 Coillard opened a Bible school. After that, there was a continual growth of the number of Christians. The king never converted to Christianity, although he let himself be influenced by Coillard for almost twenty years. His main interest remained the economic, technical, and educational side of the missionaries' activities. The introduction of various trades as well as a literacy movement gradually changed life in the Lozi kingdom, especially of

---

[1] Also: Sundkler, and Steed, *A History of the Church in Africa*, pp.449, 459-467,473,609, 786-795, 974-981; Baur, *2000 Years*, pp.432-437.

the élite. At grass root level the pace of social and economic change was slower. At the same time, the new faith became rooted in the hearts and lives of many. Even Siwi, an influential priest of the local cult, turned to Christ. Also, Litiya, the king's son, and Mokamba, his chief minister, became Christians. These conversions contributed to the formation of the new self-conscious mission-educated élite that during the rise of the *Ethiopian Movement* tended to independency and disagreement with the missionaries.

Mainly through Methodist missionaries, Christianity also spread among the Lomba and Ila-speaking peoples, although they were slow to accept because they tended to identify the Christian faith with the interests of the Lozi who dominated them.

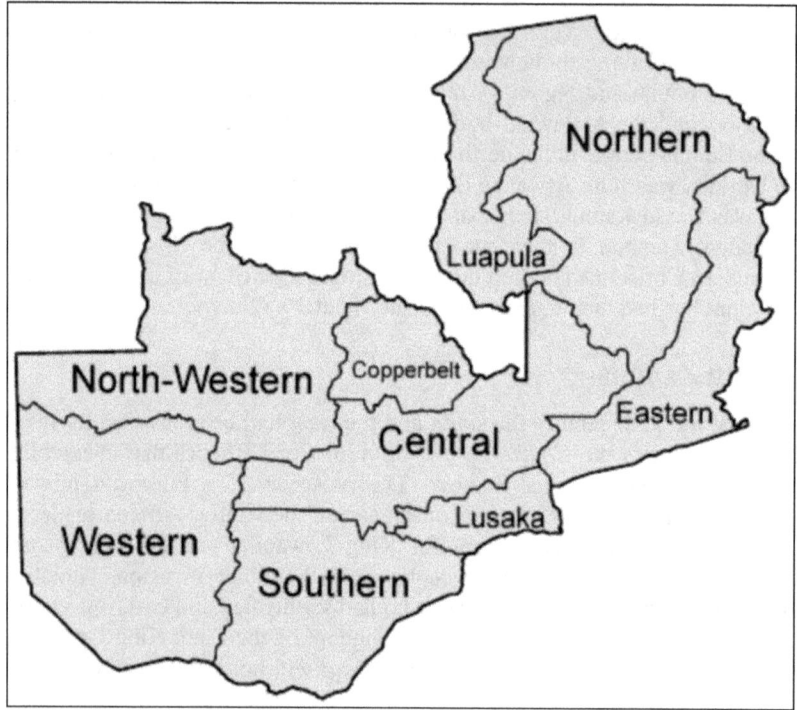

Map of Zambia.

58.3. The Copperbelt

The London Missionary Society (LMS) were the first to start, in 1878. They established churches, schools, industrial training and medical services.[2] The discovery of copper in the North West changed much of the social and economic position of many Zambians. Changes were also induced by Zambia's becoming a British Protectorate in 1924. Like South Africa at the Rand and Zaire in Shaba, the new colony opened mines, and cities emerged with Ndola as an important centre. These urban communities, classed together as the *Copperbelt*, consisted of a majority of black labourers who had migrated from the Bemba country or from great distances, quite often from Malawi, and a minority of whites mainly from South Africa.

---

[2] Cf.: Hildebrandt, *History of the Church in Africa*, p.178.

Before the mission organisations entered the Copperbelt, an African Christian movement had already prepared the ground. In the country as a whole a second generation of missionaries became active. The missionary organisations started the formation of various denominations. In this Copperbelt region of Zambia's West Anglicans, Methodist, Paris Mission, Roman Catholics, Brethren, and others formed their churches.

58.4. Unity and Dissent

Common concern about the needs of the masses in the Copperbelt led to some cooperation between missionaries of various backgrounds. Among some missionaries this also stimulated debate on Church union, which by 1965, led to the formation of the *United Church of Zambia*, a combination of Congregationalist, Methodist, and Presbyterian-Reformed Churches. Plans for church unity in Zambia were greatly stimulated by the *Mindolo Ecumenical Institute* in the Copperbelt. Here also the *All Africa Church Conference* was stationed before it was removed to Nairobi. For various reasons a considerable number of churches and missions in Zambia did not join the Union: the Roman Catholics, Anglicans, the *South Africa General Mission*, the *Plymouth Brethren*, the Baptists, and the Dutch/African Reformed Church. Generally, the Zambian proceedings to union were inspired by a specific white theological thinking in bodies like the *International Missionary Council* and later the Geneva based *World Council of Churches*. Kenneth Kaunda, Zambia's first president, was one of the advocates of the ecumenical programme. The United Church of Zambia has spread to nearly all parts of the country and is relatively big, yet much of Zambia's church life continued to develop outside this 'Genevan' ecumenical climate.

In 1891 the Roman Catholics started work in Zambia. On their side there were the *White Fathers*, who worked in the extreme north, establishing stations near those of the LMS, and had much response among the Bemba people.[3] The later spreading of Bemba about the whole country helped a nationwide growth of Roman Catholicism. Although at Mindolo the Africa expert Adrian Hastings served as a representative of Rome, his church kept itself outside the ecumenical structure, like it had always done. This does not mean that the Roman Catholic Church in Zambia found it easy to identify with the Roman world church in all aspects. Lusaka's Archbishop Emmanuel Milingo resisted Rome when he began healing sessions in 1982. Immediately the Archbishop was called to Rome. The Pope tried to use him because of his popularity. But Milingo did not fit nicely in the Euro-Roman system. Even in his 'exile' he went on with prayer-healing meetings and found acceptance in charismatic Roman Catholic circles. From Roman Catholics in Zambia complaints reached the Vatican about the absence of their leader. Two decades later Milingo created a new crisis by marrying a member of the Moon sect. Unlike the Protestant missions who mainly concentrated on urban areas, Roman Catholicism especially developed in the countryside. Baur's suggestion that the Roman Catholic Church in Zambia is 'twice as large as all Protestants together',[4] seems to have no foundation when compared to the 2004 figures of the Website of *Catholic-Hierarchy*.[5]

---

[3] Vezeau, *The Apostolic Vicariate of Nyasa*, pp.19-45.

[4] Baur, *2000 Years*, p.432.

[5] Of the 11.7 million inhabitants 3 million are said to be Roman Catholics, i.e. 26 percent [www.catholic-

In the north west there was the successful *Open Brethren* Kalene Hill mission among the Lunda, started by Walter Fisher in 1906. This work initiated great spiritual and social change among the Lunda. Although the Brethren do not recognise an ordained ministry, the work in Zambia has led to the church-like formation of hundreds of 'assemblies' of baptised believers shepherded by elders.

The *Seventh Day Adventists* started their presence in Zambia in the south at Rusangu in 1903. Under the control of missionaries a thriving farming community developed. Later an African group, under the influence of Ethiopian thought, withdrew from the missionaries at Rusangu and settled at the Kemba Hills under African leadership. The Adventists contributed much to the formation of the *Northern Rhodesian African Congress* in 1937 and therefore to the ensuing nationalist movement in Zambia.

In the 1950s, initiated by black American missionaries, the *African Methodist Episcopal Church* (AMEC), one of America's largest black denominations, started a branch in Zambia. The church had close links to the nationalist Congress Party. Sundkler claims that even the party's general secretary and later state president Kenneth Kaunda was a local preacher and choir leader of the Lusaka AMEC, before he joined the *United Church* in 1965.[6] Although the AMEC claimed to be African and black, it still depended on American leadership. This led to a break, and consequently to the establishment of an independent parallel church (*African Methodist Independent Church*).

Emmanuel Milingo (born 1930), R.C. Archbishop of Lusaka.

58.5. Reformed and Presbyterian Churches

There are three denominations of Reformed-Presbyterian character in Zambia.[7] First, there is the Zambian Synod of the *Church of Central Africa Presbyterian* (CCAP). The other CCAP Synods are in Malawi and Zimbabwe; there are also congregations in Mozambique. The Zambian CCAP originates in missionary activity under the responsibility of the *Free Church of Scotland*. The Free Church began its work in Malawi by the end of the 19th century. Later the work was extended to Zambia, where a mission was established at Lubwa, with congregations in the north and the centre of the

---

hierarchy.org/country/zm.html].

[6] Sundkler and Steed, *A History of the Church in Africa*, p.795. Kenneth Kaunda may have had some connection with the AMEC during his years in Lusaka, but he is of Presbyterian descent. He was raised at Lubwa mission in North Zambia, where his father worked as a Presbyterian missionary. Father David Kaunda came from North Malawi. He was sent to Zambia by the *Free Church of Scotland*, which had already established the *Livingstonia Mission* in Malawi, and which developed into the Livingstonia Synod of the Church of Central Africa Presbyterian (CCAP).

[7] For the information in this paragraph I am indebted to: G.Verstraelen-Gilhuis, *From Dutch Mission Church to Reformed Church in Zambia: The Scope for African Leadership and Initiative in the History of a* 59. *The Church in Zimbabwe Zambian Mission Church*, Franeker, 1982, and to Mr. Burnett Muwowo's study of this book.

country. The *Zambian Free Church* that was produced by this mission had its members mainly among the Bemba-speaking people, whereas there are also Tumbuka and Nyanja (Chewa)-speaking members, the main vernacular languages of neighbouring Malawi. In church services these languages are used alternatively. In 1965 this *Zambian Free Church* joined the *United Church of Zambia*. At that time especially the Bemba in the North felt more at home in that church. Later, however, the United Church grew less popular. Some of its members together with immigrants from Malawi formed congregations and established the Zambian Synod of the CCAP, thus joining the General Synod of the CCAP and through this the three main Presbyterian churches in Malawi. Its congregations are to be found in the Copperbelt, the Eastern Province and in Lusaka. Ministers are trained either at Justo Mwale Theological College in Lusaka or at Zomba Theological College in Malawi.

Secondly, there is the *Presbyterian Church in Zambia*. This Church originated from groups of Malawian CCAP immigrants who were not accepted by the United Church in 1965, because their leader, Khowani, was a suspended minister. This denomination and the Zambian CCAP are two equally strong churches, each having about 9 presbyteries and some 45 congregations. The Presbyterian Church in Zambia has its congregations mainly in Lusaka; it also has some membership in the Copperbelt and in the Eastern Province. The majority are members who speak Tumbuka and Nyanja (Chewa), the main vernacular languages of neighbouring Malawi.

The Presbyterian Church in Zambia is not independent, but a part of the *Uniting Presbyterian Church in South Africa*. It has two presbyteries under the Synod of that church, and students for the ministry are sent to Justo Mwale Theological (University) College and to South Africa.

Thirdly, there is the *Reformed Church in Zambia*.[8] It originated in missionary work by the Orange Free State Synod of the Dutch Reformed Church of South Africa. It is the largest of the three denominations discussed in this paragraph. The earliest Dutch missionary arrival in Zambia was in the 1890s through the Orange Free State Synod, which opened stations at Fort Jameson, Madzimoyo, Nsanje, and Nsadzi. The station at Magwero station was established in 1908.[9] These days congregations of the Reformed Church can be found in Lusaka the Copperbelt, and in the Eastern Province, especially in the Chipata region. A great majority of the members are Chinyanja (Chichewa)-speaking. Future ministers have been trained at Justo Mwale Theological College (now: University) in Lusaka and in South Africa.

58.6. Independent Zambia

The British-inspired and dominated federation of Zambia, Malawi and Zimbabwe met with much African opposition, and was a prelude to these countries' independence. In 1964 Kenneth Kaunda became president of independent Zambia. He wanted to introduce a kind of humanism with socialist characteristics, coloured by Christianity. These ideals were put to the test by the movement of the prophetess Alice Mulenga Lenshina, and by the *Jehovah's Witnesses*.

---

[8] Cf.: Verstraelen-Gilhuis, op.cit.
[9] Cf.: Hildebrandt, *History of the Church in Africa*, p.178; J. du Plessis. *The Evangelisation of Pagan Africa*, p.308.

Lenshina came from Lubwa-Chinsali, the same district as Kaunda. She went through a death-and-resurrection experience in 1953. Then, according to Sundkler, she was baptised in the Presbyterian Church by Paul Mushindo, a Bemba minister who had worked at Lubwa mission where Kenneth Kaunda had grown up.[10] She started a millennarian preaching sharply focussed against sorcery, witchcraft, and beer drinking. At a later stage she and her movement were accused of using the evils that they condemned, like mobilising the power of magic and the condoning of sexual orgies.

Memorial of Alice Mulenga Lenshina (1953-1991) at Chinsali.

In the beginning the prophetess cooperated with nationalist leaders because of their joint hatred of the British-founded federation. Until 1959 her movement, called Lumpa, attracted many followers, even Presbyterians, Roman Catholics and Traditionalists. Then, the tide turned. Many left the movement when the announced return of Christ did not take place. Lenshina's attitude towards the outside world changed. In 'another Bible' given to her by Jesus – so she said – the remnant of her followers were called upon to flee the world and go to Zion, i.e. to Lenshina's villages that tended to behave as a separate state. The movement lost much of its voluntary character as the inhabitants of her closed settlements were sometimes forced to join and to remain. Lenshina was said to behave like a traditional sorcerer who pushed her followers into things like murder and having people eat faeces. From 1963 there were violent clashes between her Lumpa movement and Kaunda's United National Independence Party. Lenshina's movement was crushed by the troops of Kaunda in the months before the day of Independence, 24 October 1964. The bloodshed took the lives of many of Lenshina's followers and would not easily be forgotten.

The beginnings of the *Jehovah's Witnesses* of Zambia were in Malawi. The movement was started by Elliot Kenan Kamwana (see chapter 57, sections 3.a. and 5.a.), who was educated at the Overtoun Institution of the Livingstonia Synod of the CCAP. Kamwana left Overtoun and Presbyterianism and was drawn to the *Watchtower Movement* through Joseph Booth. In 1908 migrant workers brought the movement to Zambia. In a later period influences from the south were added. Labour migrants from the Southern Rhodesian (Zimbabwean) mines carried the Watch Tower teachings with them when they returned to their homes in Zambia. In 1968 the Watch Tower movement was violently attacked by the youth wingers of Kaunda's party. The president stopped the persecution, but agreed to the expulsion of foreign *Jehovah's Witnesses*.

In 1972 Malawian *Jehovah's Witnesses* entered Zambia as refugees, after the regime of Kamuzu Banda had started to persecute them. More than 20,000 of these refugees were placed in a camp at Sindamisale. Again the Zambian state did not show much of

---

[10] Sundkler and Steed, *A History of the Church in Africa*, p.790.

its humanist or Christian ideals. Although according to Sundkler the churches provided help through a combined committee[11], Fiedler reports on miserable circumstances in the camp.

> 'Nsindamisale (or: Sindamisale – S.P.) was a place of refuge but also of death. The camp was ill-equipped, the number of people was too large, and the sanitary conditions terrible. Hundreds died of waterborne diseases'.

The Zambian state only very reluctantly allowed refugees to enter. In spite of responsibilities given by the United Nations, Kaunda's government did not like to keep them. Some were humiliated and beaten, and finally all were forced to go back to Malawi and to new persecution.[12]

---

[11] Sundkler, *A History of the Church in Africa*, p.975

[12] Klaus Fiedler, 'Power at the Receiving End: The Jehovah's Witnesses' Experience in One Party Malawi', in: K. R. Ross (ed.), *God, People and Power in Malawi: Democratization in Theological Perspective*, Blantyre: CLAIM, 1996, pp.163,164

59. The Church in Zimbabwe

59.1. Jesuit and Dominican Attempts

The earliest history of Zimbabwean Christianity[1] is written in blood. It began with the successful missionary work of the Portuguese Jesuit Gonçalo da Silveira in December 1560 and January 1561. It took him little time to baptise King Mwene Mutapa, the king's mother and hundreds of his courtiers and other subjects. However, this victory soon changed into disaster. A witchdoctor saw his influence increase, and he told the king that Da Silveira was a spy for the Portuguese army, and that the water of baptism was a magic poison. This made the king turn round, and decide to have Da Silveira strangled. Because of the discovery of gold the Portuguese government did indeed try to establish its power in Mwene Mutapa's territory. At the same time, the order of the Dominicans succeeded Da Silveira in attempting to spread Roman Catholicism. In the years 1628-1633 the Dominican Luis do Espirito Santo combined the political and the religious aims by militarily interfering in favour of one of the contenders for the throne of the Mwene Mutapa kingdom. He organised an army headed by armed Dominicans and eliminated the army of the other contender. After this action the successive kings of the Mwene Mutapa Kingdom were Christians. They depended on the power of the Portuguese who soon shared out large portions of land to landlords and started using slaves.

In the 19th century the circumstances for spreading the Gospel in Zimbabwe were much more favourable than before. Sundkler says that 'there was a preparedness on the part of marginal people or leading men and women to break with the guardians of the ancient cult'. He refers to different kinds of 'territorial cults' in Central Africa that were relating 'to what is seen as a High God' or to 'divinised human beings'. These cults, like the Mwari cult and the Mhondoro cult in Zimbabwe and the Mbona cult in Malawi and Zimbabwe, underwent important changes that made them seem parallel to Christianity or a stepping stone to it. The central figure in the Mbona cult, a martyred prophet, was even said to be the 'Son of God' or the 'Black Jesus'.

Part of the Ruins of Great Zimbabwe, built by Bantu people from 11th to 14th century. See: chapter 42.c.

---

[1] For the History of the Church in Zimbabwe, also: W.J Van der Merwe, *From Mission field to Autonomous Church in Zimbabwe* (A Publication of the Institute for Missiological Research of the University of Pretoria, NG Kerkboekhandel, 1981); cf. Sundkler, and Steed, *A History of the Church in Africa*, pp.68-69,93-94,398,402,408, 445-449,800-816,981-983; Baur, *2000 Years*, pp.417-428.

59.2. Mission before 1890

In the 19th century Zimbabwe was opened up for mission through various routes from the south to the north. Even in the pre-colonial period before 1890, there was much missionary activity in the country. The main route ran from Kuruman to Bulawayo. Through it hunters and explorers approached the north. It was called 'the missionary road' because it was originally used by missionaries like Moffat, Livingstone and MacKenzie. Mzilikazi and Lobengula, the Ndebele kings, only allowed those strangers who had travelled through 'the missionary road', to enter their kingdoms. There were also other routes. The eastern route was especially used by African Evangelists. The Dutch, Paris and Swiss missions organised many expeditions to Zimbabwe using almost exclusively African personnel. Some expeditions started in Lesotho.

King Lobengula of the Matabele, who was misinformed about the meaning of the Tati Concession, by which he was disowned.

A permanent mission station was started in 1859 when Robert Moffat from Kuruman led a group of missionaries into the region.[2] Missionary expeditions from North Transvaal are also connected with the name Stephanus Hofmeyr, a Dutch Reformed missionary. Hofmeyr had successfully worked among the Buys people, a group of coloured people of mixed race at Goedgedacht in North Transvaal, and was ready to extend his work beyond the Limpopo River. In the period 1872-1887 he trained no fewer than seven groups of Africans, especially from the Buys clan, to enter the land that now is known as Zimbabwe, effectively carrying and spreading the Gospel. After Hofmeyr's death, his work was continued by J.W. Daneel, his son-in-law. Likewise, hundreds of Zimbabweans who had become Christians while working in the mines at the Rand, returned home as missionaries of various denominations.

Among those who crossed the Limpopo were Wesleyan Methodist preachers at the Rand, including David M. Ramushu. On their way they established new Methodist centres in Zimbabwe.

From their centre Tshakoma in Vendaland the Lutheran *Berlin Mission* organised mission to Zimbabwe. Missionaries Johannes Schwellnus and C.P.G. Knothe had trained Africans, among whom Johannes Madima, who himself together with other Africans made several expeditions to Zimbabwe.

Not all missionaries were welcomed. François Coillard of the *Paris Mission*, who had planned to work among the Shona, was refused and sent back by Lobengula because he had not travelled by 'the missionaries' road' and because the king considered the Sotho people who accompanied Coillard as his enemies. Later Coillard returned to the north, but then to Zambia.

---

[2] Cf.: Hildebrandt, *History of the Church in Africa*, pp.176f.

59.3. The Era of Colonialism

In 1889 King Lobengula had to submit to Cecil Rhodes' *Chartered Company*. In 1890 this was followed by Rhodes' military invasion of Mashonaland and the hoisting of the British flag at Fort Salisbury (now Harare). In the wake of this invasion many settlers and also missionaries entered the country. Two risings against the British, the Matabele war in 1893 and wars by the Shona and the Ndebele in 1896-1897, sometimes called the *First Chimurenga* (First Liberation War), could not change the situation of complete British military supremacy.[3] Baur explains the violent character of the beginnings of colonialism in Rhodesia. 'Everywhere else in tropical Africa European powers entered into some contracts with chiefs before they occupied a country, but Mashonaland was invaded by settlers abruptly without any previous notice.'[4] The integrity of the missionaries, especially of the British among them, was put to the test. On which side was their loyalty? In 1923 Southern Rhodesia became a colony. The relationship between colonialism and mission would continue to be a problem. Although the first years of colonialism saw many new missionary groups, who were offered large plots of land, the number of conversions slowed down, especially among the Ndebele.

Cecil Rhodes (1853-1902), an Architect of British Colonialism.

However, the above mentioned Dutch Reformed and Lutheran missions successfully continued their evangelisation among the Southern Shona. Methodism also continued its progress after 1890. Beside the British Wesleyans with centres in e.g. Harare, in 1898 the American United Methodists entered and started work mainly in the east of the country. The United Methodist missionaries were blacks. Both branches started early to Africanise the leadership of the church. The Methodists produced important figures in the movement for independence, like Abel Muzorewa, Canaan Banana, Joshua Nkomo, and Ndabaningi Sithole.

The Anglican Church in Zimbabwe was established after the beginning of the Protectorate. Its first bishop was George Knight-Bruce. It progressed considerably in the period when Edward Paget was bishop in Salisbury (1926-1957). After independence, Africans were nominated (1981) as archbishop and as bishops in the dioceses of Gweru and Mutare.

After earlier attempts in the 16th and 17th centuries, the Roman Catholic Church entered Zimbabwe again in 1890 together with Cecil Rhodes' expedition. The first mission workers were German Dominican Sisters from South Africa. Soon the Jesuits followed. After 1927, English Jesuits were responsible for Roman Catholic Mission in the whole of Southern Rhodesia (Zimbabwe). Their method of Christian villages seemed to fit to the situation. They were active in agriculture and education.

---

[3] Cf.: D.N. Beach, *War and Politics in Zimbabwe 1840-1900*, Gweru: Mambo Press, 1994².
[4] Baur, *2000 Years*, p.417.

59.4. The Reformed Church of Zimbabwe

The origin of the Reformed Church of Zimbabwe is in the mission of the *Dutch Reformed Church* of South Africa which had reached Zimbabwe (Mashonaland) in 1891.[5] Its first establishment was at Morgenster near the Great Zimbabwe court building of Mwene Mutapa, the King, where in 1894 for the first time a minister was ordained.[6] The founder was Andrew Louw. Right from the beginning he cooperated with African evangelists.[7] Jozua Masoha, Lukas Mokoele, Jeremia and Petrus Morudu, David Molea and Izak Kumalo who were trained by Stephanus Hofmeyr. They contributed much to the missionary work of the DRC in Zimbabwe. Louw and his wife Cinie Malan translated the Bible into Karanga and they started theological courses for evangelists. This work was later developed into a full training of ministers at Murray Theological College in Morgenster. New centres were opened in Dete in 1995 and in Binga among the Tonga people in 1996. At present there are plans for evangelising the Shonga and Venda peoples near the southern border of Zimbabwe. Today the *Reformed Church of Zimbabwe* has about 85,000 members, and 50 ministers. It has 47 congregations subdivided into smaller units to suit pastoral work.[8]

59.5. The CCAP in Zimbabwe

Although the *Church of Central Africa* (CCAP) is mainly a Malawian church, offshoots of it took root in Zimbabwe. The imposition of hut tax in Malawi forced many to go abroad and seek work. Soon groups of Malawians were found as far away as Harare[9] and Johannesburg. Regular labour migration from Malawi to Zimbabwe dates from 1903. In the same year the Mission Council consisting of various Protestant missions in Malawi emphasised the urgent necessity to begin work in Harare in conjunction with the work in Malawi. They saw the need of providing for the spiritual welfare of the large number of Malawians who had gone to Harare. In 1905 a delegation of these migrants walked from Zimbabwe to Mvera mission in central Malawi to ask for a missionary who would minister to their spiritual needs in Zimbabwe. The delegation comprised Joseph Mandovi from Livingstonia, Yonamu from Nkhoma, Yeremiya Mwalo from *Zambezi Industrial Mission*, and a person from Blantyre whose name has remained unknown.

Five years later a general Missionary Conference at Mvera decided to send a European missionary to Zimbabwe[10] for the purpose of looking after and ministering to Malawian migrants. Because none of the missions indicated a person, finally Teunis Vlok of the Dutch Reformed Mission, by then a veteran of 23 years' experience in Malawi, offered to go, and he started this work in November 1912. The following year Vlok began to employ African evangelists to enlarge the scope of the activities. This marked the beginning of the CCAP in Zimbabwe. Actually, Vlok was sent by the Synod of the Western Cape of the DRC through the Nkhoma Synod of Nyasaland. Vlok, also

---

[5] Van der Merwe, *From Mission Field*, 47-57; cf. C.M. Pauw *Mission and Church in Malawi* p.48.
[6] Adrian Hastings. *Church in Africa*. p.455; Jonathan Hildebrandt, *History of the Church in Africa* p.177.
[7] Cf.: Louw's biography: A.A. Louw, *Andrew Louw van Morgenster*, 1965.
[8] Enos Chomutiri during a workshop in Liwonde, Malawi in June 2004.
[9] At that time named: Salisbury.
[10] At that time named: Southern Rhodesia.

called Foloko or Voloko by the migrant population, travelled all over Zimbabwe meeting zealous Nyasas who agreed to establish a separate Reformed Church branch in Zimbabwe.

The first Nyasa affiliated church was established in 1935 operating under the Nkhoma Synod and after the number of congregations had grown, they were divided into several Presbyteries. The Synod of Rhodesia gained autonomy in 1965. After the Civil war, the name of the capital city changed from Salisbury to Harare. The Rhodesia Synod also changed to be called the Harare Synod.

In 1965 the Harare Synod became a fourth constituent synod of the *Church of Central Africa Presbyterian* (CCAP).[11]

59.6. Independence

Right from the beginning white settlers in Southern Rhodesia (Zimbabwe), Northern Rhodesia (Zambia) and Nyasaland (Malawi) expected economic advantages from a federation of these regions. In general, the Africans, however, resisted the idea, because a federation would strengthen white domination, and would consequently lead to more discrimination. Despite the opposition by emerging African nationalism, and resistance by Garfield Todd, ex-missionary and Rhodesian prime-minister, the federation was forced through in 1953.

Abel Tendekayi Muzorewa (born 1925), a Methodist Bishop who was prime minister of a coalition government of Zimbabwe in 1979 for a few

In Rhodesia this event led to a sharp division between the blacks in the *African National Congress* and the whites in the *Rhodesian Front*. In 1964 the white minority, led by prime minister Ian Smith, challenged Britain and the West and the African majority by announcing a *Unilateral Declaration of Independence*. The Roman Catholic Church and the Ecumenical Protestant bodies clashed with the white minority regime. The ensuing civil war was called the *Second Chimurenga* (Second War of Liberation). It was aimed at majority rule for the Africans, and it ended in 1978 by a provisional agreement, which made the Methodist bishop Abel Muzorewa president. However, this *Internal Settlement* did not work. In 1980 the *Lancaster House Agreement* gave Rhodesia complete independence under majority rule. Robert Mugabe was elected prime minister. The division of land is one of the difficult problems that the new government has never adequately solved. The invasion of white farms by 'war veterans' by the end of the millennium, dubbed by the government the *Third Chimurenga*, was universally criticised, and has damaged Zimbabwe's economic and social stability.

Although Mugabe moderated his Marxist-Leninist stance, he and President Canaan Banana tried to introduce a kind of socialist Christianity with a church for and of the proletariat. Generally, the new government had a policy of 'forgive and forget'. However, this reconciliatory attitude did not apply to the relationship between the Shona and their pre-colonial overlords, the Ndebele. Mugabe's Shona security forces caused tremendous bloodshed and suffering among the Ndebele. Despite this

---

[11] Cf.: Isabel Apawo Phiri, *Women, Presbyterianism and Patriarch*, Zomba: Kachere, 2000, p.50.

Zimbabweans have been voting him into power for many years. Reconciliation between the Shona and the Ndebele was achieved in 1987 when the parties of Mugabe (largely Shona) and Joshua M.N. Nkomo (largely Ndebele) joined to form one party. However, with the death of Nkomo in 1999 the relationship became uneasy again.

Map of Zimbabwe.

60. Pentecostals and Charismatics

60.1. Five Streams

In African Protestant Christianity there are (a) *Classical* mainline churches, (b) *Post-Classical* churches, (c) *Pentecostal* churches, and (d) the groups and churches of the *Charismatic Movement*. Besides, there are (e) the *Independent* churches who directly or indirectly derive from the above mentioned types.

The *Classical* churches originated in the missionary movement, which was a product of the 18th and 19th-centuries evangelical revival or awakening in the mainline churches in Europe and America bringing them in line again with the 16th-century Reformation. In Malawi there are the *Presbyterian, Lutheran,* and the *Anglican* churches.

The *Post-Classical* churches have their roots in the evangelical awakening of the mid 19th-century holiness revival that led to the formation of interdenominational faith missions and denominational evangelical missions. Examples in Malawi are the *Zambezi Evangelical Church*, the *Nyasa Industrial Mission*, the *Africa Evangelical Church*, the *Providence Evangelical Church*, the *Seventh' Day Adventists, Free Methodists,* and the *Baptists*.

In this chapter, we will deal with the Pentecostal Movement, and with the Charismatic Movement.[1]

60.2. Beginnings of Pentecostalism

Pentecostalism is a distinct variant of Protestantism, born out of the 16th-century Reformation. As such, it is a relatively young phenomenon. It started in America and soon touched Africa. In some cases there was an interaction between Pentecostalism and Independency, but the two movements remained distinct. After its American beginnings, Pentecostalism spread to Africa. There were various ways.

First there were the 'solo entrepreneurs', such as Clyde Miller, who founded the Nyang'ori Mission in Western Kenya.

Secondly there were the sponsored missionaries from Pentecostal groups, such as the Azusa Street ministry, who sent Lucy Farrow and Henry M. Turner to South Africa in 1908. Generally, Pentecostal Churches are rooted in the Pentecostal revival that began in Azusa Street in the Californian city of Los Angeles in 1906. Soon the movement spread to other parts of the world. The missionaries that arrived in 1908 founded the *Apostolic Faith Mission*, at first mainly among the whites. Instrumental in this cross-ocean movement were the South Africans David du Plessis, called 'Mr. Pentecost', and P.L. le Roux.

Thirdly, there is the influence of the radical American-Scottish/Australian Pentecostal preacher J.A. Dowie (†1907) of the *Christian Catholic Apostolic Church*. He was at the cradle of many Pentecostal Churches in Africa, especially in South

---

[1] Apart from this chapter, also: A. B. Anderson, *African Pentecostals in South Africa*, Pretoria, 1991; A. Anderson, *Zion and Pentecost: The Spirituality and Experience of Pentecostal and Zionist/ Apostolic Churches in South Africa*, Pretoria, 2000; K. Fiedler, 'The Charismatic and Pentecostal Movements in Malawi in Cultural Perspective', in: *Religion in Malawi*. 9, (1999). Fiedler, *The Story of Faith Missions*, 116-121; K.Ward, 'Africa', in: Hastings, *World History*, pp.234, 235.

Africa. Near Chicago he founded a *New Jerusalem* which he called *Zion City* and a *Zion Tabernacle* where healings and miracles took place. Dowie considered himself 'Elijah the Redeemer', the last prophet before the coming of the Messiah. At the time of his death his church had spread to South Africa. Dowie's message was taken over by P.L. le Roux, who was a missionary to the Zulus and had left the DRC. Le Roux re-established the *New Jerusalem* among the Zulus. Soon the *Zion Apostolic Faith Mission* was formed, consisting of blacks.[2] One of the original leaders was Edward Lion from Lesotho. By 1990 the Zion movement claimed to have more than 2000 black churches with about 4 million members in South Africa alone. A distinctive variant of the Zionists is the *amaNazaretha Church* of Isaiah Shembe (†1935), who unlike other Zionist leaders developed a personality cult by calling himself the new David and a black messiah, even the 'Promised One' himself. The Zionists featured healing, speaking in tongues, purification rites and the handling of various fetishes. Like the contemporary Ethiopianist movement, the Zionists operated an 'Abyssinia-theology', which was a mythical conception of Biblical Zion (*Hebrews* 12:22) drawn near into African reality. At the same time, the Zionists differed from the Ethiopians because they did not exclude non-Africans from leadership.[3] There was also a Pentecostal breakthrough among the Indian community in Natal, mainly through the work of J.F. Rowland. In 1931 in Durban a centre was founded, called 'Bethesda'.

David du Plessis, an Afrikaner of South Africa who was a traveller for the Pentecostal Movement.

In Southern Africa there was a flowering of Zion churches. Only a few can be mentioned. A Malawian migrant worker from Likoma Island, John Philips, settled at the Rand, where he founded the *Christian Catholic Apostolic Church in Zion*. In 1925 the Zion movement split because Ignatius Engenas Lekganyane formed his own Zion Christian Church. His follower Samuel Mutendi, a Shona from Zimbabwe, founded the church in his home country. Mutendi's Zion Church experienced many schisms. Other famous Zimbabwean Zion leaders were Yohane Masowe and Yohane Maranke. They travelled extensively. That is why their influence was not limited to Zimbabwe. In the 1920s the *South African General Mission* at Rusitu in Zimbabwe witnessed Pentecostal enthusiasm, often induced by Western preachers like Rees Howells. There was also a Pentecostal awakening in the Methodist Episcopal Church at Mutare.[4]

Fourthly, Africa was also reached by a Pentecostal wave from the Swiss Herisau community led by Johannes Büchler, who founded his own Zion church in Johannesburg. One of his disciples was Edgar Mahon, an ex-Salvation Army officer.

Let us look at important events in the history of Pentecostalism some parts of Africa. In 1914 the majority of American Pentecostals joined together in the denomination of

---

[2] Gregory Chawanangwa Mvula and Enson Mbilikile Lwesya, *Flames of Fire: A History of the Assemblies of God in Malawi*, Limbe: Assemblies of God in Malawi, 2005, pp.360,361.

[3] Sundkler and Steed, *A History of the Church in Africa*, pp.426,427.

[4] Sundkler and Steed, *A History of the Church in Africa*, pp.809,813.

the *Assemblies of God* (AOG) under leaders like James Mullan Africa, and Nicolas Bhengu (†1985) with his influential *Back-to-God Crusade*. The AOG started its ministry in Sierra Leone in 1914, Burkina Faso in 1920 and Dahomey in 1947. In the meantime, in 1939, missionary W.L. Shirer and his wife had started work in Eastern Nigeria. The road for Pentecostalism was paved by Apostolic preachers, first whites from the *Bradford Apostolic Church*, like the brothers Daniel P. and William J. Williams, and George Perfect, and then by African preachers like Joseph Babalola, whose work extended the *Christ Apostolic Church*.[5] Since 1964 the American *Assemblies* have formed a separate organisation with branches in Africa as well. Other denominational brands of Pentecostalism were established in various parts of Africa, beside South Africa, especially in Western Kenya, Burkina Faso, and Benin. They include the *Church of God in Christ*, the *Pentecostal Holiness Church*, and later the *Foursquare Gospel Church*.[6]

Sundkler refers to the Swedish Pentecostal influence in Burundi, which coloured Burundi Protestantism. When ethnic clashes forced Hutu refugees to 'settle in their hundreds of thousands in South-Central Tanzania', they brought with them their Pentecostal enthusiasm, and established 'an intense Pentecostal community'. Earlier the Swedish Pentecostals had already started work in Tanzania among the Sukuma, and about 1960, they were represented all over the country.[7] At an early stage the Swedish Pentecostals also sent missionaries to South Africa, e.g. Mary Johnson and Ida Andersson to Durban in 1904, and in 1915 they opened stations in the Congo and Egypt.

Interacting with the historical *Pentecostal Movement* were some ecstatic or charismatic movements most of whom we discussed before. They were revivals within or outside existing churches, like the *Aladura Movement* in West Africa, the revival in the *Qua Iboe Mission* among the Ibibio people in Southern Nigeria (1925-1947), the one among the *Quakers* in Kaimosi in Western Kenya in 1927 and 1928, referred to as *Abarohi* (= people of the Spirit), and the one that started at Swedish mission centres in Kimpese in the Belgian Congo and Ngouedi, near Brazzaville in 1946, the *Jamaa Movement* among the Roman Catholics in the Congo, the *Balokole Movement* in Eastern Africa, the *Ngunza* (= prophetic) movements of Kibongi, Kimbangu and Matswa in the Congo region. These groups are sometimes very different from one another. In them there was some indirect influence by Pentecostalism, but even more they are expressions of the movements of *African Instituted Churches*, or of *Evangelical Revival* in Classical churches, while others signal the advent of the modern expressions of the *Charismatic Movement*.[8]

60.3. Pentecostal Churches in Malawi

In 1923 the *Zionist Churches* reached Malawi via South Africa. They were not conscious of their affinity to the Pentecostal Churches which would reach Malawi by the same route. In other words the Zionists behaved as independent or African Instituted

---

[5] Duncan and Kalu, 'Bakuzufu: Revival Movements', in: Kalu et al. (eds), *African Christianity*, pp.295,296.
[6] Kalu, 'African Christianity', in: Kalu et al. (eds), *African Christianity*, pp.346,347.
[7] Sundkler and Steed, *A History of the Church in Africa*, pp.878,911,1015.
[8] Duncan and Kalu, 'Bakuzufu: Revival Movements', in: Kalu et al. (eds), *African Christianity*, pp.296-300.

Churches.[9] Malawian workers in South Africa brought the two oldest Pentecostal Churches to Malawi. After having founded their 'native controlled missions', foreign missionaries followed.

First there was the *Apostolic Faith Mission,* originating in the Azusa Street revival, founded in Zomba near Jali by Robert Chinguwo in 1933.[10] Later it spread considerably in the Lower Shire area, where the work was begun by Jim Phiri. Early missionaries were Erasmus, Cooksey and Wendland. Foreign missionaries played a role, the AFM in Malawi, with its African style of worship and emphasis on healing. That is why – according to Fiedler – it qualifies as an African Church, but not as an AIC.[11]

The *second* Pentecostal Church to reach Malawi, also through returning migrants, was the *Assemblies of God*. It started in Igali in Tanganyika where Paul Derr, a missionary of the Assemblies of God, had worked since 1928. Derr 'influenced Noah Siwale, an itinerant evangelist who went back to his home, Kameme, Nyasaland and influenced a group of people who relocated and followed him'.[12] In 1934 Lyton Kalambule started in the Misuku Hills (Mubulu) and Elliot Nkunika in Dedza (Gilbert Village). Later they moved to Lilongwe, where there is now also a Seminary. Foreign missionaries from Tanzania and South Africa followed. In the following decades several other Pentecostal Churches settled in Malawi.

Generally, the new Pentecostal Churches are more thriving than the older ones, a phenomenon that is also apparent in the faith mission Evangelical churches. Their comparative growth might be explained by their ability to answer certain African needs. According to Ward:

> 'The *Pentecostal Movement* tends to be even more condemnatory of compromise with paganism than the old established Churches, and consequently more hostile to those *African Instituted Churches* which are arrogantly dismissed as pagan. On the other hand, the Pentecostal Movement does focus on, rather than shy away from, the realm of spiritual powers, and so (like the older Independent Churches) can be seen as dealing with this important area of life in more honest and direct ways, helping people to cope with the struggle which defines and circumscribes day-to-day life for so many'.[13]

In comparison to Pentecostals and Evangelicals, the Classical (mainline) churches are declining worldwide. Fiedler might be mistaken in his opinion that this process 'does not show clearly in Malawi yet'. There is hope, though, that new revivals including rediscovery of the spiritual riches of the *Reformation* will reverse their decline, at the same time strengthening the orientation on the Word and the Spirit in Pentecostalism and Evangelicalism.

---

[9] Ulf Strohbehn, in his PhD dissertation, University of Malawi, found that there are now 33 different Zionist denominations in Malawi.
[10] Mvula and Lwesya, *Flames of Fire*, pp.362-365.
[11] Cf.: Chapter 57.4.b; Ulf Strobehn, *Pentecostalism in Malawi*, op. cit.
[12] Mvula and Lwesya, *Flames of Fire*, pp.72-76.
[13] Ward, 'Africa', in: Hastings, *World History*, p.234.

60.4. Features of the Charismatic Movement

The *Charismatic Movement* as such is much less a variant of the churches that go back on the Protestant *Reformation* of the 16th century, although like the Pentecostals it is related to some characteristics of the Radical or the Left Wing of the Reformation.[14]

In African Christianity there are early examples of charismatic expression. Enthusiast expectations of the speedy outpouring and miraculous working of the Holy Spirit can be noticed in the 2nd-century movement of *Montanism* of which North African Church Father Tertullian was a follower later in his life. Early Christianity in sub-Saharan Congo witnessed the enthusiastic utterances of prophetesses like Maffuta and Kimpa Vita (Donna Beatrice, †1706).[15] Some African Charismatics in the first half of the 20th century are Simon Kimbangu in the Congo, Isaiah Shembe in Natal (South Africa), William Wadé Harris in Liberia and the Ivory Coast, George Khambuli in Johannesburg (South Africa), and Ma Nku in Evaton (South Africa). In chapter 41.6.c we dealt with the birth of the *Charismatic Movement* and at the end of section 2 of the present chapter we referred to its modern expressions in ecstatic and charismatic phenomena in Africa.

Isaiah Shembe (1867-1935), founder of the amaNazaretha Church; he combined Traditional African Religion with Christianity.

The modern *Charismatic Movement* is a loose worldwide 'network' that began in California in 1960, started by Dennis J. Bennett, an Episcopalian priest. The movement was not affected by missionaries or by a worldwide organisation. Charismatic groups began to emerge in the 1960s as a reaction against secularisation in the Western countries. The Charismatic Movement started in the Protestant, Roman Catholic and Eastern Orthodox mainline churches in America, and then it spread to Europe and the other continents. Initially it remained a movement inside existing churches, but after a time 'independent' charismatic churches came into being.

Although the modern *Charismatic Movement* in Africa was connected to previous ecstatic stirrings and movements, it entered Africa from abroad, by external spiritual forces in the white western Christian community. This external origin is one of the reasons why the movement is different from the movements for African Independent Churches or African Instituted Churches. Modern Charismatic churches are not just 'New African Independent Churches'.[16] Duncan and Kalu point to the *Scripture Union* (SU) as a 'signifier' demonstrating the start and the early history of the *Charismatic Movement* in Africa.

---

[14] Cf.: chapter 27.

[15] Sundkler and Steed, *A History of the Church in Africa*, pp.59,60.

[16] The term 'New African Independent Churches' is used by: Kibutu Ngimbi, *Les Nouvelles Églises Indépendantes Africaines (NAIC): Un phénomène ecclesial observé au Congo/ Kinshasa et auprès de ses extensions en Europe occidentale: Approche historico-missiologique*, Heverlee (Louvain/ Leuven): Faculté de Théologie Evangélique (Evangelical Theological Faculty), 2000, although he admits that 'all those New Churches came from the Charismatic Movement and could all be dated from 1980 and not earlier' (English Summary, p.2).

Benson Idahosa (1938-1998), founder of Church of God Mission International, based in Benin City, Nigeria.

The SU began as an interdenominational agency for Bible study and prayer in British Protestant Schools in the 1950s. It spread to Africa, first to the West, and became radicalised under the influence of social, political and economic challenges. In this process it influenced existing organisations and churches. Other igniting agencies were the *Hour of Freedom* ministry, the work of Benson Idahosa, founder of *Church of God Mission International*, and Welsh missionary Pa G. Elton of the *Apostolic Church*, and movements within the *Student Christian Movement*, especially a break-away group, the *Christian Union*. More recent groups such as the *Rhema Bible Church* of South Africa like to use foreign preachers and televangelists, e.g. Kenneth Hagin, Oral Roberts, Morris Cerullo, and Rheinhard Bonnke. The foreign white origin of these groups and churches is apparent, which makes them different from the older movements for *African Instituted Churches*. Asamoah-Gyadu points out other differences between these charismatic movements and the *African Instituted Churches*. In comparison to the AICs, charismatic groups are said to be more Spirit-centred, less hierarchical, more 'Afro-optimistic', more involved at all levels of society including education, more friendly to ruling politicians, and more open to supernatural possibilities. Charismatics stress the possibilities for empowerment against evil powers, leading to transformation and freedom, including health and prosperity.[17]

Re-evangelising the mainline churches and winning new souls is the charismatic goal. The charismatic objectives were adopted by representatives of the youth and of the leadership of some mission churches.

The *Charismatic Movement* has undoubtedly become part of African Christianity. Whether it has really changed the character of African Christianity – as Duncan and Kalu claim – remains to be seen. According to them, the *Charismatic Movement* has been so much Africanised that it shows 'continuity with the traditional past, embedding African Christianity into the deep structures of all *African Traditional Religions*'.[18] If it is true that in a way the *Charismatic Movement* is a continuation of African traditional religions, then critical questions on its Biblical orthodoxy could be rightly asked. The features of the *Charismatic Movement* can be defined in comparison to those of the *Pentecostal Movement*.

The *Charismatic Movemnent* is related to *Pentecostalism*, but at the same time it strongly differs from it 'in terms of origin, social context, and spiritual appeal':

(a) The Charismatic Movement started within mainline churches. Pentecostalism started at the fringes of historical Protestant Christianity.

---

[17] J. Kwabena Asamoah-Gyadu, 'Born of Water and the Spirit: Pentecostal/ Charismatic Christianity in Africa', in: Kalu et al. (eds), *African Christianity*, pp.403-406.
[18] Duncan and Kalu, 'Revival Movements', in: Kalu et al. (eds), *African Christianity*, p.306.

(b) The Charismatic Movement started in middle and upper classes. Pentecostalism started in poor and lower classes.
(c) The Charismatic Movement was started by whites. Pentecostalism was started mainly by blacks.
(d) The Charismatic Movement generally did not start its own churches. Pentecostalism soon separated from mainline churches and established its own churches.
(e) The Charismatic Movement was to a degree accepted by Evangelical interdenominational agencies. Pentecostalism was rejected early by Evangelical churches and missions.
(f) The Charismatic Movement mixes Protestants and Roman Catholics. Pentecostalism is conscious of differences from Roman Catholicism.
(g) The Charismatic Movement is open to Theological Modernity. Pentecostalism is historically connected to Protestant Orthodoxy.

Apparently, the historical, social, and ecclesiastical and theological features of the *Charismatic Movement* and the *Pentecostal Movement* differ considerably, although at the same time they interact and run parallel in aspects of Pneumatology.[19] Charismatics are not just *New Pentecostals*.[20]

60.5. The Charismatic Movement in Malawi

The *Charismatic Movement* in Malawi started in the 1970s. Some interdenominational para-church organisations, such as the *Scripture Union*, the *Students' Christian Organisation of Malawi* (SCOM), and the *New Life for All*, provided a breeding and teaching ground. Further developments have left SU and SCOM with an internal struggle between Charismatics and Evangelicals. From abroad Malawian charismatic expressions were stimulated by people like Barbara Tippet, who in 1980 founded the *Blantyre Christian Centre* in Blantyre. Although the Charismatic Movement has 'no inbuilt intention to start new denominations', and many groups remained in the existing churches, these beginnings also led to the formation of charismatic churches, like *Agape* (1982, Mgala), *Faith of God* (1984, Matoga), *Living Waters* (1985, Ndovi),[21] *Glad Tidings* (1986), *All for Jesus* (1993, Zalimba), *Flames of Victory* (1993, Katchire), *Calvary Family Church* (1994, Mbewe),[22] *Vineyard* (1994, Gama), and the *Charismatic Renewal Ministry* (1997, Kambalazaza). Their membership comprises about 250,000, according to Fiedler, which would indicate that the Charismatic Movement is stronger on that side than in the established churches.

Mark Kambalazaza, founder of the Charismatic Renewal Ministry, who broke away from the Roman Catholic Church in Malawi.

---

[19] *Pneumatology* is derived from the Greek word *pneuma*, which means: breath, soul, spirit. In theology it is the study of the Holy Spirit, the third Person of the Trinity.
[20] Asamoah-Gyadu, 'Born of Water and the Spirit', in: Kalu et al.(eds), *African Christianity*, pp.389-409, in general classifies both movements together as 'Pentecostal/ Charismatic Christianity', and uses the term 'New Pentecostal' for newer phenomena of Charismatic expression.
[21] Cf.: Mvula and Mbilikile, *Flames of Fire*, pp.373,374.
[22] Cf.: Mvula and Mbilikile, *Flames of Fire*, pp.375-378.

Originally, these groups were *fellowships* of active members of existing churches, but they consolidated themselves into denominations over the years. The fellowships organised themselves around a *'ministry'* group consisting of a leader and helpers. Members are recruited on an interdenominational or even nondenominational basis. Gradually the fellowship is meeting at the times of worship of existing churches, members calling themselves 'born agains'. Formalisation of this new status takes place as the sacraments are being administered, to which is added the baptism with the Holy Spirit and the sacramentalisation of weddings.[23] Fellowships started *outside* existing churches, and later they developed into separate denominations. Generally, the fellowships that started *inside* the structures of the existing churches remain there, but in some cases, like that of the *Presbyterian Church of Malawi* (PCM), and the *Charismatic Renewal Ministries*, there have been secessions.

Stanley Ndovi, founder of the Living Waters Church, in Malawi.

The *Charismatic Movement* has been interpreted in sociological, economic, and political terms. However, Fiedler sees the *Charismatic Movement* as a 'quest for a deeper Christian life' going beyond attending catechism classes, church services, and behaving properly. As such, the Charismatic fellowships and churches are a necessary challenge for the older churches, although he does not expect them to replace the mainline, evangelical and independent churches.[24]

The Charismatic Movement generally does not thrive in rural areas, but mainly reaches the urban and middle class. How far it still is a Western phenomenon remains to be seen.[25] Charismatic Churches are less African than the Pentecostal churches, although their African leaders might develop them in the direction of more 'Africanness'.

60.6. Politics

Originally, *Pentecostals* and *Charismatics*, just like many *Evangelicals*, have not mixed in politics. They define their vision of the Kingdom in eschatological terms as a future hope. This can lead to condoning oppression and social injustice. Shaw mentions the example of Liberia in 1980 where 'charismatic preachers and evangelists avoided any confrontation with the oppressive regime of S.K. Doe, by blaming poverty and injustice on territorial demons that hovered above Liberia'.[26] He says that sometimes Charismatics restrict themselves to casting out demons, 'while their nation goes to the

---

[23] Cf.: R.A. van Dijk, *Young Malawian Puritan Preachers in a Present-Day African Urban Environment*, University of Utrecht, 1992, who gives a sociological interpretation of the emergence of the 'born again' movement.

[24] K.Fiedler, 'The Charismatic and Pentecostal Movements in Malawi in Cultural Perspective', in: *Religion in Malawi*, 9, (1999); See also: Rhodian G. Munyenyembe, 'The Church and Socio-cultural Issues: An Evaluation of the Charismatic Movement's Contribution towards the Centralisation of the Gospel in Malawi', 2006 [unpublished MA dissertation of the University of Malawi].

[25] Munyenyembe, 'The Church and Social Structures, op. cit., stresses the Africanness of the movement.

[26] Shaw, *The Kingdom of God*, p.265.

devil'.[27] However, Pentecostals in South Africa took their stance against 'apartheid'. Parallel to the *Kairos Document* (1985), produced by the South African Council of Churches, and the *Evangelical Witness* by 'concerned Evangelicals', the Pentecostals issued their *Pentecostal Witness* (1986).

Charismatics in Malawi seem to be 'invariably apolitical', tending to support the ruling powers of the country. Pentecostals, however, have started to realise that political justice and the struggle against corruption and poverty belong to the message of the Kingdom of God and the responsibility of Christians.[28]

---

[27] Shaw, *The Kingdom of God*, p.292.
[28] Lazarus McCarthy Chakwera (b.1955): from 1989 to 2013 President of the largest Pentecostal denomination in Malawi, the Assemblies of God. In 2013 he was elected President of the Malawi Congress Party (MCP) and for that party he became the presidential candidate in the general elections for the Presidency of 2014.

61. The Position of Africa's Women

61.1. Biblical Pattern

a. Together with Man

A description of the position of Christian women in Africa[1] needs a wider perspective than Africa alone. Christians believe that the Word of God has the final say in teaching and life. That is why the norm for the position of women in Africa and anywhere is to be found in the Bible.[2] Scripture pictures the position of the woman within the relationship between man and woman. Men and women are one another's counterparts. They are partners. In a very special way this is true in marriage and in family life. In a more general way it is also true in the Church and in society as a whole. One cannot get a balanced and truthful vision of the position of women without realising how they relate to men. In the same way the position of men becomes clear when we see how it is situated within the framework of men's interaction in partnership with women. In some philosophies or theologies either women or men are looked on as independent entities, disconnected from this partnership. They are doomed to distort the positions of either women or men in married life, in the Church and in society.

One of the many ways the African woman tries to sustain herself and others.

---

[1] Here is a selection of recent titles that can be helpful in studying the subject in a Central African setting: Isabel Apawo Phiri, *Women, Presbyterianism and Patriarchy: Religious Experience of Chewa Women in Central Malawi*, Blantyre: Kachere/ CLAIM, 1997; Isabel Apawo Phiri, Devarakshanam Betty Govinden, Sarojini Nadar, *Her-Stories: Hidden Histories of Women of Faith in Africa*, Pietermaritzburg: Cluster, 2002; Janet Y Kholowa, and Klaus Fiedler, *In the Beginning God Created them Equal*, Zomba: Kachere 2003; Helen E.P. van Koevering, *The Lakeshore Nyanja Women of the Anglican Diocese of Niasa*, Zomba: Kachere, 2005; Rachel Nyagondwe Banda, *Women of the Bible and Culture: Baptist Convention Women in Southern Malawi*, Zomba: Kachere, 2005; Rachel Nyagondwe Fiedler, *Coming of Age: A Christianized Initiation among Women in Southern Malawi*, Zomba: Kachere, 2005; Clara Henderson, *Rolling Away the Stone: The Africanisation of Christian Music by Presbyterian Mvano Women in Southern Malawi*, Zomba: Kachere, 2008. See also: Seodi Venekai-Rodo White et al., *Dispossessing the Widow: Gender Based Violence in Malawi*, Blantyre: Kachere/ CLAIM, 2002; Klaus Fiedler, *The Story of Faith Missions*, pp.292-309; C.M.Pauw, *Mission and Church in Malawi: The History of the Nkhoma Synod of the Church of Central Africa Presbyterian, 1889-1962*, 1980, pp.199-204; T.O. Ranger & J.Weller (eds), *Themes in the History of Central Africa*, London: Heineman, 1974, pp.256-268.

[2] Among the many Bible studies on this issue I recommend here: George and Dora Winston, *Recovering Biblical Ministry by Women: An Exegetical Response to Traditionalism and Feminism*, Xulon Press, 2003; Alexander Rattray Hay, *The Woman's Ministry in Church and at Home*, Audubon: New Testament Missionary Union, 1962; Cf.: C. den Boer, *Man en Vrouw in Bijbels Perspectief: Een Bijbels-Theologische Verkenning van de Man-Vrouw Verhouding met het oog op de Gemeente*, Kampen: Kok, 1987².

b. Equal to Man

In Biblical thought, God created man and woman in close relationship to one another and to Himself. He created them in His own image. That is why they are equal[3] and to a great extent similar. In their equality and relative similarity they reflect their Creator to Whom they are related. This togetherness as equal and relatively similar beings dependent on their Creator and reflecting Him is one of the most central ideas in Scripture. This togetherness in equality is meant by God as the basic structure of any human relationship. Divisions of responsibility including labour and family care, or positions of leadership, power and authority are to fit in the pattern that relates woman and man to one another and both to God. The threads that hold its elements harmoniously together are made by the supreme authority of the Word of God. In faithful acceptance of that

African woman pounding maize.

Divine authority, man and women are called on to cooperate when performing the tasks of life, sharing one another's burden and challenges.

c. Different from Man

Man and woman have many characteristics in common. In this relative similarity they are images of God. At the same time, they are not uniform. They are not similar in an absolute sense. There are distinct differences. In this they are also images of God. Their differences from one another are parallel to the differences between the three Persons in God. In marriage, church, and society men and women have many similar roles and responsibilities, but at the same time they represent different aspects of life and act in different role patterns.

61.2. Cultural Patterns

a. Philosophy

Of course, African Christianity is a product of the Word of God, and so is the position of women in marriages, churches and societies that have fully accepted the authority of the Bible. However, the reality of daily practice is more complicated than this. Unfortunately, there is the reality of sin that corrupts or even obliterates Biblical patterns. Even Christians have no perfect understanding of God's will, neither are they perfectly obedient to Him.

Moreover, like societies anywhere on this globe, African societies, including churches and Christians, are influenced by culture. The term culture comprises the way in which humanity builds up life, using the means given by human capacities and by surrounding nature. Traditions and customs belong to it, also traditional religions. The

---

[3] Cf.: Janet Y Kholowa and Klaus Fiedler, *In the Beginning God Created them Equal*, Zomba: Kachere 2003.

term culture is closely related to the term philosophy, referring to man's love of wisdom. Philosophy is the rationalising power of man. It enables human beings to reflect on their own being and existence. Through philosophy human beings can organise their thinking on culture and their knowledge of it in an orderly way.

The perception that African Christians have of the position of women is influenced both by Western Culture and by African Culture.

b. Western Culture

In Western Culture at least two different strands can be distinguished. There is the Biblical line, focusing on God, which led to the plantation of God's Church, through Paul, Augustine, the Reformation, and the Evangelical or Reformed and Jansenist Revivals and Awakenings in modern times. This line leads from and to the Cross of Jesus Christ, through Whom there is salvation for anyone who believes in Him. Sometimes pharasaistic and heterodox Jewish Culture weakened this line, e.g. by its one-sided emphasis on perfect obedience to the Law, presented as a feasible way for mankind to be saved. Another strand is the wisdom of pre-Christian Greek and Roman cultures, focusing on man and nature.

Literacy project for African women (Mariotschool).

On the one hand, through Humanism, Enlightenment, Industrial Revolution, Positivism, and Emancipation, they contributed immensely to the development of science and technology. On the other hand, they undermined Christian life. Gnostic ideas misrepresented the relationship between matter and spirit, body and soul, which distorted the view of Western man on his own life, including his sexuality. This also led to the replacement of God by a mistaken faith in the power of human progress. This blinded man to the limitations of economic and technical development. In post-modern thought there is again a realisation that man cannot live by bread alone. By the end of the 20th century transcendental religiosity took the place of unlimited materialism. However, in general, this has not led people back to faith in Christ and to acceptance of the salvation through His victory over sin and death on the cross of Golgotha.

The position of women in Western Culture has changed as history continued. In the Jewish-Biblical climate women were respected and were not always completely dependent on men. In marriage, however, they were under the leadership and authority of men. But the New Testament shows that discriminatory differences between men and women fade out when people are living near to Christ. In the classical Greek and Roman Cultures women were positioned at a very low level. They were not much different from slaves, assigned to act as workers and sex tools. Only as religious prostitutes and priestesses at the pagan temples, and sometimes in queenship positions could some of them have independent power.

The arrival of Christianity fundamentally changed the position of women. The number of women among the first Christians was disproportionately large. Consequently, many played an important role in the Church, especially in prophetic and charismatic ministries. In the *Middle Ages* the position of women deteriorated. Their influence did not fit well in the male-oriented feudal organisation of society and hierarchical rule of the Church. At best, they were given honour by noblemen, through the courtly songs of bards, or by the Church, by elevating them to a special religious position as inhabitants of a convent. A Gnostic view of marriage and sexuality was maintained.

The *Reformation*, as a back-to-the-Bible movement, tried to restore the Biblical pattern of the relationship between men and women. The Reformers re-appraised family life as the cornerstone of society. In the family the wife played a key role, so indirectly her position in society was elevated. In the churches of the *Reformation* women were given an opportunity for various activities, especially diaconal work. In marriage, church and society, men were considered to be the leaders, having final authority. However, a Biblical reform of man-woman relationships, taking into account equality, similarity, and difference, did not take place. Gradually the promising perspectives of the *Reformation* on real Christianisation of the man-woman relationship patterns grew dim, and later developments were less inspired by Biblical thinking than by cultures that had started outside and before the birth of Christianity.

Changes in the position of women in the *Modern Era* were mainly the result of views that had revived in the periods of *Renaissance* and *Humanism,* then been taken over by the movements of *Enlightenment, Romanticism* and *Positivism*. These movements were not necessarily anti-Christian, yet they took their criteria from earthly realities considered without the Bible or God. In this way much of Western society was secularised. Also, the view of the relationship between men and women was secularised to a high degree. In the Modern Era of Western history, as a result of philosophical revolutions, the position of women changed in two directions.

First, there was the ever growing tendency of emancipation. This tendency gathered momentum, especially after the French Revolution, and it came to a climax after the *Second World War*, getting to extremes in movements of feminism and women's lib. Its ultimate objectives are beyond reaching equality, it aims at removing all differences between the two sexes.

The second tendency seems to go against the first one. In the agrarian and early capitalist societies, which had started to erode before 1800, to a certain extent women could be economically independent from men, because they had access to land and commerce. This does not mean that men and women in rural societies had equal power, but the economic factor strengthened women's influence in a culture that for the rest was dominated by men. Man's overlordship was balanced by the fact that in rural family life, wife and husband only could survive by being one another's cooperating partners.

This situation began to change as a result of the technological and industrial revolutions of the 19th century. The heartbeat of economic life shifted to the cities, where factories, ports and civil service attracted many people that thus far had lived in the countryside. As a result, farm life and home industry declined, together with the relatively independent position of women. More and more the kitchen and the delivery room were the only areas where women could be of significance. In general, the churches did not try to counteract this tendency to diminish the space in which a woman could operate. Absolute male dominance seemed a matter of course.

In the meantime, mainly from the secular world outside the churches, movements for women's emancipation grew stronger. To many Christians, the campaigns for women's emancipation seemed to aim at anti-Biblical objectives. In this polarised situation, although in theory accepting women's equality, the churches would defend the contemporary situation in which there were practically no similar responsibilities for women and men. Yet sometimes in the church there was a powerful wave of influence by women. The evangelical revivals and awakenings of the 18th and 19th centuries had revived the churches, and had given more room to women in various activities.

European and American missionaries who came to Africa were very much products of the cultural situation in their home countries. They brought with them not only Biblical views, but also Western cultural perceptions of the relationship between women and men. Among them there was a wide spectrum of views: some were on the progressive side, but most of them were conservatives. Some were under the influence of liberal thought; most of them were children of the evangelical revivals and awakenings. That is why there was no uniformity in their ideas on the position of women. Missions of the mainline churches (classical missions) did not send women as missionaries in their own right. But the post-classical missions did. (See chapter 55).

c. African and Islamic Cultures

African Culture. In the traditional African context women have always been subordinated to men. Women obey, men are in command.[4] Besides, they were considered as a segregated group, because of their specific female roles, e.g. in pregnancy and childbirth.[5] There was total submission to the husband. Girls were taught not to argue with the husband and treat him as king. They were prepared to live with a man at a very young age. Initiation ceremonies for girls were considered very important as they were regarded as moral and religious education. However, sexual rites were often performed between the initiates and unknown men, called in Chichewa *afisi*,[6] to mark the end of puberty initiation. Widows were sometimes forced into the custom of *kuchotsa fumbi*,[7] which means that they have to sleep with a brother of the deceased husband.[8]

On the other hand, there have been areas where women dominated. Like in classical Greek Culture, certain women-dominated fields were often related to religion, fertility (including rain-making), prophecy and priesthood.

Here is an example of the Chewa women in Malawi, described by Phiri. Women known as spirit-wives were the controllers of the territorial rain shrines.[9] When in ecstasy, they were said to receive messages from god. The shrine for Chisumphi in Central Malawi was served by a succession of women known as Mangadzi or Makewana. In the south there was the shrine of the Mbona cult.[10] There a human

---

[4] Cf.: Phiri, *Women*, p.17.

[5] Rachel Banda, *Women of the Bible and Culture*, pp.169-189.

[6] Paas, *Chichewa/ Chinyanja: English Dictionary*: the word *afisi* is plural for *hyena*:

[7] Paas, *Chichewa/ Chinyanja: English Dictionary*: 'kuchotsa fumbi' literally means: *to remove dust.*

[8] Phiri, *Women*, pp.38-40.

[9] W.H.J. Rangeley, 'Two Nyasaland Rain Shrines: Makewana, the Mother of All People', in: *The Nyasaland Journal*, Vol. 5, No. 2 (July, 1952), pp. 31-50; also: W H Rangeley, 'Mbona the Rain-Maker', in: *Nyasaland journal*, 6 (1) January 1953, pp.8-28.

[10] J.M. Schoffeleers, *River of Blood: the genesis of a martyr cult in SouthernMalawi c. AD 1600*, Madison: University of Wisconsin 1992; idem, 'The Interaction between the Mbona Cult and Christianity' in: Ranger, T.O. and J. Weller, *Themes in the Christian History of Central Africa*,(1975).

woman was provided as wife for the spirit who was believed to visit the shrine. The woman was known as Mbona. Makewana had female attendants. These were young virgins between the age of five and eight. At a shrine, it was believed that God would not be present if the woman was producing menstrual blood. Makewana and her female attendants were not allowed to marry or to become pregnant. Yet Makewana was involved in ritual sexual intercourse at the shrine with a special functionary, called Kamundi, as a way of marking the end of the initiation ceremony for girls.[11] The example shows that women could have complete control of religious shrines, and that their position was connected to cultic prostitution.

As priesthood and kingship were closely related, women could also be leaders in a wider political sense. Traditionally quite a number of Chewa chiefs are female. In a matrilineal situation women could also be in a stronger position because of the marriage arrangements that forced the husband to move to the village of the wife, thus making him dependent on the family of the wife. Economically the wife used to have independent access to land and commerce, adding to her relative independence.

On a negative note, a number of women would enlarge their power by witchcraft. Many witches are female,[12] and with their manipulations they definitely influence many people, including men.

Islamic Culture. The arrival of Islam in Africa did not improve the status of women. Islamic tradition puts the woman lower than the man. A man is allowed to marry four wives, and room is created for extra-marital sex by men. Islam offers perceptions that are offensive to women, for example the expectation that in heaven man 'enjoys' the presence of virgins ready for him. On the other hand, Islamic law regulated the position of women, giving them probably more protection than the unstable structures of *African Traditional Religions.*

d. Christ is more than Culture

We have noted that philosophy is a consciously designed system of principles of wisdom for reasoning on our way of life, i.e. on our culture. This applies to any culture, including Western, African, and Islamic Cultures. Cultures and religions that preceded the arrival of Christianity or cultures and religions that operate outside the scope of Biblical faith may harbour some august philosophical insights and noble ethical values that confirm Scripture. Yet they do not focus on Christ.

Now the question is, what value do we attach to our philosophy, our culture, our system of thought, our tradition, and our wisdom? If compared to the faith in Jesus Christ, which position does our natural wisdom take? We cannot completely separate the two. They are related. But there is a certain order. What is the order of these things in our lives? There are basically two positions. In the first position our wisdom and culture dominate our faith. In the second position wisdom and culture are dominated by faith. In the first position faith in Jesus Christ is the first thing in our lives and everything else is second. In the second position our culture and philosophy are first. They are dearer to us than Jesus and the faith in Him. In this case our own wisdom and the wisdom of the world want to rule over our faith in Jesus. Here we have to make a choice. This choice has great consequences. When you put your wisdom higher than

---

[11] Phiri, *Women*, pp.23-33.

[12] R.J.Gehman, *African Traditional Religion in Biblical Perspective*, Nairobi: East African Educational Publishers, p.73.

your faith, then in the end you will find that your wisdom fails you, and that you have no faith at all. When you put your faith first, then it will 'colour' everything in your life, including your wisdom.

Only those who believe in Him will find real wisdom. They find real understanding of sin and grace and of the ways of the Lord. Being in the faith produces a culture, customs, and a philosophy that are Christ-oriented. Faith precedes philosophy and produces it. Because of the faith in Christ wisdom becomes real wisdom. Faith produces a wisdom that is both disciplined by the Word of God and derived from the Word of God. The centre of the Word of God is the Cross of Jesus Christ. That is why we can say that Jesus Christ is the wisdom of God. Christ's saving work on the Cross is the ultimate wisdom.

61.3. Christian Women Today

a. Situation before Independence

It is apparent that today's position of Christian women in Africa has been influenced from various sides. First, by the work of the sovereign God himself through his Word and Spirit. Secondly, by the effects of the Jewish-Biblical, the Western, the Traditional African and the Islamic Cultures. At some point all these cultures show a break with the Word of God, although many of their phenomena may run parallel to it.

In general, missionaries from the West were sincere Christians, ignited by revivalist movements. They professed the final authority of the Bible in all issues, including man-woman relationships. As such, they looked at African society, and made comments on it. Often they did not favour African traditions, and they wanted to bring the lives of African men and women in line with the Biblical patterns.

Yet at the same time, they were influenced by their own Western Culture, which means that unconsciously they may have defended views that do not necessarily agree with Scripture. They may also have condemned certain features of traditional African gender too rigidly or in the wrong way. In a way Phiri could be right when she says that the coming of the missionaries and the colonial governments did not create a favourable environment for improvement of the position of women. According to Phiri, the missionaries attacked traditional female cults, matrilineal privileges for women, and royal positions for women. In the vision of the missionaries, defined by a 19th-century rural tradition in Europe and America, women particularly belonged to the spheres of housekeeping and childcare.[13]

African women, carrying water.

---

[13] Cf.: Phiri, *Women*, p.23.

There may be some truth in this, yet it cannot be denied that there is an important other side. Missionaries realised that women should participate fully in developments in family, church and society. That is why they had to be educated. Western missions included women and girls in their education programmes.

On the other hand, attempts for uplifting women were hindered by factors of change due to the effects of Western economic and social influence. There was a parallel here with 19th-century Europe and America when they experienced the effects of the industrial revolution. The social and economic infrastructure of African family and village life changed when traditional barter economies in an agricultural environment were replaced by a cash economy depending on an urban environment. The new economy had not much use for women participating independently in the economic process.[14]

b. Present situation

What is the Greatest Problem? Today African women operate in societies and churches that are independent of Western rule. Yet forms of dependence on the West have continued ever since the end of colonialism. Moreover, modern Africa has become part of the global community. How have these changes affected the position of African women? A description of the present situation was offered at a conference in Dakar in 1994 and more especially in 1995 at the *Fourth Women's World Conference* in Beijing.[15] In a report made by Takyiwaa Manuh, the growing recognition of the contributions of women is noted, but also the enormous obstacles that they face. The report exclusively deals with social, economic and political aspects of the position of women. According to the World Conference, the greatest problem of African women is that they are not given sufficient access to resources, and decision-making powers. This is said to have affected their general position in a negative way. Here is a summary of the main points of the report.

Religious Sisters in an African Independent Church in Zimbabwe.

Three Developments. The report says that in recent decades women's lives have been profoundly affected by three main developments: *First*, the structural adjustment programmes. By placing greater emphasis on export crops, which are usually grown by men, the domestic terms of trade have tended to shift against food production, where women predominate. *Secondly*, there has been increased civil strife and conflict. The majority of refugees, displaced persons and post-conflict returnees were women and children. *Thirdly*, many African countries are grappling with the AIDS crisis, high

---

[14] Cf.: Fiedler, *The History of the Faith Missions*, pp.292-298.

[15] Takyiwaa Manuh, 'Women in Africa's development: Overcoming Obstacles, Pushing for Progress', *Africa Recovery Briefing Paper*, Number 11, April 1998.

and increasing rates of HIV infection and the costs in human lives. Just over half of the estimated 20 million cases of HIV in Africa are female.

Marriage and Family Life. In the countryside and in the cities women perform all domestic tasks, while many also farm and trade. They are responsible for the care of children, the sick and the elderly, in addition to performing essential social functions within their communities. While today women rarely have the same access to resources as men, in the past some resources were available to them, especially land. Wives in many societies were not fully economically dependent upon their husbands. Women's power and spheres of influence largely disappeared under the impact of colonialism and external religions, which upset existing economic and social complementarity between the sexes. Women have profited from improved education, employment, health care, and nutrition, but in general their position has deteriorated. Development plans were made and executed without an adequate understanding of women's contributions to African economies. That is why they have tended to be marginalised. New marriage laws transformed the previously fluid and negotiable relations between them into rigid duties and obligations of wives and women. Women came to be regarded as primarily dependent on men, making it unnecessary to plan and provide for their needs; they were to work in the fields and home to produce food and other crops to support their men, who worked in visible, documented activities. About half of all women in Africa are married by the age of 18 and one in three women is in a polygamous marriage. Estimates of average total fertility rates in Africa were 5.7 children per woman in 1995.[16] Women head about 31 per cent of households in urban and rural areas across Africa, often with no working resident males.

Labour. In many rural areas, women contribute unpaid labour to the household's agricultural production and spend up to 50 hours a week on domestic labour and subsistence food production, with little sharing of tasks by spouses or sons in the household. Studies have documented that women work 12-13 hours a week more than men, as the prevalent economic and environmental crises have increased the working hours of the poorest women. In some areas, women may have separate access to land and work independently in farming or in some other income-generating activity. But in general they have fewer opportunities to earn income. They combine their unpaid labour with independent production to meet the needs of their families and to attain some measure of autonomy and self-reliance. Their income is indispensable for family survival regardless of the presence of men, since the system of allocation and distribution within many African households usually imposes individual responsibilities on men and women to meet their personal needs.

Women provide the backbone of the rural economy in much of sub-Saharan Africa. About 80 per cent of the economically active female labour force is employed in agriculture and women comprise about 47 per cent of the total agricultural labour force. Food production is the major activity of rural women and their responsibilities and labour inputs often exceed those of men in most areas in Africa. Women also provide much of the labour for men's cultivation of export crops, from which women derive little direct benefit. Food security in Africa cannot be assured without improving the situation of women producers.

---

[16] Ann R. Breneman and Rebecca Mbuh, *Women in the New Millennium: The Global Revolution*, Oxford: Hamilton Books, 2006, p. 140.

Education and training. Although a number of women profited from education, for very many there is still a lack of access to formal education and training. This has been identified as a key barrier to women's employment and advancement in society. In Africa, female illiteracy rates were over 60 per cent in 1996, compared to 41 per cent for men. In many African countries, parents still prefer to send boys to school, seeing little need for education for girls. In addition, factors such as adolescent pregnancy, early marriage and girls' greater burden of household labour act as obstacles to their schooling. In 1993, only about 40 per cent of school-age girls were enrolled in primary or secondary schools.

Health and sanitation. For women, as for men, inadequate potable water, sanitation

Members of the Women's Guild (Amayi a Mvano) of Mulunguzi CCAP, Malawi.

and waste disposal in urban and rural areas in Africa leave populations vulnerable to water-borne and other environmental diseases. Malaria, lung and other respiratory diseases are still major killers in Africa.

Maternal and infant mortality remain high. Up to 40 per cent of pregnant women in many countries have no access to antenatal care, while the percentage of births attended by trained personnel has declined. In 1994 the infant mortality rate in Africa was estimated at 92 deaths per thousand. High rates of infant mortality, the opposition of male partners and religious and cultural factors result in levels of contraceptive use of only around 15 per cent.

The health of women and girl-children is also jeopardised by female genital mutilation (FGM). It is estimated that about 2 million girls are subjected to the practice each year. The high and growing incidence of AIDS also highlights women's lack of power over their own sexuality. Research in West and Central Africa has shown that because of cultural and economic reasons, many women feel unable to refuse the sexual advances of partners even when they know they risk infection. Issues of rape, sexual assault and domestic violence also are beginning to receive due attention in discussions of women's health. In situations of conflict, refugee and displaced women and girls often have been sexually assaulted.

Political power. Many governments have been negligent in enacting women's rights into national law. Moreover, many women are ignorant of the existence of laws that recognise their rights and which can be invoked for their protection. Traditional women leaders have not been given the same recognition as male chiefs who after independence have been co-opted into new positions of power in their societies.

61.4. The Way Forward

This report of the *Beijing Conference* reflects the views of many African leaders in Church and Society. They like to depict the problems of Africa's women mainly from an economic and social angle. This general acceptance is also true for the solution suggested in the *Beijing Report*. It boils down to one demand. Give to women the same access to resources, and decision-making powers as to men. In other words, remove the gender bias and realise gender equality. The philosophical starting point for this description of problems and solution is not explicitly given, but is reminiscent of a Western or globalist approach in the line of the *Enlightenment*. Possession of economic means and power is supposed to solve all women's problems.

Can this thought determine the vision of Church and Christians? I think it can't. Christians have more to say, and they have to say it differently. In the conclusion of the *Beijing Report* the reality of the Biblical patterns of relationship between men and women to God and men and women to one another are not taken into account. Secular thought pays no attention to the fact that the similarity of men and women is limited, and that differences between them necessarily play an important and positive role. Realising this Biblical reality is required when Church and Christians want to fathom the economic and social misery of so many women in Africa. Christians should prophetically encourage political leaders to develop their economies and social structures for the benefit of the people, giving also to women their rightful place.

In the light of Scripture, Church and Christians in Africa have to make a diagnosis of the deepest causes of the crisis. Secularist approaches are blind to spiritual dimensions. The basic Biblical guidelines for marriage, for sexuality, for family life, and for role patterns of men and women in church and society are meant to prevent problems and to heal relationships that have got broken and lopsided. Having found the spiritual diagnosis of the problem, the Church and the individual Christians should also derive from Scripture the method of healing. They are called to proclaim and apply the Gospel of Jesus Christ, and show that He is able to touch and heal in any broken relationship.

What does this mean for the Church? Traditionally in the African churches women are conspicuously present, often more than men. Women were among the first to receive the message and they were very influential as local evangelists. Philomena Mwaura explored how the planting and growth of Christianity in Africa has been facilitated by female agency. She concludes that especially in *African Instituted Churches* women played an essential role as spirit-filled initiators of revival, as church founders, as prophetic figures, as healers, and as evangelists.[17] In *Classical Churches* too women have played pivotal roles in initiating, upholding and extending the life of faith in family and congregation. In the light of this situation and by the influence of

---

[17] Philomena Njeri Mwaura, 'Gender and Power in African Christianity: African Instituted Churches and Pentecostal Churches', in: Kalu et al. (eds), *African Christianity*, pp.410-445.

female-oriented and feminist theologies the role pattern for Christian women in the church has become an issue for renewed discussions.[18] Like Christian men, female Christians are kings, prophets and priests in Christ (1 *Peter* 2:9). What does this mean for the position of women concerning the leadership in the Church? This challenging question has to be answered with an open mind, in obedience to Scripture.

---

[18] Cf.: Nyambura J. Njoroge, 'A New Way of Facilitating Leadership: Lessons from African Women Theologians', in Kalu et al. (eds), *African Christianity*, pp.446-468.

62. Conversion

62.1. Conversion in Context

The Expansion of Christianity and *The Planting of Christianity*. Under these headings Latourette and Groves wrote their extensive accounts of *African Church History*. They made their books during the three decades before, in and after the *Second World War*. It was evident to them that much of sub-Saharan Africa was in the process of conversion from *Traditional Religions* to Christianity. However, at that time they could not know that the most spectacular increase of the number of Christians in Africa was still ahead of them. The growth of Christianity in Africa is called by Bonk 'one of the most astonishing phenomena of the 20th century'. He 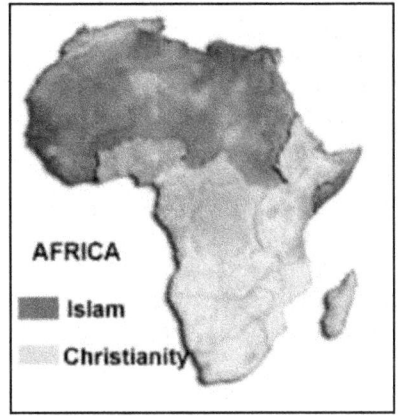 quotes figures from recent publications showing that during the 40 years since the beginning of independence, about 1960, the 'number of Christians in Africa has multiplied by six to nearly 380 million', that is nearly fifty percent of the total population of Africa. The numerical progress of Christianity has overtaken the growth of Islam, to which another 41 percent of Africans are said to belong.[1]

There are many reasons why Africans become Christians. According to Walls,[2] an important reason is that becoming a Christian is a means of access to the desirable things of Europeans, especially to *power*. The writer thinks it a mistake to call this reason secular. He uses the example of Igboland, where 'religion always was directed at the acquisition of power'. When the British came and subdued them, for the Igbos there was every reason to abandon traditional religion, because it had been shown not to be of any value for the acquisition of power. There were two movements in Igbo Christianity: first, vigorous adhesion to Christian worship, understanding it as a kind of *Deuteronomic Theology*, and secondly in a later generation a new emphasis on the cross and the taking up of the cross. So, first they 'accepted Christianity in terms of traditional world view' and then, 'it entered deep into the traditional system and interacted with it'.

Generally, Western influences contributed to the many changes in African society. If tradition has no answer to the changes, then there is the danger of disintegration, disturbance, and confusion, unless a new *rule* of life, a *key* to conduct, can be found. Evangelical preaching can provide such a key, but sometimes it got stuck in the attitudes of *legalism*.

---

[1] Jonathan J. Bonk, 'The Dictionary of African Christian Bibliography: Ecclesiastical Cartography and the Invisible Continent', 2004 [DACB Website], who quotes: Lamin Sanneh, *Whose Religion is Christianity: The Gospel Beyond the West*, Grand Rapids: Eerdmans, 2003, p.15, Patrick Johnstone and Jason Mandryk, with Robin Johnstone, *Operation World: Twenty-first Century Edition*, Carlisle: Paternoster, 2001, pp.20,21; cf. Isichei, *History of Christianity*, p.31.
[2] Walls, *Missionary Movement*, pp.89-93.

62.2. God and the African Past[3]

Unlike African converts, the first Greek Christians did not give God a personal name; for them he was just *ho theos* (= the God), who replaced their polytheism. The Africans, however, generally recognised a creator god, the moral governor of the universe, a supreme being. They tended to use the name of this being for the God of the Bible.[4]

A Diviner leaving a religious shrine in Burkina Faso.

The question is: Was God thus part of the African past? Can God be found in the African heritage? Or is this Christianising African traditional religion? Okot p'Bitek, a non-Christian, says: 'the process of seeking God in the African past will render the Christian revelation unnecessary'. But the other side is: no one can have an identity without his or her past. Kwame Bediako, who paralleled ancient Hellenistic and modern African identity questions, says that the first question on the African theological agenda is: Where was God in Africa's past? He answers: The Supreme Being of Africa's past with its many names is the God of Scripture, in a way that Zeus and Odin never were!

But is this answer true according to Scripture? And if so, does this help Africans to get saved?

62.3. New Perspectives on an Encounter[5]

Some approach these questions from a nationalistic and political angle, stressing the usefulness of Christian mission for modernisation and political independence of Africa. This approach neglects the deeper religious reasons why Africans found Christianity 'appropriate or useful in their campaign with the new and wider world that was intruding upon them'.

Horton observed a change in the way Africans appreciated their traditional religious hierarchy of the *Supreme Being* as the highest level, together with subordinate deities, and the lower local spirits. He says that of late the cult of the *Supreme Being* became more important, whereas the lesser *spirit cult* declined. Modern developments drew people more into the realm of the *macrocosmos* of the *Supreme Being*, whereas the realm of the *microcosmos* with its spirits became less important. This development would have facilitated the acceptance of the Christian God who was considered to give power for coping with the advancing macro-world of modern life. Horton thinks that African Christianity borrowed features of these two levels of *African Traditional*

---

[3] Walls, *Missionary Movement*, pp.94-97.

[4] NB 1: Muslims were very reluctant to do this. NB 2: Sometimes this practice contributed to neglecting God the Son.

[5] R. Strayer, 'Mission History in Africa: New Perspectives on an Encounter', in: B. Carmody, *African Conversion*, Ndola: Mission Press, pp.1-15.

Religion. This would mean that to some Mang'anja and Sena Mbona-worshippers of Southern Malawi Mbona became a black Christ,[6] and that to some even anti-witchcraft cleansing would be identified as an aspect of Christian sanctification. Whether Horton observed rightly remains to be seen. On the ground, the worship of territorial cults and spirits, like the Mbona cult, may still be active, but they have declined and have a limited appeal only. Moreover, there are examples of remaining Mbona-worshippers, who are far from mixing with Christianity, and even publicly declare hostility towards the Christians and their 'alien god'.[7] At the same time, it cannot be denied that in the perception of many people the 'lower' spirits, ancestors etc. still play important roles.

According to Horton, the change in African religious concepts was not only brought about by the advent of Christian mission, but also by changes in African traditional religious systems that had begun before the coming of the missionaries and by which these systems retained their vitality. The vitality of African traditional religion, as expressed in the new emphasis on supernatural healing, witchcraft cleansing, and spirit-possession (often denounced and neglected by the missionaries), partly became assimilated into Christianity, and partly it expressed itself in anti-mission protest, as can be seen in the ridiculing of Christianity by the *Nyau Societies* and their *Gule Wamkulu* by adopting pseudo-Christian forms like *Mpingo wa Aroni* in Malawi.[8]

Many became disappointed with the inability of mission Christianity to meet with African needs for explanation, prediction, or control and practical problems like life-healing, unemployment, sterility, and casting off evil as a real and personal power. This disappointment contributed to an ongoing interest in aspects of traditional religion and to the growth of independent separatist churches that gave room to traditional approaches. On the other hand, however, Christian mission in Africa has been extremely successful, and churches have grown in influence and number, at the expense of traditional religion and independent churches. There are a number of reasons for this:

a. Adaptation

There has been an adaptation of Christian mission to the African situation and needs, which did not provoke schism.

First, the missionaries often expressed their message as instruments to overcome 'this-worldly problems', like praying for rain, reading as a magic art, the power of modernisation. In the changing and secularising world of Africa, to many, the missionaries seemed more effective than traditional religion and later independent churches.

Secondly, the missionaries, especially the Roman Catholics, allowed adaptation in African religious and cultural terms. Examples are Roman Catholic leniency in matters of polygamy, bride wealth, and the veneration of ancestors. This gave them an advantage over Protestantism. In working among the southern Shona the *Dutch Reformed Mission* was less successful than the *Roman Catholic Mission*. There are few separatist churches in Tanzania probably because of strong adaptation by Roman

---

[6] Cf.: J.M. Schoffeleers (ed.), *Guardians of the Land: Essays on Central African Territorial Cults*, Gweru: Mambo, 1992, pp.147-186.

[7] Cf.: Deogratias Mmana, 'Asking for Rain through Libations at Khuluvi', and 'Otsatira Chipembedzo cha Makolo apempha mvula kwa Mbona ku Khuluvi', in: Malawi News, October 1-7, 2005.

[8] Cf.: J.W.M. van Breugel, *Chewa Traditional Religion*, Zomba: Kachere, 2001, pp.125-168.

Catholic missionaries. Acceptance of female circumcision by the Anglicans gave them more influence among the Kikuyu than the Presbyterians and the *Africa Inland Mission*.

Thirdly, missionary absolutism from above by the foreign missionaries was often balanced by pragmatism from below by the African helpers, catechists and clergymen. In practice, allowance was made for the wearing of protective charms, consulting traditionalist religious specialists, and interaction with traditional religious communities.

Fourthly, in the mission churches there was reinterpretation of Christian rites and practices in terms of traditional belief within mission, for example Dominican Sisters as the equivalent of the *Mbonga-Virgins* at the shrine of the Mwari, the Shona high god, baptism became a healing rite, and miraculous healings and exorcism were incorporated.[9]

b. Functions in Society

Mission churches came to perform important functions in society. Acceptance of Christianity was strengthened when these functions helped to underline valued traditional views. For example, the Roman Catholic missions especially emphasised male dominance. Mission churches also gave expression to political and economic aspirations of peoples and tribes.

c. Mediators of Modernity

Mission churches came to be viewed as important mediators of modernity, both progressive and consonant with tradition, whereas the members of mission churches sometimes regarded independent churches as backward and ignorant. Mission schools played a very important role in this respect.

d. Position towards the State

In the colonial era the mission communities functioned as a link between the culture of subordinate groups and the rulers. In some cases missions were instruments of the colonial administration. At the same time, there were contradicting interests, and ensuing struggles between mission communities and the colonial establishment. There was a cleavage that was based on class, education, values and Evangelical convictions. Generally, missions tried to avoid close association with the state. As children of their time missionaries were imperialists, but they aspired to a different empire than the colonialists. They resented increasingly strong government control, because they feared the secularising effect of government policy, for example in the field of education, where the colonial governments gradually opted for secular schools free from mission influence. Missions often clashed with governments on the issue of defending African interests. The link between mission communities and the colonial state weakened to the extent of disengagement when the nationalist mass movements challenged the missionaries to opt for independence of African states against colonial rule.

e. Agents of Cultural and Social Change?

The alleged Westernisation as a result of the work of the missions has been both damned and praised by Africans. Were the missions agents of Westernisation?

---

[9] Cf.: Isabel Mukonyora, *Women and Ecology in Shona Religion*, Harare: Univ. of Zimbabwe, 1999.

Missionaries cannot be considered as friends of contemporary Western Culture, simply because they have denounced some aspects of African Culture. Strayer points to 'a deep missionary ambivalence regarding modern Western Culture'. Many missionaries wanted to safeguard Africa from the secularising effects of rationalism, materialism, and urbanisation that were undermining Christianity in the West.[10] Strayer quotes Horton, who claims that the process of cultural and social change was not at all brought about by missions, and that the process of religious change only partly originates in the activities of missions. Further Strayer points to 'recent studies' suggesting that Roman Catholic and Dutch Reformed Mission in Malawi 'simply did not generate anything akin to a modernising élite'.[11]

Missions did not always disrupt the existing political, social, and psychological patterns of society. Christians were not separated from other members of their communities. Christianisation did not break political unity and it did not lead to 'detribalisation'. Of course, there were instances of conflict and discontinuity, but often they were in a 'subtle relationship with continuity'.

62.4. African Conversion[12]

Horton describes the 'typical traditional cosmology' or worldview of Africans, originating in pre-modern life, that is in pre-Christian and pre-Islamic times. It is a two-tiered system of ideas about unobservable personal beings which provides an instrument for explanation, prediction, and control of ordinary daily events.

> (a) The lower level of the *microcosmos*: lesser spirits, who are concerned with local things. Most events are attributed to them. There are many ideas about their modes of action. Some deal with human morality. There are many ideas about approaching and manipulating them.
>
> (b) The higher level of the *macrocosmos*: a Supreme Being, who is concerned with the world as a whole, and who controls the lesser spirits. Ideas about his modes of action, the events that he controls, the techniques to address him, are much vaguer and less developed.

In a pre-modern situation the *microcosmos* of the lesser spirits plays a much bigger role than the *macrocosmos* of the *Supreme Being*. The former are constantly approached, whereas the latter has no direct association with daily events and morality; hence, he is rarely addressed. In Horton's view this religious system has persisted in modern times. It has continued to be the basis of the African worldview, irrespective of the presence of Christianity and Islam. It has been able to adapt itself to the cultural and social changes in modern times. Instead of abandoning it, African people remoulded it, so that it still is an instrument of explanation-prediction-control. In the situation of modern change the macrocosmos of wider life becomes more important to people than the microcosmos. This means that the lesser spirits are being regarded irrelevant or even evil, whereas the *Supreme Being* is taking over control. New techniques of addressing him are being developed. As daily life is becoming more and more part of the macrocosmos, the *Supreme Being* is becoming the direct controller of morality. In the traditional setting man's relationship with the spirits already differed greatly from man's relationship with

---

[10] For examples from Tanzania and how Tanzanians reacted to such missionary attempts, see: Fiedler, *Christianity and African Culture*, especially pp.136ff.

[11] Strayer, 'Mission History', in: *African Conversion*, p.13.

[12] Horton, 'African Conversion', in: *African Conversion*, pp.19-26.

the *Supreme Being*. This difference becomes much bigger in the modern situation. Depending on the degree to which individuals have left their *microcosmos*, the rudimentary cult of the *Supreme Being* has been expanded in response to cultural and social change. The more an individual lives 'modern', the more the cult of the spirits is likely to be overshadowed by that of the *Supreme Being*. Even diviners and other 'philosophers of traditional religion' tend to adapt themselves to this new religious situation.

Horton concludes that the acceptance of Christianity (and Islam) is *'as much'* due to this development in *African cosmology* as it is to the activities of the missionaries. He says that Africans in accepting Christianity both *added* their own cosmology and *omitted* those elements in mission Christianity that that do not fit in with this African cosmology. Consequently, this acceptance was 'highly conditional and selective'. Christianity and Islam were accepted because of the adaptation of traditional religion to modern cultural and social challenges. This view reduces Christianity and Islam to the role of *catalysts*, 'stimulators of changes that were in the air anyway'. In Horton's view, missions who refuse to accept this humble role produce 'very meagre results'. Having added Christianity to the adapted traditional cosmology, Africans reject the other-worldliness of Christianity, and they use Christianity as an instrument for explanation-prediction-control, just as they used religion in the pre-modern situation. They accept the monotheism, and the moral concern of Christianity, just as they valued the *Supreme Being*. In Horton's view, the 'so called converts' in church (or mosque) form a *'continuum'* with the cult of spirits and the *Supreme Being*.

Early baptisms in Lake Malawi.

Because Islam has been 'fairly content' with this role of catalyst, it has expanded without having many breakaway sects. Missionary Christianity, however, has never been content to play this role. Therefore, many members of its churches are dissatisfied, which results in many breakaway sects.

62.5. The Character of the 'Continuum'

What can we learn from the writers summarized above? In comparing pre-modern society, modern society, and mission Christianity, they see continuity. In our opinion this view is one-sided. Christianity did more than continuing African tradition. There is *continuity*, and there is also *discontinuity*.

Scripture characterises the position of heathen peoples, whether they are pre-modern or modern, in two different ways. On the one hand the *demonic character* of their existence is stressed:

> They follow 'the ways of this world and of the ruler of the kingdom of the air, the spirit who is now at work in those who are disobedient'. They are 'gratifying the cravings of our sinful nature and following its desires and thoughts'. They are 'objects of wrath' (Eph.2:2,3).

> They are 'without hope and without God in the world' (Eph.2:12).

They are 'darkened in their understanding' (Eph.4:18).

They have 'lost all sensitivity, they have given themselves over to sensuality so as to indulge in every kind of impurity, with a continual lust for more' (Eph.4:19).

On the other hand, it is admitted that the non-Christian cultures have elements of *knowledge of the Law* of God:

> 'When Gentiles, who do not have the Law, do by nature things required by the Law, they are a Law for themselves, even though they do not have the Law, since they show that the requirements of the Law are written on their hearts, their consciences also bearing witness, and their thoughts now accusing, now even defending them' (Rom.2:14,15).

John Calvin (1509-1564), the most influential representative of the 16th-century Reformation.

This natural knowledge of God that is planted in the hearts of people does not lead them spontaneously to Christ. Something else is done by it to men. It stresses their personal responsibility for their own iniquity. The Reformer John Calvin says:

> 'In the human mind there is a certain consciousness of God, that is to say through natural inspiration. God himself has laid in everyone a certain understanding of his Divinity, so that no one could resort to the pretense of his ignorance ... because all without any exception understand that there is a God who is their Creator, and they would be condemned by their own witness, because they have not served Him'[13]

People do not come to Christ *spontaneously* or *voluntarily*. They come because God calls them. Mission work is not done because missionaries are invited. Mission work is done in obedience to a command. Neither is the missionary message an invitation to people of good will. The message is the proclamation of God's command, although the hearers themselves bear the responsibility for their reaction to it. They are chosen, *not because of* their continuity with the past, but *notwithstanding* their continuity with the past. The old creature, including his cultural or religious 'sparks' of divine light, is called to new birth, so that it is renewed to be a new creature in Christ.

62.6. Lessons from History

God's call to turn to Christ for salvation is the basic reason for conversion in Africa, or in any other part of the world. This call created the Church, and it is proclaimed by the Church through the spreading of the Word, and the answer to it is worked by the Holy Spirit. Only by being faithful to this command can the Church be established, survive and expand. This is what Hildebrandt means when he sums up some lessons from history for the Church in Africa. First, the history of persecutions and attacks by heresy has taught that loyalty to Christ and the Scriptures is a necessity for the Church and for all individual Christians. This implies that the Scriptures be made available to all people

---

[13] John Calvin, *Institutes of the Christian Religion*, Grand Rapids: Eerdmans, 1998 [Translated from the edition of 1559 by Henry Beveridge in 1845], Book I, chapter 3, section 1 (p.43).

in their local languages. Secondly, the Church needs faithful pastors and elders; by their care and by their example they build and continue the Church. Fourthly, evangelism and missionary outreach have been a priority, otherwise the Church could not continue to deploy. Fifthly, the Church has to 'be careful about how much it adapts itself to the national culture in which it is practised'.[14] In history many have mixed the Gospel with their traditional religion. This has weakened or taken away the witness of the Church. We can use good aspects of our culture for the expression of our faith in Christ, but glorification of humanity, superstitions, magic and witchcraft cannot be part of that.

Finally, the writing and learning of *Church History* reflects the teaching of a lesson, the conveying of a message, the stressing of a reality. Because it is part of Theology, the lesson or the message or the reality of *Church History* is Christ. In the *Covenant* of his Grace ultimately expressed in the sending of his Son, God planted the Church and commanded it to spread the Good News and to being deployed unto the ends of the earth, so that anyone who surrenders to Christ in faith, will have eternal life in his Kingdom. Proclaiming the Good News of the King and his Kingdom that saves and changes people's lives is the best contribution which the Church and the Christians can give to Africa and to the world. In the realisation of the Kingdom, the history of the Church finds it goal and its end.

---

[14] Hildebrandt, *History of the Church in Africa*, pp.38-42.

Bibliography: South Central-Africa

a. Zambia

Bolink, P., *Towards Church Union in Zambia*, Franeker: Wever, 1967.

Chilenje, Victor, 'The Origin and Development of the Church of Central Africa Presbyterian (CCAP) in Zambia 1882-2004' [PhD dissertation] Stellenbosch 2007 [Internet].

Hinfelaar, Hugo, *History of the Catholic Church in Zambia 1895-1995*, Lusaka: Bookworld Publ., 2004.

Lehmann, D., and J.V. Taylor, *Christians of the Copperbelt*, London: SCM, 1961.

Mwamba, Musonda T.S., 'The evolving role of the Church: the case of democratization in Zambia', in: Daniel O'Connor (et al.), *Three Centuries of Mission: The United Society for the Propagation of the Gospel 1701-2000*, London/ New York: Continuum, 2000, pp.382-394.

Verstraelen-Gilhuis, G., *From Dutch Mission Church to Reformed Church in Zambia: The Scope for African Leadership and Initiative in the History of a Zambian Mission Church*, Wever: Franeker, 1982.

Websites

Religion in Zambia, http://en.wikipedia.org/wiki/Religion_in_Zambia

b. Zimbabwe

Beach, D.N., *War and Politics in Zimbabwe 1840-1900*, Gweru: Mambo Press, 1994^2.

Dachs, A.J. (ed), *Christianity South of the Zambezi*, Gweru: Mambo, 1973.

Daneel, M.L., *Old and New Southern Shona Independent Churches,* volume 1: 'Background and Rise of the Major Movements', The Hague, 1971 (a), volume 2: 'Church Growth: Causative Factors and Recruitment Techniques', The Hague, 1974, volume 3: Leadership and Fission Dynamics, Gweru: Mambo Press, 1988.

Daneel, M.L., *Quest for Belonging: Introduction to a Study of African Independent Churches*, Gweru: Mambo, 1987.

Daneel, M.S., *Mbiri ya CCAP Sinodi ya Harare 1912-1982*, Harare: CCAP, 1982

Mandivenga, E.C., *Islam in Zimbabwe*, Gweru: Mambo Press, 1983.

Merwe Van der W.J, *From Mission field to Autonomous Church in Zimbabwe*, The Institute for Missiological Research of the University of Pretoria: NG Kerkboekhandel, 1981.

Mukonyora, Isabel, *Women and Ecology in Shona Religion*, Harare: University of Zimbabwe, 1999.

Wallis, J.P.R. (ed), *The Matabele Mission: A Selection from the Correspondence of John and Emily Moffat, David Livingstone and others 1858-1878*, London: Chatto & Windus, 1945.

Zoobgo, C.J.M., *The Wesleyan Methodist Missions in Zimbabwe 1891-1945*, Harare: University of Zimbabwe, 1991.

Websites

Religion in Zimbabwe, http://en.wikipedia.org/wiki/Religion_in_Zimbabwe

c. Malawi

Alpers, E.A.,'The Role of the Yao in the Development of Trade in East-Central Africa 1698-c.1850', unpublished PhD thesis, London University, 1966.

Anderson-Morshead, A.E.M., *The History of the Universities Mission to Central Africa*, London: UMCA, 1953.

Anonymous, *Mbiri ya Chipani cha Atumiki a Maria Virgo Woyera 1925-1975*, Limbe: Montfort, 1975.

Baker, Colin, *A Fine Chest of Medals: The Life of Jack Archer*, Cardiff: Mpemba Books, 2003.

Banda, Kelvin, N., *A Brief History of Education in Malawi*, Blantyre: Dzuka, 1982.

Banda, Rachel Nyagondwe, *Women of Bible and Culture: Baptist Convention Women in Southern Malawi*, Zomba: Kachere, 2005.

Bilima, Jaspine D., *The Life of K.M. Malinki*, Andrews University, 1993.

Bilima, Jaspine D., *The Seventh-Day Adventist Church in Malawi 1900-1980*, Andrews University, 1987.

Birmingham, David, and Phyllis Martin (eds), *History of Central Africa*, 2 vols, London: Longman, 1983.

Bismarck, Joseph, 'A Brief History on Joseph Bismarck', Occasional Papers of the Department of Antiquities, no. 7, Zomba, 1968, pp.49-54.

Blood, A.G., *The History of the Universities Mission to Central Africa*, 3 vols, London: UMCA, 1962.

Bone, D.S. (ed.), *Malawi's Muslims: Historical Perspectives*, Blantyre: CLAIM-Kachere, 2000.

Booth, J., *Africa for the African*, Baltimore, 1897 [reprinted: CLAIM, Blantyre 1998].

Boucher, Claude, *When Animals Sing and Spirits Dance: Gule Wamkulu, the Great Dance of the Chewa People of Malawi*, Kungoni Centre of Culture and Art, 2012.

Breneman, Ann R., and Rebecca Mbuh, *Women in the New Millennium: The Global Revolution*, Oxford: Hamilton Books, 2006.

Breugel, J.W.M., *Chewa Traditional Religion*, Blantyre: CLAIM/ Kachere, 2001.

Brough, Beryl, *St. Johnson of Lake Malawi*, Zomba: Kachere, 2004.

Campbell, G.H., *Lonely Warrior*, Blantyre: CLAIM-Kachere, 1975 [a short biography of William Koyi].

Chadwick, Owen, *Mackenzie's Grave*, London: Hodder and Stoughton, 1959.

Chakanza, J.C. and K.R. Ross, *Religion in Malawi: An Annotated Bibliography*, Blantyre: CLAIM/ Kachere, 1998.

Chakanza, J.C., *Voices of Preachers in Protest: The Ministry of Two Malawian Prophets: Elliot Kamwana and Wilfred Gudu*, Blantyre: CLAIM-Kachere, 1998.

Chaponda, Orison, 'Gule Wamkulu in the Catholic Church, Lilongwe Rural: A Cultural Phenomenon and a Pastoral Problem', Zomba: University of Malawi, 1998 [unpublished MA module].

Chimulu, F.M. (ed.), *The Universities' Mission to Central Africa: A Bibliography in Progress*, Zomba: University of Malawi, 1980.

Chiphangwi, Saindi D., *Why People Join the Christian Church: Trends in Church Growth in the Blantyre Synod of the Church of Central Africa Presbyterian 1960-1975*, University of Aberdeen, 1978 [PhD thesis].

Chirwa, Devlin, 'The History of the African Methodist Episcopal Church in Malawi: The Karonga Branch (1943-2000)' [unpublished thesis].

Church, Henry, *Theological Education that Makes a Difference*, Blantyre: CLAIM-Kachere, 2001.

Crosby, C.A., *Historical Dictionary of Malawi*, Metuhen and London: The Scarecrow Press, 1980.

Dicks, Ian D., *An African Worldview: The Muslim Amacinga Yawo of Southern Malawi*, Zomba: Kachere 2012.

Du Plessis, J., *Evangelisation of Pagan Africa: A History of Christian Missions to the Pagan Tribes of Central Africa*, Cape Town, 1919.

Elmslie, W. A., *Among the Wild Ngoni: Being Some Chapters in the History of the Livingstonia Mission in British Central Africa*, Edinburgh/ London: Oliphant Anderson & Frerrier, 1899.

Fiedler, Klaus, 'Christian Missions and Western Colonialism: Soulmates or Antagonists?', in: Kenneth R. Ross (ed), *Faith at the Frontiers of Knowledge*, Blantyre: CLAIM-Kachere, 1998, pp.218-234.

Fiedler, Klaus, 'Power at the Receiving End: The Jehovah's Witnesses' Experience in One-Party Malawi', in: K.R. Ross (ed.), *God, People and Power in Malawi: Democratization in Theological Perspective,* Blantyre: CLAIM-Kachere, 1996, pp.149-176;

Fiedler, Klaus, 'The Charismatic and Pentecostal Movements in Malawi in Cultural Perspective', in: *Religion in Malawi*, 9 (1999).

Fiedler, Rachel Nyagondwe, *Women of Bible and Culture: Baptist Convention Women in Southern Malawi*, Zomba: Kachere, 2005.

Fraser, A.R., *Donald Fraser of Livingstonia*, London: Hodder and Stoughton, 1934.

Garner, Judy, *History of the Baptist Mission in Malawi: A Rambling Remembrance of Some People and Events in the History of the Baptist Mission in Malawi*, Lilongwe: Baptist Publications, 1998;

Gray, Ernest, 'The History of the Churches of Christ Missionary Work in Nyasaland, Central Africa 1907-1930', in: *Churches of Christ Historical Society Occasional Paper*, no. 1, Cambridge, 1981.

Henderson, Clara, *Rolling Away the Stone: The Africanisation of Christian Music by Presbyterian Mvano Women in Southern Malawi,* Zomba: Kachere, 2008.

Hetherwick, Alexander, *The Romance of Blantyre: How Livingstone's Dream Came True*, London: James Clarke, nd [c.1931].

Hetherwick, Alexander, *The Gospel and the African: The Croal Lectures*, Edinburgh: T & T Clark, 1932.

Jackson, Bill., *Send us Friends*, Blantyre: CLAIM, nd [c.1997].

Jeal, T., *Livingstone*, New York: Putnam, 1973.

Johne, Harold, R., and Ernst H. Wendland, 'To Every Nation, Tribe, Language and People', in: *A Century of WELS World Missions*, Milwaukee: Northwestern Publ. House, 1993^2, pp.169-221.

Kalilombe, P.A., *Doing Theology at the Grass Roots: Theological Essays from Malawi*, Zomba: Kachere, 1999.

Kamnkhwani, H.A., *An Evaluation of the Historiography of Nkhoma Synod, Church of Central Africa Presbyterian*, D.Th., University of Stellenbosch, 1990.

Kaplan, S., 'The Africanization of Missionary Christianity: History and Typology', in: *Journal of Religion in Africa* (16), pp.166-186.

King, M. & E., *The Story of Medicine and Disease in Malawi: The 130 Years since Livingstone*, Blantyre: Montfort, 1992^2.

Kishindo, J.H.A., *Mbiri ya Ecclesia Anglicana ku Nyasaland 1860-1960*, Cape Town: Oxford UP, 1960.

Koevering, Helen E.P., *Dancing their Dreams: The Lakeshore Nyanja Women of the Anglican Diocese of Niassa*, Zomba, Kachere, 2005.

Kwiyani, Harvey C., 'Coming of Age: Pentecostalism and Umunthu in Malawi', in: Vinson Synan, Amos Yong and J. Kwabena Asamoah-Gyadu, *Global Renewal Christianity: Spirit-Empowered Movements Past, Present, and Future,* Vol. Iii of *Africa and Diaspora*, Lake Mary, FL: Charisma House Publishers, expected 2016.

Langworthy, H., *Africa for the Africans: The Life of Joseph Booth*, Blantyre: CLAIM, 1996.

Laws, R., *Reminiscences of Livingstonia*, Edinburgh/ London: Oliver and Boyd, 1934.

Linden, Ian, *Catholics, Peasants and Chewa Resistance in Nyasaland 1889-1939*, London: Heinemann, 1974.

Linden, Ian, *Mponda Mission Diary 1889-1891*, Lilongwe: White Fathers, 1989.

Livingstone, D., *The Last Journals: David Livingstone in Central Africa* (vol. 1), Westport: Greenwood, 1970 [first 1874].

Livingstone, David, *A Popular Account of Dr. Livingstone's Expedition to the Zambesi and its Tributaries: And the Discovery of Lakes Shirwa and Nyassa 1858-1864*, Gutenberg, e-book # 2519, 2005.

Longwe, Hany, *Christians by grace – Baptists by choice : a History of the Baptist Convention of Malawi*, Zomba: Kachere theses no 19 / Mzuni Books no 3, 2011 [PhD thesis].

Lwanda, J., *Politics, Culture and Medicine in Malawi*, Zomba: Kachere, 2005.

Macdonald, Duff, *Africana: The Heart of Heathen Africa*, 2 vols, London: Dawson 1882.

Macdonald, Roderick J., 'Reverend Hanock Msokera Phiri and the Establishment in Nyasaland of the African Methodist Episcopal Church', in: *African Historical Studies*, Vol. 3, No. 1 (1970).

Macheta, Harry K., *Blantyre Mission: Nkhani ya Ciyambi Cake*, Blantyre: Hetherwick Press, 1951.

Macpherson, F., *North of the Zambezi: A Modern Missionary Memoir*, Edinburgh: Handsel, 1998.

Makondesa, Patrick, *Moyo ndi Utumiki wa Mbusa ndi Mai Muocha wa Providence Industrial Mission*, Blantyre: CLAIM-Mvunguti, 2000.

Makondesa, Patrick, *The Church History of Providence Industrial Mission 1900-1940*, Zomba: Kachere, 2006.

Matemba, Yona Hisbon, *Matandani: The Second Adventist Mission in Malawi*, Zomba: Kachere, 2003.

McCracken, J., *Politics and Christianity in Malawi 1875-1940: The Impact of the Livingstonia Mission in the Northern Province*, Cambridge UP, 1977.

McIntosh, H., *Robert Laws: Servant of Africa*, Carberry: Handsel & Blantyre: Central Africana, 1993.

Mgawi, K.J., *Mbiri ya Mpingo ndi mudzi wa Nkhoma 1896 mpaka 1996*, Nkhoma Press, nd. [1996].

Michongwe, Nelly, *Meet the Daughters of the Blessed Virgin Mary in Malawi Africa*, Zomba: Kachere, 2005[2].

Moir, Fred L.M., *After Livingstone: An African Trade Romance*, London: Hodder and Stoughton, 1924.

Monjeza, Joshua, 'Distinctives and Polity of the Evangelical Brethren Church in Malawi, including Church History', nd. [about 1995].

Msiska, S.K., *Golden Buttons: Christianity and Traditional Religion among the Tumbuka*, Blantyre: CLAIM, 1997.

Munyenyembe, Rhodian G., 'The Church and Socio-cultural Issues: An Evaluation of the Charismatic Movement's Contribution towards the Centralisation of the Gospel in Malawi', 2006 [unpublished MA dissertation of the University of Malawi]

Murray, Andrew, *Moyo Watsopano: Mawu a Mulungu kwa Ophunzira Ongoyamba a Yesu Khristu*, Zomba: Kachere, 2006 [transl. of *The New Life*, ed. by Steven Paas; first published 1885].

Mvula, Gregory Chawanangwa, and Enson Mbilikile Lwesya, *Flames of Fire: The History of the Assemblies of God in Malawi*, Lilongwe: Assemblies of God in Malawi, 2005.

Mwimba, H.Z., 'The Establishing of the Evangelical Lutheran Church in Malawi', Tanzania, Makumira, 1992 [unpublished B.Div. paper of Makumira Lutheran Theological College].

Ncozana, Silas S., *Sangaya: A Leader in the Synod of Blantyre Church of Central Africa Presbyterian*, Blantyre: CLAIM/ Kachere, 1999.

Ncozana, Silas S., *Spirit Possession and Tumbuka Christians*, PhD dissertation, University of Aberdeen, 1985.

Newell, J., 'Not war but Defence of the Oppressed?: Bishop Mackenzie's Skirmishes with the Yao in 1861', in: K.R. Ross (ed.), *Faith at the Frontiers of Knowledge*, Blantyre: CLAIM, 1998, pp.129-143.

Nthara, S.Y., *Mbiri ya Achewa*, Limbe: Malawi Publications and Literature Bureau, 1965.

Nthara, S.Y., *Namon Katengeza*, Nkhoma Synod, 1964.

Nthara, S.Y., *The History of the Chewa*, Wiesbaden: Steiner, 1973.

Nurse, G.T., *The Physical Characters of the Maravi* [PhD Thesis], University of Witwatersrand, 1974.

Nzunda, M.S. and K.R. Ross, *Church, Law and Political Transition in Malawi 1992-1994*, Gweru: Mambo Press, 1997^2.

Pachai B. (ed.), *Early History of Malawi*, London: Longman, 1972.

Parrat, J.K. (ed.), *A Bibliography of Traditional Religion in Malawi*, Zomba: University of Malawi, 1983^2.

Pauw, C.M., *Mission and Church in Malawi: The History of the Nkhoma Synod of the Church of Central Africa Presbyterian 1889-1962*, PhD dissertation, University of Stellenbosch, 1980.

Perry, L. (ed.), *Joseph Booth: Africa for the African*, Blantyre: CLAIM, 1997 [first 1897],.

Phiri, D.D., *From Nguni to Ngoni: A History of the Ngoni Exodus from Zululand and Swaziland to Malawi, Tanzania, and Zambia*, Limbe: Popular Publ., 1982.

Phiri, D.D., *History of Malawi: From Earliest Times to the Year 1915*, Blantyre: CLAIM, 2004.

Phiri, D.D., *History of the Tumbuka*, Blantyre: Dzuka, 2000.

Phiri, D.D., *Let Us Die For Africa: An African Perspective on the Life and Death of John Chilembwe of Nyasaland/ Malawi*, Blantyre: Central Africana, 1999.

Phiri, I.A., *Women, Presbyterianism and Patriarchy: Religious Experience of Chewa Women in Central Malawi*, Blantyre: CLAIM, 1997.

Phiri, Kings M., 'Wealth and Power in the History of Northern Chewa Chiefdoms 1798-1895' [unpubl. MA Thesis], Wisconsin University 1972

Phiri, Kings M., and K.R. Ross (eds.), *Democratization in Malawi: A Stocktaking*, Blantyre: CLAIM, 1998.

Phiri, Kings M., *Chewa History in Central Malawi and the Use of Oral Tradition 1600-1920* [unpubl. PhD Thesis], Wisconsin University, 1975.

Pike, J.G., *Malawi: A Political and Economic History*, London: Pall Mall, 1968.

Ranger, T.O., and J. Weller (eds.), *Themes in the Christian History of Central Africa*, London: Heinemann, 1975.

Rangeley, W.H.J., 'Two Nyasaland Rain Shrines: Makewana, the Mother of All People', in: *The Nyasaland Journal*, Vol. 5, No. 2 (July, 1952), pp. 31-50.

Rangeley, W.H.J., 'Mbona the Rain-Maker', in: *Nyasaland journal*, 6 (1) January 1953, pages 8-28.

Reijnaerts, H., and A. Nielsen, and M. Schoffeleers, *Montfortians in Malawi, their Spirituality and Pastoral Approach*, Blantyre, CLAIM-Kachere, 1997.

Retief, M.W., *William Murray of Nyasaland*, Lovedale Press, 1958.

Ross, Andrew C., 'Wokondedwa Wathu: The Mzungu who Mattered', in: *Religion in Malawi* 7: 3-5 (1997).

Ross, Andrew C., *Blantyre Mission and the Making of Modern Malawi*, Blantyre: CLAIM, 1996.

Ross, Andrew C., *David Livingstone: Mission and Empire*, London: Hambledon and London, 2002.

Ross, Kenneth R. (ed.), *Christianity in Malawi: A Source Book*, Gweru: Mambo/ Zomba: Kachere, 1996.

Ross, Kenneth R. (Ed.), *Faith at the Frontiers of Knowledge*, Blantyre: CLAIM/Kachere, 1998.

Ross, Kenneth R. (ed.), *God, People and Power in Malawi: Democratization in Theological Perspective*, Blantyre: CLAIM-Kachere, 1996.

Ross, Kenneth R., *Here comes your King: Christ, Church and Nation in Malawi*, Blantyre: CLAIM, 1998.

Rowley, H., *The Story of the Universities Mission to Central Africa from its Commencement under Bishop MacKenzie to its withdrawal from the Zambezi*, London: Saunders, 1867[2].

Saunders, D.L., 'A History of Baptists in East and Central Africa', Southern Baptist Seminary 1973 [unpublished PhD thesis].

Schoffeleers, M., 'The Meaning and Use of the Name Malawi in Oral Traditions and Precolonial Documents', in: B. Pachai (ed.), *The Early History of Malawi*, London: Longman, pp.91-103.

Schoffeleers, J.M., 'The Religious Significance of Bush Fires in Malawi' in: *Cahiers des Religions Africaines*, no 10, pp.271-287.

Schoffeleers, J.M., and I. Linden, 'The Resistance of the Nyau Cult to the Catholic Mission in Malawi', in: Ranger and Kimbambo (eds), *The Historical Study of African Religion*, London: Heinemann, 1972.

Schoffeleers, J.M., *River of Blood: the genesis of a martyr cult in Southern Malawi c. AD 1600*, Madison: University of Wisconsin 1992.

Schoffeleers, J.M., *In Search of Truth and Justice: Confrontation between Church and State in Malawi 1960-1994*, Blantyre: CLAIM, 1999.

Schoffeleers, J.M., *Pentecostalism and Neo-Traditionalism: The Religious Polarization of a Rural District in Southern Malawi*, Amsterdam: Free University Press, 1985.

Schoffeleers, J.M., *Religion and the Dramatisation of Life: Spirit Beliefs and Rituals in Southern and Central Malawi*, Blantyre: CLAIM, 1997.

Scott, D.C., and A. Hetherwick, *Dictionary of the Nyanja Language: Being the Encyclopaedic Dictionary of the Mang'anja Language*, London: United Society for Christian Literature, Lutterworth Press, 1929 [reprinted 1951, 1957].

Selfridge, J.C., *Jack of All Trades Mastered by One*, Fearn: Christian Focus, 1989.

Shelburne, C.B., 'History of the Church of Christ in Malawi', np, nd [A brief factual account of the history of the Church of Christ in southern Malawi].

Shepperson, G. and Th. Price, *Independent African: John Chilembwe and the Origins, Setting and Significance of the Nyasaland Rising of 1915*, Edinburgh UP, 1958 [re-edited: Blantyre: CLAIM, 2000].

Smart, Y.J., Msinkhu, 'Zionism in Malawi: The History and Theology of Zion City Church in Ntcheu District', Unpubl thesis University of Malawi, 2005.

Strohbehn, Ulf, *Pentecostalism in Malawi: A History of the Apostolic Faith Mission 1931-1994*, Zomba: Kachere, 2005.

Stuart, R.G., *Christianity and the Chewa: the Anglican Case 1885-1950*, unpublished PhD thesis, University of London, 1974.

Stuart-Mogg, David, *Mlozi of Central Africa: Trader, Slaver and self-styled Sultan: The End of a Slaver*, Blantyre: Central Africana 2010.

Tembo, Masiye, *Touched By His Grace: A Ngoni Story of Tragedy and Triumph*, Zomba: Kachere, 2005.

Thiessen, Anne, *The Warm Heart of Africa*, Winona: Choate Publ., 1998.

Thompson, T.J., 'African Leadership in the Livingstonia Mission 1875-1900', in: *Malawi Journal of Social Science*, vol.2 (1973), pp.76-91.

Thompson, T.J., 'Xhosa Missionaries in Late Nineteenth-century Malawi: Strangers or Fellow Countrymen?', in: *Religion in Malawi*, no 8 (1998), pp.8-16.

Thompson, T.J., *Christianity in Northern Malawi: Donald Fraser's Missionary Methods and Ngoni Culture*, Leiden: Brill, 1995.

Thompson, T.J., *Touching the Heart: Xhosa Missionaries to Malawi 1876-1888*, Pretoria: Unisa, 2000.

Tindall, P.E.N., *History of Central Africa*, London: Longman, 1997 [first 1968].

Van Dijk, R.A., *Young Malawian Puritan Preachers in a Present-day African Urban Environment* [PhD-dissertation], Utrecht UP, 1992.

Vezeau, R., *The Apostolic Vicariate of Nyasa: Origins and First Developments 1889-1935*, Rome: Missionari d'Africa, 1989 [re-edited by Kachere: Zomba, 2006].

Vezeau, R., *The Church in Malawi: The History of Bembeke Parish*, Dedza: Private, 1982.

Wendland, Ernst R., *Buku Loyera: An Introduction to the New Chichewa Bible Translation*, Blantyre, CLAIM/ Kachere, 1998.

Wendland, Ernst, H., *A History of the Christian Church in Central Africa: The Lutheran Church of Central Africa 1953-1978*, Wisconsin: Mequon, 1980.

White, L., *Magomero: Portrait of an African Village*, Cambridge UP, 1987.

Wills, A.J., *An Introduction to the History of Central Africa*, London: Oxford UP, 1964.

Wilson, G. Herbert, *The History of the Universities' Mission to Central Africa*, Westminster: Central Africa House, 1936.

63. Europe and Africa in the Post-Modern Age

63.1. Minority and Majority positions

a. Shift of appearances

It is hazardous to conclude a history book like this with a glance at the future. Yet past and future touch each other. That is particularly true for the history of the Church of Christ. It embodies the reality of the Kingdom of God, which belongs to the past and to the present, and which will come in its fullness. For this chapter the meeting point is imaginary, because our description of the history of the Church in Europe and in Africa ends in the decades around the turn of the Millennium. In an account of history the meeting point between past and present already belongs to history itself.

On the eve of the 21st century the institutional appearance of the Church in Europe, and to a lesser degree in North America, found itself in a process of erosion, at least in terms of membership. In the Modern Age, particularly from the time of the Enlightenment and more conspicuously since the 19th century, the Church had gradually moved from a majority to a minority position, gaining momentum dramatically after the *Second World War*.[1] The Church in Africa, on the other hand, moved after the war and especially after the end of Western colonialism, approximately 1960, from a minority to a majority position. In terms of formal allegiance the Church left African Traditional Religions far behind and by mid-1960s it had also overtaken Islam numerically.

b. Post-Christian culture

The process of secularization of the Modern Age has weakened the mother churches in Europe to such an extent that they have lost their powerful influence in society. Consequently, Europe in the Post-Modern Age again has become a mission field. Many believe that Biblical revelation and the Christian faith are not unique and that in the end all religions lead to the same goal. This misleading idea has influenced various post-modern theologians.[2] Fortunately, new missionary activities have been developed by church-denominations and Christian agencies that have not bowed down to this idea. But it must be doubted whether their impact is sufficient to reach the mass of secularized city-dwellers, who have no Bible knowledge and have grown up in all kinds of post-Christian cultural settings. What makes their missionary task harder is the presence of millions of Asian and African Muslims, who for various reasons have settled in Europe, and in many respects have become conscious and active or even radicalized agents of their own religion.

---

[1] Cf. chapter 41.5.: Church in Crisis
[2] In post-modern theology Einstein's adage has been influential: 'All religions, arts and sciences are branches of the same tree'. Cf. Paas, *Liefde voor Israël nader bekeken*, op. cit. pp.33,34.

63.2. The Faith Moves North

a. The Blessed Reflex

In this situation of the African and European branches of the Church the question arises: Who needs who? There are two sides, the European one and the African one: (a) Where the European churches are concerned, does Africa still need their help, financially, spiritually, and theologically? Are they still in a position to continue their classical role of assisting African churches? Are they welcome as such?
(b) Where the African Church

Nigerian-born Matthew Ashimolowo, charismatic and widely known Pastor of Kingsway International Christian Centre (KICC), a mega church based in London.

is concerned, is it able and willing to assist in re-evangelizing Europe? Does Europe welcome African missionary activities? Do Africans find access to the modern 'heathen' in the European cities? Do European churches entrust this task to their African brethren? Let us first look at (b).

African Christian presence in Europe does not need to wait for the first missionaries to be sent. Since the 1960s millions of African refugees, among them many Christians, have entered Europe. Poverty, dictatorial regimes, war, and repression by radicalized Islamic movements have made people decide on flight. They accept the risk of losing their lives at the hands of traffickers on the dangerous land and sea-routes that lead to the gates of 'fortress' Europe. Many of those who do not perish are allowed to stay. Consequently, almost all European cities have congregations of African Christians. This means that African 'reverse missionaries'[3] are already present in the heartlands of the secularized Western society. For Harvey Kwiyani[4] the reality of African immigrants in Europe is part of 'the blessed reflex', a fulfilment of the vision of 19th-century missionaries, who expected a day in which Christians from Africa and other parts of the non-western world would travel to Europe to strengthen Christianity there and to re-evangelize the European peoples.

After moving south, the Faith is now in the process of moving north. Kwiyani shows, however, that the start of African mission is much older than that. He writes: 'Historically African Christianity has held missionary impulse since the days of the

---

[3] The term 'Reverse Missionaries' became more widely known through American and British TV broadcasts. Non-European missionaries were followed as they travelled to the West to find out about the historical roots of their faith and tried to address secularized Americans and Europeans with the Gospel of Jesus Christ. Cf. Ruth Giedhill, 'How reverse missionaries built the UK's fastest-growing church': on the establishment in 1952 and the growth to almost 300 congregations in 2014 of the Redeemed Christian Church of God [Internet].

[4] Harvey C. Kwiyani, *Sent Forth: African Missionary Work in the West*, American Society of Missiology Series, No 51, Mary Knoll N.Y.: Orbis Books, 2014.

Early Church, one that continued throughout history in many contexts, including the United States'. For him the 'blessed reflex' is the belief that the continued evangelization of the world needs 'the energies of the African churches'. Europe can also profit from the communal characteristic in African philosophy and spirituality, the 'ubunthu' or 'umunthu',[5] the idea of 'we are and therefore I am' as opposed to the individualistic Western individualism of 'I think, therefore I am'.

In general, African Christianity is more orthodox than European Christianity. The movements of Humanism and Enlightenment do not spring from African soil. The consequences are both negative and positive. Africa profited less than Europe from the fruits of science and technology, which came from these movements. At the same time, the Enlightenment has had less opportunity in Africa to undermine the Christian faith in God and Scripture than it has had in the West. Africa has kept its own spiritual perspective, which has enabled it to make its own choices. This means that African Christians in Europe in their own way have a Gospel-message about Christ and salvation to tell that most Europeans have lost sight of. However, in evangelistic communication, racial and cultural differences and contradictions should not be underestimated.

Pastor Sunday Adelaja is a the founder and pastor of the 30,000-member strong Blessed Embassy of the Kingdom of God for All Nations in Kiev, Ukraine. This is the largest African-led church in Europe with most of its members being Europeans.

African Christianity has appeared in Europe in its many flavours. While the Pentecostal/evangelical stream dominates, it is not difficult to find African versions of Western denominations in many cities in Europe and North America; for instance, congregations identifying themselves as Ghanaian Methodists, Tanzanian Lutherans, Malawian Presbyterians, and Nigerian Anglicans can be found in London today. In addition, there is also a significant presence of African independent churches in Europe. Zionist and Kimbanguist Christians can be seen in large numbers in Brussels while the church of the Brotherhood of the Cross and Star has its largest temple (known as Bethel) outside Africa in Elephant

A church building of the Brotherhood of the Cross and Star in Elephant and Castle, London. The Brotherhood is a Nigerian African Independent Church

---

[5] *umunthu* (Chichewa) comes from *munthu*, which means 'human being'. *Umunthu* refers to the essence of being a human of good moral qualities. Cf.Harvey C. Kwiyani, 'Coming of Age', op.cit. p.12.

and Castle, London. All these 'types' of African Christianity hope for continued presence in Europe. However, they pose a challenge to Western Christians, how do they relate with them?[6]

b. Racist tensions

Harvey Kwiyani notices that the African missionary potential in Europe has not yet become really effective. African missiological impact is marginal, despite the functioning of a few African bishops, priests, ministers and pastors in some European mainline churches. One reason is that Africans often do not understand the European mission field and therefore do not see how to be effective. As a more important reason he detects racial tendencies in the attitudes on both sides. They are sometimes unconscious, sometimes consciously hidden, but always harmful to the process of the two sides finding one another. Although there are notable exceptions of African presence in European churches,[7] Kwiyani is right in arguing that in general Western Christians have not yet welcomed African Christians and encouraged them to live and work in their midst as members of their own churches. African immigrant Christians often miss hospitality and spirituality in the mainline churches. That is one of the reasons why they join or constitute their own African congregations of immigrants. There are also mutual misunderstandings on what hospitality really means.[8] Kwiyani points out tensions between African and Western Christians. 'Both camps need to slow down and engage each other in thoughtful conversations, listening to what God may be saying through the other. Such conversations are good for the entire enterprise of theology.'[9] Considering the multi-ethnic and cultural diversity of Europe and North America, Kwiyani thinks that 'God's preferred future for mission' is a multicultural missionary movement with emphatic African participation.[10]

Stefan Paas discusses African participation in the new situation of world mission, in which any place can be mission base and mission field at the same time. In his view, the success of African Christian mission in the West depends on whether African Christans will really understand the characteristics of the modern culture of the urbanized peoples of Europe (and America), and for an explanation of their lack of missionary fruits will look beyond the classical reproach of Western racism. In that modern culture Christianity has been replaced by a completely different set of beliefs, which are disconnected from traditional faith in the God of Scriptures. Consequently, in secularized Westerners the old faith cannot be revived or restored. Simply because there is nothing to be restored or revived. The modern culture of urbanized Europe has become a non-Christian culture that should be treated as the early missionaries did with the cultures of Hindu India and Confucian China. African immigrant Christians who feel a responsibility for the European mission field should take this to heart.[11]

---

[6] Harvey C. Kwiyani, "The Mission of God Belongs to Africa Too: The Emerging Story of the African Missionary Movement", in: *Journal of Contemporary Christian Studies* 1, no. 1 (2014): pp. 80-98.

[7] A popular example is the Ugandan John Tucker Mugabi Sentamu (b.1949), who has been the Archbishop of York since 2005.

[8] Kwiyani, *Sent Forth*, pp.162, 188-190.

[9] Kwiyani, *Sent Forth*, p.158.

[10] Kwiyani, *Sent Forth*, pp.168,169, 204.

[11] Stefan Paas, 'Mission from Anywhere to Europe: Americans, Africans, and Australians Coming to

Apart from the African immigrant churches in the West, the churches of the African continent are called on for doing mission work. Peter Vumisa stresses that the Church in Africa should 'change from seeing herself as an object of missions to becoming a subject of missions'. He points to a lack of missionary vision and strategies while the Lord calls His people to the mission fields both inside and outside Africa. The Church, he says, 'must respond by creating an enabling environment for young people to be trained, sent and supported as cross-cultural missionaries'.[12]

Preoccupation with racial differences or ethnic characteristics is not only to be found among tribal Africans. In general, the white race has been notorious for expressions of racism, especially since the 19th century when the evolution theory of Charles Darwin (1809-1882) was misused for the invention of theories of racial superiority. There is a link to the ideology and practice of *apartheid* in South Africa. But there is also a connection with the phenomena of Christian Zionism or Israelism and its counterpart Antisemitism.

A meeting in Leeds of African Pentecostal pastors who live and work in Great Britain.

c. Christian Zionism and Antisemitism

Study of the Scriptures and of Church History has led me to the conclusion that Christian Zionism or Israelism is an excessive fascination with the people, the land and the religion of post-Biblical physical Israel, which particularly in its reaction against the shameful Holocaust events, in contradiction to Scripture, gives today's physical and ethnic Israel key roles in the history and the order of salvation, thus decentralizing Christ and undermining the Church's universal mission. The movement has distorted the definitions of Christianity and Judaism, and has failed to avoid antisemitism and philosemitism, despite its objective of combating the former.[13]

Amsterdam', in: Brill, *Mission Studies* 32 (2015), pp.4-31 [pp.11-17: 'African Mission in Europe'].

[12] Peter Vumisa (ed.), *Evangelical Christian Missions: An African Perspective*, Bloemfontein: African Sun Media, 2012, pp.9,91-115.

[13] Steven Paas, *Christian Zionism Examined: A Review of Ideas on Israel, the Church and the Kingdom,*

Originally, like Antisemitism or hatred against Jews, Christian Zionism is a Western phenomenon. One of its causes is the mixing of religious and political power. In Israel before the period of captivity king and temple-religion were closely connected to one another. In Christ this connection was fulfilled and given its final meaning. His Kingdom is not of this world. The Church should not be in alliance with the political rulers but has an independent task of its own. Unfortunately, ever since the adoption of Christianity by the State, Church and State in Europe have very often disobeyed this rule. With the first Christian Emperor, Constantine the Great, the *Corpus Christianum* or the Christian Empire began to put itself in the place that had been occupied by Biblical Israel in the plan of God. Contrary to the Gospel-meaning of Scripture the rulers of Church and State acted as if after Christ the specific character of the covenant with Israel had been continued and given to the Roman Empire and its successors. The Jews, who rejected Christ and the Church, consequently continued to claim a special position for Israel and Judaism in God's plan. As such, they behaved as competitors of the Roman Empire, which unleashed anti-Jewish hatred and persecution. The European tradition of Antisemitism among some Christians continued until the position of Christianity began to erode and the institutional Church could no longer derive power from its relationship with the State. After the Holocaust, among Christians the opposite philosemitic position became popular, with one-sided sympathies for present-day Israel and the religion of Judaism. Strikingly in it the same mistaken idea of ethnic or racial preferences and conditions in God's plan of salvation is adhered to that led to antisemitism in the past.

One should notice that Antisemitism and Christian Zionism have not existed at all times and at all places. Outside Europe, for example in sub-Saharan Africa and China, these phenomena have never been known. Present-day expressions of Antisemitism in the Islamic world are heavily influenced by Western antisemitic ideologies.[14] Extraordinary preoccupation with post-Biblical Israel, either in love or in hate, is a consequence of literal reading of isolated Old Testament pericopes and especially of a hermeneutical approach that is not centralised in Christ and not enveloped by the light of the New Testament. The Reformer Martin Luther is one of the representatives of classical theology who emphatically opposed this method of understanding the Scriptures. His Christocentric exegesis took a principled stand against any explanation of a Bible verse that does not 'drive' its readers to Christ.[15] Unfortunately, Luther's criticism of Judaism, because of its rejection of Jesus as Son of God and the Messiah, was sometimes misunderstood as Antisemitism.[16] Christian Zionists do not distinguish Antisemitism and Anti-Judaism. It all boils down to hatred of the Jews. They accuse the Church in the whole of its history from the New Testament onwards of Antisemitism and complicity with those who committed the Holocaust-genocide and other crimes against the Jews. Therefore, they want to redefine classical theology in its entirety and purify it from anti-Jewish elements. This is an impossible and dangerous enterprise that necessarily will have to declare the New Testament and parts of the Old Testament as antisemitic.

Nürnberg, Verlag für Theologie und Religionswissenschaft, 212, pp.55,105-114.

[14] Steven Paas, *Liefde voor Israël nader bekeken: Voor het Evangelie zijn alle volken gelijk*, Kampen: Brevier, 1015,pp.125-131.

[15] Paas, *Idem*, chapter 2 ('Luther en Christus'), pp.31-53.

[16] Paas, *Idem*, chapter 3 ('Luther en de Judaïsten'), pp.54-84.

Also at this point African missionaries have an important role to play. They are completely free of the Holocaust tradition. Their defence of classical Christocentric hermeneutics cannot be suspected of having a double agenda, hiding antisemitic motivation.

d. Enlightenment suspicions

Many African missionaries tend to think that they are called to correct Western Christianity. Especially they suspect the effects of the Enlightenment on Western Christianity.They think the Enlightenment and its succesors of philosophical Modernism and Secularism have relegated spiritual values to the private domain and have reserved the public domain for reason, logic and science. This has influenced Western Christianity so that it has not only segregated the head and the heart but it has also overemphasized both in being focused on man at the detriment of the knowing and feeling that man depends on God. Especially among African Pentecostals there is a feeling that Western systematic theology is ruled by humanistic logic and less by the Holy Spirit. According to them, there is a serious deficit of pneumatology in American and European theology. And that is why they think African missionaries in the West need to be careful how they negotiate their relationship with the the traditions of the Enlightenment and Western Christianity/theology.[17]

63.3. European Christians and Africa

a. Hospitality

In the global village with almost unlimited opportunities for travel and internet communication Europeans and Africans have not only become close neighbours, but also frequent guests. Our age of increased mobility has brought many immigrants to Europe. This has created serious problems, but has offered new opportunities too. A very important task for European Christians is being hospitable and showing love to the Africans who for various reasons either permanently or temporarily have settled in their midst, especially to the Christian brethren among them. Such a welcoming attitude is an expression of basic Christianity. It also facilitates missionary activity by African Christians in their new environment. In this way African and European Christians strengthen one another when they meet with the enormous challenge of re-evangelizing Europe.

b. Muslim Mission

What about other responsibilities of European Christians with regard to Africa? In several respects Africa has become a Christian continent. Of course, that is not true for Muslim North Africa and for the regions immediately south of the Sahara, where Islam is numerically in the lead. Yet this means that the classical task of mission in Africa by European churches has practically ended. These days traditional mission fields in Africa are limited to the regions where Muslims live. However, it is not the European churches

---

[17] Harvey Kwiyani, 'Conversations with African Pastors in the Diaspora', at his blog http://harvmins.com/2013/11/16/conversations_intro/.

but their African sisters who are responsible for Muslim mission in their own countries. Here Western churches can assist, not only financially, but also with their specific expertise that has been shaped by their work among Muslims in the Middle East and in the Far East.

c. Harmful influences

Taking into account the complex reality of mutuality between Europe and Africa, what can European churches contribute to African Christianity? There are both negative and positive answers to this question. European churches add nothing, rather harm African Christianity, if they have distanced themselves from the roots of Biblical faith. African criticism of the Enlightenment is justified in so far its effects have led to a secularized humanism that has introduced the fiction of the autonomy of man and has no room for the supremacy of God. Only those Western churches which operate from the classical Christ-centred confessions of Christianity can meaningfully assist sister-churches in other parts of the world. Christianity is not assisted by gradually dying liberal denominations, which propagate the abandonment of the authority of Scripture as God's revelation and consider other religions, apart from Jesus Christ, as equally valid ways of salvation. Africa is not being helped by churches which do not realise that Western Christianity has dwindled because its mainline representatives unfaithfully allied themselves with the philosophical systems and hedonistic self-centred ideologies and practices of the modern world. Instead of being self-critical, modest and showing respect for God's work in flourishing and growing African Christianity, they force their own liberal ethics on African Christians, including the acceptance of marriage of homosexuals and lesbians, abortion, and euthanasia.

d. Conditions

On the other hand, faithful confessing European churches continue to be important and welcome sources and tools for assistance to their sister churches in Africa. Of course, there are conditions. One should realise that African churches have had their own history in their own political, cultural, linguistic, economic and social setting. European Christians cannot offer Columbus's egg as if African Christians had not also themselves experienced a process of learning ways and methods. Any neo-colonial attitude, racist preference, Western cultural or linguistic arrogance and disinterest in African culture and people, found in European 'fraternal helpers', despite possibly good intentions, is immediately detected by the African context and closes doors to meaningful cooperation in the Kingdom of God. European workers in Africa should not look down on African Christianity with its often comparatively brief history as they admit it is like a very wide river, but disparagingly add that it is only one foot deep. European newcomers who are rash to observe 'shallowness' in African Christianity often do not realise the danger of being biased and one-sided in their judgments. African Christian spirituality can be very deep and real, although for Western standards not connected to a lot of rational knowledge of Scripture and theology.

e. Education

Yet Bible knowledge and theological training are important. Without knowledge African Christians are exposed to the dangers of superficial pseudo-beliefs, particularly to the attractiveness of the 'prosperity gospel',[18] and to syncretism with African Tradition Religions and Islam. Therefore, Africans can profit from being taught by Western Christians who are thoroughly trained in the various subjects of theology. In the teaching of basic Reformation theology and fundamental Patrology, e.g. for hermeneutics, exegesis, dogmatics, and church history, Western churches can give a lasting contribution to African Christianity. However, this teaching of the African church must involve African teachers of theology who are emerging across the continent. Western Christians have also to expect to be taught by and learn from African Christians. This teaching goes both ways.

f. Church and Mission

Besides, African churches need to be assisted in the fields of mission and diaconal work. African churches cannot continue to rely on Europe or America for activities in these fields. Mission is a natural responsibility of any church. Making Africans more aware of that missiological truth can be a task for Western Christian expatriates in Africa. If the sending out of African missionaries is hindered by poverty and lack of funds, by mutual agreement a plan can be devised in which Western churches assist the financing of African missionary enterprises, for example by contributing to the upkeep of African workers, who are sent to their cities or to the Muslim world.

g. Church and Diaconia

Africans should also realise that despite relative poverty African churches, like the Church in general, are naturally responsible for organising and carrying out diaconal activities for their own members, and in cases of emergency for others as well. Of course, when comparatively rich Western churches point to this important issue and contribute to the teaching about it, they have their own diaconal responsibilities as well, which can lead to relief campaigns in assistance of the diaconal outreach by African sister churches in cases of earthquakes, floods, epidemics, famine and war.

63.4. The Militant Church

The Church in Europe and America and the Church in Africa are in different positions. But both should remember how Jesus saw the future of the Church. The Gospel will reach to the ends of the earth,[19] so that the Church will consist of all the elect of all places. Then, He will come back to take her as His bride to eternal glory. This is a very hopeful perspective. At the same time, however, the Lord says that His Church will be powerless in worldly terms, disrespected and persecuted. That is the most 'normal' situation for the Church in this world. The history of the Church shows that in many places and at many times, Christians have been discriminated against or hunted down because of the Name of Jesus: Christians in the Roman Empire until 313, Christians of

---

[18] Viateur Habarurema, *Christian Generosity according to 2 Cor.8-9: Its Exegesis, Reception, and Interpretation Today in Dialogue with the Prosperity Gospel in Sub-Saharan Africa*, Protestantse Theologische Universiteit, Groningen, 2015, compares the prosperity gospel in Sub-Saharan Africa with the medieval belief in the selling and buying of indulgences that were supposed to give sinners the remission of their sins, which triggered Martin Luther to start the Reformation [cf. chapter 23.4].

[19] Mt.24:14; Acts 1:8; cf.: Ps.22:27; Is.45:22.

the Eastern Churches in the Persian Empire, the Lollards, the Waldenses, the Hussites, the Anabaptists, the Huguenots, and others in the time of the Reformation, Christians under Buddhist, Hindu, Muslim, communist and national-socialist regimes, the Ugandan Martyrs, and the victims of Boko Haram and Al Shabaab. The Church before the Second Coming of Christ is not yet a glorious Church; she lives by the Cross and like Her Master she is suffering. However, like He, in her weakness she is victorious and is winning the hearts of all who God has destined for salvation. Ultimately the powers of hell and Satan will be powerless in their attempts to conquer the Church.[20]

Since the time of Constantine the Church in the West has been closely connected to the vestiges of political power and respectability. At times this has helped her to grow. But modern secularized people have withdrawn themselves from her message and influence. They have come to mistrust a church that has been glorified because of her all-embracing religious and cultural image and her relationship to political dominion. Now the Church in Europe and America is being stripped of the many nominal members she has harboured. Denominations are becoming small. Consequently, the Church has to go back to her New Testament origin, the image of the weakness of the Cross of Christ, who said: 'My power is made perfect in weakness'.[21] That is the message of the Gospel, which through the Holy Spirit will convince future generations of genuine believers.

The Church in Africa still is numerically large and influential, not only spiritually strong but also in cultural and political terms. In African public opinion it is fashionable to be a Christian. However, we should not be silent about the fact that many members do not know Christ as their personal Saviour; their membership is just nominal or not founded in faith. Nominal Christians are spiritually dead, they cannot stand in the battle against the looming danger of syncretism, the modern grasp of atheist globalism, and the radicalisation and growth of the religion of Islam, which 'will likely surpass Christians'[22] in numbers again. It is wholesome for Africans to be taught by the history of the birth, the growth and the downfall of Western Christianity and by the example of how in these days a Church has been guided by the Word and the Spirit to repack herself and to find her way, following the crucified and risen Lord, in the struggle of faith in a secularised society.

---

[20] Mt.16:18.
[21] 2 Cor.12:9.
[22] Michael Lipka and Thomas Hacket, 'Why Muslims are the world's fastest-growing religious group' [Internet]: 'Muslims will grow more than twice as fast as the overall world population between 2010 and 2050 and, in the second half of this century, will likely surpass Christians as the world's largest religious group.'

O God, our help in ages past

Isaac Watts, 1674-1748

1. O God, our help in ages past,
 our hope for years to come,
 our shelter from the stormy blast,
 and our eternal home.

2. Under the shadow of thy throne,
 still may we dwell secure;
 sufficient is thine arm alone,
 and our defense is sure.

3. Before the hills in order stood,
 or earth received her frame,
 from everlasting, thou art God,
 to endless years the same.

4. A thousand ages, in thy sight,
 are like an evening gone;
 short as the watch that ends the night,
 before the rising sun.

5. Time, like an ever rolling stream,
 bears all who breathe away;
 they fly forgotten, as a dream
 dies at the opening day.

6. O God, our help in ages past,
 our hope for years to come;
 be thou our guide while life shall last,
 and our eternal home.

Register

A

Abarohi movement, 407, 488
Abbasid dynasty, 298
Abdallah Marshambo, King, 309
Abelard, Peter, 128, 148
Abeokuta, 342, 343
Abgar, King, 68
Abraham, 92, 110
Absolutism, 243
Abu Bakr, 111
Abun (of Ethiopia), 311, 314, 315, 316, 317
Abyssinia, 110, 111, 131
Acco, 139, 140
Accommodation Theory, 237
Accrediting Council for Theological Education (ACTEA), 438
Achamoth, 76
Actium, 42
Acts of Martyrs, 63
Ad Fontes, 163
Adeodatus, 93
Adeyemo, Tokunboh, 418
Adoptionism, 79, 123, 315
Adowa, battle of, 318
Adrianople, 102
Adriatic Sea, 131
Aedesius, 310
Aeon, 76
Afghanistan, 113
Africa Evangelical Church of Malawi, 465
Africa Inland Mission (AIM), 347, 365, 372, 399, 400, 401, 424, 427, 428, 437, 510
Africa, James Mullan, 488
African Baptist Assembly, 465
African Congregational Theology, Network for (NetAct), 438
African Greek Orthodox Church, 405
African Independent Churches Association (AICA.), 439
African Instituted Churches (AIC), 401, 405, 408, 411, 412, 416, 420, 488, 489, 490, 491, 505
African Lakes Company (Mandala), 454
African Methodist Episcopal Church (AMEC), 262, 404, 468, 476, 516, 518
African Methodist Independent Church, 476
African National Congress (ANC), 415, 484
African Synod of 1994, 392, 393
African Theology, 269, 416, 420
African Traditional Religion (ATR), 296, 300, 324, 395, 405, 418, 419, 433, 434, 435, 491, 500, 507, 509
Africanisation, 344, 345, 411, 457, 468, 470
Afrikaner Volk, 351, 353, 448, see: Boers
Afrikaaner, Jager, 360

Afscheiding, 255
Agaja, King, 302
Agape, 492
Agathangelos, 69
Agbebi, Mojola (David Brown Vincent), 404
aggiornamento, 392
Aggrey, J.E.K., 398, 404, 405
Agnosticism, 282
Ahmad al-Mansur, King, 299
Ahmad, Imam, 313, 314
Ahmed, Muhammad, 318
Ahura Mazda, 70
AIDS, 435, 503, 504
Akan, 302, 321, 323, 416
Akinsowon (Christiana Abiodun Emmanuel, 407
Akinyele, Isaac, 407
Aladura movement, 401, 405, 407, 412, 488
Alaric, King, 102
Albert (King of Belgium), 407
Albertus Magnus, 129, 148
Albigenses, 95, 125, 129, 137, 150, 195, 214
Alcuin, 119, 122
Alembert, Jean le Rond d', 236
Alexander of Alexandria, 79
Alexandria, 48, 52, 59, 70, 71, 79, 84, 85, 99, 142, 292, 297, 309-311, 314- 317, 319
Alexandrian School, 52, 81, 84
Alexius, Emperor, 138
Alfonso I (Mvemba Nzinga) of Congo, 323, 402
Algeria, 53, 112
All Africa Conference of Churches (AACC), 437
Allah, 110, 111, 112
Allegorical Method, 52, 59
Almohad Empire, 299
Almoravid Empire, 298
Altizer, J.J., 269
Alvarez, Francisco (Portuguese diplomat), 314, 328
Alypius, 93
amaNazaretha Church, 408, 487
Amayi a Chifundo, 472
Amayi a Chigwirizano, 459
Amayi a Dorika, 472
Amayi a Mvano, 471
Amayi a Tereza, 472
Amayi a Umodzi, 471
Ambrose of Milan, 85, 94, 101
Amde-Zion of Ethiopia, 313
American Baptist Missionary Union, 381
American Bible Society, 270
American Board of Commissioners for Foreign Missions, 368, 343, 389
American Civil War, 261, 262
American Council of Churches ACC) , 271, 436
American War of Independence, 261
Amharic language, 316, 317, 319

Amin, Idi, 411, 415
Amsterdam, 192, 268, 271, 274, 275
Anabaptists, 31, 176, 178, 181, 183, 185, 186, 188, 190-193, 200, 205, 235, 531
Andel, Gerard van, 333
Andersson, Ida, 488
Anglican Church, 125, 130, 205, 206, 247, 256, 257, 259, 261
Angola, 304, 323, 324, 325, 329, 331, 347- 350, 373, 378-380, 390, 391, 414, 421, 422
Angra Mainyu, 70
Anselm of Canterbury, 146, 147, 148, 163
Anskar, Missionary, 119
anti-clericalism, 367
Antioch, 51, 52, 58, 59, 68, 70, 71, 85, 138, 140, 142
Antiochene School, 52, 81, 292
Antisemitism, 140, 282, 526, 527
Antislavery Society, 270
Antoninus Pius, Emperor, 84
Antonio I, King, 324
Antony, the heremite, 98, 99
Antwerp, 199, 200
Anund Jakon, 120
Anzanea, 303
Aoko, Gaudencio, 410
apartheid, 352, 415, 417, 418, 494
Apollo, 43
Apologeticum, 84
Apologists, 83
Apostles, 43, 57, 59, 68, 83
Apostolic Church, 255
Apostolic Confession of Faith/ Creed, 80, 185
Apostolic Faith Mission, 467, 486, 487, 489
Apostolic Fathers, 57, 58, 59, 83
Apostolic Succession, 58, 247
Apostolus Armatus, 123
Aquinas, Thomas, see: Thomas Aquinas
Arabs/ Arabia, 68, 71, 97, 110-114, 131, 136, 268
Aramaic, 68
Arbil, Chronicle of, 69
Archaeology, 25, 30
Arckel, Johan van, 333
Arethas, 71
Arianism/ Arius, 54, 65, 73, 75, 79, 80, 81, 95, 101, 102, 190
Aristides, 84
Aristotle, 46, 146
Armenia, 51, 68, 69, 70, 95, 131
Arminianism/ 202, 249, 254, 256, 261, 262
Arminius, Jacobus/, 199
Arnaud, Antoine, 242
Arnaud, Jacqueline, 242
Ascesis/ Ascetism, 82, 98, 126, 133, 151
Ashanti people, 302, 376, 396
Ashmun, Jehudi, 345
Asia/Asia Minor, 50-52, 73, 74, 101, 112, 131, 136, 138, 162, 189, 238, 249, 267
Assemblies of God, 350, 383, 468, 472, 487-489

Association of Evangelical Churches of West Africa (AECWA), 438
Association of Evangelicals of Africa (AEA), 418, 438
Assyrian Christians, 131
Astruc, Jean, 265
Athanasian Confession of Faith, 80
Athanasius, 52, 80, 98, 99, 292, 310
Aufklaerung, 234
Augsburg Interim, 181
Augsburg, Creed of, 173
Augustine (missionary), 203
Augustine of Hippo, 22, 29, 53, 54, 77-79, 82, 83, 86, 87, 92-97, 101, 104, 117, 142, 146, 147, 164-173, 203, 241, 293
Augustinian order, 130, 328
Augustus, Emperor, 42, 43
Auma, Alice, 414
Auricular Confession, 125, 169
Auschwitz-syndrome, 268
Australia, 189
Austria, 73, 113, 125, 195, 198, 238, 240, 252, 278
Averroes, 146
Awakenings, 25, 31, 237, 249, 257, 260, 270
Axum, 309, 310, 311, 312, 313
Ayyubid dynasty, 297, 309
Azariah, Samuel, 272
Azusa Street (start of Pentecostalism), 283, 486, 489

B

Babalola, Joseph, 402, 407, 488
Babylonian Captivity, 143, 169
Bachmann, Traugott, 366
Bacon, Francis, 236
Baeta, Christian, 420
Baeta, R.D., 386
Bagamoyo, 365, 366, 390
Bagster, W.W., 349
Baily, A.W., 349
Baius, Michel, 241
Bakker, Jan de, 199
Balano, Alfonso de, 322
Balokole (East Africa Revival), 409, 410, 411, 412, 488
balubaala cult, 366, 367
Banana, Canaan, 482, 484
Banda, Hastings Kamuzu, 468, 469, 478
Banda, John Afwenge, 473
Baptism/ Baptists, 59, 60, 65, 96, 118, 121, 135, 169, 171, 173, 178, 190-193, 205, 241, 247, 260, 262, 278
Baptist Convention, 350, 465, 470, 471, 495
Baptist Foreign Mission Society (BFMS), 389
Baptist Missionary Society (BMS), 257, 339, 343, 346, 347, 348, 389, 421, 463
Baptist World Alliance, 271
Baqt, Treaty of, 308

Bar Kokhba, Simon, 49
Bartholomew, Night of St.,196
Bardaisan, 69
Barmer Declaration, 281
Barnabas, 51, 59
Barnabas, letter to, 59
Barnabas, Pseudo-, 83
Barrett, David, 26, 374, 403, 420
Barron, Edward, 346
Barrowe, Henry (Martyr), 205
Barth, Karl, 266, 267
Bartle Frere, Henry, 364
Basel Evangelical Missionary Society, 343, 346, 386, 399
Basel, Council of, 144, 151
Basilius The Great, 80
Bauern Mission, 319, 355, 389
Baviaan Kloof (Genadendal), 334
Bayle, Pierre, 236
Bayudaya, 412
Beaton, James, 209
Bediako, Kwame, 26, 32, 418, 420, 508
Belgian (Belgium), 381, 382, 383, 391, 392, 396, 399, 407, 488
Belgium, 73, 195, 198, 199, 200, 213
Bemba people, 304, 473, 474, 475, 477, 478
Benedict of Aniane, 126
Benedict of Nursia, 99, 126
Benedict XII, 143
Benedictine Rule, 99, 126
Bengel, Johann Albrecht, 252
Benin (Dahomey), 302, 321, 323, 324, 385, 488
Bennett, Dennis J., 284, 490
Berbers, 92, 96, 299, 102
Berlin Conference (1884/ 1885), 348, 371, 373, 375, 381, 384, 386, 389, 395, 396
Berlin Mission, 355, 366, 481
Bernard of Clairvaux, 127, 128, 138, 148, 151, 195
Berwick On Tweed, 209
Bessieux, Jean, 347
Bet Abba Libanos, 312
Bethel Mission, 366
Betsileo people, 368
Bevan, Thomas, 369
Beyers Naudé C.F., 415
Beza, Theodorus, 187
Bhengu, Nicolas, 488
Biddle, John, 249
Biko, Steven Bantu, 417
Bingham, Roland V., 428
Bismarck, Joseph, 457
Bismarck, Otto von, 365, 386, 457
Black Theology movement, 269, 403, 417
Blandina, 54
Blantyre Mission, 450, 456-458, 463, 467
Blaurock, George, 192
Blessed Reflex, 523
Blood Council, 200
Blyden, Edward Wilmot, 18, 344, 345, 405

Board of Commissioners for Foreign Mission, 346, 349
Boers, 331-333, 337, 351-359, 368, 373, 375
Boesak, Allan, 269, 415, 417
Boethius, 146
Bogomils, 95
Bokwito, Tom, 453, 456
Bolsec, Jerome, 186
Bonhoeffer, Dietrich, 281
Boniface IV, Pope, 75
Boniface VIII, Pope, 143, 154, 164
Boniface, Missionary, 99, 117-119, 122
Bonnke, Rheinhard, 491
Book of Common Order (Book of Geneva), 210
Book of Common Prayer, 182, 204, 210, 211, 223, 228
Book of Discipline, 211
Book of Geneva (Book of Common Order), 210
Boom, Corrie ten, 280
Booth, Joseph, 397, 404, 425, 463-465, 478
Booth, William, 255
Bora, Katherina von, 171
Boru Meda, Council of, 318
Bossuet, Jean Bénigne, 240
Bourget, Pierre, 461
Bowes, Marjorie, 209
Bradford Apostolic Church, 488
Braide, Garrick Sokari Daketima, 344, 406
Brainerd, David, 260
Brakel, Wilhelmus à, 250
Branch, Mable, 464, 465
Bremen Mission, 346, 386
Brent, C.H., 272
Brethren (brothers) of The Common Life, 152, 179, 199
Brethren (Plymouth Brethren.), 334, 349, 353, 354, 359, 421-424, 428, 468, 475, 476
Briggs, Charles, 266
British Council of Churches, 271
British/ Britain, 306, 317, 318, 333-337
Broad Church, 248
Brown, Samuel, 342
Browne, Robert, 205
Brudergemeinde, 252
Brunner, Emil, 267
Buber, Martin, 267
Bucer, Martin, 165, 172, 173, 176, 179, 180-193, 215, 271, 436
Büchler, Johannes, 487
Buganda (in Uganda), 304, 366, 367, 377
Buku Lopatulika (Holy Book), 459
Bulgaria, 95, 132, 134, 137, 278
Bultmann, Rudolf, 267, 268
Bunyan, John, 206, 228, 230, 235, 369, 370
Buren, Idelette van, 186
Burkina Faso, 385, 418, 488
Burundi, 304, 383, 386, 387, 388, 488
Bushnell, Horace, 265
Busskampf, 252
Buthelezi, Manas, 269, 417

Butscher, L., 342
Buys people, 481
Byzantine/ Byzantium, 101, 102, 104, 110, 112, 132, 134, 138, 140, 150

C

Caecilian, Bishop, 96
Caesaro-papism, 132
Caius Octavianus, Emperor, 42
Cajetanus, Thomas de Vio, Cardinal, 168, 179
Calixtus, Bishop, 90
Calvary Family Church, 492
Calvin, John, 96. 165, 172, 173, 178, 182-199, 204, 205, 210, 215, 251, 271, 436, 513
Calvinist/ Calvinism, 178, 187, 189, 194, 195, 199, 200, 205, 215, 247, 254, 262
Cameroon, 346, 378, 385, 388, 399
Candace, 307, 403
Canon Law, 122, 127
Canons of Dordt, 202, 249
Canossa, 124, 127
Canterbury, 117, 143, 182, 204
Cape General Mission (CGM), 357
Cape Maclear, 453, 456, 458
Cape of Good Hope, 321, 326, 337
Cape Town, 306, 331, 337, 355, 450, 453, 465
Cape Verde, 322, 379
Capitein, Jacobus Eliza, 329, 330
Cappadocian Fathers, 52, 80
Capuchin order, 317, 322, 324, 325, 330, 331, 347, 348, 391
Cardobo, Antonio, 460
Cardoso, M, 324
Carey, Lott, 345
Carey, William, 257, 271, 338, 389, 421, 436
Carmelites order, 369
Carolingian Law, 190
Carolingians, 121, 122
Carr, Burgess, 437
Carr, Henry, 404
Carta Caritatis, 127
Cartesius, see: Descartes
Carthage, 53, 58, 86-90, 93, 96
Cartwright, Thomas, 205
Castellio, Sebastian, 186
Catabaptists, 178, 190
Cathari, 150
Catherina of Siena, 151
Catholic Reformation/ Resortion, 213
Celibacy, 93, 95, 99, 100, 127, 179
Celtic Church/ Celts, 51, 73-75, 99, 100, 116-121, 203, 208
Cerulanius, Patriarch, 133
Cerullo, Morris, 491
Chad, 385, 428
Chagga people, 304, 366
Chakachadza, Mark, 465
Chalcedon, Council of, 35, 53, 81, 292, 308
Chao, T.C., 274

Charismatic Movement, 283, 284, 408, 411, 439, 471, 475, 486, 488, 490-493, 498
Charlemagne/ Charles The Great, Emperor, 112, 118, 122, 123, 132, 142
Charles I, King, 206, 211
Charles II, King, 206
Charles Martel, 112, 117, 118, 122
Charles V, Emperor, 169, 170, 180, 181, 195, 198, 203, 215
Charles X, King, 244
Chaza (Mai Chaza), 410
Cherubim and Seraphim, 407
Children's Crusade, 139
Childs, Gladwyn M., 348
Chilembwe, John, 397, 398, 404, 423, 457, 463, 464-469, 519
Chiluba, Frederick (President), 415
Chimurenga, 482, 484
China, 72, 112, 131, 216, 238, 257, 258, 268, 269, 273, 274, 279
China Inland Mission (CIM), 422, 424, 463
Chinguwo, Robert, 467, 489
Chinunu, Charles, 455
Chinvat Bridge, 70
Chisumphi Cult, 499
Chitsulo, Cornelio, 470
Chiwere (Ngoni Chief), 458
Chiwona, James, 470
Chiyanjano cha Azimayi, 472
Chrischona Lutherans, 317
Christ Apostolic Church (CAC), 407, 488
Christaller, Johann Gottlieb, 346
Christian and Missionary Alliance (CMA), 427
Christian Catholic Apostolic Church in Zion, 452, 486, 487
Christian Council of Malawi, 467
Christian Hospitals Association of Malawi (CHAM), 470
Christian Mission in Many Lands (Brethren), 349, 422
Christian Reformed Mission, 390
Christian Students' Society of South Africa, 357
Christian Zionism, 282, 283, 288, 422, 445, 448, 526, 527
Christology, 52, 53, 81
Christoph da Gama, 314
Christotokos, 81
Chrysostom, Johannes, 101, 131
Chuma/ Juma (Livingstone's servant), 452
Church Fathers, 25, 52, 77, 83, 104, 146, 147, 164, 184
Church Missionary Society (CMS), 256, 257, 298, 316, 340-344, 346, 362-367, 359, 387, 389, 396, 397, 399, 402, 404, 409, 437
Church of Central Africa Presbyterian (CCAP), 352, 421, 450, 458-460, 466-471, 476-478, 483, 484, 495
Church of Christ in the Congo, 383
Church of England, 204, 210, 247, 254
Church of God Mission International, 488, 491

Church of Scotland, 208, 210, 258, 352, 354, 356, 365, 386, 399, 453, 456, 459, 473, 476
Church Order, 196
Church Session(s), 186, 188, 199, 205
Church, Joe, 409
Churches of Christ, 410, 422, 464, 472
Cistercians, Order of the 127, 151, 239
Clapham Sect, 256, 257, 338, 339, 341
Classical Missions, 339, 389, 401, 421, 424, 425, 427, 463
Claudius, Emperor, 61, 74
Clement of Alexandria, 52, 292
Clement V, Pope, 143
Clement VI, Pope, 144
Clement XIV, Pope, 245
Clericalism, 115
Clermont, Council of, 137
Clovis, King, 75, 121
Cluniacs/ Cluniac Spirit/ Cluniac Movement/ Cluny, 126, 127, 151
Coillard, François and Christine, 354, 473, 481
Colenso, John William, 355
Coligny, Gaspard de, 196
Colonialism, 110, 114, 337, 338, 350, 371-375, 383, 384, 389, 393-398, 402, 404, 410, 417, 482, 502, 503
Columba, Missionary, 75, 208
Columbanus, Missionary, 75, 99, 119
Comber, Thomas, 347
Communion of Saints, 173, 183
Communism/ Communists, 135, 192, 245, 269, 276-281, 380, 413, 437
Conceptualism, 147, 148, 149, 163
Conciliar Movement, 144, 151, 164, 214
Concordat of Worms, 125
Cone, James, 417
Confessing Church, 281
Congo, 216, 257, 304, 321-325, 329-331, 347, 349, 373, 381-385, 390, 391, 396-399, 402, 407, 416, 421, 422, 427, 428, 488, 490, see: Zaire
Congo Free State, 337, 375, 381-383, 391-397
Congregationalists, 205, 235, 257, 259, 262, 418
Conrad, Joseph, 381
Consensus Tigurensis, 178
Consistory, 188
Consolata Fathers, 365
Constance, Council of, 144, 151, 153, 271
Constantine The Great/ Magnus, 66, 76, 70, 79, 99, 80, 101, 122, 136
Constantinople, 70, 80, 101, 102, 112, 113, 116, 120, 131-142, 161, 297
Constantinople (Council of C.), 35
Constantius Chlorus, 66
Consubstantiation., 169
Cooke, Thomas, 253
Cop, Nicolas, 184
Copernicus, Nicolaus, 234
Coptic Church/ Copts, 52, 53, 131, 292, 297
Cordier (Corderius), Mathurin, 184

Counter Reformation, 129, 195, 198, 204, 213, 238, 239, 314, 391
Covenant, 41, 211
Covenant (of Grace), 312, 352, 419, 514
Cox, H., 269
Cox, Raymond G., 468
Cranmer, Thomas, 182, 188, 204, 210, 271, 436
Cromwell, Oliver, 212, 206
Crowther, Samuel Ajayi, Bishop, 342-345
Crummel, Alexander, 345
Crusades/ Crusade, 95, 104, 110, 125, 128-130, 134-141, 152, 162, 163, 256, 293, 309
Cugoano, Ottobah, 339, 402
Currie, W.T., 348
Cyprian, 53, 58, 62, 66, 83-91, 104, 164, 293
Cyril, Missionary, 134

D

Dahomey (Benin), 302, 385, 386, 488
Damascus, 113, 138
Daneel, J.W., 481
Daneel, M.L., 408, 420
Danquah, Joseph B., 269, 416
Darby, John, 255
Darwin, Charles, 526
David of Basra, 71
Davies, Richard, 342
Davies, Samuel, 261
Debre Damo monastery, 311
Debre Libanos monastery, 313
Decius, Emperor, 61, 88, 89
Deification of Man, 135
Deism/ Deists, 235, 236, 249, 261, 263
Denmark/ Danes, 73, 102, 117, 119, 143
Derr, Paul, 489
Descartes (Cartesius), Rene, 236
Dialectic Theology/ Dialectics, 175, 267
Diaz, Bartholomew, 321, 326
Dickson, Kwesi, 417
Dictionary of African Christian Biography (DACB), 29
Didache, 59, 83
Diderot, Denis, 236
Difaqane (Scattering), 332
Dingane of the Zulu, 305, 333, 352
Diocletian, Emperor, 62, 66, 95, 96
Diognetus, 59, 83
Dissenters, 205, 206
Divinity of Christ, 54
Docetism, 77, 78, 81, 133, 193
Doe, S.K., 414, 493
Domingo, Charles, 397, 464, 468
Dominican order/ Dominicans, 125, 128, 129, 143, 146, 152, 179, 214, 239, 241, 327, 480, 482, 510
Domitian, Emperor, 44, 61, 88
Donatism/ Donatist(s)/ Donatus, 54, 66, 78, 79, 87, 91, 96, 97, 190, 293
Donna Beatrice (Kempa Vita), 325, 490

Dowie, J.A., 283, 408, 486, 487
Doxology, 132
Doyle, Arthur Conan, 382
Driver, Samuel R., 265
Dualism/ Dualistic, 59, 65, 70, 76-78, 85, 94, 95, 133, 147, 148
Duns Scotus, John, 148
Dusen, Henry P. van, 274
Dutch, 184, 192, 198-207, 234, 238, 249,-261, 274, 306, 323-325, 329-337, 351-360, 368, 373, 376, 390, 458-461, 473-476, 481-483, 513, see Netherlands
Dutch Confession of Faith, 202
Dutch Reformed Church Mission, 333, 458-460, 467, 473, 483, 509, 511
Dwane, James M., 404
Dwight, Timothy, 261

E

East Africa Revival, 400, 409
East London Training Institute, 422, 425
Eastern Christianity, 120
Eastern Christianity, EC, 104, 120, 130, 131, 134, 268
Eastern Orthodox Churches (EOC), 81, 131, 134, 150, 195
Eastern Religions, 269
Ecclesiology, 25, 96, 165, 205
Echege (of Ethiopia), 315-317
Eck, Johann, 167
Eckhart (Meister), 151
Ecumenical Movement, 28, 32, 267, 270, 271, 279, 280, 283, 419, 416, 436, 437, 435
Edessa, 51, 68, 138
Edinburgh, 22, 259, 266, 271, 272, 273
Edinburgh Missionary Society (EMS), 389
Edward VI, King, 182, 204, 209
Edwards, Jonathan, 235, 257, 261, 338, 421
Église Réformée De France, 197
Église Réformée Evangelique Independente, 197
Egypt, 44, 48, 52, 53, 68, 80, 98, 103, 104, 112, 113, 131, 139, 140, 257, 292-300, 307-309, 311, 319, 370-377, 402, 403, 427, 439, 488
Eichorn, Johannes G., 265
Elders, 57, 58, 65, 90, 186, 188, 205, 211, 259
Election, 125, 128, 173, 236
Eliot, John, 256, 260
Elizabeth I, Queen, 204, 205, 210
Ella-Amida of Axum, 310
Elmina, Fort, 322, 329, 330
Elmslie, Walter, 454, 455, 458
Embden, Synod of, 200
Engels, Friedrich, 245
England, 73, 74, 117, 119, 124-126, 137, 143, 144, 150, 181, 182, 194, 197, 198, 203-211, 236, 237, 247, 252-254, 259, 260, 270, 272
Enlightenment, 22, 148, 165, 234- 237, 243, 244, 249, 250, 252, 256, 263, 265, 268, 270, 327, 338, 340, 393, 497, 498, 505, 528

Ephesus Council of, 81
Epicureans, 46, 183
Episcopal Church Government, 65, 89, 142, 211, 212
Equiano, Olaudah, 339
Erasmus, Desiderius, 151, 165, 171, 173, 175, 179, 184, 199, 234
Erhardt, Jakob J., 362, 376
Ericzoon, Barent, 329
Espirito Santo, Luis do, 480
Esschen, Johannes van, 199
Estifanites order, 313
Ethiopia, 51, 68, 71, 104, 131, 216, 294, 295, 297, 303, 304-320, 327, 328, 373-377, 402, 403, 415, 427, 428
Ethiopian Evangelical Church Mekane Yesus, 319
Ethiopianism, 18, 26, 318, 346, 397, 403, 404, 405, 410, 474
Eugenius III, Pope, 128
Eusebius, (of Caesarea) 6, 68, 69, 71, 85, 101
Eva (Krotoa), 333
Evangelical Alliance, 436
Evangelical Awakening/ Revivals, 235, 247, 250, 253, 256, 339, 402, 436
Evangelical Brethren Church, 468
Evangelical Church of Malawi (Nyasa Industrial Mission), 464
Evangelical Lutheran Church, 275
Evangelical Lutheran Church in Southern Africa, 355
Evolutionism, 263
Ewostatewos order, 313, 315
Exeter Hall Group, 256
Exsurge Domine (Papal Bull), 170
Ezana of Ethiopia, 310

F

Faith and Order Movement, 271, 436
Faith and Reason, 146, 147, 148, 163
Falashas, 316, 403
Fambidzano, 408
Fante, 321, 329, 330, 376
Faras, 307, 309
Farel, Guillaume, 185
Farrow, Lucy, 486
Fashoda incident, 375
Fasilidas of Ethiopia, 314, 315
Fatimids, 297
Faulding, Jennie (Taylor), 424
Faulkner, Swam, 349
Felicissimus, 89
Felicitas (Martyr), 61
female circumcision, 504
Feminist theology, 417, 269
Fernando Po, 346
Ferrara, Council of, 15, 185
fetishism, 324
Feudalism, 123, 177, 198

538

Fichte, Johann Gottlieb, 237
Filioque, 81, 123, 132
Filpos, Echege of Ethiopia, 315, 316
Finish Missionary Society, 73, 387
Finney, Charles G., 262
Fire Worshippers, 69, 70
First Book of Discipline, 211
First Vatican Council, 246, 266
First World War, 113, 266, 271, 366, 375, 377, 386, 387, 398, 399, 465, 470
Fisher, Walter, 476
Flacius, Illyricus Matthias, 122
Flad, Martin, 316
Flanders/Flemish, 198
Florence, Council of, 134, 144, 152
Flower-power Movement, 268
Forerunnetrs of the Reformation, 153
Form-criticism, 265
Dauphin (Fort), 368
Fort Hare University, 354
Fort Jesus, 326, 328
Jesus (Fort), see: Fort Jesus
Fort Nassau, 329
Nassau (Fort): see Fort Nassau
Fourah Bay College, 342, 343, 344
Foursquare Gospel Church, 488
Fox, George, 260
France/ French, 54, 73, 75, 95, 102, 112, 117, 119, 121, 124-127, 137, 139, 143, 144, 150, 179, 184, 187-189, 194-198, 209-216, 236-238, 240-244, 260, 316, 317, 335, 337, 346, 348, 353, 368-377, 382-399, 406, 416, 461
Francis I, King, 184, 185, 186, 195, 215
Francis II, King, 210
Francis of Assisi, 128, 195, 294
Franciscans Franciscan Order, 125, 128, 129, 143, 146, 148, 214, 239, 294, 322, 391
Francke, August Hermann, 235, 251, 252
Frankish Empire/ Franks, 115, 117, 121, 122, 123, 132
Fraser, Donald, 357, 358, 455
Frederick Barbarossa, Emperor, 138
Frederick II, Emperor, 139, 143
Fredrick The Wise, 168, 170
Free Church of Scotland, 258, 352, 354, 356, 389
Free Grace, 65, 96, 241, 254
Free Presbyterian Church, 471
Free Will, 82, 96, 173, 241, 254, 263
Freeman, Thomas Birch, 343, 346
Freemasons, 236
Freetown, 342, 343, 376, 404
French see: France (France),
French Revolution, 130, 197, 234, 237, 243, 498
Frere Town,363, 364
Frigga, 116
Frisia/ Frisians, 75, 102, 117, 118, 122, 191
Froude, R.H., 247
Frumentius, 310
Funji people, 309

G

Gabon, 346, 384, 385, 390
Gad, Prince, 71
Gaisaric, King, 102
Galawdewos (of Ethiopia), 314
Galilei, Galileo, 234
Galla people, 316
Gallia, 121, 240
Gallican Articles, 240
Gallicanism, 125, 238, 240, 241
Gallus, Missionary, 75
Gambia, 300, 336, 378, 390
Gansfort, Wessel, 165
Garanganze Mission, 349
Garcia II of Congo, 330
Garcia III of Congo, 330
Garcia V of Congo, 347
Gare Maskal, 312
Gatu, John, 400, 437
Gaul, 52, 54, 74, 99, 102, 121
Gaulle, Charles de, 399
Ge'ez language, 310, 311, 317
General Methodist Society, 257
Geneva, 150, 182, 185, 186, 190, 210, 211, 240, 280
Genevan Academy, 187, 195
George, David, 299, 310, 342, 453, 464, 495
Georgia, 253, 254, 260, 261
Georgios II of Nubia, 308, 309
Gereformeerde Kerk (GK) - Dopper Church, 352
German Order, 138
Germany/ German, 42, 54, 72-75, 94, 100, 102, 115-118, 121-127, 137-139, 143, 150, 151, 164-168, 170-176, 179-184,189-195, 198-201, 209, 213, 214, 234-238, 244, 246, 250-252, 256, 260-263, 265, 316, 334, 347, 356, 364-366, 374-377, 385-387, 397, 399, 482
Ghana (Gold Coast), 275, 298, 301, 303, 322, 329, 336, 346, 376, 377, 386, 388, 396, 399, 402-406, 411, 416, 418, 428, 437
Glasgow Missionary Society (GMS.), 354, 389
Glorious Revolution, 207, 212
Gnosticism/ Gnostics, 54, 59, 65, 76, 77, 78, 84, 85, 86, 88, 95, 497, 498
Gobat, Samuel, 316, 317
Godfrey of Bouillon, 138
God-is-dead Theology, 269
Goethe, Johann Wolfgang von, 237
Gold Coast see: Ghana
Gomani (Ngoni Chief), 462
Gomer, Joseph and Mary, 345
Gomez, Diogo, 322
Gonakumoto, Justin, 471
Gordon, Charles, 374
Goths, 51, 72, 73, 102, 121
Govan, William, 354
Graf, Karl H., 265
Graft, William de, 346
Gratian (Decretum of), 127

539

Gray, Robert, 324, 331, 355, 360, 464
Great Awakening, 235, 250, 261, 337, 338, 352, 421-423
Great Schism (in The West), 144
Great Trek, 337, 352
Great Zimbabwe Ruins, 305, 483
Grebel, Conrad, 192
Greek Orthodox Church, 68
Greenwood, John (Martyr), 205
Gregorius'/Gregory the Great, Pope, 99, 103, 116, 142
Gregory Illuminator, 69
Gregory IX, Pope, 139
Gregory of Nazianze, 79, 80
Gregory of Nyssa, 80
Gregory VII, Pope, 124, 127, 137, 143
Gregory VII (Hildebrand), Pope, 142
Gregory XI, Pope, 144
Grenfell, George, 257, 347, 396
Grote, Geert, 165
Grubb, George, 358
Gudnaphar, King, 71
Guinea Bissau, 379
Guinea Coast, 322
Guinness, Grattan and Fanny, 347, 381, 390, 422, 425, 427
Gutierrez, G., 269
Gutmann, Bruno, 366

H

Habsburg Empire, 173, 176, 177, 186, 194, 198, 213
Hagin, Kenneth, 491
Haile Selassie I (Ras Tafari Makonnen), 318, 319, 320
Hakon, King, 119
Hamilton, Patrick, 208, 209
Hannington, James, 366, 367
Harald, King, 119
Harare, 450, 467, 482-484, 510
Harare Synod (CCAP), 467, 484
Haroldson, King, 119
Harriot, Thomas, 259
Harris, William Wadé, 385, 402- 406, 490
Hartfeld, P., 342
Harvard, John, 260
Hauranne, Jean-Ambroise Duvergier de, 242
Hausa, 300, 302, 342, 344, 414
Hawkins, William, 336
Hayford, J.E. Casely, 404
healing, 312, 325, 406-411, 475, 487, 489, 505, 509, 510
Hegel, Georg Wilhelm Friedrich, 237, 264, 265
Heidelberg Catechism, 80, 201
Helena, Queen, 66, 136
Hellenbroek, Abraham, 250
Hellenist Superstitions, 44
Helm, Charles, 397
Henderson, Henry, 348, 456, 495, 517

Henrique, Prince of Congo, 323
Henry (Tudor) VIII, King, 203
Henry II, King, 138
Henry IV, Emperor, 124, 127
Henry of Navarre, King, 196
Henry of Portugal (Infante Dom Henrique, Prince Henry the Navigator), 321
Henry VIII, King, 203
Herbert, Edward, 236
Heremite(s), 98
Herero people, 332, 387
Hermas of Rome, 59
Hernhuters, 252
Hesychasm, 132, 133
Hetherwick, Alexander, 457-459
Heyling, Peter, 317
Hierarchicalism, 58, 78, 85, 115, 131, 142
Hieronymus, see: Jerome
Hildebrand, see: Pope Gregory VII, 124, 127, 143
Himyar (Yemen), 71
Hinduism, 32, 273, 531
Hippo Regius, 93, 167
Hippy-movement, 268
Hitler, Adolf, 276, 281
Hodge, A.A., 262
Hodge, C., 262
Hoen, Cornelis, 178, 199
Hoffmann, Melchior, 192
Hofmeyer, F., 368
Hofmeyr, L., 459
Hofmeyr, Stephanus, 481, 483
Hogg, A,G, 274
Holiness Movement/ Revival, 358, 421-427, 455
Holiness Revival, 421, 423
Holland, see: Netherlands, Dutch
Holocaust, 280, 282, 527
Holy Ghost Fathers (Congregation), 325, 345-348, 365, 366, 385, 386, 390, 399, see: Spiritans
Holy Sepulchre, 137, 138
Holy Spirit, 22, 25, 32, 42, 50, 51, 55, 66, 76,-81, 86, 93, 109, 132, 134, 135, 167, 171, 172, 185, 186, 190, 250, 252, 262- 267, 269, 270
Horton, W.H., 274
Hova people, 368
Howard, J., 256
Howells, Rees, 487
Hubmaier, Balthasar, 192
Huguenots, 196, 197, 200, 238, 260, 333, 334
Humanism/ Humanists, 148, 151, 163, 165, 171, 172, 175, 178, 179, 195, 199, 234, 263
Hume, David, 236, 237
Hungary, 113, 120, 137, 189, 238, 278
Huns, 51, 72, 73
Huntingdon (Countess of)/ Selina Hastings, 256, 271, 436
Hupfeld, Hermann, 265
Hurlbert, C.E., 347, 428
Huss, John, 153, 165

Hussites, 531
Hutter/Hutterites, 193
Hutu people, 488
Hyper-calvinism, 253

I

Ibibio people, 488
Iceland, 120
Iconoclastic Controversy, 132
Icons/ Iconography, 25, 132, 135
Idahosa, Benson, 491
Idowu, Bolaji E., 419
Idris Alooma, King, 302
Igbo people, 344, 399, 405, 406, 414, 507
Ignatius of Antioch, 52, 58, 59, 83, 85
Ignatius de Loyola, 129
Imasogie, Osadolor, 418
Immens, Petrus, 250
Independents, 205, 206, 212
India, 51, 68-72, 113, 114, 131, 216, 256-258, 268, 273, 274
Individualism/ individualisation, 147, 148, 164, 165, 235, 263, 268
Indulgences, 137, 140, 164, 165, 167, 176, 215, 530
Infallibility(of the Pope), 240
Inge, Queen, 120
Ingeborg, Queen, 143
Initiativniki., 278
Innocent II, Pope, 128
Innocent III, Pope, 125, 129, 137, 139, 143, 152
Innocent VI, Pope, 144
Inquisition, 95, 129, 143, 195, 199, 200, 213, 214
International Council of Christian Churches, 271, 275, 436, 438
International Missionary Council (ICCC), 271, 273, 436, 475
Investiture Controversy, 124, 127
Iran, 69, 70, 268
Iraq, 70, 268
Ireland, 73-75, 99, 117, 119, 195, 197
Irenaeus of Lyons, 54, 58, 59, 77, 84
Irving, E., 255
Isa bin Tarif, 361
Islam, 70, 71, 102, 104, 109-114, 125, 128-130, 135, 136, 140, 150, 273, 294-310, 313, 314, 316, 321, 345, 367, 393, 396, 414, 415, 429, 435, 438, 500, 507, 511, 512, see: Muslims
Israelism, 282, 526
Italy, 42, 50, 73, 75, 93, 95, 99, 102, 103, 112, 119, 122-127, 144, 194, 214, 240
Ittameier, Max, 366
Ivory Coast, 385, 402, 406, 490
Izhaq (Martyr), 69

J

Jacobis, Justin de, 317, 318
Jamaa Movement, 488
James Stuart II, King, 207
James Stuart I, King (Scottish James VI), 206, 211
James V, King, 209, 210
Jansenism, 238, 240, 241, 242
Japan, 216, 238, 257
Jefferson, Thomas, 237
Jehovah's Witnesses, 80, 190, 464, 470
Jerome/ Hieronymus, 85, 101
Jerusalem, 48, 50, 51, 57, 78, 138, 139, 142, 192, 273
Jesuits/ Jesuitism, 129, 199, 213, 215, 216, 235, 239, 240, 241, 245, 314, 317, 322- 328, 347, 367, 368, 381, 473, 480, 482, see: Societas Jesu
Jews/ Jewish Religion, 44, 48-52, 55, 61, 65,76-78, 83-85, 96, 110, 111, 137-140, 214, 280, 281
Joachim of Fiore, 152
Johannes Chrysostom, 73
Johannesburg, 483, 487, 490
Johanssen, Ernst, 366
Johera movement, 410
John of The Cross, 151, 239
John, Order of St., 138
John The Persian, 71
John XXII, Pope, 143
John, King, 143
Johnson, James ('Holy Johnson'), 344, 345, 397, 404, 452
Johnson, Mary, 488
Johnson, William Percival, 452
Jones, David, 369
Jones, William, 364
Jönsson, Anton, 319
Josephinism, 125
Judaism, see: Jews
Julius II, Pope, 322
Jupiter, 43
Justification, 47, 170, 173, 178-182, 186, 187, 190, 209, 215, 261, 270, 272
Justin Martyr, 69, 84
Justo Mwale Theological College, 477

K

Ka'ba, 110, 111
Kagame, Alexis, 269, 416
Kairos Document, 415, 417, 494
Kalambule, Lyton, 489
Kalden, Petrus, 334
Kaleb of Ethiopia, 311
Kalilombe, Patrick, 470
Kalonga Masula, 305
Kambalazaza, Mark, 492
Kamwana, Elliot Kenan, 464, 468, 478
Kanem-Borno Kingdom, 302
Kant, Immanuel, 237, 263, 264
Kaparidze, Mutapa , Emperor, 326
Kapeni (Chief in Blantyre area), 456
Karanga language, 483

Karlstadt (Andreas Rudolph Bodenstein), 171
Kasavubu, Joseph, 383
Kato, Byang, 28, 418, 419, 438
Kaunda, David, 473
Kaunda, Kenneth, 411, 415, 473, 475, 476, 477
Kazembe dynasty, 304
Kebra Nagast text, 311
Kelly, John, 347
Kemp, Johannes Theodorus van der, 353, 357, 359, 360, 389
Kempis, Thomas à, 165
Kenya, 304, 317, 319, 342, 352, 354, 362-365, 375-378, 387, 390, 399, 400, 405, 409, 410, 419, 427, 428, 437, 438, 458, 486, 488
Kepler, Johannes, 234
Keswick Convention, 255, 357, 358, 409, 455
Khadija, 110
Khambuli, George, 490
Kharijite Movement, 298
Khoikhoi people (Hottentots), 305, 331-335, 353, 359, 360
Khoisan People, 257
Kibongi movement, 488
Kierkegaard, Sören, 267
Kigozi, Blasio, 409
Kikuyu people, 304, 377, 399, 510
Kilham, Hannah, 342
Kimbangu, Simon/ Kimbnguists, 383, 384, 407, 412, 439, 488, 490
Kimpa Vita (Donna Beatrice), 325, 402, 490
Kitchener, Horatio, 375
Kitombo, battle of, 330
Klerk, Willem de, 415
Knight-Bruce, George, 482
Knight's Templars, 128
Knothe, C.P.G., 481
Knox, 209, 210, 211
Knox, John, 209-211
Knut, King, 119
Koelle, S.W., 343
Koelman, Jacobus, 235, 250
Kohlbrugge, Hebe, 109, 112
Koi, David, 364
Koine Greek, 45
Kok, Arie, 274, 275
Kololo people, 473
Konrad (Poor K.), 190
Koran, 110, 111, 112
Koyi, Isaac William Ntusane, 453, 454
Kraemer, Hendrik, 274
Krapf, Johann Ludwig, 316, 317, 361-366, 376, 441, 444
Krio language, 342
Krotoa (Eva), 333, 334
Kufa, John Gray, 457
Kühnel, Johann Christian, 334
Kuijper, Abraham, 352
Kulturkampf, 246
Kumalowno, Izak, 483
Kumm, Karl, 428
Kumm-Guinness, Lucy, 428
Kunibert (Missionary), 117
Kush, 307, 403
Kuunikira, 234
Kuypers, G., 250

L

laager- mentality, 352
Labadie, Jean de/ Labadists, 250
Lakwena (or: Lekwana), Alice, 415
Lalibela of Ethiopia, 312
Lambeth Conference, 271
Lancaster House Agreement, 484
Lany, Emma de, 466
Lapsi/ Lapsus, 62, 64, 66, 89-91, 96
Lateran Council, 125, 143
Lausanne Conference (1974), 419
Lavigerie, Charles Martial Allemand, 365, 390, 391, 397, 460, 461
Laws, Robert, 354, 453-455, 458-460
Lay Investiture, 124
Lazarists order, 239, 369, 391
Lebna Dengel of Ethiopia, 314
Lefèvre d'Etaples, Jacques, 185, 195
Legion of Mary/ Legio Maria, 462, 472
Leibnitz, Gottfried Wilhelm, 236
Leiden, Jan van, 192
Leipzig Mission, 366, 387
Lekganyane, Ignatius Engenas, 487
Lena (Moravian convert), 334, 402
Lenin (Vladimir Ilyitsh Ulyanov), 276
Lenshina, Alice, 410, 411, 477, 478
Leo III, Pope, 123
Leo IX, Pope, 127
Leo 'the Great',Pope, 142
Leo X, Pope, 164
Leo XIII, Pope, 246, 266
Leonard Kamungu Theological College (LKTC), 470
Leopold II of Belgium, 373, 381, 382, 391
Lessing, Gotthold Ephraim, 237, 265
Lettow-Vorbeck, Paul Emil von, 387
Lewanika of the Lozi, 473
Libellatici, 64, 89
Libellus Pacis, 89
Liberalism, 245, 249, 263, 266, 267, 271, 274, 352, 379, 410-416-420, 433, 436, 438, 499
Liberation Theology, 269, 417, 420
Liberia, 345, 373, 406, 414, 428, 437, 490, 493
Libermann, François, 345, 346, 390
Licinius, Emperor, 66, 76
Life and Work (l.W.), 272
Liguori, Alphonso de, 239
Lijadu, E.M., 405
Lincoln, Abraham, 260
Lindsey, Theophilus, 249
Lion, Edward, 487
Litiya (Prince of the Lozi), 474
Living Waters Church, 471

Livingstone Inland Mission (LIM), 347, 427, 381
Livingstone, David, 257, 326, 339, 347, 349, 353, 354, 365, 390, 422, 427, 450-457, 481
Livingstonia Mission (Free Church of Scotland), 397, 398, 450, 452, 453, 455, 458, 467, 473, 476
Lobengula, King of the Ndebele, 397, 481, 482
Locke, John, 236
Lodensteyn, Jodocus van, 250
Loisy, Alfred Firmin, 246
Lollards, 164, 203, 208, 531
Lolo, Dede Ekeke, 405
Lomwe people, 462
London Missionary Society (LMS), 257, 339, 343, 352-354, 359, 369, 370, 387, 389, 397, 450, 451, 474, 475
Longobards, 75
Lord's Supper, 65, 169, 172, 178, 181, 186, 188, 199, 210, 271
Louis III, King, 138
Louis IX, King, 139, 140
Louis Napoleon, Emperor, 244
Louis Philippe, King, 244
Louis VII, King, 138
Louis XIII, King, 197
Louis XIV, King, 197, 238, 240, 333
Louis XVIII, King, 244
Louw, Andrew, 483
Louw-Malan, Cinie, 483
Lovedale College, 354, 365, 404, 452-454, 458, 464
Low Lands, see: The Netherlands
Loyola, Ignatiius de, 129, 215, 231, 232
Lozi people, 473, 474
Luba people, 304
Lull(ius), Raymond (Missionary), 294, 298
Lumpa Church, 410, 478
Lunda people, 304, 476
Lusitanianism, 378, 391
Luther, Martin/ Lutheranism/ Lutherans, 96, 130, 149, 151, 165-181, 184, 187-195, 199, 204, 208, 209, 220, 222, 251, 260, 261, 271, 283, 357, 436, 527, 530
Lutheran Church of Central Africa (LCCA), 468, 471
Lutheran World Federation (LWF), 271, 436
Luwum, Janani, 411, 415
Lyons, Council of, 134

M

Maarsveld, Hendrik, 334
Macdonald, Duff, 457
Macedo, Henry de, 460
MacGoye (Oludhe), Marjorie, 361
Mackay, Alexander, 367
Mackenzie, Charles Frederick, 365, 451, 452
Mackenzie, John, 257
macrocosmos, 508, 511

Madagascar (Malagasy), 60, 332, 368-372, 384, 385, 390, 427
Madima, Johannes, 481
Maffuta, 325, 490
Magister Reformers, 190, 191
Mahon, Edgar, 487
Maimonides, 146
Majorinus, Bishop, 96
Makarios, Bishop, 72
Makewana, 500
Makololo people, 354, 396, 450, 453
Makuria, Nubia, 307, 308
Malagasy, see: Madagascar
Malawi, 18, 19, 296, 300, 304, 333, 352, 354, 356, 365, 375, 378, 387- 392, 397, 398, 404, 418, 425, 433-435, 450-474, 476- 495, 499, 509, 511, 517, see: Nyasaland
Mali, 301, 302, 322, 385
Malikebu, Daniel, 422, 466
Malinke people, 301
Mamluks, 297, 309
Mandala (African Lakes Company), 454
Mandela, Nelson, 415
Mandovi, Joseph, 483
Manes/ Mani, 77, 88, 95
Mangadzi, 499
Manichaeism, 65, 77, 93, 94, 95
Communist Party (Manifesto), 245
Mankadan, Sybrand, 333
Manning, Henry Edward, 248
Mansfeld, 166, 174
Mansfield, Lord, 339
Manuh, Takyiwaa, 502
Manz, Felix, 192
Maples, Chauncy, 452
Maranke, Yohane, 487
Maravi Empire, 304, 305
Marcion/ Marcionism, 65, 76, 77, 84, 85, 88, 94, 133
Marcus Aurelius, Emperor, 61, 88
Mario Legio of Africa, 405
Mariology, 325
Marists (Congregation), 462
Maroons, 342
Marot, Clément, 186
Martin V, Pope, 144, 321
Martyrdom/ Martyr, 55, 58, 59, 64, 66, 69, 78, 87, 90, 98, 137, 199, 209
Marx, Karl, 245, 276, 277
Mary of Lotharingen, 210
Mary Stuart, Queen, 209, 210, 211
Mary Tudor, Queen, 182, 204, 210
Maskal Kebra, 312
Masoha, Jozua, 483
Masowe, Yohane, 487
Mass, 134, 150, 153, 169, 196, 199, 209, 215, 248, 262
Massaja, G., 317, 318
Matchona Churches, 467
Matecheta, Harry, 457

543

Mather, Cotton, 260
Matipwiri (Chief in Mangochi area), 460
Matthijsen, Jan, 192
Mattita, Walter, 402
Mau Mau movement, 400, 411
Maurice (St. Mauritius), 103
Maurists (Congregation), 239
Mauritania, 292, 298, 321, 385
Mauritius, 364, 370, 385
Maximian, Emperor, 103
Maximilla (Prophetess), 78
Maximus, Emperor, 88
Mayflower, 259
Mazarin, Jules Raymond, Cardinal, 240
Mazdaism, 70
Mbanza Congo, 323, 324
Mbele (Ma Mbele), 410
Mbelwa (Ngoni Chief), 454
Mbila, Yohana, 399
Mbiti, John S., 269, 417, 419
Mbona Cult, 296, 433, 480, 500, 509
McIntire, Carl, 271, 436
Mecca, 110, 111
Medina, 111, 112, 113
Meerhof, Pieter van, 334
Meister Eckhart, see : Eckhart
Melanchthon, Philip, 170, 172, 181, 215
Melkite Church, 52, 292
Melville, Andrew, 211
Melville, James, 209, 211
Mendez, Alfonso, 314
Mendicant Orders (Friars), 128, 129, 143, 146, 151
Menelik I, King of Ethiopia, 311, 312
Menelik II, Emperor of Ethiopia, 318
Mengistu Haile Mariam, 320, 415
Mennonites, 193, 260, 262, 383, 401
Mercator, Isodore, 122
Merina people, 368, 369
Merkurios of Nubia, 309
Merovingians, 75, 121, 122, 126
Mesihafe Qedir book, 314
Methodism, 250, 253, 254, 256
Methodius, Missionary, 134
Mfecane (Crushing), 333
Milan (Edict of), 66, 70, 76, 79, 86, 93, 99, 115, 196, 238, 260
Milingo, Emmanuel (Bishop), 475
Militant Church, 34, 530
Mill Hill Fathers, 365, 392
Miller, Clyde, 486
Miller, Samuel T., 349
Miller, William, 262
Mindolo Ecumenical Institute, 475
Missionary Movement/ Mission, 25, 31, 50-52, 55, 68, 71-75, 99, 115-118, 126, 129, 131, 142, 173, 195, 203, 208, 215, 238, 239, 249, 253, 255-261, 265, 267, 270-274, 338, 340-342, 401, 402, 408, 411, 412, 421, 507, 508
Mliwa, Shadrack, 399

Mobutu Sese Seko, 407, 414
Modernism, 148, 246, 263-266, 269, 270-274, 420, 433, 437, 492, 510
Moerbeke, William of, 146
Moffat, Robert and Mary, 353, 354, 357, 481
Moir, John and Alfred, 454
Mojtahids, 112
Mokamba (Prince), 474
Mokoele, Lukas, 483
Mokone, Mangena M., 404
Molina, Luis de, 241
Molinists, 235
Molinos, Michael de, 240
Moltmann, Jürgen, J., 269
Mombasa, 304, 317, 326, 328, 362, 364, 366, 377, 399, 427, 428
Monasticism, 25, 31, 78, 98-100, 116, 126, 127, 130, 133, 143, 150, 164, 165
Monism, 77
Monjeza, Joshua, 468
Monnica (Augustine's mother), 93
Monophysitism/ Monophysite(s), 53, 81, 131, 132, 292, 307, 308, 311, 315, 316, 318
Monotheism, 44, 48, 70, 110, 264
Montaillou, 95
Montanism/ Montanists/ Montanus, 66, 78, 81, 85, 86, 87, 88, 96, 190, 490
Montesquieu, Jean Louis de etc., 236
Montfort Fathers/ Missionaries, 460, 461, 462
Moody, D.L., 255, 262
Moore, H., 256
Moravian Mission/Moravian Brethren, 193, 252, 257, 330, 334, 335, 353, 359, 366, 387, 402, 421
Morel, Edmund Dene, 382
Morocco, 53, 112, 293, 298, 299, 373, 385
Morudu, Jeremia and Petrus, 483
Moscow, 134, 277, 279
Mott, John, 358
Mozambique, 304, 305, 322, 326, 332, 333, 352, 367, 368, 373, 378-380, 390, 391, 414, 461, 462, 470, 476
Mponda (Chief in Mangochi area), 453, 460, 461
Mtekateka, Josiah, 470
Mtuwa, Harry Apika, 457
Mueller, Richard, 468
Muftaa, Dallington, 367
Mugabe, Robert, 484, 485
Mugambi, Jesse, 420
Muhammad, 71, 110, 111, 112
Muhammad bin Abdullah, 375
Muhammad Mahdi, 112
Mulago, Vincent, 269, 416
Müller, George, 255, 423
Müller, Ludwig, 281
Müntzer, Thomas, 171, 191, 192
Muocha, Leonard, 466
Murphy, J.B., 381
Murray Theological College, 483
Murray, Andrew, 349, 352, 356, 357, 358

Murray, Andrew Charles, 352, 356, 458
Murray, Annie, 358
Murray, Charles, 356
Murray, William Hoppe, 458, 459
Musa, King, 301
Museveni, Yoweri (President), 415
Mushindo, Paul, 478
Muslims, 54, 80, 97, 109-111, 114, 122, 137-140, 161, 214, 297, 364, see: Islam
Mussolini, Benito, 276
Mutapa Empire, 305
Mutendi, Samuel, 487
Mutesa I, Kabaka of Buganda, 366, 377
Muzorewa, Abel, 482, 484
Mvemba Nzinga (Alfonso I) of Congo, 323
Mvera, 458, 459, 467, 483
Mwalo, Yeremiya, 483
Mwanawasa, Levy (President), 415
Mwanga, Kabaka of Buganda, 367, 377
Mwari Cult, 295, 480, 510
Mwase, Edward, 471
Mwene Mutapa, 305, 327, 480, 483
Mwinyi Mkuu, 304
Mysticism, 59, 109, 128, 151, 164, 167, 238, 239, 240
Mzilikazi, King of the Ndebele, 333, 481
Mzimba, Pambani J., 404

N

Nadere Reformatie, 235, 250
Nagenda, William, 409, 410
Nama people, 387
Namalambe, Albert, 454, 458
Namibia, 305, 332, 352, 386, 387
Nantes (Edict of), 196, 238, 260, 333
National Association of Evangelicals, 271
National Black Evangelical Association, 271
National-socialism, 276, 280, 281
Navigator, Prince Henry the (Infante Dom Henrique), 321
Ndebele people, 333, 397, 481, 482, 484, 485
Ndovi, Stanley, 471, 492, 493
Neau, Elias, 260
Necessitades, Francisco, 326
Nederduitsch Gereformeerde Kerk (NGK), 352
Nederduitsch Hervormde Kerk (NHK), 352
négritude movement, 399
neo-colonialism, 529
neo-evangelicalism., 267
neo-nazis, 279, see: national-socialism
oeo-orthodoxy, 263, 266, 267, 268, 274, 275
neo-platonism, 77, 93-95, 146
neo-reformed theologies, 267
Nero, Emperor, 49, 52, 61, 88
Nestorianism/ Nestorius, 81, 131
Netherlands, The (The Low Lands)/ Holland, 73, 150, 189-205, 214, 235-238, 241, 242, 249 - 257, 259, 260, 329, 334- 337, 351-353, 359, 389, 392, 471, see: Dutch

Neuberg, Hermann, 366
Neukirchener Mission, 365
New Age Thinking, 269
New England, 260, 261
Newman, John Henry, Cardinal, 231, 247, 289
Newton, Isaac, 234
Ngola of the Ndongo, 304, 325
Ngombe, Nguana, 473
Ngoni people, 305, 332, 333, 454, 455, 458, 461, 462, 467, 473
Ngunana, Shadreck, 453, 454
Nguni, see: Ngoni
Ngunza (=Prophetic) Movement, 488
Nicaea (Nicene Council, Nicene Creed), 35, 71, 74, 80, 81, 85, 101, 123, 132, 142
Nicolas I,Pope, 143
Nicolas V, Pope, 321
Niebuhr, Reinhold, 267
Niemőller, Martin, 281
Niger/ Niger mission, 144, 344
Nigeria, 28, 339, 343-345, 352, 376, 377, 388, 390, 396, 397, 402-407, 414, 417-419, 427-429, 437, 488
Ninian, Missionary, 208
Njobvuyalema (Ngoni Chief), 462
Nkhoma Synod (CCAP), 352, 354, 438, 450, 458, 469, 471, 483, 484, 495
Nkomo, Joshua M.N., 482, 485
Nkrumah, Kwame (President), 399
Nku (Ma Nku), 410, 490
Nkunika, Elliot, 489
Nobatia, 307, 309
Nominalism, 147-149, 163
Nomiya Luo Mission, 405
Nonconformism, 205, 235, 247, 259
Noo, Ishmael, 410
Norsemen/ Vikings, 119, 123, 124, 127
Norway/ Norwegian Missionary Society, 73, 119, 355
Novatianism/ Novatian, 62, 66, 78, 85, 90, 96, 190
Novatianus, 90
Novatus, 89, 90
Nsibambi, Simeoni, 409
Ntintili, Mapas, 453
Ntsikana, 360, 405
Nubia/ Nubian Christianity, 51, 68, 103, 104, 110, 294, 297, 300, 307-310, 402
Numidia, 53, 96
Nyang'ori Mission, 486
Nyasa Industrial Mission (Evangelical Church of Malawi), 464, 467, 486
Nyasaland , 356, 357, 363, 375, 378, 396-398, 404, 423, 442, 463-467, 483, 484, 489, 517-520, see: Malawi
Nyasaland Christian Council, 467
Nyau Societies, 433, 462, 509
Nyerere, Julius (President), 415
Nyimbo za Mulungu, 404, 467
Nyländer, M., 342

Nzambi, Mama, 325

O

Oakely, Frederick, 247
Obote, Milton (President), 415
Ockenga, Harold J., 267
Ockham, William of, 148, 149, 163
Odoacer, King, 102
Odubanjo, David, 407
Ojukwu, 414
Old Catholic Church, 242
Olevianus, Caspar, 201, 202
Olowala, Cornelius, 418
Omar, 111
Onitsha entre, 344
Oppong, Sampson, 402
Opuku Ware, King, 303
Orange Free State Synod (of the DRC), 473
Oratians, 239
Ordo Fratrum Minorum (OFM), 128
Ordo Predicatorum (OP), 129
Organisation of African Instituted Churches (OAIC), 439
Organisation of African Unity (OAU), 413
Origen, 52, 79, 84, 85, 292
Original Sin, 81, 96, 169, 215, 236, 241, 247, 265
Orimolade, Moses Tunolase, 407
Oromo people, 304, 314-319
Orthodoxy/ Orthodoxism/ Orthodox Church, 135, 150, 235, 249, 277-279, 338
Oschoffa, Samuel Bilewu, 407
Osei Tutu, King, 303
Ositelu, Josiah, 407
Oswy, King, 117, 208
Ottoman Empire (Turkish), 113, 136, 297
Overney, Abraham, 333
Overtoun Institution, 455, 464, 473, 478
Oviedo, Andrew de, 314
Oxford Movement, 247, 248, 256

P

p'Bitek, Okot, 417, 508
Pachomius, 98, 99
padroado, 321, 328
Paderborn Synod, 118
Paez, Pedro, 314
Paget, Edward, 482
Paine, Thomas, 237
Palestine, 42, 48, 50, 51, 68, 74, 112, 113, 130, 136, 138-141, 258
Palladius, 74
Palli-vanavar, King, 71
Palmer, Phoebe, 423
Pannenberg, W, 269
Pantaenus, 71, 84
Pantheism, 151, 236
Panther/ Ben Panthera, 84
Paolo, Vincentius de, 239
Papal Infallibility, 246, 266

Papal State, 116, 169
Papias of Hierapolis, 59
Paqida, Bishop, 69
Paris Mission Society, 347, 354, 371, 386, 389, 399, 473, 475, 481
Parthian Empire, 68, 69
Pascal, Blaise, 241, 242
Patrick, Apostle of Ireland, 74
Patripassian Monarchianism, 84
Paul III, Pope, 214
Paul V, Pope., 241
Paul, Apostle, 46, 52, 56, 171, 265
Paul, of Samosata, 79
Paulicians, 132, 133
Pax Britannica, 396
Pax Romana, 42
Pelagius/ Pelagianism, 65, 81, 95, 96, 165, 167, 173
Penn, William, 260
Penry, John (Martyr), 205
Pentecostal Movement, 24, 31, 41, 50, 283, 284, 407- 412, 467-471, 486-494, 505
Pepin III, King, 122
Perfect, George, 488
Perkins, William, 235, 250
Perpetua (Martyr), 61
Persia/ Persian Empire, 45, 51, 68, 69, 70, 71, 77, 95, 112, 131, 258
Peter The Hermit, 137
Peters, Thomas, 342
Phelps-Stokes Commission, 398
Philadelphia Missionary Council, 428
Philafrican Mission, 349
Philip IV (Augustus) II, King, 138, 143
Philip II, King, 198, 199
Philip, John, 257, 353
Phillip of Hesse, 172
Phillips, John George, 452, 467, 487
Philo, of Alxandria, 84
Phiri, Hanock Msokera, 468
Phiri, Jim, 489
Phiri, Moses, 467, 471
Phiri, Wyson Chitsulo, 471
Photinus (Martyr), 54
Photius, Patriarch, 132-134
Piarists, 239
Pierson, A.T., 262
Pietism/ Pietismus, 235, 249-252, 257
Pilgrim Fathers, 205, 259
Pilkington, George Lawrence, 258
Pinto, Serpa, 460
Pirquet, Charles du, 348
Pisa, Council of, 144, 151
Pius II, Pope, 140
Pius IV, Pope, 137
Pius IX, Pope, 245, 246, 266
Pius VI, Pope, 246
Pius VII, Pope, 245
Pius XI, Pope, 246
Plato, 46, 77, 94, 95, 146

Plessis, David du, 283, 286
Pliny (Plinius), 61
Plymouth Brethren, 255
Pocahontas, 259
Poland, 120, 189, 195, 213, 214, 238, 278
Polemicists, 83, 84, 85
Polycarp (Martyr), 54, 59, 61, 83
Polytheism, 44, 46, 48, 69, 79, 111
Pombal, Marquis of, 324
Portugal/ Portuguese, 129, 150, 195, 216, 238, 240, 294, 297, 299, 303-305, 314, 321-331, 334-337, 347-350, 367, 368, 373, 376-380, 391-393, 396, 397, 414, 460, 461, 480
Post-Apostolic Fathers, 83
Post-Classical Missions (Faith Missions), 389, 427, 463
Post-Modernism, 18, 263, 269, 275, 284, 433, 497, 522
Praxeas, 84
Predestinatianism, 109
Presbyterian Church in Kenya, 437
Presbyterian Church in Zambia, 477
Presbyterian Church of Malawi (PCM), 493
Presbyterian(s)/ Presbyterial/ Presbyterianism, 142, 188, 189, 196, 202, 205, 206, 210-212, 235, 249, 257, 259, 260, 262, 418
Presbyteros/ Presbyter, 57, 87, 90, 142, 183, 188
Prester John, 294, 327
Pretorius, J.L., 459
Prezeau, Auguste, 461
Price, W.S., 364
Priestley, Joseph, 249
Princeton College, 261
Probabilism, 239, 242
Process Theology, 269
Prophet-Healing Churches, 403, 405, 422
prosperity gospel, 530
Protten, Jacob, 330
Providence Industrial Mission (PIM.), 398, 423, 465, 466, 467, 471
Pseudo Isidorian Decretals, 122
Public Affairs Committee (PAC), 469
Purgatory, 116, 134, 150, 165, 168, 209
Puritanism/ Puritans, 205, 235, 250, 253, 257, 259
Pusey, E.B., 247, 248

Q

Qallabat, battle of, 318
Qaradushat, Bishop, 72
Qua Iboe Mission, 488
Quaicoo (Quaque), Philip, 336
Quakers, 235, 250, 260, 342
Quesnel, Pasquier, 242
Quietists, 235, 240
Quinn, Edel Mary, 462
Qur'an, see: Koran

R

Radama I, King of Madagascar, 369
Radama II, King of Madagascar, 370
Radbod, King of Frisia, 117
Radical/ Radical Reformation/ Radical Reformers/ Radicals, 32, 178, 181, 187-193, 205, 235, 268
Rafaravary, Mary, 370
Ragot, Miriam, 410
Raikes, R., 256
Ramushu, David M., 481
Ranavalona I, Queen of Madagascar, 369, 371
Ranavalona II, Queen of Madagascar, 371
Ranavalona III, Queen of Madagascar, 371
Raqbakht (of Adiabene), 69
Rasalana, Rafavavy, 370
Rasolerina of Madagascar, 370, 371
Rationalism/ Rationalists, 190, 234, 235, 237, 252, 263, 264
Rauschenbusch, Walther, 265
Ravensbrück, 280
Raymond Lull, see: Lullius
Rebmann, Johannes (Missionary), 361-366, 376, 445
Redemptorists (Congregation of the), 239
Reformation (of the 16th century), 26, 31, 32, 80, 110, 128-295, 314, 329, 338, 391, 401, 412, 418, 421, 486, 489, 490, 497, 498
Reformed Church in Zambia, 477
Reformed Church of East Africa, 438
Reformed Church of Zimbabwe, 483
Reformed Ecumenical Synod, 437, 438
Reformed Mission League, 390, 418
Reformed Presbyterian Church of Malawi, 471
Reformed-Evangelical Movement, 420, 270, 330, 416, 418
Regensburg (Ratisbona), 180, 181, 186, 223
Reimarus, Hermann S., 265
Reinhard, Anna, 176
Religious Tract Society and The British and Foreign Bible Society, 256
Renaissance, 148, 150, 163, 165, 199, 234, 244, 263, 264
Renner, M., 342
Rerum Novarum, 246
Restoration, 206, 212, 238, 239, 244, 250
Restorationist Revival, 422
Reveil, 255
Revival(s), 237, 247, 249, 253, 255, 260, 263, 268, 270, 285
Revolutionary Theologies, 268
Rhema Bible Church, 491
Rhenish Missionary Society, 387, 389
Rhodes, Cecil John, 375, 397, 473, 482
Richard II, King (Lion's Heart), 138
Richelieu (Aman Jean du Plessis) Cardinal de, 240
Riebeeck, Jan van, 331, 333
Riggs, Stephen, 261

Ritschl, Albrecht, 264
Ritzema van Lier, Helperus, 334
Roberts, Oral, 491
Robinson, John A.T., 157, 205, 228, 229, 230, 267, 268
Rogers, Cyrill, 465
Roman Catholic Church/ Roman Catholicism, 31, 68, 73, 82, 94, 124-128, 131, 135, 144, 169, 173, 179-182, 199, 200, 203, 207, 213, 215, 234, 235, 238-248, 259, 266, 268, 280, 283, 317, 379, 385, 390, 416, 420, 460-462
Roman Empire, 25, 42, 43-45, 48, 50- 54, 61, 62, 66, 68-73, 76, 88, 92-95, 98, 100-104, 110, 112, 113, 115, 121, 123, 131, 136, 138, 161
Romanticism, 234- 237, 249, 263, 498
Roosevelt, Theodore, 382
Rose, H.J., 247
Rousseau, Jean Jacques, 237, 243
Roux, P.L. le, 283, 408, 486, 487
Rowland, J.F., 487
Rufinus, 310
Rumania, 278
Russia, 81, 120-135, 150, 193, 195, 244, 245, 252, 269
Russian Orthodox Church, 275
Rwanda, 304, 383, 386-388, 409, 416

S

Sa'art, Chronicle of, 72
Sabellianism/ Sabellius, 79
Sabiti, Erica, 410
Sacramentarians, 199
Sadoleto, Jacopo, Cardinal, 186
Saint-Cyran, 242
Saker, Alfred, 346, 386
Saladin, Sultan, 139, 297
Sales, Francis de, 239, 240
Salesians (Congregation), 239
Salimini, 363
Salvation Army, 255, 428, 487
Sambani, Sam, 453
Samson, Bernhardin, 176
Samsun, Bishop, 69
San (Bushmen), 305, 332, 359
Sanders, W.H., 349
Sankey, I.D., 255, 262
Sanneh, Lamin, 420, 507
São Salvador, 323-325
São Tomé, 322-326, 379
Saracens, 122
Sassanid Era, 70
Saudi Arabia, 110
Savimbi, Jonas, 380
Savonarola, Girolamo, 152, 165
Sawyer, Harry E., 417
Sawyer, John S., 292, 293
Saxons/ Saxony, 75, 102, 117-119, 122, 150, 166-170, 175, 177, 203
Sayyid Said, 361

Scandinavia(n), 73, 119, 173, 194, 256, 260, 261
Scheut, Society of, 381, 391
Schiller, Friedrich von, 237
Schleiermacher, Friedrich D.E., 237, 263, 264
Schleitheim Confession, 192, 193
Schlettstadt, 179
Schmidt, George, 257, 334, 335, 402
Scholasticism, 128, 146, 235
Schortinghuis, Wilhelmus, 250
Schweitzer, Albert, 347
Schwellnus, Johannes, 481
Schwinn, Johann Daniel, 334
Scotland, 73,-75, 99, 117, 119, 144, 189, 194, 206,- 211, 255, 265
Scott, David Clement, 457
Scott, Peter Cameron, 365, 427
Scottish Confession of Faith, 211
Scramble (The Scramble for Africa), 373, 374, 383, 385, 389
Scripture Union (SU), 411, 490, 492
Sechele of the Bakuena, 354
Second Book of Discipline, 211
Second Coming of Christ, 338, 397, 406, 422, 531
Second Vatican Council, 31, 283, 392, 416, 420, 436, 439
Second World War, 112, 114, 271, 274, 277, 375, 377, 383, 410, 428, 435, 437, 498, 507
Secularisation, 235, 255, 268, 269, 274, 276, 281, 283, 284, 393
Selama, Abun, 310, 316, 317, 318
Seljuk Turks, 113, 136, 137, 138
Semi-pelagianism, 82, 96, 150, 240
Semler, Johann Salomo, 237
Seneca, 184
Senegal, 301, 302, 346, 384, 385, 390
Senghor, Léopold Sédar, 399
Sentamu, John Tucker Mugabi, 525
Septimus Severus, Emperor, 61, 88
Septuagint, LXX, 48
Sergeyi (Metropolitan), 277
Servet, Michael, 187, 190
Seton, Alexander, 209
Seventh Day Adventists, 262, 350, 383, 399, 464, 467, 476
Seventh Day Baptist Church, 464
Shaftesbury, Lord, 236, 256
Shaka (Chaka) of the Zulu, 305, 332, 333, 352
Shanahan, Joseph, 399
Sharp, Granville, 339, 341
Shaw, William, 354
Sheba, Queen of, 311, 312, 403
Shekanda, King, 309
Shembe, Isaiah, 408, 412, 487, 490
Shembe, Johannes Galilee, 408, 412
Shembe, Londa, 408
Shenouda III (Coptic Pope), 439
Shi'at Ali/ Shi'ites, 111
Shimbra-Kure, battle of, 313
Shimun, Bishop, 70

548

Shirer, W.L., 488
Shona people, 305, 327, 408, 481-487, 509, 510
Shonga people, 483
Siberia, 193, 276, 279
Sidi, Abe, 364
Sierra Leone, 258, 337, 339, 341-345, 376, 377, 390, 402, 404, 427, 488
Sigismund, Emperor, 153
Silbereisen, Elisabeth, 179
Silveira, Gonzalo da, 326, 327, 480
Simond, Pierre, 333, 334
Simons, Menno, 193
Simony, 123-127, 150, 164
Simpson, A.B., 424, 427, 428
Sioux-people, 261
Sithole, Ndabaningi, 482
Siwale, Noah, 489
Siwi (priest), 474
Slaves/ Slavery/ Slave trade, 45, 55, 60, 63, 114, 116, 137, 140, 141, 162, 209, 243, 252-262, 300-306, 313, 322-325, 328-331, 337-342, 352, 354, 360, 365, 367, 373, 376, 369, 381, 394, 397, 402, 403, 457
Slessor, Mary M., 344, 345
Slötkonung, Olaf, 120
Smith, David M., 269
Smith, Edwin William, 416
Smith, Ian, 354, 484
Smith, Joseph, 262
Smyth, Joseph, 346
Social Gospel, 265, 273
Socialism/ Socialists, 245, 415
Societas Jesu/ Society of Jesus, see: Jesuits
Society for the Propagation of the Gospel (SPG), 336
Socinianism/ Socinians, 190, 235
Söderblom, Nathan, 272, 273, 274
Solzhenitsyn, Alexander, 279
Somalia, 375, 414, 428
Songhay country, 299, 302
Soninke kingdom, 298, 301
Sonni Ali, King, 302
Sontonga, Enoch Mankayi, 404
Sotho people, 305, 332, 333, 355, 473, 481
South Africa, 19, 197, 249, 257, 283, 284, 305, 306, 368, 374, 375, 388, 390, 396, 399, 403, 404, 408, 410, 415, 417, 418, 427, 438, 447, 452, 453, 458, 460, 465, 467, 468, 473-475, 477, 482, 483, 486-491, 494, 526
South Africa General Mission (SAGM), 350, 357, 465, 467, 475
South African Missionary Society, 334
Soviet Union, 268, 276-280, 379, 380, see: Russia
Soyo Congo, 324, 325, 330
Sozomen, 69, 70
Spain, 42, 94, 95, 102, 112, 122, 137, 144, 150, 163, 194-200, 211, 214, 216, 238, 240, 243
Spanish Inquisition, 214
Spartas, Reuben, 405

Spener, Philipp Jakob, 235, 251
Speratus (Martyr), 61
Spinoza, Baruch, 236
Spiritans, see: Holy Ghost Fathers
Spiritualists, 190, 235
Spurgeon, Charles Haddon, 255, 262
Stalin, Joseph Joseph Stalin (Vissarionovitsh Dzugashvili), 277
Stanley, Henry Morton, 339, 354, 367, 381
Staupitz, Johann von, 166
Stellenbosch University, 333, 352, 356, 438, 450, 458
Stephanos Foundation, 471
Stern, H.A., 316
Stewart, James (of Lovedale), 354, 365, 452, 453, 458
Stober, M.Z., 349
Stoffels, Jan, 360
Strasbourg, 150, 172, 180-188, 192, 209
Straton, David, 209
Strauss, David, F., 265
Stuart, C.E., 409, 410, 451
Studd, C.T., 347
Student Christian Movement (SCM), 491
Students Volunteer Movement (SVM), 270, 357
Students' Christian Organisation of Malawi (SCOM), 411, 492
Stuurman, Klaas, 360
Sudan, 51, 114, 299-302, 307-319, 374-377, 384, 385, 391, 400, 409, 414, 421, 428, 429, 465
Sudan Interior Mission (SIM), 319, 428, 465
Sudan United Mission (SUM), 428
Sukuma people, 488
Sulayman, King, 301
Sundiata, King, 301
Sundkler, Bengt, 269, 295, 309, 417
Sunnites, 298, 111, 112
Susenyos, King of Ethiopia, 314
Sutherland, William, 454
Suze/ Susi (Livingstone's servant), 452
Svane, Frederik Pederson, 330
Svend I, King, 119
Swahili, culture, 114, 300-305, 322, 326, 362
Sweden, 73, 119, 272, 362
Swedenborg, Emanuel, 262
Switzerland, 32, 73, 75, 99, 172, 175-177, 180, 189, 191, 194, 238, 240, 256
Syncretism, 28, 116, 118, 311, 324, 419, 433, 434, 435
Syria, 42, 50, 52, 112, 138
Syriac Language, 68, 69, 71, 72
Syrian-Jacobite Church, 131

T

Tafari Makonnen, Ras (Haile Seleassie I), 318
Taffin, Jean, 235, 249
Tantalus, 43

Tanzania (Tanganyika), 304, 333, 364- 366, 375, 378, 386-388, 391, 400, 409, 415, 428, 467, 468, 488, 489, 509, 511
Tatian, 69, 84
Tauler, Johann, 151, 176
Taylor, James Hudson, 258, 423, 424
Taylor, Maria, 424
Taylor, William, 348, 349
Teilhard De Chardin, P., 269
Tekle Haymanot, 313, 315
Tembo, Ephraim, 471
Tembo, Mawelera, 455
Tempel, Placide, 400, 416
Templars' Order, 138
Temple, P., 269
Temple, W.(Archbishop), 272, 273
Tennent, Gilbert, John and William, 338
Teresa of Avila, 151, 239
Teresa of Lisieux, 239
Tertullian, 53, 60, 63, 77-79, 81, 83-88, 104, 293, 370, 490
Tetzel, Johann, 168, 176
Tewodros II of Ethiopia, 316-318
Thembu National Church., 403
Theodora, Byzantine Empress, 307, 308
Theodore of Mopsuestia, 101
Theologia Crucis, 179
Théologie Nouvelle, 268
Theologies of Reconstruction, 420
Theologies of the AIC's, 420
Theology of Crisis, 267
Theology of Hope, 269
Theotinus (Bishop) 71
Thirty Years' War, 213
Thole, Peter, 455
Thomas Aquinas, 129, 148, 149, 163, 299, 432
Thomas Christians, 131
Thomas The Merchant, 71
Thomas, Acts of, 71
Thomas, Apostle, 71
Thomist philosophy, 432
Thompson, Thomas, 336
Thorgilson, Steven, 120
Three Forms of Unity, 202
Tiénou, Tite, 418
Tikhon (Vasili Ivanovitsh Byelavin), 277
Tile, Nehemiah, 403
Tillich, Paul, 267
Tippet, Barbara, 492
Todd, Garfield, 484
Togo, 385-387, 399
Tolbert, William R., 414
Toledo, Council of, 123, 132
Tomani, 458
Tonga people, 454, 455, 473, 483
Tordesillas, Treaty of, 321
Torwa State, 305
Tozer, William, 365, 452
Tractarian Movement, 247

Traditional Religions, 295, see: African Traditional Religion
Trajanus, Emperor, 61
Translation Theologies, 420
Transubstantiation, 125, 135, 153, 169, 172, 199, 203, 204, 215, 247
Trappists, (Congregation), 127, 239
Trent, Council of, 199, 213-215, 240, 241, 266, 272
Triangular Trade:, 336
Trinity, 23, 52, 79, 80, 81, 84- 86, 109, 187, 190, 262, 270
Tripmaker, John, 192
Trotha, Adrian Dietrich Lothar von, 387
Trypho (Dialogue with Trypho), 84
Trygvason, King, 119
Tshatshu, Jan, 360
Tshibango, Tharcisse T., 269, 416
Tswana, 305, 332, 352, 353, 357
Tübingen, 146
Tubman, William, 414
Tucker Theological College, 410
Tucker, Alfred, 258
Tucker, John T., 348
Tunisia/ Tunis, 53, 92, 112, 140, 293, 385
Ture, Muhammad, 302
Turkey/ Turks, 45, 52, 72, 101, 112, 113, 134, 136, 140, 161
Turner, Harold, 420
Turner, Henry M., 404, 486
Tutu, Desmond Mpilo, 269, 415, 417
Twain, Mark, 382
Tyndale, William, 208, 250
Tyrrell, George, 246, 266

U

Ubangi-Shari, 385
Ufilas 'Apostle to the Goths'), 73
Uganda, 258, 304, 362, 365-367, 376-378, 383, 396, 400, 402, 405, 409-412, 415, 424, 428, 531
Ugandan Martyrs, 367, 531
Ukpabio, Esien, 345
Union of South Africa, see: South Africa
Union of Utrecht, 200
Unitarianism/ Unitarians, 79, 80, 190, 235, 249, 272
United Church of Canada, 275
United Church of Zambia, 475, 476, 477
United East Indies Company, 257, 331, 337
United Presbyterian Church, 275
United States, 193, 205, 262, 275
Uniting Presbyterian Church in South Africa, 477
Universities' Mission to Central Africa (UMCA), 258, 365, 389, 451, 467
Urban II, Pope, 137
Urban V, Pope, 144
Urban VI, Pope, 144
Ursinus, Zacharias, 202

Ursinus, Zacharias, 201
Uthman, 110, 111

V

Valentinus, 76
Valerianus, Emperor, 62
Vandals, 54, 94, 102, 293
Vanneste, Alfred, 416
Varley, Henry, 358
Vasco da Gama, 314, 322, 326
Vatican II, see: Second Vatican Council
Venda people, 483
Venn, Henry, 343, 344, 395, 397, 404
Verlichting, 234
Vermeulen, Dick, 471
Vernon, W.T., 468
Vespasianus, Emperor, 49
Vikings, see: Norsemen
Villa-Vicencio, Charles, 420
Vincent, David Brown (Mojola Agbebi), 404
Visigoths, 92, 102
Vlok, Theunis C. Botha, 356, 458, 483
Voes, Hendik, 199
Voetius, Gisbertus, 250
Volta, 385
Voltaire (François-Marie Arouet), 236, 243, 244
Voluntarism, 148
Vulgate, 215

W

Waldenses, 152, 195, 214, 531
Waldo, Petrus, 195, 152
Wales/ Welsh Revivals, 73, 75, 99, 117, 119, 255
Wallonian Churches, 197, 198
Walton, Spencer, 357
Ward, W.G., 247, 248
Warren, George, 342
Washington, Booker T., 357, 382
Waterboer, Andries, 360
Wauchope, Isaac, 453
Wellhausen, Julius, 265
Wesley, John and Charles, 235, 253, 260, 338, 375, 421, 467
Wesleyan Methodists' Mission, 343
Westminster Abbey, 452
Westminster Assembly, 206, 212, 250
Westminster Catechisms, 206
Westminster Confession of Faith, 80, 206
Westphalia/ Münster, Peace Treaty of, 200, 213, 234, 238
Wezel, Synod of, 200
Whitby, Synod of, 117, 208
White Fathers (Congregation), 365, 367, 390, 397, 460, 461, 462, 475
White, Ellen G., 262
Whitefield, George, 235, 253-257, 261, 338
Wilberforce, William, 256, 339
Wilkinson, Moses, 342
William III of Orange, 206, 207, 212

William I of Orange, 199, 200
Williams, Daniel P., 488
Williams, G., 255
Williams, William J., 488
Willibrord, Missionary, 117, 118
Windekind, 118
Winnen, Antoine, 461
Wishard, Luther, 357
Wishart, George, 209
witchcraft, 44, 116, 296, 325, 405, 407, 408, 434, 478, 500, 509, 514
Wittenberg, 166, 167, 170, 171, 191, 208, 209
Wolff, Christian, 237
Word of Life Evangelical Church (WLEC), 319
Work and Life Movement (WL), 436
World Evangelical Fellowship (WEF), 436
World Alliance of Reformed Churches (WARC), 436
World Christian Fundamentals Association (WCFA), 271, 436
World Council of Churches (WCC), 267, 271, 274, 279, 283, 379, 407, 417, 436-439, 475
World Evangelical Fellowship (WEF), 271
World Methodist Council, 271
World Mission Conference (Edinburgh 1910), 357
World Pentecostal Conference, 271
World Presbyterian Alliance, 271
World's Evangelical Alliance (WEA), 270
World's Student Christian Federation (WSCF), 270
Wurmbrand, Richard, 279
Wycliffe, John, 152, 153, 164, 165, 203, 208
Wylant, Willem, 333, 334

X

Xhosa people, 305, 332, 333, 353, 359, 360

Y

Yao people, 305, 365, 399, 457, 465
Yaqob (Abun), 313
Yekunno-Amlak of Ethiopia, 313
Yemen, 71
Yohannes I, King of Ethiopia, 315
Yohannes IV, King of Ethiopia, 318
Yoruba people, 302, 342, 343, 344, 404, 414
Young Men's Christian Association (YMCA), 255, 270
Young Women's Christian Association (YWCA), 270
Young, E.D., 453, 493
Youth For Christ, 270
Yugoslavia, 278
Yusuf bin Hasan, 328

Z

Za-Dingil, King of Ethiopia, 314
Zagwe Kings of Ethiopia, 311, 312

Zaire, 346, 383, 414, 474, see: Congo
Zambezi Evangelical Church (ZEC), 464, 486
Zambezi Industrial Mission (ZIM), 464, 467, 483
Zambia, 304, 333, 354, 375, 378, 410, 415, 419, 422, 452, 455, 467, 470-478, 481, 484
Zanj (Zenji) Empire, 303, 304, 377
Zanzibar, 304, 317, 326, 328, 339, 364-366, 371, 377, 386, 415, 452
Zar'a-Ya'qob, Emperor of Ethiopia, 313, 314
Zarathustra, 69
Zimbabwe, 295, 300, 305, 327, 352, 354, 375, 378, 408, 410, 467, 470,-487, 510
Zimmerman, Johann, 346

Zinzendorf, Nikolaus Ludwig, Count of, 252, 253, 257, 271, 334, 436
Zionism, 401, 405, 407, 467, 486-489
Zomba Theological College, 18, 335, 434, 470, 477
Zoroaster/ Zoroastrianism, 69, 70
Zulu people, 305, 332, 333, 352, 353, 355
Zwangendaba of the Ngoni, 333
Zwickau Prophets, 171, 191
Zwingli Huldrych/ Zwinglianism, 165, 172, 175, 176-180, 187, 188, 190, 193, 199, 204, 209, 215, 436

Other Books by the Author

Oxford Chichewa Dictionary, fifth edition

Cape Town: Oxford University Press, 2016; 1158 pp.
ISBN: 978-0-19-041659-1

Christian Zionism Examined: A Review of Ideas on Israel, the Church and the Kingdom

Nürnberg: Verlag für Theologie und Religionswissenschaft, 2012; 135 pp.
ISBN: 978-3-941750-86-9

Israëlvisies in beweging; gevolgen voor Kerk, gloof en theologie

Kampen: Brevier, 2014; 316 pp.
ISBN: 978-94-91583-35-3

Liefde voor Israël nader bekeken: Voor het Evangelie zijn alle volken gelijk

Kampen: Brevier, 2015, 207 pp
ISBN: 978-9-49158-372-8

Johannes Rebmann: A Servant of God in Africa Before the Rise of Western Colonialism

Nürnberg: Verlag für Theologie und Religionswissenschaft / Bonn: Verlag für Kultur und Wissenschaft, 2011; 274 pp.
ISBN: 978-3-941750-48-7/ ISBN: 978-3-86269-029-9

Digging Out the Ancestral Church: Researching and Communicating Church History, 3rd edition (revised, enlarged, and illustrated)

Zomba: Kachere, 2006 [2000, 2002]; 114 pp.
ISBN: 99908-76-66-5

Beliefs and Practices of Muslims: The Religion of our Neighbours

Zomba: Good Messenger Publications, 2006; 183 pp.
ISBN: 99908-909-2-7

A Conflict on Authority in the Early African Church: Augustine of Hippo and the Donatists, 2nd edition

Zomba: Kachere, 2005 [2000]; 68 pp.
ISBN: 99908.76.07.X

Ministers and Elders: The Birth of Presbyterianism,

Zomba: Kachere 2007; 195 pp.
ISBN: 978-99908-87-02-0

A Conflict on the Church and the Sacraments: How Rome and the Reformation Differed at Regensburg in 1541

Zomba: Kachere, 2006; 41 pp.
ISBN: 99908-76-64-9 (ISBN 99908-76-60-6)

Thomas Aquinas on Church and Office

Zomba: Kachere, 2007; 24 pp.
ISBN: 978-99908-87-01-3

www.ingramcontent.com/pod-product-compliance
Lightning Source LLC
Chambersburg PA
CBHW071448250426
43671CB00042B/477